FUNDAMENTAL THEOLOGY

Heinrich Fries

FUNDAMENTAL
THEOLOGY

Translated by Robert J. Daly, S.J.

With an Epilogue by Thomas M. Kelly

The Catholic University of America Press
Washington, D.C.

Originally published as *Fundamentaltheologie*
© 1985 by Verlag Styria, Graz, Austria

English translation copyright © 1996 by
The Catholic University of America Press
620 Michigan Ave, NE
Washington, D.C. 20064

Printed in the United States of America

Library of Congress Cataloging–in–Publication Data

Fries, Heinrich, 1911–
    [Fundamentaltheologie. English]
    Fundamental theology / Heinrich Fries; translated by Robert J.
Daly, S.J.
        p.   cm.
    Includes bibliographical references and index.
    1. Faith. 2. Revelation. 3. Church. I. Title
    BT771.2F7313   1996
    230'.01--dc20
    96-17346
        ISBN 0-8132-0862-9 (cloth). -- ISBN 0-8132-0863-7 (pbk.)

CONTENTS

TRANSLATOR'S FOREWORD

Why publish in 1996 the translation of a book written over 10 years ago? A comparison of the contents of this work and situation of contemporary Roman Catholic theological education reveals the answer.

Catholic theology in North America is in a very different place than it was three or four decades ago. It is no longer just a seminary affair. It is taken up by women as well as men, by laypersons as well as clerics and religious. It is studied in preparation for professional and academic as well as ministerial work. And increasingly, it is undertaken in a variety of institutes, colleges, and universities, some of which have limited ability to mediate to their students the wealth of the Catholic theological tradition.

The seminary has also changed. One could say that seminaries used to educate future priests as if they were all destined to be scholars, and then, somewhat as an afterthought, "declared" them to be prepared for ministry. The seminaries offered a heavy diet of scholastic philosophy and theology, often in Latin, along with significant attention to the ancient biblical languages and the other languages of theological scholarship. The more promising seminarians were often sent to Rome or Louvain for significant parts of their training. This made them more or less at home in the international world of Catholic theology. In effect, the major seminaries of Western Catholicism used to provide basic training for an ever replenishing supply of theological scholars. Now, because of the decline in seminary vocations, and because of changes in seminary education itself, this is no longer the case.

Not all these changes have been for the worse. Seminaries now do a better job of preparing students for pastoral and ministerial work, and the Church in general is responding better to the call of the Second Vatican Council to be attentive to the signs of the times. But this improvement has been accompanied by a general decline in the level of traditional theological education. For a Church which, even in its progressive forms, has always drawn much of its life from tradition—as for example in the reforms of Vatican II—this is a cause for concern.

Some of the influences which are at work in Catholic theology in the waning years of the 20th century, and which help explain this complex situation of both improvement and decline, can be enumerated as follows.

1. Neothomism. Let this term stand in general for the great scholastic system which "reigned" in Catholic theology in the first half of this century. This was the common base for the theological minds both "conservative" and "progressive," which guided the Church up to and through Vatican II. This system formed people who were at home in the rich intricacies of the scholastic philosophical and theological tradition, who were at least incipiently aware of historicity, who were at home in Latin, the traditional language of the Western Church's intellectual heritage, and who enjoyed functional familiarity with many of the other theological languages, ancient and modern.

2. Transcendental Thomism. Commonly associated with the names of Bernard Lonergan and Karl Rahner, this can be described as the marriage of Thomism with historicity, hermeneutics, and phenomenology. It may once have been possible to identify this narrowly with the "progressive" element in the Church, but no longer. Many of its positions have become part of mainstream Catholic theology.

3. The Reform of the Church (sometimes called *aggiornamento*). For centuries, the post-Tridentine Church had lived with very little change. When, under the leadership of Pope John XXIII and the Second Vatican Council, the Church finally opened its windows and set itself on the road to reform and renewal, a great deal of pent-up energy was released and not always constructively channeled. The thirty years since Vatican II have settled down into a phase of ongoing reform and renewal with no end in sight. This ongoing phase will probably have its ebbs and flows, but a return to the stasis that characterized pre-Vatican II Catholicism seems unlikely.

4. Liturgical Reform. *Sacrosanctum concilium*, on the sacred liturgy, was the first constitution produced by Vatican II. Appropriating developments already under way in some parts of the Church, this constitution set in motion a process that has revolutionized Catholic life: Major elements in this process have been: the translation of the liturgical and sacramental rituals into the vernacular; the introduction of an expanded lectionary, subsequently also adopted by many of the other Christian churches; the purification, adaptatation, and, increasingly, inculturation of these rites; the recovery of the kerygmatic and salvation-history nature and structure of the Eucharistic Prayer. In sum, the faithful are now encouraged to experience themselves as active participants in the universal priesthood of Jesus Christ. The revolutionary or reformational consequences of this development are still being worked out, indeed perhaps just beginning to be felt.

5. Liberation Theology. Quickly developing in the years following Vatican II, especially in the less developed countries of Latin America, liberation theology has brought something of a cultural revolution to

some parts of the Church. No longer automatically identified with the
established ruling classes, as it generally had been since colonial times,
the Church now often sides specifically with the poor, expressing and
exercising a "preferential option for the poor." Much of the spiritual
force for this movement has come from the small local cells called "base
communities." But because it has not always been easy to distinguish
Communist revolution and Marxist critique from authentic Christian social reform, the history of liberation theology has often been characterized by conflict, confusion, or at least tension, the effects of which
can be found even in the highest Vatican and papal pronouncements.

6. Political Theology. This arose at the same time as liberation
theology, but in the specifically European context of Christianity's
appropriation of the political and social implications of *Gaudium et
spes*, the Council's Pastoral Constitution on the Church in the Modern
World. In some ways, it is the first-world equivalent of liberation
theology.

7. Feminist, Womanist, and Mujerista Theology. By the early
1970's, some of the women entering into the theological disciplines formerly ruled almost exclusively by men, began to expose the patriarchal
structure and bias that has traditionally characterized Christian
theology, and to call for a reconceptualization of theology in terms that
were inclusive of women's experience, and which did not assume the
natural or spiritual superiority of women over men. Proponents of feminist theology represent a full spectrum of positions, from those that
are entirely faithful to the Church and to traditional understandings
of Christianity, to those that are sharply critical or antagonistic.
Women's ordination is only one of many questions raised. In recent
years, Black women and Hispanic women, increasingly aware of the
particular characteristics of their own experiences, and also wanting to
separate themselves from the anti-Christian affect of some of the more
radical feminist theologians, have begun to stake out their own Black
Woman Christian (i.e. Womanist) and Hispanic Woman Christian (i.e.
Mujerista) areas of theology.

8. Inculturation and the Shift from an Eurocentric to a World
Church. For the past two decades, Catholic Christians have become
increasingly conscious that their Church is in the process of developing
from an Eurocentric to a World Church. The task of evangelizing the
world, formerly conceived of in terms of adapting (i.e. merely translating) Christianity and its forms of worship to different cultures, is now
seen as the vastly more demanding task and responsibility of allowing
the gospel to be experienced and expressed more naturally in cultural
forms that are often quite different than those of Western Europe. Many
of the cultural assumptions and theological presuppositions which inspired the missionary efforts of the colonial and even postcolonial

periods have been superseded. The resulting efforts to inculturate Christianity in different parts of the world is proving, along with other recent developments, to be a source of both enrichment and tension. We have barely even begun to work out the religious and theological ramifications of this process.

9. Ecumenical Movement. In the earlier part of the 20th century, Christian ecumenism, usually associated with the World Council of Churches, was predominantly a Protestant movement. After Vatican II, Roman Catholicism, which had hitherto largely looked in from the outside, became a major player. Some of the Catholic contributions, for example in the areas of liturgical scholarship and reform, have helped contribute to the promising situation in which, for the first time, the major Christian churches are using the same lectionary and celebrating the Eucharist with an increasingly common understanding of what is happening in that central mystery. Major bilateral agreements on broad ranges of formerly divisive issues have been reached, even to the point of some Protestant churches recognizing a certain spiritual primacy in the Roman Pontiff. In recent years, however, a plateau seems to have been reached in which the striking advances of earlier years have become less frequent. However, Christians can rejoice that Catholic-Protestant relations have transcended much of their traditional antagonism. Looking ahead, the major long-term leavening effects of Catholics and Protestants beginning to worship in substantially the same way are probably still to be felt

10. Interreligious Dialogue. Vatican II carefully distinguished Christian ecumenism from interreligious dialogue by devoting separate documents to each. Nevertheless, apart from the still incalculable benefits of Christianity's progressive recovery and reappropriation of its Jewish roots, especially in its forms of ritual and prayer, interreligious dialogue has remained something of a stepchild in comparison with Christian ecumenism. However, the increasing attention which scholars of different faiths and cultures have been giving to themes relating to interreligious dialogue, especially in the last decade, suggests that this may soon change.

11. Traditionalism. Originally, "traditionalism" referred to the teaching of some Catholic philosophers and theologians of the 18th and 19th centuries who, against the Enlightenment, insisted that divine revelation is passed down within a tradition that provides instruction through the written and spoken word. In contemporary usage it has also become a (sometimes polemical) term to designate those opposed to the central reforms of Vatican II. That there are traditionalists in this sense is a matter of fact. What is harder to agree upon is the precise meaning of terms like: revolutionary, radical, progressive, moderate, conservative, reactionary, traditionalist, etc.

That the definitions of these terms are fluid, depending on who is doing the defining, is a matter of common experience. Such fluidity is, among other things, a sign of vigorous health. But when that fluidity makes it difficult, as it often does, to distinguish clearly and fairly between those who support and those who oppose the central reforms of Vatican II, it also becomes a danger.

12. Progressive Movements. At the other end of the spectrum from the traditionalism we have just mentioned are a number of movements, some of them ongoing, others ad hoc, whose purpose, generally, is to accelerate or go beyond the reform developments introduced by Vatican II. Again, the existence of such movements is a sign of vigorous health. But also again, the difficulty, indeed practical impossibility, of deciding where the precise boundary lies between healthy criticism and challenge and unhealthy opposition means that contemporary Catholics are being asked to live with much more ambiguity than characterized the decades immediately preceding Vatican II.

13. Rapprochement with Modernity. For most of the 19th and much of the 20th century, the Catholic Church found itself, more often than not, in opposition to those developments in the social and natural sciences which most characterized modernity. This was a position untypical of most of the history of the Church which generally patronized or at least tolerated developments in the arts and sciences. In recent decades, especially since Vatican II, and following the guidance of *Gaudium et spes*, The Pastoral Constitution on the Church in the Modern World, the Church has been making something of an alliance, albeit an uneasy one, with many of these developments.

14. Postmodernism. While much of the Church is still struggling to come to terms with modernity, the world itself, especially Western civilization which still supplies the Eurocentirc base for much of Christianity, has been exploring new ways of understanding itself which call into question some of the most basic presuppositions that have been common to both radical modernity and conservative Christianity. This may well be the most significant development for fundamental theology in the past decade, which explains why we have added an additional chapter on this theme at the end of the book. This chapter, § 61, was written by Thomas Kelly who assisted me with much of the work of this translation.

15. The Collapse of Soviet Communism. It may not be possible to foretell the precise theological implications of this recent development. However, since great cultural and historical turning points of this kind have generally signaled eventual religious and theological changes, and since Christian theology is in the process of becoming much more aware of the eschatological dynamics of Christian faith, we should be alert to what may be developing from the fact that for

the first time in a century, the words of Karl Marx: "A spectre is haunting Europe—the spectre of Communism," no longer sound very threatening.

One could easily extend this list, but this is more than enough to make the point that the current world of theology is an exceedingly complex one. Students entering into theological studies characteristically have some familiarity with the contemporary side of many of the issues we have just listed. But just as characteristically, they have little knowledge of their historical background, even in the relatively recent past. Thus, in their efforts to understand what is now going forward, as Lonergan used to put it, in their efforts to read the theological signs of the times, they are at a crippling disadvantage.

Heinrich Fries (b. 1911) grew up in the years of Catholicism's conservative reaction against the ventures of Modernism, cut his teeth as a theologian when Neothomism reigned supreme and when the Church, unknown to itself, was being guided by the Spirit towards the Second Vatican Council. As a young theologian, and especially in his middle years, he personally helped contribute to the great achievements of the Council, and since that time has played a leading role in the contemporary development of the Catholic theology of revelation and ecumenism. His personal appropriation of that brand of Transcendental Thomism associated with Karl Rahner, with whom he worked closely on a number of issues, places him at the center of those theological developments which have most characterized post-Vatican II Catholic theology. In addition, his earlier work on and continuing discussion with the modern European philosophies of religion has significantly contributed to his unique qualifications to write a fundamental theology which will give to younger students a chance to understand what is now going forward.

About This Translation

This translation, which in many ways amounts to a revised English edition of the German original, is designed to meet the basic background educational needs of English-speaking students of Catholic theology in college, seminary, and graduate school. Our aim has been to produce an English edition and not just a translation. Thus, the footnote documentation has been expanded to include the commonly accessible English equivalents to German theological reference works. Unless otherwise noted, the translations of quoted texts and documents are from Fries's German text. However, as an aid to the English-reading student, we have generally provided page references not to the original German works but to their English translations, when such existed and could be identified. English works quoted by Fries in German translation, have been quoted in their original English, unless otherwise noted. The Name Index is basically a translation from the original. The Subject Index is designed to be an English adaptation of the original *Sachregister*. The Select Bibliography has been added as an aid to the English-speaking reader, and thus also includes works which have appeared since the original 1985 publication.

Finally, this work is much indebted to several Research Expense Grants both from Boston College itself and from the Jesuit Community at Boston College. Much of what is of quality in the editing and produc-tion of the book is due to the conscientious copy editing of Susan Needham of The Catholic University of America Press, and also most especially to the generous technical and scholarly assistance of John Boyd Turner, Thomas M. Kelly, and Tiffany Israel Shiner, theology graduate students at Boston College.

Boston College, August 1996   ROBERT J. DALY, S.J.

ABBREVIATIONS

BZ — *Biblische Zeitschrift*, Paderborn 1957ff.

Cath — *Catholica.* Jahrbuch für ökumenische Theologie, Münster 1932ff.

DS — H. Denzinger — A. Schönmetzer, *Enchiridion symbolorum definitionum et declarationum de rebus fidei et morum,* Freiburg, 33d ed. 1965

DT — *Dictionary of Theology,* ed. K. Rahner and H. Vorgrimler, 2d ed., New York 1981

DFT — *Dictionary of Fundamental Theology,* ed. R. Latourelle and R. Fisichella, New York 1994

ER — *Encyclopedia of Religion,* ed. M. Eliade et al., New York, MacMillan 1987

FZThPh — *Freiburger Zeitschrift für Theologie und Philosophie,* Fribourg 1955ff.

HerKorr — *Herder-Korrespondenz,* Freiburg 1946ff.

HThG — *Handbuch theologischer Grundbegriffe,* ed. H. Fries, Munich 1962f.

LThK — *Lexikon für Theologie und Kirche,* ed. J. Höfer and K. Rahner, 2d ed., Freiburg 1957ff.

MThZ — *Münchener Theologische Zeitschrift,* Munich 1950ff

MySal — *Mysterium Salutis. Grundriß heilsgeschichtlicher Dogmatik,* ed. J. Feiner and M. Löhrer, Einsiedeln—Zurich—Cologne, 1965ff.

NCE — *New Catholic Encyclopedia,* ed. Catholic University of America, New York 1967

NDT — *New Dictionary of Theology,* ed J. Komonchak, M. Collins, D. Lane, Collegeville, Minn. 1991

RGG — *Die Religion in Geschichte und Gegenwart,* ed. K. Galling, 3d ed., Tübingen 1956ff.

SM — *Sacramentum Mundi,* New York—London 1968

StdZ — *Stimmen der Zeit,* Freiburg 1871ff.

STh — *Summa Theologiae* (Thomas Aquinas)

ThGl — *Theologie und Glaube,* Paderborn 1909ff.

ThQ — *Theologische Quartalschrift,* Tübingen 1819ff., Munich

ThW — *Theologisches Wörterbuch zum Neuen Testament,* ed. G. Kittel, continued by G. Friedrich, Stuttgart 1933ff.

ZKG — *Zeitschrift für Kirchengeschichte,* Stuttgart 1878ff.

ZSTh — *Zeitschrift für systematische Theologie,* Berlin 1923ff.

FUNDAMENTAL THEOLOGY

FOREWORD

In a number of earlier works I argued that a contemporary fundamental theology could be produced only by a team, so comprehensive
and so differentiated are the themes of this basic theological
discipline. In addition, the specialization that now characterizes
theology, leaves no individual adequate to the job. A further
complication is that fundamental theology is the place where most of
the challenges and opportunities for theology to be up to date are
located. It is not enough, therefore, just to repeat old truths; there has
to be translation in the truest sense of the word, from shore to shore,
from the past to today; there has to be a merging of horizons. It is
precisely fundamental theology that has the duty of being both true to
origins and adapted to contemporary situations, or attending to the
message of faith as well as to the needs of concrete human beings. For
they are the ones to whom the message must be mediated in such a way
that they can understand and experience it as an answer to their
questions as well as a challenge to their own attempted answers.
Where there are no questions, answers useless.

The magnitude and complexity of the tasks that constitute
fundamental theology make a good case for making the treatment of
this theological discipline a team project. This was how it was done
in the quickly sold-out *Handbuch der Fundamentaltheologie* edited
by Walter Kern, Herman Josef Pottmeyer and Max Seckler. The
advantage of this model is that individual themes are treated with
both thoroughness and variety. But the inner relationships of the
individual parts to the whole remain problematic.

This is why it makes sense to attempt a fundamental theology as
the work of a single author. It has the advantages of unity, consistency
and continuity. My qualifications for such an attempt can be found in
the many years I have taught fundamental theology. This book has
grown out of that teaching and has gone through many stages. It owes
much to the lively cooperation of my students.

Even in its present form, this volume of fundamental theology is an
incomplete work. How could it be otherwise? It is like speaking of a
forest while leaving the details of every individual tree uninves-
tigated.

As for the structure of the book, the question of religion and the critique of religion are not given their own thematic development. This is not just because the book would otherwise have become too large, and also not just because a great deal is now being written on these questions—one could mention Bernhard Welte, *Philosophy of Religion*, (Freiburg/Basel/Wien, 1978); Hans Küng, *Does God Exist?* (München, Zurich 1978); Walter Kasper, *The God of Jesus Christ* (Mainz 1982), but also because these themes are taken up in our treatment of faith and of revelation. I myself have repeatedly gone into print on these questions, such as in the book edited by me: *Gott—die Frage unserer Zeit* (Munich 1973); and together with Peter Glockmann: *Ich sehe keinen Gott* (Freiburg 1971); and together with Aloys Buch: *Die Frage nach Gott als Frage nach dem Menschen* (Düsseldorf 1981).

In the treatment of fundamental-theological problems, I devoted special attention to contemporary ecumenical questions. Ecumenical theology is not a discipline within theology but a dimension of all of theology.

In spite of everything, I would never have dared to publish this work of fundamental theology if the editorial director of Styria Press, Dr. Gerhard Trenkler, had not repeatedly requested and encouraged me to do so. I owe him therefore special thanks. I am likewise grateful to Herr Josef Helmut Machowetz, who in a thoroughly helpful way assumed the task of reader and produced the Index of Names. The lengthy and not always easily readable manuscript was typed by Frau Hildegard Förschner. For that, my heartfelt thanks.

Herr (Ministerialrat) Dr. Otto Martz assisted in the reading of proofs. My colleague Johannes Brosseder, together with his institute through Frau Katharina Altmeier and Frau Roswitha Mombauer, produced the comprehensive Subject Index. For all this help I would like to express my thanks.

Munich, January 1985   HEINRICH FRIES

INTRODUCTION

Fundamental theology treats the fundamentals, the foundations of theology. Under "fundamental" and "foundation" is meant the presuppositions and conditions for the possibility of theology. Such presuppositions and conditions are not invented or constructed arbitrarily, or brought in from outside; they are rather required by the subject itself, theology.

Theology is the methodical reflection on faith in God which is witnessed, communicated, and revealed in many ways, but definitively, and in a way that cannot be superseded, in Jesus Christ, whose presence, word and work is alive in the Church.

The *foundations of theology* deal thus with the question of faith itself, and especially with its correlative: revelation as the principle of all theology and its specific contents. These foundations also deal with the question of the mediation of revelation as a question of [about] the Church, insofar as it is the bearer and traditor of revelation. These foundations, in the fundamental-theological perspective, are not objects of belief in themselves; they are rather the object of human understanding and rationality.

In this way, it should become possible to make the same demand of faith and of the believer which is already found in the New Testament where one finds the classical description of the purpose of fundamental theology: "Be always ready to answer the question of anyone who asks about the hope with which you are filled" (1 Pet 3:15). Hope is a synonym for faith; hope is the future form of faith.

The question of the *believability of faith* is the special characteristic of fundamental theology and its specific mode of questioning, at least in the understanding of a Catholic fundamental theology.[1]

1. Cf. the introductory reflections in the different presentations of fundamental theology. In addition: G. Söhngen, Fundamentaltheologie, in *LThK* 4, 452–59; H. Fries, Fundamentaltheologie, in *SM* 2, 140–50; Zum heutigen Stand der Fundamentaltheologie, in: *Glaube und Kirche als Angebot* (Graz—Vienna—Cologne 1976) 154–71; die ökumenische dimension der Fundamentaltheologie, in: ibid., 172–86; H. Stirnimann, Erwägungen zur Fundamentaltheologie, in: *FZThPh* 24 (1977) 291–365; J. Schmitz, Die Fundamentaltheologie im 20. Jahrhundert, in: H. Vorgrimler—R. van der Gucht, eds., *Bilanz der Theologie in 20. Jahrhundert II* (Freiburg—Basel—Vienna 1969) 197–245; R. Latourelle—G. O'Collins, *Problemi e Prospettive di Teologia fondamentale* (Brescia 1980); H. Wagner, *Einführung in die*

The term "fundamental theology" has taken the place of *apologetics*.[2] This does not mean that the "business" of apologetic—the readiness-to-give-answer of the Christian faith, in the sense of giving an account, of defending, of taking a position over against the questions directed against it—is done away with or outmoded. Apologetic is already found in the Old and New Testament, and the first theological efforts in the Early Church were produced by the apologists. Apologetic remains an ever-valid dimension of theology which, for its own sake, must attend to its encountering and creatively coming to terms with the spirit of the historical epoch in which it finds itself. The term "fundamental theology" is intended to express that the apologetic task can and should be integrated in a comprehensive theological reflection: in the believing reason's self-examination of its foundations and presuppositions. Fundamental theology is, in this sense, a transcendental-theological reality.

This clarifies how fundamental theology is the foundation of theology. This claim would be excessive if it were saying that fundamental theology, in the questions it asks and the answers it gives, was the one and only foundation of theology in the sense that the Christian faith would follow—like a conclusion from premises—with logical necessity or psychological compulsion from the grounds of believability.

In that scenario, faith would no longer be faith. It is more accurate to say that the grounds of believability create the presuppositions and conditions under which faith becomes something that is responsible, or perhaps even binding. This is the significance of what Thomas took from Augustine: *"Nemo crederet nisi videret esse credendum"*—no one would believe if (s)he did not see that (s)he should believe. On the other hand, it is also true that no believability, no intelligibility of

---

Fundamentaltheologie (Darmstadt 1980); "Fundamentaltheologie," in: *Theologische Realencyklopädie* 9.738–52. Zur Fundamentaltheologie innerhalb der evangelischen Theologie (G. Ebeling, W. Pannenberg, W. Joest) vgl. M. Seckler, "Evangelische Fundamentaltheologie. Erwägungen zu einem Novum aus katholischer Sicht," *ThQ* 155 (1975) 281–99; H. Petri, "Die Entdeckung der Fundamentaltheologie in der evangelischen Theologie." *Cath* 33 (1979) 241–61; H. Wagner, op. cit., 109–24.

2. Still classical are: J. S. Drey, *Die Apologetik als wissenschaftliche Nachweisung der Göttlichkeit des Christentums in seiner Erscheinung* (Mainz 1938–1947, reprint: Frankfurt 1967; F. Hettinger, *Apologie des Christentums* Freiburg 1863–1967; A. M. Weiß, *Apologie des Christentums* (Freiburg 1878-1889) ; P. Schanz, *Apologie des Christentums* Freiburg (1887–1988 [sic]); H. Schell, *Apologie des Christentums* (Paderborn 1901); K. Aland, *Die Apologie der Apologetik* (Berlin 1948); E. Kamlah—C. Andresen—H. H. Schrey—C. G. Schweizer—H. Fries, "Apologetik, in: *RGG* 1.477–95; H. Lais—W. Lohff, "Apologetik" in: *LThK* 1, 723–31; E. Seiterich, *Die Glaubwürdigketiserkenntnis. Eine theologische Untersuchung zur Grundlage der Apologetik* (Heidelberg 1948): H. Lais, *Probleme einer zeitgemäßen Apologetik* (Vienna 1958); J. B. Metz, "Apologetics" in *SM* 1.66–70.

On the history: K. Werner, *Geschichte der apologetischen und polemischen Literatur der christlichen Theologie* (Schaffhausen 1861–1876); A. Lang, *Die Entfaltung des apologetischen Problems in der Scholastik des Mittelalters* (Freiburg 1962).

faith dispenses from faith or can replace faith. It is, and remains, a new act of its own.

As for the presuppositions and conditions for the possibility of Christian faith, i.e., grounds for believability, there are many. With regard to the theme: "Faith and the Science of Faith," I would propose as a fundamental thesis: Whatever has to do with the act and the content of Christian faith, that faith is possible, is capable of being responded to, and is fulfillable only when it has a *relationship to human being*. This is not just any old relationship, or an external or alienated one, but an original and inner relationship to the human and to what essentially belongs to it: namely, world and history. In other words, Christian faith, on which theology reflects, is only possible when there is in human beings and in the conditions which make them such, the possibility and disposition for Christian faith, when human beings are so constituted that they can believe (also and precisely in the sense of Christian faith). When such conditions of possibility are not present or cannot be detected, the Christian faith becomes, both in general and in particular, unrealistic, external, and ideological. Indeed it doesn't even seriously come into question.

The themes of fundamental theology are precisely those which people of today talk and argue about. That gives this theological discipline a high degree of actuality. For today's questions are not about this or that individual aspect of Christian faith, today's questions are about the foundation of faith that precedes everything, and about the faith as foundation.

It is no longer enough merely to proclaim or solemnly assert the Christian faith. One has to lay out its grounds in the face of the overwhelming power of the contemporary experience of world and existence and of the challenges which accompany this experience. It is a massive task, but also a great opportunity.

BOOK ONE

FAITH AND THE SCIENCE OF FAITH

PART ONE

FAITH

What we will now present under the theme of faith is basic to all aspects of fundamental theology. We encounter it along with the theme of revelation. In other words, faith is the *subjective correlate of revelation*. Faith signifies revelation which has reached its addressees and thus its goal. Without faith, revelation ceases to be what it should be and is intended to be: revelation for human beings. If *Church* belongs to the theme of fundamental theology, the question arises whether and in what *sense* the Church has to do with the presuppositions and conditions of the possibility of faith, and what function it assumes as the official locus for the mediation of faith.

Generally speaking, it can be said that whatever has to do with faith, with revelation, with Church, or with simply being a Christian, can be traced back to some basic structures. The confusing variety and complexity found in theology take on a context and a simple transparent structure when one opens up these fundamental structures. What often looks like overlap or repetition is actually an indication of a pervasive form one will encounter again and again. The theology of a theologian, when it is not the synthesizing of material from elsewhere, is characterized by large patterns such as these, patterns typical of and specific to that theologian.

That these fundamental structures repeatedly recur in relation to many different subjects is not a sign of carelessness; it is rather an indication that what is being done is appropriate not just to the particular subject being treated but also to numerous others.

I

The Anthropological Specifications of Faith

We cannot today, any more than we could previously, begin with faith and its contents as from an obviously accepted reality and then go on to further developments or derivations. We must first open up access to God, to God's revelation, and to the faith that is ordered to God. Otherwise our theological enterprise runs the risk of appearing as some strange, foreign body, and of having no relationship to reality, above all to the activity and behavior of human beings. Thus, we look to the realm of the anthropological for possible starting points for theological faith.

When we speak of faith in the theological and anthropological sense, that indicates there is something common to them. Otherwise, we wouldn't be able to use the same word, unless we assumed that we were dealing with a mere equivocation. This indicates where we must begin.

This doesn't mean that we could thus commit ourselves to the Christian faith in this way without noticing it; but rather that we can thus become aware of connections which nowadays need to be specifically spelled out. It is quite possible for these connections to become something which goes along with Christian faith, which, indeed, consists of inner connections.

§1

FAITH AS PERSONAL ACT

The concept and the word "faith" are extraordinarily many-sided and ambiguous.[1] Should one ask by questionnaire what ideas individuals connect with the word faith, one would get the most varied of answers. In everyday language one encounters the following conceptions.

The Meanings of Faith / Belief

I believe. This could have meanings such as: I don't know; I think; it could be, but so could the opposite. Faith in this *sense* has only a very small degree of reliability and certainty; it really means something like *don't know*. One comes to a somewhat higher level with phrases such as "I believe that XY has gone away." Those who speak this way mean that they have reasons and indications for such an assertion, but that these reasons are not sufficient for a firm and sure statement. This form of belief is higher than vague assumption, but belief in this *sense* is less than a knowledge and recognition based on sufficient grounds. In this manner of speaking faith means more or less: *to know this only approximately*.

Thus measured, faith is from the outset a provisional or deficient mode of knowing and recognizing. It can, at best, serve as a kind of mid-

---

1. Literature on the theme of faith is so comprehensive that one cannot even come close to listing it all. Reference has to be made to the corresponding articles in the theological dictionaries, lexicons and handbooks.

For the formulation of the question treated here, one can mention: J. Mouroux, *I Believe; The Personal Structure of Faith* (New York: Sheed and Ward, 1959); A. Brunner, *Glaube und Erkenntnis* (Munich, 1951); G. Søhngen, *Einübung in die Theologie* (Freiburg–Munich, 1955); C. Cirne–Lima, *Der personale Glaube* (Innsbruck, 1959); Heinrich Fries, *Glauben—Wissen* (Berlin, 1960); Josef Pieper, *Belief and Faith A Philosophical Tract* trans. Richard and Clara Winston (Westport: Greenwood Press, Publishers, 1975); H. Gollwitzer—W. Weishcedel, *Denken und Glauben* (Stuttgart, 1965); Henry Bouillard, *The Logic of Faith* (New York: Sheed and Ward, 1967); H. Fries, *Faith Under Challenge* (New York: Herder and Herder, 1969); *also Was hieft glauben?* (Düsseldorf, 1969); Walter Kasper, *Einführung in den Glauben* (Mainz, 1972): H. Beck, *Anthropologischer Zugang zum Glauben* (Sazburg, 1979); B. Welte, *Was ist glauben?* (Freiburg–Basel–Vienna, 1982).

dle status between mere supposition and exact, grounded insight. But in terms of knowledge and cognition, it never escapes its inferior position. If this is where one starts, faith in the theological sense is inevitably something quite suspicious and vulnerable. It is easy to see why the connection of faith with the science of faith seems like the union of irreconcilables.

In everyday language, faith has still another form. We find it in sentences like "I believe in you—I believe you." In this form, faith is related to a person. Faith is primarily an act of *encounter* and of trust; it embraces understanding, will, and feeling in primordial union. The form "I believe in you" is radical and comprehensive. It goes to the totality of the person, more than does the formulation "I believe you," which is subject to a possible reservation. In any case, faith in this form operates primarily not in the realm of I and it, of I and the world of objects, but in the realm of encounter between I and You. It is a *personal act*.

In the German and English languages, faith has the same word root as *geloben* and *lieben*, believe and love. The Latin *credere* comes, as one possible derivation suggests, from *cor dare*: give one's heart. The Hebrew word for believe—it is taken up in the word "Amen"—means stand fast, set firmly, or make firm.

In the form of "I believe in you" and "I believe you," faith is not only an act of encounter but an eminent *mode of cognition*. This holds above all for personal cognition. So true is this that one has to say: Faith, understood as "I believe in you—I believe you," is the mode and manner in which I gain knowing access to the person of the other: Without this faith, the person as person, in its own reality, in its depth, in that which moves it, in its self, remains shut off from me.

That this is the case is clear from the following consideration. How can I come to know the persons of others in their own selves? Much of this is accomplished by the fact that I observe and analyze those persons, that I do with them what I will, that I subject them to experiment, test, and control, and from all this I get the results and conclusions that I draw about the persons themselves, from their words, actions, gestures, and dreams.

Without doubt, a broad and deep knowledge of the person is possible in this way. We know much more than we used to know about the many factors and conditions on which the human being is dependent. But the question has to be asked: Isn't it now a fairly widespread idea that human beings are only the product, only the ensemble of the kind of psychological, biological, societal, and economic conditions that determine them, and thus just the results of the factors influencing them, and that human beings are known when one knows the factors that determine them? If earlier anthropological theories ran the risk of not giving enough attention to the external conditions that shaped human beings and had the tendency to determine what human beings are only from their own metaphysical nature, we have today the opposite, no less one-sided tendency to forget this self of the human being as its own reality. Our tendency today is to underestimate this reality, to banish it into the realm of the "extraterritorial," and from there to explain the human being as a being directed from without.

Note this too: When I, in order to come to know the human being as person, restrict myself to analysis, test, and external observation—i.e., when I work according to scientific, exact method—I obtain a more or less foreground knowledge of the person, a perhaps average or typical knowledge, or a knowledge of certain qualities, abilities, and modes of reaction, but in no way do I gain a proper, individual knowledge. But precisely this is what is important and needed for personal knowledge.

When depth psychology seeks to illumine this "depth" as the individual and/or collective unconscious of the person—the depth that lies within and is perhaps suppressed within this unconscious—it frequently bring to light some astonishing and previously unknown things. But one still has to ask: Is that a knowledge of the person in its real individual, conscious, and personal self and not just in its impersonal and unconscious self? But more important is the fact—and herein lies the distinction of the knowledge of a person from the knowledge of a nature or a thing—that person is not an object like other scientific objects. A knowledge that, from the external and from observed expressions, draws conclusions about the person, presupposes that the person expresses itself, that it doesn't close itself off and refuse to communicate. It could decline and refuse to express anything about itself, it could remain dumb, closed and defensive; it could even energetically forbid all attempts to observe and test it. Of course, even that would be an expression, and that too would result in an important bit of knowledge. But could one maintain that such a knowledge had grasped the essence, the uniqueness, the depth of a person in its innermost self?

It would, in addition, be possible that the persons who are expressing themselves, and about whom one could make conclusions from their expressions about their selves and their natures, are misrepresenting themselves, that they are deceiving the one making the observations, that they are presenting themselves as something quite other than what they are. One can perhaps recognize that a person is doing that; but could one thereby also recognize what that person now is, in his/her own proper being and depth? This kind of knowledge is possible only when one can believe the person and believe in the person. In addition, we have to keep in mind that we are not talking here about knowledge of persons such as is possible to the professional psychologist, but knowledge of person in the everyday, average sense.

From all this we can conclude: the knowledge of person that comes from the external remains confined to the realm of external expression, and thus reveals nothing at all about the person itself. But if this knowledge wants to move beyond the external, and would like to understand and interpret the expressions as expressions of an inner, unique, and essential aspect of person, this presupposes that the person is giving himself to be known, that she is revealing herself in the manifold modes of her possibility, i.e., in expression and bearing, in work and deed, in gesture, but above all in word, in conversation. It is further presupposed that one can give credence to the person, and that the external corresponds to the internal from which it comes. In other words, persons themselves can be known as persons themselves and in their uniqueness only when they gives themselves to be known, when they reveal themselves. Persons can do this because they possess themselves, because they have the capacity to exist in and for themselves.

That persons show themselves in self-revelation is their own free decision and will; they can also close themselves off in silence. At the same time such self-revelation is an act of their readiness to open themselves, indeed—one must say—an act of their self-giving. They could also refuse to do this; they could dissemble or deceive.

I become part of this revelation of the person when I believe the person and believe in the person. The act of faith and the understanding in faith that is opened and laid before one corresponds to the revelation of the person. But this act too stands under the sign of freedom. I do not have to believe, but I can and may do so.

The Implications of Faith

What happens in the act of faith in the form of the "I believe in you—I believe you"? What is included in this? First and foremost: I confirm and value you, I acknowledge and affirm you, I love you. We believe because we love, says John Henry Newman. But what we are also saying—as becomes clear above all in the "I believe you"—is that we, in our acknowledging, gain access to the person. We have communion with it and take part in it and in its life, in its thinking, knowing, recognizing, and willing, and in the way in which it sees itself, and the world of things, and human beings. We take over the person who reveals him/herself to us and to whom we—believing and in faith—give ourselves.

Through the "I believe in you—I believe you" something new grows in me that I didn't have before, a new possibility, a new seeing and recognizing. I see with the eyes of another, and thereby, to a certain extent, something new comes into existence. I am grounded in another.

From this comes, in the realm of knowing, a with-one-another in the form of intersubjectivity; it is knowledge through communication.

With faith as encounter with the person and as mode of knowledge of the person, something further is given and expressed: The higher a person stands in human rank, the more does that person have to say and to give, and so much the more am I, for my knowledge of this person and for my encounter with it, dependent on its self-opening revelation and on its "I believe in you" and "I believe you." But it is also true that the more that happens, so much the more has this person a right and claim on my faith in this way. Thus, such a faith with its respective intensity and depth becomes a sign of the high estimation and an expression of the respect, honor, and reverence I have for the person in whom I believe and whom I believe. If I say to someone, I don't believe you, I don't believe one word of yours, this refusal is the strongest expression of a low estimation and disrespect, of offense and insult. Finally, the more deeply and the more uniquely I would like to have experience and knowledge of the person whom I revere, value, and love, the more am I dependent on that person's "I believe in you—I believe you." In this connection, one can make sense of what authority means as source and origin, and one can make sense of the dictum: Authority has to do not with subjection, but with recognition.[2]

Consequently, when faith is really understood and seen as it is in itself, nothing would be more wrong and inappropriate than to see in it only a lesser or unimportant kind of knowing, as if faith meant not to know, or only to half know, or to know only approximately, or only to surmise, or merely to have an opinion about something. Faith, in the form we are describing here, means *knowing* in the fullest meaning of the word. Faith, like love, makes one blind, but seeing. The knowledge made possible in faith has its fulfillment precisely where it concerns knowledge of the person. Without faith, persons and their world remain closed and inaccessible. But it is just as clear that faith, as a means of knowledge, has no place and no rights in the realm of the exact sciences, of mathematics, and of logic.

The modes of knowledge in all the realms and dimensions of the human are not hindered or limited by faith; they are instead led to new possibilities that would otherwise be closed to them. A rejection of faith in this sense is thus no liberation for knowledge but a loss of knowledge, or at least the lessening of the possibilities of knowledge, and precisely of those forms of knowledge that are vitally important and even of existential significance for human beings as persons and for their lives. No human being, and above all no community and society, can live humanly without faith.

2. Hans–Georg Gadamer, *Truth and Method,* trans. Joel Weinsheimer and Donald Marshall, 2nd ed. (New York: Crossroad, 1989) 277–85.

Affirmational (Propositional) Faith

Faith in the form of "I believe in you—I believe you" comes to fulfillment only when it is ready to accept its consequences, that is when the personal You-faith, the faith of trust, is unfolded and given shape in so-called affirmational faith. You-faith would not be fulfilled and brought to its full potential if affirmational faith were not recognized as part of it. This means: to believe someone and to believe something go together. The "I believe in you—I believe you" includes the individual, the concrete, and the definite, somewhat in the form: I believe what you say, what you promise, what you entrust to me, what you give me to believe.

Faith thus takes on that shape under which it is most often presented: It becomes the taking over of contents of quite definite and concrete form; it becomes affirmational faith. These affirmations—and this is decisive for faith—are not accessible to me, or at least not primarily through my own insight and experience. Instead, I take them over from, in, and whom I believe, on the basis of that person's witness, cognition, knowledge, and vision, and on the basis of the authority inherent in them. Through this taking over, there takes place that which we have already mentioned: I have community with him/her; I enter into the seeing, thinking, cognition, and knowledge of him whom I believe; I am taken up into the community of her spirit and heart. The other becomes the surety, the guarantee, and the witness for truth and cognition. From this it follows that if there were no one who had cognition, no one who saw, and knew, and who was ready to disclose this, there would also be no faith.

Through the coordination of affirmational faith with faith as trust, it turns out that faith in something, in propositions, in truths, is no longer an isolated, relationless and freely suspended act; it becomes rather grounded, borne, and encompassed by the Greater and the More Encompassing. It becomes grounded in the Person of the One in whom I believe.

Thus is disclosed the *fundamental structure of faith*. Its core is the trust, the affirmation, and recognition of the person, and the cognition that is manifested therein. Thereby and therein is also affirmed what comes from this person by way of individual proposition and expression: first and foremost as proposition of the person about itself, about its sentiment, about its intention, about its self. Person-related *affirmational faith* has its foundation in the *you-faith*. The affirmation, which has to do with the person involved, is affirmed because the person in whom I believe and whom I believe is affirmed.

I can also give my yes to affirmations that have to do not with the disclosure of the person itself, but with affirmations which the person makes, thus affirmations of a factual nature, and do this—in the first

instance—for the sake of the person, for the sake of the person's qualification and competence, on the basis, therefore, of authority. Thus begins the process of learning. But here one immediately sees the possibility, indeed the necessity, of freeing such affirmations from the person.
To accept in principle propositions of a factual nature only, completely
and always because of the person in whom and whom I believe, would
leave affirmational faith on the level of immaturity and would, on the
other hand, grant to the persons whom I believe a qualification or authority no longer appropriate to them.

The dependent child believes what its mother says for no other
reason than that she says it. But the fact that for the child there is no
other reason to hold something to be true—that precisely is what
constitutes its dependency. The human being can and should move
beyond this stage. This process of separation begins quite early;
it begins when the child starts asking, "Why?" Since proof from
authority is the weakest proof, as Thomas Aquinas says, human beings
should not accept factual propositions and knowledge of factual situations just from authority, even though the actual process of cognition
might have begun with authority. Human beings should cognitionally
appropriate something because, through a learning process which is
oriented to factual reality, they have gained an insight into and an
understanding of the factual situation confronting them.

At this point of the phenomenon of faith, of the intertwining of
you-faith and affirmational faith, of you-faith and that-faith, the
boundaries set for the human being in the inner-human realm become
clear. This clarification of boundaries does not, however, exclude but
includes, on the basis of this anthropological model, the attempt to
enter into an understanding of faith which encompasses faith in God
and in God's revelation. Why? Because, for the cognition of the person
as person, there is, through faith, a cognitional access for which faith
remains indispensable.

Faith in God is an act that is encountered not primarily in the relation subject-object, I-it, but in the relation I-You. God, the all-determining reality, cannot stand beneath the level of the personal to which be-
ing-self, spirit, self-possession, freedom, and love primarily belong.
Belief in God is primarily a personal act which is situated in the relation of I and You. It is therefore reasonable and appropriate to emphasize this perspective of faith. It is, in addition, to be surmised from the
outset that the content of a possible revelation of God has a whole lot
more to do with God and God's mystery, and remains inseparable from
God, than is the case with factual assertions of an empirical kind,
which are communicated from human beings and are accepted initially
in faith but then are separated from faith and become aspects of independent insight and knowledge on the part of the subject. The earlier

theological distinction between *credere in Deum/believe in God* (as personal faith), *credere Deo/have faith in God* (as ground of faith) and *credere Deum/believe God* (as expression for the content aspect of this faith) makes this differentiation both clear and vivid.

From what has been said so far we can conclude: The question of God and of a dependent orientation of the human being to God is not only a question of rational cognition but a concern of the whole human being.

Martin Buber, who in his book *Gottesfinsternis* [*The Darkness of God*] describes the "extinguishing of the light of heaven," the extinguishing of the reality of God in our time, says: The question of the reality of God will, for the individual human being, be decisively determined by whether the I-You relation takes its appropriate place next to the I-it relation in that individual's life without being absorbed by the I-it relation. *The question of God is not so much a question of capacity for cognition as it is of capacity for encounter.* The question of God, the infinite You, will awaken, according to Buber, when the encounter of I and You in the inner-human realm once again prevails, in the acts of inter-human faith and trust, of speaking and loving.[3]

Credibility

One important question still needs answering. Doesn't personal faith itself as inter-human encounter still need to be grounded? Can I, may I, affirm the other completely and unreservedly just as s/he is? Doesn't that mean that I affirm that person's limits, mistakes, and weaknesses? Doesn't that mean delivering myself thoughtlessly and unquestioningly to error and deception? Is faith grounded only in the rationally ungraspable freedom of human beings, in their even less rationally graspable sympathy and love for the You of the other person? Doesn't that place faith once again on an extremely shaky basis? Can not faith then turn into mere child's faith, into an irresponsible blind faith and a blind decision?

And further: Can my "I believe in you—I believe you" be said to anyone at all, even to those who do not know anything and have nothing to say, to those who misuse and mislead me, who deceive and blind me? Doesn't this threaten the end, even the perversion of all the knowing that is or can be included in faith—and with that the end of trust, love, encounter, and community? Even if we don't push the questions to the limit—are there not stages of faith, of personal faith?

This question must of course be answered affirmatively. It is precisely from this question that the thought naturally arises: It depends on those in whom I believe and to whom I give belief. It depends on whether those in whom and whom I believe, can or should themselves

3. M. Buber, *Werke I* (Munich—Heidelberg, 1962) 505–603.

believe, whether they themselves are worthy of belief and can be believed. My "I believe in you" presupposes the *credibility* of the one whom I believe, in whom I believe. But this credibility cannot, in principle, be itself believed; it must be known and recognized: *I must know the one whom I believe*; I must be acquainted with the one in whom I believe. The old proverb *"Trau, schau, wem*—trust, but check the credentials" expresses this connection clearly and pregnantly.

Those in whom I believe, those whom I believe, must be legitimized. They must be made believable, be made recognizable, and give themselves to be recognized as worthy of belief. Being worthy of belief belongs thus to the presuppositions of faith, just as being worthy of love belongs to the presuppositions of love. It is not a part of what the believer believes; it belongs rather to what the believer knows or at least must be able to know. If everything is supposed to be faith, there is no faith at all. The credibility of a person belongs to the conditions and presuppositions of faith/belief in that person.

How this "Trust, but check the credentials," that is, how this knowledge of credibility, is precisely constituted is not easy to say. This knowledge is in any case not a conceptual, abstract knowledge culminating in a definition, but a knowledge oriented to the concrete. It is also not a logical conclusion from evident premises, but a knowledge in the sense of a synoptic view of the whole which is all-inclusive, and takes into account and considers many signs and indicators. John Henry Newman dealt with this problem repeatedly, especially in his major work *An Essay in Aid of a Grammar of Assent.*[4] Assent is for him a description of faith. Newman spoke of argumentation as a *convergence of arguments* and attributed to it a special intellectual sense and faculty, the so-called "illative sense" which is not related to abstract concepts but looks to concrete experiences, individual facts, and individual observations. It is their convergence into knowledge which makes it possible to give and to justify that assent which is faith.

The argument from the convergence of data[5] is grounded in the fact that human beings have different kinds of experience and sources of experience, but are unable to grasp everything at once. The convergence of proofs is dependent on the working together of several elements and factors. An individual phenomenon is not enough to come to a knowledge of the "real" in this area. Yet this process brings about that security which is as necessary as it is sufficient for our concrete life and decisions. We undertake this operation, e.g., in our decisions about a vocation or for the lifelong joining with another human being in matrimony, for important decisions in political, juridical, and especially ethical questions. The doctor, the judge, the politician, the pastor—they are

4. C.f. H. Fries, *Die Religionsphilosophie Newmans* (Stuttgart, 1948).
5. Karl Rahner and H. Vorgrimler, "Argument of Convergence," *DT* (1981) 26–27.

all dependent on "convergence of data" and cannot do their job without it. As Newman explains it: "What I mean can be best illustrated by a cable that is assembled from a number of wires, each of which is weak, but together are a strong as a rod of iron."[6] A rod of iron embodies, in his view, mathematical or strict demonstration; a cable represents the non-mathematical, the so-called moral demonstration and the moral certitude—i.e., necessary and sufficient for action—that comes from it. He adds the important bit of experiential wisdom: If we required a mathematical or logically stringent proof for all decisions, we would never get to do anything, never come to a decision. To this law we must also add: it makes no sense to want to do everything *more geometrico*—in a geometrical way."

Regarding this knowledge of credibility, it must be emphasized that it cannot be forced. "There may well be cogent arguments for the credibility of a human being, but no argument can force us to accept it. It stands in the horizon of freedom and will: *Nemo credit nisi volens*—no one believes unwillingly."[7]

The "I believe in you—I believe you" thus presupposes the credibility and the proof of the credibility of the one whom I believe; the "*trau*—trust" is conditioned by the "*schau, wem*—check the credentials." But while this proof is provided as it always is, in the faith-preceding and faith-conditioning knowledge of credibility, we also find that the space is opened and the condition created for the possibilities and for the realization of my "I believe in you—I believe you."

This proof of credibility is also the reason why there are levels and degrees of personal faith. It is due to the differences between persons and the differences between their respective qualifications and competence, which come to light in the proof of credibility. This knowledge of credibility also grounds the fact that my "I believe in you—I believe you," has limitations. These limitations are also due to individual persons; for not everything that comes from an individual person is taken over and accepted in faith, but only those things in which the person is specifically qualified and proven to be credible. The knowledge of credibility that precedes faith can also be the very reason belief is not achieved, or cannot be achieved, why belief must be refused. That would be because the one whom I know or have come to know does not deserve belief.

---

6. John Henry Newman, "Briefe und Tagebuchauszeichnungen aus der katholoschen Zeit seines Lebens," in: *Ausgewählte Schriften*, ed. M. Laros and W. Becker, Bd. II and III (Mainz, 1957), 378; On this theme, prominent in Newman's *Grammar of Assent* and numerous other works, see Thomas J. Norris, *Newman and His Theological Method* (Leiden: Brill, 1977) 19–22.

7. Pieper, *Belief and Faith A Philosophical Tract*, 25–26.

The Transcending Dimension

From this previous knowledge of the person, which precedes belief as its condition and presupposition, something extraordinarily important becomes clear: The complete, unlimited, and absolutely perfect exercise of faith is neither possible nor permissible in the realm of human existence and action. The very knowledge of credibility makes one aware of the weaknesses, imperfections, and limitations inherent in humanity both in general and in particular, which prevent human beings from carrying out in the act of belief what they want and are striving for: an "I believe in you—I believe you" that is complete and without limitation.

Wherever, in the relationship of human being to human being, belief is demanded or given in the radical, extreme, unlimited sense, something inhuman is taking place, something that is reconcilable neither with the limitedness nor with the dignity of the human being. For no mature human being is by nature so inferior or superior to another that one can stand over against the other as an absolutely valid authority.

This means that faith in the full and unlimited sense is possible only on the condition that "there is someone who stands incomparably higher than mature human beings as they stand over the immature, and that this Someone has spoken in a way that is understandable to human beings."[8] Thus belief, which is so much a part of human beings and their intersubjectivity, in both its fundamental structure and its finality points beyond human beings. This is not because they construct an artificial superstructure, but because they take themselves seriously. This gives us a starting point and a kind of mediation for our reflection on faith/belief in the theological sense .

Naturally, such considerations neither prove or even sufficiently indicate that God exists as the infinite You, nor that God does reveal and has revealed Godself to human beings. But it is affirmed, and that is important enough, that in human beings themselves, in the fundamental living out of faith/belief as a personal act, as an act of encounter and trust, there is already a presupposition, a condition of the possibility of faith in God and God's possible revelation. This is because faith points beyond every finite You, because faith, in its radical execution, cannot be infinitely fulfilled. Of course, the presupposition for a reality is not the reality itself; the awaited or hoped-for is not the fulfillment. But without expectation and hope there can be no fulfillment, any more than there can be an answer without a question.

The "I believe in you—I believe you," related to the You of God and to a possible revelation of God, would not in any case be something

8. Ibid. 23–24.

alienating to human beings; it would, rather, represent their highest fulfillment, insofar as encounter, trust, faith, and love, which transcend the human, belong to the human.

Such an indication is no proof of facticity but a dismantling of fences and barriers that often, especially nowadays are obstructions to faith and its full and genuine understanding. It is a positive preparation for the horizon of questions for which a possible revelation on the part of God comes into question.

§2

FAITH IN THE HORIZON OF THE QUESTION OF MEANING

The purpose of this theme is to work out a further access to faith in the theological sense. This is done under the conviction that, for theological faith, personal faith is insufficient, however important and broadly inclusive it may be. For while personal faith is of vital importance for the inner-personal and inter-human sphere, it is so only for those immediately affected by it. Faith thus understood is limited in its sphere of application; it is privatized, so to speak, into just the "I and You," however much it would like to spread out into the sphere of persons. But if faith in the theological sense applies to all human beings, which we do presuppose, and if, beyond that, it makes a public claim, if it is supposed to have a relationship to the whole of reality and to the whole experience of reality, then yet another dimension of faith than just the personal-dialogical must be brought into play.

There is a further important consideration: In the inner-human realm, the personal thrust as encounter of I and You may seem limited— although this need not mean a closing off—but can be an opening to the greater and to the whole. For the personal concretization does not exclude but includes the possibility of a comprehensive universality. This is true especially in the relationship between the human being and God. For human beings, all human beings, are dependently oriented totally to God, totally to the infinite You as the all (including themselves)-determining reality. God is the infinite You for every human being; and God would not be that if God were only my God, the *"je meinige Gott*—God just for me" (K. Jaspers). What is specific for belief in God lies in the fact that, in contrast with the human sphere, the personal is connected with the whole and the whole with the personal.

It is nevertheless correct and appropriate also to bring expressly into play and to articulate the other anthropological specification of faith, that dimension that is connected with the word *Sinn*—sense.[1]

---

1. On this theme: R. Lauth, *Die Frage nach dem Sinn des Daseins,* (Munich, 1953); B. Welte, *Auf der Spur des Ewigen* (Freiburg—Basel—Vienna, 1963); H. Gollwitzer, *Krummes*

This brings in the whole of reality, also the whole of human existence. *Sinn* (*sense/meaning*)—which will be further explained—has to do with the whole. God, who as "You" is encountered in faith and as "You" is spoken to in the language of faith, in prayer, is both the all-determinative and the *sense/meaning*-giving reality. Thus the question of *sense/meaning* (*Sinn*) becomes an important context for understanding faith.

The Meaning of "Sinn" (Sense/Meaning)

First we will attempt a description of *sense/meaning*. When one looks at the German word [*Sinn*], *sense* belongs together with "path" or "journey," and it signifies the direction of the "whither" and the "what for," the goal of a journey—as, for example, is also suggested by the related French word, *sentier*. *Sense* is originally the determination of direction in an all-encompassing system of relationship, and thus the ordering of the individual to the whole, in and with an obvious connection. We talk of *meaning* in this sense when something is "just right," when we ascertain that it is good this way, that something is turning out the way it should. *Sense* is thus the agreement between what is and what really should be. I find *meaning* when something works out well and successfully, when an awareness of the sense and interconnectedness of things illuminates my mind and fills my heart with joy. I find *meaning* when I can say, so to speak, Yes and Amen to what is, to what I encounter, to what I do: as confirmation and agreement, as peace, as happiness, as fulfillment and joy.

Sense is connected with the experience of being healthy and whole, with the true reality of human beings in and with their world. The often-described and often-reproached, but secretly longed-for whole and healthy world ("*heile Welt*") would be the world that is filled

---

Holz—aufrechter Gang. Zur Frage nach dem Sinn des Lebens (Munich, 1970); Walter Kasper, *Möglichkeiten der Gotteserfahrung heute, in: Glaube und Geschichte* (Mainz, 1970) 120–43; P. L. Berger, *A Rumor of Angels: Modern Society and the Rediscovery of the Supernatural* (Garden City, N.Y.: Double Day, 1969); Viktor Frankl, *Der Mensch auf der Suche nach dem Sinn* (Freiburg—Basel—Vienna, 1972); *Man's Search for Meaning: An Introduction to Logotherapy* (Boston: Beacon Press, 1962); Heinrich Fries, "Gott und der Sinn des Lebens" in: Heinrich Fries (ed.) *Gott—die Frage unserer Zeit* (Munich, 1973) 160–70 (Conference Papers); A Paus, ed., *Suche nach Sinn—Suche nach Gott*, (Graz—Vienna—Köln 1978); Hans Küng, *Does God Exist?: An Answer For Today* (Garden City, N.Y.: Double Day, 1980); R. Spaemann—R. Loew, *Die Frage Wozu?* (Munich, 1981); *Nichttheologische Texte zur Gottesfrage im 20. Jahrhundert. Mit einer Einleitung von L. Kolakowski* (Berlin, 1981); H. Döring—F. X. Kaufmann, "Kontingenzerfahrung und sinnfrage," in: *Christlicher Glaube in moderner Gesellschaft* IX (1982) 7–67; Karl Rahner, "The Question of Meaning as a Question of God," *Theological Investigations* 21.196–207 (New York, 1988); Wolfhart Pannenberg, *Anthropology in a Theological Perspective*, trans. Matthew J. O'Connell (Philadelphia: The Westminster Press, 1985).

with *meaning* and that is revealed in its quality of being filled with *meaning*.

Experiences of Sense/Meaning (Sinn)

Sense/meaning is experienced in the moments of success and good fortune. Expressions of this experience of sense are an answer that has been found; insight and knowledge that has been gained; a hope fulfilled; a good deed; a perfect piece of work; a goal reached; a deep, understanding, self-squandering and thereby self-winning love; a forgiveness given; but just as much also the experience of the beautiful in nature and art.

But the question of meaning is concretely and primarily encountered much more frequently and even more intensively by negative experiences: there where sense seems to be concealed, disturbed, or broken; in the experiences of unhappiness in its various forms and shapes; in pain and suffering, in loss, in plans gone awry, in failing to reach one's goal, in the destruction of life's work, in the unhappiness of innocent suffering. Here we experience the absence of meaning, senselessness/ meaninglessness, because we cannot make sense of what has happened, because what has happened cuts across our thinking and our concepts, the causal and correlational schemata we have of ourselves, of human beings, and of the world. These formulations of questions are articulated in the questions: "Why? Why must I . . . ? Why me? That we find or receive no answer constitutes the experience of the senseless.

The question of meaning also becomes particularly acute when we meet human beings who have been, as the expression goes, "written off": human beings and human destinies that are, so to speak, explained and legitimated by no achievement, by no work, by nothing useful. These are the seriously incapacitated, the ones who cannot care for themselves, the incurably ill, the intellectually extinguished, where no sensible "What for" that makes any sense to the reason can be detected.

There is still another experience of senselessness as the deprivation of meaning or as the absence of sense in the form of satiety, boredom, revulsion. Along with the other signs of prosperity, this can be one of the byproducts of technical civilization: human beings unfulfilled because their existence remains without happiness and excitement, without depth, without center. It is the fate of human beings who don't know what to do with themselves, who do their thing and perform their job without becoming part of it, without inner relation to the whole or even to themselves, who, as they say, live carefree lives, who while away time, who, according to a well-known saying of Pascal, couldn't stand to be alone in a room. This is what, in the, mind of this philosopher, constitutes the unhappiness of human beings.[2] It is the situation of human beings who are consumed in pure superficiality, indifference, or bustling about, or in constant flight from themselves into activities, into numerous "diversionary maneuvers," or into the consciousness-extinguishing and illusion-producing world of drugs, which results only in a more wretched disillusionment. The symbol of this experience and condition is yawning boredom and, often enough, the ending-of-it-all in the form of suicide. For, as the reports often say: it's all senseless. The experience of meaninglessness as "existential vacuum" is numbered among the principal causes of neurosis. Viktor Frankl has pointed this out emphatically, and, in contrast to S. Freud and C. G. Jung, but with A. Adler as well, he spoke of *noogenen neuroses—noogenous neuroses*" and turned them into a field of penetrating diagnosis and therapy.

The most extreme form of meaning-experience in the negative sense is the experience of death—not that death which is the end of a mature life that has been satisfied with life, a so-called natural death, or as the end of an incurable disease, which is the experience of death as redemption (wherein the problem of incurable disease still remains the problem of death as radical departure from everything), but the unexpected death, the death that snuffs out a young, blossoming life and all the expectations connected with it, the death that makes parents look into the grave of their child, the death that robs children of their mother, the death which in war, in extermination camps, in the form of crime and brutality. This death is the end of everything, the end of expectations, of hopes, of life's dreams. Dust and ashes are the surviving remains of a life that struggled with all its might against death, that drove death from consciousness, kept it at a distance, and didn't want to admit its existence.

In the face of death, said the Second Vatican Council:

The riddle of human existence is at its strongest. Human beings experience not only the pain and the progressive breaking down of the body, but also, and even more, the fear of everlasting extinction. But they are judging correctly in the instinct of their heart when they reject with revulsion the complete destruction and final ruin of their person. The kernel of eternity in human beings cannot be reduced to mere matter and struggles against death. But all the precautions of technology, however useful, are unable to assuage human anxiety. The temporal extension of biological life is unable to satisfy that longing for a further life which lives unconquerably in the human heart.[3]

Our experiences of sense/meaning, seen positively and negatively, are, however, not just soberly rational observations. They are, rather, connected with a vivid longing and a passionate emotion. Our articulation of this is at first negative: we sense that the irrational and the

2. Pensées No. 184.
3. Pastoral Constitution on the Church in the Modern World (*Gaudium et Spes*) no. 18.

meaningless, that, above all, evil, hate and injustice, egoism and brutality, the might of the stronger, and even death, cannot be allowed the final victory. We sense that the conquering of all these darknesses and our "longing after the totally Other"[4] is not just utopian longing. And there is also the readiness not to let it remain with mere wishes, but to resist injustice and help tear down the power of evil piece.

We have the hope—and that is part of our experience of meaning—that the piercing questions will find an answer, the torturing doubts a solution, that anxiety will disappear in a sense of security, that we will no longer suffer and be consumed by our defects and lack of so many things—and that eventually the unsolved question of meaning will be answered. But we also have the hope that love does not die, that true life is still to come.

We have a variegated experience of *sense* in the form of the experience of negativity and meaninglessness. Those who reject the question of meaning as irrelevant also use the term senselessness or meaninglessness. But whoever speaks about senselessness always presupposes a certain knowledge and understanding, a preunderstanding of meaning from which sense lessness is set apart or distinguished as the contrast or opposite of meaning. Otherwise one wouldn't be able to speak of senselessness.

Those who explain: Everything is senseless; those who see in this a legitimate, eloquent, and even sensible statement, have no easy task of it in grounding their decision for non-meaning as the fundamental option of their life, in making non-sense that which gives meaning to the world, to history, to life, and in professing allegiance to this [non] meaning. Whoever explains: Everything is non-sense, is unable to explain why human beings fight against senselessness in all forms, shapes, and manifestations, why they attempt to overcome it and are unwilling to concede, especially to it, the last word or final victory. This means that the in-tune comes before the out-of-tune [Der klang kommt vor dem Mißklang (Th. Haecker)], the Yes comes as preliminary sign before the No, the No is borne by a Yes, not vice versa.

How Is It That Human Beings Have an Experience of Sense/Meaning ?

The answer lies in the specific human characteristic of *openness to the world*. Human beings are not like animals fitted into an already established environment ordered to them, in which they move in the security of instinct. On the contrary, the human being is, as they say,[5] a

---

4. M. Horkheimer, "Die Sehnsucht nach dem ganz Anderen." An interview with commentary by H. Gummnior (Hamburg, 1975).

5. A. Gehlen, *Der Mensch. Seine Natur und seine Stellung in der Welt*, 12th ed. (Bonn, 1978); W. Pannenberg, *Anthropology in Theological Perspective*.

"biologically defective being," poorly equipped and in need of many artificial limbs. But the world of human beings is not the "environment"
but the world as a whole. The human being is open to the world as a
whole as a questioning, thinking, shaping, planning being. What human beings lack biologically and in instinct, they more than make up
for by intellect and freedom, by spirit and will. In that way the human
becomes, in a certain sense, everything: "*Homo quodammodo est omnia.*"
In their capacity of knowing, human beings appropriate the world,
make this knowledge serviceable, and, shaping and changing, intervene in the world. They turn the world they find into their own world,
a world which serves them, and for which they are responsible.

Their questioning cognition does not allow human beings to be satisfied with information about this or that, to be content with the factual
or with what happens to be, and simply to acknowledge, affirm, and
legitimate what is there, what happens to be the case in any situation,
particular or general. Human beings want to know the whole, they
want to see through to connections, they want to get behind things. In so
doing they repeatedly come to know that their thinking, as also their
willing and their longing, finds no satisfaction in individual things,
that every answer is the beginning of a new question, that every finished work lays the foundation for a new one, that every goal achieved
becomes a point of transfer to new goals, that every successful encounter
holds open the longing for the totally Other, that the quest of human
beings for meaning is a quest for the whole as its ground in the limitlessly open human spirit which documents its limitlessness in its questioning.

That human beings articulate and specify the question of meaning
in this way, that they protest against evil, against letting hate, violence, and injustice have the last word, that they want the victory of
the good and the triumph of justice, which has its ground in the conscience of human beings and in the determination of their will by the
good. The good as such, unconditioned and in itself, is the horizon
within which the human being does the individual good. And every
individual good deed points to the good as such. The question of meaning in human beings is determined by spirit and conscience; that is
where it is grounded.

Bernhard Welte has this situation, this *"condition humaine,"* and
these unavoidable consequences of the "sense/meaning postulate—
Sinnpostulat" of existence in mind when he speaks. Our existence as
such presupposes sense/meaning, even demands it, without needing an
explicit act to do so. Take away this presupposition and human existence is done in. This is clearly recognizable in the negative mirror image. Welte asks: If everything should fall into nothingness, if every-

thing should one day turn into an endless nothing, would then those immanent fulfillments of meaning be really and truly relevant?

[Do] then, e.g., love and fidelity, still really have any meaning? Can one then still seriously maintain the distinction between justice and injustice, between truth and falsehood, between freedom and servitude? To what does it all lead when important and pure human beings dedicate their lives in service to the sick or in the selfless service of freedom and justice? To nothing? Analogous questions are raised even more sharply on the basis of negative experiences and situations. May one think that the suffering of the innocent is senseless? May one and can one think that the great questions which both Dostoyevski and Camus have asked with regard to suffering have no answer? If everything, sooner or later, is finally nothing, then they really have no answer. And then the short-term answers are no help either. The prophesied future paradise is no authentic solution to the problem. For if only the final generation can enter into paradise and all preceding ones are given given over to nothingness, and then if—something we all need to think about—even this prophesied future paradise is also surrendered to nothingness: where does it all lead: to nothingness? If everything, bad as well as good, happiness as well as unhappiness, is finally be thrown indifferently onto the scrap heap of nothingness and there left to rot forever, does it really still make sense/meaning to commit oneself to truth and justice rather than to falsity and injustice? To commit oneself to the happiness of human beings rather than indifferently to accept their unhappiness? Nothingness, understood and interpreted as futile nothingness, puts an absolutely fundamental question mark before all meaning and thereby before every ethical attitude of human beings. There is no real way to evade this consequence. But human beings, fortunately, do repeatedly evade it. They seem to be protected from the final consequence by an ineradicable ethical instinct. But our job is precisely to look this final consequence fearlessly in the eye. If everything is absolutely and forever surrendered to nothingness, and this is only an empty nothingness, then all this truly makes no real sense.

But this solution is unbearable; it must not be be accepted. The sense-postulate of our human and interhuman existence stands in direct contradiction to it. This postulate, if one will only look it in the eye concretely enough, is indispensable. It becomes a fundamental ethical postulate. It can be expressed in the sentence: Everything has meaning. For one may not give up the distinction between good and evil. It must be firmly held that love makes sense. That the fight for freedom and justice makes sense. That the pain of the sufferer makes sense. The indispensable fundamental ethical postulate must be held valid against the absolute threat from the total and universal meaninglessness which comes from clinging to the consequences of the experience of nothingness.[6]

In this context the matter of *faith* surfaces: as option, as *decision of the whole human being for the whole of his/her life*. This decision does not take place groundlessly, but it is more than the considerable sum of the possible grounds; it is a Yes spoken in reason, freedom and courage. In the context of the totality of existence, world, and history, this decision is not the result of an exact scientific investigation made with logical cogency and irrefutable proofs. It is rather an act of faith of the human being: an act of which everyone is capable and to which

6. B. Welte, "Versuch zur Frage nach Gott" in: *Zeit und Geschichte* (Freiburg—Basel—Vienna, 1976) 124–39, here 135–36.

everyone is called, an act that necessarily concerns everyone, an act that even they perform who deny that they have faith. Even those who do not decide have thereby and therein made a decision, even if the worst of all: the decision for the non-committal, the decision of the one who wants to catch a hundred hares, but catches none.

The Question of the Giver of Sense/Meaning

We now go a step further and ask: Do we ourselves give meaning to our action, to our life, and, beyond that, to things, to happenings, events and reality? Or do we receive that meaning, receive it because it exists, because something makes sense?

Doubtless we give our action meaning when we put it at the service of a plan, when we place it within the total horizon of life, when we take what is individual, put it in some sort of ordered context, and seek to make it real as part of a whole. With these observations, however, we are already recognizing that plans and goals, horizon and context, and what we mean by "the whole," are in no way made and produced by us. We find this "whole" already there, it is "given" to us, we receive it. This moment of determining the sense becomes still more obviously recognizable in other experiences of meaning: in the experience of love, of friendship, of forgiveness, of recognition. Here is where meaning becomes illuminated, and that brings about peace, joy, harmony, and happiness. But none of that—peace, friendship, forgiveness, recognition—is made by us; nor can we force it to come. We receive it, it is imparted to us, given. Certainly we ourselves can be for others the ones who give, and who thereby bestow meaning; but the principal characteristic of the experience of meaning reads: Receiving comes before doing, being comes before having (E. Fromm).[7]

That we are not the real givers of meaning, however much we try to be, even with partial success in some instances, is also clear from the fact that we don't have before us the whole, which is what the question of meaning and the answer it requires are all about. We don't have the whole in view; we don't control it, neither the whole of the world, nor that of history, nor the whole of our life. We entrust ourselves to a making sense that doesn't come from us. The same state of affairs is demonstrated in the fact that every answer generates a new question, because in our cognition and questioning we cannot take in the whole of reality; it is always greater than our finite thinking and comprehending. We likewise experience that we often fail in our attempts to make sense of specific experiences and events, that we sometimes even fail to know and recognize any meaning, that we, with every attempt at an an-

---

7. E. Fromm, *Haben oder Sein. Die seelischen Grundlagen einer neuen Gesellschaft*, 4th ed. (Stuttgart, 1977).

swer to our question, can react allergically or with outrage, like the friends of Job.

The fact that, in the question of meaning, receiving comes before doing, is shown by the fact that, when things go well for us and we are successful, that is also of course our doing; however, we experience it predominantly as gift, as dispensation. The "Thank God!" expressed a thousand times and in all possible situations in life is perhaps a worn and thoughtless usage, but still an important indication that thinking in all forms is connected with thanking, and thanking with thinking. How little we ourselves and from ourselves are the ones who give and make sense can be seen in our inability to illuminate or counterbalance the negation of meaning which we come to know in misfortune, sickness, suffering, and death—however much we can provide meaning, help, alleviation, and prophylaxis in particular things—and that is more true today than it used to be. But more sources and fields of meaning-denial are arising. The water-mark of finiteness, the dissonances, the lack of fulfillment, the unanswered questions: "Why? Why me?" remain. Even the most beautiful theories—those, for example, like Leibnitz's theodicy, or that infer meaning from the signs of light and darkness—are no help. On the contrary, they only sharpen the question.

Further, when we attempt to create a better, more just and more free world, we ourselves often stand under conditions of injustice and violence. The great powers arm themselves in order to prevent the terrors of war. We don't break out of this vicious circle of violence and counter-violence, of injustice and revenge. We can't step beyond the borders of the senseless or meaning-negated.

And yet, strangely enough, despite all negative experience, despite failure and defeat, we start again; we begin again with life, with time, with the future; we create hope that life will go on, even begin anew; we believe that the mother can console her child without deception but full of confidence: Don't be afraid, it's going to be alright.[8]

How does the mother know that? She knows it out of an invincible and constantly renewed *primeval trust in the goodness of the whole*, in its sense, even if she cannot prove it mathematically. Mother and child live from this. It is not based on any "lie of love." This describes the situation of human beings. The truth of their trust in the meaning of the whole lies in the testing carried out and proven to be true in life. This is something different from and more than a mathematical or logical formula, for one cannot live, persevere, and face suffering and death with that. It isn't true what Max Frisch says: "Mathematics is enough for me." No, it isn't enough for him either. Viktor Frankl wrote a book about his time in a concentration camp entitled *"Trotzdem Ja zum Leben sagen! Ein Psychologe erlebt das Konzentrationslager* [Despite Every-

8. P. L. Berger, *A Rumor of Angels.*

thing, Say Yes to Life: the Experience of a Psychologist in a Concentration Camp]."[9] This book went through fifty editions in America and first appeared in German in 1977—although without much acclaim. Documents like this are important and revelatory. We have here a desperately serious case of searching for meaning, not a theoretical mind game. Frankl writes:

> While the worry of most prisoners focused on the question: Will we survive the camp? Because if not, all this suffering will have made no sense—the question that troubled me was quite different: Does all this suffering and dying make any sense for us? If not, then ultimately it wouldn't make any sense at all to survive the camp. For a life whose meaning stands and falls by whether one escapes from it or not, a life, therefore, whose meaning depends on the grace of such an accident, such a life really wouldn't be worth having lived at all.[10]

Two other sentences from this book seem to me to be important. One of them is a quotation from Nietzsche: "He who has a Why for [his] life bears up under almost any How," and: "It is not really all that important what we still have to expect from life, but rather, what life expects of us. Not life in general, but the way life, in various concrete situations, demands a concrete answer from us. Our concern was for the meaning of life in that totality which also included death, and thus accepted responsibility not only for the meaning of life but also for the meaning of suffering and dying—it was about this meaning that we struggled."[11] In other words: Life makes has meaning only if it makes sense together with death.

In these phrases and what stands behind them, as well as in the words of the mother to her child: "Everything will turn out alright," one can see that the space of the presently experienced and the horizon of the factual and the human is being transcended, that a reality with the dimension of a totality is being opened up, which *transcends the measure of the human*, the measure of human possibilities and human achievement. For a human being, of his/her own power, has no disposition over a totality that includes life, suffering, and death, and neither does humanity. An absolute primordial trust is, for human beings, neither possible nor admissible.

As Wolfhart Pannenberg says,

> Although this basic trust is directed to the nearest relational persons, by its unrestrictedness it is implicitly but always directed beyond mother and parents to an instance which can justify the limitlessness of such trust. This instance must measure up to the unique unrestrictedness of the basic trust.[12]

9. Munich, 1977, ET: *Man's Search for Meaning; An Introduction to Logotherapy.*
10. Ibid. 117.
11. Cf. Ibid. This is Fries's approximate rendition of what Frankl wrote on pp. 76–77.
12. W. Pannenberg, *Anthropology in Theological Perspective* 233.

Here the borders of the human are qualitatively transcended; there comes into view here a reality that has to do with encompassing totality, with wholeness, which can give a context and a meaning to all things in life and death, something we ourselves cannot create, but which can be given us, which we can receive. To rely on this is what it means to believe.

It is from this new and totally Other reality that human beings live, those who ask and seek for meaning, those who cannot live, suffer, and die as human beings without letting themselves be shaped by the meaning of life. It is living from a meaning which encompasses the boundless totality—of which historically living, finite human beings are not capable—of all reality. It is living from a meaning which human beings cannot generate, but can only receive and accept in order to help them through their finite life. If one is talking about meaning in this sense, then it is pointing as source and ground to a reality which is the *all-determining reality*. This "all-determining reality," is a paraphrase of what is meant by the word *God*.

Corresponding to the limitlessness of the basic trust which, beyond the mother as its primary object, points to God, is its relationship to the wholeness of the self. The basic trust is oriented, in its own proper sense or meaning to that instance which can protect and support the self in its wholeness. Thus, in the actual living out of basic trust, *God and salvation* stand in the closest possible relationship.[13]

Let us return to the beginning of this reflection: faith in the horizon of the question of meaning. Faith is the way in which human beings relate themselves to the questions of the whole of their life and of reality, how they see them, how they answer them. One can of course reject these questions as theoretical and intellectually irrelevant, as positivism does, but in praxis it is impossible to escape them. Every person lives, consciously or unconsciously, admittedly or inadmittedly, out of some kind of comprehensive view of existence. But these questions can't be answered in the manner of individual problems. The one Whole [Totality] cannot be encompassed in the same way as the individual. It encompasses all questions, and so we cannot objectify it; it encompasses us also. Where one is dealing with the decisions and basic questions of life, with sense or non-sense, hope or desperation, where the basic option and the fundamental orientation of our life are in play, there all exact knowledge of individual reality ceases, there everyone believes, even the one who does not use the word faith, even the one who denies faith. Even unbelief is a basic decision which, because of its option for the Whole, is different from exact knowledge of individual reality— that holds for science too—and cannot be simply covered by that kind of

13. Ibid. 234.

knowledge. On this level one is dealing not with knowledge or faith but with forms and modes of faith.

Faith in the horizon of the question of *sense/meaning* produces a very important context for the text of faith in the theological sense, for faith in God in which the personal and the universal, the infinite You and the ground of all reality come together.

§3

PHILOSOPHICAL FAITH

In order to come to the problem of faith in the theological sense, the overall context requires us to say something about the phenomenon of philosophical faith, i.e., about the fact that faith is also encountered in the philosophical realm, not, to be sure, in contradiction to philosophy but in its horizon. This mode of reflection will also illustrate and strengthen the idea that faith does not stand under the sign of a deficient phenomenon, because it is measured by a quite different, apparently superior, standard.

As models for philosophical faith we can mention philosophical faith in Kant and the philosophical faith of Karl Jaspers.

Immanuel Kant (1724-1804)

Kant belongs among the great figures in the history of philosophy. His insights and cognitions are decisive for philosophy to this day. "After Kant," goes the popular adage, "there is no going back."

Reminiscent of Copernicus, Kant himself speaks of the "turn" that was introduced by his philosophy, which stands so prominently under the sign of the critique of reason. On the basis of the model of natural science in modernity, he showed that the investigator does not simply take note of individual observations in nature and describe individual processes in it. Modern science has, according to Kant, become possible in that nature is forced—by repeated experiment—to align itself according to the questions and presuppositions in the subject of the investigator. Investigators approaches their investigation of nature not with the attitude of questioning and learning students, but with that of judges who force the witnesses, i.e., nature, to answer the questions which they put to it.[1]

---

1. See Immanuel Kant, *Kritik der reinen Vernunft* [*Critique of Pure Reason*]. Vorrede zur zweiten Auflage, ed. R. Schmidt, Ausgabe Meiner (Leipzig, 1930) 17–21.

The result is knowledge of the natural laws, presented in mathematical concepts, which wants to know not what nature is according to its essence, but how it works, and which verifies its knowledge by the clear reckonings and predictions and practical-technical applications of its processes that can be made.

This characterizes the fundamental thrust of Kant's "Copernican turn": the turn to the subject and the orientation to it. Cognition is, accordingly, not the copy or image of an objectively ordered reality; cognition is also not the agreement of thought and thing. Cognition is rather the possibility, produced by the subject and the subject's capability, of seeing reality objectively, of ordering, synthesizing, and thereby knowing it. Thus, cognition in the proper sense is possible only where there is an experience mediated through meaning which, through the intuitive forms of space and time, is brought to perception and conception, which is then ordered to cognition through the categories of understanding. Hence the axiom: concepts without intuition are empty, intuitions without concepts are blind.[2] Generality and necessity in cognition—that is, knowledge—are not impeded by the turn to the subject, but are made initially possible. For the subject (and its function) is the subject of all knowing human beings, it is the being of the knowing spirit. Kant speaks accordingly of the transcendental subject. It becomes clear from this that world and thing are recognized/known and determined/specified in the way in which they "appear/seem" to us.

The second meaning of transcendentality in Kantian thinking refers the ability of the subject and the capacities of the understanding prior to any perception and cognition; in other words, the aprioristic specification.

For a long time Kant and his philosophy were seen as the great adversary and the antipodes of what, in fact, theological faith was about, especially the specifically Catholic understanding of faith. For reasons we will not pursue here, but apparently because of his turn to the subject and because of his critique of reason, Kant was called the philosopher of Protestantism. But this is not an accurate characterization. Catholic theology and apologetics saw Kant as the "Alleszermalmer—he who smashes everything," because he undermined faith in God by his critique of the traditional proofs for the existence of God. Against this view, one has to agree with Gottlieb Söhngen:

If the theology of today has not yet finished working out its inner relationship with Kant the way theology previously did with Plato and Aristotle, that should be blamed less on Kant than on the fact that the generation of theologians of today no longer seem to be of the kind that is strong in faith and in science

2. Ibid. 95.

as were the theological generations of Origen, Augustine, Anselm, Albert, and Thomas of Aquinas.[3]

Against a one-sidedly negative perspective, we should remember that the *God question* comes up in Kant in other contexts. This is best seen by naming the questions that Kant himself formulated as the fundamental questions of philosophy:

What can I know?
What should I do?
For what may I hope?[4]

The God question cannot, according to Kant, be answered positively in connection with the question: "What can I know?" For, according to his presuppositions and conditions, true human cognition is, strictly speaking—as necessary and generally valid cognition—found only in natural science and mathematics in the specifically modern sense of these words. For only there, according to Kant, are found the conditions necessary for knowledge and cognition: experience, intuition mediated by the senses, and the conceptuality fashioned by the categories of the mind.

If, according to Kant, there is cognition only under these conditions—if thus no cognition beyond our experience is possible—then it is clear that there can be no cognition of God, *no proof of the existence of God* in the strict sense.

But this critique of pure reason is only the answer to the first question: What can I know? The other questions remain open: What should I do? For what may I hope? What is the human being? They are proclaimed in the famous words of Kant from the Foreword of the second edition of the *Critique of Pure Reason:* "I had to get rid of knowledge in order to make room for faith."[5] This means: because God cannot be known in the sense of theoretical reason, the matter of faith is not done away with, but—on the contrary—opened; it must be thought out anew. Kant expressly emphasizes that the fact that the theoretical reason cannot know God does not say that the reality of God as "highest Being and foundation of everything" does not exist. Theoretically, the inability to prove God by no means confers the right to deny God. Kant intends by his critique to bar the way to dogmatic atheism.

The other way to make sure of the reality of God and to gain access to it for human beings is what Kant called *practical reason,* which comes into play with the question: What should I do? which is actualized in the practical, above all, in the moral action of human beings. In

3. G. Söhngen, "Die Theologie im Streit der Fakultäten" in: *Die Einheit in der Theologie* (Munich, 1952) 12.
4. I. Kant, *Critique of Pure Reason* 635.
5. Ibid. 29.

the moral action of human beings, something unconditioned and absolute, according to Kant, makes its appearance. Kant calls it the *categorical imperative,* which makes apodictic claims and imposes obligations on human beings, and of which they are certain. It is a law of action residing in human beings which affirms the will as the absolute law of their being. Kant says of it: It contains a determination of the will which is unavoidable and forces itself on us, although it doesn't rest on empirical principles.

The imperative is called categorical in distinction from hypothetical because it is motivated by no other intention, neither by desire nor by inclination nor by any material outcome. The categorical imperative is motivated only by itself through the law of morality recognizable in human beings; they feel obliged to follow it. Kant gives this so-called categorical imperative not a specification as to its contents but a formal specification when he says: "Act in such a way that the maxim of your will could serve as a general or universal law."[6] This does not mean that nothing is said about content, for content is, in fact, specified, namely all those things that, in modern terms, make possible life in human society—or negatively: the prohibition of what destroys human community: violence, oppression, lying, injustice, hate, etc.

That becomes even more clear in another Kantian formulation of the categorical imperative: "Act in such a way that you use humanity, as well in your own person as in the person of everyone else, always as purpose, but never merely as means." — "In the whole of creation everything that one wishes and over which one has any power can also be used merely as means. Only human beings, and with them all rational creatures, are ends in themselves. Human beings are the subjects of the moral law, which is holy."[7] The human being experiences the demands of the categorical imperative as unconditional, absolute demands—as "holy obligations." The organ and faculty for this is practical reason, another word for conscience.

This brings into discussion areas of inquiry which are not encountered in that of theoretical, pure reason and which, nevertheless, are no less real and, for human beings, are even more important. Further, the area of the ethical, with which the quality of the unconditioned and absolute, even holy, is connected, needs confirmation and grounding. This comes about not through the theoretical knowledge of categorial cognition through reason, but through thinking of the unconditioned as a postulate of the practical reason which is directed to action. Without this postulate, moral action, practical reason, doesn't have its condi-

---

6. I. Kant, *Critique of Practical Reason,* trans. Lewis White Beck, 3rd ed. (New York: Macmillan Publishing Company, 1993) 30; *Groundwork of the Metaphysic of Morals,* trans. H. J. Paton (New York: Harper & Row, Publishers, 1964) 88.
7. I. Kant, *The Metaphysic of Morals,* trans. Mary Gregor (New York: Cambridge University Press, 1991) 255.

tion of possibility. This thinking of the unconditioned as postulate of moral action Kant also calls faith.

Along with the categorical imperative experienced in the conscience with unconditioned obligatory character comes, according to Kant, the fact also experienced in conscience that the action of human beings is judged, it is put on trial as if in court, with roles for defendant and judge. He gives the following analysis:

> All human beings have a conscience and find themselves watched over by an inner judge, threatened, and kept in line; and this power watching over the laws within them is not something that they themselves arbitrarily make, but is embodied in their being. It follows them like their shadow, when they think about escaping. . . . This condition . . . called conscience, has this special characteristic in itself that, although its business is a business of human beings with themselves, they are still forced by their reason to attribute it to the bidding of another person. For the action taking place is the conduct of a trial in court. But since the defendant, through his/her conscience, is presented as one and the same person with the judge, we have an absurd concept of a trial court; for in that case the plaintiff would lose every time. Thus the conscience of the human being will necessarily have to think of someone other than itself as judge of its actions, if it is not to stand in contradiction with itself.[8]

About this someone Other, Kant says:

> Since such a moral being must also have all power in heaven and on earth, because it otherwise would be unable to give its laws their appropriate effect (which necessarily belongs to the office of judge), and since such a being is called *God*, conscience will thus have to be thought of as the subjective principle of a responsibility to be carried out before God for its deeds.[9]

With that, Kant comes to the idea of God as highest *guarantor of morality*, who has the attributes of justice and holiness, who thus has personal traits: "At the basis of the imperative is the idea of someone imperating."

When Kant speaks of the idea of God, he doesn't mean that God is in reality only an idea to which no reality corresponds; he means only, and quite decisively, that access to God does not come about by way of theoretical cognition, but through thinking, through the postulate of practical reason, through faith. The fact of the really experienced unconditioned obligation, and the, for Kant, likewise given connection of morality and happiness, lead inevitably to the acceptance of God distinct from nature and from human beings as the real supposition of moral action. "The moral law has to postulate the existence of God as necessarily belonging to the possibility of the highest good."

When Kant describes the acceptance of the reality of God as a postulate of reason, he means that it is the real presupposition of moral action. Kant speaks of the objective reality of God, different from that of

8. Ibid, 233–34.
9. Ibid. 234.

human beings, which is postulated by the practical law, which is accepted, which—in other words—is believed. But *faith* is accordingly—and this is the real point—not a deficient mode of knowledge but a specific way of perceiving the reality of the ethical and its presuppositions, a mode that has its own methods. It is a faith that Kant also calls philosophical faith: the faith grounded in and taken from practical reason.

If one follows this line of thought, then theoretical reason prepares the way for practical reason. Knowledge, in this scientific sense, in which cognition takes place, does not have the last word about the meaning of the world and of life. Science cannot give final answers to the questions: What should I do? For what may I hope? What is the human being? Thus understanding cannot provide the final insight into the nature of the human being. Over and above the conditioned, which is uniquely accessible to science, arises an unconditioned, which is thinkable by reason but not objectively knowable in its objectivity through reason. But it doesn't merely arise as a continuation, so to speak, beyond the empirical world; it also is the ultimate meaning of all reality; nature must ultimately serve the spirit. Knowing must yield its primacy to another, to willing, i.e., for Kant, moral reason. Ethics is the heart of Kantian philosophy, for that is where Kant's ultimate longing and the deepest motive for his thought is fulfilled: finding room for faith. For the sake of faith, i.e., for the sake of the practical reason's belief in the convictions about God, freedom and immortality taken over from the Enlightenment, he had to sublate knowledge.[10]

This is the positive side of the boundaries established by Kant, of the limitation of cognition he carried out: the goal of his philosophy. It gives to science what belongs to science, but also to faith what belongs to faith.

It follows that the concept of God belongs not to science, to natural science, but to ethics. Human beings believe in God because they believe in the sense or meaning of the ethical, which contains in it the idea of the highest good, the unification of morality and happiness, which would be sense-less if there were no God to make it real.

In Kant's system, ideas bear the characteristic of a subjective freedom which actually belongs to every subject. That is how and where ideas get their guarantee, their objective and, though only practical, still indubitable reality. God's existence is adequately assured in the moral reason's idea of the highest good. With the fact of the freedom and existence of God, immortality is given a warrant which is valid in

10. Cf. Th. Steinbüchel, *Immanuel Kant I. Einführung in seine Welt und den Sinn seiner Philosophie* (Düsseldorf, 1931); G. Krüger, *Philosophie und Moral in der Kantischen Ethik* (Tübingen, 1931).

practical intention. And this practical intention is also the only one religion needs.

In order to evaluate properly the seriousness and the significance of this belief of reason, one must understand Kant's concern also to remove moral reality from the realm of individual opinion, to say nothing of arbitrariness.

The "subjectivism" of Kant is, in ethics as in the theory of knowledge not an individualistic subjectivism but a subjectivism of consciousness as such, of reason as such. It is the structure proper to its being and the internal law of the spirit, of reason itself, on which Kant grounds the general validity of cognition as well as morality. To say this does not prevent one from expressly pointing out that the content of philosophical faith in Kant is clearly different from the content of the Christian faith, and even stands in contrast to it. Kant sees in philosophical faith, in the faith of reason, the superiority over and the victory over what he calls dogmatic church faith.[11] But this brings up a theme to be treated not here but later on (§27).

Karl Jaspers (1883-1969)

The second—representative and still current—model of philosophical faith is to be found in Karl Jaspers.[12] The theme of philosophical faith runs through his whole work from the beginning: from his major work *Philosophie* (1933, ET *Philosophy*, 1969) to *Philosophischer Glaube*—Philosophical Faith (1947), and one of his last publications: *Der philosophische Glaube angesichts der Offenbarung* (1962, ET *Philosophical Faith and Revelation*, 1967). Jaspers took over quite a bit of his thematic of philosophical faith from Kant, but he also gave it his own, more comprehensive shape.

Philosophy as doing philosophy belongs, according to Jaspers, to humanity and to being human, if being human is not to remain beneath its own level. Already in this definition one encounters the word *faith*: in doing philosophy a faith is expressed, "appealing to him/her who

11. Cf. B. Jansen, *Die Religionsphilosophie Kants* (Berlin—Bonn, 1929); J. L. Bruch, *La philosophie religieuse de Kant* (Aubier—Montaigne, 1969).

12. Major works of Karl Jaspers on this theme: *Die geistige Situation der Zeit* (Berlin, 1931); *Philosophy* trans. E. B. Ashton, 3 vols. (Chicago: University of Chicago Press, 1969–1971) (the later editions are unchanged); *Philosophical Faith and Revelation*, trans. E. B. Ashton (New York: Harper & Row, Publishers, 1967); *The Way to Wisdom: An Introduction to Philosophy*, trans. Ralph Manheim (New Haven: Yale University Press, 1951); *Reason and Existenz; Five Lectures*, trans. William Earle (New York, Noonday Press, 1955) 11.

Taking issue with Jaspers: B. Welte, "Der philosophische Glaube bei Karl Jaspers und die Möglichkeit seiner Deutung durch die thomistische Philosophie" in: *Symposion. Jahrbuch für Philosophie II* (Freiburg—Munich, 1947); W. Lohff, *glaube und Freiheit. Das theologische Problem der Religionskritik von Karl Jaspers* (Gütersloh, 1957); Heinrich Fries, "Karl Jaspers und das Christentum, *ThQ* 132 (1952) 157–287; "Der philosophische Glaube: Karl Jaspers" in: *Ärgernis und Widerspruch*, 2nd ed. (Würzburg, 1968) 41–99.

is on the same road; it is not an objective guide in the confusion; each one takes only what (s)he is as possibility through him/herself. In a world that has become questionable in everything, we seek in philosophizing to keep to the right way."[13] This "seeking in philosophizing to keep to the right way" is the act of philosophical faith and takes place through it.

From these remarks something further becomes clear: Jaspers's philosophy is *philosophy of existence*; for he doesn't see philosophy as only theory, nor existence as an objectifiable object. Existence is always origin and subject. Existential philosophy would in no sense be philosophy if it were to do without reason and thinking, but it would never be philosophy of existence if it wanted to be emancipated timelessly, apparently purely objectively, from existence, i.e., from the subject, from the individual who thinks and asks and who, in philosophical thinking, clarifies him/herself. Without reason, "Existence," according to Jaspers, would be "blind; without existence,s reason would be without obligation; in this, existence wants its own, reason wants the whole." Through such philosophizing out of their origins, human beings should have not so much objective cognition; they should rather come to themselves.

Existence, according to Jaspers, is always connected with *transcendence*. Transcendence means, first of all, orientation beyond oneself, over and beyond existence. Existence is open, limitlessly open; it is possible only in relation to an over-against that is not itself. It is open to the world, without which relation it would remain empty and, as thinking existence, continually running up against its own limits. This is because it can never comprehend the whole of the world. A further transcending relationship of existence is history, situation. Through history, through the shapes and intellectual movements encountered in it, human beings are to be not primarily taught but awakened and inspired, struck with impulses. The over-against of the other person in You and We represents another form of transcendence, to which belongs existence in dialogical form.

In all these relationships, which represent a kind of transcendence as a kind of over-against, no real essential knowledge of existence is produced; instead the manner is described in which existence is actualized: "I am not what I know; I know not what I am."

The true mode of transcendence is transcendence in the specific sense as *origin of origin*, as existence understands itself. Jaspers says of this: "No existence without transcendence." The definition of existence is thus expanded: "Existence is the self-being which is related to itself and through that to transcendence, through which it knows itself to be

---

13. *Philosophy* 1.v.

gifted and on which it is grounded."[14] Existence is gifted, received existence. In the same way in which I am certain of the existence which I am, I am certain of the transcendence through which I am. From the indubitable That of existence, the *That of transcendence* becomes immediately certain.[15]

This is for Jaspers so certain that he declares that a proof for transcendence is not necessary. To be sure, it is also not possible, because transcendence goes beyond the dimensions of the orientation of the world and cannot be the object of actual objective knowledge.

But what is not possible to cognition is supplied by *faith*, i.e. through the faith of human beings philosophizing, thinking, illuminating existence, questing after the origins and conditions of existence, and fulfilling existence. For Jaspers as for Kant, philosophical faith is that act of thinking human beings in which transcendence as existence-grounding and existence-determining reality becomes conscious to them, that act in which the assurance one has about transcendence and about existence comes about as godsend and gift: "I cannot think God, and yet cannot stop thinking Him."

Pursuing this more deeply, Jaspers sees faith in God as coming not so much from the limits of the experience of the world but from the *human experience of freedom*. Freedom which, in modern thought, especially in N. Hartmann and J. P. Sartre, is used as an argument or postulate against the possibility of a Transcendent God—atheism is a postulate of freedom—becomes for Jaspers an intensive confirmation that God is: the more human beings are free, the more certain is God for them. For the freedom of human beings is a freedom that is given. Of this I am certain: in my freedom I am not the one who gives, but the one who receives. I cannot take freedom by force; I receive it. But I do not receive it from the existing orientation of the world, for there is no freedom here, but only the compulsion of things. Thus the freedom through which I am raised beyond the compulsion of things, through which I strive for what is new, and through which I create, cannot be mediated through the world. I receive it from the ground of my existence, from transcendence, from God.

This is why Jaspers explains: God is certain for me with the decisiveness in which I myself freely exist. God is not certain to me as content of knowledge but as presence of freedom for existence. This yields the consequence: If the certitude of freedom includes in itself the certitude of God's being, there is a connection between the denial of freedom and the denial of God. If I do not experience the miracle of myself being,

---

14. K. Jaspers, *Reason and Existence*, First Lecture: "Origin of the Contemporary Philosophical Situation" 19–50.
15. See Jasper's treatement of transcendence in, *Philosophy* 3. 3–112.

then I need no relationship to God but am satisfied with the existence of nature and things.

There is on the other hand a connection between the assertion of a freedom without God and the idolizing of human beings. It is the mock freedom of arbitrariness, which understands itself as the supposed absolute independence of the "I will." But this deception about myself, that I myself am through myself alone, changes freedom into the perplexity of emptiness.

Freedom as freedom from arbitrariness, as decision for the unconditioned, needs guidance. But this can happen only through the transcendence that determines me, that is the ground of my existence. On the other hand, it remains true: Freedom is the place where transcendence becomes perceptible.[16]

Philosophical faith is, according to Jaspers, a faith that is not articulated objectively, but is enlivened in many kinds of encounter. It is a faith without dogmas, without confessional content. But what seems to be its weakness is precisely its strength and greatness: Philosophical faith is connected with breadth, openness, oscillation, swinging, which never comes to rest and for that precise reason remains living and existential.

That is why Jaspers can make only a few concrete, content statements about transcendence. But this much he does articulate: "God is"—"There is unconditioned demand"—"The world has a disappearing existence between God and existence"—"If everything disappears, God remains."[17]

Jaspers loves the word about the *hidden God*. He holds it as irreconcilable with transcendence that it should reveal itself: in word, history, or persons. Jaspers allows only the ambiguous cipher to stand as language of transcendence, as indicator and trace. "Cipher is the sign that transcendence is hidden but not disappeared."[18]

However ambiguous the cipher and writing of about transcendence might be, the attempt must be made to read this writing. It is read, according to Jaspers, not through science, but through laying claim to the whole of existence. "Just as the organs of sense must be intact so that the world can be perceived, so must the being self *[Selbstsein]* of possible existence be present in order to be struck by transcendence. If I am existentially deaf, so too, in the object, is the language of transcendence inaudible."[19] "I take from transcendence only as much as I myself am and become." All remains dark to those who are not themselves, i.e., who

16. K. Jaspers, *The Way to Wisdom: An Introduction to Philosophy* 45.
17. K. Jaspers, *Der philsophische Glaube* (Munich, 1984) 29–31, 82. Jaspers revisited this theme in the 1962 book translated as *Philosophical Faith and Revelation*, trans. E. B. Ashton (New York: Harper & Row, 1967)
18. K. Jaspers, *Philosophy* 3.180.
19. Ibid. 132.

do not exist in openness, freedom, readiness for communication, in the courage to face disquiet and oscillation. Doubt about transcendence is possible only out of a failure of existence. This transcendence—to repeat again—is for Jaspers indubitable reality, the true being, it is the reality that grounds the world and existence as creative free origin. Transcendence is the reality in which rest and stability is to be found; it is ultimately that "from which I live and towards which I die."

Thus it is possible for Jaspers to speak of the subjective and objective side of faith. "If I took only the subjective side, faith would remain, as piety, without object, a faith which, so to speak, believes only itself, faith without contents. If I took only the objective side, the content of faith would remain as object, a dead something as it were." Faith is the one and the whole; it encompasses subject and object.

A series of questions from the side of theology can and must be put to this conception of philosophical faith, especially since Jaspers sets philosophical faith over against content-articulated revelational faith in the Christian sense, and sets it in direct contrast with it. This brings us to the question: revealed or hidden God? We will look into this alternative in another context (§ 27).

What concerns us in this contest is this: The phenomenon of faith as philosophical faith takes on, in Jaspers's model, a central position, even more, more comprehensively, and more existentially than the faith encountered in Kant. The phenomenon of faith in the theological *sense/meaning* is given through this context the irreplaceable and thereby also unsurpassable rank that is its due. In this way faith is from the outset freed from the false, pejorative perspective and related disparagement which is still associated with it.

Let us conclude these observations with an appeal from Jaspers: Revelational faith and philosophical faith should not stand over against each other as enemies. They can, according to Jaspers, be in agreement over what one can know and cannot know. They can be in agreement about the limits of scientific cognition, in defense against scientific superstition and scientific contempt, and in the will for truth. "We should come so far in understanding others in faith, without following them in it, but precisely thereby to put ourselves all the more in that union with them which unites us against all the vanities there are as powerful forces in the world, physically and psychologically almost overwhelming: in union against godlessness and nihilism."[20]

20. K. Jaspers—H. Zahrnt, Philosophie und Offenbarungsglaube. Ein Zwiegespräch (Hamburg, 1963) 101–2.

THE LOGIC OF ACT AND TRANSCENDENCE
THE THEORY OF MAURICE BLONDEL (1861-1949)

In our efforts to gain access to faith in the theological sense, let us present the ideas contained in the work of the French philosopher Maurice Blondel.[1] He is one of the most important inspirations for theology to this day, especially in France. The fundamental theologian H. Bouillard has highlighted the significance of Blondel and made it extensively accessible. Blondel's significance lies in the fact that he resisted the reigning split in his time between believing and thinking, and the claim that serious thought could only be unbelieving. He sought to illuminate and to ground philosophically the coordination and the relationship of believing and thinking.

Important for the question we are asking is Blondel's philosophy of *"Action"* —as his major work is called, a philosophy of human action, praxis. Blondel's purpose was to provide an analysis and a phenomenology of action, and an exposition of its internal logic.

The Analysis of Act

"Action" or act, for Blondel is not praxis in the emphasized or in the socio-political sense, i.e., praxis with which human beings change nature, society, and structures, but action, deed, activity of the kind encountered in the many everyday radii of action, in the ordinary activity of human beings. Blondel seeks to gain knowledge about the inner determination and dynamic of activity and praxis. In doing so he first notes something of fundamental importance: Reflection over praxis

1. Major works: *Action: Essay on a Critique of Life and a Science of Practice* (Notre Dame, IN: University of Notre Dame Press, 1984); La Pensée I and II, Paris 1934, German translation (R. Scherer): *Das Denken* 2 vols. (Freiburg—Munich, 1953/56); *Exigences philosophiques du christianisme* (Paris, 1950), German translation (R. Scherer): *Philosophische Ansprüche des Christentums* (Vienna—Munich, 1954); Henry Bouillard, *Blondel and Christianity*, trans. James M. Somerville (Washington: Corpus Books, 1970); *The Logic of Faith* (Dublin, 1967).

shows that there is no substitute for praxis, action. The problem of life is to be solved only by living. Never to say or to prove anything does not dispense one from action. Through act and activity, a reality is disclosed and an experience mediated which one can then theoretically represent. But the experience itself and the reality contained and disclosed therein are not won by way of knowledge (i.e., scholarship/research). The theory of magnanimity is a long, long way from one act of magnanimity. But it is quite true that the act of magnanimity can, for a subsequent reflection, disclose what magnanimity is. Praxis is never only application of theory; it can become the foundation of theory.

In the analysis of act and the logic needed for it, Blondel observes this remarkable discrepancy: Human beings want and strive for more than they ever attain or realize in act and praxis. They never arrive at the full identity of what they originally wanted and sometimes realize. Wanting and act turn out to be similar to asking and knowing, in that human beings infinitely surpass human beings. The perfection of the human act, of human action in terms of its goal, succeeds—as far as we can see—not through human beings themselves and not through any activity in the course of human life. Blondel examines this point more deeply. It is impossible, he says, not to recognize the inadequacies of the whole natural order, and not to experience a need reaching far beyond it; it is impossible to find in oneself the fulfillment of this neediness. It is necessary, and it is unachievable."[2] This means: *The perfection of the human act* is unreachable through human action itself. This results in the dialectic set up by Blondel—it is the pivotal point of his thought: the perfection of our action lies in its logic; but the perfection of action is at the same time—and this is the other side of the dialectic—unattainable by human beings and their action.

According to Blondel, this situation is experienced above all in the fact of failure. The failure of human action in its most manifold dimensions wouldn't come into the consciousness of human beings if there were no human will [with its "mind"] set on perfection, to which will the factually attained—or rather, not attained—stands in contrast or in no satisfactory correspondence. The failure of the act willed testifies to the indestructibility of the intentional act, i.e., that act which is from the will of human beings themselves and which they, nevertheless, are unable to produce from themselves.

This is the situation as Blondel sees it: I cannot withdraw myself from the necessity of willing myself, and at the same time it is impossible for me wholly to attain myself. The natural act of the human being thus contains in itself an *inner dynamic*, which is borne by and connected with the element of the unconditionally necessary. This explains the

2. See H. Bouillard, *Blondel and Christianity* 8, 62.

impulse and the specific logic of human act and activity. In their act human beings point beyond themselves and verge on the horizon of a perfection which they strive for and need, which is constitutive of their act, but which they cannot reach with their own power.

This situation leads to Blondel's thesis: Human beings cannot make themselves perfect in their activity unless perfection is bestowed on them: through an act which is not their own, which they can only receive, but which nevertheless appears as the perfection of their action.

From these presuppositions Blondel derives the concept of the *supernatural (surnaturel)*[3] as distinguished from the natural order in whose field the human act is carried out. The analysis of act shows, according to Blondel, that the supernatural is the "cry of human nature," that the supernatural necessarily belongs to human beings and their act and is demanded by them and their logic; but on the other hand it is not attainable by human beings themselves. The supernatural is for human beings absolutely impossible and, at the same time, absolutely necessary—this is the specification and characteristic of the supernatural according to Blondel. But because all this has to do with the perfection of human action, with the human act, the supernatural itself cannot be understood as a dumb, passive, lifeless reality; it must be living, it must be able to be active, it cannot lie beneath the level of the human being as *person*. This supernatural—understood as personal and active— which, in activity, turns out to be the reality of transcendence, is for human beings the both necessary and unattainable condition and presupposition of their "action," their act.

Faith

Faith enters into this view of things in the sense of the *option of the whole human being*, in the sense of a *basic decision*, similarly to the thematic of the experience of meaning. Human beings are, as acting and through their action, given a choice. They must choose for or against the acceptance of the transcendence of the supernatural. They can choose the possibility that they remain totally masters in their own house, closed in on themselves, and restricted to the empirical realm of their action. But in so doing they contradict the infinite dynamic of their will, or the dynamic of their act towards infinite perfection and fulfillment. But it is also possible—and in this, human beings remain true to themselves in their activity—that they open themselves for the transcendence to which their conscience gives witness,[4] for supernature and its possible act as gift, as perfection and goal of their own activity.

3. Ibid. 47–102.
4. Cf. Ibid. 8, 73.

About such an act and gift, Blondel as philosopher says nothing, or at most this: that it cannot be forced, but can indeed be expected. Whether the expectation is or has been fulfilled cannot be determined philosophically. Blondel wants only to open up an approach for such a possibility precisely through the reflection that the analysis and the logic of human action has on this theme. The act that brings about this decision is an act of faith, and this is encountered in a horizon similar to that of the question of sense: It is more than exact knowledge of particulars. It is at the same time a free act. The philosophical reflection that poses the problem of faith does not force one to faith.

Against these considerations one could raise the obvious *objection*: It seems that a hidden postulate could lie behind this way of thinking. Is not the dissatisfaction of the human will with the finite and its orientation to a naturally unattainable goal presupposed rather than proven?

This was precisely the objection raised against Blondel in the public defense of his thesis: Is the orientation of the will towards the infinite not the starting point of your investigation? And does not this involve a *petitio principii* (begging of the question)? Blondel's answer was:

> The will for the infinite is not the starting point but the result of the philosophical investigation of act. But precisely this led to the knowledge that the will for the infinite is the real principle of human activity.

> If one wishes to avoid an impermissible prejudgment, it should first of all be neither accepted nor rejected. In those cases where, through education or history, it is offered to the consciousness as a hypothesis, one will first try to resist it. I tried that—from that comes the negative character of the method which seemed to me to have a purely scientific rigor. I check out the number of objections which could be raised against my secret postulate; I take pains not to be influenced by this postulate, to repress it; I think up possibilities of ridding myself of it. But from all these attempts comes a system of positive indicators showing that, before conscious reflection and before the decision of the will, one still finds that what one was fleeing from at the beginning of the process was already present: the will for the infinite. The a posteriori established and recognized fact of the will for the infinite is the a priori factual presupposition of human act and activity.[5]

Several things come from this analysis. It shows that human beings in their act and activity are oriented beyond themselves and to *transcendence*, the supernatural. It shows, further, that transcendence, the supernatural, is not a mere accident of nature, that it must be understood not as static and dumb but as dynamic and living; free act and unforced—indeed unforcible—initiative are its characteristics. It also shows how much this "supernatural" act of God—which thought does require but which human beings look for—really fits in with what human beings are. Thus the call, act and action of God upon their actions

5. Ibid. 10.

is, with the supernatural as gift and act being so much the fulfillment of an expectation, the realization of a disposition. It thereby signifies not alienation but perfected human realization.

The terminology frequently used today, above all by Karl Rahner, of the supernatural existential of the human being, and the attempts to understand theology existentially, i.e., from the existence of the human being and as an interpretation and realization of the human being seen individually, socially and historically, all these are anticipated in Blondel's theses.[6] Against the reservation or objection of numerous theologians that he immanentizes or "naturalizes" the supernatural, that he turns free grace into a postulate of the human being, Blondel responds with the statement that what is absolutely necessary for human beings and their act is at the same time something that is unachievable by them, but [only] granted them in grace.

The call of human nature for the Messiah—this is Blondel's image[7]—does not turn this call into a human creature; but such a call can recognize and acknowledge him [the Messiah], when he appears, as sent by God. But it can and should be pointed out that the Messiah, when he comes, that the word and the act of God, when they become real, correspond to a disposition, an expectation, and an a priori of the human being, because the human being can and must be described as one who is by nature and essence open for this. Or, put another way: If transcendence, if the supernatural, has a universal claim on human beings and should correspond to them, then an echo of this claim must be recognizable in human beings themselves; "a trace of this" must "be found in the logic of the human act."[8] Otherwise the claim cannot be known and mediated.

To find and to name this trace was the goal of the philosopher Blondel, who, in so doing, intends to remain faithful to his philosophical goals, but who, precisely in an unmasked philosophy, makes room for revelation and faith, and manifests this faith in its *humanity*. From this position Blondel can formulate the proposition: The more unique, independent, and autonomous philosophy is and so understands itself, so much the more is it, in the *sense* of a presupposition, appropriate for revelation and the Christian faith. Or still more pointedly: "The only philosophy which Catholicism allows is philosophy itself."

It can certainly be said that, without the fact of Christian revelation, and the faith that responds to it, and the history of faith that has come from it, Blondel would never have written such a philosophy.

---

6. Cf. H. Fries, "Theologie als Anthropologie" in: K. Rahner—H. Fries, *Theologie in Freiheit und Verantwortung* (Munich, 1981) 30–69.

7. H. Bouillard, *Blondel and Christianity* 64, 66.

8. Ibid. 18, 56.

Blondel doesn't deny this, but that doesn't prevent or exclude the thought awakened by such an impulse from being philosophical thought, which, as such, flows from human thought and behavior. Blondel's thought and method remain in the philosophical horizon and in the human realm.

When Blondel says of himself that he has done the work of a philosopher as a believer—and that is his claim—then his intention is to make a philosophical contribution that can remain true to the believer and to the philosophizer, without intellectual dishonesty, without a bad conscience, without inauthentic compromises. The philosophy Blondel represents consists in the fact that it, as unadulterated philosophy, rests on those presuppositions and names those conditions that are there and must be there for a possible revelation, if revelation, even if it is only hypothetically accepted, is going to reach human beings. Blondel's philosophy does not require God's self-revelation, it only uncovers the a priori in which a revelation can be grasped and recognized.[9]

In addition, Blondel shows that the "supernatural," which speaks to and encounters the human being in revelation, is a concretion of the philosophically not sufficiently specified idea of the supernatural; it is a concretion in the sense of personality, initiative, gratuity, historicity, and bodiliness. In the personal self-disclosure of God in Jesus Christ it has found its absolute and unsurpassable final form, and is thus, seen in terms of the phenomenology of religion, incomparable.[10]

This self-disclosure has a human, subjective a priori which is theologically, as one would expect, presupposed. But this presupposition has to be illuminated philosophically and, for its part, described in the possibilities and modes of its perfection that come from the supernatural. Thus the philosopher cannot have knowledge of any ground to forsake faith for the sake of philosophy, or to become unfaithful to philosophy for the sake of faith.

9. Ibid. 59, 96.
10. M. Blondel, *The Letter on Apologetics and History and Dogma,* trans. Alexander Dru and Illtyd Trethowan (New York: Holt, Rinehart and Winston, 1965).

FAITH IN GOD IN THE LIGHT OF THE
ANTHROPOLOGICAL CHARACTERISTICS OF FAITH

These reflections on the anthropological characteristics of faith, of faith in God, of faith in the theological sense were directed to the question of presuppositions and conditions. If—as is the case today—faith as such is questioned, if it is described and thus rejected as intellectually deficient, alienating, or unwarranted, we then have to ask about its anthropological characteristics, i.e., about whether and how the human being, humanly and existentially, has anything to do with what is called faith in God.

In addition, we must also, by order, relation, and correlation, bring faith in God into relationship with anthropological characteristics. This correlation can take the shape of question and answer, of answer and question, or the shape of expectation and fulfillment, of probability and event, of fragment and whole, of inauthentic and authentic. In any case, it has to do with the mode of the connection without which faith in the theological sense cannot be mediated. The mere assertion and exhortation, the loud adjuration "We believe," is not enough these days.

Theology in our day is possible only in its anthropological form, in relationship to human beings and human society—one could also say, only in a fundamental-theological basic orientation.[1] This brings us to the question: How does one get from anthropological presuppositions to God? Some things that can be said about this have already been mentioned. We will now, on this basis, once again specifically take up this theme.

The manner in which belief as *personal* act contains an indication of belief in God has already been described. We pointed out that the radical and unlimited practice of faith in the horizon of the human person and persons is not possible, however much the faith itself intends this.

---

1. The basis for this can be found in K. Rahner, *Foundations of Christian Faith: An Introduction to the Idea of Christianity*, trans. William V. Dych (New York: Crossroad, 1994).

The full realization of faith repeatedly fails because of the intellectual and ethical limitation of human beings, because of the deficiency, the weakness and unreliability, because of the very different and to-be-differentiated credibility of the person and persons in whom I believe and whom I believe.

The highest level and intensity of personal belief is found between persons who are bound to each other in love. But here too, faith is often disappointed or broken by failure, narrowness, infidelity, fickleness, and questionability. So also, precisely those human beings who strive in faith and love for their fulfillment know best and most painfully that they will not succeed in actualizing their faith unbroken and undisturbed, uncurtailed and unconditioned. Thus it becomes clear not only from the deficient modes of faith but also from its most authentic and highest human realizations that faith points beyond the horizon and beyond the possibilities of its interhuman relationship, that as personal faith it seeks a mode of realization free from and raised above these limits and inadequacies.

Thus, from its interhuman and interpersonal actualization, faith creates space in which it gains the genuine fulfillment of itself. This fulfillment is not possible in the interhuman realm; it is found when and where faith can be related to a personal You that is different from every finite personality, and possesses not less but more personality; that is person in the absolute sense, in the *sense* of freedom, love, knowledge, word, self-disclosure, inability to be used as an object; that allows and makes possible an unlimited "grounding of myself in another." On the other hand, this fulfillment of human faith in a personality transcending the human is the fulfillment of the deepest intention of faith as human actualization.

One cannot of course say: From this conception of faith follows the reality of a transcendent and absolute You in which faith is radically realized and wholly fulfilled. But this conception does provide a horizon of expectation and hope. It is therefore true that when the transcendent, absolute You is encountered in any form of self-disclosure, there resides within the faith related to it the fullness of the possibility of faith. For there the limitations and hindrances which determine faith as an encounter of one human being with another fall away. It becomes immediately manifest how human and existential such an encounter is when human beings believe in this transcendent personal reality and find therein the fulfillment of the sense of their being, and how, on the other hand, human beings and their deepest intention in faith and the love connected to it would be nothing but failure and vanity if the idea of transcendence were an illusion.

In connection with these reflections on personal faith, let me add a remark on the phenomenon of *word,* which is of central significance in the field of faith. The "I believe You" is articulated in the spoken word. The opening up of what is to be believed also takes place in word: "I believe what you say." Gerhard Ebeling addressed this question in many of his works.[2] The whole of theology, the whole of revelation is described by him as word-event, as speech-event. He develops the following ideas: So comprehensively can human beings bring everything to actuality in word, even be able to create reality in the performative word—they experience again and again that they do not have power over their word, that they have neither the first nor the last word, that often enough they are speechless in the face of many actualities and events. Because their own human word is an inadequate, often lying word which one cannot trust, on which one cannot build, they hunger after another word that does not come from human beings, from which word they can live, in which are truth, light, and fidelity. Thus, according to Ebeling, human word as articulation of personal faith points not only to the dialogic aspects of shared human existence, but also beyond, to a deeper dimension of human beings and human word, not as mere extension on the same level but as the deepest ground, as origin and goal of word that stands out in the word of human beings and is at the same time awaited by them, over against which the "I believe in You" has its absolutely limitless right. It is that You to which the human You points, and the ultimate ground for that is that the human being encounters and is encountered as You.

God is encountered also in the context of the *question of meaning* which is connected with the question of faith. If *meaning* points to the whole and to the ground of reality, and if, in addition, the whole and its ground are not encountered in this world and in history, this points to the existence of an unobjective, all-determining, transcendent reality which is called God.

If it is established that we ourselves, in many human experiences, are not really the ones who are the source of meaning, if it is established that we, in the midst of all experiences of meaninglessness and the absence of meaning, nevertheless entrust ourselves to a meaning, draw new assurance and hope, and therein realize a fundamental and primordial trust to which, after all empirical experiences, we have no right at all, but from which these same experiences do not keep us, this reveals a dimension of reality that is qualitatively new, that comes from another origin and is directed towards an "over-against" that is quite different from the many possible origins and goal-forms that arise from within world, life, and history.

2. G. Ebeling, *The Nature of Faith*, trans. Ronald Gregor Smith (Philadelphia: Muhlenberg Press, 1961); *Word and Faith* (London, 1984); *Gott und Wort* (Tübingen, 1966); *Introduction to a Theological Theory of Language*, trans. R. A. Wilson (Philadelphia: Fortress Press, 1973); *Dogmatik des christlichen Glaubens I* (Tübingen, 1979).

This reality that surpasses the world and inner historical experience is what that thematic of meaning runs up against, even when and where human beings themselves can find no meaning but still believe in a meaning and act accordingly. There are concrete instances of this, as we have indicated, even among people where no immanent practical value, no identifiable benefit, no obvious or even discernible achievement or usefulness seems to be found.

Where there is no longer any kind of use and function, there still remains a characteristic of *sense* which, coming from someplace else, extends like a strange dignity over these human beings, even when we do not know this *sense*. Precisely these human beings also have a dignity that does not allow them to be used or encroached upon. They are creatures who point to the Creator and are related to the Creator and thereby receive their "infinite value" which raises them to the dignity of human beings, to the level that human beings are never a means to the goal and purpose of another but are themselves goal and purpose.

If this guarantee for the right and dignity of human beings should disappear, where could one then get protection and hope for those who don't or who no longer come up to the norms of achievement and productivity demanded by society? To the question: "For what do you really need God?" Heinz Zahrnt answers:

In the *sense* of what is effectively useful to get through life well, to support the state or to change society, the human being has no need of God.[3]

God is rather that which is completely and wholly unnecessary in the life of human beings, and precisely that reason, the only thing they need. For only this Not-necessary protects them from being calculated, used, and sacrificed to the considerations of usefulness and necessity.[4]

To remember God for God's sake and thereby help human beings to preserve their true measure and dignity—for that Christianity is good. In doing this it contributes to the balance of the intellectual economy of the time and thus makes an original contribution to the life of the individual and of society.[5]

Belief in God is expressly thematized in the *philosophical faith of Kant and Jaspers.*

For Kant, God is the security, guarantee, and ground of the moral, which as categorical imperative makes its demand on human beings and is effective both as command and sanction, as judgment and court. According to Kant, God is different from nature and human beings. God is not to be known categorically, but to be thought of as a being with reason and freedom, whose basic characteristic is holiness as the cen-

3. H. Zahrnt, *Wozu ist das Christentum gut?* (Munich, 1974) 59.
4. Ibid. 70.
5. Ibid. 245. Cf. also H. Gollwitzer, *Krummes Holz—aufrechter Gang. Zur Frage nach dem Sinn des Lebens*, 7th ed. (Munich, 1976); also *Von der Stellvertretung Gottes. Christlicher Glaube in der Erfahrung der Verborgenheit Gottes* (Munich, 1967).

tral concept of the moral and the happy. Belief in God as a postulate of practical reason holds a very distinguished place in the thinking of Kant. Faith does not stand under the sign of a defective intellectual faculty. Instead, place is to be made for faith. In faith human beings are given sure answer to the most important questions: What should I do? For what may I hope? What is the human being?

For Jaspers and for the philosophical faith he sketched out, transcendence is the ground of existence. Existentially actualized faith is the assurance of transcendence, which neither requires nor is capable of proof. Transcendence is, according to Jaspers, necessarily hidden transcendence; its language is only the ambiguous cipher, not revelation.

In Jaspers's philosophical faith, which can be defined as the possibility of human beings to be certain of their transcendence, it is most impressive how he connects the ideas of transcendence and of God with the freedom of the human being—as the ability of the human being to decide for the unconditioned and for the new. Freedom has its place not in the world of laws, compulsions, and repetitions, in the world of the conditioned, but in the origin of subject and existence which Jaspers calls transcendence or God. Denial of God leads to atrophy and to the loss of freedom.

The *philosophy of act* in Blondel's reflections on human action is characterized by the fact that it makes one conscious of the discrepancy between what is willed and what is done, i.e., the non-identity of willing and the completed. Blondel sees in this an indication of transcendence, of the supernatural, which cannot be any lifeless and dumb reality, but action itself; thus not only word—that too—but act is activity in the most comprehensive sense. This act of transcendence, the gift of the supernatural, is bestowed on human beings as the perfection of their human willing. This act presses for its realization in act and activity. In this process the human will makes demands that far surpass its capacity and its own power. In view of this situation, Blondel talks about faith as the unavoidable option, as the decision of human beings over the whole of their existence and their action. This involves the alternatives, whether human beings open themselves to transcendence and its possible supernatural application in faith in the mode of openness and expectation, or whether they decline to do this, whether they withdraw into themselves and make the empirical horizon the only and ultimate horizon of their life. The consequence of the latter is, according to Blondel, that human beings become unfaithful to all that they experience as the strongest dynamic of their will and act: perfection in the absolute and infinite sense.

In this concept faith in God is clearly and expressly given its place. This is so much the case that, according to Blondel, the human act without this dimension of the transcendent and the supernatural becomes incomprehensible in its logic and in its actualization condemned to failure. All this produces the condition of the possibility for faith in God, for faith in the theological sense.

Faith in God unites for faith critical dimensions, the way they are encountered in faith as inner- and inter-human reality, but without coming to their radical and ultimate fulfillment there.

In conclusion we add another reflection in view of the fact that the word "God" seems today to be overworked, and misused, and to have become superficial. Some have recommended that we do without the word "God" entirely, or at least for a while. However much one can understand this recommendation and the reason for it—the same holds true for the words "love, freedom"—it is not to be accepted. For if the word "God" disappears, i.e., the absolute personal identity which is not identical with the human being and the world, but is what grounds it, disposes it, questions it, and calls it to responsibility, the reality of the world and of human beings will then be falsified; it will be deprived of its deepest truth and ultimate mystery. When God is not or no longer talked about, when the word "God" disappears, an irreplaceable anthropological dimension then drops out: the reality of human beings—and of the world—will be lost.

"God" is not to be replaced by any other word; God is the all-determining reality and as such is the absolute and free over-against of the human being. If one does without the word "God," one runs into the danger of giving up and losing the reality that is intended by "God" and can be replaced by nothing else. One should rather try everything in order to rescue the word "God" from superficiality and the trash heap, from the thoughtlessness into which we have brought it, and to speak it freshly and authentically. Karl Rahner reflects: What would happen if the word "God" disappeared without trace and clue, and without even a visible gap being left in its place? He answers: Human beings would have forgotten the whole and its ground and at the same time have forgotten that they had forgotten. What would happen then?— We can only say that the human beings would have ceased to be human. They would have crossbred themselves back into being clever animals.[6]

In this context we can share a text of Martin Buber from his book *Eclipse of God*. He is reminiscing about a visit with a professor in Germany—it was the famous philosopher, Karl Jaspers. In the morning Buber corrected proofs of a book and read to his host what was printed. Buber's account then reads:

He listened in a friendly manner, but obviously astonished, even with growing alienation. When I had finished he said, hesitatingly, and then, driven by his deep concern, more and more passionately: "How can you go on like that, saying

6. K. Rahner, "Meditation über das Wort 'Gott'" in: H. J. Schulz, ed., *Wer is das eigentlich, Gott?* (Munich, 1969) 18; *Foundations of Christian Faith* 47–48.

'God' time and time again? How can you expect your readers to take the word in the meaning which you intend? What you mean by it is elevated far beyond all human concept and understanding; and you mean precisely this elevation; but in saying it you throw it into human clutches. What word in the human language is so misused, so stained, so desecrated as this one! All the innocent blood that has been shed for it has robbed it of its luster. All the injustice which had to be brought in to cover it has wiped away its character. When I hear the name of the Most High God, it sometimes sounds to me like a blasphemy."

The kindly, clear eyes burned. The voice itself burned. We then sat there for a while in silence, across from each other. The study lay in the fluid brightness of early morning. It was as if I was drawing power into myself from the light. What my response was I am now unable to repeat exactly, but can only give an indication of it.

"Yes," I said, "it is the most heavily loaded of all human words. No word is so befouled, so tattered. That is precisely why I cannot do without it. Generations of humans have loaded the burden of their anxious lives onto this word and pressed it to the ground; it lies in the dust and bears all their burden. Generation of humans with their religious factions have torn this word to pieces; they have killed for it and died for it; it bears all their fingerprints and all their blood. Where could I find a word like it to characterize the Most High! If I took the purest, most sparkling concept from the innermost treasure chamber of the philosophers, I could pick up there only a non-committal thought-image, but not the presence of the One whom I mean, of the One whom generations of humans, with their monstrous living and dying, have honored and degraded. . . . Of course, they draw caricatures and underneath write the name of God; they murder one another and say: 'In God's Name.' But when all madness and deceit has crumbled away, when they stand over against God in lonely darkness and say no longer 'He' but 'You,' groan 'You,' cry out 'You,' all saying that single 'You,' and when they then add 'God,' is it not the real God upon whom they all call, the one, living God, the God of the children of men?! Is it not He, God, who hears them? To whom they—listen? And is it not that, precisely that way, the word 'God,' the word of our crying out, the word that has become Name, in all human languages and for all times become holy? We must pay attention to those who prohibit/despise it because they are protesting against the injustice and mischief for whose authorization they so readily appeal to God; but we still dare not give it up. What many propose makes a lot of sense, i.e., to keep silence for a while about the last things, so that the misused words can be redeemed! But that is not the way to redeem them. We are unable to wash clean the word God, and we cannot make it whole; but, stained and tattered as it is, we can lift it from the ground and raise it above a time of great trouble."

It had become bright in the study. The light was no longer following, it was there. The old man stood up, came to me, laid his hands on my shoulders and said: "We want to say 'you' to each other." The conversation was finished. For, where two really are together, they are there in the Name of God.[7]

We have by now established the presuppositions and set up the context that will enable us to speak of *faith in the theological sense.* By this we mean faith as the act and behavior of human beings, acts that are personal and engage the totality of those persons, acts that are

---

7. M. Buber, "Gottesfinsternis" in: *Werke* 1.508–10.

related to the personal reality that is indeed the all-determining reality called by the name "God."

Corresponding now to this possibility on the part of human beings is a fact: it is the fact of *religion*, the religions of human beings, the history of religions in the world. They all speak and treat of human behavior that is expressed in relationship to God and can be described as religious faith. This faith has a universal and unmistakable expression in that mode of expression called prayer (in part also sacrifice)[8] which is typical of all religions and at the same time characteristic of them. Prayer is the language of faith. In prayer is found all those characteristics that are specific to faith. First there is the personal characteristic: In prayer, human beings turn towards a personally understood You, but a You that is not identical with any human being. They turn to this You as a reality that can hear and see, that has sovereign disposition over human beings, to whom they entrust themselves, to whom they take flight, where they seek protection, from whom they expect help, consolation, and the key to the meaning of things, and also answers where human beings can no longer find any answers.

All the prayers in the world, with all their differences, mean the one mystery: The Holy, the Transcendent, the Divinity, God. They are a sign that the orientation of human beings to transcendence is one of their indestructible characteristics, that there are no human beings who, in this comprehensive sense, do not believe. The only question is whether, in this faith, they acknowledge transcendence, the true, personal over-against, or break off their infinity-oriented intention, that is, divert it to a finite, earthly instance: a person, a collective, or some immanent value.

The differences in religion and prayer comes from the differences in human beings, in nations, and from the many different experiences human beings have. The difference also comes from the richness and multiformity of the divinity to whom the one praying turns. But with all this difference there are also many common melodies as contents of prayer: praise, honor, thanksgiving, petition, dedication. Nicholas of Cusa speaks of the *"una religio in rituum varietate*—one religion in a variety of rites."* This also holds when the religion one is talking about is not a composite of the world religions or a hybrid form from them, but also an actual religion that, however, has a relationship with the other religions and cannot be understood without them.

---

8. Still important: F. Heiler, *Prayer: A Study in the History of Psychology of Religion* , trans. Samuel McComb and J. Edgar Park (New York: Oxford University Press, 1932); O. Karrer, *Das Religiöse in der Menschheit und das Christentum*, 3rd ed. (Freiburg, 1936); Th. Ohm, *Die Liebe zu Gott in den nichtchristlichen Religionen. Die Tatsachen der Religionsgeschichte und die christliche Religion* (Krailling, 1950); P. W. Scheele, *Opfer des Wortes. Gebete der Heiden aus fünf Jahrtausenden* (Paderborn, 1960); H. R. Schlette, ed., *Alter Gott, höre! Gebete der Welt* (Munich, 1961); F. Mildenberger, *Das Gebet als Übung und Probe des Gebetes* (Mainz, 1970).

That holds also for the specifically religious characteristic in the form of *Christian faith*. If we, then, concern ourselves primarily with Christian faith and not with the religions of the world, it is not to declare everything outside of that faith, i.e., the religions of the world, to be irrelevant or false. Our purpose is, by way of reflection on the Christian faith, also to consider what the discussion is about in world religions.

This idea is strengthened by the fact that the Christian faith, the religion represented in being Christian, makes the claim and the promise of being "for all": to be there for all, thus to be what is called a world religion. One cannot, to be sure, maintain what Adolf Harnack meant: Whoever knows the Christian religion knows all religion. But one can indeed say: Whoever claims to know the Christian religion really cannot do this without knowing the universal context in which the Christian faith, as religion, exists.

II

The Theological Characteristics of Faith
A Correlate of the Anthropological Theory

The following considerations will take up the other side of our theme: the question of whether and how—in the matter of the anthropological characteristics of faith, the indicators which point beyond itself—the expectations and openings that lay therein are factually and historically verifiable in the actual and radical practice of faith. It is the question of whether these expectations have a correspondence and answer which give assurance of fulfillment.

There is, as we have already indicated, an answer in a universal sense: in the fact of religion, of religions, of the history of religions. They are all characterized by behavior that transcends the immanent anthropological horizon and is related to transcendence, to the Divinity, to the Holy, to holy things. This relation is documented in religious faith, whose language is prayer and sacrifice, which turn out to be basic and universal phenomena of all religions.

This more universal answer, which is grounded in the very fact of the existence of religions, should not be superseded by the following considerations. It is, rather,to be specified and concretized through the correspondences found in the horizon of biblical faith and the reality of revelation ordered to it.

§6

FAITH IN THE OLD TESTAMENT

It is a questionable venture when a non–Old Testament scholar, a non-exegete, sets out to say something about such a huge and demanding theme. The suspicion could arise that the one who attempts this has no inkling of the multiplicity and breadth of what the Old Testament is, that such a person could talk only in general terms.

But when such a person—to look at the other side of this problem—speaks systematically, in a context of fundamental theology, about faith without going into the original witness of the Bible, then (s)he cannot speak of faith in the theological sense. But (s)he cannot, on the other hand, wait until all individual aspects of this question have been treated in scholarly exegetical monographs. This is a dilemma we constantly encounter, one we cannot avoid. One can evade the dilemma, to some extent, when the specialist is open to the whole and when the systematician remains open to the particulars without getting lost in them. Karl Rahner discusses this when talking about a first level of reflection which he describes with the, admittedly problematical, concept "evasive maneuvre—*Umgehungsmanöver*."[1]

Despite the breadth of time and content comprised in the Old Testament, something binds the differences into a unity. But it can bring these differences together only if, through all the different historical events, there actually is a thread of commonality, a real connection. In addition there are in the Old Testament unchallenged starting points, high points, and pivotal points which are determinative for the individual [aspects]. Old Testament scholarship itself points this out. A theology or theologies of the Old Testament are possible only on the basis of a connection existing in the Old Testament which overlaps the individual element, however such a connection is specified: covenant, revelation, salvation history. All these conceptions intend to show, and to show factually, that there are not only trees but also a forest. To see

---

1. Cf. preliminary remarks on the theory of knowledge in: *Foundations of Christian Faith,* 8–10.

a forest and to talk about a forest is also possible and allowable for someone who doesn't know or hasn't investigated all the trees in all their details.

This is the situation of systematicians who, when they treat a theological theme, cannot prescind from the biblical witness, and yet must do more than simply summarize the countless details. But in their desire to get to a ground or whole, they do not do away with the individual element as if this were unnecessary. But they are concerned to poiont out that every individual element is not a random erratic block but is encompassed by a whole. One needs to be aware of this for the way we approach the problem.

It is incontestable that faith is a fundamental concept of the Old Testament.[2] Faith has this characteristic because there is beneath it an experience which runs through the whole Old Testament and is one of the decisive reasons why one can speak of a unity. Martin Buber speaks of the history of Israel as *faith history*. The fact that the Hebrew word for faith varies is no argument against this: the reality remains. The basic word for faith is formed from the stem *häämin*—the familiar "Amen" comes from the same root. The meaning of this word is first of all of a formal kind and says that a thing is firm, reliable, that one can stand on it, build on it, live with it. This characteristic is carried over into Israel's relationship with the God of Israel.

The Faith of Abraham

We begin our brief analysis where the phenomenon of faith is found in the Old Testament in an exemplary and model form—in the figure and history of Abraham.[3] The story of Abraham forms the center of the so-called patriarchal history, which represents the transition from primitive history to the history of the People of Israel.[4] In the patriarchal histories or stories of the patriarchs, the beginnings and origins of the People of Israel are described. This means not just the natural, genealogical origins, but also the origins of the faith that is

---

2. On the theme "Faith in the Old Testament": M. Buber, *The Prophetic Faith*, trans. Carlyle Witton-Dans (New York: Harper and Row, 1960); "Zwei Glaubensweisen" in : *Werke I*, 651–782; A. Weiser, *"The Old Testament Concept,"* TDNT 6.182–96; F. Stier, *Geschichte Gottes mit den Menschen* (Düsseldorf, 1959); Gerhard von Rad, *Old Testament Theology* (New York: Harper, 1962); W. Eichrodt, *Theology of the Old Testament*, trans. J. A. Baker (Philadelphia: Westminster Press, 1967); L. Wachinger, *Der Glaubensbegriff Martin Bubers* (Munich, 1970); W. Zimmerli, *Old Testament Theology in Outline*, trans. David E. Green (Atlanta: John Knox Press, 1978); A. Kolping, *Fundamentaltheologie II* (Münster, 1964) 74–234; A. Deissler, *Die Grundbotschaft des Alten Testaments* , 6th ed. (Freiburg–Basel–Vienna, 1978); Claus Westermann, *Elements of Old Testament Theology* (Atlanta: John Knox Press, 1982); J. Scharbert, *Sachbuch zum Alten Testament* (Aschaffenburg, 1981).

3. F. von Trigt, *Die Geschichte der Patriarchen* (Mainz, 1963).

4. H. Renckens, *Urgeschichte und Heilsgeschichte* (Mainz, 1959).

the actual foundation of the existence of the People of Israel and its history.

Abraham's behavior, his life, his history, the fate that befalls him are, according to the witness of the Old and—quite remarkably— also of the New Testament, raised to a representation of what faith is. Abraham is called by Paul (Rom 4:11) *Father of Faith.* Abraham's faith is repeatedly praised and presented as a model. All who believe like Abraham are, for that reason, Abraham's children (Gal 3:6f). According to the Gospel of John, faith in Jesus Christ is the fulfillment of the faith of Abraham (John 8:33). In the praise of the fathers (Sir 44:19–21) and the "heroes of faith" (Heb 11:1–12:3), Abraham is given the highest rank. The way of his faith is described in the most thorough way and in its high points in the Letter to the Hebrews.

The source of our presentation is the book of Genesis, chapter 12 and following. Abram—that is his original name—a nomadic shepherd or nomadic chief, leaves his homeland in Ur, Chaldea (in Mesopotamia). In doing so he leaves behind his land and his relatives. He does this, according to the witness of Genesis (which is not a protocol and direct reporting but the writing down of a long narrative tradition and has to be interpreted as such) not on the basis of a decision of his own, but at bottom against his intention, against his will. He does it on the basis of an order which became for him an experience. The Bible interprets it and says: "The Lord spoke" to Abraham. This order tells him to: "Go from your country and your kindred and your father's house to the land that I will show you. And I will make of you a great nation, and I will bless you and make your name great, so that you will be a blessing. . . By you all the families of the earth shall bless themselves" (Gen 12:1–3).

A breaking loose, as described here, and a wandering into the unknown are, for human beings in antiquity, an almost unfulfillable demand. It could, according to the expectations of the time, lead only to destruction. But Abram nevertheless decides to do this; he bases his life and his future on it, and precisely this is described as his faith. The faith of Abraham is subjected to severe testing—first with respect to the land that is promised him, the land of Canaan, which is already in the possession of a population, and then with respect to the progeny promised him in his old age, and then—most difficult—in the testing (Gen 22:2–19) that orders him: "Take your son, your only son, Isaac, whom you love, . . . and offer him there as a burnt offering upon one of the mountains of which I shall tell you." We cannot here go into detail about the problem of the sacrifice of Isaac and its possible meaning, e.g., as narrative representation of the prohibition of child sacrifice; rather, we want to see it in connection with the faith thematic graphically presented here: the faith demanded of Abraham and lived by him means giving up the past ("Go from . . . ") and giving up the future ("Take your son . . . ").

From this merely cursory witness several things become clear: The faith of Abraham is reaction to an action, to an order; it is an answer to a word, however experienced and perceived by him, a word directed to him and imposing an obligation on him, and which for him is a word of God: "God spoke." In his believing, Abraham is ready to rely on word, order, and promise, to ground himself in these, to set his life and future on them, and to them to say the Yes of his amen: "So is it, so be it."

The faith of Abraham was, accordingly, a personal faith; he was obedient to a call experienced. This call was at the same time very concrete and required his "I believe that . . . " It was in addition a fundamental decision which determined his whole future life; it was faith in the form of an all-encompassing *making sense (Sinngebung)*, even if this *sense* was at first withdrawn from all human understanding.

For the faith of Abraham, the possible death of his son Isaac did not mean the contradiction and destruction of all the promises, but became a motive to leave *making sense* to the one to whom he had believingly entrusted himself. that is the way Paul in his Letter to the Romans saw it and wrote about it. Abraham is

" . . . the father of many nations"—in the presence of God in whom he believed, who gives life to the dead and calls into existence the things that do not exist. In hope he believed against hope, that he should become the father of many nations, as he had been told. "So shall your descendants be." He did not weaken in faith when he considered his own body, which was as good as dead because he was about a hundred years old, or when he considered the barrenness of Sarah's womb. No distrust made him waiver concerning the promise of God, but he grew strong in his faith as he gave glory to God, fully convinced that God was able to do what he had promised. That is why his faith was "reckoned to him as righteousness." (Rom 4:17–22)

This faith of Abraham bears in all the sign of the "Nevertheless," of the "In spite of everything"—against all appearances. Thus faith, according to the model of Abraham's faith, is a unique *form of existence of the human being:* a setting-oneself-outside-the-world, a being-grounded-in-God, a being-bound-to-God. Faith understood in this way—in any other way, it is not faith—is significantly elevated beyond the anxiety and fear that befalls human beings, as well as beyond all false self-confidence and vain glory; but it is also stronger than all doubt that can rise up against faith from appearances and the factual.

We must also specifically point out that, even according to the witness of the Old Testament, the magnificently described faith of Abraham was itself not realized so magnificently in every instance (cf. Gen 12:10-20). The prayer "Lord, I believe, help my unbelief!" is not foreign to him.

A further remark in this context: It concerns the *name of God* in the Abrahamic history. The God who moves through the events of the patriarchal histories is called Yahweh. This is, historically, an anachronism, or the pre-Mosaic ancestors of Israel did not yet know Yahweh-faith. The revelation of this name comes in the much later time of Moses (Exodus 3) and is described as a new beginning of the history of faith.

The God of the fathers had various names: El-Elohim. These are related mostly to persons and are respectively called, e.g., the God of Our Fathers, the God of Abraham, the Fright of Isaac, the Strength of Jacob. Because the later Yahweh-faith is related to the earlier God of the Fathers, and because the later history of Israel was brought into an inner relationship with the earliest history of the Fathers, the connection that is made between the earlier God of the Fathers and the later Yahweh, the God of Israel is, chronologically speaking, false. The connection can, however, be factually grounded; both are brought together into a grand inner relationship.

The Faith of the People of Israel

The Abrahamic and patriarchal histories point beyond themselves to a greater fulfillment than was given to the fathers themselves. Abraham takes possession of Canaan only to a small extent, and temporarily. The fulfillment given to him is interrupted as a result of the Egyptian interlude introduced by Joseph. The descendants of Abraham, the sons of Jacob, move to Egypt where, in the course of some 400 years, they become a large group. Even if we cannot give exact numbers, the Israelites did apparently seem to be so strong that the king of Egypt, apparently Ramses II, saw in them a threat to his own people. He thus ordered the repression of the Israelites. They had to provide slave labor in the brick factories, in agriculture, in the building of military installations and fortifications. The goal was—in modern terms—annihilation through work. As a last measure, it was finally ordered that all new-born baby boys should be killed. Thus Egypt became for Israel the land of bondage, repression, and slavery.

In this situation occurred a second great thrust in the history/faith-history of Israel. It is again an *emigration*, although in another form than with Abraham. The new emigration is connected with the *call of Moses*, first with his miraculous rescue by the daughter of Pharaoh, then with the theophany granted to him (Exodus 3).[5] This is described as follows:

---

5. P. Weimar—E. Zenger, *Exodus. Geschichten und Geschichte der Befreiung Israels* (Stuttgart, 1975).

"I am the God of your father, the God of Abraham, the God of Isaac, and the God of Jacob. . . I have seen the affliction of my people who are in Egypt, and I have heard their cry because of their taskmasters; I know their sufferings, and I have come down to deliver them out of the hand of the Egyptians, and to bring them up out of that land to a good and broad land, a land flowing with milk and honey, to the place of the Canaanites ... I will send you to Pharaoh that you may bring forth my people, the sons of Israel, out of Egypt." (Exod 3:6,7–8,10)

Moses takes on this task and carries it out. The events connected with it—the night of the escape, the Egyptian plagues, the rescue at the Sea of Reeds, the wandering in the desert, the event on Sinai, the making of the covenant, the taking over of the land in Canaan—cannot and need not be described here. For our thematic is important: All these events are no accident, and they are also not achievements of the leader, Moses, and his band; they are, rather—this is ineradicably stamped on the consciousness of Israel—they are the act, the providence, the guidance of the God of Israel. The one acting so powerfully is a *living God*, to whom one can call, to whom one can turn. The word and the manifestation of this God are shown in historical facts and events, in the language of facts—grouped around the great theme of Exodus and liberation. And these facts—that's the other side—are not to be seen as mere facts, but to be understood as language, word, and act of God. As such they are knowable only in faith.

The answer to this was the readiness of the people to acknowledge this God, Yahweh, in faith, to entrust themselves further and always to his powerful guidance, and to see in this trusting faith the grounding of their own existence and history. The history of Israel thereby becomes faith history. Faith is the illuminating interpretation of the external history. Israel is the People of God—Yahweh is the God of this people.

From this larger horizon the *meaning of the name of Yahweh* described in Exod 3:14 becomes understandable. 'Yahweh' does not mean, as the Vulgate translates and as scholasticism has interpreted it: "I am who I am" or I am the *ipsum esse*, being itself. The name 'Yahweh' contains no definition but a message. It goes: "I am there/here," "I will be there/here." The verification of this message takes place in the historical events of the rescuing of Israel. Thus, 'Yahweh' also means, concretely: I will be there for you as the rescuing, redeeming, liberating God of My People. This means: Israel's existence, historically seen, is grounded in the liberation from Egypt. But this is the proof of the power and love of the God who chose and called Israel. To assure itself of this is the task of the faith of the People of Israel; in this faith is grounded its history. This is what is meant by the phrase "Chosen People."

This makes once again clear what significance there is in the proclamation of the name of Yahweh. It doesn't serve, as is the case in other religions, to gain power over God in order to put God at the disposition of human beings. In Israel, calling on the Name should rather open up the possibility of assuring oneself of the presence and nearness of Yahweh; to call upon the name is to let oneself be made use of by Him, and to heed his instructions in his guiding and controlling of history.

Further, in all the external historical changes of this people—in the transition from nomadic to sedentary life, in the establishment of the kingdom, in the division of the nation after the death of Solomon, in the destruction of the northern and then the southern kingdoms, in captivity, in exile, in the return, in the new foundation and subsequent foreign domination—this faith remains as light on the way. This faith history is no simple history of progress in which faith grows and becomes more deep, but an extremely dramatic history of ups and downs, of turning to, of falling away, of readiness, of recalcitrancy. Faith is a path.

But Israel's history, with and under all the political factors that move its history, remains a faith history and vice versa: It is from the history of faith that Israel's external history is determined. And it is important to remember that not only victories and successes, but also defeats, captivity, and exile are for Israel the voice of God, a work, a revelation of Yahweh. This is what constitutes the special character of the faith of Israel in contrast to many other religions.

Faith and Existence

The history of Israel as faith history cannot here be gone into in detail. We will point out only one scene which, in the opinion of Old Testament scholarship, represents a high point in this history and, at the same time, describes in a highly concentrated way what faith means for this people.

The scene develops as follows: Judah's King Ahaz (739–734 B.C.) is in a difficult political situation. The neighboring kings of Samaria and Damascus want to force him, by besieging Jerusalem, into a coalition against Assyria. But Ahaz, for his part, is playing with the idea of asking Assyria for help against this threat. In this situation, the prophet Isaiah appeals to the ambivalent and anxious king neither to be afraid of the neighboring kings—he calls them "pieces of firewood" and "smouldering stumps" (Isa 7:4)—nor to ally himself with Assyria against these kings, but to set himself on the ground of faith and thereon to take his stand. He does this with the words: "If you will not believe, surely you shall not be established ("have no stability" or "not survive") (Isa 7:9). To have stability is the fruit of faith. Not to have faith means to fall, not remain, be unable to survive.

Thus, for Isaiah, faith and being are identical. Therefore, faith is the fundamental question for the survival and being of the People of Israel, who are in danger of falling away from this ground of existence into unbelief and non belief, and who, both in their fear of the peoples and powers threatening them as well as in their union with and trust in them, are betraying their faith and thus moving toward destruction.

This basic understanding of faith as existing in and grounding in God is repeatedly emphasized in the Old Testament and called up, as both demand and gift, into the consciousness of the people (the Psalms). This basic understanding unfolds the richness which comes with this fundamental sensitivity of faith: the trusting in and hoping in God, the being safe and protected in God, the freedom from anxiety and self-glory, the new power of existence and life-energy opened up therein: "They who wait for the Lord shall renew their strength, they shall mount up with wings like eagles, they shall run and not be weary, they shall walk and not faint (Isa 40:31). No less a part of this, given with and in this faith, is the power and the obligation to the "Nevertheless" in spite of all appearances, in spite of all the hiddenness of this God (Job).

The points of reference of faith are thus brought out in all clarity. It becomes recognizable that the faith of Israel means a double exclusivity: *God alone*—exclusively God—nothing outside of God. *The whole human being*—human beings with all their powers, human beings with whole and undivided hearts.

In the agitated history of Israel, in its history of faith, the fundamental sources and motivations of this faith are named and presented again and again: the great acts that took place in the calling, the history, and the leading of the People of Israel. In them Yahweh demonstrated his fidelity and power which obligate the people, in its turn, to fidelity. There are, further, the promises which Yahweh has given, which he fulfilled and will always fulfill anew on the basis of the already fulfilled, which obligate and encourage to faith and trust. There are, in addition, the concrete demands and instructions, above all in the Law, in the Torah, which are perceived not as burden but as help and light, and in the word and mission proclaimed by the prophets, which call to the obedience of faith: in general and in the concrete here and now of an historic hour, and which always make possible and require a new decision for this living God, for his word and his will.

There is no question about it: In the witness of the Old Testament, faith has the fundamental form: "I believe in you, I believe you." Faith is meant as *credere in Deum, credere Deo*, as belief in God—in the *sense* of existential and total grounding in God and towards God and at the same time as an unconditioned acceptance and recognition of whatever God says, promises, orders. Faith is a You-faith and a propositional faith, which in the concrete and individual recognizes the You that is revealing itself, and which makes possible and demands believing dedication to the You of the living God, of the guiding God, of the God who can be called upon. At the same time, this faith is the *sense*-giving power for the whole of its history.

The history of Israel is faith history mediated by secular history. The historical happenings and events are the actual language in which Yahweh speaks; that is the sense in which they are interpreted by the prophets.

The Confession of Faith (Creed)

The sources of faith were at the same time also the contents of the so-called creeds, the propositional faith found in the Old Testament. These are related to the fundamental developments in the history of this people. Biblical scholars often point to—as does Gerhard von Rad[6]— the fundamental Old Testament creed as described, e.g., in Deut 26:5–9 or Jos 24:2–13. The creed reads:

A wandering Aramean was my father; and he went down into Egypt and sojourned there, few in number; and there he became a nation, great, mighty, and populous. And the Egyptians treated us harshly, and afflicted us, and laid upon us hard bondage. Then we cried to the Lord and God of our fathers, and the Lord heard our voice, and saw our affliction, our toil, and our oppression; and the Lord brought us out of Egypt with a mighty hand and an outstretched arm, with great terror, with signs and wonders; and he brought us into this place and gave us this land, a land flowing with milk and honey. (Deut 26:5–9)

The content of this *credo* does not consist of doctrines or propositions which one must hold as true; *the credo consists of a history* which one narrates, hands on, which one remembers and out of which one can meet the present and the future. The history of Israel began with the fact that helpless people cried out to God and had the experience of being heard and saved. They knew this God not only in reality; they could even cry out to him.

The Old Testament recounts on the whole a history in which there are many changes, even in the image of God, in the worship of God, and in the way one spoke of God. But this content of the faith doesn't change; God is always the God who is open to the suffering of human beings, and that is how God is experienced in faith.

Thus, also belonging to the history of Israel is a *history of lamentation*, a history of the oppressed in Egypt, a history of suffering. We hear the lament arising from all kinds of need of the individual

6. *Theologie des Alten Testaments 1* (127–34); taking a critical position on this point: W. Richter, "Beobachtungen zur theologischen Systembildung in der alttestamentlichen Literatur anhand des 'kleinen geschichtlichen Credo'" in: *Wahrheit und Verkündigung*, hrsg. von L. Scheffczyk, W. Dettloff, R. Heinzmann (Festschrift M. Schmaus), (Munich—Paderborn—Vienna) 1967, 175–212.

and of the whole people (Psalms); we hear the laments over the fall of Jerusalem and the destruction of the temple. Lamentations stemming from the personal suffering of the individual come to their high point in the Book of Job: a man accuses God from the depth of his desperation, and, in doing precisely that, holds fast to God.

But in answer to the experience of being rescued come the jubilation and praise of the liberated. The oldest song in the Old Testament, Exod 15:1–21, comes after the account of the rescuing from Egypt.

No less than lament, *praise* runs through the whole Old Testament from the beginning. Praise signifies the joy coming out in words that cannot but recount—and this with exuberance—what the liberated experienced. The Old Testament credo has the literary form of the narrating praise of God, and vice versa: Israel's tradition of history is rooted in the praise of the great deeds of God, which is, for its part, an expression of faith.

The contents of another confession of faith is represented by the *prayer* that Israelites must recite daily: "Hear, O Israel: the Lord our God is one Lord" (Deut 6:4). A still further side of the faith, in terms of content, are the *Ten Words* (known as the Ten Commandments, although never called this in the Old Testament), which begin with the sentence "I am the Lord your God, who brought you out of the land of Egypt, out of the house of bondage. You shall have no other gods before me. You shall not make for yourself a graven image, or any likeness of anything that is in heaven above, or that is in the earth beneath, or that is in the water under the earth." (Exod 20:2–4) God alone—the whole human being: here too an indication of the exclusivity of Old Testament faith.

This is the fundamental pillar of the *Law* which, for the faith of Israel, is perceived not so much as burden but as light on the way of life, as orientation and instruction (cf. Psalms 18 and 119). The fundamental characteristic attributed to the Law with these words was that of peace-creating justice. For that, praise and thanks are given: "The heavens are telling the glory of God; and the firmament proclaims his handiwork" (Ps 19:1). This means: Yahweh, the God of Israel, is also *the creator of heaven and earth,* the Lord of the world.

In the course of the history of Israel, above all after the exile and with the continued growth of diaspora Judaism, the Law, the word was the only faith-orientation of the people, there begins a process in which the Law became an absolute reality. It stepped out beyond its serving function and became dictation which demanded verbal and literal obedience and laid claim to timeless validity, which therefore saw in obedience to the Law the proper realization of faith. A further fundamental characteristic of this faith is its form in terms of promise and hope, in other words, the fact that, for the faith of Israel, which is so connected to history and the present, the future opens up even greater dimensions.

Summing up: Faith is described according to the Old Testament as a comprehensive characteristic of the existence of human beings and of a people. No situation is excluded from this. Faith is trust, getting involved, grounding oneself in the God of the fathers, the God of Israel, the God who has a name and can be called upon, the God who has manifested himself through magnificent events and deeds attributable only to him, through his calling and guiding of human beings, and who makes himself, i.e., his being God and Lord, known in the history of a people, in the language of facts—so much so that this history is understood as a faith history.

The same Hebrew root ('mn') underlies the Hebrew words which are translated as the verb to believe, and Amen. This word is never used in the Old Testament in order to describe the relationship of human beings to the gods. It remains restricted to the relationship to the God of Israel as the only God.

It is not a projection into the Old Testament but the exegesis of its findings and witness when we say: Faith is encountered here in the form of personal faith, of "I believe in you, I believe you." To this is added affirmational faith as encountered in the forms of the Old Testament credo. Faith understood this way assures and establishes a making-*sense* in the existence of an individual human being and in the history of a people.

None of this was supposed to be a privilege of just this nation; it was supposed to become a sign for the other nations. But it is characteristic of other nations that they do not describe their relationship to God and to the Divinity with the attitude of faith.

From time immemorial, the religion of the Greek people flowed from the idea that the depth of the world is divine, that everyone can perceive by reflection, and that faith is not needed to do this. Even the cult of the sovereign was not based on faith. The fact that a sovereign was divine was obvious to anyone who could see, because of the sovereign's authority, which disseminated order, peace, and prosperity for all. In popular Stoic philosophy, the divinity was proven through rational conclusions from nature and history. In the mysteries and in gnosis it was ecstatically experienced or mystically contemplated. Thus, in Hellenistic religion, there was no talk of faith.[7]

7. L. Goppelt, *Theology of the New Testament* (Grand Rapids, Mich.: W. B. Eerdmans Publishing Co., 1982) 149–50.

§7

FAITH IN THE NEW TESTAMENT

Continuity with the Old Testament

The faith[1] which is found in the synoptics in Jesus' preaching of God's rule and kingdom is in the form of Old Testament faith. Its central expression is found in the double form: "Repent, and believe in the gospel" (Mark 1:15). Faith is encountered as surrendering to and trusting in the God to whom and through whom everything is possible: "All things are possible to him who believes" (Mark 9:23). Hence the requirement: "Pray and ask for whatever you will; believe that you have received it, and it will be yours" (Mark 11:24). Faith is, metaphorically speaking, a mountain-moving faith (Mark 11:23). It is also the overcoming of fear: "Do not be afraid, but believe." Hence the significance of the plea: "Lord, I believe; help my unbelief" (Mark 9:24).

These statements are not talking about an explicit faith in Jesus. They are about faith in the God who can rescue, who is good and merciful, the God of Abraham, Isaac, and Jacob, the God of the People of Israel, who now speaks and acts through Jesus. Faith is the opposite of faint-heartedness, fear, despondency. It is faith in the form already mentioned: the whole human being—God alone. In the New Testament, faith is not described with *one* word and concept, but is co-signified in

---

1. Cf. the theological dictionaries, lexicons and reference works: RGG C.2.1588–1611 (F. Baumgärtel—H. Braun—A.A. von Ruler—H. Graß); *Theological Lexicon of the New Testament* (Peabody, Mass: Hendrickson, 1994) 3.110–16; *TDNT* 6.182–228; P. K. Meagher, "Faith," *NCE* 5.792–804; M. Seckler, *HThG* 1.528–48; J. Alfaro, *SM* 2.310–409.

See also the presentations of the theology of the New Testament: Hans Conzelmann, *An Outline of the Theology of the New Testament* (New York: Harper & Row, 1969); K. H. Schelkle, *Theology of the New Testament* (Collegeville, Minn.: Liturgical Press, 1974); R. Bultmann, *Theology of the New Testament*, trans. Kendrick Grobel (New York: Charles Scribner's Sons, 1970); Leonhard Goppelt, *Theology of the New Testament* (Grand Rapids, Mich.: W. B. Eerdmans Publishing Co., 1982). Monographs: A. Schlatter, *Der Glaube im Neuen Testament*, 4th ed. (Stuttgart 1927); Rudolf Schnackenburg, *Christian Existence in the New Testament* (Notre Dame, Ind.: University of Notre Dame Press, 1968) 67–98.

the following field of words: trust, confidence, being unafraid, rejecting care and anxiety; but above all in the command to love God "with all your soul, with all your strength."

It is precisely this same form of faith that is found in the gospel healing stories: If you believe you will be whole, you will be healed, you will be helped. This is affirming that the well-being and the becoming well of human beings is opened up by means of faith in this broad, open sense. Where this faith is lived, one finds a healing of existence and of the whole human being, the sign of which is the external healing: "Your faith has saved you."

When this faith is not there, Jesus appears unable to work signs and miracles, as was the case in Nazareth, his native city (Matt 13:58), apparently because specification of meaning connected with the sign as sign and language of God is absent in this case. It is something that can be perceived only in the believing sense; the sign degenerates to a mere miracle or sensation. Equally significant is the other moment in the synoptics: Faith saves, in the sense that the forgiveness of sins is connected with it. "When Jesus saw their faith, he said to the paralytic, 'My son, your sins are forgiven'" (Mark 2:5).

A conceptual and formal characterization of faith understood in this way is given in the well-known ("classical") text of Heb 11:1: Faith is the hypostasis, i.e., the foundation of reality for what one hopes for, the rock of conviction of things one does not see: "Faith is the assurance of things hoped for, the conviction of things not seen."

Jesus and Faith

In the synoptics—with the exception of Matthew 18:6: "Whoever causes one of these little ones who believe in me to sin,"—the formula "believe in Jesus" is never found.

This raises the question: Is Jesus also a believer?[2] Is he to be ranked among the crowd of the "heroes of faith"? Does the fulfillment of faith take place in him as it did with Abraham and Moses? Jesus is the son of Abraham, the father of faith. In the letter to the Hebrews, after the enumeration of the Old Testament heroes of faith, Jesus is apostrophized as "Pioneer and perfecter of our faith" (Heb 12:2). Can this be said of Jesus because he makes faith perfect in his person, in that he proclaims the message of God's rule and kingdom and himself stands believingly in the service of this message, and thus is a radical believer in the *sense* of "the whole human being—God alone"?

2. Thomas of Aquinas, *Utrum in Christo fuerit fides* in: STh 3.7.3; Karl Rahner, "The Eternal Significance of the Humanity of Jesus for Our Relationship with God," *Theological Investigations* 3.35–46; Hans Urs von Balthasar, "Fides Christi" in : *Sponsa–Verbi* (Einsiedeln, 1960) 45–79, ET: *Spouse of the Word* (San Francisco, 1991); Gerhard Ebeling, "Jesus and Faith" in: *Word and Faith* (Philadelia: Fortress Press, 1963) 201–46.

Is Jesus, therefore, as Martin Buber and Shalom Ben Chorin say, the continuation, indeed the perfection of the Old Testament line of faith and faith history? If so, then Jesus is for believing Jews—past and present—their great brother in faith, of whom Buber said that he had revered him from his youth.

Or is it the case that, as traditional Catholic Christology affirms, Jesus is not a believer because he, as son of God, as God-human, possessed immediate knowledge of God, yes the vision of God, and thus was not a believer but a knower? To say of Jesus that he believes would be to bring him down in everything to the level of the mere human. But that is apparently inconsistent with the—God-human—mystery of his unique person: for Jesus sees and knows what we believe.

Over-against that comes the opposite question: What is to be made of the fact and the truth: *Jesus is true man*? Perhaps the following ...consideration can help: If Faith is primarily what we said it was: a mode of existing understood as grounding in God, a dedication of the whole person to God, an unshakable and unreserved trusting and living from this ground, then Jesus is *a radical believer*. He is the perfecter of faith because in him, in his person and in his whole existence, faith has found its perfection: Jesus lives from the God whom he calls his Father. Jesus' existence is dialogue with his Father, he lives from the Father's word, to do his will is his food (John 4:34).

If prayer is the language of faith, then it is precisely in and from the prayer of Jesus to his Father, from his prayer of thanks, of petition, of readiness, of obedience, but also of need, of anxiety, of loneliness, of powerlessness as in Gethsemani and on the cross, that the life of faith in the *sense* of the perfection of faith becomes discernible. All this is confirmed and intensified by statements like the following:

In the days of his flesh, Jesus offered up prayers and supplications, with loud cries and tears, to him who was able to save him from death, and he was heard for his godly fear. Although he was a Son, he learned obedience through what he suffered. (Heb 5:7–8)

With faith understood in this way, Jesus is now seen as being a part of Old Testament faith history. Jesus is a Jew; he belongs to his people and is—as a long-time lost son—finally being taken home; he has come home. Jesus moreover represents a real culminating point in the history of faith. In this connection one could repeat with variation a word from Karl Jaspers, who not only ranks Jesus among the influential figures of world history, like Buddha, Confucius and Socrates, but speaks of Jesus as the most definitive. For, as Jaspers explains: "Jesus led humankind to a frontier which is the most revolutionary in all history. He has broken through to that place where there is nothing but love and God. This place, conceived like a place in the world, is in fact no place."[3] In place of "love," one could also say "faith," remembering that both words come from the same root.

If, in a one-sided view "from above," the reality of the faith of Jesus understood this way is not attended to, it is a loss for Christology, because it is a curtailment of Jesus' humanity. For human faith is part of the mysteries of the life of Jesus. The situation becomes even more serious if, as we see sometimes happening in contemporary Christologies, attempts to do this are qualified as unorthodox, and there are facile accusations of "Nestorianism." That there is also the Christological heresy of monophysitism, and that it is still alive today, is far less noticed, let alone challenged.

The Discontinuity: Faith in Jesus Christ

If there were no other witness in the New Testament regarding faith and the revelation corresponding to it, then the New Testament would be only the final act of the Old, and the line of continuation of its promise. The logical consequence of this perspective would be that the only thing of abiding value in the New Testament would be what was conformed to the Old, turning the New Testament, so to speak, into the last book of the Old Testament. Martin Buber formulated the consequences of this position:

> What is creative in Christianity is not Christianity but Judaism, and we don't need to establish contact with that. We need only to recognize it in ourselves and take possession of it, for we bear it unforgettably in ourselves.[4]

But this perspective doesn't do justice to the New Testament, to the differences, to the discontinuity in, with, and under the continuity. The specific difference can be illustrated in one sentence from Buber: "*Belief in Jesus unites us, belief in Christ divides us.*"

What is specific in the faith we encounter in the New Testament is the Christian faith. This is understood as faith in a final and definitive revelation of the God witnessed in the Old Testament, the God of Israel. It is the revelation in Jesus of Nazareth who is the Christ. The event connected with Jesus of Nazareth is not related to the history of a people but to the person, way, word, and deed of an individual.

Faith thus understood is, accordingly, oriented not just to the proclaiming and believing Jesus, the man from Galilee, not just to the

---

3. Karl Jaspers, *The Great Philosophers* (New York: Harcourt, Brace & World, Inc.) unable to find precise location of this quote.

4. Martin Buber, "Die Erneuerung des Judentums" in: *Reden über das Judentum* (Berlin, 1923) 54; on this: H. U. von Balthasar, *Martin Buber and Christianity: A Dialogue Between Israel and the Church*, trans. Alexander Dru (New York: Macmillan, 1961).

message of God's rule and kingdom; it is oriented above all to the Jesus who is proclaimed as the one in whom the message of God's rule and kingdom was fulfilled and made present, as the one who is witnessed in Old Testament terms as the one who has come, as the one—and this is the decisive point—whom God has authenticated through acts and works, and above all through the resurrection from the dead: as Messiah and Lord. There is where the power of God's rule and kingdom has made its appearance. In this sense, New Testament faith is Christian faith, faith in Jesus Christ, or, more precisely, in Jesus the Christ.

Basically, this is the theme of the New Testament as a whole. It is most clearly expressed by Paul and, in his own way, by John. Paul[5] formulates his own confession of faith: I live in faith in Jesus Christ, "the son of God, who loved me and gave himself for me" (Gal 2:20). This sentence affirms that Christian faith is a personal faith ("faith in Jesus Christ") as well as an affirmational/propositional faith, i.e., faith in the Son of God who "loves me and gave himself for me." It is important to note that this affirmation intends not only to inform but also to move, to effect, to make an impact.

The repeatedly emphasized difficulty of actualizing faith in God as personal encounter is now overcome. It is realized in a unique way through faith in the person named Jesus Christ. This is also the way by which we come also to the other dimension: that of affirmational faith with concrete content which is inseparably connected with, and is the revelation of, the person of Christ.

This content of faith is described, like Old Testament faith, in credal formulas, which are connected with a history. We cite two well-known texts:

For I delivered to you as of first importance what I also received, that Christ died for our sins in accordance with the scriptures, that he was buried, that he was raised on the third day in accordance with the scriptures, and that he appeared to Cephas, then to the twelve. (1 Cor 15:3-5)
If you confess with your lips that Jesus is Lord and believe in your heart that God raised him from the dead, you will be saved. (Rom 10:9)

It is clear from these texts that, according to Paul, faith as faith in Jesus, the Messiah and the Lord, finds its high point and ultimate grounding in confessing Jesus whom God raised from the dead. Thus, the resurrection of Jesus from the dead is the pivotal point of specifically Christian faith. The extent to which faith in God, Abrahamic faith, is concretized and at the same time transcended in this event, Paul makes clear by his coordination of creation and resurrection from the dead. He speaks (Rom 4:17) of faith in God who raises the dead and calls into being that which is not. This concentration is so strong in Paul that, for

---

5. O. Kuss, "Der Glaube nach den paulinischen Hauptbriefen" in: *Auslegung und Verkündigung 1* (Regensburg, 1963) 187–202.

him, the preaching of Jesus, indeed the earthly Jesus as such, hardly makes an appearance.

Paul further characterizes faith as *obediential faith* and as confession in its manifold possibilities of articulation: as praise, witness, thanksgiving, public testimony. Through faith in Jesus, the Christ and the Lord, a new personal and existential situation which is characteristic of faith is created. Faith bestows a new being, "being in Christ." This is actualized in that the believers co-consummate the life and fate of Jesus in their own lives. In other words, faith as suffering with, being crucified with, being buried with him, faith as resurrection and as glorification further signifies entering into the knowledge and comprehension of Jesus Christ, which transcends all reason (Phil 4:7). Faith means having the Spirit of Christ (1 Cor 2:16). Faith is the acceptance of the wisdom of God, which, in view of the folly of the cross, is foolishness for the world (1 Cor 1:18). Faith means the surrendering of the human being to the God who was in Christ and who reconciles the world with himself (2 Cor 5:9).

Faith in Jesus Christ is, in Paul, the repudiation of the self-glorification and self-justification that tries to gain salvation by its own power and thus denies Jesus Christ and the act of God living within. Justification takes place, therefore, by faith alone. For only in faith does that which happens for me in and through Christ become accessible, mediated, and appropriated.

The Earthly Jesus and the Christ of Faith

From this starting point, let us go again to the Synoptic Gospels, which, in their witness to the proclaiming Jesus, do not mention faith in Jesus the Christ. But these Gospels are also written in the light of the Easter message and resurrection faith. They make the statement "Jesus is the Christ" in the form: "Christ is Jesus of Nazareth" in order to give witness to the identity of the earthly Jesus with the proclaimed Christ, with the Christ of faith, in order thus to protect the Christ-kerygma from the suspicion of an unhistorical myth.

The problem "historical, earthly Jesus—Christ of Faith" is thus not a new theme, but is already the basic theme of the New Testament itself. There is no contradiction between these two aspects and dimensions; what there is instead is that continuity and discontinuity, that connection and radical break which are found in the way and the fate of Jesus: death and resurrection from the dead.

All the writings of the New Testament proceed from faith in Jesus the risen, the Messiah and Lord. The Synoptic Gospels look from this horizon back to the earthly Jesus and recognize, already in the life and deeds of the pre-Easter Jesus, the traits of his coming glory. Important for them is the affirmation and confession: The Christ is Jesus of Nazareth. Paul speaks hardly at all of the earthly Jesus. His whole concern is to speak of the salvation opened up in Christ the crucified and risen, to speak of the justification and atonement granted to human beings in Christ, to speak of the new creation. Jesus is the *Christ*. That is the witness of Paul and, for him the decisive affirmation. There is no contradiction between Paul and the synoptics, but the respectively different accenting of the one gift of God to human beings in Jesus, the Christ.

The Synoptic Gospels show that Jesus demands conversion and faith in the royal rule of God, which was not only proclaimed by him but already breaking in and coming near in his person and in his deeds. They show how Jesus also claims faith for himself and how he articulates this claim by his "But I say to you"; "Amen, I say to you"; "Here is more than" the temple, prophet, king, more than Moses; "Today that word has come to fulfillment"; "One is your teacher"; "One is your Father." The verification of this claim and the words associated with it is found in the acts of Jesus, not least the act of forgiving sins.

From this claim come consequences like: "Follow me!" This demand is placed above even love for father and mother (Matt 10:34–39) and includes the readiness to leave everything. This radical following is related to the appeal to do and suffer "for my sake." With this also comes the demand for a clear decision in the sense of being for or against Jesus himself: "He who is not with me is against me, and he who does not gather with me scatters (Matt 12:30; cf. Mark 9:40). Confessing Jesus is, according to the synoptics, decisive for the position of human beings in relation to God: "Every one who acknowledges me before men, I [the Son of Man] also will acknowledge before my father who is in heaven; but whoever denies me before men, I also will deny before my Father who is in heaven" (Matt 10:32f; Luke 9:26; 12:8f; Mark 8:38).

These words correspond to the affirmation that can be described as the high point of the synoptic gospels: "All things have been delivered to me by my Father; and no one knows the Son except the Father, and no one knows the Father except the son and any one to whom the Son chooses to reveal him" (Matt 11:27).

Thus, already present in the framework of the earthly image of Jesus is that condition which is necessary for faith: Faith presupposes someone who has seen and knows. Corresponding to this position is the fact that Jesus is the judge, that he exercises that act which establishes the absolute and definitive truth about human beings and their existence. The criterion of the court and the definitive judgment, however, is not a general norm; it is Jesus himself: What you have done to the least of my brothers—or not done—that you have done to me—or not done (Matt 25:34–44). Jesus is the definitive what and why of the action. These words not only contain an utmost kenosis [emptying] in the sense of solidarity with the least of human beings, they are at the same time an exorbitant, superhuman claim: Who can claim that what was done or not done to human beings was done to him/her?

It follows from this that, precisely from the witness of the first three gospels, Jesus can be understood as the one who believes in a radical manner, and thus is the perfecter of faith, and at the same time the one to whom the faith of human beings—and its implications in discipleship, confession, and decision—are related. If God's rule and kingdom are claimed as present in Jesus, if the Jesus who proclaims also proclaims himself and the mystery of his person in the parables, then there is also in the Synoptic Gospels an implicit Christology whose distinct development takes place after the resurrection of Jesus from the dead. Thus is built the bridge from the proclaiming Jesus to the proclaimed Christ, from the faith of Jesus to faith in Christ.[6]

The Gospel of John

The significance that faith has in the Gospel of John[7] becomes clear from the statement of its goal. We read: "that you may believe that Jesus is the Christ, the Son of God, and that believing you may have life in his name" (John 20:31).

The Gospel of John does not, for the most part, use the substantive "the faith," but rather the verb "to believe" and describes faith as a doing. This gospel says expressly: To believe means to believe in Jesus. "Believe in God, believe in me" (cf. John 14:9-12). This is possible because Jesus is he in whom the Logos has become flesh, in whom the doxa of God can be seen as the doxa of the "only begotten son of the Father" (John 1:18). This doxa already shines in Jesus' earthly life, through which shines the glory of God.

Believing in Jesus is possible and indeed commanded because Jesus, as Son, knows and sees the Father and on that account—"No one has ever seen God" John 1:18)—has brought tidings from him. Believing in Jesus is possible because he comes "from above," because he "comes from God," because he "speaks the words of God," because he is the revealer.

6. H. Ristow—K. Matthiae, ed., "Der historische Jesus und der kerygmatische Christus. Beiträge zum Christusverständnis" in: Forschumg und Verkündigung (Berlin, 1960); K. Rahner, Ich glaube an Jesus Christus (Einsiedeln, 1968); cf. Walter Kasper, Jesus the Christ, trans. V. Green (New York: Paulist Press, 1977).

7. Rudolf Bultmann, The Gospel of John; A Commentary, trans. G. R. Beasley–Murray (Philadelphia: Westminster Press, 1971); H. Schlier, "Glauben, Erkennen, Lieben nach dem Johannesevangelium" in: The Relevance of the New Testament (New York: Herder and Herder, 1968) 156–71; cf. R. Schnackenburg, The Gospel According to John, trans. Kevin Smyth (New York: Herder and Herder, 1968) esp. 1.558–78 (Excursus: Johannine Faith).

Believing means to believe that it is Jesus by whom the "I am" statements are made. I am the shepherd, the door, the bread, the light, the vine, the resurrection, the life, the way, the truth—statements that are not parables but images taken from human life and therefore have their relationship to human beings, and to their being as existence. The Johannine statements are understood as answer to the question of who the human being actually is. Believing means, in John above all, to accept the absolute claim that Jesus is the absolute predicateless "I am he," words reminiscent of the theophany of Exodus 3:14. That is why Jesus can say: "Whoever has seen me has seen the Father" (John 14:9).

Faith, according to the Gospel of John, is, as faith in Jesus, a You-faith. It is at the same time an affirmational faith: Faith in Jesus' words and, above all, in the works that give witness of him, witness that the Father has sent him. They are works such as "no human being can do." At the same time, these works point to the mystery of His person, as bread, as light, and as resurrection. Their intention is to affirm what Jesus Christ meant for human beings.

Faith encompasses and moves all that human beings are and all that is in them. This is shown in the fact that faith is connected with the "coming to Jesus," with "receiving him," "loving him," and "abiding in him." But the extent to which faith is knowing becomes clear in this Gospel; *believing and knowing* are seen as almost identical: "We have believed and have come to know, that you are the Holy One of God" (John 6:69).

All believing is, according to John, also a coming to know; all coming to know is a believing coming to know. And yet, between believing and knowing there is a difference, which gets expressed by the fact that the relationship of Jesus to His Father is always described with "knowing," never with "believing." In the Gospel of John, accordingly, there is no faith of Jesus. But that is no contradiction to the synoptic gospels because knowing is the faith that has come to perfection. Knowing in the biblical sense signifies more than a "knowing about"; knowing is community between persons as the highest personal unity; it is community of life and exchange of life with the one who is known—in the sense of the "I and the Father are one" (John 10:30). For the one who believes in Jesus, the Christ, a knowing is possible in which the faith will be made perfect. Whoever believes is taken up into the community of knowledge of the Son and the Father.

The effect of faith being expounded here helps one to understand that faith is a crossing over into new existence. Being grounded in "He who believes in the Son has eternal life" (John 3:36; 6:40,47; 20:31), "he is born again," has "passed out of death into life" (1 John 3:14), "will not be condemned." In faith, eternal life has already broken in. Faith takes part in the new beginning of existence opened up in Jesus, while in unbelief judgment has already taken effect (John 3:14,21; 5:24). In faith, decision is made between life and death, light and darkness, truth and lying, a decision in favor of life, light, and truth. This does not refer to "cosmic powers" but to characteristics of existence.

Finally, it is said that faith is a gift of God: "No one can come to me unless the Father who sent me draws him" (John 6:44). That means neither that the human being has no part in it nor that unbelief is free of guilt—quite the contrary. Unbelief is the No to Jesus spoken against one's better knowledge, to the Jesus whom the Father attests in unique "signs" and "works." The role of human beings in all this is to let themselves be drawn in, not to refuse or close themselves off. Their receiving becomes their greatest act.

Our intention in these reflections has been, in order to complement the phenomenologically developed "a priori" of faith, to present its biblical "a posteriori." We hope that no artificial construction has been presented, for we have been attempting to describe what arises from the matter itself. This description is both an application and a verification of faith in its fundamental form: as personal act, as content-specific relationship, as option of human beings for the whole of what they are, for their existence, their act, their history, and their world.

FAITH AS HEARING AND SEEING

In the Old and New Testaments

It has often been pointed out that the difference between the revelation of the Old and New Testaments and other religions consists especially in the fact that other religions, especially in their highest forms, e.g., the Greeks, are primarily concerned with contemplation of the divinity. The divine is not something to be believed or heard, but to be seen. It thus reveals itself in contemplation, in theophany, in hierophany, in image and in form. Consequently, cult, mysteries, and initiations are all at the service of this contemplation.

In contrast, the revelation of the Old and New Testament is predominantly characterized by hearing: "Thus speaks the Lord"; "Hear, O Israel"; "Land of the Lord, hear the word of the Lord"; "Hear, you heavens and the earth, hearken to it"—that is the fundamental tenor of revelation in the Old Testament and its daily admonition to the people of God. The Law and the Prophets proclaim the word of the Lord, and all the promises for the future are likewise given in the word. This word is to be heard; it is to be obeyed, believed; this word is to be done. Out of this ground of the word and of faith the People of Israel are to exist and historically live and work. The real sin of the people consists in not hearing, in not having heard, thus in its "obstinacy" and hardness of heart. Word and image really do come together frequently in the Old Testament, especially in its earlier history, and the idea of "seeing God" is not foreign to it. The same is true of the notion of the seeking for and gazing upon the face of the Lord and the longing for this. But this wanting to see happens for the sake of the word, and in the visions of the prophets it is the frame for the word that is entrusted to them. Image and sight especially need the interpreting word. The unveiled vision of God is withheld from human beings. No living human being can look on God as God is; whoever looks on God dies. The Old Testament prohibition of images is the correlation and the consequence of this faith perspective: "You shall not make for yourself a graven image" (Exod 20: 4).

This is how Israel's faith was distinguished from the religions of its surrounding world, from the temples, idols and cults, which were concerned with a bodily presence as well as with seeing, initiation, ecstasy, and rapture. The Temple of Jerusalem, however, contains no images. Its only image is light.

In the New Testament too, word and hearing along with its manifold forms obviously predominate, even if no longer with that obvious emphasis found in the Old Testament. The classical description of the phases of revelation (Heb 1:1) speaks explicitly of God speaking through the prophets and finally in His Son. "The Word" is not by accident a decisive name for the majesty of Christ. Jesus is the Word of the Father from whom he brings the decisive and definitive word. Therefore Jesus knows he is sent to preach the good news. His messianic task consists essentially in announcing the message of God's rule and kingdom: "Repent, and believe!" (Mark 1:14).

The gospel also gives witness to what Jesus did and experienced, witness to the decisive salvific activity in Jesus, and above all, witness to who he is. The answer, given in the language of Scripture: Jesus is the Lord and the Christ (Paul). "The Word has become flesh—we have seen his glory"; "Whoever has seen me has seen the Father" (John).

Nevertheless, the deeds of Jesus and the events in his life, as saving events, have to be proven and interpreted through the word. Jesus himself interprets his death and resurrection as saving events (Luke 24:25–27). When the synoptics hand on the gospel of the proclaiming Jesus, and John hands on the gospel of the Christ proclaiming himself, and when Paul and the Acts of the Apostles are witnesses of the proclaimed Christ, of Jesus the Christ and Kyrios, all this stands under the sign of the word, under the sign of hearing, and of believing, especially of believing in him whom they have seen and whose works and deeds they have seen. But for the event—above all the cross—to be seen and interpreted as act and revelation of God, for that the word is needed, the word from the cross. What is seen and what takes place are, by themselves, not enough; they allow ambiguity. The cross is folly and scandal. Faith comes from hearing, hearing from proclaiming, proclaiming from being sent (cf. Rom 10:14–15).

However much the New Testament speaks of what we have heard and seen, and however much are the eyes that see what the disciples saw called blessed (Matt 13:16), so much does the witness of the New Testament nevertheless know that Jesus is not just the revealed but also the hidden God, God in the form of a servant in whom one does not immediately see the form of God, whom one does not know even though he stands in the midst of all (John 1:26).

But even more: In the New Testament the desire to see and contemplate is often expressly rejected, and seeing and wanting-to-see is rejected as lack of faith, as flight and evasion from the true message. The desire for miraculous signs in the sense of spectacular miracles is rejected by Jesus because they do not lead to faith. "They have Moses and the prophets; let them hear them. If they do not hear Moses and the prophets, neither will they be convinced if someone should rise from the dead" (Luke 16:29–31). This is the reason for the principle: "Blessed are those who have not seen and yet believe" (John 20:29). For "faith is the conviction of things not seen" (Heb 11:1). This is the understanding of the emphatic antithesis: "For Jews demand signs and Greeks seek wisdom, but we preach Christ crucified, a stumbling block to Jews and folly to Gentiles" (1 Cor 1:22). All who were not eye- and ear-witnesses to Jesus, all whom the Risen One did not appear to and encounter, are dependent on the word of the disciples: Through the word, through hearing the word, they come to faith in Jesus, the Christ.

If, despite all this, we can legitimately talk about human beings of faith seeing and contemplating in this life, that is no contradiction, nor is it an inappropriate incursion of Greek ideas and Greek religion into the realm of biblical revelation. It is, rather, a witness to the fact that the eschaton, the last things, have already broken in and made an appearance in Jesus Christ, that they thus can be seen in his person, in his deeds, in the events of the life of Jesus, and that what is to come at the end is only the perfection/fulfillment of what has already become event in Jesus Christ, the last word which God has spoken to us, his incarnate Word. Christ is "the image of the invisible God" (Col 1:15). Therefore, seeing now has a legitimate place; it points to the last things and is, in a certain sense, their anticipation: the seeing from face to face, "seeing God as he is." Hans Urs von Balthasar's major work, *Herrlichkeit*, builds on this characteristic. It is called a theological aesthetic, a theological "theory of perception"; its first volume has the significant title *Seeing the Form (Schau der Gestalt.)*[1] Christ is spoken of as the "center of the form of revelation." This vision, however, is made visible not through images but through the word.

The union of hearing and seeing is the legitimate appropriation of the concerns of religion. It is an expression of the existence and history brought about through Jesus Christ, an expression of the "already" and the "not yet," which is characteristic of Christian faith. That is why there is, in the name of the revelation of God in one person, Jesus Christ, no longer any absolute and rigorous prohibition of images. It is superseded by the "image of the invisible God" in Jesus Christ. It is notable that the representation of Jesus Christ came about first in

---

1. Einsiedeln 1961, ET: *The Glory of the Lord. A Theological Aesthetics. I: Seeing the Form* (San Francisco: Ignatius—New York: Crossroad, 1982).

images and symbols: shepherd, alpha and omega, above all the cross. Only later was the representation of the figure of Jesus added.

In the Tradition of the Origin

This fundamental law of the origin of revelation applies also, and most significantly, to the time of the *tradition of revelation*, which is a tradition of the origin, because revelation itself is the origin of the tradition. Tradition in the community of believers, the Church, takes place corresponding to the origin, revelation, not only in the audible word but also in the *visible sacrament*; but these two modes are bound together in a higher unity: The proclamation is also proclamation and *mysterium fidei, verbum visibile*. But only through the word is it disclosed what reality is being referred to. The sacraments are signs of faith. Baptism is not "mere water, it is water encompassed in God's word."[2] This comes out even more emphatically in the events of the Last Supper. The signifying words of the Eucharistic words of institution disclose the reality of the visible forms of bread and wine. One can likewise say that proclamation stands in the horizon of the sacramental, effective sign. It is *"sacramentum audibile,"* audible sacrament, a sacrament of life.

There follow from this some conclusions that are important : for the Church, for its life and activity.[3]

If the Church is founded on Jesus Christ, if it is to make present and equally available to all times the word and work of God, which has in Christ become event and person, then the Church that is understood as such must be, originally and in its essence, both word-church and sacrament-church. Only as *primordial word* and as *primordial sacrament* can the Church have part in Jesus Christ, in the truth and love of God which has become history and person through him.

If Jesus Christ is *the* Word of God, if "Word of God" is a full and comprehensive description of the mystery of Jesus Christ, then Word is that comprehensive reality in which the sacrament is also taken up and into which it can be integrated. If, in the self-disclosure of God and in communion with him, grace comes about through Jesus Christ in the Holy Spirit, then its application to human beings is not something that happens to things; it is a personal process. As such, it must ultimately come about through word and, if it comes about as sign, be determined by word. For word is uniquely and essentially ordered to person and to self-communication. The reformational cry *"Verbum solum habemus—*we

2. Martin Luther, *Dr. Martin Luther's Small Cathechism* (St. Louis, Concordia Publishing House, 1943) 170.

3. Cf. Heinrich Fries, "Wort und Sakrament" in: *Wort und Sakrament* (Munich, 1966) 21–22.

have only the word," when seen this way, can no longer be a cry that divides the confessions; rather, it is a confession that all Christians can profess. But precisely because the Word of God entered into the visibility and bodiliness of the human, precisely because it became flesh, there is, consequently, sacrament.

But sacrament stand's not outside but inside the word of God and appears as its special form and mode of intensity. On the other hand, sacrament is the highest realization of the word of God definitively and victoriously spoken in Jesus Christ. Thus one can, indeed must say: Because the Church is Church of the theologically correctly understood word, it is the Church of sacrament; and because the Church is Church of sacrament, it is Church of the word. The sacraments do not say anything other than the word, but they say it in their specific way: in sign, in act, in execution.

The sacraments make clear what in word can be overlooked or remain hidden: that one is dealing with the healing, effective, and graced word of God. Sacrament is the highest realization of the essence of the effective word of God as a making-present of the saving act of God in the radical engagement of the Church in the decisive salvific situations of the individual. Under this aspect, the Eucharist is the sacrament of the sacraments, and, at the same time, the absolute instance of the word of God.

From this come the practical consequences which Karl Rahner formulates: If the Church were only to preach, without the courage to speak its most radical, creative word in sacrament, then its preaching would unavoidably be theoretical and ultimately empty talk about something, instead of being the word that does the thing it is affirming. If the Church were to neglect the proclamation of the word in bare confidence in the *opus operatum*, that would leave out what the sacraments point to and intend to bring about: personal faith and personal love.[4]

Correct Hearing and Seeing

We will now speak again of how the hearing and seeing of faith should be done. As dimensions of faith, hearing and seeing must be *existential* and *existentiell*.[5]

Existential hearing and seeing is an act in which human beings understand and interpret themselves and present themselves as human beings. It is a hearing and seeing in which the whole human being is

4. Karl Rahner, in: *Handbuch der Pastoraltheologie I* (Freiburg—Basel—Vienna, 1964) 329; see Bernard L. Marthaler, "Creeds," *NDT* 259–64.

5. H. Fries, Vom Hören des Wortes Gottes. Eine fundamentaltheologische Überlegung in: Joseph Ratzinger—H. Fries (Hrsg.), *Einsicht und Glaube* (Freiburg—Basel—Vienna, 1962) 15–27.

present with the whole "awakedness" and truth of his/her "I am." It is a hearing and seeing that takes place in full openness of the spirit and heart and in which this openness finds its ultimate goal, its true whence and whither. It is a hearing in the sense of a genuine listening to, in the sense of a living readiness for a word which is not and cannot be my own word springing out of myself, but which is said to me and for me, and which I can perceive and receive. It is a hearing in the sense of a willingness to step out of oneself and one's shell, to transcend oneself, to be "all ears," to be attentive with one's whole understanding being. The same is true of seeing, which is an open, unobstructed seeing, which is "all eyes" and thereby "existential." Becoming adept in such a hearing and seeing takes place in the everyday, in the way in which human beings can hear, listen to, and see each other.

Existential hearing and seeing is the kind of hearing and seeing in which the ground and origin of my self, of my existing, is just as present as the whither, the goal of this existing. That is the meaning of the Psalm verse: "Thy word is a lamp to my feet and a light to my path" (Ps 119:105). Word is supposed to illuminate, spread light, open up understanding for and of the path to be taken. The reality coming to us is expressed in a new way. The word of God is accordingly not a light which God beams out, but which beams out from God and illuminates the place of human existence and historical reality.[6]

Because there is such an existential hearing and seeing, there is also an *existentiell* hearing and seeing. This is hearing and seeing in the sense of commitment, of being "hit" or personally "struck": "You are the man" (2 Sam 12:7), "*tua, mea res agitur.*" This *res* is not separable from me, this *res* I am myself. It is about me, about the sense and salvation of my existence, for it is about God, who belongs to the definition of my self. It is about the salvation of which I have need, towards which my being strives, and in which it is to be fulfilled and made perfect.

From this it follows: I can correctly and truly hear and see only if I act in a manner that is both *existential* and *existentiell*, out of the fundamental structure and fundamental constitution of my existence as an existence opened towards God because grounded in God and related to God. The fundamental presupposition of this act is, biblically seen, metanoia, conversion from the false way, from the false direction, and getting pointed towards and set out on the right course, the reversal of poles, so that my existence is understood as existence before God and is actualized as such. I can hear and see correctly—in Johannine language—only if I am "of the truth" (John 18:37). Truth in the *sense* of the Gospel of John is true reality: the reality of God and the open, human, historical reality unveiled before the reality of God. If human

6. G. Ebeling, *The Nature of Faith* (Philadelphia: Fortress Press, 1967) 189–90.

beings are characterized by their origin, then they are of the truth because they are of God, and they are of God because they are of the truth. Only as such do they hear the word of God. They who do not hear don't hear because they are not of God, because they are not of the truth (John 8:46–47).

Next to this authentic existential and existentiell hearing and seeing is inauthentic hearing and seeing, unsubstantial and decadent hearing, inexistentiell hearing. There are always, especially prevalent in today's human beings, deficient modes of hearing, of which we become daily aware in ourselves and in converse with the world and others around us: the prejudiced, deluded hearing, that is not a listening to someone else but only a hearing and listening to oneself; the undeveloped hearing, which only incidentally hears; the cold, uninvolved hearing; the bad, mistrustful hearing; the hearing that lurks, seeking out failures and weaknesses, wanting to catch someone in the act. Add to this the diminishment of hearing, because there is no room left where anything can be heard: no space of quiet and silence, because the backdrops of the stage on which we play our play and our role are backdrops of sound and without them we can hardly continue to play at all. We drive away and banish the stillness. These phenomena are well known and have been described often enough.

Such a deficiency of hearing has a real effect on hearing as a dimension of faith. It is even worse here, because the word of faith is not to be found in noise, but needs the stillness in which it can be heard and perceived, and because this hearing is not about anything arbitrary or irrelevant but is about the decisive reality of my existence and its relationship to meaning.

The same is true of seeing. There is the narrow, one-sided, the loveless and inimical seeing, the nasty, hate-filled glance, there is the "overlooking" and the looking away, the seeing with a blind spot, the seeing through blinders. These deficient modes are multiplied and strengthened in our optic age in the overflow of the images daily brought before our eyes, which leave behind no lasting impression.

Scripture speaks extensively of the deficient modes of hearing. We will mention only the key words: "Hear, and yet not hear"; "hearing they do not hear, nor do they understand" (Matt 13:13); and the words about slow and non-comprehending hearing. Recall the parable of the different types of earth which receive the seed (Mark 4:1–9; Matt 13:1–9; Luke 8:4–8) and the interpretation given in the gospel itself which above all is also to be understood in the sense that the different kinds of ground not only refer to the different types of hearers, but also to the individual hearers and the different kinds of ground in one's own heart. Recall too the repeated call to awakening: "They who have ears to hear, let them hear," which is found in the synoptics as well as in the seven letters of the Apocalypse. Recall that text about correct hearing: "If any man has ears to hear, let him hear." And he said to them, "Take heed what you hear; the measure you give will be the measure you get, and still more will be given you. For to him who has will more be given; and from him who has not, even what he has will be taken away" (Mark 4:23–25). Finally, recall the drama of the speech of Stephen, which speaks about the "stiff-necked people, uncircumcised in heart and ears" who "always resist the Holy Spirit" (Acts 7:51) and of whom is said: "They cried out with a loud voice and stopped their ears and rushed together upon him and stoned him" (Acts 7:57–58).

The New Testament describes a similar situation with regard to seeing. It speaks of seeing and yet not seeing, of not seeing with seeing eyes (Matt 13:13), of the blind leading the blind (Matt 15:14), of people who with seeing eyes are blind, of people who see disproportionately (speck and log) (Matt 7:3).

A fundamental analysis of the phenomenon of inauthentic, obstructed hearing and seeing reveals its cause to be an *existentiell and anthropological deficiency*. It goes back to human beings refusing to hear, or receive anything, to their wanting to hear only their own word, to hear and listen only to themselves; to their refusal to let anything be said. This behavior is based on human beings not wanting to be indebted, not wanting anything to be given them, not wanting to receive anything, but demanding to be autonomous lords of themselves and the measure of all things.

It is the same with seeing. Human beings want above all to see themselves and what has been brought about and achieved by themselves. It is in this that they see their own significance or what is useful and helpful to themselves, their "reputation." The selfless and free glance of the gift given, the tranquillity and fulfillment that come from this and from an unhurried gaze have become quite strange to them. It is in themselves and in their own doing that they recognize the source of all light and every illumination. Doing comes before receiving.

It is obvious that the contemporary world offers an especially rich field for such behavior. This is the world which human beings make, have made, and will make. Human beings fancy themselves as the creators of all things. They have the feeling of being able to make and produce everything. They are convinced that there is no right and no boundary that would prevent them from doing this. This claim and will of human beings is both factually and impressively confirmed everyday. Human beings today manage and organize the world so that it is more and more their own world, at their—and only their—own disposition, indebted to no one and received from no one but themselves. Human beings in this world of their own making consume and use it as its absolute lord, as the ones who give the orders and pull the strings.

They plunder it—unaccountable to anyone—for themselves, and their own needs and purposes. So true is this that even the human person in the world is used and consumed and takes its worth from its "consumption value." Human beings in this world have insured themselves for everything and against everything possible: against sickness, accident, death, fire, and flood, and they have ways and means for everything. They no longer need any help, any providence, any blessing, or any prayer of petition.

Much more could be added to this description of a manufactured, managed, organized, and insured world of human beings, a world which is claiming and threatening to become something that it is sufficient for itself; and that in becoming part of this world these human beings are endangering their nature and the true structure of their being; that, immanently and monologically caught up in themselves, they are losing the openness, the power that transcends them, that quality which brings them out of themselves, and in which they recognize their true whither and whence, and which lets them become what they truly are: hearers of the word, receivers of the light.

This line of thinking can be pushed by pointing out that this described anthropological deficiency can also be conditioned by external political and social factors: by systems or conditions of exploitation and oppression that lead to pauperization, poverty, and hunger. It is especially from here that the lack of the hearing and seeing that characterize faith can come. Metanoia under these conditions cannot take place without a change which helps human beings towards a humanly worthy subjectivity and freedom. Before one can say to these people: "Man shall not live by bread alone" (Matt 4:4), one should consider the imperative and its consequences: "Give them to eat!" Luke 9:13).

However, this description of the situation would be incomplete without indicating how, along with these incontestable signs of deterioration, new possibilities for an open and authentic hearing and seeing are also opening up. In the overflowing of sound and image, a new longing for "stillness in the noise," for meditation, for self-discovery is awakening. This is so because the nature of the human being, which is open, seeking, asking, and characterized by receiving, can indeed be covered over and damaged, but it can never be destroyed.

The question of existence and its sense, of well-being and ruin, of living and dying, of happiness and joy, of anxiety and security, of truth, justice, and peace, cannot be choked off or replaced. Nor can these problems be solved solely by science and technology. This is exactly what human beings in today's world are experiencing. The more they use up, manage, and insure, the more obvious it becomes how little all this can fulfill them. There is awakening the hunger for a new world and reality, which is not made but which is there and abides. The desire for a new word is being stirred up, a word that comes from somewhere else than the ephemeral words of the day, a word that is quite different from the words one hears everyday to the point of boredom. What the prophet Amos said is coming true: "Behold the days are coming," says the Lord God, "when I will send a famine on the land; not a famine of bread, nor a thirst for water, but of hearing the words of the Lord" (Amos 8:11). In addition, the longing is awakening for the one who is light and the source of all light, the longing for the totally other.

Let us also add that the made, administered, and insured world reveals how little it can rely on itself and reach fulfillment in itself. Do not all insurances owe their existence to the fact that we cannot do away with what we are insuring ourselves against: sickness, age, accident, death? And do we not, especially today, have the question, the anxiety and worry, about how we human beings are going to deal with this mighty world we have constructed and organized for ourselves? Do not we human beings of today know that the answer to this question can be drawn from no computer and that power over power must be drawn from a source totally other than the world of motors? The questions of technical reality press beyond the purely technical and seek a word and a light which they themselves cannot give. Haven't we already gained the experience that a world which is even more managed and organized will cause human beings and what is characteristic of them—encounter in word, love, and personal communication—to suffer more and more deprivation?

Along with all the perfection of technology, its boundaries are discernible: the boundaries of growth which, left to itself, lead to destruction. To that comes the a priori of the perfect means and the confused end. The irremovable limit situations of human existence remain. Contemporary anthropology has spoken of the decadence and finitude of human beings and also in a positive way, about their indebtedness and dependency, and thus opened that flank which offers the openness of human beings for the possibility of faith and for the hearing and seeing present in them.[7]

---

7. Wolfhart Pannenberg, *Anthropology in Theological Perspective*, trans. Matthew J. O'Connell (Philadelphia: The Westminster Press, 1985).

§9

FAITH AND CONFESSION

Their Coordination

Confessing as activity and expression, confession as form of what gets verbalized in confessing, is the voice, answer, and witness of faith.[1] Confession is a sign that faith and its contents have been heard and perceived, that its word has reached its goal and can be made perceptible. But confession is not, be it noted, *the* voice of religion in general, nor of those religions of which it is characteristic that the Divine manifests itself in manifold forms and in which the dependency of human beings on God and the Divine is witnessed in all imaginable forms. These religions, e.g., the nature religions, come to no clear propositional affirmation, to no historicity, to no decisiveness, and thus also to no confession. This is the way it was in Greek and Roman religion. In the pantheon of the gods, they see the legitimate representation of themselves. The pantheon is not closed off and can be constantly increased. It is limitlessly assimilable; everything has its place in it. It even accepts and gives place and voice to the contradictory. The obligatory veneration of the emperor as divine, which caused conflict with the Christians, was primarily something political which, religiously, was pushed to excess. It is likewise characteristic of these religions that they are oriented to and connected with no time, no historical event, no historical person, but are found in the circle of constant recurrence so that, of the content of the religion it can be said:

---

1. H. Dörries, *Das Bekenntnis in der Geschichte der Kirche*, 2d ed. (Göttingen, 1947); R. M. Speight and B. A. Gerrish, "Creeds," *ER* 4 (1987) 138–50; F. X. Murphy, "Creed," *NCE* 4 (1967) 432–38; N. Brox, *Zeuge und Märtyrer. Untersuchungen zur frühchristlichen Zeugnisterminologie* (Munich, 1966); P. T. Camelot, "Creeds," *SM* 2.37–40; Helmut Gollwitzer, "Die Bedeutung des Bekenntnisses für die Kirche," in: *Hören und Handeln*, Festschrift E. Wolf (Munich, 1962) 153–90.

"It happened nowhere, but always is." There is no confession here because there is no clear statement.[2]

The same can be said of the religions of the East with their flowing, seeing-everything-in-one conceptions of the divine and with the infinite form of expression which the divine takes—the one light in thousands of waters, which consciously does not explain or define itself. These religions are quite ready to plant even Christianity as a flower in their garden, but they refuse to acknowledge in Christianity anything other than what they acknowledge in the other flowers. For the special place of what is Christian, or even for Christianity's claim to be definitive or unique, they have no understanding; indeed, they expressly resist this and see in it a lessening of religion itself.[3]

Consequently, confession as voice, as expression and witness of faith, is found only where faith is articulated, where faith says and has something to say, where something historical took place, where historical persons are encountered as bearers and mediators of faith, where faith is not the echo of one's own self-reflection but is an answer to a word which is not a human word, an answer to an historical event which human beings themselves have not designed and brought into being.

Confession as confession of faith is found preeminently within *biblical revelation*, which culminates in the self-disclosure of God in Jesus Christ, and also in those religions which, like Islam, stand in the horizon and under the influence of biblical revelation. Confession as confession of faith in the proper sense is, accordingly, possible only where there is *faith in the precise and specific sense*: within what is witnessed by the Bible of the Old and New Testaments, and within the historical radius of influence determined by it, as this is realized through the community of faith and believers. Confession as an answer of faith is really possible only where there is faith as an answer.

That is why confessions as professions of faith in the clear, circumscribed sense are found in the Old Testament. One finds there the profession: "Hear, O Israel, the Lord our God is one Lord" (Deut 6:4); there is the profession of Yahweh who led Israel out of Egypt (cf. Exod 12:17; Deut 25:5–9; Jos 24:2–13); there is profession of the most important events in Israel's history which, as acts of God in the past, provide the guarantee of God's fidelity in the present and future. There are further the professions of Yahweh, "the creator of heaven and the earth." In all these instances there is a clear affirmation as well as simulta-neously a clear rejection of the other gods, of the other nations. Not to

2. Cf. Heinrich Fries, "Mythos und Offenbarung," in: *Fragen der Theologie heute*, ed. J. Feiner—J. Trütsch—F. Böckle (Einsiedeln—Zurich—Cologne, 1960) 11–43; "Neudruck" in: J. Bernard, ed. *Offenbarung. Phänomen—Begriff—Dimension* (Leipzig, 1981) 106–42.
3. Walter Kasper, *Dogma unter dem wort Gottes* (Mainz, 1968) 36.

be like the other nations, not to do what the other nations do, that was Israel's destiny and election. That does not exclude but includes that Israel had a special vocation and mission *for* the other nations.

The coordination of confession and faith continued and intensified in the New Testament and concentrated on what is witnessed to there. The confession of Simon Peter as answer to the question of Jesus: "Who do men say that I am?" . . . . "You are the Christ," is a high point in the gospel (Mark 8:27–29); likewise the words of Jesus: "Every one who acknowledges me before men, I also will acknowledge before my Father who is in heaven" (Matt 10:32; Luke 12:8). The reflection of Paul over the state and content of the Christian faith is formulated in the sentence: "If you confess with your lips that Jesus is Lord and believe in your heart that God raised him from the dead, you will be saved. For man believes with his heart and so is justified, and he confesses with his lips and so is saved" (Rom 10:9–10). In the hymn of the Letter to the Philippians (2:11) it is said in response to the way of Jesus: "Every tongue [shall] confess that Jesus Christ is Lord." The First Letter of John says: "Whoever confesses that Jesus is the Son of God, God abides in him, and he in God" (1 John 4:15).

Confession thus contains a clear, content-specified and articulated affirmation. This confessional affirmation, however, does not describe everything possible, but expresses the center, the decisive core of that to which faith relates and to which it answers. From this core of the biblical confession have come the expanded confessions of the faith: the so-called *Apostles' Creed* and the subsequent symbols of the faith.[4] Symbols come from throwing together, binding together. In the case of the symbols of faith, this means not an accretion of articles but an inner interweaving, a cohesion of contents.

In addition, confession means that one does not have a mere affirmation, and also not just a committed affirmation, but an act of homage, glory, and praise. Confession honors and praises the God who has made himself known and present to human beings in word and act, in event and person, especially in Jesus Christ, who is the salvation of humankind. The place of confession is worship,[5] more precisely, the response of the gathered community after they have heard the message of the revelation of God in the gospel (confession as confession of sins does not need to be mentioned in this context).

---

4. Oscar Cullmann, *Die ersten christlichen Glaubensbekenntnisse* (Zurich, 1949); Joseph Ratzinger, *Introduction to Christianity* (San Francisco: Ignatius Press, 1990); Wolfhart Pannenberg, *The Apostles' Creed in the Light of Today's Questions*, trans. Margaret Kohl (London: S. C. M. Press, 1972).
5. H. Schlier, *Die Verkündigung im Gottesdienst der Kirche* (Köln, 1958).

The Function of Confession

Confession is supposed to make clear that faith, which can and should be made known, is *distinguished* from what it itself is not.[6] Its purpose is to make clear that, concretely expressed, the Christian faith is set apart from religion in general and from the religions in particular, as well as from ideologies. The purpose of confession is to articulate that its uniqueness, differentiation, and clarity are characteristics of the Christian faith. This also affirms that Jesus Christ, whom this faith confesses, is not the founder of a religion after the manner of other religions. He and his work cannot be confused as happens, for example, in Lessing's *Parable of the Ring*, where the authentic ring cannot be distinguished from the inauthentic, and even gets lost. The purpose of confession is, thus, demarcation over against possible misinterpretations and one-sided interpretations of faith; confession also means demarcation against unbelief.

But that is not the only perspective that is represented in the confession of faith. In the Christian confession of faith the *universality* of this faith can and should come to expression: the openness of Christianity towards the world, towards humanity, towards the other religions and world views. In the Christian confession, therefore, there should be not only the articulation of what and whom the demarcation and consequent exclusion concerns, but also an expression of that which can be included in this faith, which is represented in the confession.

There is not just the text: "He who is not with me is against me" (Matt 12:30); there is also the other, less often cited statement: "He that is not against you is for you" (Luke 9:50). We have, as biblical affirmation, not only the text about the folly of the cross (1 Cor 1:23), but also the quite different "What therefore you worship as unknown, this I proclaim to you" (Acts 17:23).

This universality is based not on the supposition that everything is equal or equally valid, but in the fact that the concrete center of Christian faith, Jesus Christ, has a universal dimension: as the second Adam, as that person to whom creation and humanity are related (Col 1:16-20).

From these points come a number of things: First, that the Christian faith is not a private matter and cannot be privatized, but is oriented towards the public, towards community, and is represented in it. This is a consequence of the fact that the revelation that the faith in its response confesses, is revelation for all. Faith as answer to the word of God is thus that which founds the community of believers, which is called by the word from the world; and this is the biblical term for Church (*ecclesia*). Those who believe and want to come to faith must be

6. H. Gollwitzer, *The Existence of God as Confessed by Faith* (Philadelphia: Westminster Press, 1965).

joined to this community of believers, become part of it, be accepted into it, and be brought into harmony with it.

Confession, however, whenever it is not just formal, thoughtless lip service, makes and becomes in itself the foundation of new community, keeps it alive, and brings it together ever anew as community of believers and confessors. Confession as elucidation, confession as demarcation over against another as well as power of universal integration, presupposes the possibility that the community of faith can find and speak this clear word, that—in other, concrete words—the community of those who believe abides in the truth and the truth abides in it.

The confession that is in the community of believers as expression, witness, and voice of faith must be an abiding one if this community is to be an abiding one. The confession is elucidated on the occasion of certain situations, events, challenges, critical and sceptical questions, controversies, difficulties, attacks.

The confession of the faith and of the believers has *to be actualized* in view of these realities. The confession—as becomes clear from the fact of the situation—has to emphasize those accents which are especially needed or called into question. The confession must do this in its concern to protect and not to falsify the matter of faith—above all, the matter of its normative origin. But it is not enough simply to repeat the old formulas and words with which the confessions are made. It can be necessary, for the sake of abiding continuity, to say the old, true things in a new and different way, so that they can be said to human beings who live under other conditions of understanding, who speak another language. The confessions need interpretation that is constantly being renewed.

The history of faith is also stamped by the history of its confessions. In them is expressed the faith, the understanding of faith, insight into faith, and growth into faith. It is characteristic of the confessions that they stand and wish to stand under the sign of continuity, that they make possible not only a horizontal community, i.e., the community of brothers and sisters in faith, but also a community in the depth dimension of history, i.e., community with those who have gone before them in faith, who are to be honored and respected because we are indebted to them and would not even exist without them.

Because the confessions have to do with a genuine history, continuity cannot be the only element of the historical path. That would lead to fixations and ossifications. To historicity belongs the upwardness and future of the ever new. For the confession of faith this cannot mean simply that more and more new revelations are given, but must mean rather that faith, through historical challenges, gives new answers to the questions being asked here and now. It must give these answers, but it also has the ability to do so.

Through confession and through the confessions, therefore, there is expressed not just what faith used to be, but an opening up of what faith is, what aspects and dimensions it has, what wealth it can produce. *The historical* does not bring about the relativization of what is valid or the repeated dissolution of the things of yesterday; it turns into that comprehensive time-space in which faith unfolds, interprets and makes itself and its perspectives current. The historical path of faith, to be sure, should not be seen in a highly uncalled-for triumphalism as constant progress towards ever greater perfection; but even less is this path a mere history of decline. The path of faith is characterized by the dialectic of continuity and discontinuity that characterizes the history of faith and of the faith community and requires from every present reality its respective appropriation.

Finally, included in the meaning of confession is that it must speak out and be answerable before the public, before the neutral as well as the hostile, the scholarly as well as the societal and political. This corresponds to the demand "Always be prepared to make a defense to anyone who calls you to account for the hope that is in you" (1 Pet 3:15). Confession means that the persons confessing can be brought to court, that they will have to represent their confession there, that the scenes will be repeated that are sufficiently known from history and from the present; that for the sake of this confession, scorn, mockery, prejudicial treatment, exploitation, and—in still more serious cases—punishment, persecution, and finally death, is to be expected.

That is why believers and confessors stand in the discipleship of him of whom the First Letter to Timothy says that Jesus Christ under Pontius Pilate "made the good confession" (1 Tim 6:13); they stand in the great line of figures and witnesses of the faith described in the eleventh chapter of the Letter to the Hebrews. They stand in the discipleship of him "that is spoken against" (Luke 2:34), whose cross represents the answer of the world to the offer of God. Martyrdom represents the utmost extreme case of confession.

Faith and Confession Today

Confession nowadays means, first of all, that if faith is to be and to be abiding, confession too must be abiding—and, to be sure, all that implies, i.e., content, expressibility, binding character, answerability, public character, relationship to community and authority, definition, specificity, and differentiation. Confession nowadays means to stand in continuity with the confession from yesterday and with the confession in the beginning. Confession today means that we must not start from the beginning, making nothing out of nothing; rather, we are to accept the given and the handed on in order to make it our own. Confession today means to stand in the tradition as the real history of faith. Confession today also means not to fall back into the greater uncertainty that lies behind what has been recognized and expressed in faith; but confession today also means not just repeating the past; it means leading the past over into today, into the possibility, into the understanding and into the language of the present. Confession today means having the courage to accept the content character and objectivity of faith, it means knowing that escape from what is binding is likewise, in principle, a decision, even if a bad one. For human beings are oriented to the concrete and to something binding; they don't have to decide for anything and everything, but at least for something concrete, in life, in vocation or profession, in encounter with others, in the question of God and salvation. Corresponding to this tendency to concreteness is the articulated content character of Christian faith and Christian confession. Or perhaps it is the other way around: To the concretization of revelation in its supreme form in Jesus Christ corresponds the concretization of our answer in faith and confession.

Confession today also means knowing about that situation of the Christian faith and Christian confessions which, through historical events and decisions, have brought it about that out of the creed have come creeds, out of the confession have come confessions, and that from this have come such different understandings of faith as the decision of one confession against another, which has led to separation in the community of believers. Confessions of faith have become counter-confessions.

Confession today means knowing that separation in faith is set over against the demand for unity in faith. Confession today means knowing that what has happened cannot of course be made not to have happened, but that it can be changed because it is human, i.e., an event situated in human freedom. This change becomes obligatory when the event is something that is not supposed to be, an event involving guilt and scandal.

In view of this, confession today means to place oneself in this painful situation and to attempt, in the power of faith and love, in the confidence of hope, to change it: *Counter-confessions* should become *co-confessions*. In this question of confession, a highly unusual observation can be made these days: there is in our time revaluation of the reality and the word "confession" in the realm of modern ideologies (the confession of Marxism and Leninism), but likewise in the realm of religion. And we are learning every day about the kind of intensity of confession of which contemporary Islam is again capable.

Whether one can discover the same kind of thing within the Christian community of faith is not easy to decide. The confessions made on "Church Day" or "Catholic Day" or at other public events is indeed impressive. But it is difficult to decide whether such gatherings can as a whole be judged to be confessions *of* the Christian faith or as confession *to* the Christian faith.

The value and position that confession held in earlier times in the community of Christians is well known. Recall the respect which the word "confessors," who in crisis became martyrs, aroused in the realm of Christianity and, one hopes, will continue to arouse. The word "Confessing Church" in connection with the Barmen Declaration was and is a glory of the Evangelical Lutheran Church in the time of National Socialism [Nazism].

If today the word and the matter of confession within the Christian community of faith, within the Church, no longer has the same significance and high value, one can ask whether we have here a change of nomenclature, a play on words, or a breakdown in reality and behavior which is a dubious development for Christian faith. This raises some questions. Are there not some worrisome causes behind what is recognizable today as a devaluation of confession? Is it not because one is no longer sure and can no longer exactly say to what one can and should confess? And is that not due to the fact that there is no longer any abiding content or valid orientation, because everything has been sucked into the wake of the relative and non-binding, because there is apparently nothing that abides in all changeability because everything is said and adapted in new ways through interpretation? Isn't there a connection between the devaluation of confession and the inclination to do without the truth and content factor of affirmation according to the motto "What is truth?" to put no value on orientations, to maintain consciously a balancing act of the more-or-less, of the possible, of the open, and even cultivate oscillation in order to be always able to plead for the "could be," for the "it depends," for the "it's possible"?

Isn't this low estimation of confession also connected with the other attitude of shying away from what is binding, of refusing to set any kind of a course, make a concrete decision, commit oneself to accomplish something, undertake something venturesome? One wants to stand "outside," one wants to be totally uninvolved, an "objective" onlooker standing in the distance.

To push these considerations further or illustrate them, one would really have to say that the very death of Jesus, that the serious case of a confession to Jesus, the true Lord, that the refusal to offer sacrifice to the Roman Caesar or any contemporary Caesar, and the readiness to take on oneself the resulting consequences including the giving of one's life—one would really have to say that all this was, to put it mildly, a misunderstanding. One could argue these things could and perhaps even should actually have been put aside by interpretation and enlightenment.

Are we not in danger these days of qualifying a serious intention or even the clarity of an affirmation as fanaticism, intolerance, and narrowness? Aren't we in danger of avoiding, or at least smoothing out, all rigor in decisive questions, and, in Christian terms, tearing down enough of the content of faith and confession that the folly and scandal of the cross can be avoided, that it can be gotten rid of by hermeneutics and dialogue? Doesn't it sometimes seem that what people, especially the people of today, think is possible is made into the yardstick of faith? Isn't modernity, contemporaneity, being up-to-date, the first commandment, even for the Christian faith, when it wants to avoid the risk of being only a tail light?

Aren't we in danger of turning dialogue into a dialogism in which everyone talks uncommittedly about anything? Isn't that what consitutes true brotherliness? Isn't it possible that such important and helpful theological expressions as "anonymous Christian," which describe a critically important way for Christians to see and value non-Christian people, can be misused and misinterpreted into a leveling universal principle in whose horizon one has to leave everything the way it is?[7] Aren't we in danger of tearing down or leveling out all Christian differentiations, and thus turning every profile and contour into something faceless?

These remarks are intended as motivating questions to help us deal with the matter of faith and confession, in order to clarify the now-recognizable difference between "is" and "should" and in order to indicate the problems and difficulties with which confessions of faith have to deal in our day. These difficulties do appear to be surmountable, and are perhaps already being surrounded. After all, why should Christians leave to others the possibility and the chance of confession? Would we not then be pushing the matter of our faith into a corner and putting our light under a bushel, which of course we shouldn't do (cf. Mark 4:21; Luke 8:16)?

---

7. On this cf. H. Fries, "Der anonyme Christ—Das anonyme Christentum als Kategorien christlichen Denkens" in: E. Klinger, *Christentum innerhalb und außerhalb der Kirche* (Freiburg—Basel—Vienna, 1976) 25–41; N. Schwerdtfeger, *Gnade und Welt. Zum Grundgefüge von Karl Rahners Theorie der "anonymen Christen"* (Freiburg—Basel—Vienna, 1982).

FAITH UNDER THE SIGN OF
DOCTRINE, DOGMA, TRUTH, AND PRAXIS

Doctrine

Like the relation of confession to the content of faith, doctrine is related to what can be affirmed about faith and to what is communicable in the form of instruction, information, communication. Doctrine does not have the same existential dimension as confession. Doctrine brings out the content aspects of faith and seeks, by way of thorough reflection, to establish a connection, a relationship.

The form and linguistic character of faith formulated in doctrine is already found to an impressive degree in the doctrinal writings of the Old Testament, among which one can list the books of Job, Wisdom, Proverbs, Qoheleth (Ecclesiastes), Sirach, and many Psalms. That the doctrinal writings come from the later period of the Old Testament and, like the Book of Wisdom, reach into the second century before Christ, is an indication of the level of reflection which presupposes the proclaimed, the narrated, and the actualized, and turns it into the content of a new mode of reflection—i.e., doctrine.

Another reason for this late development is to be found in the fact that these writings of the Old Testament are influenced by the intellectual milieu of Hellenism. Many Jews lived in the Diaspora. In the doctrinal writings, an attempt is made to translate the faith of Israel into a language in which the people of the time, and also they themselves, lived: into the language of Greek thought, of the logos, to which wisdom and teaching belong. In this way a new mediation of the faith was to be made possible.

In the New Testament we find the fact that Jesus appears in the form of a teacher whose teaching was above all interpretation of Scripture, and that his preaching is presented under the concept of teaching (Matt 7:28; Mark 6:2). One must note here that the doctrine and teachings of Jesus are characterized as a speaking and teaching "in power" (Matt 7:28; Mark 6:2), and thus distinguished from the teachings of the scribes. This characterization comes about in Matthew after the so-called Sermon on the Mount, in which the teaching in power becomes visible: in the Beatitudes, for example, but above all in the multiple antitheses: "You have heard that it was said to the men of old but I say to you, in the matter of killing, of adultery, divorce, swearing, revenge, love of enemies" (cf. Matt 5:21-48). This goes far beyond the differences in teaching customary among the Jewish rabbis. Jesus sets himself above the otherwise unchallenged authority of Moses.

Accordingly Jesus also says: "You are not to be called rabbi, for you have one teacher, and you are all brethren. . . . Neither be called masters, for you have one master, the Christ" (Matt 23:8,10). "Teacher" did not, to be sure, become a Christological title. In his trial, Jesus is questioned by the high priest about his teaching (John 18:19).

None of this keeps Jesus, as we read in the synoptic gospels, from sending out his disciples to teach (Mark 6:30). The mission command of the Risen One, "Make disciples of all nations" (Matt 29:19), includes the moment of teaching. The teaching of the disciples and apostles is a teaching of the teaching of Jesus and a teaching/doctrine about him as the Christ and the Kyrios. In the writings of Paul, teaching is described as a special charism, as a gift of the Spirit for the building up of the community (Rom 12:7). In the Acts of the Apostles (1:1) Luke describes the contents of his gospel with the words that he has written down everything "that Jesus did and taught." The Acts of the Apostles describes life in the community of Jerusalem and mentions first the holding fast to the teaching of the apostles (Acts 4:2).

In the late New Testament writings, above all in the Pastoral Letters where the expectation of the parousia is ebbing, where the concern is to be prepared for the continuation of history, in the letters to Titus and Timothy, the word and the reality of teaching take on a towering significance. The proclamation is presented primarily in the form of teaching. The Apostle is the teacher; the disciples of the Apostle, Titus and Timothy, have primarily the task of attending to "right," "true," "sound" teaching, warding off heresy, of guarding and protecting the treasure of a precious heritage mediated and entrusted to them in the form of teaching.

Such a process, *the way from kerygma to teaching*, is important in two ways: first, as information and instruction about the content and context of faith—that supplied an element of stabilization—and second, as rejection of the false teachings about the faith, the heresies. These are described even in the New Testament, especially in the late writings, the Pastoral Letters and the letters of John. The true and sound teaching was set apart from these heresies.

The significance of teaching as figure and language of faith became important in subsequent times in the encounter and controversy of the Christian faith with the intellectual tendencies of a particular time and with the teaching mediated there. In the beginning of Christianity this encounter was above all with Greek thought in the form of colorful, glittering gnosticism.[1] Thus it is not surprising that Greek thought, concerned as it was with logos, with essence, and with insight into essence, also asked the Christian faith about its logos, its essence, and that the representatives of this faith, on their side, represented the matter of faith in an objectifiable form, in the form of truth, of teaching. From that grew the form of *orthodoxy*, right teaching as sign and expression of faith. In that way the faith became knowable, ascertainable, capable of being questioned. Its literary form is the catechism in the form of important propositions and dogmas. Thus truth is related to true propositions, to agreement of the teaching with the reality, and it is then said: "The word is reliable."

All this is a legitimate, necessary process, part of the reality of faith and its historical development. Teaching is a sign that the content of faith has an inner relationship to reason and understanding. Teaching, orthodoxy, has its right, as long as it does not push aside the other languages of faith: prayer, praise, proclamation, narration, or even want to replace them. The word, doctrine of the faith, is just as legitimate as that of confession of faith. It is constitutive of faith and the community of faith.

Orthodoxy, however, becomes dubious when it makes itself autonomous and absolutizes itself as the central concept of true teaching. Orthodoxy becomes objectionable when it reduces the faith to statements and propositions, and when the act of faith as option of the whole human being in freedom, when the life of faith and the fruits of faith, become secondary to it: Orthodoxy becomes a problem when the only question asked is: Are you orthodox?, and when this is tested only for the important propositions of dogma. When orthodoxy becomes the only and exclusive criterion of being truly Christian, then orthodoxy can become a weapon. It leads to suspicion, persecution, and condemnation. Without consideration for concrete human beings and for the freedom to which their faith lays claim, it attempts to win the day with all means in the name of the true faith. That the customary punishment of heretics in the Middle Ages was death—a worse punishment, they say, than for money counterfeiters, who deserved death—was a consequence of this attitude. Here ruled that principle which

1. Hans Jonas, *The Gnostic Religion; the Message of the Alien God and the Beginnings of Christianity*, 2nd. ed. (Boston: Beacon Press, 1963); E. Peterson, *Frühkirche, Judentum, Gnosis* (Freiburg, 1959); R. Haardt, "Gnosis," *SM* 2.374–79; N. Brox, *Gnosis und gnostischer Mythos bei Irenäus von Lyon* (Salzburg, 1966).

was applied against Jesus, but was certainly no Christian law: "We have a law, and by that law he ought to die" (John 19:7).

The other consequence consists in thinking that, in the matter of faith and of being Christian, it is best when orthodoxy, the true teaching, is accepted in the most literally faithful and externally controllable way by all the faithful and without reservation or limitation.

In the Reformation of the sixteenth century, Erasmus diagnosed as a sign of the times the fact that the articles of faith, doctrine, were increasing, but love was continually decreasing. He correctly saw in that a loss of faith; at the same time he pointed out that the most correct preservation of the articles of faith had not prevented the arising for the sake of faith, of a movement able to burst the unity of Western Christianity. The popes and bishops of that time were doubtless blameless as far as their orthodoxy was concerned. It wouldn't have occurred to them to deny a truth; they just kept multiplying them with new additions. But if they had really been serious about living from faith, doing the truth, and drawing from their orthodoxy the consequences of orthopraxy, how much would Christianity and humanity have then been spared!

Generally it can be said: a correct answer to a doctrinal and catechism question is still no indication of personal dedication in faith. An incorrect answer is still no indication of a lack of faith. The *fides quae*, faith as doctrine [the faith which is believed] can be preserved only if it is believed by human beings and handed on to others in a living way. We have today picked up an awakened feeling for this important dimension and with it also new criteria for the "measure of faith," which is more than just holding firmly to doctrines.

Dogma

In distinction from doctrine or teaching as representation of the whole content of faith, dogma[2] has a more specific meaning. It signifies that part of Christian doctrine which was formulated by the Church at a particular time and in response to specific questions or challenges. It is the expression of a clearly recognizable intention to formulate something as an authentic and binding expression of the Church's faith to be held and believed by all the faithful.

The concept and word "dogma" did not at the outset seem appropriate as an expression of this state of affairs. Originally, "dogma," a word from the Greek, meant: the opinion, then conclusion, instruction or

---

2. E. Schlink, "Die Struktur der dogmatischen Aussage als ökumenisches Problem in: *Der kommende Christus und die kirchliche Traditionen* (Göttingen, 1961) 24–79; N. Ring, "Dogma," *NDT* (1991) 293–95; Karl Rahner, "Dogma," *SM* 2. 95–98; Walter Kasper, *Dogma under dem Wort Gottes* (Mainz, 1968); J. Finkenzeller, *Glaube ohne Dogma?* (Düsseldorf, 1972).

doctrinal view of a philosophical school. There was, accordingly, considerable scepticism against the reception of the word "dogma" in the realm of Christian belief. One couldn't recognize in this word precisely what was meant in the name of the faith: i.e., a binding statement and decision in questions and matters of the Christian faith.

In the ancient Church, "dogma" meant disciplinary, juridical determination. The Eastern Church understood under "dogma" those traditions of the Church not explicitly spelled out in Scripture; there in the East, liturgy, dogma and doxology remained very closely connected. Among the theologians of the Middle Ages, the concept "dogma" played hardly any role at all; they spoke of *"articuli fidei"* [articles of the faith] and understood by that the individual parts of the confession of faith. Only in more recent times has the concept "dogma" become accepted in its now customary sense. The theologian Chrisman (1751-1810) specified dogma as a truth revealed by God which is so presented by the public judgment of the Church as (truth) to be believed with divine faith, that its contrary is condemned by the Church as heretical doctrine.[3]

Dogma as binding articulation of the faith qualified with its claim to truth is, so to speak, a *line of defense*, a reaction to a recognizable emergency: to attacks, confusions, and falsifications in the area of faith. Dogmas should thus, as John Henry Newman thought in looking towards Vatican I (1870), not be a luxury and not involve indulging in submissiveness.[4] Dogmas should also come not just from finding pleasure in the unfolding of the faith; they should rather, like the dogmas of the ancient Church, grow out of a necessary decision to be made.

Because of this characteristic, dogma always represents an articulation and interpretation of the truth of faith that has become necessary in a particular historical period. One can understand dogmas properly only when one knows the questions (and addressees) they intend to answer. Dogmas should thus neither be seen in isolation nor be considered as exhaustive statements. That would mean turning one aspect into the only aspect. When one, e.g., separates the anti-reformationally determined dogmatic definitions of the Council of Trent from their addressees and turns the statements of this council on priesthood, Mass and sacraments into exhaustive, comprehensive statements, one does not do justice to the historicity of these dogmatic decisions. For a long time, attention was not paid to this in post-Tridentine theology. Ecclesiastical and theological development thus became one-sided. It remained antireformational, and this was made to

---

3. W. Kasper, *Dogma unter dem Wort Gottes* (Mainz, 1968) 36.
4. Briefe und Tagebuchaufzeichnungen aus der katholischen Zeit, Mainz 1957, 543.

equal Catholic. Only quite recently has history-of-doctrinal hermeneutics, with its often liberating tendencies, consciously been applied.[5]

There is a second consequence: Dogmas are formulated with the help of the language and conceptuality of a specific time; until now this has been above all with the help of Greek and scholastic philosophy. How a dogma can be grasped in the linguistic and conceptual form of a quite different way of thinking, as, e.g., of the Far East, is a problem both open and difficult. When concepts and language have a history, it can then become necessary, if the concepts change, to say a thing in a different way so that the reality of faith remains the same. One must ask, for example, whether concepts like nature, essence, substance, etc. can simply be repeated today in dogmatic formulations in order to preserve the identity of faith. These concepts, intended earlier in a metaphysical way, have become physical and chemical concepts in today's language and thought, and have thus taken on a quite different meaning.

For this reason it has been rightly said, with regard to the understanding and evaluation of dogmas, that they are a matter of *language regulation*. The language of dogmas as language regulation makes *sense* and is in some instances necessary for the questions of faith itself and for a faith community in a concrete historical situation. This language regulation is a foundation of its unity.

But let it be said at the same time that a language regulation must take place in another sense when the language field as a whole is changed, whether by history or by a changed social and cultural milieu. The fact of language regulation is an indication that a dogma bears the sign of obligation as well as of public character, that dogma is a sign of the historical form of faith. Some attempts to understand the medieval dogma of eucharistic transubstantiation in another conceptual world are an (obviously controversial) illustration of that.

For the most part, dogmatic decisions also represent a *compromise*, a compromise in the sense that an attempt is made to find a way between the different theological opinions and orientations that were the occasion for a dogmatic decision, a way that took pains to take up the justified concerns of the different perspectives.[6] This is recognizable in the ancient councils, e.g., of Chalcedon with the situation there between Nestorius and Eutyches. This "law" also came into play in

---

5. K. Rahner, "Considerations of the Development of Dogma," *Theological Investigations* 4 (1974) 3–35; K. Rahner and H. Vorgrimler, "Historicity," *DT* (1981) 209–10; A. Darlap and J. Splett, "History," *SM* 3.31–39; Joseph Ratzinger, *Das Problem der Dogmengeschichte in der Sicht der katholischen Theologie* (Cologne, 1966) Summaries in English and French; Wolfhart Pannenberg, "Die Geschichtlichkeit der Wahrheit und die ökumenische Diskussion," in: M. Seckler—O. Pesch—J. Brosseder—W. Pannenberg, *Begegnung. Beiträge zu einer Hermeneutik des theologischen Gesprächs* (Graz—Vienna—Cologne, 1972) 31–43.

6. M. Seckler, "Über den Kompromiß in Sachen der Lehre" in: *Begegnung* 45–57.

Vatican I with regard to the radical papalists and episcopalists. For a dogmatic decision in a specific situation is not already established from the outset, even if there have been repeated tendencies at councils, as in Vatican I and at the beginning of Vatican II, which wanted it that way. A dogmatic decision is the result of a struggle and search where dialogue, discussions, and argument play a role, and of course other factors too, and where, as everyone knows, a vote is taken—without prejudice to the necessity of a final approval by the pope.

For the most part, therefore, a compromise is no matter of captivating brilliance but the result of a laborious struggle, traces of which can often still be seen in the records. The result is that no side is completely happy with the result. Yet it is true that, without this result achieved as a compromise, there would be no common foundation. The compromise is not a sign of weakness. It is, when it comes about honestly, much more a sign of recognition of others and of their justified intention, a sign of humility and modesty.

Dogma is a dynamic functional concept. It is the result of previous experiences of faith in converse with Scripture and in dialogue with the respective historical hour. But this result is at the same time the opening for experiences of the faith in the future in and with new dimensions.

Truths and Truth

In the contents of confession, doctrine, and dogmas, one repeatedly runs up against the concept of truth.[7] Truth of faith means the disclosure of reality found in it. Truth of dogmas means the articulation of this disclosure of the reality of faith found in them. But when faith is specified by history as past and future, then the concept of truth which is ordered to faith must also be stamped by this. And when faith's disclosure of reality is related to events and persons, when the word and act of truth is met in the realm of faith, when Jesus claims to be the truth, then the truth must also be affected by all these moments which are met in the realm of Christian faith. The truth spoken of in Christian faith can also be merely philosophical or logical truth involved only with knowing or understanding; but the truth of Christian faith involves comprehensive encounter with the reality of the historically and personally self-communicating God.

---

7. H. von Soden, "Was ist Wahrheit? Vom geschichtlichen Begriff der Wahrheit" in: *Urchristentum und Geschichte I* (Tübingen, 1951) 1–24; *TDNT* 1.233–51; Emil Brunner, *Truth as Encounter* (Philadelphia: Westminster Press, 1964); Rudolf Schnackenburg, *The Truth Will Make You Free* (New York: Herder and Herder, 1966); Wolfhart Pannenberg, "Was ist Wahrheit?" in: *Grundfragen systematischer Theologie* (Göttingen, 1967) 200–222; W. Kasper, *Dogma unter dem Wort Gottes* 65–67.

There is an *exposition of the contents of faith* as truths of faith that moves into ever-new unfoldings. These help in disclosing the dimensions and perspectives of faith. Along with them is the "infolding" (*Einfaltung*), the *concentration* of the contents of faith: concentrated on its center, which is not an idea but an event, a person. The purpose of this infolding is not only to count the truths but also to evaluate them according to their proportion with respect to their position in the framework of revelation and for the question of salvation. A brief formula [of faith] attempted according to this principle will express not a part but the whole of Christian faith, even if not all the consequences that flow from it are mentioned.[8]

In these investigations there is a tendency to differentiate between fundamental or nonfundamental articles of faith, between truths that concern the center and such contents as unfold out of this center.

Against this has been and still is raised the often-heard objection and disagreement expressed in the well-known image: Whoever takes the truth of a single dogma as less important, or overlooks or even opposes one, endangers the whole system, the well-assembled structure of Catholic dogma, doctrine, and faith possibly even to the point of collapse. Hence the demand that all truths are to be believed in the same way, for behind all of them stand the promise and authority of God. Whoever calls them into question in one place denies them all.

But we need to recall what has already been said about the manifold dimensions of faith: as personal and existential act, as option for the whole, as affirmational/propositional faith imbedded in the greater reality of personal faith. One must add, in addition, that faith itself stands under the sign of the incomplete and the partial. It follows from this that faith is not a closed system but a way, that faith has a center, that it is characterized by history and person. If this is true, then, with respect to the demand that all truths of faith are to be believed in the same obligatory manner, it can be determined along with Walter Kasper:

> One-sided emphasis on the formal obligatory character of each dogma on the basis of the authority of God and of the Church inevitably has an especially fatal effect in the modern age with its emphasis on subjectivity. Can I hold the Christological central truths with the same subjective intensity as the Marian dogmas? They don't concern the question of salvation and damnation in the same way. Accordingly, the same degree of subjective engagement is also not possible. Furthermore, in preaching and in devotional praxis, this conception has led to a fatal shift of balance. The image of the Church in the modern age is extensively stamped by the secondary and tertiary characteristics of its teaching. In defending against Protestantism, the antireformational truths were overly emphasized; that led to an overemphasis on truths that concern the means of salvation (Church, sacraments, office) over against the real Christological and soteriological truths of salvation. In the last century and this one there have appeared more encyclicals

---

8. K. Lehmann, "Kurzformeln des christlichen Glaubens" in: *Gegenwart des Glaubens* (Mainz, 1974) 175–99.

on questions of Mariology than on questions of Christology or of modern atheism. Such disturbances of equilibrium are a sign that heart and circulation are no longer functioning properly. One-sided insistence on verbal and formal orthodoxy bears some of the guilt for the fact that faith is reaching people in the modern age less and less.[9]

If this is not kept in mind, then orthodoxy is no longer what it should be, but is getting derailed.

An important aid in finding one's way through this question is provided by a text from Vatican II. In the decree on ecumenism we read: "When comparing doctrines, they [Catholic theologians] should remember that in Catholic teaching there exists an order or 'hierarchy' of truths, since they vary in their relationship to the foundation of the Christian faith" (no. 11).

Add to this that this foundation consists in the riches of Christ (Eph 3:8). In the Modus accompanying explanation (*Modus*) which led to the acceptance of this text it says that truths must be weighed rather than counted. In this text of the council, therefore, what we have is the replacement of a quantitative and formal understanding of truth by one that is qualitatively determined, i.e., according to content. There would indeed be a misunderstanding of the doctrine of the hierarchy of truths and a return to quantitative rather than qualitative thinking if one were to so understand them as if one could number, so to speak, the individual truths of faith and in this way distinguish the important truths from the less important. Properly understood, the doctrine of the hierarchy of truths is based on the realization that the content of faith represents not just the sum of individual propositions, but a whole edifice of teachings which has definite, established proportions. The principle of the hierarchy of truths is not a principle of choice but a principle of interpretation. Its purpose is to assist in understanding and explaining the truths of faith in the proper way.

Connected with this description of hierarchy of truths is another experience. It is psychologically not possible for the believer to hold fast to all the contents of faith, all developments from the center of faith, with the same constant and undifferentiated intensity of conscious affirmation: the believer will necessarily set accents. The same holds true for the Church as community of faith and of the faithful. Here too, in the course of history, there have been accentuations and shifts; there has also been a certain becoming silent, a submerging of what was once the raging question in an epoch. This is all determined according to different factors and motives, which are not only of inner-Church origin but are often brought up as a question or challenge from outside, as a question or challenge to the Church.

---

9. W. Kasper, *Einübing in den Glauben* (Mainz, 1972) 93; cf. also "Kirchliche Lehre—Skepsis der Gläubigen" in: *Kirche im Gespräch* (Freiburg—Basel—Vienna, 1970) 82–83.

The Common Synod of the Bishoprics of the Federal Republic of Germany formulated this idea as follows: "Neither for the Church nor for the individual Christian is it possible to be equally conscious of all the historical unfoldings of faith. There will always be centers of gravity. Of course, the accentuation that one finds must be tested for its reliability. But differences in the understanding of the one faith are unavoidable."[10] These processes are legitimate when that which is not expressly and consciously affirmed or can be affirmed, is not expressly denied or contested.

If it is right that one cannot believe all truths of faith in the same way, then it is also not to be demanded that all truths of faith, for the sake of the church community, must be believed in the same way. Nor can one demand from other confessions more than one expects from the members of one's own community of faith.[11] The text of the Synod of the Dioceses of the Federal Republic of Germany, "Pastoral Cooperation of the Churches in the Service of Christian Unity" has said the following in its "Theological Reflections" on this question:

It is to be asked how far it is necessary for the unity of faith that all developments and derivations, which in the history of faith and of dogmas have been drawn from revelation, must be affirmed by all Christians in the same way. The Catholic Church does not even demand that of its own members, but is satisfied with an inclusive assent to the faith of the Church. A union in faith is, to be sure, not possible where one church sees it necessary to judge a binding doctrine of the other church as contrary to the gospel. In dialogue between churches and church communities it is to be tested whether a union in faith is possible in such a way that one church can respect and recognize the special tradition of the other as a legitimate unfolding of revelation, even if it does not want to take it over for itself (e.g., veneration of saints, sacraments, indulgences).[12]

The Doing of Truth: Orthodoxy and Orthopraxy

Today the problem of orthodoxy and orthopraxy, i.e., correct doctrine, correct theory and practice of the faith, is under intensive discussion. It is a legitimate question. But today it is often seen alternatively, or even solved, in the *sense* that orthodoxy is unimportant and it is orthopraxy that really counts. This would turn orthodoxy into a marginal problem or into an outmoded stage in the history of faith. Of course, the question has to be asked right away: "Wherein lies the "Ortho," i.e., the criterion of correctness for correct action as the way in which faith is articulated? It has to be an action coming from faith,

---

10. *Gemeinsame Synode der Bistümer in der Bundesrepublik Deutschland, Offiziele Gesamtausgabe* (Freiburg—Basel—Vienna, 1976) 782 (Beschluß Ökumene 3.3.2).

11. On this, cf. H. Fries—K. Rahner, *Unity of the Churches—an Actual Possibility*, trans. Ruth C. L. Gritsch and Eric W. Gritsch (Philadelphia: Fortress Press, 1985) esp. 25–42.

12. Gemeinsame Synode, 780f. (Beschluß Ökumene 3.2.3).

motivated by faith, and giving witness from faith, an action, a praxis in which faith makes an appearance.

But first let us give some *indications* of this dimension of faith called orthopraxy. Recall the text: "Not everyone who says to me, 'Lord, Lord,' shall enter the kingdom of heaven, but he who does the will of my Father who is in heaven" (Matt 7:21). This will is recognizable in what constitutes God's rule and kingdom: justice, peace, reconciliation, mercy, love, the overcoming of injustice, hate, and oppression. Recall, too, what is expressed in the New Testament as including the unity of love of God and love of neighbor: "He who does not love his brother whom he has seen, cannot love God whom he has not seen" (1 John 4:20). Recall the absolutely decisive criterion for the definitive determination or characterization of human beings: "As you did it to one of the least of these my brethren, you did it [or did not do it] to me" (Matt 25). Recall the New Testament statement about the faith that must bring forth fruit by which it will be measured (Matt 7:22); about the faith which, without deeds, is dead (Jas 2:14–26); about faith that is effective in love (Gal 5:6). Recall the text in the Gospel of John about "doing the truth": "He who does what is true comes to the light" (John 3:21). From the doing of truth comes its verification.

Faith does indeed mediate a disclosure of reality with regard to the reality of God and of human beings. But faith is not just illumination of existence, it is also a *renewal and transformation of existence*. It is new praxis, which naturally cannot dispense with seeking after that illumination which can show one in what way and direction renewal and transformation are to take place. Johann Baptist Metz says this in a concentrated formulation: Christianity is not in the first instance a doctrine that must be kept as pure as possible but a praxis that must be lived more radically.[13]

The relationship between theory and praxis is nevertheless not simply to be determined in such a way that out of theory, in the form of a conclusion, a practical case of application is made. If that were the case, "out of sheer theory and reflection on theory," one would hardly come to action. There is still a difference between praxis and reflection. In praxis, theory is manifested. From the realization, i.e., from the praxis of friendship, love, self-giving, and forgiveness, is disclosed what friendship, love, self-giving, and forgiveness are, what they contain, what they mean. From bearing, accepting, or resisting suffering, one can come up with what suffering is more than in a theory of suffering with little connection to praxis. The doing of truth is a way to come into the light of truth. That is the way it also, and especially, is in the realm of faith and the truth of faith. Only they who love God

13. Johannes Baptist Metz, in: *Gott nach Auschwitz* (Freiburg—Basel—Wien, 1979) 136.

know God. The reason for this lies simply in the fact that the truth, which is what faith is about, is not a theory that prescinds from the person or existence, but is truth as way and life, as existential characteristic of the whole human being. Thus theology can be characterized as the self-consciousness of a specific praxis.[14]

Schillebeeckx points out that orthopraxy is not simply the consequence of a theoretical insight, but is the way in which a common conviction is concretely realized.[15] From the unity of praxis, even with a pluralist understanding of faith, the unity of the same faith can be recognized. The symbol of faith, the creed, was the theoretical model of an ecclesiastical action: baptism. The saying, the proclamation, was contained in the act. The celebration of the Lord's Supper is expressly seen as the proclamation of the death of the Lord until he comes (1 Cor 11:26).

Thus, according to Schillebeeckx, gnosis is *the* Christian heresy. It narrows Christianity down to a doctrine that changes nothing and presents itself as orthodoxy. The criterion of orthodoxy, therefore, lies less in a correct answer to a catechism question than in the question of what the truth of faith means as motivational power for life. Schillebeeckx cites in this context a word of the American theologian Paul van Buren, a representative of the so-called "God is Dead" theology: Talking about God is senseless. But Christ is my only rule in life." The real orthodox meaning of this profane statement depends, according to Schillebeeckx, on the influence of this word on life. One's behavior in life will show whether van Buren is in truth affirming something unique in Christ, even though he presents this statement in theologically deficient thematizing.

Consequently, a living praxis radically oriented to Christ can Christologically, i.e., according to the theoretical implication of such a praxis, come closer to orthodoxy than the merely verbal theoretical statement: Christ is one person in two natures, if this statement remains without consequences or confirmation in the praxis of living behavior. The sense of such a profane, worldly statement as "Christ is my only rule in life" is ultimately and really an appropriate, comprehensive Christian and Christological statement. For the sense of what is said in a specific play of language is determined by the totality of human behavior and cannot be expressed purely theoretically. Heresy, accordingly, does not mean saying something different from the Bible, but to speak of something different from the Bible and then to represent this as speaking true to the Bible. New interpretation means to speak

---

14. Edward Schillebeeckx, *The Understanding of Faith: Interpretation and Criticism* (New York: Seabury Press, 1974) 143.
    15. Ibid. 59.

in a different way about the same thing while preserving the biblical intentionality.[16]

A further dimension in the question of theory and praxis comes from the fact that the matter of Christian faith and the salvation connected with it is not only a private matter played out between "God and the soul." It also involves the public and society, and has in this sense a *political dimension.*[17] This means that the already-mentioned contents and demands of faith—justice, peace, freedom, reconciliation—have their realm of application not only in the I-You relationship but also in the public domain: for society, as justice in conditions and structures, as peace among nations, as freedom for all.

The sense and the mission of faith are, accordingly, not fulfilled if the relationship to the world is lacking, if one doesn't move beyond the exclusive concern: "If only I am at peace with God, if only I find a gracious God," it is enough, regardless of how the world turns out. The biblical content of peace, justice, and freedom grow instead into a critical instance over against a—political—public reality of state and society where these biblical contents are not realized or where they are repressed.

The existence of unjust, repressive conditions is a contradiction to the faith. Such conditions must be not only be recognized but also vigorously opposed. For however strong the motivating force of the ultimately invincible freedom of the imprisoned and oppressed can be— often equal to even the heaviest burdens—one may not derive from that massive power any legitimation of conditions supported by imprisonment and oppression.

Under the sign of this orthopraxy today stands the so-called *liberation theology.*[18] There is no disagreement that societal, social liberation from conditions of unfreedom and oppression are a direct consequence of faith understood as praxis, but only whether, in saying this, everything is said that is meant biblically and theologically by freedom. The other question is: By what means should this social

16. Ibid. 68–69.

17. This is developed above all in the political theology of J. B. Metz: *Theology of the World*, trans. William Glen–Doepel (New York: Herder and Herder, 1969); "Political Theology" in: SM 5.34–38; *Faith in History and Society: Toward a Practical Fundamental Theology*, trans. David Smith (New York: Seabury Press, 1980); W. Peukert, *Diskussion zur politischen Theologie* (Mainz—Munich, 1969); S. Wiedenhofer, *Politische Theologie* (Stuttgart, 1976).

18. Major work: G. Gutierrez, *A Theology of Liberation: History, Politics, and Salvation* , trans. Sister Caridad Inda and John Eagleson (Maryknoll, N.Y.: Orbis Books, 1988); K. Lehmann, ed., *Theologie der Befreiung* (Einsiedeln, 1977); L. Boff, "Eine kreative Rezeption des II. Vatikanums aus der Sicht der Armen. Theologie der Befreiung" in: E. Klinger — K. Wittstadt, *Glaube im Prozeß. Für Karl Rahner* (Frieburg—Basel—Vienna, 1983) 628–54; C. Boff, *Theology and Praxis: Epistemological Foundations* , trans. Robert R. Barr (Maryknoll, N.Y.: Orbis Books, 1987).

liberation take place? With force, which can create new injustices, or with nonviolence?

One thing must still be kept in mind and said in this context. In the New Testament, salvation is expected primarily not from the changing of societal structures—which was at that time perhaps not even possible—but from change through the conversion of human beings. That a change of structures can and should come from this is not denied but expressly affirmed and accepted. Jesus associated with human beings, entering into solidarity with those whom society and the social order of that time had rejected. But he rejected every offer to become a political messiah. The revolution intended by him is one of personal disposition, a revolution of the heart, not the overthrowing of social conditions.

An especially interesting and moving example is the question of slavery in the New Testament.[19] As an institution of that time it is not directly opposed in the New Testament, nor was its dissolution sought after as a goal of the Christian faith and its requirement of justice, freedom and familial love. Paul expressly took up this theme and dealt with it in this way: Even as slave you are a free person in Christ; Christ has freed you too. Christ himself took on the form of a slave. In Christ the distinction between slave and free no longer holds. The socially free, the citizen, has become the slave of Christ. "But if you can gain your freedom," counsels Paul in his First Letter to the Corinthians which, to be sure, stands under the sign of imminent expectation of the parousia, "make use of your present condition instead" [N.B.: a textual variant preferred by the RSV reads: "avail yourself of the opportunity"]. "For he who was called in the Lord as a slave is a freedman of the Lord. Likewise he who was free when called is a slave of Christ" (1 Cor 7:21-22).

Certainly, with words like this, one can create legitimizing theories for existing unjust conditions, with the well-known consoling effects—that has indeed happened and often enough. But when one takes seriously the truth Paul spoke, there turn out to be not just practical consequences for the behavior of masters towards slaves, whom they can no longer treat as disposable goods, but must respect as brothers and sisters. The Letter to Philemon is a beautiful, personal illustration for this praxis. With these themes was also introduced and disseminated a process at the end of which stood, and necessarily, the abolition of slavery as an institution. That this process took so long is due partly to the weakness and negligence of Christians, and also to the Church's lack of power; but it is also due to the resistance that came

---

19. Cf. J. Vogt, *Sklavenfrage und Humanität im klassischen Griechentum* (Mainz, 1953); ferner die Kommentare zum Philemonbrief von P. Stuhlmacher und J. Gnilka.

from outside which, politically, socially, and economically, was interested in the preservation of the institution of slavery.

Some final words on the theme of orthopraxy: The concrete realization of orthopraxy takes on many forms. It has two points of orientation: one, the reality, challenge, and inspiration of the Christian faith, and two, the concrete situation in a society for which the praxis of faith, orthopraxy, must be concretely found and done. Thus it is true, for the most part, that there is a broad consensus regarding the knowledge and condemnation of what is negative in the human sphere, of evil in the form of injustice and lack of freedom, but that for the concrete and positive solution and answer, numerous ways are possible. Here, exclusivity is to be avoided; here, a tolerance is to be striven for which has the power to outlast tensions and differences. The fulfillment of the Christian command of love can no longer consist only in binding the wounds of someone who, as in the well-known parable of Jesus (Luke 10, 25-37) fell in with robbers, but that one does one's best to prevent someone from falling in with robbers, to prevent wounds from being inflicted. In other words, the realization of love includes also the changing of conditions and structures that hinder justice and love. But to this must be added that the changing of structures does not automatically produce love, justice, and new human beings, for the human being is not just the ensemble or result of structural conditions, but, as person and individual, is a center of nondisposable reality. The changing of the human being and the changing of consciousness must go hand in hand with the creation of better conditions.

The intention of these reflections was to bring out the dimension of orthopraxy as a constitutive dimension of faith. False alternatives—such as orthopraxy instead of orthodoxy, service of humanity instead of service of God, developmental assistance instead of preaching, kindergartens instead of places of worship—are to be avoided. Only the togetherness and interrelationship that come from the intertwining of theory and praxis can do justice to the whole of faith in its various gifts and requirements. Only the whole is the true. But the main thing remains: orthopraxy has to begin with human beings themselves. Then it can and should bear its manifold fruits.

PART TWO

THE SCIENCE OF FAITH

§ 11

FAITH AND UNDERSTANDING

This theme brings to mind the specific interrelationship of the ex–
pressions "standing in faith" and "understanding in faith," as Söhngen
would put it. This interpenetration of "faith and understanding," this
core of the analysis of faith will now be the object of a brief reflection
which we shall present by way of some important instances of it from
biblical times to the present day.

The Biblical Data

The word for understanding is not a specifically biblical word, but a
common word of human language (gnosis). With respect to its use the
following can be said. In the Greek, understanding and cognition mean a
kind of seeing-in, a comprehension on the basis of seeing. Cognition is
the seeing of the spirit. Corresponding to it is the thing seen: the idea,
the eidos, the truth in the form of aletheia, of inobscurity. The seeing/
gazing of the spirit stands for the Greeks as the perfection of human
activity, the seeing of the divinity as the state of happiness.

In contrast, the cognition found in the Old Testament is ordered to
the realm of hearing. It is understanding on the basis of a heard word or
call. Understanding is not, as in Greek, ordered to a timeless idea but to
an historical experience, to the word and will of persons. Hence, cogni-
tion/knowing does also mean to take cognizance of, but in a way that
presses towards recognition; knowing turns out to be a kind of encounter,
the event of a living community.

In the New Testament we find, corresponding to the already-
mentioned unity of hearing and seeing, a connection of the two aspects of
cognition as a mode of spiritual hearing and seeing, cognition and
recognition. In the synoptics one finds the characterizing word of Jesus
to the Twelve: "To you it has been given to know the secrets of the
kingdom of heaven, but to them it has not been given" (Matt 13:11).

These words don't stand isolated in the New Testament, but are taken up above all in the proclamation of Jesus as the Christ and Kyrios. Paul speaks of the gnosis connected with pistis, faith. Gnosis as knowledge is a gift of the Spirit of God granted to believers to enable them to grasp God's gift of grace. "Now we have received not the spirit of the world, but the Spirit which is from God, that we might understand the gifts bestowed on us by God" (1 Cor 2:12). Gnosis is often mentioned by Paul together with sophia, wisdom. It mediates a penetration into the mysteries of God, it opens up a reality that remains closed to merely natural human beings and their capability. Even when the wisdom of God is presented in the form of the cross and hence is folly in the eyes of the world, it is and remains wisdom. If it requires a conversion of human wisdom, it also provides new wisdom from this new source. For knowledge in faith, it is decisive that it, as knowledge, remain in the horizon of faith. Faith may not be dissolved and absorbed into that form of gnosis which Paul already knew in Corinth: into a gnosis that leaps over faith as a primitive stage in order to absorb it and its contents as well into a higher level, that of gnosis emancipated or emancipating itself from faith. Against this kind of gnosis and its wisdom, Paul sets the folly of God, which is manifested on the cross and which, at bottom, is the wisdom of God (1 Cor 2:6-16).

On the other hand, it was important for Paul to separate the knowledge of faith, the "understanding in faith," from the highly prized but incomprehensible glossolalia: "I thank God that I speak in tongues more than you all; nevertheless, in church I would rather speak five words with my mind, in order to instruct others, than ten thousand words in a tongue" (1 Cor 14:18-19).

How the knowledge of faith is ordered to seeing in faith is shown in the statement: "For it is the God who said, 'Let light shine out of darkness,' who has shone in our hearts to give the light of the knowledge of the glory of God in the face of Christ" (2 Cor 4:6).

The hearing that is granted along with the knowledge of faith is expressed in the text: "We have not ceased to pray for you, asking that you may be filled with the knowledge of his will in all spiritual wisdom and understanding" (Col 1:19). The Christocentric perspective leads Paul to coordinate knowledge of God and knowledge of Christ: ". . . . as they are knit together in love, to have all the riches of assured understanding and the knowledge of God's mystery, of Christ" (Col 2:2); ". . . . that I may know him and the power of his resurrection, and may share his sufferings, becoming like him in his death" (Phil 3:10). This knowledge brings about community with Christ, which finds its expression in love. The whole meaning of the apostolic office consists in leading human beings to this knowledge.

The close connection of faith, knowledge and understanding found in the Gospel of John has already been mentioned: faith is the beginning of knowing, knowing is the perfection of faith.

From this we see that faith and knowledge are not contradictions but coordinates; they both relate to the same thing: to the truth of God made visible in Jesus. There is believing knowledge and knowing faith. The knowing remains in the horizon of faith; in knowledge faith comes to itself. Knowing is a structural element of faith. But knowing also means not a mere taking-cognizance-of and theorizing about; knowing means relationship to reality made perfect. Its unattained and unattainable image is the knowledge of the Father through the Son.

Pistis and Gnosis as Problem in the Early Church

From the coordination and tension between pistis and gnosis arise the constant possibility, danger, and temptation to dissolve the tension, to separate pistis from gnosis and gnosis from pistis. The result is either a blind, irrational faith not involving any kind of understanding, or a faithless gnosis which qualifies faith as an attitude proper and suitable for those who are unknowing and inarticulate, but not expected of those with knowledge and understanding.

This gnosis, rejected already by Paul, was the great danger in the time of the early Church. It was the danger of gnosticism[1] as inner concept, mixture and conglomerate of philosophy, mystery religions and elements of Christian faith. Their was a tendency to outdo faith according to the criterion of gnosis, rather than come to know faith more deeply through gnosis. The contents of faith were not understood from themselves but from the higher view and insight of the gnostic consciously separating himself from them. In addition, gnostics had the idea that they were thereby meeting the real intention and true reality of faith. It is quite remarkable how the answer to the situation and challenge of gnosticism developed.

The one answer—developed above all in the Latin Church of the West by the early Christian apologists[2]—was a decisive "no" to gnosis, the rejection of its intention and contents. This "no" found its most decisive, most impressive, and most brilliant representative in the African, Tertullian. In his writing De carne Christi [On the Flesh of Christ] he explains as a principle, so to speak: "Reason is nailed to the cross." The often-quoted, "Credo quia absurdum [I believe because it is

1. W. Völker,.Quellen zur Geschichte der Gnosis (Tübingen, 1932); Hans Jonas, The Gnostic Religion; the Message of the Alien God and the Beginnings of Christianity, 2d ed. (Boston: Beacon Press, 1963); H. Leisegang, die Gnosis, 4th ed. (Stuttgart, 1955); also Le Gnose (Paris, 1971); E. Peterson, Frühkirche, Judentum, Gnosis (Freiburg, 1959); R. Haardt, "Gnosis," SM 2.374–79;

2. N. Brox, Offenbarung, Gnosis und gnostischer Mythos bei Irenäus von Lyon (Salzburg, 1966); P. Stockmeier, Glaube und Religion in der frühen Kirche (Freiburg—Basel—Vienna, 1973).

absurd]," from him verbatim but in line with his intention, expresses this view pregnantly. The following statements from Tertullian are illustrative: "God's Son has died; this is credible because it is an absurdity. He was buried and rose again; that is certain because it is impossible." Paradox becomes the criterion of the truth of faith. Tertullian joins with this his polemic against Greek philosophy and especially against Aristotle. "What has Athens to do with Jerusalem? What has the Greek Academy to do with the Christian Church? Jesus arranged for fishermen and not philosophers to preach his message." The sign of philosophy is curiosity and humility; the sign of faith is readiness and humility. In addition one finds in Tertullian the astonishing affirmation about the human soul, which is Christian by nature (*anima naturaliter christiana* [the soul is naturally Christian]).

Nevertheless, this is not the only answer of the Christian faith and its self-understanding against the challenge of gnosis that has been left to us. Along with this radical "no" to gnosis is also a faith-inspired "yes." This "yes" sought its grounding in the fact that the questions raised by gnosis and gnosticism, the questions of understanding and knowledge, were granted their rightful importance for the faith. Believers could appeal to the legitimacy of a properly understood gnosis already witnessed in the New Testament by Paul and John. They appealed also to their own past and origin in gnosis and in Greek philosophy, which were not obstacles for their faith but preparation for it. The representatives of this direction come from the Greek Church, above all from the school of Alexandria. Its most important representatives are Clement of Alexandria[3] (150-215) and Origen[4] (185-254). These two great theologians recognized in the Greek philosophy from which they came a significance, a position, similar to that of the Old Testament. Both are "pedagogues for Christ." In the ancient religions, even in the mystery cults, they saw not just error and idolatry but prototypes and questions which came to fulfillment in the Christian faith.[5] Even in faith, according to these theologians, one cannot do without the way of gnosis. This path is to be followed to the extent that faith needs life and growth, maturity and the ability to articulate, and hence, gnosis.

But this is not something that can be done without philosophy. In gnosis thus understood, the intention of the gnostic is "superseded" in the manifold senses of this word. With false gnosis, the intention of the

3. J. Bernard, *Die apologetische Methode bei Klemens von Alexandrien. Entfaltung der Theologie* (Leipzig, 1968).
4. W. Völker, *Das Vollkommenheitsideal des Origenes* (Tübingen, 1931); H. von Campenhausen, *The Fathers of the Greek Church*, trans. Stanley Godman (New York: Pantheon, 1959); R. Gögler, *Zur Theologie des biblischen Wortes bei Origenes* (Düsseldorf, 1963).
5. Hugo Rahner, *Greek Myths and Christian Mystery*, trans. Brian Battershaw (New York: Harper & Row, 1963).

gnostic is done away with; with true gnosis, it is preserved and elevated. The Christian is the true gnostic. Christian faith is thereby distinguished from many religions and myths in that it makes room for understanding and commits itself to the fulfillment of understanding. It doesn't need, like many mystery teachings, to shy away from the light of reason. In this Alexandrian theology one finds an astonishing breadth, freedom, and boldness, far removed from all fear of adulteration or fear that the Christian faith could be mythically corrupted. Quite the contrary: the religious world of myths is given a positive interpretation grounded on faith.

This program was given its classical formulation by Augustine: *Credo, ut intelligam* [I believe that I may understand]. Faith is the beginning and impulse of a thought movement. It also knows the other formula: *Intelligo, ut credam* [I understand that I may believe]. This way describes Augustine's own path from Neoplatonism to Christian faith. He was, moreover, of the opinion that Neoplatonism and Christian faith are not different as to their goal: in both instances it is "communion with God"; the difference lies in the path to the goal.

The Program of Scholasticism

In Scholasticsim, in the time of the eleventh to the thirteenth centuries, the principle of faith and understanding was taken up under the program *Fides quaerens intellectum* (faith seeking understanding). Reason (*ratio*) as principle was placed in the service of faith. This is shown in the following noteworthy characteristic.

The methods of faith instruction and understanding previously used to gain an understanding of the faith by commenting on the authorities—the writing and doctrine of the Church Fathers—in which *auctoritas* [authority] and *sententia* [sentence/position] were the constitutive elements, were expanded by the element of the *quaestio* and by the method of the *disputatio*.[6] Not the sentence but the question and the disputation sparked by it were to set in movement an intellectual concern for the faith. This made demands on reason in a special way, above all in the search for grounds for the fittingness [*convenientia*] of faith. This way of thinking was not satisfied with the acceptance of "that which is," but was concerned with the question whether and why "that which is" is supposed to be or has to be that way. An exemplary instance of this is the *Cur Deus homo* [Why God Became Human] of Anselm of Canterbury. Anselm[7] searches for the *rationes necessariae*

---

6. Cf. A. Lang, *Die Entfaltung des apologetischen Problems in der Scholastik des Mittelalters* (Freiburg—Basel—Vienna, 1962).

7. Cf. R. Heinzmann, "Anselm von Canterbury" in: H. Fries—G. Kretschmar, *Klassiker der Theologie I* (Munich, 1981) 165–80.

fidei, the necessary reasons of faith, i.e., for the reason why what is disclosed in faith about the Incarnation of God must be that way and thus cannot be any other way.

The utilization of reason for faith within Scholasticism led also to the result that reason, even outside of faith, is conceded its own importance. Within a comprehensive horizon, namely the *Summa,* a theologically conceived overview, reason now makes it possible to know and to distinguish a twofold order, that of reason and that of faith. This was, above all, the work of Thomas Aquinas.[8] He arrived at a *theologia naturalis,* a theology of the philosophers. This was a knowledge and an affirmation about God possible to the philosopher (the representative is Aristotle), in which, by the so-called proofs for the existence of God, God can be known as the ground and goal of the world and of the self. Thomas calls the proofs "ways."[9] They proceed from the experiential world and its quality of being—finiteness, causal connection, goal orientation and order—and, with the help of the principle of causality, recognize God as the unconditioned, absolute being which is the condition of every finite being, as being itself, the *ipsum esse.* Distinguished from this was another theology called *sacra doctrina* [sacred doctrine] in which God is considered as origin of a supernatural revelation.[10] In this, God is not so much object as subject of a theology called "understanding of the faith."

The two orders which are unfolded and represented in the theological summa are bound in an inner unity. According to Thomas, this unity is given by God, who manifests [him]self in the order of creation as well as that of redemption, it thereby possesses the unity of his action. This unity is also found in human beings, who are distinguished by understanding, insight, and the ability to believe, and who thus can remain human. How the relationship of the two orders is determined is shown in the well-known guiding principles: Grace presupposes nature, perfects and completes it. Philosophy is the handmaid of theology.

---

8. M. Grabmann, *Introduction to the Theological Summa of St. Thomas,* trans. John Zybura (St. Louis, Mo.: Herder Book Co., 1930); *Die Werke des Thomas von Aquin,* 2d ed. (Münster, 1949); A. D. Sertillanges, *Saint Thomas Aquinas and His Work,* trans. Godfrey Anstruther (London: Blackfriars, 1957); J. Pieper, *Guide to Thomas Aquinas,* trans. Richard and Clara Winston (San Francisco: Ignatius Press, 1991); M. D. Chenu, *Toward Understanding Saint Thomas,* trans. A. M. Landry and D. Hughes (Chicago: H. Regnery Co., 1964); H. Meyer, *Thomas von Aquin,* 2d ed. (Paderborn, 1961); W. A. Wallace—J. A. Weisheipl, "St. Thomas Aquinas," *NCE* 14, 1967, 102–15; U. Kühn, "Thomas von Aquin" in: *Klassiker der Theologie I* (Munich, 1981) 212–25.

9. *STh* 1.2.2 and 3.

10. *STh* 1.1.

The Intention of the Reformers

This impressive conception lasted a long time. Late Scholasticism, however, did show unmistakable signs and tendencies that called into question the unity of *Summa* and *Ordo*. With regard to the contents of faith, late Scholasticsim made less use of rational reasons than it did of unprovable, unintelligible decrees of divine will. From this developed the principle of the double truth: something can be at the same time philosophically true and theologically false, and vice versa.

An express contradiction was formulated by the Reformation. In the name of faith, it rejected the form and intention of Scholasticsim. The reformers speak in the spirit of Tertullian, of the infiltration and even the falsification of faith by philosophy. Above all, Luther[11] accuses Scholasticsim of reading the Bible in the spirit and according to the criterion of Aristotle, of making theology, despite claims to the contrary, factually the handmaid of philosophy, of violating the principle of biblical hermeneutics according to which Scripture was to be read and interpreted according to the measure in which it *Christum treibet* [does Christ's business], indeed according to which Scripture, because of its clarity, is its own interpreter.[12] What is needed is to free the Church—so Luther—from this "Babylonian Captivity." What is needed is to raise up the *theologia crucis* against the *theologia gloriae*, i.e., natural theology, in order to preserve the divinity of God.[13]

From these teachings comes the scepticism of the reformers with regard to the use of philosophy in theology. They see it as a danger to the faith and to the trust and obedience ordered to faith. Theology has the task, not of erecting systems or producing summas, but of interpreting Scripture.[14]

But in this it is often overlooked that the interpretation of Scripture has its own systematic-theological presuppositions. Interpretation of Scripture is interpretation not simply of "what was written," but of how it is seen in each particular perspective—otherwise there would

11. Cf. B. Lohse, *Martin Luther: An Introduction to His Life and Work*, trans. Robert C. Schultz (Philadelphia: Fortress Press, 1986); O. H. Pesch, *Hinführung zu Luther* (Mainz, 1982); *The God Question in Thomas Aquinas and Martin Luther* (Philadelphia, 1972); Gerhard Ebeling, *Luther, An Introduction to his Thought*, trans. R. A. Wilson (Philadelphia: Fortress Press, 1970); H. Fries, "Die Grundanliegen der Theologie Luthers in der Sicht der katholischen Theologie der Gegenwart" in: *Wandlungen des Lutherbildes*, ed. K. Forster (Würzburg 1966,) 157–91; E. Iserloh, "Die protestantische Reformation" in: H. Jedin ed., *Handbuch der Kirchengeschichte IV* (Freiburg—Basel—Vienna, 1967) 3.446; J. Brosseder, "Martin Luther" in: *Klassiker der Theologie I* (1982) 283–313.
12. M. Luther, "De servo arbitrio" in: *Martin Luther. Ausgewählte Werke*, ed., H. A. Borcherdt—G. Metz, Ergänzungsband I (Munich, 1962); P. Neune—F. Schröger, "Luthers These von der Klarheit der Schrift" in: *ThGl* 74 (1984) 39–58.
13. "Die Heidelberger Disputation" in: *Ausgewählte Werke I*, 125–39.
14. W. Link, *Das Ringen Luthers um die Freiheit der Theologie von der Philosophie* , 2d ed. (Munich, 1955).

be no explanation for the great differences in the interpretation of Scripture from the beginning to this day.

Faith and the Understanding of Faith in the Modern Age

The further history of the understanding of faith was determined by the following factors. The understanding of faith itself was no longer seen, as it had been in the different schools, as a unity in multiplicity. It became a principle of separation according to the different confessions. It was a faith-understanding "against others."

With regard to the questions of the time and their relationship to the Christian faith, there was in the confessions profound misunderstandings vis-a-vis the newly developing natural sciences. The trials of Galileo and Kepler—the one carried out by the Inquisition and the other by the Evangelical Consistorium—brought about, because of the alienation of Church and World, the alienation of faith and knowledge. The result was that knowledge and science were more and more separated from faith and the understanding of faith; they became independent and entered into opposition to faith.[15]

In the autonomous, subject-grounded thinking of the modern age, this process took on an ever more comprehensive and intensive form, especially in the thought of the Enlightenment, with its exhortation to awake from "dogmatic slumber" with the program formulated by Kant: *Sapere aude* [dare to know]. Dare to make use of your own understanding and put an end to your self-inflicted immaturity."[16]

To the extent that any connection was made from this autonomous thinking to the Christian faith, it took place in such a way that revelation and faith were still affirmed as a means of introduction into the "education of the human race"; but of course they would have to be "superseded" in the stage when humanity had become articulate and mature (G. E. Lessing). Kant describes the path of this development as the path "from faith in the Bible, through faith in the Church, to faith in reason," in which the contents of faith receive their true moral significance and find their real fulfillment. The moral was turned into the hermeneutical principle of the understanding of faith.[17] Hegel, the great reconciler of knowledge and faith, of theology and philosophy, of Christianity and religion or religions, sees in the Christian faith a high point in the history of Spirit—in a form of presentation, to be sure, which is preliminary to and remained subordinate to the higher form of the concept of Spirit, and which is "superseded" in it.

15. H. Fries, *Glauben—Wissen* (Berlin, 1960).
16. "Beantwortung der Frage: Was ist Aufklärung?" in: I. Kant, *Werke IX*, Ausgabe W. Weischedel, 4th ed. (Darmstadt, 1975) 53–61.
17. Kant, *Religion Within the Limits of Reason Alone*, trans. Theodore M. Green and Hoyt H. Hudson (New York: Harper, 1960) esp. 142–55.

Space does not allow us to speak in detail of the great movements of modern intellectual history. We can say only that faith and the understanding of faith were not much affected by them. This is true of the faith understanding of the Catholic Church even more than of the churches of the Reformation. But even the great theologian D. F. W. Schleiermacher asks the worried question: should the knot of history be so loosened that Christianity goes with barbarism and science with unbelief? The very understanding of faith developed as confessions within the Church, especially with a view to each particular confessional orthodoxy.

Some theologians attempted to enter into a "creative controversy" with the "spirit of the time" and thus come to a contemporary understanding of faith. Drey, Möhler, Hirscher, Staudenmaier, and Kuhn, theologians of the Catholic Tübingen School of the 19th century, courageously encountered the Romanticism and German Idealism.[18] Other attempts such as those of Hermes in Bonn and Günther in Vienna, were condemned by the magisterium. Thus, in the second half of the cen tury, the line was drawn. It was the line of demarcation between Chris tian faith and "modern thought" which, as autonomous and above all natural-scientifically oriented thought, was emancipated from authoritatively stamped revelational faith and then was declared by this same faith and understanding to be irreconcilable with it. Modern philosophy was declared to be unusable as an instrument for the understanding of faith and, against it, NeoScholasticsim as true philosophy, as *philosophia perennis*, was recommended. Thomas Aquinas was declared by Pope Leo XIII as "universal teacher."[19]

That would in itself have been a good recommendation, above all if one took on the responsibility to work "in the spirit" and according to the principles of Thomas Aquinas.[20] Thomas had done precisely what now, under his mantle, one sought to prevent: discussion with the spirit and thought of the time. Thomas was, in modern terms, a progressive. He began something new by entering into discussion with the newly discovered and powerfully developing Aristotelianism and making it a dialogue partner of his theology. He saw it as representative of what human thought can achieve in the realms of philosophy, ethics, and politics. Taken as a whole, however, Neoscholasticsim did not have this spirit.

The affirmations of Vatican I stand wholly under the sign of this Neoscholastic understanding of faith, especially the statements in the chapter with the heading: *Dei filius. De fide catholica* [Son of God. On

---

18. J. R. Geiselmann, *Die katholische Tübinger Schule* (Freiburg—Basel—Vienna, 1964).
19. Encyclical *Aeterni patris* (1879) DS 3135–3140. In the new Code of Canon Law (§ 252) Thomas of Aquinas is still especially recommended.
20. Cf. H. Fries, "Im Geist des hl. Thomas von Aquin" in: *ThQ* 131 (1951) 139–62.

the Catholic Faith]. [21] Vatican I is an explicitly apologetic council. It treated, above all, those themes in which the opposition of modern thought to the Catholic faith is manifested, the errors already mentioned in the *syllabus errorum* [Syllabus of Errors] of Pius IX in 1864:[22] the intellectual currents of atheism, materialism, agnosticism, positivism, rationalism, and pantheism,—but also those of irrationalism and fideism. The council treats in definitive propositional form the rights and limits of human reason in the horizon of revelational faith.

It speaks on the one hand of the possibility of the rational knowledge of the existence and essence of God, and it speaks on the other hand of the fact and the function of the *alia supernaturalis via,* of the other, the supernatural way, in which God, beyond God's manifestation in creation which is accessible to all, "has communicated Himself and the eternal decrees of His will to the human race." The council was especially concerned with the credibility of supernatural revelation: it took pains to make concrete mention of motives and criteria of revelation that are fundamentally accessible and perceivable to everyone.[23] Correct as this principle is, the criteria specifically mentioned in Vatican I—miracles and prophecies, form and history of the Church—have themselves become in our contemporary situation more a difficult problem than an applicable guide to faith.

It was an important concern of the council to express the intelligibility, the reasonableness of faith. A whole chapter treats the relationship of faith and reason. We find there remarkable propositions about the understanding of faith: "When reason illuminated by faith seeks diligently, honestly, and conscientiously (*sedulo, pie et sobrie quaerit*), it gains with God's help a certain insight (a certain understanding) with respect to the mysteries (of faith) (*aliquam intelligentiam*)." Mentioned as ways and modes of this understanding of faith are the natural analogy to these mysteries and the knowledge of the "nexus mysteriorum," i.e., the connections of the mysteries of faith—and this both in their connection with each other and in their connection with the "last end of human beings" (*ultimus finis hominis*).[24]

These are affirmations that open up a broad horizon of understanding. It is said that an understanding of faith is possible with the help of a natural analogy. This should mean that between the contents of faith and the experiences of human beings with themselves and their world there are correspondences, similarities in dissimilarities—that

21. DS 3000–3045; on this: H. J. Pottmeyer, *Der Glaube vor dem Anspruch der Wissenschaft. Die Konstitution über den katholischen Glauben "Dei Filius" des I. Vatikanischen Konzils und die unveröffentlichten Voten der vorbereitenden Kommission* (Freiburg—Basel—Vienna, 1968).
22. DS 2901–80.
23. DS 3009.
24. DS 3016.

is the concept of analogy. In the mysteries of faith one meets words and concepts like father, son, grace, love, peace, reconciliation, joy, justice, light, life, but also concepts like person, substance, nature, essence; these words and concepts are taken from human language and experience. Even for faith there is no other language and conceptual world than the human. The basis of this is the *analogia entis* [analogy of being] grounded in creation, and the explicit similarity and dissimilarity therein between Creator and creature. But this means that in the experience and understanding of these words and concepts there is an understanding, or at least a pre-understanding of those concepts of the mysteries of faith which are mediated through these words and concepts. That doesn't exclude but rather includes that this understanding and pre-understanding is itself modified, surpassed or changed by the content of faith. But without this natural content there is no understanding of the supernatural contents of faith.

The second way to gain an understanding of faith is, according to the words of Vatican I, the *nexus mysteriorum inter se*, insight into the interconnection of the contents of faith, in the sense of a mutual dependence. Although no example is mentioned, what comes to mind is something like the connection between creation and covenant, between creation, redemption, and fulfillment; the connection within the history of revelation: revelation in the beginning, revelation as promise, as fulfillment, and then as final fulfillment; the connection between the earthly Jesus and the proclaimed Christ, between kingdom of God and Church, between word and sacrament. A *nexus mysteriorum inter se* also results from attending to the "hierarchy of truths." But the knowledge of the connection is caused by one's understanding in faith; it is not given of itself just with "standing in the faith."

The *nexus mysteriorum* [interconnection of the mysteries] in connection with the *ultimus finis hominis* [final end of the human being] is called a third way to come to an understanding of faith. Now this does not mean only the "ordering of the truths of faith towards their fulfillment in the hereafter,"[25] but the anthropological, existential and existentiell level and content of the mysteries of faith. It is the case that the contents of faith are related to human beings and their existence, that in them human beings truly understand themselves, that they interiorly involve and correspond to human beings, that they change and renew human beings, that they involve humans' salvation and their quest for sense, purpose, and wholeness. The *ultimus finis* [final end] is not so much a specification of time as a description of quality. Its purpose is to express what ultimately, and therefore definitively and unconditionally, involves the human being.

---

25. As in J. Beumer in: *Theologie als Glaubensverständnis* (Würzburg, 1953) 183.

It does no violence to the text to recognize in it that understanding of the faith which is today sought after in existential theology, or in theology properly understood as a comprehensive anthropology or comprehensive description of reality. The content of faith is mediated as answer to the question and the questions of human beings, to the questions human beings ask, to the question that human beings themselves are.

This doesn't mean that the answer of faith is anticipated or even predetermined and decided by the questions of human beings, but it does mean that the contents, affirmations, events, and promises found in faith are related to human beings and to their questioning, existential, and real situation. This is the motivation of such different theological conceptions as those of Paul Tillich, Rudolf Bultmann, and Karl Rahner, but also of Karl Barth in his later theological period. It is the way from dialectic to analogy.[26] Faith is in this way protected from becoming "extrinsicist"; it becomes, without becoming "naturalized" and "immanentized," that word from which one can live as from daily bread, that light which illumines the ways of existence, of the world, and of history. Faith becomes the power and the courage to go this way.

26. Hans Urs. von Balthasar, Karl Barth. *Darstellung und Deutung seiner Theologie* (Cologne, 1950).

§ 12

THE SCIENCE OF FAITH, OR, THEOLOGY

Science is qualified knowledge. It is knowledge that is methodically laid out and gives an account of how it was arrived at. Theology is the *scientia fidei* [science of faith], *fides in statu scientiae* [faith in the state of science], "the luminous and clear existence of that which is known" (B. Welte). The object of the science of faith, of theology, can thus be nothing other than faith and the reality that is disclosed in faith and in faith understanding—in other words, God and God's revelation.

From the understanding of faith to the science of faith has proven to be a long step. It is that step which leads from knowing to science. All science is knowing, but not all knowing is science. Thus, the science of faith is always an understanding of the faith, but not all understanding of the faith is science of the faith (theology) in the explicit sense of the word.

The Meaning of the Word

The word "theology"[1] is not a "theological" creation in the sense that Christian understanding of revelation and faith understanding would have created for its own reality and purpose a conceptual form taken from the Greek language. Theology is, as word and concept, at

---

1. On this, cf. the theological dictionaries, handbooks and lexicons: *RGG* 6 (1962) 754–838 A. Kremer–Marietti, "Positivism," *ER* 11 (1987) 458–60; Karl Rahner—W. Post, "Theology," *SM* 6 (1970) 233–49; B. F. Van Ackeren—P. De Letter, "Theology," *NCE* 14 (1967) 39–58; Further: G. Söhngen, *Philosophische Einübung in die Theologie* (Freiburg—Munich, 1955); C. Hefling, "Science and Religion,"*NDT* 9 38–45; Edward Schillebeeckx, *Revelation and Theology* (London, 1974); B. Welte, *Auf der Spur des Ewigen* (Freiburg—Basel—Vienna, 1965) esp. 351–426; E. Neuhäusler —E. Gößmann, *Was ist Theologie?* (Munich, 1966); K. Rahner, "Ecclesiology," *Theological Investigations* 10 (1973) 3–121; B. Caspar—K. Hemmerle—P. Hünermann, *Theologie als Wissenschaft* (Freiburg—Basel—Vienna, 1970); M. Seckler, *Im Spannungsfeld von Wissenschaft und Kirche. Theologie als schöpferische Auslegung der Wirklichkeit* (Freiburg—Basel—Vienna, 1980); "Theologien. Eine Grundidee in dreifacher Ausgestaltung" in: *ThQ* 163 (1983) 241–64.

home in Greek thought. It was only hesitatingly, and not without resistance and modification, taken up within the horizon and inner space of the Christian faith and its possibilities of affirmation and understanding. Theology as a concept in Greek thought occurs first in Plato. He understands by it the myths and the legends and histories of the gods, purified of everything scandalous, Judged philosophically and critically, demythologized, and interpreted in the sense and according to the criteria of political education. Theology thus represents the path from myth to logos, which begins with Heraclitus and Anaximander and ends with Plato. The function of logos consisted in uncovering in the mode of *aletheia* [truth] the truth hidden by the gods in mythology and myths; this was, thus, a mode of revelation. A quite different meaning of theology is found in Aristotle. There it means the philosophical-metaphysical consideration of [what has] being in its being; it forms the theme of what Aristotle called "first philosophy." Thus, what Aristotle is doing is an ontological theology: "The God of the philosophers became the end and goal of a first philosophy which has as its subject [that which has] being in its being, and which makes affirmations about its original relationships and first causes until it comes to the proof that there is a first-of-all, a first cause, on which heaven and earth depend."[2]

In these philosophical reflections, and in their treatment of religion and things religious, there is a recognizable effort to consider talk about God and the divinity as a philosophical possibility. This intention remained connected with assigning the name "theology" and "theologian" to the religious realm. Theologians are proclaimers of God; theology is religious talk about the gods. Theology is above all the talking to God that is carried out in cult. That is why Homer and Hesiod were called theologians.[3]

From these presuppositions there resulted, especially in Stoicism, the distinction of a threefold type of theology: the mythical theology of the poets and legends of the gods; the "physical" theology of the philosophers which had to do with the *natura deorum* , the true nature of the gods; and political theology, the *theologia civilis* [civil theology] of the lawgiver and the official state cult (M. Varro, 116-27 B. C.).

The definitive appropriation of the word "theology" by the Christian faith came about in the course of the fourth and fifth centuries, when *theology* became the customary name for the true study of God and specifically came to be applied to the Trinitarian and Christological affirmations. The biblical writers as a whole were

2. G. Söhngen, "Theologie" in: Staatslexikon 7 (Freiburg, 1962) 966.
3. Gerhard Ebeling in: *RGG* 6 (1962) 753.

called theologians. Some, like the evangelist John, were given the name with very special emphasis.

A further enrichment in the acceptance and use of the concept of theology is represented by Dionysius the Areopagite's Neoplatonic reflection on how God is to be spoken of; this resulted in the distinction between an apophatic (negative), kataphatic (affirmative), and mystical theology.

It took much longer before the word and concept of theology which Augustine characterized as *ratio sive sermo de divinitate*—thinking or talking about the Divinity—began to have that comprehensive sense of science of faith which is related to the whole of revelation and the faith ordered to it. This transition took place in the Latin language at the time of the beginning of high Scholasticsim. This was the time, of course, when revelational faith was being questioned as to its relationship to science, above all to philosophy, when it was coming into contact with Aristotelianism and, in connection with the founding of the universities, had to set itself up scientifically within the *artes liberales*. The whole of Christian faith was being reflected on dialectically in the form of the *quaestio*. Abelard, Gilbert of Porretania, Henry of Ghent, and above all Thomas Aquinas were important figures in this.

Theology as Science in Thomas Aquinas

The question of theology as science and of the scientific character of theology was raised and discussed principally by Thomas Aquinas (1225-1274). Central to this development was the concept of science, taken from Aristotle, and its potential application to theology.[4] In article two of the first question of the *Summa theologiae*, Thomas asks: *Utrum doctrina sacra sit scientia* (Whether sacred doctrine [theology] is a science). Thomas begins his answer from Aristotle's concept of science.[5]

According to Aristotle, science consists in the knowledge of the general essence of things and in the knowledge of their grounds. This knowledge, which at the same time makes logical connections, comes about in the form of deriving and drawing conclusions and in the proof thus produced. The ultimate grounds of these conclusions and proofs are the highest principles of being and thinking; they cannot be derived or proved but are evident, discernible and cogent in themselves: *principia per se nota* [principles known through themselves]. Principles, knowl-

---

4. W. A. Wallace—J. A. Weisheipl, "St. Thomas Aquinas," *NCE* 14.102–15.

5. Cf. the notes and commentary in the German–Latin edition (Die Deutsche Thomasausgabe), (Salzburg—Vienna, 1934); M. Seckler, "Geist der Katholizität. Thomas von Aquin und die Theologie" in: *Im Spannungsfeld von Wissenschaft und Kirche* 163–77.

edge of essence, and drawing conclusions are the framework of this concept of science.

On the basis of these presuppositions, Thomas asks whether theology is a science. At first, all indications are to the contrary, for "theology," as Thomas observes, "proceeds from the articles of faith, which are not necessary to thought, which are not acknowledged by all. For not all have faith, says the Scripture (2 Thes 3:2). Thus, theology is not science. Faith is the conviction of things not seen" (Heb 11:1). Furthermore, "Science is not concerned with the individual but with the general. But theology treats of specially particular things, e.g., the history of Abraham, Isaac, and Jacob, and the like. Thus, theology is not science."

Then follows Thomas's response:

> Theology is a science. But one has to consider that there are two kinds of sciences. One proceeds from principles that are given by the natural light of reason, like arithmetic, geometry and the like. Others proceed from principles that come from the light of another, higher, science, as perspective proceeds from the principles that geometry teaches, and as music proceeds from arithmetic realities. It is in this latter manner that theology is a science, because it proceeds from principles given it from the light of a higher science, namely the knowledge of God and of the blessed. Just as the musician relies on the principles provided by the mathematician, so theology relies on the principles of the divinely revealed faith.

These principles are evident to God; human beings share in them through faith. That which in philosophy functions as principles, in theology is faith. Theology is thus a *scientia subalternata*, a science which draws its legitimation from a "higher" science, namely the knowledge of God and of the saints. In a precise qualification, Thomas adds that, in contrast to philosophy, theology seeks to know God "as God is knowable only to Himself, and as God communicates Himself to others through revelation" (1.6).

According to Thomas, theology relates to faith as a conclusion to its principle. Consequently he says: "Theology is learned by study even though its principles flow from revelation." Thus theology is a formal, natural science, like other sciences, but in its principles in is a "supernatural" science.

If reason is the subject of the understanding of faith, this is all the more so in the qualified faith-knowledge of theology, i.e., when it is *ratio fide illustrata*, reason illuminated by faith. The ability and function of the intellect is here raised to its highest actualization. It does not lose but gains when it is placed and places itself at the service of something higher. Thomas is guided here by the conviction that the smallest knowledge that we have of the highest and most sublime things is worth more and is more worthy of our longing than the most certain knowledge of less important things.

In order to understand and correctly evaluate this characterization of the science of faith, one must recall the concept of science prevailing at that time. And indeed, as an attempt to make possible theology as science, it was an attempt, by no means uncontroversial even in its own day, in which unexplainable and artificial solutions were also to be found.

Acceptance of a "science of God" may have been possible in a situation of unbroken faith. This presupposition is no longer fulfillable in our day. What was taken for granted in another time has become a problem of the first order today. Nevertheless, the attempt of Thomas was a significant and original novelty. It is to be compared with our contemporary effort to characterize and legitimize theology from the theory of science. Thomas's contemporaries Duns Scotus and Bonaventure rejected his conception. They, instead, spoke of theology not as science (*scientia*), but as wisdom (*sapientia*), or called theology the science of the holy Scripture.

The Significance of This Concept of Theology

In his characterization of theology, Thomas sees revelation and faith above all under the sign of truth. With his construction of the knowledge of God and of the blessed, Thomas seeks to represent the principle and evidence-character of theology as science and at the same time to describe its special character. Under these presuppositions it is possible to describe the scientific aspect of theology in formally the same structure as knowledge through derivation and conclusion from the highest principles and to characterize theology as "a discerning knowledge mediated through a process of conclusions from the articles of faith as revealed and believingly presupposed warrants."[6] The discernment or insight of theology is thus related to the discernibility of its derivations and conclusions. Thus no new content is added to the articles of faith—they are instead, by their translation into the language of science and its concepts, unfolded in content, interpreted, and thus given a more precise and profound understanding. Theology thus is related to faith as a conclusion to its principle. But no distancing from faith is expressed by the conclusions; instead, faith in its substance and content is brought to understanding.

This process can be illustrated by two well-known examples: the characterization of the sonship of Jesus as "one in nature with the Father" (*consubstantialis Patri*), and the concept of "transubstantiation" in the doctrine of the Eucharist. There is no claim that these two expressions can be found as such in the apostolic, biblical message and at all times in the tradition of the Church. Nor can it be denied that

6. G. Söhngen, *Philosophische Einübung in die Theologie* 124.

the two expressions were first developed and became part of the Church's preaching only through the scientific work of theologians and through the application of concepts to the content of revelation. Without the assistance of Greek metaphysics in the first instance and, with the second expression, of the idea of a change in nature or essence derived from Aristotelian metaphysics, the emergence of both expressions in theology would be unthinkable. In other words, both expressions came as something new to the proclamation of the faith by way of theological concept-building. The expressions did not spring from divine revelation itself but from specifically theological thought. However, both of the realities to which the two expressions are related are apostolic affirmations of faith, i.e., the unique divine Sonship of Christ and the essentially real presence of Christ in the Eucharist. What is new are specific concepts, not new specific realities. It is not as if these realities were not already contained in the apostolic heritage of faith and in the Church's proclamation of the faith, and even clearly expressed there. The contents of faith are expressed, but they are said and given to us there in different, let us say pre-scientific, language, and thus leave plenty of room for working out the concept theologically.[7]

Such examples are easy to multiply, so one can well imagine how much the faith as history of faith, as dogma and development of dogma owes to the theological "stretching of concepts [*Anstrengung des Begriffs*]." This provides as an explication the internal and external clarification that is helpful for distinguishing and demarcating. That is something that is legitimate and, under certain conditions, even necessary for faith. There is, of course, danger that theology could become too concept- and conclusion-happy, that it could make itself independent, that for sheer joy at the play of concepts it could lose its hold on the original witness of Scripture and history. There is the further danger that a theology of conclusions, which comes to its results with the help of philosophy and metaphysical concepts, could forget that the concepts have a history, that they can change, and that in another context they might no longer say what they originally meant. In other words, the reality might have to be expressed differently today if the same thing is to be described.

To understand theology in this way implies that the reality of faith can and must be expressible in another philosophy than traditional Greek and scholastic philosophy. For example, theology can and must be expressible in the contemporary philosophy of modernity and the contemporary world, and even in the philosophy of the Far East something that is far more difficult and, up to now, barely even averted to by Christian thinkers.

7. Ibid. 132.

A still stronger misgiving is raised against the presuppositions of this theology. According to Thomas, these presuppositions are to be found in the phenomenon of the characterization of faith as doctrine or teaching, that is, as truth which is thought to be as eternal and as timeless as the principles of logic and mathematics. The fact that faith is connected to history, to events, and to persons, or as Thomas says, to the singular, and to the individual, represents a genuine difficulty. How can this be science if science is to be characterized as knowledge from principles, as knowledge that is determined by the universal, the general?

Thomas sees this difficulty and responds to it in the *Summa theologiae* by pointing out that the individual, the "singular," is not important in itself but only as type, as example of a general truth or rule of life, or as introduction it.

With respect to the singular within faith and theology, one must point out, against Thomas, that the singular means a great deal more than that it is simply the bearer of something common. The singular as person and history is essentially connected with revelation, the relational point of faith. Revelation cannot be separated from its historical ground, especially from its fulfillment in the person of Jesus of Nazareth, the way some other religions can be separated from their founder. The truth of which revelation speaks and at which theology aims is not a theory that calls for a closed and complete system; it consists rather of events and human beings. Accordingly, history and historicity belong not only to the presupposition or the frame, they belong to the content of that which, theologically, has to be asked about. That is why the content and truth of faith are concrete. The concrete is by no means a disturbing contradiction of the general nature, but its concrete realization. The best expression of this is the fact that Jesus Christ is the essence of Christianity. This fact does not exclude but includes the stretching of this concept of the relative importance of the singular and the general. But at the same time one can see where the relational point of these efforts lies: not in the essence of general ideas but in the concretion of history and person.

Therefore the reason that is made use of in theology is not only speculative but also historical reason. Only in the combining of these two dimensions, of these "two eyes," as I. Döllinger says,[8] can revelation as truth, event, and history, and can truth as person be mediated. This is the only way to assure that no side is overlooked or beaten down at the expense of the other. What this can mean concretely may be illustrated in the words of Cardinal Manning, who, when historical

8. "Die Vergangenheit und die Genenwart der katholischen Theologie" in: J. Finsterhölzl, *Ignaz von Döllinger*, Wegbereiter heutiger theologie (Graz—Vienna—Cologne, 1969) 227–69.

problems surfaced in connection with the discussion of the infallibility of papal *ex cathedra* decisions, said: Dogma decides history. No less one-sided would be the opposite thesis that history makes dogma impossible.

In connection with the question of whether and to what extent Thomas Aquinas actually did justice theologically to the dimension of history as a structural element of revelation, take note of the following: More recent research into Thomas has pointed out that a fundamental starting point for the historical is also present in Thomas Aquinas. Max Seckler, for example, has impressively portrayed this in his book, *Das Heil in der Geschichte. Geschichtstheologisches Denken bei Thomas von Aquin* (Salvation in History: Historico-Theological Thought in Thomas Aquinas).[9]

In this context the following two points are especially important. First, the fact that in Thomas, the singular cannot be the object of a science of the universal does not really make the singular unimportant. It is rather an indication of the limits of human knowledge and an insight into the individual and the uniqueness, incalculability, especially the freedom of the individual, which cannot be confined within an all-knowing speculation. In Thomas, the singular is not reduced to unimportance, but freed from the clutches of a science that sees in the universal the object and goal of its efforts. *Individuum est ineffabile* [the individual is inexpressibly valuable].

This shows that science cannot simply be made the measure of all things. This is visible in the work of Thomas from the fact that, along with his systematically organized *summae* are his still unfortunately little-read and studied Scripture commentaries. And ultimately, one must also talk about Thomas the mystic, whose last word was about the hidden God, about the Thomas who, months before his death completely stopped writing. As he put it: Everything I have written seems to me like rubbish.

A second critical point in assessing Thomas's concept of theology is this. The *Summa theologiae* stands under the threfold schema of departure—journey—return. This is a Neoplatonic model, which Thomas takes over in order to characterize the formal structure of revelation and faith. This schema describes the structure not of a timeless idea but of an event, which is characterized by origin and goal and the path that leads between the two. This opens up room for history. When revelation is characterized with this schema, it is specified in its historicity.

History, in its significance and positivity, is emphasized in Thomas by another motivation, which is mentioned by Seckler: as to the ground of history, Thomas answers that it lies in the inner-

9. (Munich, 1964).

trinitarian process. The God of Thomas is not the unmoved mover but the living God, God in the relation of three Persons.

Even if the moment of the historical is not done justice to in all aspects of Thomas, especially when one examines it from the point of view of the historical critical method in the modern sense, the coordination and inner-connection of truth and event, of truth and history, is indeed seen by Thomas and it is thought through in surprising profundity. As little as the Aristotelian-Thomistic concept of science may satisfy all concerns, it does contain in its elements a totally committed openness.

§ 13

THEOLOGY AND HISTORICAL THINKING[1]

The Realm of History

The affirmation that science is knowledge of something through knowledge of its causes is also applicable in the realm of history, as long as we don't forget that historical causality is different from natural causality, and also different from the causes in a self-evident principle. For in the realm of historical causality, along with causes of economic, social, and cultural kinds, the causes that predominantly come into play are those having to do with person, spirit, and freedom.

In the realm of history and the historical, therefore, knowledge is possible not in the sense of knowing how things have to be—that is the claim of a science which proceeds by way of conclusions—but in a knowledge of things as they are, indeed a knowledge that seeks to grasp the thing to be known in the causes that lead up to it, and to bring it into a context of understanding. Understanding as understanding from sense (or as getting a feel for something) is different from causal explanation.

The phenomenon of history and of the historical as object and element of theology is significant for two reasons: first that to which history relates, namely revelation, has an historical origin and thus is history in historical events; second the extent to which history is the way in which faith is both represented from its origins and interpreted in a history which can be described as tradition or trajectory. In history, therefore, we don't get something handed on to us that is timeless, formulated unchangeably once and for all. Instead of that, we get in history, through believing and thinking human beings, an inter-

---

1. A. Brunner, *Geschichtlichkeit* (Bern, 1961); F. Wiplinger, *Wahrheit und Geschichtlichkeit* (Freiburg—Munich, 1961); A Darlapp, "Geschichtlichkeit" in: *HThG* I (1962) 491–97; "History of Salvation," *SM* 5.411–19; Karl Rahner, *SM* 5.419–23; P. Hünermann, *Der Durchbruch des geschichtlichen Denkens im 19. Jahrhundert* (Freiburg—Basel—Vienna, 1967); W. Kasper, *Glaube und Geschichte* (Mainz, 1970) esp. 9–32; "Tradition als Erkenntnisprinzip. Zur theologischen Relevanz der Geschichte" in: *ThQ* 155 (1975) 198–215.

pretation of that which theology is all about: faith and the understanding of faith. Faith which sees in Jesus Christ the goal and end of
the history and the forms of revelation that went before him, also sees
in that goal a beginning, a "beginning in fullness," as Möhler put it.[2]
Nothing coming after this as effect can rise any higher than this origin,
this source, which is at the same time a critical norm of everything in
the future. But at the same time, this "origin in fullness" has need of
time as way and process in order to interpret this fullness of the
beginning and its dimensions, and thereby to unfold its richness.

Faith and History

Faith is dependent on history. Through history its contents come to
light. Through history these contents are analyzed, so to speak, in the
colored spectrum of the one stream of light. Through history, therefore,
faith, its content and its truth, are not endangered or denied but are
affirmed in themselves. Through history, the yesterday is not abrogated; rather, the yesterday is taken up and enlivened and enriched
through new things. In that sense, the historicity of faith does not
mean the relativizing of the valid but, as perspectivity, the gaining of
its aspects and dimensions whereby the individual, i.e., truths, are
related to the one Truth and thus remain protected from the danger of
isolation and disassociation. This process of faith will never come to an
end as long as there is faith and human beings with faith.

The historicity of faith takes on still further contours if we consider
the following. Historicity is, of course, perspectivity. Historicity of
truth, however, means that always only one perspective of faith can be
brought to expression as a result of the humanity and the finiteness and
the conditionedness of the ability to believe. Our faith consciousness,
and also that of the Church as the community of believers, stands under
the condition of the narrowness of consciousness. Consequently, while
other perspectives, or the whole of the truth of faith, is not actually
denied, it is nevertheless not existentially present or not present with
enough vitality. This can cause shifts and displacements, even disturbances, in the framework of faith. Faith needs history in order to find
its voice therein; the truth of faith becomes real in history. But it is
also true that no historical form or realization is the pure realization
of faith; it is always at the same time, its time-conditioned limitation.

Thus, the historically believing human being, as well as the
respective community of believers, must not consider itself and its
understanding of the faith to be whole, perfect, and definitive; they
must rather remain open for the whole of the past and the future of

---

2. *Grundgedanke des Werkes: die Einheit in der Kirche oder das Prinzip des Katholizismus,*
herausgegeben, eingeleitet und kommentiert von J. R. Geiselmann (Cologne—Olten, 1956).

faith. That they frequently do not is one of the reasons for many of the contemporary symptoms of crisis.

One of the causes of difficulty and aberration in many contemporary questions is the way in which what has developed and become valid for today is raised to ultimate validity and normativity, and turned into an insurmountable barrier, with the result that people refuse to look at new possibilities which at one time had a legitimate historical existence. Looking into history liberates one from this and opens up new possibilities.

Faith and history are intimately interconnected. But history always represents only one possible and limited realization of faith, understanding of faith, science of faith, and community of faith. Hence it falls to faith and to the art of theology as the science of faith to differentiate faith, its contents and the historicity necessarily connected with it from the time-conditionedness of its respective realizations. The truth of faith is not affected, but how it gets worked out becomes a problem.

Whoever takes all contemporary manifestations, forms, and realizations of faith to be the unbroken, uniquely legitimate, ever-valid form of faith itself, and mourns the loss of that form, turns faith into ideology; that person enslaves faith and thus makes it incapable of opening up a new hour of faith and of Church and of bringing about living, effective forms of its realization.

The coordination of faith and history is ultimately produced by the fact that faith and the community of believers not only create out of themselves a realization in time and history, but thereby and therein encounter an historical situation and constellation, a milieu that is conditioned and created not by faith but by many other factors, political, social, and cultural. Faith must stand up to this historical situation. But the same situation also puts questions to the faith, questions that are born of this hour. Faith understands itself fully and correctly only when it is in a position to give its affirmations as answers to questions that are asked today. This doesn't work when it unreflectingly and insensitively passes on old truth in its old form. That is nothing more than giving answers to questions that are not even being asked; the affirmations, while themselves true, fall into a vacuum. Faith and its truth is faced with new questions from the reality of the hour at hand. Through new questions, new claims are made of faith; it is in part understood anew and empowered to new affirmations, to affirmations that earlier and until then did not even exist, for the hour had not yet come for them.

The course of the history of faith and of theology can thus be adequately described neither with the categories of progress nor with those of decline.[3] One can only say that in every age and every generation of believers, those concerned with the science of faith seek to do their own thing. Whether and how far they succeed is not to be settled here.

Historical Excursus on the Coordination of Theology and History

The coordination of theology and history, which we have just discussed in various ways and which seems to be taken for granted today, was programmatically represented by the theologians of the so-called Tübingen School in the last century.[4]

At the outset of the nineteenth century, there awoke within the romantic movement an intensive historical consciousness, a return to the sources, a new discovery of the manifold traditions in the life of peoples, of literature and of the "national spirit" moving them. There was a related discovery of the emotional capacities of human beings, of temperament, feeling and fantasy, and a corresponding revitalization of myths and sagas, of the immanence of the Divine in the world and in history. This was a clear countermovement against the Enlightenment, which separated God and world deistically according to the idea of God as master builder and engineer of the world who, after creation, left the world to its own laws which are in force and work without God, without being dependent on God. It was also a countermovement to the extent that the Enlightenment had raised abstract, conceptual thinking to the highest norm of all activities of the human spirit. That which is true is that which is clear.

There was still another moment alive in the historical consciousness of the nineteenth century, and expressed above all in the philosophy of German Idealism, most impressively in Hegel. We have already mentioned that, for Hegel, the Absolute Spirit is the ground of all reality, that the Absolute Spirit does not present itself statically in reality but is unfolded in a dialectical process. It follows that history can be seen not only as a collection of facts—in which case history would be blind. History is much more determined by inner connections, which have their ground in ideas. Spirit and ideas are the impulse of historical movement; they create in history relationships of sense. This

---

3. M. Seckler, "Der Fortschrittsgedanke in der Theologie" in: *Im Spannungsfeld von Wissenschaft und Kirche* 127–48.

4. On this, cf. J. R. Geiselmann, "Die Glaubenswissenschaft der katholischen Tübinger Schule in der Grundlegung durch J. S. Drey" in: *ThQ* 112 (1930) 9–117; *Geist des Christentums und des Katholizismus. Ausgewählte Schriften katholischer Theologie im Zeitalter des Deutschen Idealismus und der Romantik* (Mainz, 1940); *Lebendiger Glaube aus geheiligter Überlieferung. Der Grundgedanke der Theologie Johann Adam Möhlers und der katholischen Tübinger Schule* (Mainz, 1942); *Die katholische Tübinger Schule. Ihre theologische Eigenart* (Freiburg—Basel—Vienna, 1964); M. B. Schepers, "Tübingen," NCE, 14, (1967) 339.

is all the more true when in the reality of history the Absolute Divine Spirit manifests itself.

The theologians of the Tübingen School, especially J. S. Drey, J. A. Möhler, and F. A. Staudenmaier as well as J. von Kuhn, directly faced this contemporary and intellectual-historical situation as opportunity and as challenge with much the same kind of courage as Thomas Aquinas had shown with regard to Aristotle. They believed that they were all the more allowed and obliged to do this because, as they put it, the Christian religion is an historical and positive religion, which cannot be sublimated into a timeless idea because, in historical revelation, an inner connection, an idea, a principle is given by the econ omy [divine plan] of God, by God's plan for the salvation of humankind, and finally, because Christian revelation has come to us by historical revelation.

But the Tübingen theologians were standing alone on a broad plain. Both the then-influential Roman school (under Perrone) and the Mainz faculty (under Liebermann) rejected the encounter of theology with the thought of the time. Their grounds were that Romanticism, German Idealism, and above all Hegel, did not sufficiently affirm the transcendence of God, that they drew God into the historical process in a pantheistic way, and would thus abrogate God's freedom.

The impulse and the stimuli of the Tübingen theologians were cut short.[5] The victory of Neoscholasticsim pushed the dimension of history in theology into the background again, one could even say suppressed it, in favor of an understanding of theology as a conceptual idea of the faith understood as timeless doctrine and truth. Connected with this was the idea that what was now achieved, known, and formulated was the authoritative norm. A consideration of history signified, in this view of things, the foolhardy enterprise of deciding the clear and the clarified on the basis of the unclear and the not yet clarified, of wanting to illuminate the brilliant today by the dark yesterday. Therefore the most important book and the immediate norm for this kind of theological thinking was the catechism, preferably the *Catechismus Romanus* and "Denzinger": the *Enchiridion Symbolorum, Definitionum et Declarationum de Rebus Fidei et Morum* [Collection of Symbols, Definitions and Declarations on Matters of Faith and Morals] eds. 1–6 (1854-1888).[6]

---

5. Cf. L. Scheffczyk, *Theologie im Aufbruch und Widerstreit. Die deutsche katholische Theologie im 19. Jahrhundert* (Bremen, 1965); B. Welte, "Zum Strukturwandel der katholischen Theologie im 19. Jahrhundert" in: *Auf der Spur des Ewigen* (Freiburg—Basel—Vienna, 1965) 380–409.

6. Cf. Y. Congar, Über den rechten Gebrauch des "Denzinger" in: *Situation und Aufgabe der Theologie heute* (Paderborn, 1971) 125–ß50, (Spanish and French translations); J. Schumacher, *Der "Denzinger," Geschichte und Bedeutung eines Buches in der Praxis der neueren Theologie* (Freiburg—Basel—Vienna, 1974).

But repression is not a good thing, and certainly not a good solution. For the repressed will one fine day force itself into the light with all the more intensity.

This process is playing itself out, after the interlude of Modernism, before all our eyes in the theology of today. The themes of this thinking are clearly recognizable in Vatican II, both in its constitution on divine revelation and in the affirmations about the Church as People of God on its journey and about the Church in the world of today.

If there is a science of history that makes use of the historical-critical method in the interpretation of sources, texts, and documents, asks about the sense of the text, seeks out the grounds and contexts of what has happened as well as the consequences and effects that result from the events, and gives much attention both to explaining and to understanding, this all has great relevance for the possibilities and conditions of theology as a science of faith. This historical thinking becomes a decisive, indispensable constitutive element of such a theology. The history of the faith and of the community of faith of the Church, as history of dogmas, is absolutely indispensable for theology, even if it is not at all valued but often perceived by the present-day Church as disruptive and disturbing the peace.

By reflection on the historical and on history we thus learn not just what has been and how something has been; we also come to know through history, and not by any other way, that which is and how it is. We are thus protected from the opinion that the situation of faith, theology, and Church that is before us here and now is the best—or worst—of all worlds and times, or that there is no possibility or no form of realizing faith and Church beyond what is already here. We are saved from thinking that the way things are will, or must, remain forever the way they are.

Nothing, therefore, prevents us from applying the methods of scientific history to the history of faith and the faith community, and thus, in the name of that science, to present them as science. This is preferable and in many ways more comfortably possible than with the form of science that Aristotle and Thomas Aquinas admitted only for the knowledge of general essence, which was unable to do justice to all that is meant by history and by revelation as history.

§ 14

THEOLOGY IN THE SCIENTIFIC DISCUSSION
OF THE MODERN AGE

The Objection of Positivism

The possibility of talking about theology as science became problematic once again when, in the victorious wake of the natural sciences and mathematics in the modern age, the concept and the conditions of science were oriented to the model of natural science and mathematics. The ideal was to measure everything else according to them, as was actually done, fundamentally and explicitly, by positivism as theory of science.

Positivism was prepared for by Francis Bacon, Thomas Hobbes, and David Hume, and classically represented by Auguste Comte (1789-1857).[1] In his proposed "Three-Stage Law" he makes positivism the goal of a development: from (1) theological or fictitious, through (2) metaphysical-abstract, to (3) scientific-positivistic study. In this last stage the useless questions and the fruitless problems about the essence and ground of things are done away with. Positivism asks about the laws of the world and the course of things. It asks in order to know and, through knowledge, to gain control over the things themselves and the world. As for the theme of God, Comte prophesies: God will disappear without having left behind a question. What Comte initiated is effective to this day in many variations as the model for science.

If the only things that can claim to be scientific are those that are sensibly or technically perceivable, things that can be dealt with mathematically, things that are predictable, repeatable, and controllable, then theology has no chance to be a science. But then, this is the

---

1. *Einleitung in die positive Philosophie. Deutsch* (Leipzig, 1880); *Soziologie, deutsch von V. Dorn* (Jena, 1907). On Comte: Max Scheler, *Schriften zur Soziologie und Weltanschauungslehre I* (Leipzig, 1923); Henri de Lubac, *The Drama of Atheist Humanism* (Cleveland—New York, 1966); R. O. Johann, "Positivism," *SM* 5 (1969) 60–62.

fate not just of theology but of most of the fields of the so-called intellectual disciplines: history, literature, philosophy, law, politics, art.

It is thus understandable that the attempt was made, above all in the nineteenth century, to distinguish between natural science and intellectual science, to work out the methods specific to each, and to accord to each the quality of science when they seek to give an account of their methods and to gain knowledge according to the standards of these methods. The difference between the two kinds of sciences was characterized by the difference between explaining—as the goal of natural science—and understanding as the goal of intellectual science. Explaining means to raise something out of its physical, chemical, biological causes and laws. Understanding means to be concerned about the sense of a thing, about the sense of a text, a work of art, or an event.

This brings us to the problem of hermeneutics, which was thought out by Schleiermacher and Dilthey in the nineteenth century and remains a problem to this day even if, as we will point out, under different circumstances. In this new horizon of science and scientific procedure, it was possible for theology also to regain its position as science, above all as historical theology, as theology that appropriates the historical-critical method for the interpretation of biblical texts and its historical documents.

Theology and Existential Philosophy

The philosophy of existence, especially as represented by Karl Jaspers and—in a different way—by Martin Heidegger, has become vitally important for the understanding of both the content and the form of theology today. This is an obvious development, since the "moment" of existence is a characteristic of faith. If faith did not have a foundation in humanity itself, it could not be appropriated in such a way that human beings could say their personal, existential "I believe." Certainly this connection has always been known; but conscious, explicit reflection on it has taken place especially in recent times. This connection has become a special characteristic of contemporary theology and its most significant representative, Rudolf Bultmann (1883-1976).[2] The demythologization he demanded and undertook is only the reverse side of a task understood in an eminently positive way: to interpret the text and the matter of faith in existen-

2. Major works: *Faith and Understanding*, trans. Louise Pettibone Smith (Philadelphia: Fotress Press, 1987); *Theology of the New Testament*, trans. Kendrick Grobel (New York: Charles Scribner's Sons, 1970); *The Gospel of John; A Commentary*, trans. G. R. Beasley-Murray (Philadelphia: Westminster Press, 1971).

On Bultmann: Walter Schmitthals, *An Introduction to the Theology of Rudolf Bultmann* (Minneapolis, Minn.: Augsburg Publishing House, 1968); Heirich Fries, "Rudolf Bultmann" in: *Klassiker der Theologie II*, ed. H. Fries and G. Kretschmar (Munich, 1983) 297–317.

tially interpretative and existentially relevant ways, i.e., to do theology as existential theology. Bultmann is of the opinion that the "existentials" in the philosophy of Heidegger correspond to the fundamental characteristics of biblical faith, which, in turn, are given new expression today in the philosophy of existence. Sin is the closing off and self-alienation of human beings, their inauthenticity; faith is freedom from ourselves and for ourselves; faith is the overcoming of the incommunicativity and inauthenticity of human beings, and their opening to the future.

According to Bultmann, the specific questions of theology arise from the fact that the path from inauthenticity to authenticity, from incommunicativity to freedom, is neither the work of human beings nor the result of philosophy; it is the work of God in Jesus Christ, a gift of God which can be received only through the kerygma and in faith.

Bultmann's attempt to mediate theology with existence, as expressed in the principle that to talk about human beings means to talk about God, and to talk about God means to talk about human beings, and to talk about human beings means to talk about existence, was provided with a rather broad base from the fact that theology as a whole is connected with anthropology in a theological anthropology and an anthropological theology. This is the form of the theology of Karl Rahner.[3]

Human beings are the starting point of this theological way of thinking. As questioning and loving beings in the transcendental openness of their spirit and heart, they are dependent on the absolute, infinite, incomprehensible mystery of themselves. When Rahner asks about faith, he is asking first and foremost a fundamental-theological question about the transcendental conditions of the possibility of this faith. From this perspective, faith is constituted in such a way that the "objectively" believed is always at the same time the "subjectively" expected, i.e., an answer to a question human beings have and, indeed, themselves are. This is Rahner's way of escaping from "extrinsicism" within faith and theology, i.e., that position which holds the whole of what concerns faith—as affirmation, as disclosure of reality, as grace and salvation—to be something that comes to human beings from outside. The gratuity of revelation is preserved, but this is done at the cost of the external, of what is "laid on us from outside." Without

3. Foundational works: *Spirit in the World*, trans. William Dych (New York: Herder and Herder, 1969); *Hearers of the Word*, trans. Michael Richards (New York: Herder and Herder, 1969); *Theological Investigations*, 24 vols; *Foundations of Christian Faith: An Introduction to the Idea of Christianity*, trans. William V. Dych (New York: Crossroad, 1994).

On Rahner for this particular theme: P. Eicher, *Die anthropologische Wende. Karl Rahners philosophischer Weg vom Wesen des Menschen zur personalen Existenz* (Friborg/Switzerland, 1970); K. Fischer, *Der Mensch als Geheimnis. Die Anthropologie Karl Rahners* (Freiburg—Basel—Vienna, 1974); Heinrich Fries, "Theologie als Anthropologie" in: K. Rahner—H. Fries, *Theologie in Freiheit und Verantwortung* (Munich, 1981) 30–69.

the least bit doubting or undercutting this gratuity, Rahner's intention, in view of the whole of what is meant by salvation and grace, in view of the individual contents of faith, is to find a way of expressing what these contents have to do with human beings, with their experience, with their life, with their expectations and hopes, and of expressing how, on the other hand, human beings know that they are not alienated by revelation but are brought back home to themselves.

Rahner's formulation is: Christian reality is the conscious taking possession of the mystery of being human. He does not, of course, make historical revelation derive a priori from human beings. It is positively and personally bestowed; as much as human beings as "Hearers of the Word" expect a possible special revelation in the realm of history and under the sign of the word, so much do human beings possess a transcendental openness towards the human mode of the self-communication of God to spirit-gifted creatures. Thus Rahner conceives the hypostatic union as "a truly unique realization, which takes place nowhere else and is the work of God, of that which being human really says." Beginning in this way, from existence and anthropology, the business of theology is in no way manipulated, narrowed, or determined from the outset. It is only explained that the business of faith is related to human beings and to their existence, that an existence analysis and a comprehensive anthropology can also make this clear of itself. In human beings and in human existence we find sketched out the conditions and the presuppositions of the possibility of faith and revelation. This is true above all in view of an interpretative horizon in which the human being as a whole is sketched.[4]

The Problem of Hermeneutics

In the horizon of existential theology, the already previously acute problem of hermeneutics took on new life.[5] In the hermeneutical principle of Bultmann, who placed his theological work under the sign of faith and understanding, it found a particularly impressive form of presentation.

Wilhelm Dilthey (1833-1911), who most persistently represented the methodical distinction between the natural and the intellectual sciences, dealt extensively with the question of hermeneutics, and with

4. His *Foundations of Faith* offers the comprehensive presentation of this program.
5. J. Wach, *Das Verstehen* (Tübingen, 1928–1933); V. A. Harvey, "Hermeneutics," *ER* 6 (1987) 279–87; E. Betti, *Die Hermeneutik als allgemeine Methode der Geisteswissenschaften* (Tübingen, 1962): H. G. Gadamer, *Truth and Method*, trans. Joel Weinsheimer and Donald Marshall (New York: Crossroad, 1989); R. Marlé. *Introduction to Hermeneutics* (London, 1968); K. Lehmann, "Hermeneutics," *SM* 3 (1969) 23–27; "Der hermeneutische Horizont der historisch–kritischen Exegese" in: *Gegenwart des Glaubens* (Mainz, 1970) 54–93; E. Biser, *Glaubensverständnis. Grundriß einer hermeneutischen Fundamentaltheologie* (Freiburg—Basel—Vienna, 1975).

understanding as distinct from explaining. Dilthey sees the possibility of understanding in the identity of life and experience. This identity is possible between one's own living and experiencing in the respective present and the expression of living and experiencing in the past, whereby the expression encompasses both word and wordless event. Living and experiencing are the connecting powers and elements of past and present—understanding becomes possible through them.

At the beginning of hermeneutical reflection stands the much-discussed, unavoidable hermeneutical circle. Understanding is not possible without the subjective elements which belong to the process of understanding i.e., without a preunderstanding. Thus knowing is, basically, a knowing of the already known. It is not possible to break out of this circle, out of this context; one can only see it and, so to speak, come into it.

Understanding is not blocked by this process; it is also not identified with the preunderstanding. Rather, understanding is disclosed when it is said how the process comes about. The preunderstanding can and should be modified or corrected by the process of understanding. When this is the case, the image of the circle is, strictly speaking, not accurate.

For Bultmann,[6] understanding means understanding oneself. Every text to be understood is to be asked the question, what understanding of existence is expressed in it. Understanding thus does not mean determining what is at hand, but figuring out what a text, a thing, an event or a person means for the understanding and realization of existence. To understand means to ask what understanding of existence, respectively, is presupposed. From that grows the possibility of an existential interpretation of faith, its actualization as well as its contents. Contents are not registered, but movements of existence are encountered and led from inauthenticity to authenticity. As Bultmann explains, one cannot tell people what death and life are in same way one can explain to them that there are flesh-eating plants. Unknown things are not made known in the text, but possibilities of myself are disclosed which I can understand only if I am open for my possibilities.[7] Potentially this principle, is for all practical purposes, indefinitely applicable. The only questions are whether the presupposition, to understand means to understand oneself, is really true in this universal sense, and whether every text is intended to express just such an understanding.

---

6. Cf. H. Fries, *Bultmann—Barth and Catholic Theology*, trans. Leonard Swidler (Pittsburgh: Duquesne University Press, 1967); M. Boutin, *Relationalität als Verstehensprinzip bei Rudolf Bultmann* (Munich, 1974).

7. Rudolf Bultmann, *Glauben und Verstehen* 3.5, ET: *Faith and Understanding* , trans. Louise Pettibone Smith (Philadelphia: Fortress Press) only first volume translated into English.

This leads to another consideration: If understanding means simply and exclusively to understand oneself, doesn't this lead to a narrowing of understanding? For everything that cannot be covered by this hermeneutical principle remains separated from the understanding. As much as world, reality, and history are related to existence, the content of all reality cannot be reduced to the understanding of existence that lies therein. Being is greater than the self. Understanding of being is not identical with understanding of self which, in the theology of Bultmann, is conceived in a predominantly individualistic way. In Bultmann's hermeneutical principle lies the danger that the new and unexpected, the paradoxical and the strange will be removed from understanding at the outset.

Let it be pointed out in this context that many representatives of intellectual science and philosophy have expressed themselves on the problem of hermeneutics. In some cases it was theological questioning that gave the push; in others, the reflections of the intellectual sciences worked back on theology.

Martin Heidegger[8] characterizes understanding as ability-to-be, and sees therein a "being character [*Seinscharakter*]" of human life. This brings out that existence as human life cannot mean a "freestanding self-possession of existence"; it is experienced much more as limited existence, as being and time, as being determined by history and historicity.

Hans Georg Gadamer brought this reflection somewhat further. He relates understanding to an event of tradition in which individuals live and stand, which is given to them ahead of time, to which they concede a certain advance measure of reliability, and which they must bring to conscious recognition before they apply themselves to the individual content of understanding and knowledge. They understand this content, if they know the question, to which an answer was given in the form of an historical affirmation. They gain thereby a preunderstanding, even a kind of "life relationship" to the thing. The preunderstanding, also the "prejudgment," is seen positively and also given temporary recognition. At the same time it is subjected to a broader process of the understanding of critical clarification. If a new experience comes into this process which cannot be arranged under the familiar, expected tendencies, this experience overthrows the former prejudgment, takes up the unfamiliar one, and with it expands and enriches the sphere of its own experience of the world. This brings about what Gadamer calls a "melting of horizon." The medium of such a hermeneutic as fundamental movement of human, historical, finite existence is the language in which the tradition and its conditions are preserved.

---

8. Martin Heidegger, *Being and Time*, trans. John Macquarrie and Edward Robinson (New York: Harper, 1962).

All this makes it clear that Bultmann's hermeneutical principle is significantly modified and freed from the narrowness of which we have spoken.

Political Theology

The existential-existentiell, the anthropologically oriented theology of the present, has been expanded by a further dimension, by the dimension of the public and the societal. From this arose what is today called political theology.[9] Its purpose was to respond to the yawning gap between faith and society, which is currently becoming more and more obvious.

Political theology—not a good concept, because of its historical burden—is applied critically against tendencies of "privatization" and "isolation," against a free-swinging subjectivity such as is found in many representatives of existential theology, in which Christian faith seems to be reduced to existential decision. It is likewise applied against that desecularizing (R. Bultmann) in which there is a lack of responsibility for the world and the shaping of its future.[10] This political theology is concerned not just with "understanding" and an activity derived from it, but with—to take up a word from Karl Marx— change, with a theory that comes from praxis and is mediated by it. The problem of this theology is thus not one of faith and reason but one of faith and praxis, faith and action. In all, this theology tries to do justice to the public dimension as well as to the social-critical function of faith and Church.

This theology affirms that the fundamental biblical categories cannot have meaning only in the framework of a relationship between God and the individual human being, i.e., between God and the soul. These categories also have a social and political level; they are originally connected with an event and a history of liberation: the Exodus of the people of Israel from servitude in Egypt.

Accordingly, the biblical message of redemption, freedom and liberation must today be brought into the context of the liberation movements that are also concerned with change from enslaving circumstances and oppressive conditions. Thus deeds and works, which bring about a better world of justice and freedom, anticipate what is meant by the phrase "kingdom of God."

9 Johannes Baptis Metz, *Theology of the World*, trans. William Glen–Doepel (New York: Herder and Herder, 1969); "Political Theology," *SM* 5 (1970) 34–38; *Faith in History and Society: Toward a Practical Fundamental Theology*, trans. David Smith (New York: Seabury Press, 1980); *The Emergent Church: The Future of Christianity in a Postbourgeois World*, trans. Peter Mann (New York: Crossroad, 1981).

10. B. Dieckmann, *"Welt" und "Entweltlichung" in der Theologie Rudolf Bultmanns* (Munich—Paderborn—Vienna).

Of course, a political theology as theology of liberation can fall into the temptation of legitimizing all practical measures that stand under the sign of political liberation and of perhaps even violent revolution. Theology can be put to work for concrete and powerful interests, and thus degenerate into ideology. There is not just an ideology of the way things are but also an ideology of change.

This danger cannot be eliminated. Yet that does not eliminate the just concerns of political theology and the theology of liberation. Its goals are legitimized by the Christian faith. Necessary differentiations come up with the question of ways and means to the goal. In the question of force or violence, there is the danger that the cycle of evil will not be broken.

In any case, however, one thing is clear, and it has practical consequences. If its message and promise is to be heard and accepted today in the Third World, the community of faith must set itself on the side of the poor and the oppressed. But to side with the oppressed means to be against the oppressor.

In the foreword of the book by Gustavo Gutierrez *Theology of Liberation*, Johann Baptist Metz writes a sentence which also comes up again in the Confession of Faith of the Synod of Bishops of the Federal Republic of Germany: "The Church will more easily survive its intellectual doubters than the speechless doubt and desperation of its people, than [its] disdain of the little ones who were for Jesus the privileged ones and who must also be the privileged ones for his Church."[11]

An important element of this theology is its future aspect and, connected with that, hope as the all-encompassing form of faith.[12] For this reason, it is only the future that, along with the past and present, provides access to the authentic message of Jesus about the coming, not yet fulfilled, Kingdom of God. This is what prevents faith and theology from becoming theories of legitimation for the way things are. The "eschatological proviso" offers an antidote against the temptation of taking an inner-worldly theory or an inner-historical social situation as fulfillment of the promise of faith, against the possibility that, under the sign of the "left," a new integralism, a new "Age of Constantine"—under different premises—might begin.

There are some questions that need to be asked of this conception of theology:

Can the social-political, if it is turned into the authoritative criterion for the theological, become, like the existential, a narrowing

---

11. Gustavo Gutierrez, *A Theology of Liberation: History, Politics, and Salvation*, trans. Sister Caridad Inda and John Eagleson (Maryknoll, N. Y.: Orbis Books 1988).

12. Jürgen Moltmann, *Theology of Hope: On the Ground and Implications of a Christian Eschatology* (New York: Harper & Row, 1967); W. D. Marsch ed., *Diskussion über die Theologie der Hoffnung* (Munich, 1967).

element for faith and theology? Isn't there the danger that theological expectations of salvation may turn into political realities? In political theology do not faith and the community of faith take their mission and orientations primarily from outside and from external realities instead of from their own specific motivations and directions? Under the intentions of political theology does not the community of faith turn into a rival power among other political movements? Does it not lose its independence in this way? Does it not, conversely, endanger the autonomy of the political and social realms? Is the criticism entirely unjustified that, in place of a rejected *ecclesia triumphans* [triumphant church] a "critically triumphing church" (H. Maier)[13] will be set up as a social-critical instance? If so, the question remains: To what will it be oriented in general and in particular? And will it be possible for criticism to have a continuing status, to be, so to speak, established or institutionalized? Finally, one must ask: are hope and future, central affirmations of political theology, meant in the same sense as in the New Testament? Is not the content of hope and future also what is popularly rejected today as privatization and reduction to the intimate: the overcoming of death through resurrection life, through eternal life, the overcoming of anxiety and desperation, the hope of glory, of communion with God, which is to be granted also and specifically to me personally, because the work of Christ was done for me. The "deprivatization" of the New Testament message, it has been said, is just as important as its "demythologization." But if that is supposed to mean a neglect and a curtailment of person and individuality in favor of some kind of conception of the "general," then an objection must be raised. For the fact is that subjectivity is for the benefit of all human beings. That is, to be sure, also considered as the goal of political theology itself.

With regard to the person, there is nothing to be superseded. Instead everything must be done to win the person over. The changing of structures and conditions has no right in itself but only in view of the person to whose condition they belong. Individuals are not to be torn apart but instead be enabled to realize themselves in the business of changes and functions. Future and hope can be what they promise only when they assure hope and future to the individual—also and specifically to those who, humanly speaking, have no hope: the incurably sick, the condemned, those abandoned by everybody. What help is it to these people simply to hope that it might go better with their grandchildren? If for these people there is no hope and no future, then one should not say anything about either.[14]

13. H. Maier, "Politische Theologie? Einwände eines Laien" in: P. Peukert, *Diskussion zur "politischen Theologie"* 1–26.

Furthermore, could not the dimension of the future connected with political theology also be a temptation to flee from the immediate present and begin a forward retreat? Couldn't this be the cause of a failure or refusal to attend to the present, just like the much-maligned looking back into the past?

The representatives of political theology have clearly recognized the justice of these questions and have taken account of them in their "discussion" of political theology. This is what Johann Baptist Metz is doing with his concept of the "eschatological proviso," with his *memoria* thesis, with his dangerously liberating memory of the death and resurrection of Jesus from the dead, with his narrative theology. Jürgen Moltmann is doing the same with his impressive highlighting of the *theologia crucis*.[15]

14. J. Pieper, *On Hope*, trans. Mary Francis McCarthy (San Francisco: Ignatius Press, 1986); *Hope and History*, trans. Richard and Clara Winston (New York: Herder and Herder, 1969).

15. J. Moltmann, *The Crucified God: The Cross of Christ as the Foundation and Criticism of Christian Theology*, trans. R. A. Wilson and John Bowden (New York: Harper & Row, 1974).

§ 15

THEOLOGY AND THEORY OF KNOWLEDGE

The most recent source of challenging questioning for theology is the modern theory of knowledge (*Wissenschaftstheorie*) and its representatives.[1]

Theses of the Theory of Knowledge

The theory of knowledge deals with the scientific aspect of the individual scholarly disciplines. Karl Popper, one of the most influential representatives of the theory of knowledge, formulates the problem as follows: How can general assertions and rules, in the way they are established by the sciences the experiential and natural sciences, and the legal sciences, be proven as true? The very question implies that science has to do with the knowledge of generally valid propositions and laws and that the so-called positive sciences constitute the model of the sciences. It follows from this that the problem of verification, the proving of propositions and laws, becomes the central theme of the theory of knowledge.

In contrast to positivism, which explains that the verification of a general assertion or rule takes place by induction, i.e., through the greatest possible number of individual observations, of individual cases, or through the most frequent possible repetitions in experiments, Popper explains that it is not possible in this way to arrive at the establishment of general rules that are valid always and everywhere.

1. H. Albert, *Treatise on Critical Research* (Princeton, 1985); *Theologische Holzwege. G. Ebeling und der rechte Gebrauch der Vernunft* (Tübingen, 1973); Gerhard Ebeling, *Kritischer Rationalismus? Zu Hans Alberts Traktat über kritische Vernunft* (Tübingen, 1973); Wolfhart Pannenberg, *Theology and the Philosophy of Science,* trans. Francis McDonagh (Philadelphia: Fortress Press, 1976); Karl Popper, *The Logic of Scientific Discovery* (New York: Harper & Row, 1968); H. Peukert, *Science, Action and Fundamental Theology: Toward a Theology of Communicative Action,* trans. James Bohman (Cambridge, Mass.: MIT Press, 1984); L. Scheffczyk, *Die Theologie und die Wissenschaften* (Aschaffenburg, 1979); G. Werbick, *Glaube im Kontext. Prolegomena und Skizzen zu einer elementaren Theologie* (Zürich—Einsiedeln—Cologne, 1983).

For the number of observations is always limited, but the rules are supposed to have universal validity. Between the limitation of the number of observations and the universality of general rules or formulations of law is an uncloseable gap, and it should not be excluded that new experiences and observations might change the assertions and rules.

From this it follows: All scientific theses are not irreversible certainties but conjectures, hypotheses that must be verifiable. But this is not achieved through the number of observations and experiences, because these are always limited and do not exclude surprises, and because they cannot be checked out against all possible applications. However—this is the other half of the method—the assertions are falsifiable. This means they can no longer be held as general propositions if there is even so much as one case that contradicts the accepted rule. An assertion then no longer has the strict universality of a law, but represents at best an approximation to the factual state of affairs and condition of things. The thesis "All lambs are white" is falsified, and thus refuted, by one single black sheep.

It is thus proper and necessary to expose theories to failure and thereby test the quality of their affirmation. The "critical rationalism" of Popper wants to approach the truth by exposing bold theses to severe opposition. In that way he learns most from mistakes.

Popper's philosophy is a decisive rejection of all ideologies and all forms of thinking oriented towards totality. He is thus in contradiction to all systems pretending to a comprehensive universality. This is as true for the system of Hegel as for Marxism, which in response to the cases that can falsify their system are willing to say: so much the worse for the facts. "The attempt," says Popper, "to set up heaven on earth always produces hell." The great philosophers were not architects of subtle systems, they were above all seekers of the truth; they sought for real solutions to genuine problems.

The progress of thought consists accordingly not in the gathering of propositions that are supposedly true but are ultimately proven false. Rather, progress takes place through trial and error. Therefore, we must search for a system that puts the lowest possible trust in error, abuse, and force.

It can legitimately be said of this system of verification, as Popper explains it, that if an assertion survives the attempt of its falsification, it can continue to be considered as confirmed. This holds all the more when predictions that are found to be accurate can be derived from it.

Encounter with Theology

Wolfhart Pannenberg, Leo Scheffczyk, and Helmut Peukert, in their monographs on the theory of knowledge and theology, have represented the conviction that theology cannot and may not evade the questionings and challenges of the theory of knowledge simply by arguing that theology is concerned with a completely different experience and reality than what is discussed in the theory of knowledge, by arguing that the concept of verifiability through control, through verification and falsification, is not applicable in the field of theology. Revelation as theme of theology, as the traditional view sees it, is a situation not affected either by the judgment of historical questions of fact or by philosophical questions of truth; for revelation is not history but salvation history. For faith and the theology that serves it, what is characteristic is the "nevertheless," the "in spite of" all appearances, the "despite" present countervailing experiences. Faith would lose its characteristic as venture and decision if it were to operate on the levels of argumentation and control of the theory of knowledge, quite apart from the fact that the concept of truth in theology and the theory of science are different. It follows from this, according to the representatives of this view, that theology is a special science with special methods and criteria, and that it must develop a strategy of immunization, so to speak, in order not to be infected by the pull of the theory of knowledge and thereby become confused and uncertain of itself.

Wolfhart Pannenberg finds this position especially in a number of representatives of evangelical [German Lutheran] theology, in the early Karl Barth, and in Hermann Diem in his work *Theologie als kirchliche Wissenschaft* [Theology as Ecclesiastical Science] (1951-1963). The position is unacceptable to Pannenberg. His reason: because theology is thus isolated from the other sciences and thereby turns out to be without communication and incapable of dialogue; because theology thereby puts itself into a situation that discredits it in the face of contemporary thought. Pannenberg rightly asks how faith, in such a position, can be mediated to the problems of our time, i.e., to the human beings who live in this intellectual/spiritual world and atmosphere. Connected with this is the question how such a position can be reconciled with the universality of Christian faith, with its claim to be word and answer [*Wort und Antwort*] for all times and cultures.

Pannenberg asks us to consider the following: The fact that theology as science of faith can prescind neither from the faith whether considered subjectively or objectively, nor from the community of faith—in other words, the fact that theology has its own specific presuppositions—says nothing against theology as a possible science. For every science has its presuppositions, also and particularly those

sciences which deny having them. But theology lays its cards on the
table, so to speak. For it is in the presuppositions of faith and in
revelation, that we encounter material which is about how it does its
work in its specific way: historical-critically, hermeneutically, and
systematically.

When the subjectivity of the faith of the theologian and its
intermingling with a community of faith and of believers is singled out
and introduced as an objection against theology as a possible science,
this question can be answered with the distinction (customary in the
theory of knowledge) between the disclosing function and the proving
function. The subjectivity of faith and the reality of the faith
community take over the function of the disclosing of the matter. But
disclosing is still not proving. The proving does not come from the
disclosing; but its intent is to make what comes from disclosure into a
scientific task, analogous to the other methods of historical-critical
understanding and of seeking out proofs and contexts of proof.

The second thing to be taken over from the theory of knowledge for
theology is the getting involved in the realm and the matter of reality
and experience. Theology must try to mediate its "thing"—the thing of
faith, which is the thing of God—in the context of reality and experience. This is possible if we understand by "reality" and "experience" not
only this or that isolated, really existing thing but everything that is,
as well as the connection of the individual with the whole. This
presumes, above all, that the sphere of human experience is drawn into
consideration. Then theology, as talk about God, would mean the
following: In all experience, in all possible objects, in reality as a whole
is manifested—not in a direct but indeed in an indirect way—the
reality of God, who is to be called the all-determining reality. This
affirmation about God is confirmed, grounded and verified, by the fact
that it exposes itself to the test, that this reality as a whole turns out
to be determined by this all-determining reality called God. In other
words, that reality as a whole remains incomprehensible and cannot be
comprehensively described without God as the ground of all reality.

According to Pannenberg, the reality of God is indirectly experienced with the thematic of sense [Sinnthematik], which accompanies
all individual experience and which, for its part, is always related to
the whole, to a totality of sense [Sinntotalität], to an overarching
context of meaning without which there is no experience or knowledge
of individual realities.

This totality of sense is not simply given in human, historical,
finite reality; it is rather encountered in the anticipation of the whole.
This happens everywhere where the human being as free historical
subject transcends the mere present existence—and precisely this
belongs to the reality and the experience of the human being. Thus the

freedom of the human being is no objection against the all-determining reality called God, but is a strong indication of it.

The conclusion from all this is that the affirmations of theology in the context of the conditions of the theory of knowledge do not appear in the form of thesis but in the mode of hypothesis. This does not mean the abolition of theology in favor of any old thing, but its coordination with the criteria of the theory of knowledge.

Theology, properly understood, has nothing to fear from this coordination. It can, in other words, pass the test of verification and falsification; it can stand up to the test question which asks whether the affirmations of theology can be falsified by any contrary fact, by any instance, by any event. To be able to submit to and pass this test belongs to the affirmations, claims and promises of faith whose reflection is theology. "The traditional assertions of a religion can thus be considered as hypotheses which, in the context of presently accessible experience, are to be tested to see how far, when starting from the traditional assertions of a particular religion, the pluriformity of contemporary experience can be integrated."[2]

As a result of these reflections on the question of the possibility of theology as science, Pannenberg finds that theology as a science of God is possible only indirectly: in view of reality as a whole. This is not the finished condition of a cosmos, but is found in a still-unfinished process and is as a whole accessible only in the subjectivity of human experience, i.e., as anticipated totality of sense [Sinntotalität]. This, as a making known of divine reality, comes about explicitly in religious experience; and the religious experience of the individual in one way or another always already stands in the context of the historical religions. Theology as science of God is thus possible only as science of religion, but not as science of religion as such, but of the historical religions. Christian theology would then be the science of the Christian religion. This would then have to be tested in competition with other religions. Theological affirmations "are proven true when they disclose the contextual sense [Sinnzusammenhang] of all reality in a more differentiated and convincing way than others."[3]

There are a lot of problems with this conception. There are problems, for example, with respect to the characterization of the Christian reality as Christian religion, or with the combining of elements which, among other representatives of evangelical theology from the early Barth to Dietrich Bonhoeffer, were strictly separated, namely Christian revelation or Christian faith, and religion. On the other hand is the problem whether, in this context, what is distinctively and specifically Christian can be adequately discussed at all.

2. W. Pannenberg, *Theology and the Philosophy of Science* 315.
3. Ibid. 347.

This proposal, perhaps shocking to some, to present theological affirmations as hypotheses can be brought into the proper light when one sees that it is not about a hypothetically understood faith but about theology as scientific reflection on faith within the method of the modern theory of science. Put this way, the mention of hypothesis loses the character of the theologically scandalous. It becomes rather an indication of what is to be done in theology and what theology can do. "God verifies [Him]self in that God verifies us, in that God brings our life to truth."[4]

Theologians can understand each of their theological propositions as provisional and subject to future confirmation and thus kept open to dialogue and correction. However, they cannot treat the proclamation of God in Jesus Christ as a provisional thesis which eventually could be dropped, for with that proclamation is given not just the final criterion to which theological propositions with regard to their factuality must answer, but also the basis of the dialogue in which they perform their mutual correction.[5]

4. G. Ebeling, *Gott und Wort* (Tübingen, 1966) 83.
5. W. Joest, *Fundamentaltheologie* (Stuttgart, 1974) 253.

§ 16

THEOLOGIA CRUCIFIXI
[THEOLOGY OF THE CRUCIFIED]

Description

Eberhard Jüngel, in his impressive work *Gott als Geheimnis der Welt. Zur Begrundung der Theologie des Gekreuzigten im Streit zwischen Theismus und Atheismus* [God as Mystery of the World. Foundations of a Theology of the Crucified in the Controversy Between Theism and Atheism],[1] presents a theological vision characterized by basic reformational concerns. He describes his intention as follows: "My purpose is to think about what we believe, and to that extent our task remains the solution of the question of whether or not God is thinkable—or there is danger of superstition" (144). Through the crisis of modern times, God, on the basis of the certainty of faith, is to be made thinkable again.

Jüngel describes the goal of his work even more concretely and in doing so he programmatically points out the way: "From the experience of the humanity of God to illuminate the possibility of talk about God, and on the basis of clear talk about God to learn again to think about God" (IX). Jüngel thus starts from the specifically Christian experience of faith: from the manifest humanity of God in Jesus Christ, which has found its utmost realization in the crucified Christ. Thus theology is *theologia crucis*—theology of the Crucified: "God identifies Himself with the crucified human, Jesus" (XII). From this it follows: "The Crucified is the criterion for a possible concept of God" (248). This thinkability of God and talk about God anchored in Christology and developed from it stands in total contradiction to the idea of God as the absolute, highest being, "*supra nos* [above us]," to the idea of God as *actus purus* [pure act], as reality without possibility, the way it had been thought out in metaphysics since the time of the Greeks and was

1. (Tübingen, 1977). The following quotations are taken from this book. Cf. my review in: *HerKorr* 31 (1977) 523–29.

effectively present in history up to the theism and atheism of the modern age. The destruction of such a God which runs under the motto of "God is dead" does not, therefore, affect the God of Christian theology; it is rather an opportunity for Christian theology. It opens up room for the truth of the death of God, which is something that needs to be theologically affirmed. As a consequence of these ideas, Jüngel can set up his task of working out the "fragments of truth" found in atheism, and can speak about a possibility, or a hope, or a future, since "atheism has recognized faith in the crucified God as its twin brother" (135).

According to Jüngel, this is confirmed by the manifest and profound theological emptiness and confusion of the modern age. This comes from the tension between a Christian theology grounded in the crucified Jesus of Nazareth and an idea, firmly held in a long tradition: the belief that one could think [of] God in God's divinity without having thought [of] him as crucified.

However, that concept of God—"theism"—oriented to the axiom of absoluteness was called into question in the modern age and led, when it was discovered to be unnecessary, to the rejection and denial of God as was expressed in the language of the "death of God." But that in no way applied to the Christian idea of God; quite the contrary. What resulted was the challenge and the possibility of taking up anew and in a full and proper way the idea of the death of God as an affirmation of Christian faith. Theology is thus called into question not so much by the proclamation of the death of God as by the deliberate ignoring of the problem contained in this proclamation. For what we really have to fear is that theology is rushing to destruction not on the bastions of unbelief but rather on its own sleepiness (57).

In his development of this thematic, Jüngel takes up Bonhoeffer's assessment of Hegel's interpretation of the proposition: "God is dead." He does this under the heading: "Hegel's Mediation of Contemporary Atheistic Sensitivity with the Christological Truth of the Death of God" (83). Hegel's intention is to give this theological proposition a philosophical interpretation in the framework of his Will for Reconciliation. "What faith in the crucified meant in the positive Christian religion" was not to be "left to faith alone but thought through by reason" (100). This is possible if it is recognized that— according to Hegel—God is the depth of God's own self-conscious Spirit and that the Spirit, if it wishes to come to its own depth and thus to itself, must rise up out of itself and go into that which it is not, the foreign, and appropriate it.

In this way the incarnation of God becomes philosophically understandable, speculatively thinkable, even necessary. To incarnation belongs dying. And precisely that is what God got involved in with the Incarnation and dying of Jesus. The dying of Jesus is, consequently, not the dying of the human Jesus. "It is not the human which dies, but the divine which, precisely by that becomes human" (102). "Only in that way does one get to the reconciliation of the infinite with the finite, that the infinite experiences in itself the whole severity of the fate of the finite" (103). But in death God abides as the death of death: "Because God is, death negates itself" (122).

Hegel's words about [a] speculative Good Friday intends exactly the opposite of an antitheological understanding of these words as a farewell to God. It is instead an effort to preserve the orthodox fundamental truth of the Christian, to think anew the truths forgotten by theology. Hence Jüngel sees in Hegel's philosophy "an historical-theological high point of the first order" (123). This does not prevent him from noting that in this theory the concrete difference between God and the human being, and above all the freedom of God, is threatened.

Flowing from this principle is that constantly echoing basic theological decision: The idea of God comes from the Christian faith; it is not its presupposition. "The contrary position is to be opposed" (207). Without the opening to God's self opened up by God—in Jesus the crucified—no thinking can ever find access to God (202). "Reason is reasonable when it grasps that God can be thought [about] as God only when thought as self-revealing God" (211). From this position Jüngel develops the possibility of presenting God as speaking, which in turn implies that the one thinking [of] God is already included in being the one spoken to by God, "that God is concerned with human beings." Jüngel thus connects with that play on words which is to be more than a play on words: "that God [Him]self goes ways [*daß Gott selber Wege geht*]," that God's being is in his coming (213).

With the description of this faith-appropriating certainty, a dimension is opened that lets God become thinkable in a new way. Christian faith thinks God and ephemerality together. According to Jüngel, this brings up the question to theology whether "it is ready to destroy its understanding of the divine being *supra nos* in order to conceive God as [He] reveals Godself in identity with the human Jesus" (252). For "one cannot conceive God and ephemerality together without giving up the metaphysically conceived idea of God. Ephemerality destroys that idea" (276). However, against the God of the philosophers stands not the abandonment of the conceivability of God but the newly worked out idea that corresponds to the being of God (269).

This being of God is to be thought of as love. The proposition "God is love" is so to be thought that God's truth remains narratable. However, the proposition "God is love," because love necessarily includes the over-against of lover and loved, necessarily leads to the "self-distinction of God from God" and thus to the affirmation of the triune God whose *vestigium* [trace, footstep]—this closes the circle—"can be

only the being of the human being with whom God has identified"
(430).

Assessment

In assessment of the impressive work of this Tübingen theologian
we can say: Jüngel begins with what is concrete and specific in the
Christian experience of faith. It is the path which, beginning from the
Christological center, seeks to unfold the universal center of the concept
of God presented here. This is a necessary, indispensable task of
theology, a highly valued service to believers and to the community of
believers who need not only to believe but to think/conceive what they
believe.

In contrast to this, the other task, also a necessary one for theology
at this time. How do I get from without to within? What are, within
human beings or the world, the presuppositions and conditions of the
possibility of such a faith? Where is the believability of this faith
which is so much sought after these days? How is this faith to be
verified? Jüngel expressly says that the verification of the theological
claim cannot be the task of scientific theology (391).

So the question is: Doesn't theology thus run into the danger of
becoming a theology of claims and assertions? Jüngel explains: God is
not necessary for the world [weltlich]; the human being can be human
without God. Against this stand not only clouds of witnesses in contemporary philosophy and theology—and basically the whole tendency to
understand theology as anthropology and anthropology as theology—
but above all the statements in the Old and New Testament about the
world as creation and the human being as image and likeness of God.
Even contemporary thought has retained traces of this. God belongs in
the definition of the world and of the human being.

Although there are similarities between the metaphysical concept
of an absolute God and the first article of the Creed about God the
Father, the Almighty Creator of heaven and earth, it remains quite
doubtful that the elimination of a much-maligned theism of an absolute, almighty "God over us" could, in alliance with atheism, discover
anew the mystery of God as love. Presumably, there is a description
here. What interest should atheism have in the continued proclamation of God, even in the form of the crucified? Furthermore, contemporary atheism has no particular interest in the metaphysical concept
of God as such, but only in the form of the Christian religion. Thus,
Christian theology is making things too simple for itself when it
declares it isn't affected by atheism because its concern is not with

theism but with something totally different, with the Christian expe–rience of God.[2]

Jüngel denies that the idea of God is the general anthropological presupposition of Christian faith which, "to be sure is no longer present but which, precisely for that reason, must be won back" (207). According to Jüngel, belief in God follows exclusively from belief in Jesus, in whom God has "become definitively accessible." No one can contest this; but does it follow from this that the idea of God cannot be the presup–position of Christian faith; does it mean a denial of the definitive aspect of the self-revelation of God in Jesus? By no means. But the ques–tion must be asked: How do human beings come to recognize a manifes–tation of God in the person and event of Jesus of Nazareth if they have no preunderstanding of what is meant by God? This preunderstanding and understanding is found by no means only in the metaphysical concept of God, or theism, but above all in that anthropological and social reality which is meant by religion, in which the original dependence of human beings on God comes to expression in manifold— even manifold broken—ways.

Put in the form of a concrete question: How does the Roman centurion come to confess: "This man was the Son of God" (Mark 15:39)? If Jüngel in support of his thesis brings up the text of 1 Cor 1:18 about the cross as scandal and folly, one needs to point out that different statements are also found in the same New Testament, e.g., the missionary sermons in the Acts of the Apostles in chapters 14, 16 and 17: "What therefore you worship as unknown, this I proclaim to you" (Acts 17:23). The popular reference to the failure, to the "miscarried sermon" in the Areopagus, is no argument, because "success" is not a theological category. The same theology which is quite familiar with Christian discernment and the inner contradictions of Christianity, but which, as we now put it, does not disregard the context, is found in a plethora of Christian sources. It is found in the Prologue of John, in the Captivity Letters, in the doctrine of the *logos spermatikos* and of the *anima naturaliter Christiana* [naturally Christian soul], and in the theology of the Church Fathers, especially the Alexandrians. This theology is characteristically found in all the most convincing representatives of a Christian mission. The message of the cross stood not at the beginning but at the goal of their preaching.

The preunderstanding of God labeled as presupposition certainly can and should be modified and transformed in a conversion of thought, and this should be done through faith in the God who identifies Himself with the human Jesus. But it is also not clear today how,

---

2. Cf. W. Pannenberg's reatment of "The Question of God" in: *Grundfragen systematischer Theologie* (Göttingen, 1967) 361–86; also: "Types of Atheism and their Theological Significance, ibid. 347–60.

without such a presupposition which must be explicitly made—e.g., in dialogue with anthropology—Christian faith is to be mediated in our time. Even if in faith in Jesus the Christ, even if in dealing with the gospel it should occur to someone who and what God is, this movement doesn't even get started without [a] presupposition.

One can also point out that the answer given in Jesus the Christ presupposes a question. Humanity—human beings themselves and the mystery present in them—is this question. This does not make God dependent on questioning human beings. For, from the question alone comes only the "that" of a possible answer; but its content is in no way determined. That is why attention to the presuppositions of the Christian faith is one of the central tasks of theology today. It seems to me that it is not by chance that there is an interest in fundamental theology within evangelical [Lutheran] theology today. Consequently, the call of Jüngel to get beyond theism is a dubious thesis. A grounding of the "Theology of the Crucified in the Struggle between Theism and Atheism" names two partners, theism and atheism, which are in no way to be considered equal or judged to be theologically equal.

§ 17

THEOLOGY AND THEOLOGIES

The starting points for this theme and the questions connected with it have already been given. In what follows they will now be given special attention.[1] We begin with an historical recollection.

Theology in the Singular

Until about twenty-five years ago, it was common, both within the field of Catholic theology and also outside of it, to think of theology not in the plural but in the singular. The model was: Theology is the explicit and methodically thought out reflection on faith, more specifically, the Christian faith. Theological reflection involves disclosure, understanding, grounding, coherence, accountability. Theology is to this day *intellectus fidei*: in other words faith which seeks understanding.

Take for example the theology of the Christian faith in its Catholic manifestation. For a long time it was the glory and characteristic of this faith to be faith in the form of the one faith, as relationship to the one God and to the one and only Christ in the realm of the one Church. It seemed quite appropriate to this concept of unity, apparently even required by it, that its theology as science of faith should also have the form of unity. It was thought, in addition, that the highest form of unity is uniformity. Thus developed the idea of a theology in the singular, in which unity and uniformity were its typically ideal characteristics.

In the last century, as we have already seen, this was thought to be possible in Scholasticsim, especially that of Thomas Aquinas, the universal teacher of the church. His concept of theology was recommended to Catholic theology as a universally binding orientation in the form of Neoscholasticsim. In its framework, theology appeared as a closed

---

1. Cf. Karl Rahner, "Pluralism in Theology and the Unity of the Creed in the Church," *Theological Investigations* 2 (1974) 3–23; Bernard Lonergan, *Theologie im Pluralismus heutiger Kulturen* (Freiburg—Basel—Vienna, 1975).

system which, through derivation from the highest principles, the propositions of faith, could become ever more unfolded and differentiated.

Joined to this form of theology in the singular was the idea of a *theologia perennis*, a theology that lasts through the years and is not affected by them. It served as a special characteristic sign of goodness and solidity amid the confusing spirit of the times. This confusion was to be encountered with clear answers and instructions: sovereign and helpful at the same time.

In this conception of things, theology could all the more live up to this task since it carries out its specific service to the faith within the Church as community of believers, but also because it understands itself and its service explicitly as delegation from the side of ecclesiastical leadership, the ecclesiastical magisterium, i.e., the hierarchy, the pope and the bishops.

An orientation of Catholic theology to these articulations of faith is, of course, indispensable. But the question arises: What place and what value does one assign to them? Are they the most important, perhaps even the unique orientation on the basis of which one can dispense with other orientations, such as from the normative origin of the Bible and from history, and do this with the remark that what is relevant has gone into the decisions and the praxis of the believing and teaching Church. It must come from, be interpreted from and be mediated from there. That which factually does not appear is in reality either insignificant or dangerous.

Those stamped with such ideas of theology can see, in a change represented as theology in the plural of theologies, only a lamentable erroneous development, a betrayal of a tried and true tradition, a loss of identity. Theology in the plural of theologies is—they therefore say— both cause and expression of the crisis permeating the present with its tendency to incertitude, to relativizing, to endless problematizing, to never-ending discussion, to suspecting all positions, and finally to dissolution.

So it not surprising that many people complain about and condemn the situation of Catholic theology today as theology in the plural of theologies. Along with this comes the recommendation to return to the "good old days" when theology was an impressively uniform and closed system, an organized and perspicuous, an obedient and manageable system of faith, and when, unbothered by the noise of the hour, it gave its witness: The unmodern is what is truly modern.

The "Good Old Days"

In effect we have already said that theology today—and that specifically includes Catholic theology, is presented in the plural of theologies, as theology in theologies. But before we go further into that, a word needs to be said about the thesis of theology in the singular and about the "good old days," and also about the recommendation to return to them as a cure for the difficulties and crises of the present.

But just how old is this time and tradition to which the *laudatores temporis acti* [praisers of times gone by] appeal as the good times? These old days in no way include the whole history of faith and theology. Instead it is a small part of it which, strictly speaking, stretches for a hundred years from the time before and after Vatican I (1870) to Vatican II (1963-1965).

In the long time before that we find a quite different picture, very much the picture of theology in the plural of theologies. This is already found in the fundamental and normative origin of faith and theology: in the New Testament, which is a book of [many] books. Almost every single one of them presents its own kind of theology: synoptic—Pauline—Johannine—narrative—kerygmatic—apocalyptic—argumentative—Hebraic—Greek. Patristics in the Eastern and Western churches was characterized by the theologies of great theologians: Origen, Tertullian, and Augustine, by the Antiochene and Alexandrian schools and their tensions.

Even Scholasticism, the theological school science of the Middle Ages, was not a uniform school but consisted of a plurality of schools of very marked orientation and profile, in the lively disputation of their *quaestiones disputatae*. Thomas Aquinas was a fiercely controversial innovator in his daring reception of Aristotle, the "modern" of that time, the aggiornamento needed at that time. The system of Thomas was of course a coordination of *summa* and *ordo*, but a long way from being something closed off in an ossified, fixed way. His basic conception was that of an open system capable of adaptation.

And the second question: Was that old time so often appealed to today a good time? Was it a good time at the turn of the century when, the theological awakening at the turn of the century described as Modernism was labeled as a catch basin of all heresies and administratively suppressed or held under suspicion as so-called reform-Catholicism? Was it a good time when the decisions of the so-called Biblical Commission, which have all subsequently proven to be erroneous, hindered the work of exegetes and drove its best representatives into resigning?[2]

2. Cf. Heinrich Fries, "Das kirchliche Lehramt und die exegetische Arbeit" in: H. Kahlefeld, *Schriftauslegung aus dem Glauben* (Frankfurt, 1979) 56–90.

To conclude from this sketch: the transformation in the form of theology in the plural of theologies which is recognizable also and especially in Catholic theology is indeed something new in comparison with an epoch of theology which immediately preceded it. But theology in theologies is a form of theology from its origin and in the longest and best time of its history. The leveling of this form into a theology in the singular was theological uniformity, atrophy and impoverishment, a road leading in the wrong direction.

The Change

If one were to give a date for the change in Catholic theology today, the Second Vatican Council (1963-1965) would be the most important event of the century in the Catholic Church.

The Second Vatican Council, called by the so-called transitional Pope John XXIII, was not primarily a council against something, against the errors of the time which were to be diagnosed, lamented, and condemned. Lamentation doesn't accomplish anything, thought this pope, and he added: Through the condemnations of the past the situation in the Church was not improved. Vatican II was a council for something, for the faithful, for human beings, for the world. The Church at this council encountered the world through dialogue, with the desire for cooperation in the recognition of a common responsibility for the future of humanity.

The way in which the Christian faith is to be mediated to the world should not be one-sided instruction, correction, criticism and condemnation, but the mediation of the gospel as a reality-disclosing, liberating, joy-giving message.

But this is possible only to the extent that the time and the signs of the time, that the present-day world and the human beings living in it, are accepted. That the message of the faith understood as Good News is related to human beings and to all that determines and characterizes their life: history, society, culture, structure, and language. This mediation should make it known that the Christian faith liberates human beings for the truth and reality of themselves.

The possibility of successfully fulfilling this task requires attentive listening to the content of Christian faith, and no less intensive sensitivity to human beings; concrete, contemporary human beings with their individuality, their fate, and their questions.

This intention, visible in the Council itself and expressed in many of its texts, is called its pastoral dimension. That sounds a bit sentimental, and the representatives of the "good old days" already see a deficiency there, a sign of debility. The Council was capable neither of a dogma nor of its attendant anathema. But pastoral dimension means a turning towards human beings, which is still a lot more than the embodiment of any kind of an "ism", which one can easily manipulate and condemn.

This goal and the tasks connected with it were sufficient to set free a theology in the plural of theologies. For how was a theology of uniformity to do justice, to be even able to do justice, to the comprehensive as well as many-sided and differentiated call of the present hour?

Vatican II has become effective and still remained decisive for a theology in theologies because of its express intention to be a council of renewal with the program: "*ecclesia semper reformanda* [Church always needing reform]." It was not enough for this Council to repeat and give new emphasis to the old truths in old forms; its goal was to bring the content and the truth of faith into "today" in a living way so that the faith would remain itself but at the same time find its way to human beings. This brings us to the so-called aggiornamento. This is not a false and hasty adaptation anywhere and everywhere at any price; Aggiornamento is the today, the bringing up-to-date of faith and its contents.

Clearly, a Church that understands itself as capable of renewal and needing renewal, reflection on the faith, i.e., theology, takes on great importance. The orientation points of the renewal, their coordination and their respective realization, must be considered; the manifold things needing to be done in the sense of renewal need reflection, need theory, so that a praxis in the service of renewal can become orthopraxis. These tasks can be carried out only by a theology which is a *theologia semper reformanda*, and this is necessarily theology in the plural of theologies.

The ecumenical dimension of the Council, as far as the shape and form of Catholic theology is concerned, opened up a new dimension in that the theology of the other churches was not, as used to be done in the "good old days," addressed primarily as a counter-position to be condemned and rejected as heresy. It was instead, acknowledged in its differences, as an important and helpful dialogue partner with whom a comprehensive, fruitful dialogue was to be conducted, not only about theology but also about the path and goal of ecumenism.

If our theme required us to talk this much about a Council that is now so far behind us, this is not due to a council-euphoria or to a glorifying nostalgia. It is based on the conviction that the Council remains effective to this day in the history of the contemporary Catholic Church. In the Council, the Catholic Church went through an epochal change and struck out on a way which—in spite of everything—filled one with a hope and confidence, that also included the other Christian churches and the time to come.[3]

Another reason for awakening the memory of the Council for our theme is that there are voices today, even voices of theologians, who look on the Council as a misfortune and make it responsible for the crisis of the present and of all the damage inside the Church. But the reality is quite different. The Council recognized an already existing crisis and, in its opening for a theology in the plural of theologies, pointed the way to a solution.

The Reason for the Change

What is the reason for theology in the plural of theologies? The reason yesterday when it already existed, and the reason today when we have become intensively conscious of it, and when this plurality has become much more extensive than it ever was?

The first reason is the inexhaustibility of the material treated in theology. According to Kant, the question: "What is the human being?" is the ultimate and abiding question of human beings, a question which, in the present age, in its inquiring into human beings, into human dignity and human rights, has gained a worldwide explosiveness and urgency. Hence theological inquiring, which takes the form of questions about the human being and God, God and the human being, God and the image of the human being, and God and human dignity, is both an ongoing theme and one requiring a broad range of reflection. It is a theme which human beings and theologians, in any imaginable vision of progress, will never exhaust.

The idea of the inexhaustibility of the contents of theology can also be given concrete form in the biblical text about the unsearchable riches of Christ (Eph 3:8)—a text that remains true to this day, not least in the great attention being given to Jesus Christ these days from outside the Christian Church.

Another reason for a theology in the form of theology in the plural lies in the subjectivity of the theologians who in their own way, with their perspectives, with their problems, with their intelligence, seek to disclose, to understand, to ground, and to justify the Christian faith or, even more comprehensively, Christian being.

The subjectivity of theologians and their theology always signifies historically stamped subjectivity. Every form of historical description is both a realization and a limitation of the particular contents being historically mediated. Historicity means also perspectivity. From

---

3. K. Rahner, "Basic Theological Interpretation of the Second Vatican Council" 77–89, "The Abiding Significance of the Second Vatican Council," 90–102 in : "Concern for the Church," vol. 20, *Theological Inverstigations*, 1981.

perspectivity comes plurality as richness of the concrete perspectives of the theologians looking at the matter of faith. It doesn't mean any dissolution into relativism if the perspectives remain related to the matter, if one perspective doesn't exclude the other but gives it room and even makes it necessary.

The subjectivity of theologians is also the subjectivity of those who exist in intersubjectivity, who are stamped by their situation, the intellectual, cultural, social, and political context of their time and are part of it. They have to take up the questions and doubts, the challenges, difficulties, obstacles, and chances that come from this context and bring them into the concerns of their theological work in order to be able to represent theology here and now.

These questions are being asked of theology today not only, as in the past, by philosophy, which, like theology, reflected on the whole of reality and asked about ground [*Grund*] and nature. In philosophy, the spirit of a time was conceptualized. That is why philosophy was the preferred partner of theology. But philosophy today, from the questions it asks, takes on a different face, one that puts it in the plural of philosophies, e.g., as language theory of the empirical sciences. Add to this the plurality of the other sciences, of psychology, sociology, linguistics, theory of knowledge, then further the pluralism of ideological, political and social systems, of natural science, medicine and technology, of behavioral science and, not least, the challenge from the non-Christian religions.

These questions are concentrated today in the question about human beings, about their reality, about their experience, and about their world. There is today no system and no ideology that does not solemnly declare that their concern is for nothing other than the human being, the human being as subject in this our world and time. Thus, the anthropological context to which the reality of the world of human beings belongs is the real text and the plural context of contemporary theology. Theology has acknowledged this task and challenge today and is attempting in all sorts of ways to do it justice.

The contents of the Christian faith are not drawn up by human beings, but are received by them and brought into living correlation. The connection of theology and anthropology, and vice versa, has its concentration in the innermost relational point of Christian faith, in the historical figure of Jesus of Nazareth. Anthropological theology is thereby concretized once again by the theology of Christ, by Christology. Karl Rahner has formulated this inner connection: Christian reality is the conscious taking possession of the mystery of the human. "The incarnation of God is the uniquely highest instance of the fulfillment of the nature of the human being."[4]

4. K. Rahner, "Anonymous Christians," *Theological Investigations* 6 (1974) 390–98.

This is possible because in Jesus Christ the connectedness of the human being with God, which determines human existence, was given in the mode of a unique existence, in the mode of the Son. Accordingly, Jesus Christ is also the image of the human being, the "Ecce homo" in the formulation of Karl Rahner: Jesus Christ is the highest instance of the human because this being human is oriented to God as absolute self-transcendence. As it is found in Jesus, this absolute self-transcendence becomes one with the self-transcendence of God in relation to human beings.

Theology as anthropology, Christology as anthropology—what this means in the context of the contemporary anthropological question is: Theology with its affirmations is in competition with contemporary world views and ideologies and their conception of the human being. Theology cannot evade them, but it does not need to be afraid of them either. That which is authentically Christian can stand up to reality, to the experience of human beings in life and in death, and it receives through this testing also the sign of truth as confirmation, as verification. In other words, the reality and the experience of human beings in their living and their dying is simply not adequately considered, or comprehensively known and, basically, not understood, if the all-determining reality is not considered along with them. The name of the all-determining reality is God.

The concentration of today's questions and challenges on the question of God and the human being and on Jesus Christ sets before the eyes of theology its original and real task; it points out the seriousness and the magnitude of this historical hour. It makes us recognize anew that the answer to this global and diversely motivated challenge is not to be found by a uniform theology but only by the engagement of theology in theologies, of theology in the plural of theologies.

Concluding Theses

1. The present form of theology in the plural of theologies and in its concrete models is now taking the place of a theology that primarily made assertions and claims and relied on data which was not to be questioned. Theology used to claim a special status in which it was sufficient to point to what was written, what was dogma. For such a conception of theology, the question is irrelevant whether theology in any sense can be called science and still have right of domicile in a university. In such an option theology fails itself; it increasingly succumbs to alienation from the world and finds its place in the ghetto.[5]

5. Cf. G. Söhngen, "Die Theologie im Streit der Fakultäten" in: *Die Einheit der Theologie* (Munich, 1953) 2–21; "Theologie im Haus der Wissenschaften" in: *ThQ* 157 no. 3 (1977).

2. Theology in the plural of theologies understands its task as an independent, responsible function for the Christian faith and for Christian existence with all its implications, existentially affirmed by the theologian, in the community of believers, of Christians, of the Church. To this extent every theology is church theology, for without this it loses its place and its base. Theology which recognizes in this its obligation and relationship to reality thus speaks of the presuppositions that determine it. Other disciplines are often silent about such presuppositions, or even try to disclaim that they have any.

In the community of believers, theology has the ministry of reflection. It can be an inspiring, renewing, critical, and often also prophetic ministry with the risks that the prophets of ancient and modern times knew: persecution in their lifetime, monuments after their death.

The teaching office of the theologians does not stand in opposition to the teaching office of the leaders of the Church—concretely, of the pope and bishops—but rather, as is proper, in common service to the faith and in responsibility for it. Pope John Paul II in his visit to Germany explicitly emphasized the independence of theology as science of faith which is distinct from the ecclesiastical teaching office. Theology and teaching office have, accordingly, different task, and these cannot be reduced to each other. Both serve the one totality. Cooperation and readiness to dialogue are necessary between them. In the application of its methods and analyses theology is, as science, free. But it stands in a special relationship to the faith of the Church, which is built upon the foundation of the apostles and prophets. Theology presupposes faith; it cannot produce it. Theology stands on the shoulders of its fathers in faith.[6] Cooperation is all the more necessary since, in these days, a merely formal authority, even in matters of faith and faith community, is no longer enough. To this authority must accrue the power of the argumentative, of reasoning and grounding; otherwise its instruction incurs the danger of not being received—to the damage of all, not least to the damage of the authority itself, even if its decision-making competence remains undisputed.

3. Controversies within theological discussion—they have to exist, according to the old motto: *theologia disputat* [theology argues]—should not be broken off too quickly by official action. It doesn't work anyway; the problems continue to seek out their way and force themselves into the light. Controversies should be at home in the responsibility of theology in the plural of theologies. The better arguments will win out. Theology too can be a river that purifies itself.

4. Theology in the plural of theologies does not contradict the unity of faith and the unity in the faith which we so much need. This would

6. Pope John Paul II in Germany (Bonn, 1981) 167–72 (Verlautbarungen desApostolischen Stuhls 25).

be the case only if theology itself had lost its point of relationship to faith and its clearly recognizable center, God in Christ, the salvation of the world. If it did lose this center, if it made itself absolutely the one theology in the plural of theologies, it would no longer be theology. Or if it refused dialogue and claimed itself alone as the source of happiness and declared everything outside itself to be heretical, it would no longer be theology. For it would have denied its legitimate plural self and given it up in favor of an illegitimate singular.

Theology in the plural of theologies, i.e., the contemporary form of theology, is no contradiction to but expression of a unity of faith, to whose characteristics it belongs to be living, dynamic, dialogical, and creative. Truths can live only with each other; one truth alone dies.

5. A theology in the plural of theologies has its legitimate place in a universality in the plurality of the sciences and their methods. If there are continued attempts to drive theology out of the university, the question must be asked whether the university is doing justice to its claim to think through the whole of reality methodically, whether the whole can be comprehensively thought through if the all-encompassing reality, God, is shut out along with everything associated with it in reality, experience and history. The departure of theology means a loss of knowledge and orientation, a loss of culture and tradition which have stamped and fundamentally determined us and this our time and world, even if that should be largely forgotten. The existence of theology in our faculties will and should remind us of these foundations, so that the sources and well from which we live to this day will not dry up.

Finally: With all the common that connect theology with the other sciences in the disclosure and interpretation of the reality of the world and humanity, there is one special task that theology and its subject-matter, God, has in a university, in the house of the sciences. That special task is to point out that the human being, the individual human being is a great mystery. Human beings are more than and other than simply what happens, they are, more than the ensemble of the factors that determine them, more too than all "isms" and more than what can be known, grasped and produced in the sciences. The human being lives not from bread alone.[7]

7. C. Hefling, "Science and Religion," *NDT* 938–45.

BOOK TWO

REVELATION

§ 18

THE CONCEPT OF REVELATION

The doctrine of revelation[1] follows naturally upon the expositions of faith and the science of faith. Revelation describes the point where they come together. Revelation as a theological theme, like all theology, has to do with God. The doctrine of revelation arises from the question whether the God who is sought after from the greatest variety of experiences and reflections and whose reality we run into from the various dimensions of our own reality, whether this God is indeed the distant, silent, unknown God totally withdrawn from our possibilities, and hence the unknown God, or whether this God does in fact make Himself perceptible, known, expressed, and communicated. In other words, the theology of revelation arises from the question whether this God has revealed Himself and in what way and form this has happened. J. S. Drey, the founder of the Catholic Tübingen School, described this situation as follows: "The revelation of God is the representation of God's essence in another which is not God and, to that extent, outside of God."[2]

On this question, the following point requires careful consideration. If God has revealed, communicated, and made Himself known, we could

1. Cf. R. Guardini, *Die Offenbarung* (Würzburg, 1940); *Religion und Offenbarung* (Würzburg, 1958); E. Brunner, *Revelation and Reason: The Christian Doctrine of Faith and Knowledge*, trans. Olive Wyon (Philadelphia: Fortress Press, 1946); A. Lang, *Die Sendung Christi. Fundamentaltheologie* I, 3rd ed., (Munich, 1961); Heirich Fries, *Revelation* (New York: Herder and Herder, 1969); R. Latourelle, *Theology of Revelation* (New York: Alba House, 1988); A. Kolping, *Fundamentaltheologie, vol. I: Theorie der Glaubwürdigkeitserkenntnis der Offenbarung* (Münster, 1968); H. Waldenfels, *Offenbarung. Das Zweite Vatikanische Konzil auf dem Hintergrund der neueren Theologie* (Munich, 1969); P. Tillich, *Offenbarung und Glaube (Gesammelte Werke VIII)*, (Stuttgart, 1970); *Handbuch der Dogmengeschichte*, ed., M. Schmaus—A. Grillmeier—L. Scheffczyk, vol. I: *Die Offenbarung. vol. Ia, Von der Schrift bis zum Ausgang der Väterzeit* (Freiburg—Basel—Vienna, 1971); Ib, *Von der Reformation bis zur Gegenwart* (1977); F. Konrad, *Das Offenbarungsverständnis in der evangelischen Theologie* (Munich—Paderborn—Vienna, 1971); P. Eicher, *Offenbarung. Prinzip neuzeitlicher Theologie* (Munich, 1977); M. Seckler, "Aufklärung und Offenbarung" in: *Christlicher Glaube in Moderner Gesellschaft* 21 (Freiburg—Basel—Vienna, 1980) 5–78.

2. *Kurze Einleitung in das Studium der Theologie*, 1819, ed., F. Schupp (Darmstadt, 1971) 10 (§ 16).

talk about it only if this self-communication could be perceived and received by human beings. Otherwise, it is not revelation. Revelation is disclosure to and for human beings. If this is the case, then revelation can take place only in a manner and form accessible to human beings.

Revelation must be a revelation and encountering of God, and not just a revelation of human beings and their own possibility and reality. It reveals that reality which transcends human beings and their possibilities, and also their world; it reveals that reality which cannot be figured out in the terms of the reality that lies before one's eyes. The theology of divine revelation does not deal with a piece of this divine reality itself, but rather with that aspect of it that can be humanly encountered—which, however, is quite other than the divine reality itself.

This clarifies a further point. Revelation as description of the ways and means in which God self-communicates and makes Himself perceptible, encompasses absolutely everything that is talked about in faith and in theology, in their themes and disciplines. The entire contents of theology can be summed up formally under the concept of revelation; they are all concretions and articulations of revelation. This does not mean that everything that theology talks about has already been summed up or that one must hold this concept unconditionally.

The theology of the first centuries spoke not of revelation but of the economy of salvation, i.e., of the series and coherence of God's actions for the salvation of humankind.[3] Today's theology speaks similarly of salvation history as the central concept of what theology has to talk about. *Mysterium Salutis—Grundriss einer heilsgeschichtlichen Dogmatik* [Mystery of Salvation: Basic Sketch of a Salvation-Historical Dogmatics] is the name of a modern representative presentation of Catholic doctrine. Another comprehensive characterization expressing the central concept of theology is: "Word of God." The most influential representatives of athis approach, in which theology is doctrine of the Word of God, are Karl Barth and, in his way, Gerhard Ebeling.

The "inflation" of the concept of revelation has already entered into the discussion.[4] The extensive investigation of P. Eicher, *Offenbarung. Studien zur Offenbarungstheologie* [Revelation: Studies on the Theology of Revelation] talks about an "overworked category." Nevertheless, the category of revelation, as comprehensive concept of the contents of faith and theology, is better suited than the others to become the central concept with which theology deals. It is said, to be

3. P. Stockmeier, "Offenbarung in der frühchristlichen Kirche" in: *Handbuch der Dogmengeschichte*, vol. Ia, 26–87.
4. P. Althaus, "Die Inflation des Begriffs der Offenbarung in der gegenwärtigen Theologie" in: *ZSTh* 18 (1941) 134–49.

sure, that the concept of revelation is too formal, too general, too open, and too comprehensive. But one can answer that it is precisely in its comprehensive generality that it is suited to unite in itself the greatest content. It protects against narrowness and one-sidedness.

The other proposals, e.g., to say "salvation history" instead of "revelation," also have their difficulties. For, how is salvation history different from history? Is it identical with it, or just part of it with special characteristics? Further: Can the concept "salvation history" sufficiently describe what theology and faith is about; can it do justice to the dimensions of truth, word, encounter, and person?

So too with the category "Word of God." Right away one has to explain: is it the word that God speaks—and how is that conceivable? Is it the authentic word that is spoken about God? Is there, in the concept of word, sufficient expression of the fact that faith and theology deal above all with deeds and history, with events and person? There is no denying that one can connect these contents with the concept "Word of God." But all of this is not immediately visible in the term "Word of God."

Thus the open, general concept of revelation is more suitable. For it easily takes in the different modes, the modes of the historical, of truth, of the word, of deeds, and of person. The concept of revelation makes no prior decision about its possible contents apart from the important requirement that revelation and its content are not the work and project of human beings.

If, instead of "revelation," one were to make "religion" the central concept of what theology talks about, that would be problematic for another reason. In theology and in faith, one is of course dealing with the relationship of the human being to God, as it is expressed in religion and in the religions. One can, therefore, with good reason also talk about the Christian religion. Thus, it is worth mentioning that there are representations of theology that radically set apart the Christian faith from what religion means, that criticize the religions in the name of faith, and that speak of a "religionless Christianity."[5] This position is certainly one-sided and contains many problems. But the danger no doubt exists that if religion is made the overall concept and the Christian faith is subsumed under that, the Christian faith would then have prescribed to it, in the name of religion so to speak, what its contents would be, what it could have or should not have. In the name of religion and of concepts of God connected with it, the cross, for example, would not be possible or allowed as a possibility of God and of divine revelation. It is folly and scandal (1 Cor 1:18-25).

5. D. Bonhoeffer, *Letters and Papers from Prison*, ed. Eberhard Bethge (New York: Macmillan Press, 1972); on this see: H. Fries, "Die Botschaft von Christus in einer Welt ohne Gott" in: *Wir und die andern* (Stuttgart, 1966) 273–314.

In contrast, revelation as the central concept of the content of faith is an open concept. It doesn't predetermine how God's revelation must take place. In its favor, it can be said that revelation is a transcendental theological concept, because it encompasses and transcends the individual contents of theology and because—which corresponds to what we are talking about here—all individual affirmations of faith are intended as contents of God's revelation. Faith as a fundamental act is oriented to this fundamental determination. Revelation and faith, in their mutual dependence, are an indissoluble totality.

Faith is answered revelation. Accepted revelation is faith. Faith is revelation arrived at its goal.

At the same time, revelation is the point of reference, the abiding support, and the goal of faith. If it is the task of theology to provide for the understanding of the faith according to its different contents, then it is the task of fundamental theology to consider that understanding of the faith which deals with its ground and its foundations—in other words, revelation with its presuppositions, conditions, and implications. Revelation is, accordingly, one of the specific themes of fundamental theology.

A final addition to these preliminary considerations on revelation: Revelation is a possibility and a modality that is also accessible to and given to human beings. Human beings, as we have already pointed out, have the capacity to reveal something of themselves. By virtue of their freedom, their spirit, their language, their bodiliness—and by virtue of the possibility therein of being able to make themselves perceived, heard, and understood—they can reveal themselves Human beings can communicate something of themselves, can communicate themselves, by an act, a word, an "expression," or by omission and refusal. The human being becomes present in these things. At the same time all specifically human expressions (i.e., intercommunicative expression) become transparent. Through them human beings open themselves and give themselves to be known. We say: He/she has revealed himself in them, shown her true self.

Consequently, and in contrast to what happens in revelation (the fundamental act of communication and disclosure of person), person does not become visible and it is not evident what human beings are, what they really are and what is in them. On the other hand, one can say: All talk about revelation involves person.

The analyses of faith in the human realm point out that personal self-disclosure or self-communication is an act of the spirit and of freedom, above all, an act of love and truth. Persons can close themselves off, keep silent, or dissemble. Accordingly, the faith that is coordinated to the revelation of person is an act of respect, honor, and high esteem. The refusal of faith, the refusal to believe, is the sharpest disparagement and disrespect of person there can be.

From the last remark one recognizes that the phenomena of revelation and faith, which theology is about, have a correspondence, an analogy in the human realm, in the realm of person. They are thus not exorbitant, nor do they represent an inhuman alienation or unreasonable expectation of human beings as persons. Revelation and faith in the theological sense move in structures and conditions which characterize human beings as human beings and concern them as persons. They have their *Sitz* (situation) in the realm called reality and experience. On the other hand, it is clear: as soon as one brings revelation into contact with God, personal being is ascribed to God.

The first part of our considerations is devoted to the theme "Reality and Revelation—Revelation and Reality." This theme deals with the connection between what is theologically called revelation and the reality that we are and that determines us. It is a part of the great theme of contemporary theology: Theology as anthropology, anthropology as theology—or, more comprehensively: theology and reality. We won't be able to bring up all that can be said about this, but only a few models.

PART ONE

THE REVELATIONAL
DIMENSION OF REALITY

§ 19

REALITY AND REVELATION—REVELATION AND REALITY

Everything that is, everything that happens and comes to pass, is and has not only an existence but also a being-meaning, a being-sign, a being-manifest. Everything that is and happens says something; it makes something visible. What does it make visible? Certainly, at first, the existing thing itself. But, in the existing thing, something further becomes visible something different from just the existing thing in the way it is first perceived and registered in its external appearance.

Being Manifest

Let us choose a simple, perhaps even somewhat sentimental example. What is a tear? What does it manifest? The tear can be described as a "salty fluid." Chemically, that is doubtless correct. But does that say what a tear is? What it is becomes manifest when I have occasion to ask (when I see the tears of a human being): what is expressed in a tear, what can be revealed in it? Tears are something more and different than a salty fluid. This other, this "more," I see not in the fluid of the tears but in the person who is shedding the tears. Reaching out from this, I try to understand and interpret the individual thing as manifestation of this human being. In the tears of a human being—depending on the situation—pain, suffering, joy, enthusiasm, helplessness, and anger can become manifest: invisible sentiments and emotions move the interior of human beings. Thus, in what is appearing, there also always appears at the same time that which does not appear but is most profoundly real. Human beings can perceive and come to know this.

For human beings can—and this is important for our question—not only observe, count, calculate, and analyze individual things; human beings can get a feeling for and understanding of someone. Human beings hear not just vibrations but a melody; they do not just register optic reflexes, they see a shape; they do not just take in syllables and sounds, they understand a context and a meaning.

Recognizable in all this is the special characteristic of human beings: the openness and creativity of their spirit, the spontaneity of their freedom, the receptivity of their sense, the functions of their bodiliness as instrument of their capacity for expression, and as revelation of their selves.

The being-revelation and being-meaning which transcend the being-existent is not a destruction of reality, nor an imposition of something foreign or something that obscures, but the perception of the whole, of the real, of the center, of the profundity. If in the individual reality of the tear, laugh, mimicry, gesture and hand movement, action, sign, the whole of the context along with the human being is not seen, then the existing individual thing is not seen properly and in its entirety.

Something further comes from these considerations. For human beings, everything that is can become revelation-being, meaning-being, can become metaphor or symbol: "Everything on earth is only a metaphor."

Symbol

Symbol,[1] literally a "something thrown together from external sign and inner sense," is indissolubly connected with the meaning which it represents in its sensibly perceivable givenness. For example, light, physically seen, is energy emanating from a light source passing through space with the speed of light as as electromagnetic wave. Light is perceived as brightness, color, and warmth. Light can also become a sign or symbol of a quality and characteristic of human beings. This quality can in turn be described in graphic images—images of light: brilliance of spirit, clarity of understanding, fire of enthusiasm, glow of love. External light, with its powers, qualities, effects, becomes the symbol of an "inner light" of human beings, of their invisible reality, as spirit-beings endowed with freedom and love.

A symbol is not an arbitrary sign like a traffic sign whose function and significance one can determine, make, and thus also change. A symbol is inseparable from its meaning and sense orientation which, by the nature of things, resides within it as quality of nature. Symbol is inseparable from the symbolized. This means that a symbol is more than what is immediately at hand and perceived. It is at the same time less than that to which it points, less than that for which it is a symbol.

Along with the being-symbol of things, there are also symbolic actions, which, in and with their execution, mean something: the

1. J. Splett, "Symbol," *SM* 6 (1970) 199–201; S. Wisse, *Das religiöse Symbol* (Essen, 1963); M. Becker, *Bild—Symbol—Glaube* (Essen, 1964); W. Heinen, ed., *Bild—Wort—Symbol in der Theologie* (Würzburg, 1968).

laying on of hands as a sign of commissioning, the meal as sign of a community, the symbolic actions of the prophets as representation of divine activity.

Relatedly, a symbol is a universal human possibility of seeing reality. It is never a symbol just for me; a symbol has an inner relationship to community; it has a representing, gathering and integrating function. In addition, a symbol has the power to vivify, strengthen, and deepen the community.

Furthermore, in symbol, things that are separate from each other are coordinated. Symbol, accordingly, points across to another being on the basis of a similarity proper to it.

In a way similar to light, being-manifest and being-symbol can be pointed out in other phenomena: for example, vivifying, fructifying, refreshing, purifying water becomes the symbol of processes, movements, and modes of behavior in human existence.

Symbol of Transcendence

If the thesis is correct that everything that is, is a revelational being, if we ourselves have this understanding of reality and this way of dealing with it, and if we come into contact with the dimensions of reality through this being-manifest, this being-symbol, then the question automatically arises: Is reality as being-manifest to be understood in such a way—that in it the totality and ground becomes transparent that is related not only to an inner-worldly context, to an empirical form and totality, and to human beings, but also to the all-encompassing ground and relational sense whom we call God?

If it is the case, that reality, precisely as symbolic, is indeed related to its all-encompassing ground of being, we must then ask whether the all-determining reality called God becomes manifest in the reality we have before us? Is everything earthly a metaphor also of transcendence, a symbol of God? The difficulty consists in the fact that the reality of God as such does not directly appear, that it is not identical with the present "world," and cannot be figured out from it. God is no particular object, no object like the things we encounter. God is rather the unobjectifiable ground of everything. And yet empirical reality in its totality and depth cannot be described without the ground.

In his reflection on revelation, Paul Tillich proceeds from the presupposition that revelation is not an object and not a process alongside others, but the dimension that is opened up in reality itself. In it is found also dependence on transcendence, transparency towards the unconditioned. Tillich speaks of this transparency of the conditioned towards the unconditional as follows:

The unconditioned enters into the context of the conditioned. But how can it appear where there still can be nothing conditioned, no object? It can only appear in/on/at the object, in/on/at the conditioned. This does not stop being conditioned; the context of the conditioned is not disturbed. But in this object, in this conditioned and its contexts, is hidden the possibility, and it becomes reality to point to something that does not belong to its conditionedness, that is most intimate to it and at the same time most foreign to it, that becomes manifest in/on/at it as the unconditioned Hidden.[2]

In the midst of the finitudes and relativities that surround and determine us, we discover the sign and the trace of another, which "unconditionally comes at me," which admits no "if" and "but," which categorically calls me in, over which I have no disposition, which has disposition over me.

Human beings can accept this transparency or openness of the conditioned to the unconditioned, of the individually real to the all-determining reality, as their ultimate ground because, by virtue of their spirit, they seek after connections and transparency; because they not only establish facts but pursue them to their ground; because they are open to the world in its context, i.e., as a whole, and thus also to the ground that bears it. This is the way human beings are in the openness of their quest after their ground, in the inconclusiveness of their knowing and their striving, which finally comes to rest on no finite goal. This is what human beings are in the seemingly inexhaustible possibility of their capacity for assertion and expression in language, art, culture, and poetry.

The capacities and activities just mentioned are needed for human beings to become aware of the openness of reality for the transcendence that is mediated and comes to transparency through the world, finiteness, and the conditioned. Reality is thus presented as mediation between the singleness and conditionedness of the concrete form on the one hand, and the infinity and absoluteness of the ground on the other.

This line of thinking leads to the question: How does all this get expressed? The being-manifest and being-meaning of reality, its overall being-symbol and especially its being-symbol towards the absolute, unconditioned—these come to expression and into being in word, especially in the language of poetry. The language of poetry is a language above all of images, symbols, metaphors, and stories, which express the dimension of revelation. This is done quite differently than, e.g., in conceptual, technical, natural-scientific mathematical language. In the language of poetry, reality is not distorted; it isn't run over roughshod; it has nothing foreign grafted onto it; poetry puts into words something that belongs to the encompassing meaning of things, something that can be expressed in no other language. Poetry as the voice of the real being in things that are (W. Schadewaldt) reveals to human beings the truth of their innermost beings.

The world as symbol, the symbolic form of the world, likewise makes its appearance in art and in art work in its different forms: painting, sculpture, architecture and music. According to Plato and Aristotle, art is the imitation of nature. To our present-day understanding, that seems inadequate, for the imitation of nature is today done better by technology than by art. The conception of Plato and Aristotle must thus be clarified by pointing out that Plato sees in things, not just what now exists, but the reflection of the eternal ideas; Aristotle assigns to art the task of representing the power of shaping that is at work in nature. Art is supposed to bring to perfect form what is begun in nature but is still incomplete. This corresponds to what the Greeks saw as the purifying power of the work of art, the "catharsis." Through works of art in poetry, painting, sculpture, and architecture of the kind found in Greece an achievement that has lasted even to our own day, human beings are to find themselves; they are to be led to their inner order, to their inner destiny. As Martin Heidegger said, art is the mode "whereby, in a single human work, the whole of being becomes visibly present to human beings, and whereby, vice versa, human beings through this work of art set themselves before the truth and to reflecting on their own nature."[3]

Finally, yet another way to gain access to the being-symbol and being-manifest of things is nonconceptual, wordless meditation, the silent surrender to what reality is in its depth. In this way the capacity and the readiness is awakened to listen to the word and the language of things and events right down into the mystery and the depth of their ground [of being].

---

3. "Der Ursprung des Kunstwerkes" in: *Holzwege* (Frankfurt, 1950) 7–68.

§ 20

THE WITNESS OF RELIGION AND THE
HISTORY OF RELIGIONS

Hierophany and Theophany

Religion as behavior, as deed and activity of human beings as well as central concept of specific contents (affirmations, doctrines, rites, instructions), is first a historical fact and a concrete human experience. Religion is characterized by that which the religious act—as in prayer and cult—and the history of religions calls the divine in the form of the Holy. The Holy is the over-against, the point of reference, the intention of religion. Its basic characteristic can be so described that the Holy is not identical with any object within the world as such, nor with the world as a whole; it is rather the "totally other," the "unworldly," and at the same time the reality that bears and encompasses the whole. It can in no way be inferior to what is meant by "person." Otherwise it couldn't affect the human being as person nor could it—in prayer—be addressed.

But precisely this divine, holy [thing], according to the witness of religion and the history of religions, is made manifest in the reality of the world, and nothing at all that exists is excluded from it. Everything can point to the Holy, in the sense that the Holy is manifest in it as hierophany; the divine makes itself known therein as theophany. It is made manifest in the world of experiential reality and is at the same time other than that in which it appears—and precisely this belongs to symbol, especially to religious symbol.

The most important contemporary scholars of the history of religions, Gerardus van der Leeuw[1] and Mircea Eliade,[2] come to the following conclusion on the basis of their comprehensive history of religions

1. G. van der Leeuw, *Religion in Essence and Manifestation*, trans. J. E. Turner (Princeton, N. J.: Princeton University Press, 1986).
2. M. Eliade, *Patterns in Comparative Religion*, trans. Rosemary Sheed (New York: New American Library, 1974); *A History of Religious Ideas*: vol. 3; *From Muhammad to the Age of Reform*, trans. Willard R. Trask (Chicago: University of Chicago Press, 1978).

investigations and religious phenomenological analyses: We must accustom ourselves to accept hierophanies everywhere, in every sphere of being. We do not know whether, according to the evidence of history of religions, anything at all exists—whether object, action, or event— that has not at some time and in some place been transformed into a hierophany, i.e., into a manifestation or revelation of the divine and the holy perceived by religious human beings. Religious human beings are not a special kind of human being; religious human beings are human beings to whose fundamental characteristic belong religion and religious experience.

The framework of our theme doesn't allow us to describe all of reality according to this dimension of hierophany and theophany, but one example, adapted from Eliade, seems to be on the one hand wholly modern, and on the other completely outmoded.

The firmament with sun, moon, and stars, is one of the oldest and most ubiquitous [places of appearance] of the divine, the Holy. The sky is symbol, and thereby revelation to human beings, of a fascinating power, majesty, greatness, wisdom, and reason, which is both set apart from human beings but at the same time determinative of them, the very source of light and life.

In the inaccessibility, infinity, eternity, and creative power of the heavens, the divine transcendence is revealed. The mode of being of the heavens is an inexhaustible hierophany. Further, everything that takes place in the sphere of the upper atmosphere—the course of the stars, the order of their course, the movement of the clouds, storms, lightning and thunder, meteors and rainbows—is a part of this hierophany.[3]

Nature is never just nature. Hierophany found expression in a multiplicity of heavenly divinities; in Uranus, Zeus, Jupiter, Sol. The phrase "God in heaven" shows the connection with this view of things. The most widespread and oldest Christian prayer is addressed to the "Father in heaven." It is connected with the consciousness that where the heavens are, there is God and the divine. This shows what is characteristic of the symbolic form of the religious: it transcends our experiences and makes us conscious of our finiteness; at the same time it is adequate enough to our experiences that we can say "You," that we can pray to Him.

The religious and history-of-religions data and perspectives that come with the hierophany and theophany of the heavens cannot (and don't need to) be described further at this point. But the obvious challenging question should be considered: Does the very old and widespread experience of "heaven," of sun, moon and stars, of the order and beauty of the universe as a symbol revelatory of the divine, still work today? Doesn't it seem completely anachronistic: a piece of the

3. *Die Religionen und das Heilige* 64.

past, naive mythical thinking, which, in the face of enlightened science, can no longer be taken seriously? Science has figured out and conquered the sky and made it subservient as part of reality. The laws of the universe have been put at the service of human beings and their goals. Thus, the heavens and their energy, put at the disposition of human beings and their possibilities, are more a revelation of humanity and its possibilities than a hierophany and theophany, than a symbol of the divine and the Holy.

The Russian astronaut Yuri Gagarin, upon returning from the first space flight, declared: "Space is dark. I see no God." When, some years later, the Americans landed on the moon, the captain of the space ship, Borman, took up the Bible and recited the story of creation: "In the beginning, God created the heavens and the earth . . . " These two statements were the starting point of a discussion in which I engaged some years ago with the physicist Peter Glockmann, from which came a small book with the title: *Ich sehe keinen Gott* [I See No God].[4] Glockmann declared that he found both affirmations "somewhat meaningless." Gagarin had made only one tiny step into the universe; no wonder he didn't see God. But one cannot conclude from this that God doesn't exist. That the American read the beginning of Genesis is, according to Glockmann, likewise "scientifically meaningless." He did add, however, that as a personal affirmation and expression of an inner experience, the reading of the American deserves recognition.

My answer was: these two affirmations should not be put on the same level.

I think rather that the affirmation of the American indeed is not just a pious elevation of feeling but has a real ground and inner relationship; to the extent that Borman became aware of the magnificence of the cosmos in an entirely new way, he was led to reflect. The American astronaut made a statement which is anything but meaningless, even if not formulated scientifically: i.e., at the basis of the experience of his space journey lay something that is more than technical data and mathematical calculation. His overwhelming experience gave him occasion to find new illustration and confirmation of a very old message.[5]

Present-Day Understanding of the World

In connection with this theme let me make the following observations. The laws that are made for the utility of human beings and their possibilities, also for conquering the sky, are not made and created by human beings; they are discovered, found to be already there. Recognizable in them is—this is less challengeable today than ever—a

4. Munich, 1971; (Freiburg—Basel—Vienna 1971) (Herderbücherei 469).
5. Ibid. (Herderbücherei).

logos, a reason and a wisdom, that precedes human beings, which they can "reflect."

The more the world is known in its scale and its governing laws, in its powers and possibilities, the more can one's gaze be open and free for that reality which is not identical with earth and heaven but what is becoming manifest in them, which is the ultimate encompassing ground of all things, the ultimate reason in all laws and systems. If one makes room for this perspective and speaks of the mystery of the world, that is not a concession to knowledge not yet achieved or to a primitive world view; it is the result of an insight into the deepest ground of things. This insight cannot, to be sure, be put into a mathematical formula, but it need not therefore remain speechless.

The hymn sung more than 2000 years ago, "The heavens are telling the glory of God; and the firmament proclaims his handiwork" (Ps 19:1) is a possible and sensible manner of speaking even today. It has been neither refuted nor superseded; rather, the meaning and content of the words "heaven" and "earth" have simply become more concrete.

If the heavens "tell the glory" and the firmament "proclaims," they are a revelation, a theophany, a hierophany. Let us develop these affirmations with some examples taken from the realm of natural science and technology.

For Galileo Galilei, the founder of modern natural science, nature is a book of God. Next to the Bible it contains the primeval proclamation of the salvation of human beings. Nature reveals in the language of mathematics the particulars of the greatness and wisdom of creation, which not only can be known in pious surmises, but can be exactly described, and which thus disclose the glory of the Creator more intensively than ever before.[6]

Johannes Kepler understands his work as a humble description of the work of the hands of God. He closes his work *Harmonia Cosmi* with the words: "Since I have attempted to give human understanding a glimpse into the universe with the help of geometry, may the Originator of the universe keep me from saying anything about His work that cannot stand before His glory and leads our capacity to understand into error. May God make us hasten after the perfection of His work of creation through the sanctification of our life."[7]

According to Albert Einstein, natural science reveals "so superior a reason that all meaningful human thought and arranging is, in contrast, a totally insignificant reflection."

---

6. Documentation in N. Schiffers, *Fragen der Physik an die Theologie* (Düsseldorf, 1968).
7. In W. Heisenberg, *Wandlungen in den Grundlagen der Naturwissenschaft*, 9th ed. (Stuttgart, 1959) 78.

Werner Heisenberg in his work *Der Teil und das Ganze* [The Part and the Whole][8] tells of a discussion in which he was asked: Do you believe in a personal God? He answered:

H: May I formulate the question in a different way? . . . so that it would ask: Can you or can anyone get so immediately close to the central order of things about which there can really be no doubt, can one come so immediately close to it, get so immediately in connection with it as is possible with the soul of another human being? I am expressly using the so-difficult-to-define word soul so as not to be misunderstood. If that is what you ask, then my answer is yes.

Q: You mean, then, that the central order can be present with the same intensity as the soul of another human being?

H: Perhaps.

Q: Why did you use the word "soul" here and not speak simply of other human beings?

H: Because precisely here, the word "soul" describes the central order, the center of a being which, in its external forms of manifestation, may be quite manifold and difficult to take in at a glance.[9]

With these words it is not just said that there is something over against human beings which simply towers over them and which they can nevertheless perceive. The word "soul" is a reference not to an impersonal it but to a personal reality.

It is for this reason difficult to see why—as one reads in many theological presentations these days—it is no longer allowed, as belonging to the outmoded Greek cosmic world view, to speak of the religious symbolism and transparency of nature, of the universe, of the cosmos, of the hierophany and theophany of the heavens. The anthropological and anthropocentric epochs into which we have entered do not exclude but include the consideration of nature as sign, symbol, and revelation of transcendence, because the human being cannot live without this relationship. The progress of natural science and the growing knowledge of empirical causes connected with it do not supersede the fundamental structure of nature to be symbolic of transcendence; rather, they make it more clear.

Certainly this fundamental orientation can be by limiting attention to the merely present, to what "the case is." But it isn't true what Bert Brecht formulates in his poem "Der Ozeanflug" [The Ocean Flight]:

Participate in the banishing of every god, wherever he appears. Under the sharpest microscopes, he falls. Our improved equipment drives him out of existence. The cleaning up of the cities, the destruction of misery, make him disappear and drive him back into the first millennium.[10]

---

8. (Munich, 1969).
9. Ibid. 193.
10. B. Brecht, *Werke II* (Frankfurt a. M., 1967) 576–77.

No technical invention, no piece of equipment, is a refutation of God, as if God could ever be found with pieces of equipment or in laboratories. The abolition of misery doesn't make God disappear, but one sees therein one's task. Natural science is silent about God. It is, methodologically atheistic. This justified and grounded silence is an indication that God is not a piece or part of the world, i.e., not an object that is, and also not an inner-worldly cause or substitute for it. Thus God, transcendence, cannot be expressed in the language of natural science, mathematics, and technology. In these methods and according to them there is no hierophany and theophany. But the language of natural science and mathematics is not the only language of human beings; the reality disclosed by natural science and technology and their corresponding methods is not reality as such, but only a part of it.[11]

God in Heaven

In his book *Honest to God*,[12] J. A. T. Robinson drew special attention to the theme of hierophany and theophany and the expression "God in heaven." The fact that this book is no longer making headlines is no indication that its theme is out of date. We have simply become acclimatized to it.

One main thesis of Robinson states that the language of "God in heaven," the coordination of God and heaven, stems from a mythological, now no longer reasonable image of the world and leads to representing God "as the Old Man above the clouds," as "Father over the starry tent." Speaking about the Father in heaven, talking about heaven as the place where God lives, can, in these days of the abolition of the heavens, easily lead to the abolition of what is meant by "God." Robinson is very much aware of the difficulty that the abolition of the heavens seems like a denial of God, hence like atheism. He is not, however, trying to abolish the idea of God and transcendence but to make them understandable for modern human beings and to produce the conditions of the possibility of Christian faith. Robinson expressly declares: "We intend in no way to change the Christian doctrine of God, but we want to prevent it from disappearing along with outmoded views of the world."[13]

In view of this situation, which he calls a "reluctant revolution," Robinson takes over from Paul Tillich the idea that "God is not a projection into the beyond, not some kind of Other above the clouds of whose existence we would have to convince ourselves, but God is the

---

11. Cf. Heinrich Fries, "Die Gottesfrage in der Begegnung mit der modernen Naturwissenschaft" in: H. Fries, ed., *Gott—die Frage unserer Zeit* (Munich, 1973) 19–23.

12. Munich, 1963. On this, cf.: *Diskussion zu Bischof Robinsons: Gott ist Anders* (Munich, 1964); H. Fries, in: *Ärgernis und Widerspruch*, 2d ed. (Würzburg, 1968) 101–32.

13. *Gott ist Anders* 51.

ground of our being."[14] Not nearness but depth signifies God. And depth, according to Tillich, signifies not the opposite of height but the origin of being; it signifies that which "unconditionally concerns human beings," that which they take seriously without reservation, which "is ultimate reality" for us. This word, depth, is intended to express that "God is not outside of us, and yet God is profoundly transcendent."[15] To illustrate this, Robinson quotes a few sentences from a sermon of Tillich:

The name of this endless depth and this inexhaustible ground of all being is God. That depth is what is meant by the word "God." And if that word doesn't have much meaning for you, then translate it and speak of the depth in your life, of the origin of your being, of that which unconditionally concerns you, of that which you take seriously without any reservation whatsoever. If you do that, you will perhaps have to forget some things you have learned about God, perhaps even the word itself. But when you have come to know that God means depth, then you know a great deal about God. You wouldn't be able to call yourselves atheists or unbelievers any more, for you would no longer be able to think or say that life has no depth, that life is shallow, that being is surface. Only if you could say that in full seriousness would you be atheists. Otherwise, you aren't. Whoever knows about depth knows about God.[16]

The idea of God as the transcendent depth within us and among us is protected by Tillich and Robinson from a misunderstanding. God is not another name for nature or humanity. To begin with, God is not the unconscious of which depth psychology speaks. The depth that is meant in connection with the idea of God is the transcendent depth of the encompassing ground of being. But this is not found in an empty "in itself," but in, with, and under the conditions of life and activities of existence, especially in encounters with human beings, in the readiness to be radically there for another. But here, too, it holds: the eternal You is not the same as the temporal You; that would be naturalism. God as depth means that our being has depths that naturalism and positivism of all kinds cannot recognize or will not recognize.

What is our assessment of this conception? First and fundamentally: All talk about God is talk in human language, with human images and ideas. These images and ideas may at times be historically conditioned, but they also constitute the unique possibilities of human beings and their language. The word "depth" as transparence and epiphany of God is legitimate, if the thesis is correct that everything that is can be revelation. But the word which comes from God as depth is no less an image and symbol than that of height, of the heavens. The image of depth also has its limits. This becomes clear in the steps we have to take to protect this idea from sliding into naturalism and to keep God from being turned into the equivalent of the unconscious of

14. Ibid. 31.
15. Ibid. 66.
16. Ibid. 31.

depth psychology. Nothing should be said against the image of depth—it is quite legitimate and is found everywhere in the language of religion where one speaks of God dwelling, being, living, and abiding in human beings and of God as the ground of all reality. If the image of depth helps contemporary human beings to make present the transcendent reality of God, then it is even necessary. Still, one has to keep in mind that it, like the image of height, is an image and like all images has limits; it cannot say everything, and its whole purpose is to raise up and highlight what is meant by the image and idea. Here again a distinction is to be made in view of the manifold use of "God" and "heaven" and "God in heaven."

Heaven can be image, symbol, revelation of God, indeed even a name for God in the way, e.g., it is met in the two biblical concepts "Kingdom of God" and "Kingdom of Heaven." It is different from the heaven spoken of when it is said that God created heaven and earth. In this mode of expression, God and heaven are clearly and radically different.

The phrase "God in heaven" thus needs interpretation. If by that is meant that heaven is the place where God dwells and where God thus, if God exists, can be found and even has to be met, then it does follow: if the heaven traversed by the space ship is empty, then God doesn't exist: God is not found in heaven. This is the "Sputnik argument" proposed in similar ways in East and West: I see no God. Only the double perspective of heaven as symbol and as epiphany of the invisible God can protect against misunderstandings and confusion and from having technical data or changes in one's view of life weaken or confuse the faith. The most one could do is to ask why one still holds onto the connection "God in heaven," "Father in heaven."

It must be said that the symbolic content connected with the idea of "up," height, heaven represents an elementary, fundamental human apperception. It is connected quite by itself with the idea of qualitative height, value, sublimity, and transcendence. This is so true that this image, precisely in its application to God and in the orientation of human beings to it, cannot be given up without losing a fundamental truth about God. This shows that heaven is not an arbitrary, exchangeable sign for God, but a symbol based in the thing itself.

This inner—qualitative—characterization of height is not changed by an altered scientific view of the world any more than a Copernican view of the world keeps us from talking about the sun rising and setting, although such talk, scientifically speaking, is erroneous. At most, one should consider whether one shouldn't make human beings again aware of these elementary things and help them to appropriate anew the original meaning of these ideas, and to make the sense of these elementary signs, images, and symbols live again.

Robinson accepts Rudolf Bultmann's demolition of outmoded mythological thinking and world views. Significantly, Karl Jaspers, dis-
agrees, and declares that mythological thinking is necessary and
proper to human beings of every time; the point is not to do away with
it but to regain it in its essence.[17] This idea is gaining in attention and
significance in the present age.

This opens up the possibility of accepting in a new way the word of
God in heaven, and thus of not writing off as an archaism or mythological image, but as accepting as a disclosure of reality the dimension of
revelation that goes along with the physical, cosmic reality of the
heavens and the universe, and that can now be seen better and in more
detail.

Coming back to our point of departure: Everything that is can be a
hierophany and theophany and it thus has the dimension of revelation.

From all this was chosen one model which is found in religions and
in the history of religions and which is still valid today: heaven.
Other phenomena: springs, mountains, seas, rocks, trees, animals,
because of their quality of being hierophany and theophany, have been
preferred, above all in the so-called "cosmic religions." We should not
acknowledge these phenomena simply with the attitude of someone
who is interested in the curiosities of nature religions and collects as
many of them as possible, for in these phenomena shine out the dimensions of reality: existing-being and revelation-being.

Hymn to Matter

At the end of these reflections, let us give one example of what such
a perspective could look like and how it could be expressed today.
Teilhard de Chardin, in an impressive and at times controversial way,
illuminated and expounded the facts of natural science in their character of transparency. He did this in his whole literary work, but especially in *The Divine Milieu*.[18] We quote from his "Hymn to Matter," in
which he discovers a revelation of God:

Blessed are you, powerful matter, unstoppable development, constantly becoming
reality, you who every moment explode our boundaries, force us to have to seek
the truth ever further away.

Blessed are you, all-encompassing matter, duration without limits, ether without
coasts, threefold abyss of constellations, atoms and sexes, you who spread beyond
and wipe out our narrow measure, and reveal to us the measure of God.

17. K. Jaspers—R. Bultmann, *Die Frage der Entmythologisierung* (Munich, 1954).
18. Pierre Teilhard de Chardin, *The Divine Milieu* (New York: Harper, 1968); on
Teilhard: A. Gläßer in: *Klassiker der Theologie II* (1983) 277–98.

Blessed are you, impenetrable matter, you who are spread out everywhere between our souls and the world of essences, who make us yearn to break through the seamless shell of appearances.

Without you, O matter, without your alluring, without your snatching away, we would live dull, stagnant, childish, not knowing about ourselves and about God.

I bless you, matter, not in the form in which—belittled and distorted—the high priests of science and the preachers of virtue describe you—a medley, they say, of brutal powers and lowly desires, but in the form in which you appear to me today, in your wholeness and your truth.[19]

This is not spoken by an enthusiast who has no inkling of the matter of which he speaks, but by someone with familiarity and knowledge, who in this hymn does not forget or keep silent about what he has researched and learned but brings it to new expression in these words. Teilhard's words certainly don't automatically become someone else's. Others perhaps may not be able to make them their own; not because they think Teilhard's words are false but because they are content with present existence. Because they don't let the transparency of things, manifest-being, make an appearance or come to word. So the question remains: Where will reality and all its dimensions and relations receive the answer for which they cry out: in limiting everything to the obviously perceivable reality, or in the effort and in the capacity to express the revelation-being of things?

19. In: *Wort und Wahrheit* (1958) 25.

§ 21

REALITY AS CREATION

The relation of reality to revelation becomes especially clear when we recall the fact that reality—i.e., everything that is—can be known and seen as creation, which, in its creational structure, invites inquiry into its ground. This is why there are hierophanies and theophanies, why existing-being is at the same time revelation-being.

Created Being

The world as a whole has borne from time immemorial the sign of having been created; its finiteness is the clearest clue to this. Finiteness says: something exists not by virtue of its nature, thus not essentially or necessarily; otherwise it could have no beginning or end, it would have to be, always and de facto endlessly. If something finite exists, it exists "by chance," but not by natural necessity; it could just as well not be. That something is created means that it is grounded and is understood not in and of itself, but that it presupposes a ground which can bestow and communicate being so that it can actually be. That something is created means that it does indeed have being, but that it does not possess the ground of being of itself, but has received it. This structure is not tied to any historical phase or any specific level of world theory. Therefore, because it expresses a primordial, grounding relationship, it cannot be replaced by anything; it cannot be fundamentally changed, much less done away with.

This kind of consideration becomes possible when one asks about the ultimate origin of that which is. It is necessary for human beings not to block off this possibility of their spirit, this questioning, this inquiry after the ground, but to let it come to light so that they will learn to see intellectually what Paul says in the Epistle to the Romans. He is speaking of human beings (before and outside of Christ), who by their wickedness suppress the truth. For what can be known about God is plain to them, because God has shown it to them. Ever since the creation of the world his visible nature, namely, his eternal power and deity, has been clearly perceived in the things that have been made. So they are without excuse; for although they knew God they did not honor him as God or give thanks to him. (Rom 1:18-21)

Let us attempt to highlight the elements of this affirmation.[1]

a. It is said of God that God is a hidden, invisible God. The hiddenness of God is not a part of God but the whole of God in a certain perspective. God has stepped out of obscurity into inobscurity. Inobscurity is the Greek word for truth. The truth of God is accordingly the revelation of God, God's self-disclosure, thus an action, a being active. Paul sets this true God over against the idols which are dumb, do not reveal themselves, cannot do anything, and have no self-realization in the truth (1 Cor 12:2).

b. The invisible God has revealed Himself and made Himself visible "through the works of creation since the making of the world." As their Creator, God is distinct from creatures, but this creation is related to and dependent on God; it is nothing without God. Creation is thus not nature come from itself or an eternally existing nature to which, in the Greek view of things, the gods also belong, but creature, a work that has a beginning and is dependent in origin and essence on the Creator, who stands over against the world in freedom. The world is God's; it is not God, and it is not full of gods. It is the characteristic of idols that the symbol and the symbolized are not distinguished but are made identical. Thus creation is also the counterconcept to myth as interpretation of the world, when myth means the conflation of world and the gods, of theogony and cosmogony, of history of the world and history of the gods (and fate).[2] That which is or has being is manifested as created. In this being created, God is made manifest, the hidden is revealed, the invisible becomes visible.

c. Because God—through creation—is indeed self-disclosing, God, according to Paul, can be known and indeed is known through creation. Paul does not speculate about the possibility of our knowledge of God, he declares it. What is knowable of God, namely God's power and divinity, is intellectually perceived, is "gazed upon," by reason. But power and divinity are modes of the invisible God. God's power is, as such, not directly accessible in an earthly mode of knowing, any more

---

1. Cf. the presentation of the doctrine of creation in the handbooks and textbooks of dogma. In addition: G. Söhngen, "Die Offenbarung Gottes in seiner Schöpfung und unsere Glaubensverkündigung" in: Die Einheit in der Theologie (Munich, 1952) 212–34; O. Kuß, Der Römerbrief (Regensburg, 1956) 26–46; P. Smulders, "Creation," SM 2.23–28; ibid., H. Gross, 29–33; A. Darlap, 33–34; E. Loveley, D. J. Ehr, H. J. Sorenson, O. W. Garrigan, "Creation," NCE 4.407–28. L. Scheffczyk, Die Welt als Schöpfung Gottes (Aschaffenburg, 1968); Ernst Käsemann, Commentary on Romans, trans. Geoffrey W. Bromiley (Grand Rapids, Mich.: Eerdmans, 1980); H. Schlier, Der Römerbrief (Freiburg—Basel—Vienna, 1977) 44–57.

2. Heinrich Fries, "Mythos und Offenbarung" in: J. Bernard ed., Offenbarung. Phänomen—Begriff—Dimensionen (Leipzig, 1983) 106–42.

than is God's divinity, which is reserved to God alone. God, who is known from creation, resides as its originator precisely not in the mere extension of the world but in God's own clearly marked transcendence of the world. Nevertheless, as God's work, the world gives witness of God. This witness lies in being created, in "being formed." This is not given to the world, i.e., to all that is, after the fact; creatureliness is rather the essence of all things one can and indeed does see in all things. This intellectual seeing is more than a thought asking about ground and cause; it is, rather, human beings becoming conscious through spirit and heart. In this context Heinrich Schlier speaks of the questioning and perceiving power of an illuminated heart.

d. The ideas expressed in the Letter to the Romans refer to a text found in the Book of Wisdom, the latest book of the Old Testament dating from the first century before Christ. It was composed in Egypt, apparently in Alexandria, by a Hellenistic Jew, and has Egyptian religiosity, above all the cult of animals and idols practiced there, as its obvious point of opposition. One surmises that Paul, in the text just cited from Romans, consciously relied on this text and in part took it over. After a somewhat lengthy description of Egyptian idolatry, the author says:

For all men who were ignorant of God were foolish by nature; and they were unable from the good things that are seen to know him who exists, nor did they recognize the craftsman while paying heed to his works; but they supposed that either fire or wind or swift air, or the circle of the stars, or turbulent water, or the luminaries of heaven were the gods that rule the world. If through delight in the beauty of these things men assumed them to be gods, let them know how much better than these is their Lord, for the author of beauty created them. And if men were amazed at their power and working, let them perceive from them how much more powerful is he who formed them. For from the greatness and beauty of created things comes a corresponding perception of their Creator. (Wisdom 13:1-5)

e. The knowledge of God, possible to human beings from creation, should not and indeed cannot be, anything like some objective taking note of a fact. The knowledge of God as Creator of the world, as the all-determining reality, naturally has consequences.

The knowledge must lead to recognition and affirming acknowledgment, so that human beings allow themselves to be determined by the knowledge experienced as truth. Put negatively: human beings do not voluntarily "suppress" this truth in injustice but "praise and thank God." Injustice is an offense against the right established by the God of creation and holding sway therein, which requires the veneration of the true God. If human beings do not allow the possible knowledge of God to grow to recognition, they offend against the reality of creation and succumb, according to Paul, into vacuous thinking and a darkening of the heart. This darkening becomes concrete in replacing God with idols and in the subversion of moral behavior. According to Paul, that is not "fate" but guilt, and thus also an object of indictment.

These people make a switch. They exchange the glory of the incorruptible God for the image of a corruptible human, or of animals. They turn the world into God; they turn God into the world. This switch is at the same time the deception and the folly that is seen as wisdom by these people. The further consequence is, according to Paul, a loss of orientation in ethical behavior. It consists, according to the Epistle to the Romans (1:26-32), in sexual perversity and "injustice of all kinds." People do all this and applaud others who do the same. In summation it can be said: According to Paul, the pagan has already been constantly involved with the real God. "For [the pagan's] reality is constantly experienced creatureliness and, to that extent, reality before God. If human beings do not deny their being human, they are constantly encountering the power of the invisible God: namely the knowable ground as well as the limits of their own existence."[3]

The Fundamental Structure of All Reality

Creation, being created, is the fundamental structure of all reality, its relation-being. This is not added to the reality of the world; it *is* the reality of the world in truth. God is the ultimate determination, specification, and characterization of reality. God is spoken of when one is talking about the dependence of the world understood in this way. They who want to talk about God must understand themselves as creatures—and vice versa: we say something about God when we talk about creation, i.e., about the fact that we are creatures. In this way, the nonidentity of Creator and creature come to light along with the fact of their innermost coordination.

Thus godlessness is not only a denial of God but also the denial of one's own existence as creature. Denial of God is, in this view, a denial of one's own self as indebted existence, as "existence in reception"—actually an "ontological impossibility" (K. Barth).

Reality is to be understood as creation, creation to be understood as revelation. According to Paul, one can see this quality in creation. This quality can also, as already pointed out, be specified with the category of hearing: the things of the world can say something, they can speak, they have word-character: "The heavens are telling the glory of God" (Ps 19:1).

At the basis of this assessment is ultimately the theological truth that creation came about by the word of God: "God spoke—and it came to be." By bringing every created thing back to the word, which calls forth and makes possible answer, there arises a genuine situation of encounter between the Creator and the created.

---

3. E. Käsemann, *Commentary on Romans*, 38.

This affirmation means: All being goes back to personal being, to persons—in contrast, e.g., to Eastern religions, in which the personal and particular is led back to the impersonal and general. Tracing back all reality to personal being is also a different characterization than the characterization of God as "first cause." Causality is an inner worldly quality for the explanation of the laws of activity and development accessible to observation. But the creative activity of God is not really the extension of the immanent causes and connections of events in which the Creator functions as first link of a chain. The Creator does not belong to the chain of being; the chain of being, as a whole, belongs to the Creator.

The conceptual understanding of this relationship of God and world through the conditional relation of Creator and creature has been worked out in the well-known doctrine of *analogia entis*, the analogy of being.[4] Recall the description of created being: It means to have being, not to possess the ground of being of itself, but to have received it. This affirms that between that which receives being and that which bestows it there is a similarity, a correspondence, an analogy, an analogy of being. This means that being can be attributed to the Creator and the creature—not in the same way, however, but in a different way—in accord with the relation: bestowing and receiving, original and derived, and in accord with the specification: Creator and creature. Consequently, no similarity can be greater than that between Creator and creature. On the other hand, the distinction between being Creator and being creature produces that greater dissimilarity which exists between finite and infinite being.[5]

This brings up a new question: Does not the modern, secularized world understand itself as opposite and contradictory to a world as creation, and thus to the world as a revelation of God?

---

4. E. Przywara, *Analogia Entis* (Munich, 1932); Hans Uurs von Balthasar, *The Theology of Karl Barth: Exposition and Interpretation*, trans. Edward T. Oakes (San Francisco: Ignatius Press, 1992); J. Splett and L. B. Puntel, "Analogy of Being, " *SM* 1.21–25; Eberhard Jüngel, *God as the Mystery of the World: On the Foundation of the Theology of the Crucified in the Dispute Between Theism and Atheism*, trans. Darrell L. Goder (Grand Rapids, Mich.: Eerdmans, 1983).

5. The ideas of creatureliness and createdness is what P. Knauer makes the starting point and foundation of his ecumenical fundamental theology: *Der Glaube kommt vom Hören* (Graz—Vienna—Cologne, 1978): "Createdness means a total relatedness to . . . in total difference from. . . . The object of this relationship we call God" (21).

§ 22

THE SECULARIZED WORLD AS CONTRADICTION TO THE WORLD AS CREATION AND REVELATION

This theme is connected to the previous reflection and to the theme: Reality as Revelation, Reality as Creation. We said that the creature-liness of reality is an abiding characteristic and thus cannot be superseded or changed. We take up this question once again and confront it with a theme current today: the theme of the secularized world. For this is the world that makes us what we are, the world in which we live, and which has this kind of self-understanding.

Description of the Concept

The concept "secularized world" contains two elements: "secularization" as description of a process and "secularism" as description of a condition or of a philosophy or worldview related to it.[1]

The process of secularization is to be described as "making worldly." More precisely, it can be described as the breaking loose that took place in all fields at the beginning of the so-called modern age—breaking loose of the world from its confinement and domination by faith and religion in antiquity and the Middle Ages. Secularization is the liberation of the world from these entanglements, the taking possession of itself as worldly, here-and-now, secular world. The result of this process is a world conscious of its independence, neither divinized nor bedeviled, the denumenized, dedemonized, demythologized world,

1. Freidrich Gogarten, *Despair and Hope for Our Time*, trans. Thomas Wieser (Philadelphia: Pilgrim Press, 1970); Hans Blumenberg, *The Legitimacy of the Modern Age*, trans. Robert M. Wallace (Cambridge, Mass.: MIT Press, 1983) Karl Rahner, "Theological Reflections on the Problem of Secularisation," *Theological Investigations* 10 (1973) 318–48; A. Keller, "Secularization," *SM* 6.64–70; C. Naveillan, *Strukturen der Theologie Friedrich Gogartens* (Munich, 1972); H. Blumenberg, *Säkularisierung als Selbstbehauptung* (Frankfurt, 1974); Heinrich Fries, "Die Säkularisierung der Neuzeit im Licht des Glaubens und der Theologie" in: *Glaube und Kirche als Angebot* (Graz, 1976) 35–61; U. Ruh, *Säkularisierung als Interpretationskategorie* (Freiburg—Basel—Vienna, 1980); "Säkularisierung" in: *Christlicher Glaube in Moderner Gesellschaft* 18 (1982) 60–100.

the world without taboos. This world is put at the disposition of human beings as the sphere of their planning, researching, making, conquering. Human beings take over the secularized world not as a house given to them, but as material for the house they themselves erect and furnish according to their will and taste. It is the striving for the kingdom of human beings that occasions the petition for the coming of the Kingdom of God. In addition, human beings no longer experience themselves as object of an unfathomable fate, an incalculable providence. Their highest virtues are no longer acceptance, patience, suffering, obedience, and resignation. Human beings understand themselves in a new and powerful way as doers, shapers of their own fate, planners of their future. Not gratitude but creativity and the transformation of the given into the willed, of nature into culture and history, constitute the position of human beings in their world. Secularization as emancipation is still in full course; the end of the road still cannot be seen.

Secularization as wresting possession of the worldliness of the world from the grasp and sovereignty of faith; secularization as the establishment of human beings as lords, shapers, and creators of nature over against what is bestowed by grace and providence; secularization as setting up the kingdom of human beings in contrast to praying for God's rule and kingdom; secularization as program of anthropocentricity over against theocentricity—all this turns out to be, if one asks about the relationship of Christian teaching to this process, countermovement, opposition, and contradiction.

In describing secularization, one can point out that the subjectivity that has come to consciousness in the philosophy of the modern age, and the anthropocentricity and autonomy in thinking and doing in this age, are in tune with this worldly world. It is characteristic of the secularized world to set itself off as anthropocentric against theocentric, as autonomy against theonomy.[2]

Secularization and Faith

Can it still be said of the secularized world, which is indeed our world, that it is reality as revelation, that it is God's creation, that it is possible to recognize God's traces in it? At first glance, everything seems to speak against this, since secularization as a process understood itself as opposition to religion and faith and drew its intellectual energies, in part, from this opposition.

Furthermore, the authoritative representatives of religion, faith, and theology rejected secularization and the secularized world because, in their opinion, it stood in opposition to that understanding of the world which the faith presupposed and took as its foundation. The sec-

2. Cf. Johannes Baptist Metz, *Christliche Anthropozentrik* (Munich, 1962).

ularized world, it is said, is the radical and conscious "no" to the world as God's creation. Secularization as an intellectual-historical process of the modern age is to be characterized as a history of decline. A historical law can be detected in it: After the battle against the Church, which broke out at the beginning of the modern age, came the battle against Christian revelation, and finally the battle against God. In his so-called "Syllabus of Errors" Pius IX presented a summary of the errors of the new age as a program for the future: the bishop of Rome will never be reconciled with or come to an understanding with progress, liberalism, and modern civilization.[3]

The First Vatican Council (1869-1870) drew the final line, so to speak, under this negative judgment by condemning, in its Constitution on the Catholic Faith, expressly or in fact, the many "isms" of the modern spirit: rationalism, atheism, materialism, relativism.[4]

However, this theological consideration of secularization, which attributes to Christian faith only the negative side of the page, is only one side of the matter. Next to it lies a totally other mode of theological judging and determining the role of Christian faith in the phenomenon and process of secularization. Its proposition goes: Secularization is a fruit of Christian faith. This proposition is maintained against the objection of those who call secularization the product of the battle against Christianity. It is maintained as a clarification of the intention of the initiators and authoritative representatives of secularization itself, who, one can say, would protest if anyone were to project onto them any motivation from faith and religion.

The fact that secularization may be a fruit of the Christian faith has been proposed in the most emphatic way by Friedrich Gogarten, but also by Max Weber[5] and Carl Friedrich von Weizsäcker.[6] It has been affirmed by J. B. Metz and Karl Rahner. And has become a kind of theological-rhetorical commonplace.

Such a judgment rests on the following fact and consideration. The fundamental phenomenon of secularization—namely, the understanding of the world as an immanent world with laws and functions, as a world entrusted to the use and responsibility of human beings—is the effect and fruit of belief in creation.

This thesis is not playing tricks with mirrors, much less looking towards some ultimate triumphalism of the Christian faith. Only in a faith that knows of the creation of the world by a sovereign, free, and transcendent God; that puts God and world apart from each other; that sets the world free in its own domain and qualifies it as finite world;

3. DS 2980.
4. DS 3021–25.
5. *Die Protestantische Ethik und der Geist des Kapitalismus* (Tübingen, 1934).
6. *Die Tragweite der Wissenschaft*, vol. 1, 2d ed. (Stuttgart, 1973).

that orders the world to human beings and elevates human beings as persons with spirit, freedom, and responsibility to the goal of creation; that in addition understands the world as a becoming and, historically, as a striving world—only in such a faith do we find the possbile intel-lectual conditions of secularization, the worldliness, of the world, and a "hominized world" (J. B. Metz). What God makes, God does not vio-late, does not swallow it up back into Himself. The acceptance of the world by God means its liberation. The specific importance of the world is not lessened but grows when it is understood as God's creation.

To illustrate this, we quote a passage from Carl Friedrich von Weizsäcker:

Whoever believes in God is no longer subject to the gods. The gods are the powers of the world in and outside of us. When we believe in God we are free in the world. The freedom from the gods, the demythologization of thought through faith, empowers human beings to become the shaping authority in the midst of nature. Only from this background can we, it seems to me, understand the secularization and the belief in science of the modern age.[7]

The control test shows this. Shaping and creatively intervening in the world, putting it at the disposition of human beings—these are im-possible in a philosophy that doesn't know the boundaries between God and world, lets the divine and the human flow into each other, under-stands the world as emanation of the divinity, is dependent for its part on the world, and makes the divine worldly and the worldly divine. These ideas were alive in the ancient religions, in their myths and cul-tures. The myth of Prometheus, who was punished with eternal torture for the robbery he committed against the gods, provides a well-known example. By their belief in God the Creator and in Jesus Christ as the Lord who freed the world of gods, the Christians were seen as "god-less," a reproach for which—among others—they were persecuted.

The difficulties for progress, development, and technical civiliza-tion that come up, for example, from the side of the religion of Hindu-ism and its conception of the immanence of the divine in all living beings, and the untouchability thereby postulated, is well known. Thus one can understand the thesis that the future of India lies in the further continuation of secularization. This holds, as many other missionaries and Christians living in India say, also for a possible future of the Christian faith in this land.

From another perspective, take a world view or faith in which the world is seen as a negative value or as mere appearance, as place of entanglement in suffering. This seems to be the case in Buddhism, where, in order to overcome suffering, human beings pursue the path of interiorization, of separation from the world, of breaking free from all things. In such a world view there can likewise be no real impulse for

7. Ibid. 47.

human beings to intervene actively, creatively, and controllingly in the world and to change it and its conditions. If such active intervention still happens, then it happens by prescinding from these presuppositions.

Secularization is an effect of creation faith. This thesis becomes even more concrete when one considers the great and liberating empowerment contained in the much-quoted, also often misunderstood words of Genesis, much more a blessing than a command: "Fill the earth and subdue it" (1:28). For one can see in natural science and technology a fulfilling of this mandate, the continuation of the sixth and seventh days of creation. Human beings are allowed to cooperate with God the Creator, with Christ the Lord of the Cosmos, with the Holy Spirit the Lord and Giver of Life. These words are no license for exploitation, but are intended to prevent exploitation.

The thesis of the derivation of secularization from creation faith is thus not a complacent, inner-theological assertion but a phenomenon that remains philosophically and historically provable even outside of faith. That should not, however, be the cause of any post-factum triumphalism. It should rather be the source of a faith-engendered courage to affirm this secularized world in its formal Christian fundamental structure as "flesh of our flesh." Though Church representatives initially and for centuries didn't want to recognize this legitimacy, but denied and opposed it, with the understandable result that the grown-up sons of secularization no longer have any interest in this genealogy, and even explicitly deny it.

Nevertheless, in theology and in the consciousness of Christian faith, we should draw attention to these origins and inner contexts of secularization. We should do this not to reap any unmerited thanks, but to point out the real ground from which the present-day world lives: namely, a correctly interpreted creation faith to which admittedly the Christians and the churches of the past did not give comprehensive enough and free enough witness, and which we are only today able to estimate in its immeasurable dimensions. In this way the alienations and needless fixations should be overcome that have so long burdened the secularized world and the Church and their mutual relationship. The view of reality and the path to it should be opened up, that the Church may rediscover a relationship to the world it has helped bring about. As Metz has said,

It is not making the world worldly that is really a misfortune of the Christian faith, but that way in which we Christians factually faced the world, or still do. Have we not, so to speak, failed to recognize our own child, or denied it, so that it ran away from us early and now, in a secularistically distorted and alienated [from us] form, now looks back on us? Did not Christianity at the dawn of the modern age enter into this new world horizon too hesitatingly, did we not close ourselves against it far too much, for the most part fundamentally suspected and denigrated it, so that the world, which was set free into a radical worldliness precisely by accepting the divine word, could stand before us in its own right only with a bad conscience? And not the inner incertitude and weakness of the worldly world, its lack of substantial authenticity but also its hubris and its false will to autonomy, follow as a consequence from the fact (but not as the only reason) that Christianity gave the world freedom in its own realm much too hesitatingly and only under protest.[8]

In the meantime there has been a change. The Pastoral Constitution of Vatican II, "The Church in the Modern World," is to date the Church's most convincing official document of a new, open and affirming specification of relationship between Church and "world." It is, so to speak, a "Counter-Syllabus," a text of the reconciliation of Church and world.

But today it seems as if this very constitution, which provided to many people access to faith and Church, is criticized and pushed aside not by people outside the Church, because it opened the Church for the world. Many theologians are saying that the text of this document is too naive and too optimistic, that it assumes a pre-theological concept of world, that it pays too little heed to distance, that it embraces an excessive belief in progress. The concepts of dialogue and cooperation are not sufficient to describe the task of the Church; there have to be clear distinctions and limitations. One no longer wants to admit and live by the fact that the windows and doors of the Church were once open. Uniformity is the new word, and the summons is: Close the doors! One can only give the advice not to follow this summons! For this uniformity leads to being closed off, and being closed off leads to sect, which is contradictory to a Church that calls itself Catholic.

Secularization and Secularism

This theme gets further clarified if, with Friedrich Gogarten, one distinguishes between secularization and secularism. Secularism is the transformation of a process into an idea and philosophy. Secularism, which means the absolutizing of secularization, lets nothing exist and have value except the empirical phenomena found in secularization. From anthropocentrism the abolition of theocentrism is taken to be an obvious conclusion. Because God doesn't appear in the secularized world; because one does not meet God in the fundamental sciences of the secularized world (mathematics, natural science, technology, linguistics); because in laboratories one neither needs nor can know God; therefore it is proclaimed by closed-system secularism: God is dead.

Secularism is the degeneration of secularization, says Gogarten. As an "ism," secularism wants to be understood as a total, "nothing but"

8. J. B. Metz, *Theology of the World*, trans. William Glen–Doepel (New York: Herder and Herder, 1969) 39.

system. It thereby denies its origin from creation faith and also withdraws from secularization as the liberation of the world by God the Creator, the bearing and liberating ground of itself. Thus secularism turns into the theory of a God-denying world in the sense of the Gospel of John. Secularism becomes an ideology, uncritical of itself, fixated and closed off, deaf and blind to realities other than those found in itself, thus making human beings into prisoners of their own self-manipulated world, thus killing off what is the real sense of secularization—subjectivity, spontaneity, freedom, and responsibility.

For the sake of an authentic secularization, that secularism has to be rejected which, in contrast to the methodical self-limitation possible in secularization, denies the creation, transcendence and sovereignty of God. For this reason secularism fends off from human beings the religious possibility that is theirs as human beings when they reflect sufficiently on themselves.[9] Nature comes to meet these human beings no longer as numinous divinity but as matter for the work of God's hands. Thus nature can no longer distort the view towards the true God in an erroneously understood "nature piety" or even in an apotheosis of nature; instead it sets free an immediacy of the human with the divine You and recognizes therein the ultimate realities encountered in the technical world.

The rejection of secularism, for the sake of secularization, as rejection of the total claims dominant there, is intended to assure to human beings that power of enablement which they need for the existence of secularization, of the world entrusted to human beings, and of the history to which they are responsible. Human beings are thus protected not only from titanism, but also from the not lesser danger that, in this "ism" they might become only a means to an end or a stage on the way to a process in which the individual experiences that well-known and multi-faceted fate: "You are nothing—the whole is everything."

The purpose of reflection on the secularized world is to ask whether it makes sense and whether one is justified in seeing in the secularized world, i.e., the world of today, a reality that can be connected with reality as revelation, reality as creation. There are good reasons for answering "yes." To be sure, the answer doesn't lie out in the open but is disclosed to reflection on the origin, on the conditions of possibility of a secularized world. One of these conditions, certainly not the only one, is an understanding of the world as different from God and thus as creation set free to be itself. By means of this its origin, and the secularized world, precisely the secularized world, is also reality as revelation.

9. Hans Urs von Balthasar, *The God Question and Modern Man*, trans. Hilda Graef (New York: Seabury Press, 1967).

That being the case, the secularized world is not contradiction to the world as creation, to the world as revelation. The world as creation is, instead, one of the most important conditions for the possibility and the undistorted realization of the secularized world.

In the debate about the secularized world as world of the modern age, Hans Blumenberg takes a remarkable position. The title of his work—*Die Legitimität der Neuzeit* [The Legitimacy of the Modern Age]—is consciously opposed to the concept of secularization. "Secularization" according to Blumenberg is a "theologically conditioned false category." They who connect modern age with secularization expose it, according to Blumenberg, to a false category and are thus actually speaking of the illegitimacy of the modern age. The modern age is rather something genuine and original. It is a break between epochs and signifies "human self-assertion over against theological absolutism."

Yet one can speak that way only if one equates the concept of secularization with that of illegitimacy and error. It was the purpose of our preceding considerations to show precisely that this is not the case. The modern age and the self-assertion that has awakened in it clearly possess a legitimacy that is also theological. There is no contesting that there is a theological absolutism, but we do indeed contest that theology as such is to be identified with it.

THE HUMAN BEING AS REVELATION

All that we have been saying about the world as creation and about the revelational quality of reality, all that we have been saying about the revelational quality of revelation itself—when we consider God the Creator as the ground of all reality, who is indeed distinct from creation but self-manifesting in it—all this holds true in a special way for human beings who are situated in the world. For their "being" can be described as a being-in, being-with, and being-toward-the-world. Thus it isn't just that human beings can know and express the createdness of reality and the manifestation of the divine included therein; for when human beings recognize their own creaturehood, they also recognize how they are constituted and what makes them what they are.

The Human Being as Creature

In all sorts of ways it is brought home to human beings that they are not sovereign creators of all things. Human beings are finite, by no means always and in all things masters of themselves. Many situations demonstrate to them their finiteness, before which they are powerless and speechless. It is in birth and death that human beings experience most strongly their passivity; for there they become most aware that they are not in control of themselves and their destiny. In all that they are, and in all that they have, and in all that happens to them, they are nothing but passive receptors. They are essentially dependent beings with uncertain and shaky futures.

Whatever position one may take on the question of God, one will have to take cognizance of the fact that human beings in any case are not their own creators; in that regard they have no possibility of choosing place and time and circumstances. One may take whatever attitude one wishes towards death, it remains in any case decided that human beings have to die, even if they enter death voluntarily—in which case they only execute in advance the sentence passed on them. And also in their existence between birth and death, human beings as called, as subject to account, as subject to question, are delivered up to passivity in all sorts of ways.[1]

Human beings experience their finiteness in their being part of a historical situation which is not of their own making; it is there and is given to them before they have any say in the matter. Human beings experience their finiteness in what happens to them without their say and often despite it: in failure, in things gone awry, in the destruction of their plans and projects, in the fragmentary character of their work, in the fragility of their achievements. Human beings experience creatureliness as finiteness in experiencing their limits and incapacities.

But this experience can be quite different. Creaturehood can also be experienced as happiness, as success, as gift, as help, as rescuing, as benign providence, as favorable circumstances. The "revelation-dimension" of these experiences gets expressed in the familiar exclamation, often used thoughtlessly, but also still quite loaded with meaning: "Thank God."

We are speaking of the human worth of every single human being without exception, of inalienable human rights, of the inviolability and "sanctity" of life, above all, of weak, unprotected, helpless life: in the child, in sick people, in those needing constant care, whose life is "justified" by no achievement, no usefulness, no remaining recognizable purpose, but still stands incontestably under the sign of nondisponibility. Human beings are not means to a purpose that is different from them; human beings are themselves and in themselves their own goal and purpose.

What is the ground of this inviolable dignity and nondisponibility given to each human being, which others cannot appropriate or take away? Is it enough just to point to it as fact, to point to tradition, custom, or habit, or to the progress achieved by human beings of the modern age? Or is the only ground that can explain even the extreme cases to be found in acknowledging that there is in human beings, as nowhere else, a revelation-being, and that this revelation-being points them beyond the finite realities and structures of human being to the "all-determining reality," namely the fact and reality of the transcendent Creator who transcends human beings in their finiteness and who, at the same time, is present in them as their deepest mystery? Does the deepest and unassailable ground for the worth of human beings lie in the fact that they are creatures of God—even more; image and likeness of God—that they thus have a worth not owed to human beings but a non-disponible worth that lays obligations on and makes claims on

1. Gerhard Ebeling, *The Nature of Faith*, trans. Ronald Gregor Smith (Philadelphia: Fortress Press, 1967).

human beings? That and much more is contained in the proposition: "To talk of human beings is to talk of God."[2]

Human Beings in Their Behavior

Human beings can encounter the world outside of themselves. They can encounter it in persons, events, things, conditions. They do this by knowing and acting. This world is given to and given over to human beings. At the same time human beings are, in turn, dependent on this world. Thus, one of the essential characteristic of human beings is their open, receptive exposure to the world, which is, at the same time, both different from them and necessary for them.[3]

The relationship of human beings to the world is characterized by the fact that over against human beings who know themselves as a unity we find the multiplicity and multiformity of things. This multiplicity, however, does not dissolve the unity of their selves but brings it to constantly new consciousness. This is clearly expressed in "I-consciousness" and in its unity.

Human beings experience their creatureliness in knowing, doing and acting. At the same time they experience therein the fact of their dependence over and beyond the present and the individual, on a comprehensive, universal horizon. Human knowledge and human activity have revelational quality not only insofar as human beings are revealed, externalized, and made known therein, but also inasfar as there is a relationship to transcendence here. When human beings question, when they want to know, when they strive after something, these acts are directed first to an individual something, to something, quite specific: to an object. But human beings don't stop with this individual something; they don't find fulfillment in it. All knowledge initiates further questions; everything that is achieved becomes itself a motive for new searching and striving. Knowing, willing and striving are in motion toward the unlimited, the boundless. This boundless something however is not only the intended goal, it is also the horizon from which knowing and willing arise.

Manifest here is the oft-described phenomenon of the boundless openness of the human spirit as well as the phenomenon of the immanently unquenched fulfillment of willing, striving, and loving. Manifest here is the inquietude of the human spirit and heart. The openness of human beings allows them to perceive, in the fundamental execution of

---

2. Rudolf Bultmann, "What Does it Mean to Speak of God?" in: *Faith and Understanding* I, trans. Louise Pettibone Smith (Philadelphia: Fortress Press, 1987).

3. The basic theme of Karl Rahner, *Spirit in the World*, trans. William Dych (New York: Continuum, 1994).

their actions, a reality constituted by that which it grounds: being, truth, value.

In its knowing, the individual activity of human beings is related to being in its intelligibility, i.e., in its truth; and in its striving and loving, this individual activity is related to being in its desirability, i.e., in its value. Consequently, this individual activity of human beings presupposes in an unrestricted sense—as indeed characteristic of being itself—the true and the good which transcend both the individual act and human beings, while at the same time being realized and affirmed in them.

The transcendentality opened up therein is the condition of the possibility for the individual action of human beings. This action is also open for the revelation present in it of a transcendence that surpasses world and human beings. Transcendentality is the presupposition of the categoriality in which it comes to expression.

Only because we know about being, preconceptually of course, do we give the contents of our knowledge the predicate "being." Only because we know about the good in general, do we have the capacity to do the good in particular which, as particular good, refers to the good as such.[4]

The tension and difference between known and asked, between achieved and willed, is understandable only if knowing and acting are not primarily grounded on the individual, concrete object—otherwise they would go no further than that—and only if this tension and difference, in an anticipatory way with the individual object, are awakened in human beings by a "foreknowledge" of truth and value. Coming again to the surface at this point is the transcendental horizon of the [thing with] being, of the true and good from which human beings are specified, and of which they have knowledge, however unthematically, and which they coaffirm and coconstitute in the individual execution of their act, and to which they turn repeatedly and in ever new ways.

The relationship between nonobjectifiable transcendence and objectifiable categoriality (transcendence as condition and ground of the individual) is nowhere so visible as in the acts of unconditioned decisions: in a radical, selfless, absolutely unshakeable and unfrustratable goodness and love, in a forgiving that pardons all guilt, in a reconciling that wipes away the traces of evil, in an absolutely selfless commitment against inhumanity in all shapes and forms. What must be done concretely in a given case stands under the sign of the individual and thus of the conditioned. But the radical and unconditioned that is

---

4. On the theme as a whole, cf. K. Rahner, *Hearers of the Word*, trans. Michael Richards (New York: Herder and Herder, 1969); *Foundations of Christian Faith: An Introduction to the Idea of Christianity*, trans. William V. Dych (New York: Crossroad, 1994).

being revealed therein comes out of the horizon and the ground of the unconditioned.

In this way human beings become aware of the transcendence they themselves are not but in their own action can experience as all-determining reality, which is a paraphrase for God. This also holds when, in human activity and behavior, God is not named in words. God is factually, i.e. through the action, acknowledged in the mode of an unconditioned, binding reality.

It follows that infiniteness and unconditionedness are not postulates born of the longing of human beings for the infinite and unconditioned, through a subsequently conceived projection of finite perfection into endless perfection. The infinite is rather the prior condition for the reality, knowability, and strivability of the individual object and human beings themselves. It can thus be no less real and valid than the world and human beings in their knowing and willing.

The unconditioned, the true and the good, can accordingly not be lacking in what belongs to knowing and willing persons, i.e., the self-presence [Bei-sich-Sein] in knowing and willing, hence freedom, spirit, personality. Without the living reality of the spirit, unconditioned being would be a dead reality; it couldn't be the supporting ground and the fulfilling goal of the knowing, striving, and acting human being.

The unconditioned, the absolute, who is called God, turns out in the course of these reflections to be that reality which is the ground of the knowing and willing world-affirmation of human beings, and therein the ground of human beings and the world itself. It is that unconditioned aspect of reality, truth, and value constantly aimed at by human beings, which grounds everything immanently real, true, and good, and which through its unconditionedness obligates the freedom of human beings to truth and goodness.

The steps, proofs and conclusions described here are by no means, of course, the reflections and expressions of all human beings. Human beings are quite capable of rejecting all that and contenting themselves with the surface reality even of their own action. But our task is to point out the possible reflection, to label what is implied, and to give it a name; our task is to lay open the origin of what is really there. Furthermore, it is important to show that the process of illumination attempted here is both possible and legitimate, that it expresses not only that which often happens wordlessly, silently, and anonymously, but also that which includes precisely in this process an acknowledgment and thus implicit knowledge of the absolute and the unconditioned as all-determining reality. The action of human beings has thus the quality of "revelation-being." It points to God.

§ 24

THE REVELATIONAL DIMENSION OF
WORD AND LANGUAGE

Language and Human Reality

Language discloses the reality of human beings, inasmuch as it is the sign, the expression, and the medium of their creatureliness. In the positive sense, this means that human beings possess a creative quality: creativity. This has its field of expression in language, in speaking in its varied forms. Human beings are linguistically creative.

Modern language philosophy[1] distinguishes between informative and performative speech. Informative speech observes and describes. It expresses facts, dates, and events. Through language, reality is grasped; it becomes "language." Language is language of news. This way of speaking should not conceal the fact that there is no such thing as objective news as such, and that the so-called "act of speaking" always gives to news some particular interpretation. Every reporting of news is a selection. That selection and the accents it sets already constitute an interpretation that depends on the subjective grounds and motives which do not appear in the apparently objective news report. News can be manipulated. This is most obvious in totalitarian systems, but is by no means limited to them. Manipulation of news is found everywhere in the age of the "mass media."

In contrast to informative language, performative language doesn't try to report reality; instead it creates and constitutes reality. Language becomes reality-creating, reality-changing activity. In expres-

---

1. H. J. Green, *The World and Spiritual Realities* (Ann Arbor, 1981, Microfilm); L. Wittgenstein, *Tractatus Logico–Philosophicus* (Atlantic Highlands, 1975); H. B. Müller-Schwefe, *Die Sprache und das Wort* (Hamburg, 1961): Martin Heidegger, *On the Way of Language*, trans. Peter D. Hertz (San Francisco: Harper & Row, 1982); Gerhard Ebeling, *Gott und Wort* (Tübingen, 1966); F. X. Mayr, "Language," *SM* 3.268–74; *Introduction to a Theological Theory of Language*, trans. R. A. Wilson (Philadelphia: Fortress Press, 1973); J. L. Austin, *How to Do Things with Words* (Cambridge, Mass.: Harvard University Press, 1962); B. Casper, *Sprache und Theologie* (Freiburg—Basel—Vienna, 1972).

sions like: I promise, I forgive, I love, I believe you, I give you my "yes," or when passing judgment, it isn't so much that something different from word and language is established or named; instead, reality is constituted and opened up. Language creates reality, which, without language and apart from it, simply would not be. This becomes most clear in sacramental action. Sacraments receive their "form" and their reality through word, e.g., "I baptize you," "I absolve you," or the pronouncing of the words of institution at the Lord's Supper. Thus one can say with Karl Rahner that sacrament is the supreme instance of word.

Language discloses and reveals the reality of human beings, and to that extent makes them free. Freedom, says Ebeling, [2] is dependent on language. Through speech human beings achieve distance from the speechless compulsion of instincts and habit, from the immediately present and existing, from the apparently inevitable, and are led to the possibility of decision. Freedom is called forth by speaking to human beings in such a way that they are let into the space of freedom promised and offered to them. The freedom movements gather around the words of freedom: the Reformation with Luther's words "On the Freedom of the Christian"; the French Revolution under the sign of "Freedom, Equality, Fraternity" the Communist Manifesto: "You have nothing to lose but your chains. Proletarians of all countries, unite!"

Because human beings have to learn how to speak, language discloses their reality as indebted beings. It introduces them to an historical origin and tradition, to all kinds of relationships of belonging and communication, and they remain connected to these. Language discloses the reality of human beings as beings stamped by origin, tradition, society, and mediation, as historical beings.

Language discloses and reveals the reality of human beings insofar as, they have, through language, the possibility of making invisible, absent, past, and future things present—the very essence of what is meant by history or transcendence. Through their historicity, which is stamped by remembering, making present, and expectation, and which they can express in language, human beings are taken out of the shackling, bewitching, fixating immediacy of the present moment and liberated into the breadth of their possibilities.

Language and word disclose the reality of human beings insofar as they open up the dialogical structure and situation of human beings, their constitution as being with others, as being with one another. The fundamental form of word and language is dialogue. Language is conversation, dialogue; monologue is interrupted dialogue. No one can speak [just] out of him/herself. And no one can be satisfied with just speaking alone. Human beings speak not only because they have received

---

2. G. Ebeling, *Gott und Wort* 49.

language from others as spoken before them, but because they need to receive an answer to their own word, a resonance to what they say.

In addition, in the interhuman realm disclosed by word and speech, human beings are dependent on freedom so that the freedom of their words as mediation and representation of themselves is guaranteed: the freedom of speech. Language likewise includes the free presence of the you with whom one is speaking. And in all this, human beings become aware, in their orientation and dependence, that they cannot force the acceptance and understanding of their words.

The extent to which language as revelation of human beings is the expression and form of sociality and co-humanity, is shown in the fact that human difficulties, inhibitions, blockages, misunderstandings find their strongest expression and representation in human beings unable to speak or talk with each other: they have nothing more to say; they become aware of their barriers in the form of insuperable language barriers; they misunderstand everything that is said or they become speechless. Sicknesses and crises can result, also what is increasingly recognized today: that fact that dialogue and the things leading up to it have a healing, freeing, and often redeeming function, if the "redeeming word" is spoken at the right time.

The problem of language at this particular moment in time becomes especially recognizable where the question of the self-discovery of the human being has become a major theme. Bernhard Casper thinks that the problem of self-discovery is represented as a lack of language, as a

breaking down of the language community into many group-specific languages which no longer understand each other. The language of the older generation differs from the language of the younger generation. The language of theory differs from the language of praxis. The language of science from the language of lived life. The highly specialized languages of technicians differ from the language that is understood on the street. The language of bureaucrats differs from the language of those who are administered by them. And the language of one ideological block differs from the language of the other. Alienation is manifested immediately in the difficulty or impossibility of talking with and understanding each other. But this again shows that language is not a peripheral phenomenon for human beings, as is often thought, not something that just happens to come about with other human things. One has language not just in the way in which one possesses a house, or stocks, or a tool. Rather, language is the expression of actually being human. Insofar as anyone is human, he/she exists due to language. Insofar as we are human beings with each other, we exist with each other in our speaking.[3]

Word and language disclose the creatureliness of human beings as finite and limited reality. How often it happens that the word remains behind what it would like to make perceivable. We search for words, we struggle for the right, the proper word. All too often the word falsifies reality through error, deception, or lie. All too often word is

3. B. Casper, *Sprache und Theologie* 14.

powerless in the face of certain overwhelming or impenetrable situations and events. All too often word remains speechless, and language "ties up human beings."

Human beings come hereby to the knowledge that they have neither the first nor the last word, that they are oriented to a word that is not their word or the word of other human beings, but is a word of power, truth, love, and freedom. A word that hungers after all words and languages, is present in all words and languages, but in the form of limitedness, of inability, of brokenness, of fragmentation. In it the "word beyond words" (H. U. von Balthasar) is awaited, the word is not spoken by human beings to human beings, the word that comes from the mouth of God, the word of God.

Through the power and the powerlessness of word and language, language possesses dimensions of revelation. It opens up in very special ways the reality of human beings as creatures in power and helplessness, and keeps awake and alive the question of the ground of created being. Thus its revelational relationship is described as relationship to transcendence.

Speaking of God

If human beings can express everything through word, they can also express that all-determining reality called God. God is a word of our language. This is precisely where language manifests its greatness and its limits.

The spirit and language of human beings are related to the "world" of which they become aware through perception, observation and encounter. Human beings are Spirit in World (K. Rahner); they know nothing that they have not previously "apperceived" and ordered by concepts and categories. Thus, with regard to speaking of God, who is not an object of the world or in the world but its unobjective ground, one can talk only indirectly—mediated by the realities that have been called *world, creation, human being*. At the same time we are dependent on these in order to be able to say anything at all about God. This is again possible through the "being-manifest" of all reality which we spoke about earlier.

In other words, one can talk about God only analogously, in the form of correspondence; this correspondence is grounded in the already-mentioned *analogia entis* (analogy of being) between God and world, between Creator and creature.

As an example of analogous speech Aristotle has referred to the many uses of the word "healthy." One speaks of a healthy body, healthy medicine, healthy blood, healthy nourishment, healthy clothing. Quite different things are labeled with the word "healthy."

The connection consists in the fact that all these objects mentioned relate to one common thing. Medicine is healthy because it brings about health, nourishment and clothing because they contribute to health, blood because it is an indication of health, the body because it is healthy or has been made healthy.[4] The ground for analogy thus lies in the fact that different things have a different relationship to one common thing. It is health, being healthy, which can be said primarily of the body and then of other things.

God can also be spoken of in the mode of analogous speech, when, e.g., we say of God that God exists. That is said also of the world and of human beings. The difference lies in the fact that God, as ground of all being, possesses being and is its origin; the human being, in contrast, receives being. Analogous speech also makes it possible for God to be called Father in the sense of a relational analogy, or for the attributes of perfection to be attributed to God. The invisible, unperceivable God is spoken of with images and concepts from our world of perception.

The ground of a possible analogous way of talking about God lies in the fact that the reality of the world as a whole and in its individual parts has a relation to one common [thing]. In other words, the relational being of Creator and creature makes possible the analogy of being as a possible way of talking about God—as talk about correspondence, about similarity and dissimilarity. It is the fate and the predicament of human beings to be able to talk about God, and to have to talk about God, but without being able to do so in an adequate way.

In his work *Gott als Geheimnis der Welt* [God as Mystery of the World], Eberhard Jüngel made himself a firm advocate of analogy as a theological category. But he stakes out a noteworthy difference from our position. He says that there is only one analogy between God and human beings—and that is in Jesus Christ. Thus, talk about Jesus Christ is analogous talk; analogous talk about God can only be talk about Jesus or telling the story of Jesus. Analogy is grounded not in creation as the fundamental situation of all reality, but in Christology alone.[5]

Over against this way of grounding the analogy of God and world, the question has to be asked: How do I get to the point of bringing God into connection with Jesus, and Jesus with God, if before Christ and outside of Christ there is no access to God? And how can Jesus speak to his listeners about God and make himself understood if God were somehow not already known to them?

Only if human beings, even before and apart from Christ and the Christian message, are related to the reality of God in their being

---

4. Aristotle's *Metaphysics* G 1003a, 33–35.; on this cf. Eberhard Jüngel, *God as the Mystery of the World: On the Foundation of the Theology of the Crucified in the Dispute between Theism and Atheism*, trans. Darrell L Guder (Grand Rapids. Mich.: William B. Eerdmans Publishing Company, 1983).

5. E. Jüngel, *God as the Mystery of the World* 261–314.

human, can the message of Jesus become relevant and can communion with Jesus signify salvation. "Only for human beings moved by the question of God, or in any case for human beings touched by it, can Jesus the human take on authority grounded in reason. We must be clear about the fact that to give up the idea of God would bring us dangerously close to the end of Christianity."[6]

The Word "God"

"God," or its translations or correlates, is a word of our language and is used with surprising frequency . These phrases and expressions come from a time in which the consciousness of God as all-determining reality was still very alive and intensive. Presumably our technical world would be neither capable nor particularly well disposed to the creation of such phrases. Yet it is noteworthy that these words do come up in the language-play of human beings who, when asked for the meaning of these usages, become embarrassed. It is manifestly remarkable that there has been no success in getting rid of this connection of our language with God—or in replacing it with another word.

Ebeling asks:

What can the word God do? Isn't it in any case so full of meanings and so unclear that it no longer says anything to someone looking for clear concepts and precise definitions? The classical Christian doctrine of God has, to be sure, always held for the non-definability of God as corresponding to God's essence. But it has always seen therein the ground of that about which the word God gives endless reason to think. The apparent lack of precision of meaning is something that this word shares with all words which are not labels for ready-made goods, but are, so to speak, calls and signals which, in their content, demand of human beings an inner movement to which the word in question points out the direction.[7]

In support of this it can also be said, in an application of the distinction between informative and performative language, that God can and should also be spoken about above all in the performative mode. The word "God" discloses and bestows reality, by bringing things about, by creating change, conversion, and renewal, and by putting into words what is meant by all-determining reality and what concretely follows from that. This reality should not only be known, but also be acknowledged by existence and praxis. It should not, to use the words of the Epistle to the Romans, be "suppressed by wickedness" (Rom 1:18).

6. Wolfhart Pannenberg, *Gottesgedanke und Menschliche Freiheit* (Göttingen, 1972) 32 and 35.
7. G. Ebeling, *Gott und Wort* 63

§ 25

CONSCIENCE

Description of Conscience

Conscience[1] is the venue of action assigned to human beings. It is a constituent part of what is proper to them as human, like spirit, will, or language—qualities that have an inner dynamic towards the actualization of a specific function, namely the voice of conscience and the decision of conscience. Conscience is characterized by that to which it is related, the moral values: justice and injustice, good and evil. These are the claim of reality on the human person. The Good is thus that quality of reality which is ordered to human beings,[2] that quality within their being on the basis of which the Good can also be aspired to as the goal of their will. Every obligation is thus grounded in being. Reality is the foundation of the ethical.

If I thus want to know how I should conduct myself in marriage, family, profession, government, technology, art, science, etc., I must first know what significance these spheres of life have for human persons and their social relationships, what laws are in effect in them, what meaning-values are represented in them, what historical possibilities are open to them, and what their limitations are. Only then can it become clear to me how I must conduct myself with them so that they can fulfill their meaning and function for human existence in an optimal way. The true being of reality, the inner truth of things, becomes the measure and norm of action.[3]

---

1. Cf. the textbooks and handbooks of moral theology. Ultimately, B. Häring, *Free and Faithful and Christ: Moral Theology for Priests and Laity*, vol 2; *The Truth Will Set You Free* (New York: Seabury Press, 1978); G. Stocker, *Das Gewissen* (Bonn, 1925); Martin Heidegger, *Being and Time* (New York: Harper, 1962) 315–25; M. Hollenbach, *Sein und Gewissen* (Baden–Baden, 1954); J. Stelzenberger, *Syneidesis, Conscientia, Gewissen* (Paderborn, 1964).

2. J. Pieper, *Living the Truth: The Truth of All Things and Reality and the Good* (San Francisco: Ignatius Press, 1989).

3. A. Auer, *Autonome Moral und sittlicher Glaube* (Düsseldorf, 1971) 16.

The function of conscience is described as follows. Conscience is a knowledge of being insofar as being is a value which can be aspired after, insofar as it is a "should-be," a knowledge of moral value, the moral values themselves. This doesn't have to be reflexive knowledge; a knowledge of the morally good or morally evil in general, and of its concretization in a specific action is enough. Moral value is affirmed by conscience, moral disvalue rejected. This is where the moment of obligation, the moral imperative, comes in. Good is to be done unconditionally; evil and injustice is to be refrained from, to be rejected, avoided, and resisted.

Conscience has, finally, the function of a sanction, of a court of judgment on action and on what has been done, on the deed done, on the action not undertaken. In this function of conscience, witnesses, prosecutors, and judges have their moments. The judgment made by conscience after a deed of action can be approval and acquittal or disapproval and condemnation. These phenomena are generally described as a good or bad conscience. Conscience thus embraces all the dimensions of human beings: recognition and knowledge, willing and aspiring, joy and pain.

Conscience is a co-knowledge, is con-scientia. The knowledge that comes about in conscience cannot prescind from the subject, and the subject cannot in any distancing way "hold itself out." Conscience is related to living unity: to the "I" of the human being as person. The co-knowledge of conscience includes self-consciousness in responsibility, and this co-knowledge found in conscience includes still more: it includes, internal to the process of conscience itself, an other as co-knower, as witness, as plaintiff, and as judge.

The Dialectic of Conscience

On the one hand I experience conscience as identical with myself. Nothing is so much my own, indeed my "I," as my conscience. I cannot get rid of the consciousness that ultimately I am responsible, not someone else for me. When conscience speaks, I always answer myself. So much am I one with my conscience that it would be more proper to say "I am my conscience" than "I have conscience."

On the other hand, I experience the speaking of my conscience just as intensively as something else: as the representative of a "not I," of something else in me. I experience the venue of responsibility like the ambassador of another power and reality, of a power located outside of my "I-sphere." I have to bend to it because it is right. Even if I act against it—and especially then—I concede it its right in that I feel guilty.

As Martin Heidegger points out, the call of conscience is both something that is in me and at the same time something that comes over me.

Conscience is represented to human beings as call and hearing together.[4] Conscience can be regarded as the basic characteristic of human beings. They are characterized not by the fact that they have understanding but by the fact they have conscience and responsibility. Conscience is what makes the being-human of the human being. Human beings experience themselves in conscience as individuals not identical with themselves, but who are asked about their identity with themselves. Their identity is found in this being-asked. Conscience is thus a disclosure of the reality of human beings, of their greatness and limitations, of their disposing and being disposed, of their independence and dependence.

The Interpretation of Conscience

The direction of our interpretation is already indicated in our reference to the totality aspect of conscience, in which claims are made on human beings as person, on their self, in which they experience themselves as both called to and listened to, in which word and answer is demanded of them, since they become aware of the identity and non-identity of their self. The direction of the interpretation lies also in the fact of the personal structure of conscience as well as its transcending dimension recognizable in its obligatory and sanctioning aspects.

Finally, one interpretation lies in the observation that conscience is a call, a voice, more precisely, the echo of a voice. Call and voice, which are in me and at the same time come over me, refer to person. The person, however, to which conscience as echo refers, cannot be the person of my own "I," but another, an essentially transcendent person. An "echo" of the voice indicates intervention, possibly a "breaking" of the call of conscience. This interpretation corresponds to the phenomenon of conscience and what is observable there, and does it justice. That is not the case for an interpretation that fails to do this.

We will now present some interpretations of conscience which take these experiences as their foundation. The reflections of Immanuel Kant on this question have already been presented in our analysis of his so called philosophical faith (see above § 3).

John Henry Newman[5] interpreted the experiences of conscience as follows. He calls conscience a primordial human experience. He speaks of conscience as a moral instinct. Conscience is a moral sense and a sense of obligation, a judgment of reason and an authoritative command. Conscience does not rest in/on itself but touches on a reality beyond itself and recognizes an approval of its actions that is higher than

4. Gerhard Ebeling, "Theological Relections on Conscience" in: *Word and Faith* (Philadelphia: Fortress Press, 1963) 412–14.

5. Cf. Heinrich Fries, *Die Religionsphilosophie Newmans* (Stuttgart, 1948); J. Schulte, "Das Gewissen in seinen sittlichen und religiösen Funktionen nach J. H. Newman" in: *Newman-Studien VII*, ed. J. Fries—W. Becker (Nuremberg 1968) 127–246.

itself. This becomes knowable in the consciousness of unconditional obligation and responsibility.

If, as is the case, we feel responsibility, are ashamed, are frightened, at transgressing the voice of conscience, this implies that there is One to whom we are responsible, before whom we are ashamed, whose claims upon us we fear . . . . we have no remorse or compunction on breaking mere human law: yet, so it is, conscience excites all these painful emotions, confusion, foreboding, self-condemnation; and on the other hand it sheds upon us a deep peace, a sense of security, a resignation, and a hope, which there is no sensible, no earthly object to elicit. 'The wicked flees, when no one pursueth;' then why does he flee? whence his terror? Who is it that he sees in solitude, in darkness, in the hidden chambers of his heart? If the cause of these emotions does not belong to this visible world, the Object to which his perception is directed must be Supernatural and Divine; and thus the phenomena of Conscience, as a dictate, avail to impress the imagination with the picture of a Supreme Governor, a Judge, holy, just, powerful, all-seeing, retributive, and is the creative principle of religion, as the Moral Sense is the principle of ethics.[6]

The phenomena of ontic flight, of ontic acquaintance [*Bekanntsein*] and of ontic guilt (G. Stocker) have their roots here.

Max Scheler in his treatise *Reue und Wiedergeburt* [Repentance and Rebirth] took the following position on the phenomenon of conscience.

The stirrings of conscience seem like a wordless, natural language, which God speaks with the soul and whose instructions concern its salvation. It is a question whether it is even possible to separate the unity and sense of the stirrings of conscience from this interpretation as a sign language of God, and to do that in such a way that their unity, which we call conscience, would still exist. It seems to me to require no real interpreting act in order to give to the psychological material of these stirrings the function by which they present such a judge. They themselves exercise of themselves this God-presenting function, and vice versa; it requires a closing-of-the-eyes and a looking-away in order not to experience these functions in themselves.[7]

Scheler makes these fundamental considerations concrete with his phenomenology of remorse. He says:

If there were nothing else in the world from which we were to form the idea of God, remorse alone could make us aware of God's existence. Remorse begins with an indictment. But before whom do we indict ourselves? Isn't it essential of an indictment, even a necessary essential, that there be a person who hears it and before whom the indictment takes place? Remorse is, in addition, an inner confession of our guilt. But to whom, then, do we confess, when lips are externally silent and we are alone with our soul? And to whom is this guilt, which presses on us, owed? The remorse comes to an end with the clear consciousness of the removal of guilt, of the eradication of guilt. But who took the guilt from us; who or what can do that? Remorse speaks its judgment according to a law felt to be holy, which we have not given ourselves but which nevertheless lives in our heart. And yet it releases us almost in the same breath from the consequences of this law for us and

6. John Henry Newman, *An Essay in Aid of a Grammar of Assent* (Notre Dame: University of Notre Dame Press, 1979) 101.

7. Max Scheler, *On the Eternal in Man*, trans. Bernard Nobel (Hamden, Conn.: Archon Books, 1972) 35.

our activity. But where is the lawgiver of this law, and who other than the law-giver could restrict the consequences of the law for us? Remorse gives us a new power of purpose and—in certain cases—a new heart out of the ashes of the old. But where is the source of power, and where is the idea for the construction of this new heart, and where is the power that causes its construction?

Thus from every partial stirring of this great moral process there is an intentional movement aimed into an intentional sphere, a movement which, left only to itself and not diverted by any hasty interpretation, also sketches out as if by itself before the eyes of our spirit the mysterious lines of an infinite judge, an infinite mercy and an infinite power and source of life.[8]

We say that conscience is not just a representation of the reality of human beings, but that it makes this very reality intelligible as the revelation-being of human beings, as the revelation of a transcendent instance which has power of disposition over human beings, makes claims on them, and passes judgment on them. But is it then too much to claim further that, since its dispository power over human beings is so radical and unconditional, this instance cannot be beneath the level of being of what is meant by person?

Conscience is thus the revelation of a reality transcending human beings, profoundly affecting them, and with dispository power over them. Thus considered, conscience is the place and the realization of religion, in which the religion of human beings and God is represented and realized.

Paul speaks explicitly about conscience in the Epistle to the Romans when he describes the condition of human beings before and apart from Christ. He says:

When the gentiles, who have not the law, do by nature what the law requires, they are a law to themselves, even though they do not have the law. They show that what the law requires is written on their hearts, while their conscience also bears witness, and their conflicting thoughts accuse or perhaps excuse them (Rom 2:14-15).

Ernst Käsemann interprets this passage as follows:

Paul is trying to say that even the pagans experience the transcendent claim of the divine will. They have a sense that human beings are challenged with questions and demands from outside of themselves, and they experience it paradoxically from within, from the law written in their hearts. Human beings are thereby brought up against the unconditionally obligatory. Pagans experience the will of God not from the Torah (the Law) like the Jews, but reflected, as it were, from the law written in their hearts. Paul introduces the concept of conscience into the New Testament as a perception of a claim made on human beings. In the same way, conscience is—in a kind of forensic process—witness, plaintiff, and defendant.

In the *actio* of their decision for that transcendent claim which human beings experience in their own heart, and in the *reactio* of their self-criticism, as in the unceasing dialectic of their judgments on themselves, it becomes clear, in Paul's

8. Ibid. 61.

view, that human beings have and live by criteria that do not come from themselves. As far as they, in general, turn against him, they might deny them or fight against them. But they don't silence them. Precisely in their innermost being, human beings are not their own masters. They don't give themselves the criteria directed against them, and each of them would, if possible, put an end to the splitting of their own I. An other is looking at us when we have to be critical of ourselves, and that other contradicts us in the contradiction of our life. The shadow of the judge falls on our innermost being and turns us into the tribunal.[9]

From this understanding of conscience involving the whole human being and orienting him/her to transcendence, it is understandable that conscience is the last, highest, and unconditional instance for human action and behavior, and that there can be no higher obligation than to follow one's conscience. In conscience the whole human being with all his/her powers and capacities and all his/her dimensions is present. The need to follow conscience unconditionally is, to be sure, possible only—and only then rational and permitted—if and because a claim is made on the conscience by that absolute, unconditioned reality whom we call God, only if—however mediated—God makes Himself known, manifest and perceivable in the conscience. This also holds true for the so-called "errant" conscience, i.e., for a conscience that can be in error with regard to a particular good required and right called for; but conscience is incapable of error in its demand that the good recognized should be done.

"Conscience stands up"—is the title of a documentary volume in which the deeds of the men of July 20, 1944, and their insurrection against Hitler are described. The actions of the Scholl sister and brother, of the White rose, of Professor Kurt Huber [Germans executed for resisting Hitler] and many others were, according to their own witness, confirmed in death, legitimated and demanded by their conscience: as resistance against the person-enslaving power, against the lie and the evil in its embodiment at that time. To follow the call of conscience was worth more to them than life. This explains why it was that Hitler made it his job, as he himself said, to take conscience away from human beings on the grounds that conscience is a fantasy, a Jewish-Christian invention. In fact, conscience is a constant counter-instance and counter-force against all forms of humanity-confiscating, yes humanity-destroying totalitarianism. A conscience decision is the highest instance of human freedom.

Freedom is the contradiction of all forms of dictatorship. That is why dictatorship sees in conscience its greatest enemy, which is to be fought against with all means and which, if at all possible, must be rooted out.

9. Ernst Käsemann *Commentary on Romans*, trans. Geoffrey W. Bromiley (Grand Rapids: Mich.: William B. Eerdmans Publishing Company, 1980) 65–66.

Other Interpretations of Conscience

The interpretation of conscience we have presented is, these days, not without challenge. Other interpretations and derivations of conscience have also sprung up. It must be asked, however, whether they correspond to and take account of what conscience is overall and not just in certain aspects.

For example, there is the thesis that conscience has been formed from individual and social experiences of usefulness, which it then validates. Against this is the fact that the voice of conscience and the judgment of conscience often enough speak explicitly against considerations of usefulness and purposefulness, because what is good and just is in no way identical with what is useful. Every martyr is an example of that.

Much more serious in its consequences, and more effectively widespread, is the theory presented by Sigmund Freud in his critique of religion. It comes under his program: *The Future of an Illusion*.[10] According to Freud, it is primarily conscience that belongs to the religion-supporting illusions. Freud describes it according to both its obliging and guiding as well as its indicting and exonerating aspects. He describes conscience as an inner perception of the rejection of certain wish impulses within us. This rejection needs no appeal to anything else; it is sure of itself. On the basis of his observations, Freud can see this inner perception, called conscience, not as in inborn quality of human beings; it arises from the ground of a feeling-situation specific to childhood: ambivalence. According to Freud, there is no primordial human decision-making capacity regarding good and evil. Good and evil arise much more from foreign influences. They determine what good and evil are supposed to be. This becomes manifest above all in the life of the helpless child bonded to and dependent on its parents, the most important persons in its relationship.

For the child, good is what is willed and commanded by its parents and for which the child is rewarded with recognition, praise, love, and protection. Evil is what these relational persons explain as evil, what one is not allowed to do. Evil is something that is punished by the withdrawal of love. Accordingly, good and evil are to be determined for the child originally and concretely by the bestowal or withdrawal

10. Albert Görres, *The Methods and Experience of Psychoanalysis*, trans. Nicholas Wharton (New York: Sheed and Ward, 1962); Joachim Scharfenberg, *Sigmund Freud and the Critique of Religion*, trans. O. C. Dean, Jr. (Philadelpia Fortress Press, 1988); J. Zahrnt, ed., *Jesus und Freud* (Munich, 1972); Heinrich Fries, "Die Gottesfrage in der Begegnung mit der Psychoanalyse" in: H. Fries, ed., *Gott—die Frage unserer Zeit* (Munich, 1973) 61–74; P. Ricoeur, *Hermeneutics and the Human Sciences: Essays on Language, Action, and Interpretation* (New York: Cambridge University Press, 1981); Hans Küng, "God—an Infantile Illusion? Sigmund Freud" in: *Does God Exist? An Answer for Today*, trans. Edward Quinn (Garden City, N. Y.: Doubleday, 1980) 262–340.

of love or protection. Good is that for which one is rewarded, evil is that for which one is punished. For this reason it doesn't make much difference whether, e.g., the evil has already been done or is still to be done; in either case it becomes dangerous only when the authority of the parents, of the father, discovers it.

When one calls this condition bad conscience, that is not, according to Freud, an accurate description. On the child's level, consciousness of guilt is nothing but anxiety over the loss of love, i.e., social fear.

Social anxiety as real consciousness of guilt or as bad conscience continues to exist when, in the course of one's life and development, other human beings take the place of the parents. This takes the form of the respective society or milieu, or of public opinion with its patterns of behavior in the form: one does this, one does not do that; this is becoming, this is expected. This sets up new instances for good and evil. Up against this new authority of society, public opinion, and milieu, the most important moral rule and behavioral norm of so-called conscience consists in the matter, the act, the behavior not becoming known. If there is no danger of this, there are also no moral restraints of any kind. This means that it is not morality but possible scandal that becomes the deciding voice and criterion of "conscience." Evil is scandal; scandal, not the deed, brings the pangs of conscience and causes remorse.

A decisive change in the development and life of human beings takes place when Freud's so-called "superego" takes over in place of parents, father, society, and milieu. This eliminates the external influence. I myself am/become the relational person in the establishment of the "superego," of the better "I," which still remains wholly in the realm of the human. This lifts the phenomena of conscience up to a new level. Basically—according to Freud—one should only at this point begin to talk about conscience and guilt-feeling. In the realm of the ego and superego, fear of discovery disappears and with it the distinction between willing evil and doing evil. For I can hide nothing from my ego and superego, not even intentions and thoughts. Still, the pangs and anxiety of conscience remain. The influence of formation makes the past of human beings live on from the earliest levels of development. Thus the origins of human beings live on in them even when they are grown up; things remain the way they were in the beginning. The "superego" torments the sinful ego with the "same feeling of anxiety as in childhood, and lies in wait for opportunities to make it suffer punishment from the outer world."

At the final level of development, conscience manifests, according to Freud, a peculiarity that is not easy to explain. It acts more strictly and more mistrustfully the more virtuous the human being, is so that, in the end, precisely those who have made the greatest progress in holiness accuse themselves of the worst sinfulness.

As long as things go well for human beings, their conscience remains mild and allows the ego all kinds of things; but when they suffer misfortune they enter into themselves, acknowledge their sinfulness, increase the claims of their consciences, impose deprivations on and punish themselves with penance. Whole nations have acted and continue to act this way. But this is explained by the original, infantile level of conscience, which, after its interjection into the superego, is not left behind but continues to exist beside and behind it. Fate is seen as substitute for the judgment of parents; if one suffers misfortune, this means that one is no longer loved by this highest power and is threatened by this loss of love.[11]

From his analyses of conscience, Freud comes to the conclusion: to interpret conscience and its functions and reactions by appealing to God as all-determining, transcending, personal reality is an illusion. The God of human beings is in truth the exaggerated figure of a father who threatens, who forbids, who also comforts and can reconcile human beings with the hardness of life. But this father is not a god different from human beings; he is a human being—as individual or community or as superego. This connection should, according to Freud, be made conscious; for that means the end of the illusion. According to Freud, this illusion can be dissolved only by the "God Logos"—science,—which destroys the wish-principle and acknowledges its allegiance to the reality-principle.

For Freud, therefore, it is unimaginable that our "poor, ignorant, unenlightened, unfree ancestors could have found the answer to this difficult world riddle in their religious affirmations. That really can't be true! Only the weak and the ignorant will hold on to this conception of wishing and wish-world. The wishful thinking that gets expressed in religion is, according to Freud, so patent, infantile and estranged from reality that it becomes painful to think that the great majority of mortals will never be able to raise themselves beyond this conception of life. Against this Freud calls for an educational attitude to reality, to insight, to enlightenment. Human beings cannot remain children forever; experience tells us: "The world is not a children's room."[12]

In his last work, in his lectures "Zur Einführung in die Psychoanalyse" [Introduction to Psychoanalysis], Freud is still writing:

Religion is an attempt to control the sense world [Sinnenwelt] with the wish world. But it is unable to do this. Its doctrines bear the mark of the times from which they come: the mark of ignorant children and of the ignorant childhood of humanity. When one attempts to locate religion in the course of development of humanity, it turns out to be the counter-piece of the neurosis that individual cultured human beings have to work through and overcome on their way from childhood to maturity.[13]

---

11. Sigmund Freud, *Civilization and Its Discontents*, trans. James Strachey (New York: W. W. Norton and Company) 73.

12. *Gesammelte Werke* XIV, 6th ed. (Frankfurt, 1976) 356.

13. *Gesammelte Werke* XV.

Also taking place in this process, according to Freud, is the procedure, carried out with full commitment by human beings of withdrawing their expectations from transcendence and turning them to earthly reality. This takes place through the "God Logos," through science, through the power and the mandate to open up reality.

> Our God Logos will turn into reality that part of these wishes nature gives us. Scientific [i.e., scholarly] work is the only way that can lead to the knowledge of reality outside ourselves. This science is no illusion. It would be an illusion to believe that we could get from some place else what science cannot give us.[14]

How far the power of the God Logos extends is made clear by the following consideration. Taking off from the thesis of Wittgenstein that, when all scientific problems have been solved, not a single problem of life has yet been solved, we can say: when the problems of neurosis are solved, the decisive problems of life make their appearance. Freud asks himself the following question:

> When I ask myself why I have always striven, honestly, to be ready to be sparing of others and to be as kind as possible, and why I haven't given that up when I noticed that one gets hurt in so doing, I really don't know what to answer.[15]

Reflections on Sigmund Freud's Analyses of Conscience

What do we have to say about the phenomenon of conscience and its development? Conscience takes part in the life, being, growth and maturing of human beings and goes through the stages of conscience based on custom, conscience based on authority, and mature, independent, personal conscience. Thus it is no wonder that a role is played here by those elements which characterize the life of human beings on their journey: the authority of the father, of the parents, the milieu, society and the system of norms which are dominant in it. It is similar to the other processes of life, for example speaking and language.

The Freudian so-called "superego" which, according to him, replaces the early phases but maintains the patterns of behavior determined by them, can participate in the maturing of the person as a kind of psychological structure. It works in the manner of an easing of the burden in situations which are predetermined by custom, taste and convention. For all that we would still have to explain or give the reason why, in situations of conventional action and behavior, there is not only a formal aspect but also a consensus regarding content, above all of a negative kind: i.e., this or that should not be done in any case: hatred, lying, violence, oppression, terror, torture.

14. S. Freud, *The Future of an Illusion*, trans. W. D. Robson-Scott (Garden City, N. Y.: Doubleday, 1964) 55–92.

15. Ernest Jones, *The Life and Work of Sigmund Freud* (New York: Basic Books, 1981) location of quote unavailable.

But in the life and development of human beings there are also situations in which conscience relativizes parents, authorities, and conventions, and even abrogates them. The independent, mature, and articulate conscience doesn't ask whether its voice and decision will bring with it a loss of love, bad feelings, disadvantages, or punishment; instead it asks above all whether "it's okay," whether the deed to be answered for fits in with one's sense of being, or, more concretely, whether it does or does not do justice to the claim of what is authoritative reality for human beings. The determining proposition is: the known good is to be done under all circumstances independently of whether or not it pleases the authorities of childhood or the present. This unconditional imperative of conscience admits of no limitation or relativization, although it does require specification with regard to the respective deed. In the realm of conscience, therefore, there are aspects of unchangeability as well as changeability. There is also misuse, when the appeal to conscience is made to serve unconscientious purposes and interests. Still, what is there that cannot be misused! And of course, *corruptio optimi pessima* [the corruption of the best is the worst corruption of all]. But these facts constitute no refutation of the matter of conscience itself and of the authoritative ethical directive given in it.

The criterion is the serious case: the situation of the confessor, the witness, the martyr. The Freudian interpretation of conscience by father-image, society, milieu, and superego cannot explain the extraordinary, exemplary decisions of conscience: i.e., the decision of conscience made against the power of tradition or milieu, against the norms of the respectively existing society. Decisions are made here where neither earthly loss nor external gain come into question, but only the matter itself: the overcoming of evil, its forms and powers, and commitment for the known good thing, for justice.

Examples of such decisions are in good supply: Socrates, the prophets, the confessors and martyrs of the Christian faith, Luther in Worms, Thomas More, Alfred Delp, Dietrich Bonhoeffer, Graf Moltke, Maximilian Kolbe, and Oscar Romero. These decisions of conscience cannot be explained by Freud's theory of conscience.

But whoever is unable to do justice to a phenomenon in its most outstanding form and realization, "at its best," to use the words of von Hügel,[16] doesn't do justice to the phenomenon as a whole, i.e., even in its everyday manifestations. Such a person is not in a position to explain the phenomenon with the depth and the power of reality proper to and required by it.

There is an undeniable fascination that comes from the analyses and interpretations of Freud which can indeed uncover many things in

---

16. On this, cf. P. Neuner, *Erfahrung und geschichtliche Offenbarung. F. von Hügels Grundlegung der Theologie* (Munich—Paderborn—Vienna, 1977).

human action and behavior that claim to be decisions of conscience. These decisions must be examined as to whether or not they correspond to the human reality expressed in the word "conscience."

When the transcendental reality of God, which both differs from human beings and profoundly affects them, enters into the discussion (when we attempt to interpret conscience and examine its ground and background, its depth and content), that entrance of God into the discussion is neither an illusion, nor a flight from experience, nor an obfuscation of reality. It is actually an indication of the deepest ground of a reality which, as ground of reality, cannot be illusion, but is reality in the paramount sense.

It is not apparent that a nonreligious interpretation, which prescinds from the personal transcendence of God, corresponds better to the phenomenon and reality of conscience than the interpretation of conscience as place and realization of religion where human beings become aware of the internal inner weaving of existence and transcendence which characterize them. This is expressed in the words of Newman: Conscience is not a long-sighted selfishness, nor a desire to be consistent with oneself; but it is a messenger from Him, who, both in nature and in grace, speaks to us behind a veil, and teaches and rules us by His representatives. Conscience is the aboriginal Vicar of Christ, a prophet in its informations, a monarch in its peremptoriness, a priest in its blessings and anathemas, and even though the eternal priesthood throughout the Church could cease to be, in it the sacerdotal principle would remain and would have a sway.[17]

17. J. H. Newman, "Conscience" in: *A Letter Addressed to His Grace the Duke of Norfolk* (London: B. M. Pickering, 1875) 57.

§ 26

THE REVELATIONAL DIMENSION OF HISTORY

What Is History?

The possible interrelationship of revelation and history comes from the fact that history[1] involves human beings. Every event could, in itself, be described as history. We can speak of the history of the earth, or the history of nature. But history in its true and specific sense is distinguished from those necessary events that are explainable from the laws of nature and are instances of nature's law and their effects. History in the true sense concerns events brought about by the activity and decision of human beings. Of course, human action also stands under the necessities and laws of nature, and in addition under the influence of social, cultural, and economic factors; but these too are not natural forces but factors caused by human beings. But human action carried out and manifested in history has its roots essentially in the free decision of the human spirit and will. The event caused and decided by human beings, in which one also encounters new, unforeseen and unexpected things, is what one calls history. History involves human beings as persons. The human being has history, has his/her history. Human beings interpret their existence in the successive events of time, in history.

But because human beings live in being with each other, in intersubjectivity, in community, history is accordingly always related

---

1. J. Bernhart, *Der Sinn der Geschichte* (Freiburg, 1931); Th. Haecker, *Der Christ und die Geschichte* (Leipzig, 1935); K. Löwith, *Meaning in History* (Chicago: University of Chicago Press, 1949); Hans Urs von Balthasar, *A Theology of History* (San Francisco: Ignatius Press, 1994); Wolfhart Pannenberg, ed., *Revelation as History*, trans. David Granskou (New York: Macmillan, 1979); M. Seckler, *Das Heil in der Geschichte. Geschichtstheologisches Denken bei Thomas von Aquin* (Munich, 1964); Heinrich Fries, "Die Zeit als Element der christlichen Offenbarung" in: *Interpretation der Welt*, ed., H. Kuhn—H. Kahlefeld—K. Forster, Festschrift R. Guardini (Würzburg, 1964) 701–12; Walter Kasper, "Grundlinien einer Theologie der Geschichte" in: *ThQ* 144 (1964) 129–69; James M. Robinson—John B. Cobb, *Theology as History* (New York: Harper & Row, 1967); M. Müller, *Erfahrung und Geschichte* (Freiburg—Munich, 1971); G. Mann—K. Rahner, "Weltgeschichte und Heilsgeschichte" in: *Christliche Glaube in moderner Gesellschaft* 23 (Freiburg—Basel—Vienna, 1982) 88–125.

to something above the individual. History is always history of a community, a family, a tribe, a nation, history of humanity. The superindividual event both caused by and related to human beings is at the same time the context and the given situation, it is the space and the time in which the individual exists and within which individuals realize their existence, and to which they in turn take a position and thus a relationship of responsibility.

The space and time that belong to history understood in this way are not the external framework for an unchanging essence of human beings; history is part of their inner constitution. Thus history is not just involved in the contemporary interrelationships of human beings; it is also related to their succession. This involves relationship to the past as the place of an earlier event which, however, is not simply past but is active in the memory and looks ahead to new possibilities of the event in the future. The comprehensive event that involves individual human beings and human beings in general, the present, the past, and the future, and that at the same time describes the context of an event, this is what is called history in the proper sense of the word

History is the coming together of this event as the characterization and the work of human beings. This event receives special accents through epochal deeds or happenings which especially accentuate the human aspects, which introduce new things in the sense of transformation and change. One speaks of historical, world-historical events which are then apostrophized in a special way when they bring about a transformation in the plan of human beings or of the world: e.g., the rising of the Roman Empire, the migration of nations, the alliance of pope and emperor, the Crusades, Renaissance, Reformation, French Revolution, October Revolution, Second World War, atomic age. The point is this: transformation, what is new, is reserved to the realm of history—in contrast to the cycle, to the hard and fast circle of events which characterize nature in the sense of "every year the same."

History and Revelation

The question connected with our theme is: Is history, as the predominant way in which the reality and activity of human beings is made manifest, a revelation in the sense of an indicator pointing beyond the observable event, in the sense of an indicator of a reality other than inner-human, inner-worldly reality? Does history have a revelational dimension in the theological sense? And if so, to what extent?

A preliminary remark is necessary. That history be brought into connection with God is by no means an obvious move. If God is conceived, as in Greek thought, as timeless, eternal, static divinity, as the unmoved mover, history can in no way be an indicator of God. For history is the inner concept of the ephemeral, the passing, and the futile, and thus the counter-image of the divine as incorruptible. History is, in the Greek conception, the moved image of an unmoved eternity, separated from and extraneous to the divinity. That is why history can turn up no positive trace of God. History can be brought into connection with God only if the concept of God as the unmoved mover, as the *Deus otiosus* [inactive God], the timeless God, is replaced by the knowledge of the living God already knowable from creation. Then history becomes the image of a moved eternity.[2]

We repeat the question. Does history have a revelational dimension? One could say right off that it does to the extent that a revelation is given in human beings themselves, who are characterized by history. In historicity it becomes particularly clear that human beings live in the dialectic of what is given to them and taken from them, and at the same time of what is given up to them and becomes responsible to them.

History has a revelation-being to the extent that it, as history of human beings, takes part in the revelation-being of human beings. For history involves the quality of being usable, the finiteness and the dependence, but also and above all the freedom, the responsibility— one could almost say the conscience—to the extent that human beings in history bring about things that are specifically human.

If there is in the phenomena of disponibility, finiteness, freedom, responsibility, and conscience a mode of transcendence towards revelation, then history can be called a reality that has a revelational dimension and is oriented to and connected with revelation. But is there beyond this a dimension of revelation that belongs to history in the specific sense?

It has been said that history is present or felt in its intensity above all in so-called special historical events, which bear the signs of a great turning point, renewal, or transformation. From this has come and still continues to come the idea that such events point beyond themselves in a special way, that in them something of a transcendent reality, something of the reality of God, of a divine guidance and providence, is knowable and can be perceived, and that therefore history is a place of the revelation of God.

Recall the way people talk about "god's activity in history" (Arnold Toynbee). To take an example from ancient and modern times, warring conflicts have been appealed to for the revelational quality of history, and a "super-worldly governance," the "beating of the wings of eternity" recognized in them. This is largely because history is mainly understood as the history of wars and victories. Wars have been the dominant, epoch-making historical events. It was believed that the events of war could and should be brought into connection with God, and

2. M. Seckler, *Das Heil in der Geschichte* (Munich, 1964).

that a divine communication was to be perceived in them, since one connected the risk and uncertainty of the events of war with divine providence, with the reality of God as the decider of battles. One cried to God for the victory of one's own forces by connecting, even identifying one's own cause with the right cause and thus with God and God's cause, and, further, by describing the outbreak of war as a characteristic of existence in which individuals transcended their earthly goals. The victory of arms was interpreted as a language in which God made Himself clearly perceptible and which argued for the cause of victory and the victors: God is "with us"—with the strongest battalions. Success was the criterion of the revelation of God: here God has spoken.

Defeat was—according to this interpretation—no less a pronouncement of God: the pronouncement of wrath, punishment, judgment on the vanquished: woe to the vanquished!

These statements are not exaggerations or figments of the imagination. They can be documented in many ways. That an ideology is at work in these attempts has become more clearly recognizable today than in earlier times. The supposed revelation and speaking of God has been used both to legitimize events and reject them. The fact that wars, warlike events, and victories are progressively less subject to such interpretations—all the more so in the present age of a possible atomic war—this is a genuine step forward that has been taken in our time and of which we are the witnesses.

Let us quote some examples from the work of K. Hammer, *Deutsche Kriegstheologie 1870-1918* [German War Theology 1870-1918],[3] above all, from war sermons. "The war [1914] has come. It is speaking to each one of us. Through it the Lord God is speaking."—"If Russia appeals to God, it is blasphemy. But it is allowable for us to do so."(37). "God is pressing his sword into the hand of his people. We must draw it in order to defend the holiest of goods. God is marching through the German country with new revelations of his power" (98). "Hail to the war which has brought us internal peace, social peace. This has been done by the Lord, and it is a miracle before our eyes" (101). "It is a holy war in which the holy God stands on our side and in which our watchword is: Immanuel is here" (158). "Our cause is God's cause" (220). "If God is for us, who can be against us?" (209). "You can't fight against God. On the side of the Germans falls blow upon blow, victory upon victory, and with each one the unavoidable impression in our heart: here is the finger of God, here God is acting and speaking, he is speaking in the thunder of battle, when consuming iron goes forth before him" (284).

The German victories at the beginning of the Second World War were likewise qualified as signs of a visibly ruling providence and special blessings bestowed on Adolf Hitler. Especially the war against

3. Munich, 1971.

Russia was apostrophized as holy war, as a crusade against Bolshevism. And as the end drew near under apocalyptic signs, Goebbels was talking about our soldiers "marching into battle as if into worship."

Claiming God for war and victory, or the interpretation of war as a revelation of God, has its grounding not only in a natural religious feeling about divine power but also in the Old Testament, in the experiences of Israel. Its founding experience, the Exodus from Egypt and subsequent taking possession of the land, is an experience of liberation and success, a grounding of and confirmation of their faith in Yahweh. God thus turned out to be the God of this small nation, since the constellation of circumstances, the passage through the Red Sea, and the destruction of the super-powerful enemy, was represented as revelation and proclamation of Yahweh. In the words of the victory song of Moses and Miriam:

I will sing to the Lord, for he has triumphed gloriously; the horse and rider he has cast into the sea. The Lord is my strength and my song, and he has become my salvation; . . . The Lord is a man of war; the Lord is his name. Pharaoh's chariots and his host he cast into the sea; and his picked officers are sunk in the Red Sea. . . . Thy right hand, O Lord, glorious in power, thy right hand, O Lord, shatters the enemy. In the greatness of thy majesty thou overthrowest thy adversaries. (Exod 15:1–21, here 1–7)

In the Exodus event the presence of Yahweh turns out to be his "I am here." This becomes more evident as the power relationships between Moses' crowd and Pharaoh's army were wholly unequal, and everything pointed to victory for Pharaoh. In the later history of Israel, this model is repeated. Israel's wars are Yahweh's wars, holy wars; Yahweh is Israel's standard, Yahweh is the commander of his warriors, whom he consecrates. The priests march into battle along with them; the ark of the covenant is the guarantee of victory. The victories of the people are victories of Yahweh. In victory and success, Yahweh's might, his presence, his covenant with his people are made manifest. And because it is Yahweh, the booty of war is considered as belonging to him. This means complete annihilation of the enemy, including women and children, as in the conquest of Jericho, and the victory over the Philistines by Saul, who is punished because he—certainly for his own benefit—did not carry out the ban of war with sufficient completeness.

These biblical passages are hard to swallow. The problem is not how they reflect on a certain epoch of the People of Israel, but how the Exodus and its theological interpretation are turned into the liturgical present—in the celebration of the Easter Vigil. And the rubrics emphasize that precisely this reading may not be left out under any circumstances. It is indeed said by way of introduction and commentary that all this is to be understood typologically: as prototype of baptism. But precisely in our own day can be heard the question: How can one expect

Christians to make sense of such a story? The reference to baptism is pushed aside by the poetically magnificent and extremely graphic victory song about the annihilation of the enemy.

Of course, one can say that the whole thing is not a historical description but a hymn; one shouldn't weigh every single word; this is story and song. The hymn also comes from a much later time than the actual event. Israel took over the customs of the peoples of the time and did what all did—but this wasn't supposed to be. One can point out that Israel was in a position of oppression, that it had a right to freedom—even if this was bought with the destruction of its enemy. But through all these explanations there still remains the untouched problem: the victory, success, and annihilation of the enemy constitute a revelation of Yahweh, a revelation of Yahweh's power and glory. Yahweh, who grants Israel the victory, proves in battle over his enemies to be the strongest and most powerful of the gods.

In the commentary of one of the best Old Testament exegetes [N. Lohfink] one finds the following on the Exodus event: "War can become a genuine experience for the consciousness of that time. We can no longer experience the same. But we shouldn't shrink from respecting our text when it, in astonishment, takes note: Yahweh is a war hero, Yahweh is his name."[4]

I must confess, I find this respecting difficult. I grant the text its value as an experience from an earlier time and as document of an understandable reaction, but at the same time as document of a situation that is for me neither authoritative nor to be imitated. But to tell the whole story it must be noted that this war and victory-theology did not win out in the course of the later history of Israel and in the witness of the Old Testament, at least not in a dominant position.

If our explanation has just made reference to Israel's environment and to the other peoples, we must also note (and this is extraordinarily important as a corrective and differentiation): the destruction of Jerusalem, the road to captivity, the exile, the victory of Israel's enemies, the defeats of the People of Israel are, in contrast to the ideas of the world around Israel, not seen as defeats of Yahweh and as signs of his weakness; they are instead revelations of Yahweh's judgment on his people. Here is manifest the non-identity of war and victory in Israel with Yahweh's present power. Astonishingly, Israel preserved its faith in Yahweh, the God of his people, through the most varied phases of its history.

In the New Testament the connection of war and victory as sign of the revelation of God is completely abandoned, transformed into the paradox of the presence of God in weakness, in suffering, in the cross.

---

4. Norbert F. Lohfink, *The Inerrancy of Scripture and Other Essays*, trans. R. A. Wilson (Berkley, Calif.: Bibal Press, 1992) 67–86.

The *theologia gloriae* in the form of victory, power, and success is re-placed and revoked by the *theologia crucis*—a process without analogy in the history of religions and phenomenology of religion.

This introduces a totally new perspective. Suffering, weakness, and death become signs of the presence of God. This paradox is borne by the faith: If God is God, the all-determining reality, then suffering and death cannot be limits for God. Then in the folly and weakness of the cross the wisdom, the power, of God become knowable, which is a power of love.

These fundamental affirmations and determinations have, how-ever, been unable to prevent ideas about the coordination of power and success as revealer of the governance of God—ideas found in the Old Testament as well as in the history of religions—from becoming effec-tive again and again in history since Christ. Examples are the interpre-tation of the victory of Constantine, of Charles Martel, the battle at Lechfeld or the battle of Lepanto, to say nothing about other manifes-tations of the history of this idea.

A second, quite different, example of an attempt to see in world-historical events a manifestation of God and to interpret them in this sense, was Hitler's seizure of power in 1933. This was the "breakout of the nation," which he conjured up from abasement and humiliation, from the shame of Versailles. The rise of the unknown soldier from the First World War to the leader of the nation is something he himself considered or proclaimed as the working of providence, and many acknowledged him as being sent by God. The visible external success of the early years was declared, not just by him, to be a blessing of the Almighty; likewise, the victories at the beginning of the war. When the situation turned bad, the constant assurance was given that the war could not be lost, the Almighty could not leave in the lurch the people and the leader which had been blessed with so many signs of excel-lence. Repeated unsuccessful assassination attempts only strengthened this impression. In the events of the year 1933 many saw a sign, the voice of God speaking. This interpretation found its way even into many areas of theology. There was at that time a theology that saw its task as accepting and interpreting the realities that lay there for all to see. The time and the signs of the time, *vox temporis, vox Dei* [voice of the time, voice of God], were providing the hermeneutical principle for the understanding of revelation and faith. This often took place as an uncritical legitimation and with the imperative to become part of the realities created at that time.

A third example is pressing on us even today and is influencing the present situation. It also has a relationship to history. It is being said: God is disclosed, revealed in the revolutionary event—and this, to be sure, is the dynamic, the acting, the all-changing God. Revolution is brought into a positive relationship to God and God's work. Following upon the theology of war, of national elevation, we have today a theology of revolution. All affirmations and contents of faith are to be interpreted in the horizon and context of the politico-revolutionary principle. Changing, overthrowing, getting rid of the existing structures are becoming categories of revelation. Jesus as Messiah is becoming a political, revolutionary figure. His activity is characterized by the text: "He has put down the mighty from their thrones, and exalted those of low degree; he has filled the hungry with good things, and the rich he has sent empty away" (Luke 1:52-53). If this is the case, then the theological and also the Christian is to be made present, above all, in the revolution event. The contribution of the Christian consists in the task of humanizing, which, in revolution, is connected with the service of justice and reconciliation.[5]

Critical Distance

Different as these models of history and revelation are in their contents and points of relationship, they are similar with regard to their structure and method. Over against all of them critical distance is needed. Why? The historical events they pick out are made into a direct revelation of God and held onto with quite apodictic assertiveness. These models and conceptions are quite sure of the fact: here and in this way God has spoken and acted. The factual event, or the success, or what one wants to have happen, is used as a criterion.

There is a second reason. Only one part of the historical reality, a subjectively chosen excerpt meant for practical application, is lifted out as the place of revelation and transparency. The divine [aspect of it] is understood as the ground of this and only this historical development. In this way the divine is itself particularized and seen as ground only of a partial reality. The rest of historical reality that is not determined by war, victory, breakout, or revolution—the everyday of history or the negativity of history, the experience of suffering, unhappiness, failure—is, with the exception of the theology of liberation and the *memoria* of the death of Christ recalled there, removed from the possibility of relationship with the divine or brought into a merely negative relationship. In other words: many fields of historical happening are closed out. It is claimed that no positive transparency toward the divine is to be found there. There is thus a rejection of that characteristic which is connected with the divine: that it is the all-determining reality.

5. T. Rendtorff—H. E. Tödt, *Theologie der Revolution* (edition Suhrkamp 258), (Frankfurt, 1968).

A using of God for historical events and deeds, a one-sided interpretation of one-sided historical processes as transparent of the divine does not go back only to the early stage of the Old Testament; it comes nowadays very close to what one calls ideology: theoretical superstructures about events and things desired in order to ground, legitimate, and justify them. When it takes place with an appeal to "God wills it," then history take on a sanctioning, a kind of transfiguration and a legitimation to which it has no right.

Suspicion of ideology is also there because such theological reflections proceed from specific interests and purposes and are tied to them. God and God's revelation are brought into play not to open up reality or to interpret and make it transparent, but to take some event that will strengthen or change something, some event motivated by anything but religious grounds, and charge it up with God's word and action. A difference perceived under the sign of God, a genuine over-against, a theological proviso, a critical distance—none of these are recognizable. God and God's activity are used without scruple and as taken for granted. In order to ward off, from the outset, criticism and opposition to what is taking place, theological affirmation is put to use.

Meaning of History

If we want to talk about history in the dimension of God's revelation in the sense of a reference to God and to the possibility, in so doing, of speaking of God, a new starting point needs to be sought. This is not to be found in individual events and processes, as in the views just described, but in that aspect of the whole which is connected with history when one speaks of the meaning of history. Meaning, already spoken of as the opening to and place of manifest-being [*Offenbarsein*], returns once again here in the realm of history. But this turns up a considerable number of difficulties and problems.

The question of the meaning of history seems at first to be unanswerable. There are many reasons for this. First, we don't have at our disposition the whole of history to which the sense of its significance, which overarches the individual, is related. We take over the whole in the form of anticipation and expectation and in the form of the action inspired by it. Second: history does not take place according to the laws of necessity.

History is made by human beings; it is decisively co-determined by human freedom. Consequently, there is not to be found in history any straight-line progress to the ever better and more perfect. Again and again we are disappointed; again and again best intentions come to naught, best opportunities are missed. Stupidity and depravity, injustice and hate, have always been the strongest experiential objections against the acceptance of one overarching sense of history. Evil and suffering in the world are still first and foremost the strongest obstacles and challenging questions for faith in a comprehensive sense.[6]

It has often been said that, after Auschwitz not only is poetry dead (Adorno), but also praying and singing.[7] This darkness has extinguished the light of God and all meaning. For some, this may be so. But it is not the whole story. For in Auschwitz itself, there was praying and singing in the face of death, in the faith and confidence that Auschwitz cannot be the last word in the fate of human beings, that the executioner does not have the last word, that God cannot be refuted by Auschwitz and has not died in Auschwitz, any more than God was and is refuted by the event on Golgotha.[8] The theology of the cross comes into effect here in all its depth. There is a striking verification of this: Auschwitz and the other extermination camps of Birkenau and Maidanek are in Poland. There, even in Auschwitz, people pray, sing, believe today— after Auschwitz. Auschwitz in Poland is no indictment against God but an indictment against human beings. Auschwitz is, according to a statement of Pope Paul VI, the Golgotha of our time.

Although the idea of the meaninglessness of event and history recurs as a constant temptation, one must turn it away and deny it. For if everything were meaningless, we would then, basically, be unable to live any longer. In every act of life we affirm at the same time that this life has a meaning, that being is better than not being. There is a something within us that keeps us from simply giving up on ourselves, on others, on the world, on history and its possible shape and shaping.

When one is troubled by the constantly repeated question, If God is, why is there evil and the contradiction of meaning connected with it?— *Si Deus est, unde mala?*—one can with the philosopher Boethius in prison waiting for death answer with the counter-question, *Bona vero, unde, si Deus non est?* If there is no God, where, then, does good come from, where does even partial meaning come from, to say nothing of initially comprehensive, possible, and real meaning?

Meaning [*der Sinn*] is not only the goal of our historical activity, but also its ground and presupposition.

We experience meaning not as "something" that is merely our own idea and projection, but as "something" that already encompasses us and begins to make possible our wishes and questions about meaning. If we had never experienced meaning we wouldn't be able to ask about it. But then we also wouldn't be able to experience meaninglessness as such, still much less understand our own activity which is borne by the factual affirmation of meaning. For in that intersubjectivity

---

6. Walter Kasper, "Möglichkeiten der Gotteserfahrung heute" in: *Glaube und Geschichte* 120–43, here 135

7. T. W. Adorno, *Negative Dialectics* (New York, 1973); D Sölle, *Suffering* (London, 1976).

8. Johannes Baptist Metz, *Gott nach Auschwitz. Dimensionen des Massenmordes am jüdischen Volk* (Fribourg—Basel—Wien, 1979)

in which history takes place, it is not we who create meaning but meaning that presses in on us. We are not the ones who claim meaning for ourselves; we are claimed by meaning.[9]

Meaning/sense is spoken to us and takes us in its service. It is, in the double meaning of the word, a challenge and an encouragement for human beings. This kind of experience of meaning can be a form of transparency of history and of event towards revelation. Such an experience of meaning not only keeps meaning from being explained only from the part of human beings, it also requires reflection on the source of this experience of meaning that is inderivably there, sent and given; it is also not self-evident, but unexpected and surprising. "We cannot simply nail down meaning; it immediately escapes us. It turns out to be different and greater. When it comes out into the open it immediately goes into hiding again." This shows that every experienced meaning points to a mystery that is made known to us in traces and signs. This mystery is not somehow beyond the world; it is the truth, the depth, the non-obviousness and the mysteriousness of the experienced sense itself. Thus we could say:

This ever-withdrawing and ever self-opening depth of meaning possesses a reservedness and interiority which is not at our disposition but which has disposition over us. It encounters us analogously to the way in which persons meet. If therefore we are looking for a model from the rest of our experience from which we could give it a name, we have available only the model of the person. But even the concept of person immediately fails. It withdraws, not indeed downwards but upwards. In no case is a less-than-personal or an a-personal model enough. Thus we can characterize this experience of meaning in the language of religious tradition as experience of the Divine.[10]

It is encountered as the all-determining reality.

To affirm a meaning in history also means: it makes sense, it is proper and required to be engaged in history, to get involved for justice, peace, and freedom, and to believe in the good. To affirm a meaning in history means never to stop beginning, never to begin to stop. It means that a better realization of meaning and a comprehensive fulfillment of meaning—bestowed on us—is to be hoped for in the future. This expectation is the content of the hope grounded in the Christian faith, which has its basis in Jesus' cross and his resurrection from the dead.

It is thus understandable that hope has these days become the form of faith, and the future has been claimed as an expression for transcendence. Future actually becomes a paradigm for talking about God (J. Moltmann); transcendence and future are connected: the "God over us" and the "God for us" (J. B. Metz). The God of the future grants the future and guarantees it as "absolute future" (K. Rahner) for human beings.

9. W. Kasper, *Glaube und Geschichte* 136.
10. Ibid. 136–37.

This does not mean that God is "future," the *Deus Spes* [God Hope] (E. Bloch). God is not dissolved into the future whereby—so Bloch—God is the cipher for the hiddenness of human beings; God remains the God of the future.

This conception of future radicalizes human engagement for the world of peace and justice. At the same time, everything already achieved is relativized. It is not end and fulfillment, but new impulse and new mandate.

Let us close these reflections with some ideas from Edward Schillebeeckx. Whereas the transcendence of God surpassing all forms of time used to be represented primarily in the mode of an unchangeable or eternalized past, it is nowadays connected with the future. God is the God for us, the Coming One, the God who is our future.

Thus, a decisive shift has come about. That One whom we previously, from an older conception of humanity and the world, had characterized as the totally other, is now shown to be the totally new, the one who is our future and creates human future anew. He shows Himself as God who, in Jesus Christ, gives us the possibility of creating future, i.e., to make everything new and to climb beyond the sinful history of ourselves and all others. The new culture thus becomes the occasion to discover again in a surprising way the Good News of the Old and New Testament: namely that the God of promise gives us the mandate to get on the road to the promised land, a land which we, trusting in the promises as did Israel before us, must ourselves cultivate and build up.[11]

This provides at the same time a clear articulation of the special character of Christian hope and the daily commitment for the world and its future which springs from it.

The new concept of God, i.e., belief in the One Who Is to Come, in the totally new, who gives us the possibility even now to make human events into a salvation history, by virtue of an inner, new creation including the new creation dead to sin, this idea of God thus radicalizes our engagement for a world of more human dignity, but at the same time also relativizes every result already achieved. The believer who knows about the eschatological fulfillment promised to humanity and its history will thus find it impossible to recognize in every already achieved result the promise of the new heaven and the new earth. In contrast, e.g., to the Marxist, the believer will not even dare to give a positive name to the coming final fulfillment. Christians allow the future a greater openness than the Marxist. They also discover that the latter destroys possibilities prematurely, because for a Christian it is ideology to characterize a concrete stage as the final point.[12]

---

11. Edward Schillebeeckx, *God the Future of Man*, trans. N. D. Smith (New York: Sheed and Ward, 1968) 181–82; cf. also Wolfhart Pannenberg, "The God of Hope" in: *Basic Question in Theology*, vol. 2 (London: S. C. M. Press Ltd., 1971) 234–49.
    12. E. Schillebeeckx, *The Future of Man* 187.

PART TWO

SPECIAL HISTORICAL REVELATION AS GROUND AND HORIZON OF THE CHRISTIAN FAITH

I

The Possibility of This Revelation

§ 27

THE OBJECTION AGAINST THE POSSIBILITY OF SUCH A REVELATION

The Objection of Modern Thought

Objections against a revelation of the kind found in the realm of Christian faith—the special revelation witnessed in the Old and New Testaments which found its culmination in the person, word, and fate of Jesus Christ—have been raised again and again in the course of history. This has been especially in recent times.[1] Basically, these objections arise wherever no possibility or room for a special revelation is allowed.

A particularly noteworthy example is the so-called *deism* of the seventeenth and eighteenth centuries, according to which the world is explained as the work and creation of God and presented and understood in the image of a precisely functioning machine. The Creator is the world engineer who, after the construction of the machine—the world—can leave it to itself, i.e., to its functions, laws, and mechanisms. All further activity on the part of God, in the sense of an historically realized revelation, would disturb the course and running of the world, would lessen, even discredit the perfection of the work of creation and thus of the Creator, would qualify creation as an incompetent job in need of correcting and perfecting. For that is unworthy of the Creator and creation.

In other words, there is no room for a special revelation if its possible contents are from the outset acceptable only if and to the extent they can be interpreted as the possible contents of critical understanding and of practical reason—*as religion within the limits of pure reason*—as everything which, encountered in historical individuality and uniqueness, can become an instance and sign of something general. In this view,

---

1. Fundamental for what follows is: M. Seckler, "Aufklärung und Offenbarung" in: *Christlicher Glaube in Geschichte und Gesellschaft* 21 (Freiburg—Basel—Vienna, 1980) 6–78; cf. also Heinrich Fries, *Die Religionsphilosophie Newmans* (Stuttgart, 1948) 19–44.

historical revelation, to which corresponds receiving by way of perception, can at most be accepted as a child's stage of a development or as "introduction." This is replaced by the stage of mature, adult thinking, which admits recognition of its own autonomous thinking, which has the courage to make use of its own understanding and overcome the immaturity for which it bears responsibility (Kant).

Based on this fundamental conception, Herbert of Cherbury, considered the father of Deism, formulated five fundamental propositions about God, freedom, and immortality: first, there is a supreme being; second, this being should be venerated; third, morality is the highest form of the veneration of God; fourth, faults and crimes are to be atoned for by repentance; fifth, there is reward and punishment after this life. According to Herbert of Cherbury, these propositions constitute the basis of the different religions; they all agree on them. They are at the same time the critical criterion for the concrete religions, including Christianity. Additions are either priestly deceit or allegory. The truly catholic church consists of the consensus of creatures endowed with reason in matters of religion.

For John Locke, the content of the Christian religion is "so simple that it is immediately intelligible to human reason, and so general that it doesn't include a special confession." Christianity is not merely rational, it is identical with the religion of reason; the gospel is the summation and confirmation of the *lex naturae* (law of nature), the *lex rationis* (law of reason).

Kant used the same basic ideas for the interpretation of the Bible.[2] "Ther are writings which contain certain doctrines that are not only theoretically proclaimed as holy, but also surpass every (even moral) concept of reason—such writings and doctrines which contain propositions contradictory to practical reason must be interpreted to the advantage of the latter." Kant mentions in this connection the doctrines of the Trinity and the Incarnation. "The gradual transition of church faith to the sole domination of pure religious faith is the approximation of the Kingdom of God."

There is no room for a special revelation if, as in the system of idealism, above all of Hegel, everything is revelation because the human being (more precisely, the spirit of the human being) is the place of the presence, the working, and the history of the Absolute Divine Spirit, and because, further, world history is the movement of the Absolute Spirit through and in the human spirit, because the way of its "revelation" is the way in the form of dialectic with thesis, antithesis, and synthesis.

---

2. Immaunuel Kant, *Religion within the Limits of Reason Alone* , trans. Theodore M. Greene and Hoyt H. Hudson (New York: Harper & Row, 1960).

One of Hegel's primary concerns was the rigorous reconciliation of faith and knowledge; specifically he insists that the content of the Christian faith should not be left in the hands of faith but should be carefully thought through by reason. This is possible if it is recognized that God is the depth of the Spirit certain of itself, and that the Spirit, when it wishes to come to itself, must go out of itself and go into that which it is not, to what is strange, and make it its own. That holds also for God, who must go into the world, into being human and into history, in order to be able to be Himself. In this way the incarnation of God becomes philosophically understandable, speculatively thinkable, even necessary.[3]

In this great vision there is an objection against a special revelation (such as Christianity as it is traditionally understood) for this universalizing philosophical vision sees everything as revelation. If, in addition, God and human beings are connected in the way that Hegel's thought presupposes, the distinction between divine and human, finite spirit is wiped out. This dismisses the possibility of speaking of a revelation of God as distinct from a revelation of human beings. If history is ultimately the path of Absolute Spirit in the form of dialectic, then revelation as act of the freedom of God is not possible; it is rather a path of necessity.

There is no room for a special revelation of God because such a revelation would not be accessible to human beings—but then it wouldn't be revelation. This is the case when, as *empiricism* and *positivism* represent it, the only things accessible to human beings are what they can experience and perceive with their senses, what therefore is immanent, objective, what the case is, what can be lifted up and verified by observation, repetition, experiment, and control. Natural science is accordingly the only form of human knowledge. All knowledge stems from experience, is limited and restricted to experience. Neither God nor any kind of a revelation belongs to this. To bring reality into relationship with such things is not an explanation but a camouflaging of reality.

That there is no room for a revelation in *materialism* of all shades, above all in historical and dialectical materialism, is obvious. Everything connected with revelation incurs the suspicion of being wishful thinking, projection, or the ideological superstructure growing out of certain economic and social conditions, and in that way working as opium.

The attempt is made to subsume the modern age under the rubric of the *Enlightenment* and its consequences; and to arrange under that category all those "isms" mentioned here. The enlightenment is considered

---

3. Cf. Hans Küng, *The Incarnation of God: An Introduction to Hegel's Theological Thought as Prolegomena to a Future Christology,* trans. J. R. Stephenson (New York: Crossroad, 1987); cf. also H. Fries, *Die Religionsphilosophie Newmans* (Stuttgart, 1948) 19–44.

above all as criticism of revelation, as the core concept of what is inimical to revelation. In a penetrating analysis, Max Seckler has shown
that the enlightenment was really concerned with the *reconciliation of
revelation and reason*, that the enlightenment's critique of revelation
is to be understood in a differentiated way

as critique of a supernaturalistic understanding of the revelation which, as contrasting counterpart of naturalism, understands revelation as an irrational superadditum which is not mediated through reason and to it as truth, but which can
be believed only in an act of giving up oneself. [The Enlightenment's critique of
revelation is to be understood in a differentiated way] as critique of a revelational positivism which demands belief for what is legislated and said by tradition and authority, and demands this only because of itself, by equating positivity
and validity; and finally as critique of a revelation-theological absolutism which
attributes the deficit of proof for revelational assertions to incomprehensible decrees of the will of the *potentia absoluta* of God and demands an unquestioning
subjection for which only extrinsic grounds—i.e., relying on the externals and the
external circumstances of revelation (*criteria externa revelationis*)—are possible.[4]

The discussion carried on in the enlightenment was a genuine theological challenge. It led to the result that revelation was recognized as
a key concept of faith and theology, that revelation constitutes the
transcendental specification of what is Christian, that the original
and essential dimension of Christianity is to be characterized by revelation.

On the level of language this gets expressed in the fact that Christian theology is
henceforth seen and characterized as revelational theology. This means factually
that revelation is recognized as both solid foundation and ontic dimension of
Christianity as a whole, and is also reflected on by knowledge theory as condition of the possibility and ontological specification of theology and faith.[5]

The Objection of Karl Jaspers

We will now treat the objection against the revelation witnessed in
biblical and Christian faith that comes from a contemporary philosophical position: that of Karl Jaspers. He more than any other
philosopher in the recent past took up the issue of revelation, especially in his book *Der philosophische Glaube angesichts der
Offenbarung* [Philosophical Faith in View of Revelation].[6] This thematic makes an especially strong impression because in the fundamental traits of his philosophy, in his "existential philosophy," Jaspers
seems to have set up all the presuppositions for a possible revelation: In
the already mentioned fundamental principles: "No existence without

4. M. Seckler, "Aufklärung und Offenbarung" 33.
5. Ibid. 54.
6. (Munich, 1962). On the issue as a whole: H. Fries, "Der Philosophische Glaube Karl
Jaspers" in: *Ärgernis und Widerspruch*, 2d ed. (Würzburg, 1968) 41–99.

transcendence"—"No true image of human beings without God," in which God is the encompassing reality distinct from human beings and warrant for the ground of existence. Not from a denial of transcen dence but with explicit appeal to its acknowledgment, Jaspers rejects revelation in the biblical, above all, in the Christian sense. His position merits treatment also because it can be called representative in its seriousness and urgency.

We now present Jasper's reflections on the theme of revelation, but include our critique of them along with their description.

a. Revelation is, according to Jaspers "the immediate, temporarily and spatially localized proclamation of God through word, demand, action, event. God gives his commands, he establishes community, he appears among human beings, he sets up the cult."[7] Revelation is, in itself, a phenomenon and a claim of every religion. But Christianity does not understand itself as one type of such a grouping, as revelation alongside other revelations; it claims rather to be the unique, absolute, universal, and thus *exclusive revelation*.

But it is contradictory to the existence of human beings, so answers Jaspers, that transcendence does not reveal itself clearly. This means a one-sided and premature fixation of human beings on one definitive situation, and thereby a limitation of their possibilities. But an exclusively understood revelation also and above all carries with it as consequence an improper drawing of boundaries for transcendence. Jaspers explains: "To deny oneself revelation faith is not the result of Godlessness but the consequence of belief in existence as freely created by transcendence. Philosophical faith . . . must dispense with real revelation in favor of the cipher in the movement of its multiplicity of meanings."[8] It is not about the alternatives, denial of God or belief in God, but about the question, hidden or revealed God.[9]

b. According to Jaspers, revelation faith implies *authority*. This is for Jaspers an undeniable human necessity. "One human being alone cannot live. In community, however, human beings are never without binding authority which the individual, without knowing it, follows, without feeling unfree about it."[10] Authority is for Jaspers also not in opposition to freedom. Freedom is possible only through authority, through freedom in a connection; otherwise it becomes arbitrariness. Consequently, there is authority also without revelation. The authority claimed by revelation and revelation faith, however, provokes the criticism of Jaspers, for it contradicts the essence of authority to demand what revelation demands: to be the universally valid authority bind-

7. Karl Jaspers, *Der philosophische Glaube angesichts der Offenbarung* (Munich, 1962) 49, ET: *Philosophical Faith and Revelation*, trans. E. B. Ashton (New York: Harper & Row, 1967).
    8. Ibid. 118.
    9. Ibid. 481.
    10. Ibid. 64.

ing on all. All authority is historical and thus, of itself, relative. True authority includes a multiplicity of forms: *the* authority doesn't exist; there exist only authorities.

c. Revelation faith gives the promise and makes the claim of being not just one truth among many, but the absolute truth, truth in itself. Included in this is the other claim, to be *truth for all*, for all human beings, for all times, for all conditions. One is valid for all, and all are held and bound to the one, to one authority, to one church, to one book, to one faith, to one God who is the God of all.

In the name of human beings it must be said in opposition that within human existence, within reason, freedom, and history, there is no universally valid, no absolute, eternal and all-obliging truth. There is truth "only for me" and for each individual; there is truth only as my truth. In this sense Jaspers takes over the thesis of Kierkegaard: "Subjectivity is the truth." Truth is not universal, it is historical, relative, polar, and dialectic. The one truth is the constantly obliging but never reachable goal of all paths to truth. "What is historically, what is existentially true is indeed unconditioned, but in its having been spoken and in its manifestation it is not truth for all."[11]

The proclamation of truth for all, as it comes up in revelation, means, humanly seen, the leveling of what is individual (indeed *putting it in a coffin*), the elevation of the general over the particular, the triumph of the impersonal over the person and the individual who is threatened and snuffed out in this absolute truth for all.

d. When revelation claims to be truth for all, this leads unavoidably to the *claim to exclusivity* which admits of nothing but itself, which condemns everything that does not carry its name and sign. "One is given the alternative to follow or not to follow it. Whoever is not for me is against me."[12]

The intolerance of revelation faith means narrow-minded fanaticism and brutal will to power, even to world dominance, which undertakes to bring all human beings to the faith and to make them Christians, which forces them to worship what it has worshiped and to burn what it has burned. Politics, persecution, inquisition, and compulsion become means of the faith, means of which the church, in a praxis that dishonors it, has made historical use down to the last refined details.[13]

Such exclusivity, intolerance, and inability to communicate are, according to Jaspers, a threat to human beings in the innermost part of their existence. For it is of the nature of being human to be in communi-

---

11. H. Fries, *Der philosophische Galube: Karl Jaspers, in Ärgernis und Widerspruch*, 2d ed. (Würzburg, 1968) 70.
12. Ibid. 72.
13. Ibid. 88–91.

cation, to come into close living contact with the "you" of other human beings both now and in history, and with the intellectual movements, impulses, powers, and ideas of all times. Only in relationship to and in encounter with that which it is not itself does existence come to its openness in breadth and freedom. The claim to exclusivity of revelation faith leaves no room and no possibility for this.

The claim to exclusivity of faith is to be rejected not only in the name of human beings but also—as Jaspers assures us—in the name of God: "The claim to exclusivity is the work of human beings and not grounded in God, who has opened up many ways to himself for human beings."[14] The assertion of an exclusive revelation of God is basically an usurpation of the truth by individual human beings and groups of human beings.

e. The truth for all claimed by revelation and by Christian faith not only excludes everything different from itself, but promises also to be the true answer to all questions and to fulfill all possibilities of thinking and questioning. Revelation faith—as Jaspers characterizes it—knows everything, knows everything exactly, knows everything infallibly. It proposes a *system of truth*, a cosmos of certainties, a structure of guarantees, a true world view in the form of a *summa* in which everything has its place, rank, order, and context, in which are gathered all the kernels of truth scattered throughout the world and history, in which all traces and parts of the truth are brought home.

According to Jaspers, this kind of thinking found its keenest conception and manifestation in Nicholas of Cusa.[15] The principles of the "*complexio oppositorum* [complex of opposites]" and of the "*concordantia discordantium* [concordance of the discordant]" developed and carried out by him open up the horizon for an absolutely universal and unlimited breadth. In a conception of revelation and faith configured and understood in this way there are no gaps and riddles left.

Should not human beings welcome with joy this promise of certitude and assurance, this chance of knowledge and cognition as the fulfillment of their very selves? No, replies Jaspers. This call is like a call of sirens. Those who follow it end up in the land of illusion and will suffer shipwreck, at best only to themselves. Faith and its promise lead human beings into a false security and peace, into the forbidden satiety of they who possess, who have, who know.

Easing the burden of existence by faith takes place at the cost of truth. Truth is there for human beings not as a system or state of being, *truth exists only as way and task*, as an ever new and original event, as an event unconditionally involving only myself. Truth doesn't come in

14. Ibid. 75.
15. K. Jaspers, *Anselm and Nicholas of Cusa*, trans. Ralph Manheim (New York: Harcourt, Brace & Javanovich, 1974).

clearly understandable and predictable sizes. Truth comes only in the back and forth of dialectic. Truth doesn't exist in timeless validity; truth exists only in historical and thus relative form. Those who say anything else are confusing human thought with divine knowledge and arrogating to themselves the status of a second Creator of the world.[16]

When Christian faith and above all the "Catholic method" gather in the scattered truths into a whole, claiming them for themselves and assigning them a place within their universality and catholicity, they do so at the cost of their own being, at the cost of life. "The cost of this Catholic unity is the loss of merit and substance in everything that was taken up, transformed, and appropriated from the outside." From the originality, freshness, and vitality of the idea in its origin comes "the corpse of something just barely objectively rational"— the whole thing becomes a cemetery.[17]

f. The special characteristic of faith in revelation brings something further with it. It is, as Jaspers says, the coordination of *revelation and history*, the conception of a salvation history as well as the concentration of all historical events in the fact of the Incarnation of God in Christ, the division of time into before and after Christ. It is the determination claimed in revelation, indeed the perpetuation of an historical fact: the life of Jesus. It is the absolutizing of an historical figure, its claim and its demand: "Follow Me!" Jaspers calls this process an inadmissible objectification of the individual, a false universalization of the factual, and speaks of the ossification into a powerful historicity of "congealed," foreign and inimical history.

Against such a conception of the historical and within the historical Jaspers draws up his criticism. As he examines the history claimed by revelation he can see only a false development, somethings which, for human beings, constitutes a danger. Now existence really does need history. But it is not acceptable to perpetuate *one* history or *one* historical event, or to elevate it to an obligation for all human beings of all times. It is not right to make one unique, historical figure into the unsurpassable criterion of existence and model for all human beings. History is unfinished and reveals no recognizable goal. What Hegel could still express in the proposition "All history moves towards Christ and comes from him. The appearance of the Son of God is the axis of world history," Jaspers can no longer affirm. For "the Christian faith is a faith, not the faith of humanity. . . . That on the basis of which all

---

16. K. Jaspers, *Von der Wahrheit* (Munich, 1948) 393. Some material from this book has been translated into English as: *Truth and Symbol*, trans. Jean T. Wilde (New York: Twayne Publishers, 1959).

17. Ibid. 844.

human beings can be connected is not revelation but must be the experience that binds all."[18]

As long as they don't fall into a bottomless vacuum, human beings live from history not in that they recognize the past as carrying, abiding, and obliging [reality]—that is "violent historicity"—but in that they, in "original historicity," are held in movement and disquiet by history and exist in view of history and its figures. This happens not as imitation of an historical "model," but by the awakening of existence in reason and freedom before unique figures of history like Jesus and Buddha or Nietzsche and Kierkegaard. They are all—both together and in their differences—necessary, not as teachers and proclaimers, but as the "stormy awakeners of existence." They "want to have their effect, but in such a way that they bring the other to himself, expect the decisive from him, not give it to him."[19]

g. The *tendency to reality, to bodiliness*, to concretion found in revelation faith has, according to Jaspers, reached its high point in the Christian confession of the God-man Jesus Christ and in the Christological dogmas. Here the absolutely real becomes detectable and touchable; transcendence is identified with a human being. "The drive of human beings towards bodiliness is satisfied here as nowhere else. God's reality is guaranteed to the believer through the bodiliness of a human being."[20]

Such positions on Christian revelation are in error and miss the mark because they offend against the fundamental understanding of transcendence. Although the THAT of transcendence may be unquestionably experienced, its WHAT remains hidden. There isn't anything at all that can be said about it, and every attempt to realize it, to make it bodily and concretely present, falsifies transcendence or extinguishes it. Transcendence remains and is only in the disappearing of the object; it is without specification and knowability, without form and figure.

But existence is also falsified. Existence-grounding behavior towards the divinity, being before God, silence and reverence before the Absolute, go for naught if human beings draw down to themselves, concretize and materialize God when they talk with God in prayer, when in dogma, ritual, and cult they dissolve the boundaries between human beings and God. That is why Jaspers can say: It all comes down to achieving "the step from slavery under bodiliness" to "freedom in the realm of cipher,"[21] and in that way to purify faith.

Against the possibility and claim of a bodily, human, personal revelation of God, Jaspers—following Kant—brings up the argument: If

18. K. Jaspers, *The Origin and Goal of History*, trans. Michael Bullock (London: Routledge and Kegan Paul, 1953) 19–20.
19. *Rechenschaft und Ausblick* (Munich, 1952) 130.
20. K. Jaspers, *Der philosophische Glaube angesichts der Offenbarung* 226 .
21. Ibid. 168.

transcendence were to show itself unhidden, this would eliminate freedom. "The divine wisdom is no less worthy of wonderment in that
which it gives us than in that which it refuses us; for if God were to
stand before us in his majesty, we would become marionettes in faith
and not remain as free as God has wanted us to be."[22]

The answer to these individual objections can and should not be
given here. It would have to anticipate all that is to come. The answer
becomes possible only when that revelation is described against which
Jaspers raises his objection.

22. Ibid. 481.

THE POSSIBILITY OF A SPECIAL, SUPERNATURAL
REVELATION AS A FUNDAMENTAL THEOLOGICAL PROBLEM

Now that we have presented the objections, we take up the question ourselves. Is there a special and supernatural revelation of God over and above the manifestation of God that is present in the reality of creation? Are there possibilities of revelation in creation and above all in human beings, or are these possibilities totally excluded? And if excluded, is this merely de facto or are they excluded in principle, in the sense that there is no possibility of any disclosure of God over and above creation simply because human beings do not possess the presuppositions for its access and reception? Our response to these questions relies in part on the thoughts of Karl Rahner in his book *Hearers of the Word*, which is still valid today and has been taken up in his *Foundations of Christian Faith*.

The Human Being as Questioner

Asking questions is profoundly and characteristically human. Question presupposes the *questionability* and thus knowability of the questioned; otherwise there would be no question. One doesn't ask about the totally unknown. The knowability of reality is, however, possible because it is the effect of a knowing: knowability presupposes being known.

The horizon of human questioning is infinite. Human beings ask about everything that is, thus about existing-being and about being as the ground of existing-being. Thus pertaining to all and to the ground of all is above all knowability, intelligibility, i.e., truth in the ontological sense. The cognition of human beings rests on the inner coordination of spirit and being. Being and spirit are ordered to each other; cognition is connaturality of being and spirit. The logos of human beings recognizes the logos of things.

Questioning contains, besides the moment of questionability [Fragbarkeit], that of questionableness [Fraglichkeit]. This gives the difference between question and questioned, and between knowing and known, the nonidentity of (human) spirit and being or existing-being. The question is accordingly also the sign of what is not completely known, or not adequately recognized. The question, which lays open the distantiation between being as such and knowing human beings, is a sign of knowing and not knowing alike. It is a sign of the greatness and limitation of human beings.

The human being as questioner, as person and subject, is the presupposition of a possible special and free revelation. For the horizon of questioning is unlimited. Human beings as questioners cannot, in their knowledge, take in this horizon; they stand at a distance from it: being and existing-being are more comprehensive than the knowing questioning and the questioning knowing of human beings. Seen this way, there is no impossibility for a revelation, in the sense of an impossibility of anything new being disclosed to human beings.

This situation is the condition of the possibility for a revelation in the special sense. One can indeed speak of the transcendence of God as the all-determining reality; but this takes place only indirectly and, in addition, primarily in the form of negation: infinitely, in an unworldly way, etc. Also the totality of the experience of reality, which we characterized as revelation-being, in which the sign of transparency is known and affirmed, has not superseded this fundamental characteristic of our knowledge of transcendence: neither our own existence, nor conscience, nor language, nor history. Nothing prevents and a great deal speaks in favor of the fact that the transcendence being referred to is proclaimed more clearly and more perceivably, that human beings are learning from it a new word about creation. As questioners, they are open for this. Our existence is characterized by "being on the lookout." To be expecting a special self-disclosure of God belongs, according to Newman, to the "likelihoods from the outset."

The Seeker of Salvation

When we consider human *willing, striving and loving*, we come up with a situation like that of the question and the questioning. Human beings, the hearers of the word, are likewise the seekers of happiness, salvation, fulfillment.

The goal and object of human striving and willing is the good, the value of everything worth striving for, and from which nothing that exists is excluded. This is the foundation of the ontology of good, of value: reality and the good, the good as conformed to reality. The striving and willing of human beings are ordered to a concrete, specific value in which they find their realization. They are not, however, exhausted therein but are open to the good as such, to the unlimited good. We can recognize this in the fact that every goal achieved becomes the beginning of some new willing and striving. No individual or categorical good is the fulfillment of human striving. The coordination of what is willed and what is striven for never becomes identity. Just as with questioning, the differentiation between transcendental and categorical remains. Thus, from the side of human willing, striving, and loving arises the possibility of a further opening to some reality in the mode of the goal, the good, the well-being, and the fulfillment for human beings that lies therein. This is not anticipated by any immanent determination of goal in such a way that there would be nothing more to expect and to hope for. *Das Prinzip Hoffnung* (E. Bloch, The Principle of Hope) lives from this impulse and is thus an indication of the condition of possibility of something new: of a perfect, unlimited form of the good, of well-being, of fulfillment.

The French philosopher Maurice Blondel has—as we have already discussed—made this phenomenon the object of an intensive reflection. He summarizes his phenomenology of action in the form of a conclusion:

"It is impossible not to recognize the inadequacy of the whole natural order and not to feel a further need; it is impossible to find something in oneself that can satisfy this comprehensive need. It is necessary; and it is unachievable. These are, put quite bluntly, the conclusions of the characteristic trait of human action." This is what constitutes the logic of action and activity.

To solve this difficulty Blondel can identify only one course of action: to make a decision. One must either make a decision for the finite and consciously exclude the infinite, or one must open oneself to the infinite and enter into the expectation that the infinite will fulfill in a new way the ultimate orientation of our fundamental willing. This happens when the infinite imparts itself and the human being receptively accepts it.

Conscience

Conscience is so constituted that it can and will perceive a rather clear articulation of the unconditioned. J. H. Newman has penetratingly shown this in his analysis of conscience. He says:

If anything is true and divine, then it is the voice of our conscience, and it would be terrible to assume the opposite. And yet there remain enough weak points to raise doubt about the authority of conscience decisions; and they who set up a critical investigation in a coldly testing way, skeptically or superficially, or in order to find an excuse for their disobedience, they will have no difficulty in bringing their reason into embarrassment and confusion until they finally begin to ask whether that which they for their whole lives took to be sinful really is a sin, and whether conscientiousness might not be a kind of superstition.[1]

The real constitution of human beings and the world requires, for the support of conscience, and the safeguarding of the natural belief in God, an *instance outside of conscience*, an authority that stands next to conscience in order to protect and affirm the authority of conscience.

Furthermore, the conscience that is not endangered by skepticism, and that can carry out a living faith in God points beyond itself; it transcends its own transcendence towards God by a still further dimension. In spite of everything the voice of conscience does for human beings,

it doesn't do enough, as we sharply and painfully feel. It thus turns out that the very gift of conscience arouses a longing for something which it alone cannot completely give. It mediates to the soul the idea of an authoritative guiding, of a divine law, and at the same time the wish to possess this in a fullness and not in mere fragments or indirect surmises. It awakens a thirst, an impatience for the acquaintance of this invisible Lord, Guide and Judge who so far was speaking only secretly to the soul, was whispering in the heart, who was communicating something, but far from what one wanted and needed. Thus, pious human beings who do not possess the blessing of the infallible teaching of revelation find it necessary to go in search of it, and indeed precisely because they are religious.[2]

Religion

The phenomenon of religion and the religions themselves, show similarly that they too are open for a further supernatural revelation. It is Newman's opinion that this expectation is one of the characteristics of religion in the religions. Speaking as a phenomenologist of religion, he says that "a revelation would be the greatest conceivable benefaction that can come to human beings." For the God of religion and of the religions is a hidden God; we don't see him, we only hear about him. He works under a veil. We know too little of his will and our obligations and prospects.

He has planted inklings of his majesty in your hearts, everywhere in creation he has left behind the traces of his presence and scattered the brilliance of his glory. You come to the place: you see, he has been there—but he is gone . . . He has taught you his law, quite unambiguously, but only by means of conclusions and suggestion, not by immediate command. He never shows himself unveiled to your yearning eyes and tortured heart; he does not step out openly before you as himself. What might that mean? An intellectual/spiritual being abandoned by its creator!

That is the situation and existence of human beings within natural religion, a limit situation in the truest sense of the word which, at the same time, points beyond the limit.

1. This and the following two citations have been translated from the German Newman anthology: *Ausgewählte Werke II* (Mainz, 1936) 300.
   2. Ibid. 321.

Thus the message of a revelation—far from being suspicious—is already born in our hearts by the irresistible expectations of reason. It would be hard to have to believe that there could be no revelation. The behavior of human beings has proven it from time immemorial, you cannot do other than wait for it from the hand of the All Merciful. Not as if you had any claim to it, but he pours the hope of it into you. It is not you who are worthy of the gift, but the gift is worthy of your creator . . . The fact that there is a creator—and a hidden one— carries you right up to the threshold of revelation and makes you seriously be on the lookout there for divine signs that there is a revelation.[3]

Of course, the facticity and reality of a revelation cannot be proven from the mere expectation of it. But it is just as unjustified to say (with Ludwig Feuerbach) that expectation and wish are a proof of nonreality. Why shouldn't reality also be able to represent itself as fulfillment of an expectation, as answer to a question? Furthermore, it is also clear that a revelation cannot be declared by human beings to be either a contradiction or an alienation.

The Supernatural Existential

These analyses can be expanded and at the same time summarized in Karl Rahner's phrase "supernatural existential."[4] Its meaning: Human beings are more than real, solely immanently structured "nature"; it belongs to their existence, and to their fundamental situation recognizable therein, to be oriented to and open to what transcends nature. Hence, they are open to the supernatural in the sense of a self-communication of God, which is a new event, a new goal in the sense of a fulfillment of existence, and all that by means of what one calls grace and salvation. "The human being is the event of the absolute self-communication of God."[5]

Karl Rahner makes this situation more precise in the following way: When the human being stands before the God of a possible revelation, something like a revelation actually always comes about: namely, the speaking or the silence of God. And human beings always and essentially hear the speaking or the silence of God; otherwise they would not be spirit and freedom. Spirit is no claim that God will speak. But when God does not speak, the spirit hears the silence of God. As spirit the human being stands before the self-disclosing or silent God as self-disclosing or silent.[6]

The whole problem, its vastness and the difficulty connected with it, can be thought through in a further way by making the following point clear. The possibilities human beings have to be hearers of the

3. Ibid. 311.

4. In: *SM* 1.1298–1300; Karl Rahner, *Foundations of Christian Faith* 126–33.

5. K. Rahner, *Foundations of Christian Faith* 126.

6. K. Rahner, *Hearers of the Word*, cf. the whole chapter: "The Free Unknown" 83–93, esp. 92–93.

word—hearers of a possible free revelation of God, receivers of a hoped-for salvation—are not only a matter of knowing but also a matter of freedom and decision. One important point of view is still to be attended to here: truths given to all human beings, as in mathematics or formal logic, are recognized by all only because they do not directly affect human beings in the innermost part of their existence, because they require no involvement, no decision of the person, indeed they are unable to require it. As Karl Rahner puts it, it is a fact that anyone with intelligence can make a mathematical truth or a process of logical reasoning intelligible, but cannot do the same for the possibility of the knowledge of God and of a possible revelation of God. That fact, however, is not a sign of the strength of the one and the weakness of the other, but a sign of the degree to which knowledge requires the actual engagement and commitment of human beings.[7]

It is an experience: Love is not merely a consequence of knowledge; love also participates in what is known and determined in knowledge. The most profound truth is thus always also the most free truth. Love enables seeing. The truth of the knowledge of God, in the way in which persons understand their God, is always also borne by the order of their love or by its disorder and inversion. An act of knowledge like this is at the same time always an engagement of the whole person in free decision. A change in knowledge is in these things always simultaneously a conversion, not just a change of opinion or a new result of investigation. These connections and laws need to be borne in mind in the questions being discussed here.

7. Ibid.: "The Free Listener" 94–110, esp. 109–10.

§ 29

THE PLACE OF A POSSIBLE SPECIAL
SUPERNATURAL REVELATION

The answer to this question is characterized by two considerations that have already been taken up. First, when one is talking about a revelation from *God*, there may not and cannot be any prior stipulation about it. On the other hand, when one is talking about a revelation to *human beings*, it has to take place in such a way that it can be received and accepted by them. This locates the answer to the question of the place of the possible revelation: the place of a possible revelation is the human being who is constituted by history and word.

History

Revelation as free act is, precisely as free action, oriented to history. History, as history of human beings, is the place of a free event, which means that it is not the place of something general or of a law that would be subject to planning and calculation. Instead, it is always something new, something unique, unprecedented and not yet existing that is being discovered and produced. Not nature and its structure determined by laws, but rather open history is the place of the special, specific, new, unexpected, not-yet-existing things that involve human beings.

Revelation as possible, new, special revelation is thus oriented to history. That is why the objection of deism that a special "supernatural" revelation would turn creation, i.e., nature, into a patchwork misses the point. Special revelation does not involve a change or correction of nature; it involves human beings who are characterized by history and freedom.

That history is the place of possible revelation is also indicated by the fact that human beings, the addressees and receivers of this revelation, are characterized by history. In history, through encounters with other human beings, through history-making events, works, and productions, human beings make their free decisions and perform their acts of responsibility which, in turn, make new history.

Accordingly, human beings are oriented to history in all dimensions of time: to the past, present, and future, to events, but above all to persons. Human beings are the constant realities against which and with which they are constituted as human beings. They cannot detach themselves from or get away from the horizon of the historical. Thus, whenever we are dealing with something that involves human beings humanly in a comprehensive and existential manner, as is the case in their orientation to transcendence, we are necessarily in the realm of history.

Finally, history is the place of a possible revelation of God because, as history of human beings, it is the *place of non-disponibility*. In historically living persons I encounter both my own limit and the non-disponibility of others, whom I cannot simply take over and through whom I let myself be claimed and get involved, gain self-recognition and fulfill myself. The non-disponibility of the other, of the You, is a constant indication of an ego-surpassing transcendence, even of a possible revelation of this transcendence. Thus it makes sense that the non-disponibility to be ascribed to transcendence is mediated through the non-disponibility of human beings, i.e., through historical mediation.

Consequently, if revelation is a free event over which I have no disposition, then this non-disponibility can be encountered only in the realm of history.

The Word

The possible place of a revelation is also the word. Thus human beings are once again spoken of as place of a possible revelation. In word, everything that is can be presented and made present and manifest: even the past, and what is not immediately objective, even the not-sensible, the intellectual, the super-worldly, unworldly, divine (the latter, however, in the form of negation).

However revelation may be described, whatever content it has, it cannot dispense with mediation through word. Word is the way in which revelation comes near to human beings, in which it can become present for them. Word, accordingly, can witness an event. Beyond that it can be an illuminating, interpreting, explaining word: for word makes visible the meaning of an event, which, as mere fact and without word, remains ambiguous. The event of the cross is represented in its meaning in the word from the cross. This meaning is not seen in the event as such: the crucifixion of a man. Quite the contrary. For the event as such makes visible something quite different: the tragic and terrible end of a human being.

If word as performative word not only witnesses to or interprets reality but creates reality, new, free, previously not existing, and not achievable from presently existing reality, then word is once again the place of a possible revelation, which is understood as new reality, as establishing a new event which moves and changes human beings. The word as word event, as dialogue, is the index of freedom, of non-disponibility, of not being able to be forced, the index of a genuine, free personal over-against. Word is, in addition, an expression of inclination, of love. It is spoken for the sake of encounter and communication. Word implies intersubjectivity, interpersonality, communication, community.

If, in this (possible) revelation, one is talking about an event between God and human beings, about a personal encounter, indeed about a community in which, human beings find their realization as hearers of the word, as seekers of salvation and happiness, but also God communicates something of Himself to us, then word is, in the multiplicity of its dimensions and "realities" (F. Ebner), the place of such revelation.

The Unconditioned Concretion

In this question regarding the place of a special, supernatural revelation, is there anything more specific to be found in the immeasurable realm of history, event, words, and human beings? Bernhard Welte has taken up this question thoroughly and extensively in his book *Heilsverständnis* [The Understanding of Salvation].[1] In it he develops the following considerations.

Human beings are indeed fundamentally open for anything and everything. It is in this openness that their humanity in spirit, freedom, and love is made manifest. But they run the danger of getting lost if they stick to this boundless openness, if they commit themselves to it and thus hold everything in oscillating suspension. Human beings have to choose, they have to decide, for one concrete thing among many, for one—their own—way, for one form of life, for one goal, for one vocation, for one human being. Welte calls this phenomenon, which is characteristic and unavoidable for human beings, the "unconditioned concretion."[2] It is grounded in the concrete individuality of human beings and represents it.

Romano Guardini took the same idea and formulated it this way:

Human beings can't have everything; they must choose certain things; they cannot live in the unlimited; they have to have a direction. The basis of their existence is

---

1. B. Welte, *Heilsverständnis. Philosophische Untersuchung Einiger Voraussetzungen zum Verständnis des Christentums* (Freiburg—Basel—Vienna, 1966).
2. Ibid. 216–31.

not the infinity of space, but the here. Not the boundlessness of the world, but the now. Not the incalculability of human possibilities, but those found in one's own ego. And the content of fruitful action is not the endless that can be accomplished but that which vocation and situation require. If human beings are satisfied with this demand, a conversion takes place. The right thing performed opens up one's glance into the whole. Those who do justice to their own situation find therein the whole given to them.[3]

A good illustration of this reality is also provided by the model, chosen by Welte, of human encounter in the realm of eros, love, and choice of partner. After going through the zone of open encounters and possibilities, eventually one human being becomes the one and only partner for me. This choice and decision in the sense of a concretion leads neither to a narrowing nor to a dissolution; it rather becomes the appropriate realization of human essence in the field of a concrete, abiding encounter anchored in responsibility and fidelity, which is grounded in faith and love and which, from the basis of this specification, finds the strength for openness, freedom, and affirmation.[4]

Applied to the possible place of revelation, this means that the revelation encountered in such a concretion of history, word, and person does not fall outside of the conditions of human existence and behavior but is in the highest way appropriate to it. It would be astonishing if the unconditioned concretion in person, history, and word were not the place of a possible revelation.

From this it follows that Lessings's axiom, "Fortuitous historical truths cannot be the foundation of eternal truths," describes a problem that can hardly be solved if it is considered in these categories—fortuitous history, eternal truth. But another aspect appears when, instead of "fortuitous" history, one says concrete history, and when, instead of using the misunderstood concept "eternal, timeless truth" in the description of revelation, one keeps in mind that one is dealing with a possible self-communication of God for human beings, which is possible only in the realm of history. One thus deals not just with the communication of theoretical truth, but with truth that is to be done, with truth as the encounter and characterization, the calling and realization of human beings.

The reference to unconditioned concretion as place of possible revelation is important and helpful, above all in view of the nowadays often conjured and appealed to situation of human beings, the *"conditio humana."*

On the other hand, the problem of revelation also raises the question as to how this possible revelation of God and the concretion or-

---

3. "Geschichtlichkeit und Absolutheit des Christentums" in: *Christliche Besinnung,* vol. 2 (Würzburg, 1951) 15–16
4. B. Welte, *Heilsverständnis* 220.

dered to it fits in with the many religions, the many religious messages, forms, figures, and witnesses.

The Problem of Exclusivity

Does not the unconditioned concretion claimed for a possible revelation lead to *exclusivity* and thus to the rejection and exclusion of everything else?

Welte formulates the problem as follows:

The unconditioned concretion is exclusive in a specific and unique way. For it must be kept in tension against other words, events, and witnesses and their differing witness. In the plurality of human existence the unconditioned concretion of faith is not possible without this at least potential tension. For there are, after all, the other witnesses whom I, in my faith, could not and have not chosen as authoritative for me, and their different voices and different forms of faith and religion. And since I, in the light of my being, am fundamentally open to all voices, I would be untrue if I did not take cognizance of them. But to take cognizance of them means to expose myself to the field of force of their claim. In principle, therefore, no messenger and no message of this kind can be indifferent to me, not even and even especially then when I, in the concretion of my faith, have not recognized them as mine. Thus the tension and its possible polemic, there at the edge, where the unconditioned concretion has its outer limits, is unavoidable. This tension is a consequence of the fundamental structure of human existence.

Hence the unconditioned concretion in its tension with the unlimited breadth of existence brings with it the danger of a break in communication. This becomes acute when I in my faith close myself off only negatively against other modes of and exhortations to faith, when I simply don't take cognizance of them, or do so only in sterile negativity, or merely combat them without really taking cognizance of them. But this break in communication would be like a betrayal of my humanity which still keeps me open to all humanities, fundamentally ready for possible communication everywhere.

However, the break in communication for the faith which understands itself in absolute concretions is not necessary, and in the essential sense not even possible. The danger can become acute only in a misunderstanding of the absolute concretion in which it collapses into a merely finite dogmatism. But if faith in the unconditioned concretion understands itself in its true sense, then it will carry, enliven, and make free the way for open communication with other forms of faith. It will then become similar to the situation of successful concretion in human existence: One's decision establishes a position, but precisely from this position comes an openness and a power of affirmation and recognition. This then is the correctly understood possibility and mode of the one and all.

In the light of the one and only I can see all in its light, and, I need to avoid no other voice. Thus I can let everything be, every voice and every witness and every possibility that may grow out of them for others. Precisely there where I have become one in the indicated sense, I can and should also become everything, if indeed I correctly understand myself in my highest and most appropriate possibility of unconditioned concretion.[5]

5. Ibid. 222–23.

This expresses an important theological principle: *Fidelity to one's own position* does not exclude but includes *openness for the other* and the whole.

"I can and should wish that all human beings might experience and find the light and its hope which shines on me from my witness and its message." But I may not do this in the form of finite subjective force. This is where we apply the principle: there is nothing to be demanded here, but everything to be expected.

The genuine possibility to which the unconditioned concretion empowers human beings with respect to other origins, and into which the tension with them can be dissolved is the possibility of essential dialogue. For those who entrust themselves to the one call and the one caller in the matter of salvation, become thereby not only open for every other call and origin that they do not want to choose, they are also touched by every other call; for this call, coming from far away and not choosable for them, nevertheless ultimately indicates the same thing. But they are not confused by these other and strange things, for they have known and chosen their basis for faith and trust; this supports them. And so there arises from origin to origin an interest and a contact of interest, and from this, transcending the strangeness, an exchange of ideas and questions. The result of this exchange of ideas is not the victory of one over the other in the finite sense, but the growth in clarity of each one. The process of this exchange is supported by freely given respect for the ways of God and for the dignity of the partner—especially there where I do not wish to share his/her ideas—and at the same time by the seriousness of my fidelity to my own origin. The unconditioned concretion in the matter of eternal salvation will assure a seriousness that will keep the dialogue from falling into the emptiness of mere small talk. However, belief in salvation for all will give the dialogue the freedom and openness and ready willingness without which the seriousness of the dialogue could easily harden into the sterile negativity of ultimate dogmatism. In such seriousness and freedom of dialogue, both partners can grow, especially where any victory by force and any demonstrable result are kept distant.

In the freedom of essential dialogue the unconditioned concretion can safely withstand and dissolve the danger of that polemic from which, because of the fundamental human situation, it can never escape, and it can nevertheless remain true to its own ground. It can, without denial and without blindness for other calls and groups of humanity, remain what it is: that in which human nature in its historical status can reach its highest understanding of itself.

As such it is the most appropriate way in which an all-encompassing sign and promise of salvation can be encountered and made understandable to human existence in the context of its historical immanence and in the horizon of its preunderstanding of its salvation. Human existence on its dark journey has every reason to examine closely whether just such a decisive and informative sign has been granted it.

This is the final and decisive determination into which the converging lines of convenience can lead the human preunderstanding of salvation and its possible signs. In it this preunderstanding comes to its culminating peak.[6]

What is the result of these reflections?

---

6. Ibid. 225–26.

The a priori preunderstanding that precedes the positivity of Christianity brings with it the possibility of humanly understanding and humanly living out Christian revelation when it appears in its divine positivity. Christian revelation can thus be allowed to become completely human without encroaching upon the divine gift in its free divine character as grace.

It produces the possibility of understanding and, with that, of human assimilation, both in view of the essential content of the Christian message and in view of the special form in which it appeared in our history, at least in its principal traits.[7]

Bernhard Welte thinks that the analyses he developed have made it clear that

human nature, as long as it correctly understands its own situation, possesses from within sufficient cause to look about itself for a binding sign of salvation within the immanence of this existence, and indeed first and foremost for a personally communicated and granted assurance of salvation which speaks to the totality of the unconditioned concretion, and requires it. If the expectations of humanity are so strongly oriented this way, its possible understanding is also mostly pointed in this direction. But the pre-understanding points to a personal bringer of salvation, and it anticipates preunderstandingly the decisive traits of the special form in which traits the Christian message positively appeared. For this message is bound to a faith-demanding person of the bringer of salvation, Jesus the Christ. From our way of looking at it, this manifestation and demand, precisely in this form, become the most understandable because they are the most human.[8]

But this analysis also shows, as a practical conclusion, that the human being, thus also the much-described and so hard to specify "modern man," is open for that which, in revelation, the ground of faith is all about. It is the task and the opportunity of dialogue, instruction, and proclamation to bring these two poles into connection.

The preceding analyses have attempted, in view of human beings and the reality that determines them, to examine that from which earlier generations could begin as from something obvious and unproblematic: from the positivity and from the fact of revelation accepted and affirmed as an unquestioned given, to which one did not need to bring anything, and from which one could work in order to interpret it in its individual aspects.

We are no longer in this situation. But what is to be seen in this new situation? Only a faith-threatening, faith-destroying crisis, or an opportunity and mandate under which many other new things are to be gained?

7. Ibid. 227.
8. Ibid. 228.

II

Special, Supernatural Revelation
according to Its Self-Witness

After so much has been said about the possibility and possible place of a special revelation, we now turn to the *fact itself*, to the positive reality of the revelation that characterizes the Christian faith. Our purpose is to see how this revelation correlates with those moments we have been discussing: history, word, and unconditioned concretion. We will further see how all this relates to human beings as hearers of the word and seekers of salvation. Our task is, by description and by argument, to give an account of this concrete, special revelation as the basis of faith.

Thus we turn to special, supernatural revelation according to its concrete self-witness in the Old and New Testaments, in other words, the matter, event, history, and content of the writings of the Old and New Testaments. In doing this, we should keep in mind the fundamental observations we have already made on the relationship of exegesis and systematic theology.

Systematic theology, to which fundamental theology belongs, must have the courage to bring things together and to connect them with and under the individual thing. It must have the courage to think of a center as origin in fullness, which does not forbid but makes it possible to speak of the individual rays that stream out from the center and of the circles that form around the center. For that which defines Christian faith is not a confusing fullness of individualities, it is really a radically simple reality that can be articulated, that can and should be unfolded in many ways. But this pluriformity is the pluriformity of the One only when it can be brought back to it. To attempt to do this, and in this sense to think through the foundations and connections of theology, this is the task of fundamental theology.

§ 30

REVELATION IN ITS ORIGIN

The Problem

Everyone familiar with the Bible knows that it begins with Genesis and its witness to the creation of the world. This (praising) witness is presented in the so-called two creation accounts.

This witness about the origin and beginning of all things comes from relatively late times, from the time of the kings of Israel and Judah and in conscious argument with contemporary conceptions of the world and its origins, above all with Babylonian myths, which can be described as theogony and cosmogony or as "battle of the Gods."

Chapters 1—11 of the Book of Genesis are called *primitive history,* although the concept of history doesn't apply, if we understand by history the concrete experience of an event recorded by observation or witnesses. But one could speak of primitive history both because it forms the basis of concrete, experienced and lived history as its presupposition and because the fact of it contains historical effects. Primitive history both precedes and forms the basis of the history of Israel. This is not only a temporal "before," but a factual ground and basis. The purpose of primitive history is to make clear in what horizon the concrete history of this people stands. It intends further to explain why the history experienced and lived in Israel became, so to speak, necessary, and in what its special significance and function consisted.

Primitive history is, in the popular and convincing contemporary description, "Israel's look into its past" (H. Renckens). The first eleven chapters of Genesis are the document, assembled from all kinds of traditions, about how Israel, on the basis of its concrete historical experience with God, thought about the beginning of the world and the human race. They are the account, born out of living experience and theological reflection, about how it was in the beginning, how it must have been in the beginning, if things are the way they are.

Genesis 1—11 is "protology" and "etiology"; account of the origins and causes and grounds for the understanding and for the being of that which now is; Genesis 1—11 is prophecy backwards into the past. The beginning of the world and history is, according to Genesis, to be interpreted antimythically: not as a process of cosmic powers, but as work of the freedom of the God calling the world into existence by God's word. This means radical difference between God and world and at the same time innermost connection between uncreated Creator and created world. The term "creation myth" is, de facto, an inner contradiction. But this doesn't have to mean that the mythical mode of speaking as a mode of narration has to be done away with. For in creation thus understood, God has revealed Himself: not only in the fact of divine existence, but also in God's being as Lord, in God's power, wisdom, and goodness.

This can be found expressed in the creation psalms—especially Psalm 104—which were composed at about the same time that the book of Genesis was being assembled into its present form (in the sixth century, following the Babylonian Exile). The Epistle to the Romans (1:19-20) also expressly refers to it. Along with affirmations about creation, we find here the outline of a *theological anthropology*. There is a description of what the human being is, and this description is projected onto the genetic level. In telling the story of how human beings used to be, it tells us what they now are.

This message does not exhaust the content of the so-called primitive history. Genesis has knowledge—especially in the so-called second account of creation in Gen 2:4b-25 and in the paradise story of Chapter 3—about a human condition that extends beyond their creation reality. Human beings are described as beings that share a special proximity, love, and friendship with God. This condition, which is described in the image of the garden of paradise and is also described theologically with the categories of original graces, belongs to the revelation of the beginning, to revelation at its origin, and is to be understood in turn protologically and etiologically: as Israel's vision into its own past and that of human beings.

The starting point and ground of understanding for this reflection in the Book of Genesis is the historical and concrete experience of this people: the experience of human guilt, of suffering, evil, grief, and death, and the related question of the ground, of the why in the history and constitution of human beings who—what a paradox!—are the most sublime work, the crown of creation, and who simultaneously find themselves in contradiction to and in dereliction of it. In the image of paradise is described the counterimage of this situation, the totally other world: the world without shadows, the world of peace, of nearness to God, of solidarity with God. The present world and situation of human beings are demonstrated as the *loss of paradise* and its special gifts. According to Genesis, this loss came about through an *act of human beings*, by their decision against their creatureliness and indebtedness. Biblically speaking, it came about through their refusal to recognize their creatureliness and indebtedness, by the presumption of wanting "to be like God," of putting themselves in God's place "knowing good and evil" (Gen 3:5), as quintessence of what belongs to God alone. When paradise was lost, human beings sank into a guilty, broken, and impaired creatureliness, in which they historically and presently and concretely find themselves, namely, human beings in contradiction, inauthenticity, and deterioration. But in the guilt of the beginning not just the past is affected; the present is also described: the constantly present option of human beings against God, happening again and again and again. The presence of sin is illuminated in the light of the past. The purpose of the text is not so much to say: this is the way human beings were, but to say: this is the way human beings are.

Chapters 4—11 of Genesis give a drastic description of an ever-darkening story, of the increase of sin: from the fratricide of Cain to the flood as sign and punishment for the universal sovereignty of evil. Of course, there are also some figures of light: Abel, Enoch, and Noah.

The Covenant of Noah (Genesis 9) is a new turning of God to the humanity represented by Noah and a confirmation and renewal of the possibility left in humanity to know God from creation, and to see creation, above all its life and fruitfulness in the rhythm of the year and seasons, as a gift bestowed, and with that to recognize this creation as revelation and hierophany, and to give expression to this knowledge and recognition in the form of religion. The Acts of the Apostles refers to this situation when Paul proclaims: "God . . . made the heaven and the earth and the sea and all that is in them. Yet he did not leave himself without witness, for he did good and gave you from heaven rains and fruitful seasons, satisfying your hearts with food and gladness" (Acts 14:15-17).

Even if all these statements are not to be regarded as factual historical descriptions, they have validity as factual affirmations in the form of narration. The reality represented in these affirmations is above all a statement about human beings—that is where it has its verification—and about their orientation to God. This is given not only by the fact of creation but also by the fact of guilt which, for its part, is an offense against a special characteristic of human beings.

Primitive Revelation

This context will help make intelligible what is meant by the concept "primitive revelation."[1] This concept was introduced into theolog-

---

1. Cf. Heinrich Fries, "Primitive Revelation," *SM* 5.355–58.

ical terminology in the nineteenth century in order to put a name to what we have just been discussing. The concept "primitive revelation" was often used not only in order to describe phenomenologically but also to explain and understand theologically the various religions about which we have been learning more and more in the modern age, along with their often astonishingly concrete common contents.[2]

In the religions of the world one finds contents like salvation, grace, the Fall, guilt, judgment, atonement, redemption, rebirth, heaven. One finds ideas of a luminous and healthy beginning (golden age) as well as of paradise lost, and also witnesses of the flood. There are also prayers, sacrifice, cults, rites, holy places, and holy times.

In these contents of religion one can recognize the continued effect of what one thought of as original revelation, namely the continued effect of primitive revelation still influencing human beings. This did not remain limited to the single point of the beginning, but lives on in the traditions, religions, and myths of the peoples. And these are traditions of an origin called "primitive revelation."[3]

Looked at more closely, this means that original revelation, primitive revelation with its contents (creation, paradise, guilt), is the *condition of religion*. This is, for its part, the presupposition and source of the many concrete religions. The common presupposition explains the remarkable agreement in their contents. The different religions of the earth can thus, theologically seen,[4] be specified according to the mode and manner in which they express the elements and contents of original revelation, i.e., of primitive revelation. At the same time, the concrete religions themselves are sign and expression of the greatness and limits of human beings.

The so-called nature religions are, in this theological perspective, both the positive and the negative answer to revelation in and from creation. The redemptive religions are characterized by elements of creation, golden age at the beginning, paradise, the Fall, guilt for paradise lost, as well as by elements of longing for rescue, salvation, redemption.

The ethical religions are authoritatively characterized by the message of God given in the conscience of human beings: the unconditioned obligation to the good, to the "voice of God" in conscience, to the experience of guilt, to the ideas of retribution and forgiveness, of judg-

---

2. N. Hötzel, *Die Uroffenbarung im französischen Traditionalismus* (Munich, 1962).

3. J. Pieper, *Tradition als Herausforderung* (Munich, 1963).

4. Karl Rahner, "Christianity and the Non–Christian Religions," *Theological Investigations* 2 (1974) 3–23; H. R. Schlette, *Towards a Theology of Religions*, trans. W. J. O'Hara (New York: Herder and Herder, 1966); Joseph Ratzinger, "Der Christliche Glaube und die Weltreligionen" in: *Gott in Welt* (Festschrift K. Rahner) (Freiburg—Basel—Vienna, 1964) 287–305; H Fries, "Das Christentum und die Religionen der Welt" in: *Wir und die Anderen* (Stuttgart, 1966) 240–272; J. Heislbetz, *Theologische Gründe der nichtchristlichen Religionen* (Freiburg—Basel—Vienna, 1967).

ment and beatitude. This consensus of the religions requires a theological explanation; it is found by going back to a so-called primitive revelation.

This fact was present to the theology of Christian antiquity in an astonishing way. Justin, picking up from the Prologue of John, spoke of the sperm nuclei of the Logos *[logoi spermatikoi]* scattered among the pagans; Tertullian coined the expression of the *anima naturaliter christiana* [the naturally Christian soul]. Along with all their criticism of religious practice, theologians like Clement of Alexandria and Origen saw in the myths a preparation for Christ, and then in Christ the answer to the questions behind the myths. From the Augustine of the Retractations comes the—especially for him—astonishing words: "The reality itself, which is now called the Christian religion, was also found among the ancients; indeed, from the beginning of the human race it has not been absent, until Christ appeared. From then on the true religion, which already existed, began to be called the Christian religion." In developing this idea, Nicholas of Cusa spoke of the *"una religio in rituum varietate* [one religion in a variety of rites]."

These ideas had been forgotten when, during the Middle Ages, the opinion was held that there were practically no more non-Christian religions, when one constructed the model of a *"puer in silvis"* [child in the forest] in order to ask what possibilities of salvation there were for him.[5] The discovery of new continents at the beginning of the new age with their religions came as a shock and was experienced as a theological problem of the first order.

Its Significance

At the beginning of our century the attempt was made to construct an historical demonstration of primitive revelation and the primitive tradition that came with it as the foundation of religion and the religions by proposing the thesis that the path of the historical religions does not proceed from polytheism to monotheism by way of an evolution, an ascending religious development, and as the result of a more profound religious reflection, but that it works the other way around. This was done above all by the ethnologist and historian of religions Wilhelm Schmidt in his ten-volume work *Der Ursprung der Gottesidee* [The Origin of the Idea of God].[6] According to this view, the high religion of primitive monotheism broke up into the many different forms of polytheism, and the whole process is to be interpreted as decline and

5. M. Seckler, "Das Heil der Nichtevangelisierten" in: *ThQ* 140 (1960) 38–69.
6. Münster, 1912–13.; "Die Uroffenbarung als Anfang der Offenbarungen Gottes" in: *Religion—Christentum—Kirche* I, eds. G. Esser, J. Mausbach (Cologne, 1911) 541–692.

fall from an original height. Wilhelm Schmidt and his school[7] attempted to prove this by investigating the religion of the oldest peoples known today. They found in them the contents of belief in an individual God or high God, as well as ideas of paradise and flood as well as relatively high ethical teachings. The further history of religion and religions is consequently to be characterized as a history of falling away.

Schmidt's thesis was not accepted in the circles of the history of religions, for they found that religion and the history of religions had a far more differentiated content than would be the case with this theory of the Fall. But even if the thesis of original religious monotheism cannot be held historically, that does not eliminate the basic idea of an original primitive revelation, even if there is no desire to take over this concept.

In more recent evangelical [German Lutheran] theology, the concept "primitive or fundamental revelation" has been taken up by Paul Althaus.[8] He understands it as a characterization of the fundamental situation or fundamental reality of human beings. The idea of a primitive revelation also came alive in the nineteenth century, because one saw in tradition as such and as a whole an indispensable element of life, of history, especially of the history of spirit, culture, and religion (traditionalism). Tradition is the handing on of what one has oneself received. Whatever a human being has or knows did not come from within, but was perceived from outside, received from others. "Whatever we are, we owe to others." A presupposition for tradition is the authority of the one who hands on. This authority is grounded in the fact that the one handing on has access to the origin or source of the tradition. This means, in the case of religion, access to the revelation that has been given to a "founder" as carrier of a religious revelation.

The concept of primitive revelation, above all what it means, also constitutes the theological presupposition and basis speaking of the *possibility of salvation for human beings* before and apart from Jesus Christ. This situation is especially applicable today. The matter was less problematic as long as one thought that the age of the human race was some 6000 years and that the Bible was the oldest book in the world and that all knowledge of God was mediated through the Bible.

With the discovery of new continents, and of new peoples, religions, and cultures, and with the discovery of a human history of millions of years before and outside of the biblical message, one began to see an explanation for the possibility of salvation thus opened up for human beings before and apart from Christ. This was becoming visible precisely in the idea of a revelation as primitive and basic revelation given to

7. W. Koppers, *Der Urmensch und Sein Weltbild* (Vienna, 1949).
8. *Die Christliche Wahrheit. Lehrbuch der Dogmatik*, 3rd ed. (Gütersloh, 1952) 37–94.

human beings and humanity right from the beginning, and in the living consciousness of God in humanity and its religions. This is also the reason that, as Karl Rahner says, *world history, history of humanity, and salvation history* are coextensive. This has to be so, if God does indeed wish all human beings to come to salvation (1 Tim 2:4). The Second Vatican Council explicitly declares:

Those also can attain to everlasting salvation who through no fault of their own do not know the gospel of Christ or His church, yet sincerely seek God and, moved by grace, strive by their deeds to do His will as it is known to them through the dictates of conscience. Nor does divine Providence deny the help necessary for salvation to those who, without blame on their part, have not yet arrived at an explicit knowledge of God, but who strive to live a good life, thanks to his grace. Whatever goodness or truth is found among them is looked upon by the Church as a preparation for the gospel. She regards such qualities as given by Him who enlightens all men so that they may finally have life.[9]

Like primitive history, primitive revelation cannot be historically proven. But it makes sense as authentic etiology. And because the ground for reality is sought, the etiology is intended to speak as reflection on the ground and cause of reality. It is the condition of a possibility, the theory of a praxis.

9. Dogmatic Constitution on the Church (*Lumen Gentium*) § 16.

REVELATION IN THE HISTORY OF ISRAEL

In our discussion of "History and (as) Revelation" (§ 26): we mentioned a number of themes—the aspects of freedom and of not being subject to manipulation or disposition of others; the experience of rugged stability, of being guided and being successful in a way that evades ultimate human explanation; the discrepancy between cause and effect; the inkling and traces of another power than merely military and political factors—all this becomes tangible in a special way in Israel's history. The theme "Revelation as History"[1] has a decisive foundation in the history of Israel because God's revelation to Israel took place in the mode of history, of historical events, actions, and experiences.

Primitive history, revelation as origin, is the framework and horizon for the history of the People of Israel created by the Old Testament itself in an astonishing conception. The beginning of this history is set down with the history of Abraham: Chapter 12 of Genesis. It unmistakably narrows the horizon from that of primitive history affecting the whole of humanity to the particularity and singularity of one people and its historical fate.

Patriarchal History

Even the beginning of this special historical revelation has an etiological intention. Its purpose is to describe the immediate origin and prehistory of the history of the People of Israel, and to come to know and establish in exemplary fashion the fate of this history: the guiding, accompaniment, election, separating out, and mandate to become different, but above all, the faith as ground of existence of this people in its patriarchal origins.

---

1. Wolfhart Pannenberg, *Revelation as History*, trans. David Granskou (New York: Macmillan, 1968).

The revelation beginning with Abraham[2] is logically and in accord with its contents described as "revelation and promise." This specifies what is new in this form of revelation. Corresponding to the promise, we have on the human side, not primarily knowledge, but faith and obedience. Promise points to history, to the future. This explains that already described characteristic, which is ascribed to the figure of Abraham throughout all of Scripture, that he is the father of faith (Rom 4:16), that all true believers are called children of Abraham, and that faith, not bodily lineage, bestows and represents the true heritage of Abraham (Gal 3:6-9: Rom 4:1-3; John 8:33).

Abram, as he was originally called, lived in Ur of the Chaldees in a milieu imbued with high culture and rich religiosity. Its most impressive figure was Hammurabi, the king of Babylon. It is possible to imagine, with Romano Guardini,[3] that Abraham would be called into solitude, led to interior liberation and illumination, and endowed with religious knowledge—knowledge about what God is, how the path and access to God become possible. This is how one can characterize the figure and way of Buddha. Raised in the royal court, he is brought, by the sight of a sick man, a beggar, an old man, and a dead man, to recognize the ephemerality of all things. He leaves his home, changes his life, and in profound meditation seeks out the paths of right action and right living. In his "thirst for existence" he recognizes the ground of all evil and, in its overcoming, sees true wisdom. In Abraham's time, similar things were taking place in India among the Brahman ascetics. The Vedas, the holy scriptures of the Brahmans, tell us about them. But in the revelation to Abraham we find nothing of the kind. Instead we find the following situation: Abram leaves his land, his home, his former milieu, and travels to one unknown to him.

This event, the decision of a human being, is—this is its uniqueness—not to be understood "naturally." The life and acts, the way and fate of Abram, stand rather under the sign of obedience to an instruction and a leading, which do not come from himself but which take control of him and lead him where he does not want to go. They stand under the sign of a power effective in him like a command, which he acknowledges in the arrangements of his life, which are not mere facts but realities in which something is said to him, in which someone else acts, in which he shows and reveals himself whom Abram calls "Lord."

According to the witness of Scripture, Abram's path and fate, his history is to be interpreted theologically, i.e., as revelation. And this is to be characterized as historical leading and guiding by another.

---

2. Emil Brunner, *Revelation and Reason: The Christian Doctrine of Faith and Knowledge*, trans. Olive Wyon (Philadelphia: Westminster Press, 1968) 81–95; Heinrich Fries, *Revelation* (New York: Herder and Herder, 1969) 54–68.

3. *Die Offenbarung. Ihr Wesen und ihre Formen* (Würzburg, 1940) 54.

Corresponding to this fate is faith, which is a moment of the revelation event, because it is through faith that this event is accepted. The quality of revelation and faith in the form of leading and guiding in the Abraham history is expressed in a very special way by the fact that these qualities stand under the *sign of promise*—thus in the future and not accessible to human calculation—and by the fact that they are connected not only with the unknown but also with the unlikely, or even the paradoxical. We have already discussed this in another context ("The Faith of Abraham" in § 6).

The activity of Yahweh with and in Abraham is sealed by the *covenant*, a covenant between unequal partners, which, again, comes from the free initiative of God and is granted to human beings. This covenant[4] includes grace and obligation in itself and likewise stands under the sign of the coming, the future, the promise: "The Lord appeared to Abram, and said to him, 'I am God Almighty (El Shaddai); walk before me, and be blameless. And I will make my covenant between me and you, and will multiply you exceedingly'" (Gen 17:1-2; cf. Gen 15:28).

As a sign of the new thing that has taken place by the establishment of the covenant, Abram receives a new name: "No longer shall your name be Abram, but your name shall be Abraham (i.e., 'father of a multitude'); for I have made you the father of a multitude of nations" (Gen 17:5). A change of name, in ancient oriental thinking, signifies a change of fate. The further sealing and guarantee of the covenant of God with Abraham and his descendants is to be circumcision (Gen 17:9ff). Circumcision is a sign of the covenant and at the same time a sign of the fact that the one who bears it is God's property.

In the Abraham event, what special historical revelation is and what dimension of reality it points to become recognizable: a life, a fate, and all paths and decisions in it are the word, will, and act of another, of a Lord and God who communicates Himself to an individual.[5] The history of Abraham also contains the model of the other patriarchal histories of Isaac, Jacob, and the Joseph story, as well as the basic structure of God's activity and guidance and the human response. The patriarchal histories describe the special way in which the People of Israel came into existence as God's own people and began its historical path. The patriarchal histories are thus not simply story but kerygma, backward-looking prophecy as well as doxology of history with a view to the present. The present is conceived as fruit of the promise; it understands itself and its task from the revelational activity of God and from faith.

---

4. The idea of covenant is the dominant idea of Walther Eichrodt: *Theology of the Old Testament*, vol. 1, trans. J. A. Baker (Philadelphia: Westminster Press, 1967).

5. H. Groß, "Zur Offenbarungsentwicklung im AT" in: *Gott in Welt*. Festschrift Karl Rahner, vol. 1 (Freiburg—Basel—Vienna, 1964) 407-22.

The founding history of the people of Israel itself contains the same traits found in an exemplary mode in the history of the fathers, especially in the Abraham event. They stand under the same sign and under the same law, only everything is greatly expanded.

The People of Israel

The second great thrust of historical revelation takes place in the call of Moses in Egypt, a highly cultivated political and religious land. It is the time of Pharaoh Ramses II (1298-1225), who had in Amenophis IV an extraordinary predecessor: the founder of the religion of the sun god, who was venerated as unique lord, creator of all life and all things. After the death of this king and at the time of Moses, the old polytheistic and theriomorphic [animal-worship] religion revived.

The call of Moses takes place in the theophany described in Exodus 3. It culminates in the communication and interpretation of the name of God, of the name Yahweh (Exod 3:14). The interpretation of the name of God, who is identified with the "God of the Fathers" (El, El Shaddai—cf. Exod 6:2) is: "I AM WHO I AM. . . . this is my name forever, and thus I am to be remembered throughout all generations" (Exod 3:14–15).

This "I am who I am," an interpretation of the special divine name of Yahweh, is a message. Its meaning:

No holy place, no mountain, no temple is the location of the God who sent Moses. He is not sedentary; he is here, he is here in the here and now of the history of Israel. I am who I am—I am means not just: I exist (existence of God); not just: I am everywhere in space (omnipresence of God); the subject is not Yahweh's existence and essence when God reveals Himself to Moses as I am who I am, but Yahweh's presence: Pharaoh will take note, even if he doesn't want to acknowledge it, that someone mightier than he now rules in his land. Israel, enslaved and condemned to extermination, will have the experience of seeing its liberator and savior at work. The Invisible One shows Himself visibly in historical deeds, reveals Himself in the everyday world of human history.[6]

However, the situation of the Israelites in Egypt had in the course of time become a genuine faith problem. Where is the God of our fathers who has allowed us to come into such tribulation? Were not the gods of Egypt in the form of animals and heavenly bodies more tangible, more mighty than the God of our fathers? The memory of their God had paled for many. If the power of Yahweh was to be demonstrated, this could happen only by Yahweh being proven mightier than the might of Pharaoh and his gods. God must be shown to be the victor.

This happened through the deeds of Moses. It happened in the actual liberation of Moses' band from the servitude of Egypt, in their be-

6. F. Stier, *Die Geschichte Gottes mit den Menschen*, 2d ed. (Düsseldorf, 1962) 22.

ing saved from Pharaoh's exterminating order, and in the crown of wondrous deeds connected with it. It happened in the affliction of the Egyptians, in the miracle of the Reed Sea and the desert journey, in the encounter with God, in the sealing of the covenant at Sinai and the taking possession of the land. These events in the history of the People of Israel are the constitutive historical realities in its coming-to-be. In their accumulated paradoxical character contradicting all human expectations, calculations and ideas, they are—this is the sense and purpose of the biblical witness—actions of divine activity, divine leading and guiding, divine election and separating out. God's revelation is realized as action and effect of that action in this history, in its events and accomplishments.

For this reason, these events are ever after "remembered" and celebrated in cult. Israel's confession expressed therein affirms the fact and glorifies it: Yahweh led Israel out of Egypt in a wondrous manner. This unique historical act is for Israel's faith the fundamental reason and the ever-new guarantee of Yahweh's rescuing help and saving power in the present and future.

The People of Israel, however—this is the other side of the coin— understands itself or should understand itself as *Yahweh's* people, as his special possession, which understands the ground of its existence in the promises and fulfilling deeds of Yahweh and in the faith directed to him. The sense of Israel's historical calling is made clear above all in the so-called "eagle saying" of Exodus:

You have seen what I did to the Egyptians, and how I bore you on eagle's wings and brought you to myself. Now therefore, if you will obey my voice and keep my covenant, you shall be my own possession among all peoples; for all the earth is mine, and you shall be to me a kingdom of priests and a holy nation. (Exod 19:4-6)

To this is added the warning:

You shall not do as they do in the land of Egypt, where you dwelt, and you shall not do as they do in the land of Canaan, to which I am bringing you. (Lev 18:3)

The further history of this people is determined by the manner and mode in which its foundations, namely God's revealing activity and the faith and obedience ordered to it, unfolded and took shape in the ebb and flow of history, and by the manner and mode in which Israel fulfilled its specific mandate of being *an exception among the nations and at the same time a ferment for the rest of the world.* The temptations that went with this distinction were assimilation, adaptation, the dispersion of Israel among the nations, thus giving up the election; and on the other hand, the exact opposite—boasting about being chosen, shutting themselves off, and closing themselves in, at the cost of universality. Again and again in its history Israel has succumbed to these two, so different, temptations. Regarding the further history of Israel, as it relates to our question of revelation, only some fundamental acts and structures still need to be mentioned.

In Canaan, Israel became a nation of the world. Expressed in biblical language, it turned away from Yahweh, abandoned its God, and forgot Yahweh's covenant. This is the judgment on the approximately five hundred years of the history of Israel from its taking possession of the land up to the second captivity in 586–539. The leitmotif of this history is *assimilation to its religious and political milieu*. In being assimilated, Israel was acting against the condition of its having been chosen. The assimilation followed from the natural course of things; what seemed to be an obvious historical development led Israel into conflict with its own special character. The land forces its law on the new settler. A nomadic people becomes sedentary and experiences the change from pasture to field, from shepherd's staff to plow, from tent to house. Canaan made the Israelites comfortable with its old culture, with its customs and laws, as well as with the indigenous religion of the land; it taught them to know and love its gods.

Another generation arose which knew neither Yahweh nor the deeds he had done for Israel. They forsook Yahweh and served the Ba'als and the Ash'taroth (Judges 2:10, 13).

Yahweh did indeed remain Israel's God in veneration. Their forebears had experienced him in Egypt, in the desert, in the battles for the land. And although the experience of their forebears might pale in the memory of the children, the story of the powerful and saving deeds of Yahweh was never silenced. But the whole realm of cultivated field, of generation and birth ruled by the cult and myth of Baal did not fit into the image of the historical God whom Israel knew from Egypt and Sinai. Nevertheless, faith puts no limits on its God; it sees Yahweh as the Lord also of this realm and transfers to him, in presumably faithful preservation of his uniqueness and field of power, attributions, cultic customs, human sacrifice, and feasts of the Canaanite fertility God. This appropriation in belief turned of course into the mistaken path by which Baal, under the name of Yahweh, could make a nest for himself in the heart of Israel. The Baalization of Yahweh went so far that the Goddess Anath, Baal's spouse, was set up as Yahweh's throne-companion.[7]

The ebb and flow between assimilation and distance, the struggle between God and idols, Yahweh and Baal, reached its high point in the challenge of Elijah to the priests and prophets of Baal: "If the Lord is God, follow him; but if Ba'al, then follow him" (1 Kgs 18:21).

The second assimilation of the chosen people took place in the political arena. The royal sovereignty of Yahweh over his people is carried out at first in the mode of immediacy. God, God's Spirit, raises

7. Following F. Stier, *Die Geschichte* 40–41.

up persons who stand by the people in its hour of need, who lead and guide it as leaders, judges, and military leaders who, as it is written, wage "Yahweh's wars." It is the time of the judges: Deborah, Gideon, Samson, Samuel. This free dominion emphasizes in a special way the sovereignty of God, who is Israel's king. This king's might and strength is to be the might and strength of the people: theocratically charismatic, charismatic theocracy.

But that is not how it all turns out. The special nature of the People of God is historically not maintained. It represents no genuine *realpolitische* possibility. From Israel's bosom comes more and more perceptibly the cry for a firm institution of power and for a visible representation of the nation. These strivings finally force from Samuel, the last judge, the decision: "We will have a king over us, that we also may be like all the nations, and that our king may govern us and go out before us and fight our battles" (1 Sam 8:19f.).

As in religion, so in politics too, the People of Israel wants to be like other nations. It looks like a natural and obvious development: the development of a group of tribes to an organized government, is, in the sight of faith, a falling away of the people from the rule of God. It is the overthrowing of God's rule, the doubting of God's fidelity and promise, of God's possibility in world and history.

And yet this breakout into the institution of the stubbornly won kingdom is taken over—and this is something new—into the law of the people of God and given a place in it. This is in fact done in such a way that the fundamental characteristics of the covenant and the promise are preserved: "You shall be my people, I will be your God." This assignment can be realized also within the kingdom: the *kingdom* is to become an *organ and instrument of the royal kingship of God.*[8] What was thus begun seems to be successful in the figure and the kingdom of David. He brings the tribes of Israel together and by successful military forays creates a powerful kingdom. The people's unity is grounded in Yahweh who is the God common to all. David expressed this tie by transferring to Jerusalem, to Mount Zion, the ark of the covenant with the tablets of the Law, the document of the covenant with God. There, next to the palace of the king, was to rise the temple in place of the former tent: the one God as king of the king of the people.

By means of the kingdom and priesthood, thought of Yahweh, the God of Israel, was to be preserved and maintained in constant remembrance—not only in words but in the living out of life for the individual, for the community, and for the people. Israel's faith in Yahweh, its remembrance of his promises and their fulfillment, its orientation to his teaching—in brief, its obligation to an existence based on faith—

8. Ibid. 46.

was to be made present, practiced, and mediated by kingdom and priesthood.

The high point in the life of David describes at the same time a turning point in the history of the kingdom of Israel. Two lines cross at this point: the horizontal line of assimilation to the milieu and the vertical line which introduces into the plan of God the historical developments of templebuilding and dynasty. These novelties lay in the natural course of things, but they had severe consequences. Both lines contain dangers. The building of the temple hides the danger of changing the "One Who Goes with Us" (M. Buber), who is "there wherever being may be," into a sedentary deity housed like the gods, the nondisponible *There* into a fixed *Here*. This novelty is avoided for a time, but is later approved for David's son. The other novelty also lies on the dangerous path of assimilation: hereditary succession to the throne. With Saul and David, the "Spirit of Yahweh" took part in deciding their choice to be king. Now, in the place of charism, in the place of the non-disponible power granted only to the one chosen, in place of the one inspired to do battle and to rule, comes the "house," the dynasty, the principle of hereditary succession to power in effect in Egypt and the other neighboring lands around Israel. And this change from the one-time choice of an individual to the continuing choice of a whole race, from "spirit" to "blood," takes place by virtue of divine dispensation.[9]

It is not possible for us here to go into the question how this new level and form of revelation in the situation of the kingdom was represented and developed in the course of history. It was—seen as a whole—not successful. Israel's playing with worldly power and attempt to preserve and represent to the world its special, its chosen, character failed. God's rule became human rule. The attempt failed visibly after David's death in the separation of the kingdom into the northern and southern kingdoms, and in the fall of both kingdoms, in the coming of the people into the Babylonian captivity—into that very country from which Abraham was once called out. Israel returns there in guilt. Through suffering, through loss of land and freedom, the People of God are to gain a deeper knowledge of its place in God's history with the human race. Power and earthly kingdom were a poor instrument and unsuitable organ for God's rule and kingdom.

The Institution/Phenomenon of Prophecy

But one phenomenon of this particular period of the kingdom (900–500 BC) must be considered: prophecy.[10] The prophets of Israel are the

---

9. Ibid. 51–52.

10. R. Rendtoff—R. Meyer—G. Friedrich in: *ThW* 6.781–863; Gerhard von Rad, *Theologie der Prophetischen Überlieferungen Israels* (Munich, 1962); N. Füglister, "Prophet,"

counterweight against the kingdom and the priesthood and against the dangers and constant temptations connected with the kingdom: forgetting and falling away from the covenant and its obligations and prophecies. The temptations of the priesthood consisted in contenting oneself with the external and ritual performance of the cult and neglecting faith and moral values. The prophets were distinguished from the prophetic figures of the other religions as Yahweh was from the gods. They are explicitly coordinated with certain kings: Elijah to Ahab, Isaiah to Ahaz, Jeremiah to Jehoiakim and Zedekiah—so also to the respective representatives of the official priesthood.

What is a prophet? A prophet is—if one starts from the primitive meaning of the word—someone who speaks in place of another, thus acts on behalf of someone. A prophet is someone who is "awakened," separated out, called and chosen. A prophet is—as is contained in the factually related word "seer"—someone who sees. But the gaze of the prophet is not first and foremost into the past and future, but into the immediate present. The prophet sees, recognizes, and says how things are in relation to God among the people, with the king, and with the priests. The eye of the prophet is not blinded by the fact that apparently everything is in order, that all services are functioning. The prophet sees the emptiness of faith and love behind the external facades, he recognizes the unwholeness in the midst of the external wholeness which the court prophets, the false prophets, praise. In addition, he is the consoler of the people in the face of misfortune, exile, and hopelessness.

A prophet is someone who, with courage and authority, says what a particular historical situation is all about: about faith and obedience, about justice and love. A prophet stands up for his word and his mission and is ready to seal his word with life and deed. The prophet is to warn king and priesthood away from infidelity to the covenant, and also from all false security. The prophet does not interpret catastrophes and afflictions as external fate but as God's punishment for incurred guilt: as a revelation event. The prophet stands interceding before God as an advocate of his people. He prays God to be mindful of the covenant, of the promises, of his "oath," so that God's own work, God's own people, may not become a subject of mockery in the eyes of the world.

From these characteristics it is also possible to pick out some criteria for the authentic prophets, in contrast to the false prophets. The most important mark of the prophetic state is its calling, on the basis of inner evidence, to speak and act in the name of God. This is often

---

HThG 2.350–72; K. Rahner, "Prophetism," SM 5.110–13; G; Lanczkowski—H. Groß—J. Schmid—K. Rahner in: LThK 7.794–802; J. Scharbert, Die Propheten Israels bis 700 v. Chr. (Cologne, 1965); Die Propheten Israels um 600 v. Chr. (Cologne, 1967).

enough expressed as contrary to personal aptitude and inclination, as an obligation imposed, as burden and necessity. The false prophet gives out his dreams as revelation and his own will as word of God.

In addition to this subjective criterion there is as an objective, although post-factum sign of differentiation: the occurrence of what has been said (Jer 28:9, 15), the consistency of the life and teaching of the prophet, his fidelity towards God, and renunciation of all opportunism. "A final differentiating characteristic is that the false prophet has an answer always and for everything, while the prophet who is called at times remains dumb because he does not have free disposition over God's word but must wait for the hour of revelation."[11]

The true prophet points from the situation of the present to a *new covenant*, the greater, universal covenant being grounded within human beings. This new covenant is frequently mentioned: Isa 19:19–21; 55:3; 61:8; but above all in the famous "new covenant" passage of Jeremiah:

Behold, the days are coming, says the Lord, when I will make a new covenant with the house of Israel and the house of Judah, not like the covenant which I made with their fathers when I took them by the hand to bring them out of the land of Egypt, my covenant which they broke, though I was their husband, says the Lord. But this is the covenant which I will make with the house of Israel after those days, says the Lord: I will put my law within them, and I will write it upon their hearts; and I will be their God, and they shall be my people. And no longer shall each man teach his neighbor and each his brother, saying, 'Know the Lord,' for they shall all know me, from the least of them to the greatest, says the Lord; for I will forgive their iniquity, and I will remember their sin no more. (Jer 31:31–34)

The words of the prophet Jeremiah are spoken during the great catastrophe of Israel: in the time of the besieging and destruction of Jerusalem. In the time of need, of exile and foreign domination, there awakens in the People of God a consciousness that lasts through the subsequent time. It is moved by the questions: What has happened? What will happen? What should we do?

After the judgment of God was carried out on Israel it would, according to the prophetic word now coming forth, also affect other nations, but then would come the time of salvation, the time of liberation and new life in the kingdom of God. This is the word of the prophets in this time, the time of Ezekiel and his vision of the field of dead bones to which new life comes (Ezek 37:1–14; cf, also 40:1). God is planning new things with his people: He will lead it into a new promised land (Ezekiel 43). There will be a new exodus like the one from Egypt. Cyrus, the Persian king, overthrows the power of Babylon—"for the sake of my servant, for the sake of Israel"—and lets Israel come home (2 Chr 36:23).

11. N. Füglister, "Prophet," 370–71.

In this world event, in Babylon's fall, Israel is supposed to recognize the rule and revelational power of God. It should grow to maturity for the new message of its God, for the new covenant, and for the coming of that figure who is called "Servant of God," for the day and the glory of the Lord.

But along with this *salvation for all nations* is brought up: The people will come and make pilgrimage to the mountain of God (Jer 16:19; Isa 56:7; Zech 2:14). God, Israel's king, shall be king over all nations. There will be a time in which the happiness of the primitive age, paradise, returns (Isa 35:1-10). All flesh see the salvation of God; the arrival of God is the epiphany of the God-king.

But the question "What shall we do that the rule of the king may come?" will move the people in new ways after their return from exile. Contributing to this new impetus will be both the experiences they had made in captivity, and that which in exile had remained the same: the memory of salvation history and the word of the prophets. The great leaders and reformers, Ezra and Nehemiah, lead the people to the path of an exact fulfilling of the Law which the nation knew from the time of Moses and which was expanded and developed in the course of the centuries, and which had been the ultimate binding power during the exile. The praise of the law (Psalm 119) the knowledge of it and zeal for the Law, the struggle to keep it pure, turn into the characterizing leitmotif and specific form of revelation.

After the overthrow of the Persian kingdom by Alexander the Great and the incorporation of the realm and dynasty of Israel into the empire of the Ptolomies and Seleucids, the struggle with Greek culture took place. In this time there developed again a dialectical situation of assimilation (cf. 1 Macc 1: 11) or the self-isolating preservation of Israel's special characteristic, the holy Law.

The Books of the Maccabees tell the story of the open religious war that broke out when King Antiochus IV (176-164) prohibited temple sacrifice, Sabbath and circumcision, ordered the Holy Scriptures destroyed and forced the Jews under penalty of death to offer sacrifice to Zeus, the God of the Greeks. These books also tell how, in contrast to the many apostates, a small band remained true, the community of the new covenant. Possibly this is the community that gathered around the "Teacher of Righteousness" and whom we have come to know more closely through the discoveries at Qumran.[12] This community was preparing itself for the day of God and the coming of God's kingly rule. What must we do that the kingdom may come? An extraordinarily

---

12. K. H. Schelkle, *Die Gemeinde von Qumran und die Kirche des Neuen Testaments* (Düsseldorf, 1960); Rudolf Schnackenburg, *God's Rule and Kingdom*, trans. John Murray (New York: Herder and Herder, 1963); P. Hoffmann, "Reich Gottes," *HThG* 2.414–28; P. Hunermann, "Reign of God," *SM* 5.233–40.

strict following of the Law and a special community rule is the answer of the people of Qumran. With the subjection of the People of Israel under the rule of the Romans, the external history of the People of God comes to an end.

In the time of Early Rabbinic Judaism the so-called apocalyptic[13] took on a growing significance alongside and often in the place of the institution of prophecy. Apocalyptic—a literary genre—was understood in a very special way as revelation that was not mediated by a calling, as with the prophets, but by dreams and visions. This revelation refers above all to the future, more precisely, to the end of the ages and the end of the world. The purpose of apocalyptic is to communicate a secret wisdom. It relativizes life on earth, speaks dualistically of two aeons, and describes in metaphorical language, often with a temporal calculation, the omens of the end time: the tribulations, the last judgment, the resurrection of the dead, beatitude and damnation. The purpose of these descriptions in apocalyptic is to give comfort and hope.

It is remarkable that Israel took into the its holy Scriptures only one work of apocalyptic literature, namely the Book of Daniel. Individual apocalyptic elements are also found in other Old Testament writings (the Isaiah-Apocalypse of Isaiah 24–27; Ezek 37:1–14;40–48; Joel 3–4). Most of the apocalyptic writings belong to the so-called apocryphal writings. Certain figures of the Old Testament were designated as their authors (Abraham, Enoch, Moses, Elijah, Baruch) to elevate the reputation and significance of the writings in question. Apocalyptic arose in a time of severe internal and external affliction of the People of Israel, in the so-called Hellenistic milieu, especially under King Antiochus IV in the second century before Christ. They belong to the time and situation called "between the Testaments."[14]

This also establishes the connection to the New Testament in which apocalyptic traits and elements are also found, specifically in the sermons of Jesus about the end of the world and the end of times. But note the marked differences from apocalyptic, for example, in the question of setting down specific times. There is, in addition, one "Apocalypse" raised to a special position: the last book of the Bible which we will treat shortly in chapter 33.

13. J. Schreiner, Alttestamentlich–jüdische Apokalyptik (Munich, 1969).
14. Ibid. 11.

THE CONTENTS OF THE REVELATION WITNESSED IN THE OLD TESTAMENT

The God of Israel

In Israel's history, God reveals Himself as Yahweh, the God of Israel. In the course of Israel's history, this path can be recognized: from the God of the fathers (Abraham, Isaac, and Jacob) and his various names and forms to Yahweh, the God of Israel; a path from henotheism to monotheism. Yahweh, the God of Israel, reveals himself as the one and only Lord, in an exclusive and incomparable sense (Exod 20:3-6). He tolerates no strange gods beside him; these are, in the concept of the Old Testament, either creatures, images of human beings, "nothings," or antidivine powers. This fundamental idea permeates the history of Israel and is articulated ever more clearly in many developments: "Hear, O Israel! the Lord your God is one Lord" (Deut 6:4), in the words of the credo to be confessed every day. It comes up again as a demand in all prophetic proclamation. Polytheistic ideas of any kind contradict this fundamental affirmation of the Old Testament. Israel has no pantheon. Israel's belief in God is a monotheism of act and praxis.[1]

The Lord of History

The God of Israel reveals Himself as the Lord of the history of this people. But one must note here that Yahweh is not so woven into the history of Israel as to risk his own fate therein and thus come to grief, as frequently happens in the form of the purely national gods of other religions. Yahweh remains the all-determining reality. Israel's victories are above all, in the beginning, a manifestation of Yahweh's

---

1. A. Deißler, *Die Grundbotschaft des Alten Testaments*, 3rd ed. (Freiburg—Basel—Vienna, 1972, 7th ed., 1979); H. W. Schmidt, *The Faith of the Old Testament: A History*, trans. John Sturdy (Philadelphia: Westminster Press, 1983).

power, which is greater than that of the Egyptians, of Pharaoh and their gods. But Israel's political downfall, its suffering, defeat, imprisonment, and Exile, are not defeats of Yahweh, not signs of Yahweh's weakness, but the answer, caused and decreed by Yahweh, to Israel's unbelief, disobedience, and apostasy. Yahweh remains the all-determining reality. Suffering and defeat are no ground to break away from Yahweh, but the occasion to ask questions, to take thought to oneself, and to return to Yahweh. The weakness of the nation did not destroy faith in Yahweh, but purified it.

The Holy One of Israel

God reveals Himself in Israel and its history as the Holy One, God is the *Holy One of Israel*. The word "holy" first of all expresses that God is other, that God is totally other: other than the world and all that is in it. Holy is the special prerogative of God, sign of the indisponibility [God can't be "used"] that is God's. Holiness is the expression of God's sublimity and glory over against all creatureliness, before all human beings, and expression of purity over against all "uncleanness" (cf. Isaiah 6). If Israel is Yahweh's people, the consequence for its behavior is: "I am the Lord . . . your God . . . be holy, for I am holy" (Lev 11:44).

The being-holy of the people is to be represented in the assembly of the people at worship, where the great deeds of God are remembered in an atmosphere of praise, belief, and hope. It is to be represented above all in *moral behavior*: concretely in behavior and action supported by justice, love, and mercy (which, in cases of doubt, count more than the cult, according to the words: "I desire steadfast love and not sacrifice" [Hos 6:6]). It follows from this that the God of Israel is no unpredictable, arbitrary God. In God's own self-describing words: the holy God is the reliable and loyal God.

Alfons Deissler sees the fundamental message of the Old Testament being given its most pointed expression in the words of the prophet Micah: "He has showed you, O man, what is good; and what does the Lord require of you but to do justice, and to love kindness, and to walk humbly with your God?" (Mic 6:8).

The Creator of Heaven and Earth

Yahweh reveals Himself as Creator of heaven and earth. Yahweh creates the world out of nothing by his free, almighty word, and preserves in being and life all that is. Israel's God transcends the People of Israel; its God is the God who from the beginning, from the time of creation in the world, was operative in humanity and manifest to human beings. By its confession of God the Creator and its affirmation of the world as free creation, Israel differs from the religions of its milieu, in which the origin of the world is connected with the genesis of the gods: cosmogony was theogony.

The Personal God

In Israel's history, God becomes manifest and experienced as personal God. This happens not by way of speculation on the concept of person but by the affirmation that Israel exists by reason of having been spoken to by Yahweh, as well as by the constant formulation of the word and the speaking of Yahweh, and finally by the emphasis on Yahweh's free action. Especially graphic is the personality highlighted in the affirmations: God has a face, God has a heart. Face signifies one's "being turned towards," the turning of Yahweh [towards us] in free mercy. With the word "heart" is described the totality of human beings and what is in them. It is said that Yahweh has a heart. This is spoken of when there is mention of Yahweh's love, compassion, mercy, and grace. More personal affirmations than these are not conceivable. The anthropomorphisms ascribed to Yahweh precisely in connection with this image are not intended to bring Yahweh down to the level of human beings, but to describe God as person. "Whoever tries to remove surgically from the Bible the I and You, the He and the Self of God as references to God's personality must be advised that their operation results in a corpse."[2]

Distance from Its Milieu

The special characteristic of the revelation which took place in Israel has as a consequence the *distance* of this nation over against its *milieu*. Such a behavior is constantly under attack by the tendency, in betrayal of its chosen statue, to a leveling assimilation, to be "like all the other nations," to be like the Egyptians, to be like the people from Canaan. But on the other hand it is also true that, in the revelation given the People of Israel and in the faith historically lived by them, that which was destined for all human beings and nations was preserved and kept safe. What happened and happens in Israel belongs not just to Israel; it is a "sign for the nations," it concerns all. The unconditioned concretion recognizable in Israel's history is oriented to universality. The law is written in the heart of every human being (Rom 2:14). The God of Israel is the God of creation and the Lord of all history.

2. A. Deiler, *Grundbotschaft* 46.

The Aspect of the Future

As clear and palpable in the revelation to Israel may be its reaching back into the past and to past history, and as unmistakably as the prophet may interpret the present as the act and decree of God, even more characteristic than this is the looking ahead, the *trajectory towards the future*, which dominates the Old Testament and is evident in many phenomena. What is to come is more important than the past and the present; it is revelation as promise. Every event, however great it may be and however strong may be its memory, points beyond itself to something still greater. Even the greatest fulfillment within Israel is still the promise of a future reality yet to come. So it is with the bearers of revelation and the figures of the faith: Moses, the judges, the kings, the prophets. They are not stopping points; they are points to be passed through. They all signify: after us comes one who is greater than we (cf. Luke 3:16). The One Who Is to Come is the Real One, to whom all words and promises point and for whom all persons are only forerunners and ones who prepare the way.

In all the promises within the Old Testament it is clear that they are oriented to something beyond the nearest immediate reality. The kingdom in which God's will rules first has to come. The king after the heart of God must first be waited for; the final, definitive prophet has not yet appeared. Nowhere does any earthly king represent the whole realization, neither David nor Solomon, not to mention the others.

Certainly the promised land, in the Exodus from Egypt and in the return from Exile, is identified with the land of Canaan. Earthly power and political brilliance were repeatedly considered the successful consequence of the promise. But the consciousness was not lost that in the earthly, factual situation, such as came about in the Old Testament, only a shadow of the future has come alive, especially when this land was again lost. In this situation, in captivity and exile, the idea of promise and hope took on new content and more profound basis. At the same time the certainty was strengthened that the promises of Yahweh to Israel are not identical with political mastery.

The same situation of pointing out beyond oneself is manifested in the many covenants and covenant agreements. They are not just confirmations and rememberances, but signs of something pointing beyond its particular self, expectations of the truly real, of the new and eternal covenant. This consciousness that what is still to come is the truly real becomes overwhelming as the political glory of the people and land of Israel is struck down, as it becomes a people that walks in "darkness and shadows," and possesses nothing more than the word and guidance of Yahweh, the Law as Torah. The great prophets of that time, Jeremiah and Ezekiel above all, are raised up not only to disclose to the people the sense of the event as judgment on the refusal and denial of faith, but to point promisingly to what is to come: the coming Day of Yahweh, the coming kingdom, the coming prophet and king, the anointed, the new covenant. In the expectation of "He-who-is-to-come" is concentrated and concretized the expectation and hope of Israel and its history.

Many elements and motifs are mixed in this figure. First the political motif: He-who-is-to-come will be a king after the model of David but will surpass him in power and glory; he will be lord over all nations. Next figures the salvation motif (Isaiah 7; 9; 11): the Messiah is the Prince of Peace who guarantees justice, mercy, and love; these, not force, are the foundations of his dominion. Ezekiel adds the motif of the good shepherd, who gathers in what has been scattered, binds up the broken, strengthens the weak (Ezekiel 34, esp. 23-31). For Second Isaiah the One-who-is-to-come is not a king but the Suffering Servant of God who atones for the guilt of the world (Isaiah 42). He-who-is-to-come appears in a new form in the visions of the Book of Daniel: the great world kingdoms will be separated from the kingdom of God and made subject to eternal dominion. This divine rule will be introduced by someone who has the appearance of a Son of Man but comes from heaven (Daniel 7). Messianic expectation and the connection of political, religious, and soteriological motifs found in it are a model and a proof of the fact that, and the great extent to which, revelation of the Old Covenant and in the Old Covenant is revelation in the form of promise.

Another view of this and at the same time confirmation of what we have been saying, is the manner in which the specification of time is seen within this form of revelation.

First, it is generally true that the decisive dimensions of revelation are not so much of a spatial as of a temporal kind. They are called not here in this world, and there in the next, but yesterday—today—tomorrow.[3] For revelation in the Old Covenant, the following specification of time is especially valid: An event takes place here and now. But what is happening now is at the same time promise of something future; the present always includes a future, and this is greater, more comprehensive, and more real than that which now is. In this way, of course, every salvation-historical moment or event gains significance for itself, but is the same time relativized with respect to what is to come. The image of time within this form and phase of revelation, revelation as promise, is not the circle—the symbol of what is closed off in itself, of what is always the same, of return, the symbol of myth,[4] but the image of a span of time or of a stream of time. In this image, history is

---

3. Cf. Oscar Cullmann, *Christ and Time: The Primitive Christian Conception of Time and History*, trans. Floyd V. Filson (Philadelphia: Westminster Press, 1964); *Salvation in History*, trans. Sidney G. Sowers (New York: Harper & Row, 1967).

4. Heinrich Fries, "Mythos und Offenbarung" in: J. Bernard, ed., *Offenbarung. Phänomen—Begriff—Dimensionen* (Leipzig, 1983) 106–42.

understood as the new and the newly arriving. But the image also expresses that, (in what is new,) something old is also given: tradition and continuity.

If it must be decided whether this span flows evenly or discontinuously, it should be noted that it flows evenly to the extent that God's word and act are operative in time and history, even if not always in obvious realization of the "mystery of His will."[5] This line or span runs discursively, up and down, if we are looking at the external course of history; success—failure, height—depth, war—peace, falling away—punishment, conversion—new falling away. Finally, one can say that span of time passes, rising and falling to the extent that, in the revelation of the Old Covenant, something coming, something greater, is promised and awaited. This coming and greater thing becomes ever more pressing and clear in the external downfall of the People of Israel. More and more, word and historical event tend towards what is called "fullness of time."

What we have described here about the significance of Israel as bearer of a special revelation of God has to this day not been abrogated. Israel is and remains the figure and the realization of the People of God. It remains the witness of God's calling, election, and fidelity; it is and remains partner of the covenant with God and embodiment of the promises of God as well as of the hope grounded therein. Israel's history is and remains history of faith.

In the moving chapters 9–11 of his Epistle to the Romans, Paul gives an account of the mystery of Israel: "I ask, then, has God rejected his people? . . . God has not rejected his people whom he foreknew" (Rom 11:1–2). and he answers further: "The gifts and the call of God are irrevocable" (Rom 11:29). Thus Paul reminds the Christian: "It is not you that supports the root, but the root that supports you" (Rom 11:18).

5. Dogmatic Constitution on Revelation (*Dei Verbum*) Second Vatican Council.

THE REVELATION OF GOD IN JESUS THE CHRIST WITNESSED IN THE NEW TESTAMENT

We know about Jesus the Christ primarily through the writings of the New Testament. These are the expression and record of the memory, the proclamation, the faith and the confession of the apostles and disciples and the first communities. The writings of the New Testament, above all the Gospels, are not a description of the life of Jesus written with any concern for particular events and minute details; they are not an exact record of his words and deeds, nor do they offer any psychology of Jesus. Whoever subjects the New Testament to these criteria will be disappointed; but above all they will be mistaking the intent and concern of these writings to give witness to Jesus Christ and to awaken faith in him (cf. John 20:31).

The New Testament is about confessing Jesus, the Christ, and about faith in him. Since an historical person, a life, a proclamation, an attitude, a claim, a fate (cross and resurrection) stand in the middle of the New Testament, these writings are most interested in the *historical reality*. The New Testament is about a faith that has historical ground and content; without these, it could not be Christian faith.

If history is connected with faith, with witnesses and testimonies, the weight and the significance of the history is not lessened by this but strengthened. A testimony as testimony of facts and truth is connected with the personal involvement of the witness who stands behind it. A testimony is more than just a record, a news report, or an announcement of which one takes cognizance. Testimony becomes the more credible and solid the more the witness for the testimony accepts dangers and risks and is ready to do so.

Therefore, proclamation, confession, and faith neither contradict nor replace history. Instead, they live from history and have their foundation in it. They are the living answer to it. The New Testament proclaims through history; history becomes present and real through proclamation. The Jesus of history is the Christ of faith; the Christ of faith is the Jesus of history.

When faith is connected with history and history with faith, it shows that a historical reality has more levels than can be contained in a narrative record. But it also lies in the nature of witness and testimony that what is testified to is personally and subjectively mediated. Thus, a better disclosure of the historical reality is brought about by the testimony of many than by the account of one individual.

That may be difficult in individual cases, but in principle, it is incontestable.

It can be maintained that only the believing witness can say what really took place in the history of Jesus. A sound film of the Jerusalem review of the week which represented the crucifixion of Jesus could indeed show us many historical details. But what happened there, whether a harmless enthusiast or a political resistance fighter was executed, and whether God was speaking a definitive word to us, it couldn't say. Only the witness, to whom we can grant or refuse to grant belief, can tell us that.[1]

The difference in the manner of seeing and representing produced in a plurality of testimony is suited to represent a reality according to its different sides. This reality is thereby neither colored nor falsified, but disclosed. The multiplicity of voices does not lessen but elevates the credibility as a whole.

The fact is that there are not one but four Gospels, and besides the Gospels there are the quite diverse Epistles, and besides the letters there are the Acts of the Apostles and the Revelation of John. Now all of this is not some embarrassing accident that must be artificially harmonized; it is in fact precisely what the New Testament is all about: the witness of Jesus the Christ. The multiplicity of the witness doesn't lead to confusion—it can be made to serve the unity given through its content; but this content is expressed in many voices.

In addition, one should note that truth is found not just in the form of history; otherwise "unhistorical things" could not be true. There is also truth in stories, parables, in teachings, poetry, legends. All these

1. Eduard Schweizer, *Jesus*, trans. David E. Green (Atlanta: John Knox Press, 1971) 7. On the same theme: Günther Bornkamm, *Jesus of Nazareth*, trans. Irene and Fraser McLuskey (New York: Harper & Row, 1975); A. Vögtle, "Jesus und die Geschichtlichen Quellen," *LThK* 6.922–32; J. R. Geiselmann, *Jesus der Christus*, vol. 1, 2d ed. (Munich, 1965); Franz Mußner, *The Historical Jesus in the Gospel of St. John*, trans. W. O'Hara (New York: Herder and Herder, 1967); Rudolf Schnackenburg, "Christologie des Neuen Testaments" in: *MySal* 3.227–388, Ernst Käsemann, "Das Problem des Historischen Jesus" in: *Exegetische Versuche und Besinnungen I*, 6th. ed. (Göttingen, 1970) 187–214; J. Blank, *Jesus von Nazareth. Geschichte und Relevanz* (Freiburg—Basel—Vienna, 1972); K. Kertelge, ed., *Rückfrage nach Jesus* (Freiburg—Basel—Vienna, 1974); Walter Kasper, *Jesus the Christ*, trans. V. Green (New York: Paulist Press, 1977); Hans Küng, *On Being a Christian*, trans. Edward Quinn (Garden City, N. Y.: Doubleday and Company, 1976); Edward Schillebeeckx, *Jesus: An Experiment in Christology*, trans. Herbert Hoskins (New York: Seabury, 1979); F. J. Schierse, *Christologie* (Düsseldorf, 1979).

literary forms are found in the New Testament. From this comes the key for the factual interpretation which asks: What was it that the particular writing wanted to bring to expression?

The writings of the New Testament are, in addition, written out of the conviction that *Jesus is no figure of the past*, but the living Lord, the Christ remaining and acting in the present, who did indeed die on the cross, but did not remain in death, but was raised from the dead. He remains connected to his faithful ones in a new way, in a new life, in a life, which has overcome death and opened up a new time and a new reality that can be described with the words salvation, rescue, reconciliation, grace, salvation, new creation, that means eternal life.

Jesus Christ's death and resurrection are the central events of his life. They are at the same time, for human beings and their salvation, the "saving events" which decide their eternal destination. The oldest writings of the New Testament, the major letters of the Apostle Paul, into which the original faith formulae and confessional formulae have already come, are so overwhelmed by this "center" that "everything else," e.g., the earthly, the pre-Easter life of Jesus, recedes into the background, although everything comes down to witnessing that Jesus of Nazareth, the Crucified, is the Christ, is the exalted-to-God "Lord."

In contrast to the letters, the four Gospels make the history of the earthly, pre-Easter Jesus the object of their witness. Their concern is to confess that *Jesus is the Christ*. Christ is not a figure of legend or myth, he is a figure and person of real history. But the Gospels too and their stories of the words and deeds of Jesus are primarily about proclamation, about confession, about belief, about the saving message. Thus the intention of the stories is not so much to tell who Jesus was but to confess who Jesus is. Or, more precisely, in that which was, the Gospels intend to express that which is. Nevertheless there is also a remarkable agreement of the Gospels with Paul. The Gospels too place the passion and the resurrection of Jesus at the central point; they are "passion narratives with an extensive introduction." The activity of Jesus is represented as the way to Jerusalem.

This is what explains the fidelity of the Gospels to the historical tradition of Jesus, as the preface of the Gospel of Luke expresses it:

Inasmuch as many have undertaken to compile a narrative of the things which have been accomplished among us, just as they were delivered to us by those who from the beginning were eyewitnesses and ministers of the word, it seemed good to me also, having followed all things closely for some time past, to write an orderly account for you, most excellent Theophilus, that you may know the truth concerning the things of which you have been informed. (Luke 1: 1-4)

In their accounts and stories, the Gospels stand in the service of the proclamation, the living and actual proclamation of the exalted Lord, who lives in the midst of those who believe in him and who speaks his word to them. This helps account for the fact that, along with fidelity to the history and its tradition, there is a remarkable measure of freedom over against the "historical" text itself. Jesus' word is preserved, not protected and fixed with anxious, archival devotion, but handed on in living tradition and actual proclamation. One can even flatly formulate it: the tradition doesn't actually repeat and hand on the word he once spoke; instead, it is his word today. This explains the manifold variations of the words of Jesus and the often-noted variants in the accounts and stories of Jesus' activity.

This is no ground for historical skepticism or a welcome opportunity to establish contrasts and contradictions in the New Testament. For everything that is there, all the variety and multiplicity, is simply an indication of the particular nature and the special purpose of the writings of the New Testament. Only when one knows these and keeps them before one's eyes is a real understanding possible.

Further, this special characteristic of the New Testament writings, of being proclamation in the form of history and through history to mediate the message of salvation, is really part of the core reality of the New Testament: to proclaim, to confess, and to give witness that Jesus is the Christ. Thus there is always the intention, in the saving message of the Gospels, to seek out the history, but also to seek out the saving message in this history. This accounts for the fact that the earthly Jesus is described with the colors of the Christ who is risen from the dead, the living and exalted Lord. The pre-Easter history of Jesus is seen and represented in the light of the Easter event. If traits of the Risen One have been brought into the picture of the earthly Jesus, then this happened not from lack of precision or from a lack of perspective, but from the plausible reason that in the light of the resurrection of Jesus one can get a better and deeper understanding of who Jesus already was in his earthly life and what his activity means.

This perspective applies to all the Gospels, most especially the Gospel of John. The interpretation of the New Testament has to take this factual situation into consideration. Certainly, in view of this situation, the questions of our historical curiosity about the when, the who, the how, and the why will not be answered. We learn nothing about how Jesus looked; we learn practically nothing about his youth and about the hidden years in Nazareth; we don't even know precisely how long the public activity of Jesus lasted. Nevertheless, a true and real history is produced whose profile and contour are unmistakable. We will now try, from this perspective, to give a precise description of the revelation that happened in Jesus Christ.

§ 34

REVELATION IN JESUS, THE CHRIST, AS FULFILLMENT

Fulfillment in the Sense of the Now, the Today

For the old covenant, the future—that which is to come and he who is to come—is the decisive category. We could add that, for believing Judaism, the future is the determining specification of time to the present day.[1]

In the New Testament conception, conversely, the determining category of time is the today, the now, the present, indeed the now that has come about and happened in Jesus, the present that has appeared in him. Mark expresses this factual situation with the words: "The time is fulfilled, and the kingdom of God is at hand" (Mark 1:15). According to Luke, Jesus says in the synagogue of Nazareth after he had read Isaiah 61:1–2: "Today this scripture has been fulfilled in your hearing" (Luke 4:21). Paul speaks in a similar manner: "When the time had fully come, God sent forth his Son" (Gal 4:4).

What is the meaning of: The time is fulfilled? According to Luke 4 it means that the messianic prophecies of the good news to the poor, the liberation of those in prison, the announcement of a year of grace of the Lord, have been fulfilled in Jesus.

"The time is fulfilled" does not mean just that a certain stretch of time or a certain date has expired. Rather, the time has reached a certain measure—not according to extension but to content. In history, the specification intended by the God of Israel as Lord of history is realized. Ephesians expresses it in a comprehensive theological perspective, "the mystery of the will of God," who in Christ wills to lead in the fullness of time "to unite all things in him, things in heaven and things on earth" (Eph 1: 9-10; cf. Col 1: 20). "The time is fulfilled," accordingly, means that the not yet actualized, but awaited and hoped for royal kingship of God, the unity of God and human beings, has taken

---

1. Cf. Martin Buber, "Zwei Glaubensweisen" in: *Werke I* (Munich, 1962) 651–782.

place in the person, word, life, and deeds of Jesus of Nazareth, who is the Christ.[2]

But there still remains for the New Testament understanding of revelation a *goal of time* at the end of time. In the New Testament the future is intensively addressed; ordered to the future is the living hope for the coming of the kingdom of God "in great power and glory": Thy kingdom come! To that extent there is "in, with, and under" the fulfillment also the promise, the resurrection from the dead, eternal life, the new heaven and the new earth. This promise had, however, another form, another sense and relationship, than the promise which characterized the Old Testament. "Maranatha"—the ancient liturgical acclamation witnessed in the New Testament (1 Cor 16: 22; Rev 22: 20) gives this New Testament expectation and petition a lasting expression: Let the Lord, who has come, come again! For this reason one can speak of a real Maranatha-Christology.[3]

So it is no contradiction but a true expression of the situation that in Jesus the Christ, the fulfillment has come about and that at the same time the end is still to come; the event that has taken place in Jesus includes in itself present reality and future expectation simultaneously: the *already* and the *not yet*. But if it is asked where the decisive point is, the answer is: in the presence of Jesus who is the Christ, and in the presence of the Christ event, of what happened/happens in Christ. Only from this is it possible to talk about the end and goal of the times. Presence is future which has already begun; future is presence which is brought to its goal. No other event, either before or after Christ, has the central significance, of that which has taken place in Him. Only from Him does the before-and-after of the times receive its correct order and position; only from Him is it really known and understood.

Without doubt the hope for the return of the Lord and the coming of the kingdom of God in power are very much alive within the New Testament. The fact that the primitive Christian hope is even more intensive than the Jewish could be the reason for the opinions of such theologians as Bernhard Weiß, Albert Schweitzer, and Martin Werner, that the New Testament placed the future fulfillment at the center of the event. But intensity and center are not the same thing and should not be confused. In reality, the heightened hope in the future is to be explained from the fact that an already real historical fact—the coming and the way of Jesus Christ through Incarnation, death and resurrection—has already taken place and that in it the future has already begun. This means: *Hope in the future is built on faith in the present.*

2. Oscar Cullmann, *Christ and Time: The Primitive Conception of Time and History*, trans. Floyd V. Filson (Philadelphia: Westminster Press, 1964) 69–80; A. Vögtle, *Zeit und Zeitüberlegenheit im biblischen Verständnis* (Freiburg, 1961).

3. Edward Schillebeeckx, *Jesus. An Experiment in Christology*, trans. Herbert Hoskins (New York: Seabury, 1979) 406–10.

What has happened is the assurance and guarantee for what will happen. Hope in the coming of Jesus Christ in power and glory is grounded in the fact that He has already come and that He was raised from the dead.

Faith in the already realized fulfillment, especially in the Easter event, is thus not a substitute for the unfulfilled imminent expectation. It actually goes the other way around. This faith has made imminent expectation possible and brought it about. It is the ground for the expectation of the return of Christ and the hope for its proximate realization. From the living presence of Christ witnessed in the New Testament, illumination falls on the paths that lead to the future. The path into the future has become visible only since the today witnessed in the New Testament, shedding its light in all directions, began to illumine the previously dark stretch. The fulfillment of revelation in the sense of now and today is also brought to powerful expression within the New Testament by the statement, above all in Paul, that what happened "once" in Christ happened "once-for-all" (Rom 6:10).

The revelation in Jesus the Christ witnessed in the New Testament, revelation as fulfillment in the Today, is thus to be distinguished from a conception such as is represented by Karl Barth.[4] He looks upon the relationship of old and new covenant through what at first seemed to be the illuminating image of the forward-looking prophets and the backward-looking apostles. Both thus see the same Christ; the prophet sees him from the front, the apostle from behind. Expectation and remembrance become identical.

There is, however, as Emil *Brunner* rightly objects,[5] some confusion in the use of this schema. Time is replaced by space. But forwards and backwards in space is something different from forwards and backwards in time. Between the prophetic looking ahead and what is said and happens in the New Testament there is a difference which lies between the promise and what was actually fulfilled and actually took place. The fulfilled is actually, in the sense of the intention, the same as the promised. Thus it has a good sense when Jesus in the Gospel of John says: "Abraham saw my day and rejoiced" (John 8:56). But the fulfilled is at the same time something other, because it, present reality, is no longer just a future to be looked to. In addition, the "fulfillment" is by no means just the calculable result of what is contained in the promises; fulfillment puts accents on the promises. In addition it brings with it other, unexpected, new, transcending things. Were that not so, then the fate of Jesus would be totally incomprehensible. Not to see this difference means not to attend to the historical steps and acts of revela-

4. *Church Dogmatics*, 4 vols., (Edinburgh: T. & T. Clark, 1956–75) vol. 1/2, 70–120.
5. Emil Brunner, *Revelation and Reason: The Christian Doctrine of Faith Knowledge*, trans. Olive Wyon (Philadelphia: The Westminster Press, 1946) 99.

tion. The Old Testament is, in the New Testament perspective, history towards Christ, the Awaited One, as question about him; but it is still prehistory, in which he is not yet there, not in the way in which he is to come hereafter. The Old Testament doesn't say the same as the New, but a different word, and precisely by that word it leads Israel and humanity towards fulfillment in the kingdom of God. Thus, despite all its connections and references, the Old Testament cannot be made the exclusive criterion of what one meets in the New Testament.

It must therefore be explicitly pointed out that the New Testament sets very great value on the *Now*, the *Today*, the *Hour*, "my hour" (cf. John 2:4; 7:39; 17:1), and sees the special characteristic and quality of what happens and takes place in the New Testament precisely in the fact that what was expected and promised is now being fulfilled. This is found most impressively in Rom 3:21. Paul is reflecting on the situation of the Jews and pagans before Christ. He describes it as a situation of being lost. This is superseded by the act of God in Jesus Christ. The Apostle characterizes this with the words: "*But now* the righteousness of God has been manifested apart from law, although the law and the prophets bear witness to it, the righteousness of God through faith in Jesus Christ for all who believe" (Rom 3:21-22).

Just as remarkable is the accent of the Captivity Letters, that the earlier, hidden mystery was now becoming manifest (Col 1:26; Eph 3:5). The beginning of the Epistle to the Hebrews impressively highlights this dimension: "In many and various ways God spoke of old to our fathers by the prophets; but in these last days he has spoken to us by a Son" (Heb 1:1-2). From this way of speaking it becomes clear that the concept "eschatological" in contemporary theology means the time opened up in Jesus Christ as end-time.

When one weighs this situation and these facts, one sees the correctness of the accentuation of the present found in the theology of Rudolf Bultmann and his understanding of revelation.[6] It accentuates the Now and Today of the Christ event as the core of the revelation of the New Testament and of what revelation as fulfillment can be, as fulfillment in the sense of the Now, the Today, the Definitive.

Bultmann makes the "now" of the Christ event even more vital and effective in a special way by raising the *now of the proclamation*, the now of the kerygma, to be the decisive theological dimension. He takes the words of the Second Letter to the Corinthians to be in support of this:

---

6. Rudolf Bultmann, "Der Begriff der Offenbarung im Neuen Testament" in: *Glauben und Verstehen* III (1960) 1–34. The first volume of the three-volume work has been translated into English: *Faith and Understanding*, trans. Louise Pettibone Smith (Philadelphia: Fortress Press, 1987).

Working together with him, then, we entreat you not to accept the grace of God in vain. For he says, "At the acceptable time I have listened to you, and helped you on the day of salvation." Behold, now is the acceptable time; behold, now is the day of salvation. (2 Cor 6:1-2)

In the Now of the kerygma, the Once of the Christ event becomes simultaneously present and effective, effective in such a way that human beings in encounter with the word of proclamation, i.e., in faith, move from the inauthenticity and alienation of themselves into authenticity. Human beings come from themselves to themselves.

This is also what makes it possible for Bultmann, in view of the concept of revelation in the New Testament, to say:

What then is revealed? Nothing at all, as long as the question about revelation is asking about doctrines, about doctrines, e.g., at which no human being could have arrived, about mysteries which, if they are communicated, are known once and for all. But everything [is revealed] to the extent that human beings have their eyes opened about themselves and can again understand themselves.[7]

Revelation in the New Testament is understood not as communication of knowledge but as an event that involves me. "To know about revelation means to know about what makes us what we are, but along with that, about our own limitation."[8]

The exclusive emphasis on the "that" of the coming of Jesus and of the Christ event (which, according to Bultmann, is the sole authoritative element), carries with it the consequence that, for Bultmann, the historical Jesus is without significance for the kerygma and the faith, and the proclamation of Jesus belongs not to the content but to the presuppositions of the kerygma.

This theological position, the radical reduction to or concentration on the "That" of the Christ event to which the That of the kerygma corresponds, stands in contradiction to the striking fact that, in the canon of the New Testament, along with the kerygma of Paul about Jesus' cross and resurrection, are also the Gospels which—certainly in the light of the kerygma—tell about the earthly Jesus. If Jesus is the proclaimed Christ of faith, then it is not a matter of indifference who Jesus was, what he proclaimed, how he conducted himself, what he did. It is supremely important, and that is the intent of the New Testament testimony itself, both how the kerygma about the Christ of faith is to be connected with the earthly Jesus, and what basis Christology has in the historical Jesus. Only through this connection will the kerygma of Jesus the Christ be maintained and protected against becoming a mere idea, doctrine, or mythology.

The time since Bultmann has been characterized by the fact that his radical skepticism with respect to the historical Jesus—articulated

7. Ibid. 29.
8. Ibid. 6.

in an exemplary way in his Jesus book—was not accepted. Ernst Käsemann with his article "Das Problem des historischen Jesus [The Problem of the Historical Jesus]"[9] introduced a new direction that has basically held to this day. The books of Günther Bornkamm and Eduard Schweizer spell out the important consequences of this new direction:

The Gospels, although in a way very different from chronicles, make visible before us the historical figure of Jesus in immediate forcefulness. Too obvious is what the Gospels relate about Jesus' message, his deeds and his stories, always characterized by an authenticity, a freshness which point back immediately to the earthly figure of Jesus. Although the Gospels don't talk about the history of Jesus in the sense of an exactly traced curriculum vitae with its fortunes and stages, its outer or inner development, they do talk about history as happening and event. The Gospels give extensive information about that.[10]

Included in Bultmann's presuppositions are the all-determining Now of the Christ event, and the kerygma as inseparably connected with it, because the kerygma is what makes the Christ event present. From these presuppositions it is understandable that, for Bultmann, all New Testament affirmations about the future—end of the world and of history, judgment and perfection—are mythological affirmations. One can no longer expect them to be accepted by human beings of a modern world view, of an enlightened historical consciousness, and of modern self-understanding. These affirmations are, according to Bultmann, to be interpreted existentially. Thus they become affirmations that involve exclusively the present in the sense of Johannine eschatology: "Now is the judgment of this world" (John 12:31), "We know that we have passed out of death into life, because we love the brethren" (1 John 3:14).

In this way Bultmann does give his theological conception an impressive consistency, but at the same time also a radicality and onesidedness which cannot be supported by the New Testament as a whole. Nevertheless, Bultmann's theological conception[11] corresponds to the revelation event witnessed in the New Testament more than those attempts which try to level out the Old Testament and the New Testament and to remain behind the Now of the New Testament, behind the *pleroma* [fullness] of times witnessed in the New Testament, behind the *kairos* which has been filled, or which make the expectation of the future into the center of New Testament revelation, and precisely in this way fail to do justice to their own fulfillment.

---

9. In: *Exegetische Versuche und Abhandlungen I,* 4th ed. (Göttingen, 1965) 187–214; *Sackgasse im Streit um den Historischen Jesus,* ibid. II, 31–68.

10. Günther Bornkamm, *Jesus of Nazareth* (Minneapolis, 1995) 24–25.

11. M. Boutin, *Relationalität als Verstehensprinzip bei Rudolf Bultmann* (Munich, 1974).

Fulfillment in the Sense of the "Here" of the Ecce

One can describe the revelation that has taken place in Jesus Christ both with the word for *hodie* (today) and also with the characterization of the *ecce* (behold), of the "here."[12] Revelation is brought to fulfillment by means of the demonstrable, concrete "here" of a person, Jesus of Nazareth, of a life, a word, a work, a happening, a fate, an event. Because there is fulfillment in the "*ecce*," there is also a fulfillment in the "*hodie*."[13]

The special characteristic and uniqueness of the *ecce* found in the person and work of Jesus of Nazareth as fulfillment of revelation is experienced, described, and reflected on in the Bible in numerous ways. In doing this the New Testament takes over a variety of categories.

1. Jesus is called *rabbi, teacher.* But when Jesus is spoken of as teacher, this is done in an unmistakably elevated manner: "What is this? A new teaching! With authority he commands even the unclean spirits" (Mark 1:27). "You have one teacher, and you are all brethren" (Matt 23:8). This sets it apart from other kinds of teaching. This difference is further illustrated in a variety of ways: that it is not the disciples who seek out their rabbi, but Jesus who calls to discipleship; that in the case of Jesus, the disciple can never be or become the master; that Jesus as teacher—in an essential difference, e.g., from Buddha—does not step back behind the teaching but is one with what he says; that the message he proclaims cannot be separated from his person. The teaching is tied to discipleship. This process is realized in the history witnessed in the New Testament by the fact that the believing Jesus— as the Christ—becomes the content of faith.

2. Jesus is regarded as *prophet.*[14] "A great prophet has risen among us" (Luke 7:16). The words of the disciples at Emmaus also belong here: "A prophet mighty in deed and word before God and all the people" (Luke 24:19). Jesus is considered a prophet in the question: "'Who do men say that I am?' . . . And they told him, 'John the Baptist; and others say, Elijah; and others one of the prophets.'" (Mark 8:27-30; cf.

12. Heinrich Fries, *Revelation* (New York: Herder and Herder, 1969),[MySal 1.213–19]
13. Han Urs von Balthasar, *Herrlichkeit I* (Einsiedeln: Johannes Verlag, 1961) 445–505, ET: The Glory of the Lord: I: Seeing the Form (Ignatius Press, San Francisco—Crossroad, New York, 1982) 463–525; Wolfhart Pannenberg, *Jesus: God and Man*, trans. Lewis L. Wilkins and Duane A. Priebe (Philadelphia: Westminster Press, 1977); Hans Küng, *On Being a Christian*, trans. Edward Quinn (Garden City, N. Y.: Doubleday and Company, Inc., 1976); Walter Kasper, *Jesus the Christ*, trans. V. Green (New York: Paulist Press, 1977) Edward Schillebeeckx, *Jesus: An Experiment in Christology*, trans. Herbert Hoskins (New York: Seabury Press, 1979); A. Schilson—W. Kasper, *Christologie im Präsens. Kritische Sichtung neuer Entwürfe* (Freiburg—Basel—Vienna, 1974).
14. Oscar Cullmann, *The Christology of the New Testament*, trans. Shirley C. Guthrie and Charles A. M. Hall (Philadelphia: The Westminster Press, 1969) 13–50; Franz Mußner, "Ursprünge und Entfaltung der Neutestamentlichen Sohneschristologie" in: L. Scheffczyk, ed., *Grundfragen der Christologie Heute* (Freiburg—Basel—Vienna, 1975) 77–113; F. Schnider, *Jesus der Prophet* (Freiburg [Schweiz]—Göttingen, 1979).

Matt 16:13-20). In John 1:21 comes the question: "Are you the prophet?" Connected with this is the idea that a final, definitive prophet is to come, like Moses, who will bring prophecy to its fulfillment and in his call for repentance make the last offer of God to His people. This expectation was all the greater since prophecy had died out in Judaism.

The image of the prophet is a suitable one to characterize the life, behavior, and activity of Jesus: his vocation and mission; his criticism not of the Temple but of the praxis done there; not of the Law but its interpretation; his symbolic actions and finally his death as culmination of a prophet's fate. This also shows how Jesus came to know his own death.

3. Along with all this is found in the New Testament, as characterization of Jesus, the picture of a prophet-transcending "surplus", a *"more-than,"* a *"greater-than."* It is reported that Jesus set himself over against all prophets, even John the Baptist (Matt 11:13). The New Testament also reports the claim of Jesus: "Here is more than Jonah" (Matt 12:41). What came to be in Jesus of Nazareth is not an increase in what was already there previously in the Old Testament; rather, he "is more than a prophet." Emil Brunner once pointed out[15] that no so-called liberal theology has yet been able to say what is meant by "more than a prophet." Jesus is more than a prophet in the sense that, like a prophet, his mission and sending surpass the measure of the prophet as a human being; Jesus, however, is identical with his mission. Thus Jesus, unlike the prophet, does not say: "thus says the Lord," but "But I say to you"—"I will, be made clean"—"I have come"—"I send you"—"I say to you, stand up"—"Lazarus, come forth"—"Your sins are forgiven you." The claim, however, to forgive sins turns out to be quite characteristic of Jesus' uniqueness in that forgiving sins is an exclusive privilege of God. It is a privilege which, according to current Old Testament ideas, is never granted to God's commissioned, not even to the Messiah. One understands, then, the protest: "Why does this man speak this? It is blasphemy! Who can forgive sins but God alone?" (Mark 2:7).

The "Amen," which otherwise serves as confirmation of something someone else has said, Jesus uses as introduction to his own words: "Amen . . . I say to you." As Heinrich Schlier sees it, this manner of speaking, which is characteristic of Jesus, includes a whole Christology.[16]

Further, the biblical "more-than" is rewritten by Jesus' claim to be more than Solomon (Matt 12:42), the representative of the divinely established kingdom, indeed more than Moses, the greatest divine messenger of the Old Testament. Jesus sets himself over him and corrects

---

15. E. Brunner, *Revelation and Reason*, 102–3.

16. In: *ThW* 1.341; with a different view: K. Berger, *Die Amen-Worte Jesu* (Berlin, 1970).

him by correcting the Law of Moses in the question of divorce. Finally he even goes beyond the Law of Moses by the authority claimed for himself: "You have heard that it was said to the men of old . . . but I say to you" (Matt 5:21-22); this authority radicalizes the Law down to the dispositions of the heart; and at the same time it simplifies and concentrates it by characterizing it as expression of the holiness of God, the will of God.

How much Jesus understands himself as fulfillment is shown by his call to the radical following of himself.[17] The following includes the readiness to let oneself be held back by nothing and by no one, the readiness to deny everything, leave everything, in order to share in the community of life and fate—the cross included—with Jesus: "Leave the dead to bury their own dead; but as for you, go and proclaim the kingdom of God" (Luke 9:60).

The following of Jesus becomes the new principle of moral action. This becomes clear in the sermon handed on at the end of the gospel, where Jesus becomes the norm of human activity, indeed, where he is the criterion of the definitive sentence of judgment: "As you did it to one of the least of these my brethren, you did it [or did not do it] to me" (Matt 25: 40).

Thus it is understandable that Jesus requires confession of his person and that in the position that human beings take towards Jesus their whole fate is decided: "Everyone who acknowledges me before men, I also will acknowledge before my Father who is in heaven; but whoever denies me before men, I also will deny before my Father who is in heaven." (Matt 10:32-33; cf. Luke 12:8; Mark 8:38)

Matthew's rewriting of "the Son of Man" (found in Mark and Luke) with "I" is already an interpretation of what the title Son of Man means.

Jesus declares that "here"—in him—is "more than the Temple" (Matt 12:6) i.e., the location of the special and grace-giving presence of God He expresses this sovereignty in the purification or cleaning out of the Temple symbolically by appealing specifically to his own authority He declares that the Son of Man is "Lord of the Sabbath" (Matt 12:8), and sets himself—as no prophet could have dared—above the authentic interpretation of the Sabbath law with the words "The Sabbath was made for man, not man for the Sabbath." (Mark 2:27) In all these formulas of going beyond, of the "more than," is expressed what the *ecce* in Jesus of Nazareth means and contains, and in which consists the fulfillment of revelation—namely, the "I" of Jesus takes the place of the God of Israel whom Jesus calls his Father.

---

17. E. Neuhäusler, *Anspruch und Antwort Gottes* (Düsseldorf, 1962) 186–214 (Baltimore, 1960) 186–214; A. Schulz, *Nachfolgen und Nachahmen* (Munich, 1962).

The "more than" found in the *ecce* of Jesus of Nazareth can further be described by the *authority*, absolute, exclusive, and derived from no human being, that Jesus claims and realizes. If the word of the prophet has and claims authority, then it is the authority of the message that is entrusted to the prophet. If Jesus is more than prophet, then this is grounded and demonstrated in the fact the authority of the word, the will, the mission and sending of God has gone over to the person of him who speaks. This happened in Jesus of Nazareth. The authority of the prophetic word as fullness of power of a person, who is present here and now—that is the fulfillment of the revelation that took place in and through Jesus.

4. Finally, revelation in the mode of fulfillment is given not only in the fact that Jesus, like the prophets and, even at the end, John the Baptist, is the proclaimer of the message of God's rule and kingdom, [18] but in the fact that Jesus makes this theme the central point of his own proclamation, that he frees the idea of God's rule and kingdom from all contemporary, earthly, political, and national misunderstandings and understands it as God's graceful turning towards us, as the establishment of the power of God against the dominion of evil, sin, and death, as grace, peace, and "eternal" life, as the salvation of human beings. God's kingdom is an exclusive gift for which human beings must seek, for the granting of which they must pray. Jesus announces in his proclamation the immediate and imminent proximity of God's rule (Mark 1:15); he describes the "entrance conditions" for the kingdom of God. These comprise not only metanoia as the tearing down of all human self-glory and as recognition of the lordship of God, readiness for self-giving and to become like a child, but above all the requirement of following him and confessing him.

If, in the actual scope of the parables of the kingdom of God in which Jesus proclaims his own mystery, it is already expressed that the kingly rule of God is present in Jesus, then the deeds of Jesus are an impressive confirmation of that. This will be treated later in another context (see below § 36).

As acts of power the deeds of Jesus are not only, as his answer to the question of John the Baptist put it, the fulfillment of messianic promises (cf. Matt 11:4–11), but also signs of God's rule already beginning in him, since sickness, death, and sin are overcome. A quite impressive documentation of the presence of God's rule in Jesus is contained in the logion accompanying Jesus' driving out of the demons: "If it is by the finger of God that I cast out demons, then the kingdom of God has come upon you" (Luke 11:20; Matt 12:28). The expulsion of the demons means that Jesus is demolishing the rule of the evil one. The rule of God

18. Rudolf Schnackenburg, *God's Rule and Kingdom*, trans. John Murray (New York: Herder and Herder, 1963); P. Hünermann, "Reign of God," *SM* 5.233–40.

present and active in Jesus drives back the power of the evil one. The power exercised by Jesus to forgive sins is an even more impressive indication than the healing of sicknesses that "the kingdom of God is in the midst of you" (Luke 17:21).

The "more than" and "greater than" present in Jesus is also shown by the way Jesus breaks through the barriers of prevailing tradition and convention and gets involved with human beings who are said to be distant from and cut off from God: tax collectors, sinners, whores. Jesus takes up table fellowship with them. He doesn't allow himself to be taken to account over this but acts in a freedom that comes from the center of his person and message: from the rule of God announced and begun in him.

Thus it is that the event that has come about in Jesus' word and deed is distinguished from the time that extended up to John the Baptist: up to John the Baptist one had only "the law and the prophets . . . since then the good news of the kingdom of God is preached" (Luke 16: 16); thus it is that the eye and ear-witnesses of the works of Jesus are called blessed: "Blessed are your eyes, for they see, and your ears, for they hear. Truly, I say to you, many prophets and righteous men longed to see what you see, and did not see it, and to hear what you hear, and did not hear it" (Matt 13:16-17).

The "more than" and the "greater than" made manifest in Jesus can also be described as unity of action with Yahweh, a unity of action which in Jesus, in contrast to the prophets, comes down to an equality of power, and even presupposes a unity in being. This opens up the path from prophet-Christology to Son-Christology.[19]

5. The unique fulfillment of revelation in the *ecce* of Jesus of Nazareth is also expressed in the New Testament by the description of the uniqueness of Jesus' being the Son of his Father. The title *Son of God* is, as such, not at all clear. It had already been used in numerous ways in the Old Testament.[20] The People of Israel, the king, the just person are called son of God. The special characteristic of Jesus' being Son is described at a high point of the Synoptic Gospels in this fashion: "All things have been delivered to me by my Father; and no one knows the Son except the Father, and no one knows the Father except the Son and anyone to whom the Son chooses to reveal him (Matt 11:27). Here Jesus claims for himself a knowledge of God that is perfectly equal to the knowledge the Father has of him. It is thus of a divine kind and consequently presupposes divine nature. All knowledge of God that human beings can possess, including that of the prophets, is, compared with

19. Cf. F. Mußner, "Ursprünge und Entfaltung," 97, n. 14.
20. M. Hengel, *The Son of God: The Origin of Christology and the History of Jewish–Hellenistic Religion*, trans. John Bowden (London: S. C. M. Press, 1976).

that which Jesus claims for himself, a non-knowing. This is grounded in the fact that he and only he is the Son.[21]

The theme "Son of God" is in a special way the content of the Gospel of John, which does not pass over the earthly Jesus but sees him totally in the light of the "more than" and describes this in the category of his special Sonship: "No one has ever seen God; the only Son, who is in the bosom of the Father, he has made him known"; he [Jesus] has, literally, "exegeted" him (John 1:18). Jesus is the exegesis, the interpretation of God; Jesus brings revelation from the Father; therefore he is, as Son, the revealer of God.

The Sonship of Jesus is represented in John as community of knowledge, of love, of life, of working with the Father. Jesus performs the works he sees the Father do (John 5:19); he brings about the same works as the Father (John 5:21, 22). "For as the Father has life in himself, so he has granted the Son also to have life in himself (John 5:26). Jesus brings the true and definitive knowledge of God—this means at the same time full community of life with him, "eternal life" (John 17:3), because he knows the Father "who has sent him," who bears witness to him in the works that no human being can do (John 15:24). Jesus speaks what he has seen and heard (John 3:11, 28; 8:26, 28). The Father is in him and he is in the Father (John 14:10f); he and the Father are one (John 10:30). "Everything that the Father has is mine" (John 10:15). And so, Jesus makes the claim: "Whoever hates me hates my Father" (John 15:23) and: "Whoever believes in me believes not in me but in him who sent me" (John 12:44f). "Whoever has seen me has seen the Father" (John 14:9).

The Gospel of John paraphrases the fulfillment present in Jesus in the sense of the *ecce* in yet another way: in the characteristic "I am" passages[22] which Jesus claims for himself: I am the shepherd, the door, the light, the bread, the resurrection, the way, the truth, the life. These formulas are neither mere allegory nor simple metaphors; they rather make a claim to exclusivity and uniqueness, which is made clear by the affirmations: "I am the door; whoever comes in through me will be saved" (John 10:9). "No one comes to the Father except through me" (John 14:6).

In these "I am" passages we have metaphorical speech. Under the sign of an image the mystery of the person is to be expressed, the answer given to the question: Who is this person? At the same time these metaphorical expressions tell what Jesus means for human beings, for me, what Jesus has to do with me and I with Jesus. For human existence he is light, bread, way, life, truth, resurrection. The high point of these "I am" expressions is, according to common interpretation, the

---

21. J. Schmid, *Das Evangelium nach Matthäus*, 4th ed. (Regensburg, 1959) 198.
22. Cf. *"egô,"* E. Stauffer, in: *TDNT* 2.343–62.

form used absolutely and without predicate: "If you do not believe that I am, you will die" (John 8:24-29). The predicateless "I am" is the self-representation of God, the conscious reference back to the Old Testament message of Exod 3:14: "I am who I am." The "I am he" belongs only to Jesus (cf. also Mark 13:6). Therefore Jesus is revelation as fulfillment in the sense of the *ecce*.

The "I am he" thus understood is the message of the New Testament as revelation of God in Jesus Christ, revelation as fulfillment. Here, in the *hodie* and *ecce*, lies the difference from the revelation as promise witnessed in the Old Testament. In Jesus, the invisible God has disclosed and communicated Himself visibly, humanly, personally: "*Deus se ipsum revelavit.*" This is fulfillment in the sense of the *hodie* and *ecce*.

Therefore, the proclaiming Jesus can become the proclaimed Christ; this is no contradiction but the consequence of the path from an implicit to an explicit Christology. The kingdom of God, the central theme of the proclamation of the historical Jesus, takes on, through Cross and Resurrection, the "face of Jesus Christ" (E. Schillebeeckx) and with that takes on its fulfillment.

The Fulfillment of the Contents and Characteristics of Revelation in the Old Testament

1. The *word* is a fundamental characteristic of Old Testament revelation. It is not just the word which treats of God and has God as its content; it is above all the word of God in the sense of the genitive of subject, the word that is attributed to God, the word that God speaks as ground of God's historical and creating activity: "the word of the Lord came forth"—"By the word of God the heavens were created." Word, in the understanding of the Old Testament, is connected with deed and work; it is act-word, history-word, event-word, performative word.

The connection of God and word, word and God, is explicitly and programmatically carried over to Jesus in the Prologue of John. Jesus is the Word (the Logos) that was with God, "and the word was God." The concept "Logos" in the Gospel of John connects the Old Testament elements of the word of God in such a way that it says: both the word about God and the Word of God have in Jesus come to concrete, personal, human manifestation, and therewith to fulfillment. In Jesus the Word of God which "already had always been in force in Israel, has become completely and definitively present for us in history. In this Word, God has expressed [his] Word, i.e., Himself, in the world."[23] The Word, which not only tells about reality but creates reality, is encountered in a special way in Jesus' activity: in his salvation and healing-producing

23. L. Scheffcyzk, "Word of God," *SM* 6.362–68; see also E. Brunner, *Revelation and Reason*, 109–11.

word, in the word that forgives sin, in the word of his self-giving unto death enacted at the Last Supper.

A further element of Logos Christology is the connection with the Greek and Stoic concept of world reason. The Logos, through whom everything is, and without whom was made nothing that was made is active in Jesus (John 1:3).

2. The name of God is, in the Old Testament, often a description of God. The name signifies a form of the self-communication of God, thus self-revelation. At the same time it signifies the divine nearness and love directed to human beings. In making use of the divine name, there was no sense of any magical control by human beings over Yahweh. Rather, Yahweh is to be called upon and blessed through his name and with his name: "The name of the Lord be praised!"

In the New Testament we find that Jesus identifies the "in-the-name-of God," "in-the-name-of-the-Lord" with himself, with his name—"in my name," "for the sake of my name"—and ties the same promise, the same power, and the same fate to it. The substitution of the name of God by the name of Jesus documents and describes in a graphic way the fulfillment of the self-disclosure and revelation of God that has taken place in Jesus Christ.

In the name of Jesus it becomes clear, in the ultimate, definitive sense, what the name of God meant from the beginning, though it was never fulfilled in full measure and meaning: God's own self as present, personal reality, as disclosed and proclaimed mystery. In the name of Jesus Christ, therefore, that name is given through which all are saved (Acts 4:12), the name in which one can call upon God, in which one can be assembled (Matt 18:20), in which God hears and will hear us: "If you ask anything of the Father, he will give it to you in my name" (John 16:23). The name of Jesus thus becomes the name "which is above every name" (Phil 2:9-10).

3. It is similar with the category: *face of the Lord*. This is the expression of divine grace and favor as well as of open access to it. In this category the character of the Old Testament as promise becomes especially manifest. For nowhere does the face that is sought become really present. It is of course said that a brilliance came forth from the face of Moses as he descended from Mount Sinai (Exod 33:18–20; 34:29–31). But his face is not the face of the Lord; his brilliance is only a reflection of the revelation glory seen by him alone. In the prophets this light turns into an eschatological reality and hope (cf. Isa 60:1–2). But in the New Testament, fulfillment has taken place: "For it is the God who said, 'Let light shine out of darkness,' who has shone in our hearts to give the light of the knowledge of the glory of God in the face of Christ" (2 Cor 4:6).

In the face of Jesus Christ, God's *doxa* [glory] shines out, but not, as with Moses, as a reflection, but as brilliance of God's own self. *Prosopon*—the word used here is the face of a person: of the incarnate Word, whose glory can be seen on earth (John 1:14). That is why Jesus says in the Gospel of John: "Whoever has seen me has seen the Father" (John 14:9). No one could say that before Christ or apart from him. He is the epiphany of God. That is why he is also the image, the icon of the invisible God (2 Cor 4:4; Col 1:15), incomparably more than the human being can be image and likeness of God. In the sense of the New Testament, image is identical with, and signifies the person present in, the image. Thus this affirmation, too, is a confession of the exclusive, personal presence of God in Christ.

If that is the case, then the element of hearing and seeing is contained in faith in Jesus Christ. The intellectual possibility of perception in human beings is thereby brought to fulfillment in its full dimension and put to use for faith. Hans Urs von Balthasar has, for this reason, no qualms about talking about a "Christ-proof" for the believing perception.[24]

God looks at human beings through the face of Jesus Christ. The face of God, often mentioned and sought in the Old Testament, is the Word that became flesh, the event in which definitive salvation came about, in which God's name was definitively revealed.

4. The fulfillment of revelation that came about in Jesus Christ is further present and expressed in the fact that Jesus is the founder of the new and eternal covenant and, as such, he brings about one of the decisive and most important promises of the Old Testament. The multiplicity of covenants, their constantly repeated renewal, the plurality of organs of the covenant, are noteworthy indications of the fact that in the Old Testament there never was a definitive covenant, but that it was being awaited (Jer 31: 31-34). In Jesus Christ—as, above all, the event of the Last Supper and the self-giving of Jesus unto death carried out there give witness—the new and eternal covenant is established and the new and definitive community of human beings, founded by God in the form of reconciliation, is grounded (cf. Matt 26:26–27; Luke 22:19–20). The definitiveness of this covenant, and with it the fulfillment of every preceding covenant-event, is made present.

The Letter to the Hebrews offers the most concentrated reflection on this, especially in the fact that Jesus Christ, the mediator of the New Covenant is the Son and thus towers over all mediating figures. Hebrews focuses this reflection by pointing out that Jesus, going beyond the Old Testament priesthood and the cult of the old covenant, is priest and sacrificial gift in one. Jesus is both of these because he offered himself up, because he is without guilt and thus need not offer sacrifice on

24. *Herrlichkeit I: Schau der Gestalt* (Einsiedeln, 1964).

his own behalf; because he—the sign of God's acceptance of this sacrifice of his—has stridden through the heavens; because his sacrifice effects not only cultic purification but the forgiveness of sins (Heb 4:14; 5:1-9; 7:24, 28; and chaps. 8—10).[25]

5. The expectation and promise of the Old Testament culminates in the expectation of *one-who-is-to-come*, the anointed, the Messiah, the eschatological mediator of salvation. To be sure, Jesus does not call himself Messiah; he is so named by others, especially in the confession of Simon Peter. But Jesus carries out messianic actions, i.e., actions attributed to the coming Messiah (Matt 11 2-6). At the same time, the confession of the Messiah is connected with a command to silence. "He ordered his disciples to tell no one that he is the Messiah" (Matt 16:20). This is not intended to refer to a kind of esotericism or arcane discipline; its purpose is to protect the messianic secret of Jesus from misunderstandings, espcially those of a political color.

What has been said thus far is intended to be an answer, gathered from many elements and grounded with many proofs and facts, to the question: "Are you he who is to come, or shall we look for another?" (Matt 11:3). Jesus himself answers this question affirmatively by referring to the fulfillment in himself of the "coming" promise (Matt. 11:4–6). All the Gospels are characterized by this purpose and attempt to realize it in their own way. The most emphatic of them is Matthew, who puts all events in the fate and history of Jesus under the category of the fulfillment of a messianic promise: "This took place so that the Scripture might be fulfilled." The Gospel of John concluded originally with the words: "These [signs] are written that you may believe that Jesus is the Christ, the Son of God, and that believing you may have life in his name" (John 20:31). The confession *Jesus is the Christ* is thus, from the beginning, a core element of Christian believing, praying, and praising, the legitimate representation and unfolding of the behavior, the message, the claim, the deeds, and the history of Jesus.

The Fulfillment of the Revelation of Creation

The revelation as fulfillment found in Jesus Christ would never do justice to its claim unless Christ were also the fulfillment of original revelation and of revelation in creation. Thus is his unique, definitive, and incomparable position once again described and completed.

According to the affirmations of Scripture, Christ is "the image of the invisible God, the first-born of all creation; for in him all things

25. O. Kuss, "Der theologische Grundgedanke des Hebräerbriefes" in: *Auslegung und Verkündigung* (Regensburg, 1963) 281–328; *Der Brief an die Hebräer* , 2d ed. (Regensburg, 1966).

were created, in heaven and on earth, visible and invisible, whether thrones or dominions or principalities or authorities—all things were created through him and for him. He is before all things, and in him all things hold together." (Col 1:15-17)

Accordingly, Christ is simultaneously the *ground and the goal of creation*. He who came in the fullness of time is at the same time he who was from the beginning and before all time.

The most convincing and strongest affirmations of this are to be found in the Gospel of John and in the Captivity Letters. The "in the beginning" of the Prologue of John (1:1) corresponds to the "in the beginning" of Gen 1:1. In Jesus comes—according to John—the Logos, the Word, which was in the beginning and through which all was made. He comes as the light which illumines every human being in the world; He comes into the world, which is his own; He comes to human beings, who are His own. Above all, the already-quoted hymn of the Letter to the Colossians, but also the Letter to the Ephesians, lift up the "cosmic position" of Christ in a special way. The same ideas resonate also at the beginning of the Letter to the Hebrews: "He [the Son] reflects the glory of God and bears the very stamp of His nature, upholding the universe by His word of power" (Heb 1:3). Therefore Christ is the head of the cosmos and the universe. Therefore He can also be called the first and the last, the beginning and the end, the Alpha and the Omega (Rev 1:17; 22:13). Here lie the sources for the Christology of Teilhard de Chardin.

From here the structure and entelechy of revelation as history and history as revelation are once again made clear. God "has made known to us in all wisdom and insight the mystery of his will, according to his purpose, which he set forth in Christ as a plan for the fullness of time, to unite all things in heaven and on earth" (Eph 1:9-10).

Similar relationships to universality are found in the concept of *wisdom*. In the Old Testament sapiential literature, "wisdom" is the representative and proxy for God in God's effective claim on the whole world, which is grounded in creation and in its order and preservation. This category is related to Christ in the New Testament: as Wisdom Christology which, in its universal, cosmic significance, stands next to Logos Christology. In Jesus the "Wisdom of God" speaks (Luke 11:49–51); in Christ God's wisdom has appeared (1 Cor 2:1–3, 4).

If Jesus Christ is wisdom in person and the recapitulation and goal of all reality, then reality as a whole and each individual reality acquires from him and for him its definitive meaning. But then too that which is centre, ground and goal of the existence of Jesus—his sonship, his being for God and for men—must intrinsically determine all reality in a hidden and yet effective way.[26]

26. Walter Kasper, *Jesus the Christ*, 188.

If Christ is not only the ground but also the goal of creation, then the revelational dimension of creation is again brought clearly to light in Him. Creation was planned towards Christ, and He Himself is the completion of creation, the final word of the words of creation, the fulfillment and completion of the works of creation, above all of human beings who have found in Christ their new and authentic image. Therefore Jesus is the true human being, the second, the real Adam; it is true of him as of no other: *Ecce homo* (cf. 1 Cor 15:21–22, 45–49). The picture of this human being is the one totally grounded in God, the one boundlessly open for God, the hearer of God's word, the obedient fulfiller of God's will, who loves God above everything and is therefore bound to human beings in selfless dedication and fraternal service. Therefore Jesus is the most authoritative among authoritative standards. In this image of the human being is expressed the fundamental anthropological law: the more human beings are with God, the more they are with themselves.

Revelation in the Cross

The revelation that has taken place in Jesus as revelation in fulfillment relates not only to creation or to individual elements one finds in the Old Testament, like word, name, face, covenant, Messiah, faith; rather, revelation happens now here, now there, here no one above all no religion, expects it. Revelation takes place in the situation of weakness, of suffering, of dying, of death.

Jesus is the fulfillment of revelation in an especially paradoxical manner. In him the following has become event: What is apparently the farthest distance from God—not the human being who is created but the human being who dies—becomes in a way the place where God becomes manifest, where God is present, where the word of the power and goodness of God does not lead *ad absurdum* but is fulfilled. The cross and the death on the cross, apparently the complete collapse of all expectations, hopes, and setting of goals, the sign of the most profound external shame and humiliation, become signs of the revelation of God.

This is where that truth comes to the fore that Luther formulated: God becomes manifest in the form of contradiction (*sub contrario*)—it is revelation in hiddenness.[27]

What Luther says, however, is only taking up again what Paul said in the First Letter to the Corinthians in an ever-so-expressive way:

For the word of the cross is folly to those who are perishing, but to us who are being saved it is the power of God. For it is written, "I will destroy the wisdom of the wise, and the cleverness of the clever I will thwart." Where is the wise man?

27. "Die Heidelberger Disputation" in: *Ausgewählte Werke I* (Munich, 1951) 125–38.

Where is the scribe? Where is the debater of this age? Has God not made foolish the wisdom of the world? For since, in the wisdom of God, the world did not know God through wisdom, it pleased God through the folly of what we preach to save those who believe. For Jews demand signs and Greeks seek wisdom, but we preach Christ crucified, a stumbling block to Jews and folly to Gentiles, but to those who are called, both Jews and Greeks, Christ is the power of God and the wisdom of God. For the foolishness of God is wiser than men, and the weakness of God is stronger than men. (1 Cor 1:18–25)

In these words, human ideas about God are, in the truest sense of the word, crossed out. If anywhere, then, it is in view of the cross that there is a "distinction of what is Christian" over against Judaism and over against the religions in the way they are prototypically represented by the Greeks, over against the thesis of God's incapacity to suffer. Paul doesn't take away the scandal and the foolishness of the cross, but insists on them. "Far be it from me to glory except in the cross of our Lord Jesus Christ" (Gal 6: 14). The cross of Christ may not be "emptied."

If we ask how it is that the cross of Christ is the special, indeed incomparable, mode of the revelation of God, the answer turns out, once again from Paul, as follows: The cross represents the highest conceivable form of the self-emptying, the kenosis of God: unto death, unto death on the cross (Phil 2:5–11). In this lies not a limiting but a manifestation of the power of God: God is so great that [he] can be small, insignificant, and lowly, that [he] can reach right to the boundaries of death. God is more powerful than the power of death. Therefore one can also say that God is nowhere greater than in [his] abasement, nowhere more powerful than in [his] weakness.

The cross is a revelation of God because it is the revelation of a love whose seriousness is shown in the fact that it is ready to give up its life for others. This "for" is to be understood as representation:[28] in the place of, and, at the same time, as a fruit that is of benefit to the many. To that extent the cross is the fulfillment of the words about the suffering Servant of God from Second Isaiah: "He bore the sin of many, and made intercession for the transgressor" (Isa 53:12; cf. 52:13–53:12). "If God suffers, then God suffers in a divine way; that is, God's suffering is an expression of God's freedom. God is not struck by suffering, but allows Himself in freedom to be struck by it. God does not suffer as a creature, because of a lack of being; God suffers out of love and from [his] love, which is the superfluity of being."[29]

Such an affirmation about the presence and revelation of God in suffering, dying, and death has transformed the situations and experiences from which no human being is spared—the suffering, dying, and death

---

28. Joseph Ratzinger, "Stellvertretung," *HThG* 2. 566–75.

29. W. Kasper, *The God of Jesus Christ*, trans. Matthew J. O'Connell (New York: Crossroad, 1984) 195.

of human beings can become manifestations of the presence of God, who, in the power of love, spared Himself from nothing human.

The revelation of God on the cross came to an extraordinarily deep and vital realization in medieval mysticism, above all in Bernard and Bonaventure. Even more impressive was Martin Luther's development of the theology of the cross, for the first time in the theses of the Heidelberg disputation 1518, where he says:

> We rightly give the name of theologian not to those who perceive and understand God's invisible nature through God's works; rather we rightly give the name of theologian to those who understand that that part of God's nature which is open and visible to the world is precisely what has been represented in suffering and on the Cross. That part of God's nature which is open and visible to the world, and contrasted to the invisible, is God's humanity, weakness, and foolishness, as we learn from 1 Cor 1:25 speaking of the divine weakness and foolishness. (Theses 19 and 20)

To this Luther adds as a corrective:

> Wisdom is, to be sure, not bad in itself, but without the theology of the cross, human beings misuse the best and turn it to the worst by ascribing wisdom and works to themselves. (Thesis 24)

It is when one keeps in mind the cross that, according to him, the knowledge of God from the works of creation becomes of any benefit for salvation.

Hegel made the attempt to recover philosophically the revelation content of the cross and the crucified and also to reconcile philosophy and theology on this point. He begins from the hymn verse: "O great sorrow, God, very God is dead," and he converts the "historical" into the "speculative" good Friday. He explains the death of Jesus as a moment of the movement of the Absolute Spirit—Hegel's term for God—on the way to itself. That is possible only if the Absolute Spirit appropriates the most alien thing—death—in such form that it [Absolute Spirit] supersedes it in the form of overcoming, preservation, and exaltation.

Because the Absolute Spirit, because God, enters into death and is in death, "God Himself is dead," death is overcome. The negation of the negation takes place, if death is to be understood and described as negation.[30]

This way of thinking has become active in contemporary theology in Jürgen Moltmann: *The Crucified God: The Cross of Christ as Ground and Critique of Christian Theology*, and in Eberhard Jüngel: *Gott als Geheimnis der Welt. Zur Begründung der Theologie des Gekreuzigten im Streit zwischen Theismus und Atheismus* [God as Mystery of the World. The Grounding of the Theology of the Crucified in the Controversy

---

30. *Vorlesungen über die Philosophie der Religion* (Ausgabe Lasson) II/2, 53–54.

between Theism and Atheism]. Hans Urs von Balthasar speaks of the death of God as a wellspring of salvation, revelation, and theology.[31] This idea has also been taken up by Walter Kasper: "The cross is the most extreme act which is possible to God in God's self-bestowing love; it is the *id quo maius cogitari nequit* [that greater than which cannot be thought], the absolutely unsurpassable self-definition of God."[32]

Transcendental Christology

Transcendental theology works from the assumption that it is not enough these days simply to proclaim and confess the truth of Jesus Christ. Christology must be mediated. Karl Rahner attempts this[33] by asking whether there are not in human beings themselves presuppositions and conditions through which they gain a knowledge and understanding of what is meant by the definitive revelation in Jesus Christ. Human beings have—Rahner says—a transcendental idea of Jesus Christ. The human being is so constituted that in questioning, willing, loving, seeking, they are constantly transcending themselves unto the deepest mystery of their selves, unto the all-determining reality, which is called God.

He adds a further idea. Jesus Christ is the highest instance of humanity. He is the unique and unparalleled realization of that towards which every human being is oriented: self-transcendence towards God, unity of the human being with God. This is found in Jesus in the most perfect way; it comes together in Jesus with the self-transcendence of God towards human beings. From this perspective, Rahner formulates the thesis that Christology is self-transcending anthropology and that anthropology can be represented as incomplete Christology.[34]

It must be specifically added that Rahner does not, as some critics claim, deduce his Christology from an a priori idea of Christ. He says: "The transcendental deduction of an idea is always the historically *posterior reflection on* a concrete experience, a reflection which explicitly sees the 'necessary' in the factual."[35]

In other words, the idea of a transcendental Christology could be hit upon only after the message of Jesus the Christ had been heard and accepted as an event of history. Then, from this event, the question is asked [back] whether, for this historical reality, there are in human beings themselves concrete presuppositions, conditions, dispositions together with their contents. This is done not in order to make Jesus into a projection of these expectations, but to make intelligible in what rela-

31. "Pachal Mystery,"*DFT* 758–76.
32. W. Kasper, *The God of Jesus Christ* 194.
33. Summed up in: *Foundations of Christian Faith*, 176–264.
34. First of all in: *Schriften* 1.184.
35. "Transcendental theology," *SM* 6.287–89.

tionship and coordination Jesus the Christ stands towards human beings, i.e., as answer to the question human beings not only have but themselves *are*.[36]

Thus Rahner believes he is opening up a way to make comprehensible to human beings what the claim and the mystery of Christ is all about, how very much what was said by Jesus has to do with human beings themselves, how Christology can be mediated as anthropology and anthropology as Christology.

There is an additional idea that is of importance precisely for the *fundamental theological question*:

The human being is that being which dares to hope that this mystery is not just the distant goal of an endless movement, but that it bestows itself as fulfillment of the highest yearnings of existence.

This most bold deed of hope seeks in history for that self-pledge of God which, for humanity, gives up its ambivalence and becomes definitive and irreversible.

The historical concreteness of the definitive self-pledge of God to the world

can only be a human being who, on the one hand, gives up in death every future in this world, and on the other hand, in this acceptance of death, ends up being definitively accepted by God. Such a human being with this destiny is what is meant by the phrase "absolute bringer of salvation."

"A transcendental Christology cannot presume to say that this absolute bringer of salvation has been found precisely in Jesus of Nazareth." But it "leads one to seek and in seeking to understand what one has always found in Jesus of Nazareth."[37]

Summing up, it can be said that the designation "Jesus is the Christ, the Messiah" is intended to describe the revelation that has taken place in Jesus as the fulfillment of revelation as promise. This takes place in the horizon of a faith and a way of thinking that is stamped by the Old Testament. The designation "Jesus is the Lord, the Kyrios" indicates first in what way Jesus is the Christ. In addition, the confession "Jesus is the Kyrios" intends to express that He is the fulfillment of original revelation and of revelation in creation. The meaning of the title *Kyrios* as translation of the Old Testament name of God (*Yahweh*) is that Jesus is this fulfillment both as messenger and bearer of God's rule (which is a sovereignty of freedom, justice, and love) and as bodily and personal presence of God.

If the proclamation of Jesus as the Christ was the appropriate proclamation for the Jews, so too the proclamation of Jesus as the Kyrios, the coordination of the Creator of heaven and earth to Jesus

36. K. Rahner—W. Thüsing, *Christologie—Systematisch und Exegetisch* (Freiburg—Basel—Vienna, 1972).
37. Ibid. 20–24.

Christ come in the flesh, was the appropriate proclamation for the Gentiles, for all human beings. That doesn't prevent the revelation in Jesus Christ from being apostrophized as scandal or folly.

The earliest Christian confession and the sum of the earliest Christian faith are brought together in the words: Jesus—Christ—Kyrios. Jesus is the Christ; Jesus is the Lord (Phil 2:11).

§ 35

REVELATION AS CONSUMMATION

By now, the most important aspects of revelation have already been mentioned. The center of everything—the revelation given in Jesus the Christ and Lord and in his saving work—is in a certain sense also the end and the consummation, the eschatological event. Nevertheless—as we have already pointed out in different ways—revelation as fulfillment still has a future, which is certainly the future of itself, but as future is not yet present, but is awaited. This future is the consummation of what has already definitively arrived and come; the future is the future which has already broken in, in the center and in fulfillment, by which it is borne, carried out, and preserved. It is grounded in the *hodie* and *ecce* of that which has taken place, and can only mean the "bringing-to-completion" of that which has already begun: the superseding of the "not yet" in the already present "already."[1]

Let us now examine how the "not yet"—and with it the future and the consummation it contains—fits into this understanding of revelation as fulfillment.

The eschatological words of Jesus are an obvious place to begin: his words about the "coming of the Son of man in great power and glory" (Matt 24:30), his words about the judgment, about the new heaven and the new earth (Rev 21:1). Further to be considered is that God's rule and

---

1. Cf. the presentation of eschatology in the dogma textbooks and in the theological reference works. Emil Brunner, *Das Ewige als Zukunft und Gegenwart* (Zurich, 1953); P. Althaus, *Die Letzten Dingen,* 6th ed. (Gütersloh, 1956); M. Schmaus, *Katholische Dogmatik* IV/2; E. Brunner, *Revelation and Reason: The Christian Doctrine of Faith and Knowledge,* trans. Olive Wyon (Philadelphia: The Westminster Press, 1946); Hans Urs von Balthasar, "Eschatologie" in: *Fragen der Theologie Heute,* ed. J. Feiner—J. Trütsch—F. Böckle, 3d ed. (Einsiedeln—Zurich—Cologne, 1960) 403–24; Karl Rahner, "Theologische Prinzipien der Hermeneutik eschatologischer Aussagen," *Schriften* 4. 401–28; A. Vögtle, *Das Neue Testament und die Zukunft des Kosmos* (Düsseldorf, 1970); Joseph Ratzinger, *Eschatology, Death and Eternal Life.* trans. Aidan Nichols (Washington, D.C.: Catholic University of America Press, 1988); H. Vorgrimler, *Hoffnung auf Vollendung. Aufriß der Eschatologie* (Düsseldorf, 1980); G. Greshake—G. Lohfink, *Naherwartung—Auferstehung—Unsterblichkeit,* 4th ed. (Freiburg—Basel—Vienna, 1982); M. Schmaus, *Der Glaube der Kirche* VI/2: *Gott Der Vollender* (St. Ottilien, 1982).

kingdom is announced and arrives in Jesus Christ. His word and deeds, above all, his Resurrection from the dead and sending of the Spirit, are the unmistakable signs of this fact. But at the same time, the coming of this kingdom is prayed for: "Thy kingdom come"—"Maranatha." The parables of growth refer to this future, as do the imperatives to watching, to waiting, to readiness, to patience, to struggle, to faith, to hope:

For in this hope we were saved. Now hope that is seen is not hope. For who hopes for what he sees? But if we hope for what we do not see, we wait for it with patience. (Rom 8:24-25)

Revelation in Jesus is revelation in servant form—in lowliness, in the folly and scandal of the cross. It is thus, despite all revelation in power and sovereignty, a hidden revelation and a revelation of the hidden God. It can be misunderstood and overlooked, it can be the occasion to take scandal and raise opposition. And this possibility is constantly becoming real. Only faith is in a position to overcome this scandal and stand up to the brightness and darkness of this revelation. This fact must be preserved in, with, and under the message and the fact of the resurrection. But to the resurrection itself we have access only through the "witnesses of the resurrection." The Risen One did not appear before the whole world but only before the witnesses chosen for it (cf. Acts 10:40). All others are to come to faith in the Risen One through their word. Thus faith is of course a gift of God and light on the way, ground, firm anchoring and security, "victory over the world" (1 John 5:4). But He, as "virtue of the journey," points beyond himself to a fulfillment which the Scripture describes as "seeing face to face" (1 Cor 13:12).

The resurrection of Jesus is the beginning of the completion; in it will be what at the end will be without end, and it is the guarantee and security of everything to be hoped for. Christ is the "hope of glory" (Col 1:27). But the resurrection too is first a beginning; its fruit is not yet effective everywhere. The signs of the anti-Godly—sickness, suffering, sin and death—are still present; creation still lies groaning, and the already redeemed await the full "redemption of our bodies" (Rom 8:23). The celebration of the saving deeds in sacrament, above all and most supremely in the Eucharist, is the proclaiming of "the Lord's death until he comes" (1 Cor 11: 26).

The work of Jesus is continued and actualized through the Paraclete; it is made present in the Church. The Church stands in its being and activity under the sign of the way, of growth to the fullness, to the full dimension of Christ: to the *Christus totus* [whole Christ]. The Church is the "wandering People of God."

All that, and more, is a sign of the "not yet." But it cannot remain that way definitively. The "already" which is present in the "not yet" must come to unbroken completion and thus to the completion also of the revelation where Christ who is the Alpha will become manifest as the Omega (Rev 1:8; 21:6; 22:13) and where that which has already happened to us and in us will be completed: "It does not yet appear what we shall be, but we know that when he appears we shall be like him, for we shall see him as he is" (1 John 3:2).

Revelation as completion means, from the side of the revealer: "Revelation in Power and Glory" for human beings means "to see from face to face," "to know as I am known" (1 Cor 13: 12).

Revelation in power and glory strips off the servant form. The divine *doxa*, the light of the glory of God, lordship, the rule, and the kingship of God will become manifest to all the world, unbroken, unlimited, without shadow. This rule will be recognized by all the world. The differences between humanity and church will be dissolved and brought to the perfected unity of the new heaven and the new earth (Rev 21:1). The Son will hand over the kingdom to the Father, "so that God will be all in all" (1 Cor 15:28). It is God's rule become complete/perfect, and therewith and therein salvation made perfect. The biblical image for this is the new Jerusalem, the holy city which no longer has a temple, "for its temple is the Lord God the Almighty and the Lamb." And this city "has no need of sun or moon to shine upon it, for the glory of God is its light, and its lamp is the Lamb" (Rev 21:22–23).

What objectively is called power and glory is called, subjectively, "seeing" as distinct from believing. To see includes the lifting of all barriers that are found in faith as an indirect form of knowing. Seeing is the most perfect form of knowing as immediate union and possession. This seeing is characterized as a seeing face to face (1 Cor 13:12). Thus, end and completion in human beings also consists in a self-presence: the more human beings are with God, the more are they with themselves. Nor does this dissolve into a person-dissolving absence of contours, for it preserves the over-against of the person face to face, which, however, in this being over-against has lost all alienation, and which connects the most profound unity with personal encounter.

This seeing face to face is further interpreted by a "knowing as we are known" (1 Cor 13:12). Knowing as partial knowing ceases, therewith and thereby, when God knows in us. When we know as we are known, then God is the knower and our knowing is a participation in divine knowing, a becoming one with that knowledge in which God knows himself, the highest perfection of the "In thy light do we see light" (Psalm 36:9). But also, in this characterization, "I will know as I am known," the boundary between God and human beings is not dissolved. Both are, and they remain who they are. Here is over against, community and unity, but not identity. The "I" remains in this knowing; and if it can know as it is known, then it is not swallowed up by the luminous Glory of God, but is quite genuinely brought to itself.

Revelation as consummation is the rule of God completed; it is, in other words, the form of life of completed human salvation.

The Synod of Bishops in the Federal Republic of Germany has made "a confession of faith in this time" under the title "Our Hope." The significance that revelation as completion has in it is shown by these words:

We Christians hope for the new human being, the new heaven and the new earth in the completion/perfection of the kingdom of God. We can speak of this kingdom of God only in images and similitudes the way they are narrated and witnessed in the Old Testament and in the New Testament of our hope, and above all by Jesus himself. These images and similitudes of the great peace of human beings and nature before the face of God, of the one table fellowship of love, of homeland and of father, of the kingdom of freedom, reconciliation and justice, of the tears wiped away and of the laughing of the children of God, they are all accurate and irreplaceable. We cannot simply "translate" them; we can really only protect them, remain true to them, and resist their being dissolved into the mystery-less language of our concepts and argumentation, which does indeed speak to our needs and our plans, but not to our longing and our hopes.

The promises of the kingdom of God which, through Jesus, has irrevocably broken in on us and is active in the community of the Church, lead us into the midst of the world of our life—with all its own plans for the future and utopias. It is into these plans that these promises break in and become clarified, even in our own time of science and technology, of great social and political changes. . . .

Our hope looks for a completion of humanity from the transforming power of God, as an eschatological event whose future has already irrevocably begun for us in Jesus Christ. We belong to him; we are grafted into him. Through baptism we are plunged into his new life, and in table fellowship with him we receive the "pledge of future glory." By placing ourselves under the "Law of Christ" (Gal 6:2) and living in his discipleship, we become, even in the midst of our world of life, witnesses of this transforming power of God: as peacemakers and merciful, as human beings of purity and poverty of heart, as mourners and strugglers, in unconquerable hunger and thirst for justice (cf. Matt 5:3-10).[2]

---

2. Gemeinsame Synode der Bistümer in der Bundesrepublik Deutschland, Offizielle Gesamtausgabe (Offical Edition) 95–97.

§ 36

THE GROUNDING AND JUSTIFICATION OF THE CLAIM OF REVELATION—THE PROBLEM OF CREDIBILITY AND CRITERIA

The Problem of Miracles

To this point, we have attempted to present both the pluriform testimonies of the Old Testament, according to the revelation in history that can be known there, and, with special emphasis, the witnesses of the New Testament in their convergence on the central figure of Jesus the Christ.

These biblical affirmations are frequently made under the sign of claim, proclamation, and confession. But already in the Old Testament, and even more clearly in the New Testament, we find significant indications that the mere claim does not suffice, however emphatically it may be raised. The claim must be mediated to those for whom it is raised. In other words, there must be a grounding, which justifies, legitimates, and confirms the claim. This brings us to the problem of the criteria of revelation, the problem of their credibility, their motives and grounds. The criteria can and should be, for human beings an introduction and guide to faith in the revelation before them. This is true even though no ground of credibility, not even the sum of grounds, replaces faith or produces faith from itself mechanically or automatically.

As we deal with this in our time, we are faced with the following dilemma. Both from within and without, the questions being asked today about the credibility of revelation and the verification of faith have a critical sharpness. It is a sign of our radically rational age, the age of a new enlightenment, of thinking oriented to experience, that insists on verification. The answers that theology and above all apologetics used to give are now of doubtful cogency. To the question, "How does special historical revelation prove its claim to divine origin and the self-disclosure of God?" the answer in traditional theology was, "through miracles and fulfilled prophecies." For these point in a special way to their origin in God and to God's special activity; they document that here God has intervened, acted, spoken.

To illustrate this, we will take a text from Vatican I, a council that dealt with specific fundamental-theological and apologetic issues. One of the themes of the council was revelation and faith. This is the content of the dogmatic constitution *"Dei Filius" de fide catholica*.

After the definition of faith as "act of obedience of human beings to the truth disclosed by divine authority" it says:

In order that the service of obedience of our faith might correspond to reason, God willed to connect, with the inner assistance of the Holy Spirit, external proofs of his revelation: namely, divine works, above all miracles and prophecies. Since they prove God's omnipotence and measureless knowledge in rich measure, they are wholly certain signs of revelation suited to the powers of understanding of everyone. Accordingly Moses, the prophets, and especially Christ the Lord himself performed many and obvious miracles and foretold future events. Of the apostles we read: "They went forth and preached everywhere, while the Lord worked with them and confirmed the message by the signs that attended it" (Mark 16:20). And in another place: "We have the prophetic word made more sure. You will do well to pay attention to this as to a lamp shining in a dark place" (2 Pet 1:19).[1]

On the same theme two other canons of the same council are important:

Whoever says that divine revelation cannot become credible through outward signs, and that it must therefore move human beings to faith through the purely inner experience of each individual or through personal illumination, let him be anathema.

And further:

Whoever says that miracles cannot happen, and that therefore all miracle stories, even those contained in Holy Scripture, are to be arranged under legends and myths; or that miracles can never be certainly known, and that the divine origin of the Christian religion can never be properly proven through them, let him be anathema.[2]

If we let these words work on us, we recognize in them a massive claim. It is the claim to *universality*. All human beings of all times are addressed by these criteria, the *facta divina*, the divine actions, especially by miracles and prophecies. It is the claim to *objectivity* and finally the claim to certitude and assurance which are stronger than all the questions and doubts brought up against them.

As necessary and helpful as this all might be for our present-day questions, we can today no longer share in the certitude and assurance expressed here, the epistemological optimism radiated from here. We have difficulty thinking this way. What is more, what is offered in this council as help and relief for the faith is precisely what makes

1. DS 3009.
2. DS 3033, 3034.

difficulties for us and represents a problem precisely for the road to faith.

If in earlier times one said of miracle that it is "the best-loved child of faith," today it must be said that it has turned into a problem child.[3] The primary source of our problems and difficulties seems to be the historical-critical method and its results vis-a-vis the New Testament miracle accounts—in addition to the well-known thesis of Lessing that mere reports about miracles are not actual miracles. Difficulties also come from the present-day view of life under the sign of natural science and technology, in which there is no more room for miracles, most especially when one, as is usually the case, understands miracle as a breaking through or lifting of laws of nature. But here too there is already an indication that there may have been a change in the concept of miracle. This could be one reason for these difficulties; but it could also open up a path towards a possible solution of the problem.

We will try to approach this problem of credibility, above all of the credibility produced by signs and wonders, in such a way that we first deal with an objection that solves the problem by not even admitting it but by rejecting it as illegitimate. This can be clarified by way of the position of dialectical theology, e.g., of Emil Brunner. He declares that revelation cannot be rationally grounded; otherwise revelation is no longer revelation but truth of reason. To want to ground revelation according to reason means not to understand and not to have understood what revelation is.

Theologians who get involved with introducing proofs for the claim of revelation are playing a lost game from the start. This is the just punishment for the fact that they don't take seriously their own ground and object. There is either faith or proof, but not both.

The doubting of faith is nothing but the intellectual form of sin. Doubt is a form of hubris; it comes from an a priori rejection of revela-

---

3. Reginald Fuller, *Interpreting the Miracles* (Philadelphia: Westminster Press, 1963); R. Guardini, *Wunder und Zeichen* (Würzburg, 1959); L. Monden, *Signs and Wonders: A Study of the Miraculous Element in Religion* (New York: Desclee Co., 1966); J. Metz—L. Monden, "Miracle," *SM* 4.44–49; R. Latourelle, "Miracle," *DFT* 690–709; C. Sant—T. G. Pater, "Miracles," *NCE* 9.886–94; Franz Mußner, *The Miracles of Jesus: An Introduction*, trans. Albert Wimmer (Notre Dame: University of Notre Dame Press, 1968); R. Pesch, *Jesu ureigene Taten?* (Freiburg—Basel—Vienna, 1970); K. Kertelge, *Die Wunder im Markusevangelium* (Munich, 1970;); M. Seckler, "Plädoyer für Ehrlichkeit im Umgang mit Wundern," *ThQ* 151 (1971) 337–45; B. Weißmahr, *Gottes Wirken in der Welt, Ein Diskussionsbeitrag zur Frage der Evolution und des Wunders* (Frankfurt, 1973); K. Kertelge, "Die Überlieferung der Wunder Jesu und die Frage nach dem historischen Jesus" in: K. Kertelge, ed., *Rückfrage nach Jesus* (Freiburg—Basel—Vienna, 1974); A. Kolping, *Fundamentaltheologie II* (Münster, 1974) 438-66; Walter Kasper, *Jesus the Christ*, 89; Hans Küng, *On Being a Christian*, trans. Edward Quinn (Garden City, N. Y.: Doubleday, 1978) 226-38; Edward Schillebeeckx, *Jesus: An Experiment in Christology*, trans. Herbert Hoskins (New York: Seabury Press, 1979) 179–200; Leonhard Goppelt, *Theology of the New Testament*, trans. John E Alsup (Grand Rapids, Mich.: W. B. Eerdmans Pulishing Co., 1981) 139-57 .

tion.[4] If faith is described primarily as a venture, as a "nevertheless," then one can see in the question of the credibility of faith only a misunderstanding of faith. Then one must even be careful to cast away the supports offered in the so-called criteria of credibility, so that faith can be realized in the most radical and pure way possible.

The reformational doctrine of justification, so explains Rudolf Bultmann, destroys every false certitude and every presumptuous desire for certitude in human beings, even though the certitude may be grounded on their good behavior or their confirming knowledge.

Human beings who want to believe in God as their God, must know that they have nothing in their hand in which they can believe, that they are, so to speak, left hanging in the air and can demand no evidence for the truth of the words being spoken to them. The ground and the object of faith are identical. Certitude is found only by those who let all certitude go, who—to speak with Luther—are ready to go into the inner darknesses.[5]

These positions are understood above all as opposed to the Catholic conception as classically presented in the texts from Vatican I.

In answer, one can say that the question of the criteria of revelation is not a presumption of human beings; instead, these criteria are contained in the testimony of revelation itself. They are connected with the revelation event and the revelation claim itself. Leaving these criteria out of consideration is not a service towards the preservation of the faith and the genuinity of revelation, but the withdrawal of an important service.

The alternative—either faith or proof, but not both—would be correct if faith were the necessary final sum resulting from a chain of proofs. The grounds of credibility, however, operate in that sphere which is paraphrased by: condition of possibility. They admit free decision, indeed even demand it.

The proposition "A theology that gets involved with introducing proofs for the claim of revelation is playing a lost game from the start" is to be answered with the "counter-proposition": A theology that refuses to make use of proofs in the sense of arguments about the claim of revelation is playing a lost game; it makes the decision of faith in revelation into a certain respectable but not grounded or groundable option; it opts for an irrational decision of faith. Further, a No to criteria of revelation doesn't do justice to the claim of revelation as a whole, especially not to the relationship to the whole human being with all of his/her powers and gifts. This relationship proceeds from and is demanded by the claim of revelation.

4. Emil Brunner, *Revelation and Reason: The Christian Doctrine of Faith and Knowledge*, trans. Olive Wyon (Philadelphia: The Westminster Press, 1946) 240–18.

5. In: *Kerygma und Mythos II*, ed. von H. W. Bartsch, (Hamburg, 1952) 207.

The other thesis of Brunner refers to the following context: Questioning comes from doubt; doubt is the intellectual form of sin; questioning comes from hubris, from the assumed autonomy of human beings, from human refusal over against God.

In reply we say, of course there are forms of questions and doubts that basically are asked or brought forward only in order to disguise the already decided No. But one must contest that these are the only forms of doubt and question. Are there not questions that come from openness, from the readiness to hear, to let something be said? Is not questioning—as was already suggested—perhaps nothing else than an expression of the greatness and the limitation of human beings, an admission of the fact that the questioner in no way already knows everything and thus had decided everything, but that human beings, precisely by their ability to ask and their need to ask gain the qualification of being hearers of the word—an absolutely irreplaceable qualification with respect to faith in revelation? Is not the question, as Heidegger formulated it, precisely the "piety of thinking"?

And it still has to be added that there is no more intensive form of closing off the self than that of not questioning or no longer questioning. It is not by questioning but by the refusal of questioning that doors for the acceptance of revelation are closed. Lacking here are all possibilities of being able to be spoken to, of the "Speak, Lord, your servant is listening" (1 Sam 3:9).

We conclude that to eliminate the difficulties that arise today from the problem of the criteria of revelation and its connected thematic of the credibility, grounding, and confirmation of revelation is not the right way to go. It is not right to eliminate these difficulties by pushing aside the whole question of criteria as theologically illegitimate. It is not illegitimate. If it were, the result would be that theology would fall into a total lack of relationship to the present situation.

The Problem of Faith and Credibility according to the Witness of the Bible

That said, we can attempt a fresh approach to the matter and ask how the Bible itself, above all the New Testament, the testimony and record of revelation, expresses itself on this theme of ours. Does it have anything to say, and if so, what, about the problems of faith and credibility, claim, and criteria of revelation?

First, the question itself is not only known to the New Testament, it is one of its important motifs. Its concern is not only to witness and proclaim the claim of Jesus, but also to ground and justify it and to produce grounds of credibility for it. This happens in many different ways, most impressively by the deeds of Jesus presented as signs, which one calls miracles. For a proper understanding and judgment on this subject, there is an important first step: what is the literary genre of the particular New Testament text under consideration? Is it an historical account, a didactic story, a legend, an interpretation of the significance of the person, behavior and words of Jesus? It is the task of exegesis to point these things out.

On the question of interpretation with respect to the question of miracles, the following guidelines have been worked out by contemporary exegesis. They are an aid to interpretation, not to have the biblical affirmations at reduced prices, but to avoid unnecessary difficulties. One must first point out that the New Testament doesn't use the concept "miracle." It speaks of "powerful deeds" or "signs." Here are some of the particular principles of interpretation.[6]

We end up with a reduction of the number of miracle stories when we take into consideration that the different Gospels have parallel accounts of the same story and that there is a tendency to elevate, enlarge, and multiply the miracles. According to Mark 1:34, Jesus healed many who were sick; according to the parallel place in Matt 8:16, he healed all. In Mark, the daughter of Jairus is still dying; in Matthew, she is already dead. From the healing of a blind man and a possessed man, there turn out to be two blind men and two possessed men. 4000 miraculously fed become 5000, and seven baskets left over become twelve. This tendency to expand and multiply, detectable in the Gospels themselves, is important for the factual question before us. The fact itself [of the miracle] is not controverted, but the kind of record-keeping precision we would like to have today is not the purpose of the New Testament. But one thing is clear: this reflection considerably lessens the material of the miracle stories.

A further clarification comes from comparison with rabbinic and Hellenistic miracle stories. The New Testament miracle stories are shaped analogously and with the help of motifs we know from the rest of antiquity. There are rabbinic and Hellenistic miracle stories about healings, driving out demons, raising the dead, stilling storms, etc. There are numerous parallels to the contemporary of Jesus, Apollonius of Tiana. Especially from the Aesculapius sanctuary in Epidaurus comes the witness of many healings. One gets the impression that the New Testament transfers motifs from outside of Christianity to Jesus in order to underline his greatness and authority. These indications have not blocked or led astray access to Jesus and the interpretation of his activity, but opened it up. There is even a quite specific technique of miracle stories, an established three-membered scheme according to which they are narrated. First, the failure of former attempts is depicted, the

6. What follows depends on the presentations of W. Kasper, *Jesus the Christ* 104–16, and H. Küng, *On Being a Christian* 226–38.

severe sickness described, in order to prepare for the greatness of the miracle; then follows the description of the miraculous process; finally the witnesses are mentioned who have seen and confirmed the miracle (chorus conclusion). Without doubt there are also characteristic differences between the miracles of Jesus and those narrated elsewhere in antiquity. Jesus performs, for example, no stipend, profit, penal or show-miracles. But in view of the clearly established parallels, one can hardly reject all Jewish and Hellenistic miracle stories as unhistorical lying and deceit, while accepting the New Testament stories in contrast as thoroughly historical.

Many miracle stories turn out, by form-critical analysis, to be projections of Easter experiences back into the earthly life of Jesus, or as proleptic [anticipated] representation of the exalted Christ. Such epiphany stories are, e.g., the miracle of rescue from the storm, the transfiguration scene, the walking on the waters, the feeding of the four thousand or five thousand, and the catch of fish by Peter. The first and foremost intention of the raising from the dead of the daughter of Jairus, of the young man of Naim, and of Lazarus is to highlight Jesus as Lord over life and death.

All this indicates that many miracle stories of the Gospels are to be categorized as legendary. Legends, however, are not fables or fairy tales but a representation of realities which, to be sure, are to be looked at less for their historical than for their theological affirmational content. They speak not about individual facts of salvation but about the salvific significance of the one saving event of Jesus Christ. The indication that certain miracles cannot be ascribed to the earthly Jesus in no way reduces to an assertion that they have no significance theologically and kerygmatically. Such nonhistorical miracle stories remain affirmations of faith about the salvific significance of the person and message of Jesus. In other words, it is of relatively little importance, in terms of the knowledge and the faith that saves, whether or not the historical Jesus can be proven to have performed this or that miracle. But taken as faith affirmations about who Jesus is as Lord and Savior, miracles stories are at the heart of the gospel message. In that sense they are true.

Nevertheless, it would be false to conclude from this thesis that there are no historically supported miraculous deeds of Jesus at all. The opposite is correct. There is practically no exegete who commands respect who does not hold fast to a basic stock of historically certain miraculous deeds of Jesus.

Even after a historical-critical examination of the miracle tradition of the Gospels, it turns out that one can hardly contest a historical kernel of the miracle tradition. Jesus performed extraordinary deeds which struck his contemporaries with astonishment. Among these are cures of different sicknesses and of symptoms which one then understood as signs of possession. But the so-called nature miracles are different. There is some plausibility in not regarding them as historical.

For Edward Schillebeeckx, the texts: "He has done all things well" (Mark 7:37) and "He went about doing good" (Acts 10:38) form the horizon of the miraculous works of Jesus. The problem is, accordingly, not the miracle as act but the question, by what power these deeds took place: the power of God or the power of the evil one. Miracles are good deeds of power which respond to the suffering of human beings. Jesus' miracles can, therefore, not be ambivalently interpreted as do Jesus' opponents: "He drives out demons by Beelzebub." Nature miracles are directed, according to Schillebeeckx, against the disciples' weakness of faith, which is to be transformed by a contrasting manifestation. Actually, faith shouldn't have any need of such a thing.

One should also add to these reflections that, with His miracles, Jesus is dealing with concrete human beings, especially with human beings to whom His message is directed in a special way: the religiously and socially discriminated against, the poor, the weak, the sinners, the lepers, the blind, the lame, the mentally ill. An involvement becomes visible here that is totally unknown among the ancient miracle workers. It is to be explained by the way in which Jesus confirms and illustrates His message by His deeds, by the way He corrects, criticizes, and intends to overturn the customary hierarchies and standards of existing society.

We will offer with these reflections no commentary on individual texts, but rather describe orientations and horizons into which the individual texts can be arranged.

One further remark of a fundamental nature is to be added here. As impossible as it may be for every individual deed of Jesus witnessed in the New Testament to have a historical proof in the modern sense, as possible as it may be for many healings to find a natural explanation, there is just as little argument in the opinion of practically all the exegetes that Jesus' word and deeds belong close together, that these deeds are to be interpreted by his word and his word confirmed by his deeds. "The great number of the gospel miracle stories would be unbelievable if corresponding processes in the life of Jesus did not stand behind them. A Jesus freed of all miracles is unhistorical."[7]

In addition, it would not be possible to talk about the claim of Jesus in the form of fulfillment, about the incomparability of his person and about the "more than" which is part of it, if absolutely nothing at all were visible on the phenomenal level of his deeds and works—however difficult it may be to say anything certain about these in each individual case. In a special deed is illuminated the special being of the person

---

7. W. Trilling, *Fragen zur Geschichtlichkeit Jesu* (Düsseldorf, 1966) 97.

who does such a deed: *"Agere sequitur esse, esse sequitur agere* [doing follows being, being follows doing]."

Some Individual Themes

After these basic remarks we now add some reflections about how this question is asked and answered: In the Gospels, how is the grounding and confirmation of the claim expressed—the claim, contained in Jesus' person, behavior, life and history, that he is revelation in the mode of fulfillment?

1. The Gospel of Matthew, directed above all to the Jews, is concerned with proving that Jesus of Nazareth is the awaited Messiah. This proof is developed according to the schema "This happened that the scripture might be fulfilled." Jesus fulfills the presuppositions of (the) Messiah-being; he is the son of Abraham, he comes from the tribe of David. Jesus is the true teacher and fulfiller of the Law. This is the proof which the great sermon cycle of Matthew 5–7 intends to produce: "He teaches as one who has power." Jesus' behavior is legitimated with reference to the Old Testament: "Have you not read?"—"It is written."

The "miracle cycle" or "works cycle" (Matt 8:1–9:34) intends to highlight the deeds of Jesus as works that attest [him as] Messiah. Even the paradox of the suffering and dying of the Messiah is fulfillment of Scripture. On this point one must note what the Tübingen theologian J. E. Kuhn emphasized against D. F. Strauss: The deeds and events witnessed in the New Testament are not projections from the Old Testament; instead, the factual event witnessed in the New Testament is interpreted with the help of the Old Testament.[8]

2. Where the addressees of the proclamation were human beings who lived outside the horizon of the Old Testament, the proof of credibility could not come only from the Old Testament. It came rather from the special emphasis put on the deeds of Jesus which accompany, illustrate, and give force to his words, and which are to justify and legitimate Jesus' claim to be the revealer, the Son, the bringer of salvation. The reference to the deeds of Jesus as deeds of power is found in all the Gospels, especially emphasized in Mark and Luke and in the thematization of the works as signs in the Gospel of John.

We see in the Bible a concept of miracle other than what we connect with the current concept of miracle: the breaking through of natural causality. This idea is not even possible in the biblical world view. For

---

8. J. R. Geiselmann, "Der Glaube an Jesus Christus—Mythos oder Geschichte? Zur Auseinandersetzung Joh. Ev. Kuhns mit David Friedrich Strauß," *ThQ* 129 (1949) 258-72, 418-31; *Die Lebendige Überlieferung als Norm des christlichen Glaubens, Dargestellt im Geiste der Traditionslehre Johannes E. Kuhns* (Freiburg, 1959).

everything that happens is done by God and is a reference to God, thus having, as we said, a revelational dimension which is suited, however it may be caused, to lead to astonishment and wonder. It is the concern of the New Testament to highlight this transparency towards the power of God.

The synoptic concept *dynamis* [power] as characterization of the deeds of Jesus is at first ambivalent.[9] Its fundamental meaning is the power, the capability, the ability. But that can be a power for any possible thing. This meaning becomes special within the Greco-Hellenistic milieu to the extent that *dynamis* becomes the world principle. *Dynamis* is the causal power from which the world comes. In various transformations it is now made equal to the cosmos, now with the divinity, or any divinity, whereby the relationship of the divinity to nature often remains unclear. But the idea of *dynamis* as cosmic divine power of nature, as divine principle of the world, but which remains entangled with the world, is an idea current at the time.

The biblical concept of *dynamis* is different from these ideas, as different as is the biblical world from the Greek world. It is to be characterized thus: In the place of the divinity stands the God who is person; in the place of the cosmic *dynamis* stands the power and might of the personal God. This is connected with the word of this God which itself is a powerful, effective, creative, performative word.

The *dynamis* of their God becomes knowable in the history of the People of Israel. It becomes a stereotype formula: "With your power and might, with your *dynamis*, you have led your people." But the God of Israel is at the same time the creator and preserver of the world, who does this with his word, which is at the same time the bearer of his *dynamis* (cf. the Creation Psalms).

The Old Testament motifs are taken up in the New Testament. *Dynamis*, the preserve of God, is transferred to Jesus; it is active in him. Jesus' deeds come from the *dynamis* of God and bear its sign. That is why they can themselves be called *dynamis*, deeds of power. In Jesus' milieu, the question was understood as: Where does he get this *dynamis*? (cf. Matt 13:54); so too the reproach of Jesus: "You know neither the Scriptures nor the *power* of God" (Matt 22:29).

The *dynamis*, the powerful deeds performed by Jesus, are signs of the rule of God, signs of its nearness, its presence. This is witnessed by the already-quoted logion: "If it is by the Spirit of God that I cast out demons, then the kingdom of God has come upon you" (Matt 12:28). The *dynamis* of Jesus is God's rule in deeds. These are for eye and seeing what words are for ear and hearing. They make visible what is heard. They are, in their way, an expression of the coming together of hearing and seeing that are required in the response to revelation.

9. W. Grundmann, *TDNT*, 2.284–317.

This brings up the question of the function and meaning of the *dynamis*, the powerful deeds of Jesus: They have an unlocking function. They are supposed to make human beings attentive, make them look up and listen attentively. They have an unlocking function in the sense that human beings are freed from the spell of the hitherto, the everyday, and the taken-for-granted, that their sense and spirit is opened in the sense of questioning and wondering: "Who is this man?" They have an argumentative, grounding function. They are to bring questioning and reflecting human beings to the consciousness that the deeds of Jesus, which stand in the selfless service of the good and overcome the power of evil, can only be signs of God. They have an advertising and inviting function. They are to provide guidance and accompaniment for faith in and the following of Jesus. They have a justifying function. They are to strengthen, support, and encourage the disciples of Jesus, especially against misgivings, doubts, and temptations. Finally, they have a judging function if, despite these deeds, no conversion results. Accordingly, the refusal to believe or to follow no longer really has any right or ground.

The faith required as presupposition for a miracle is, thus, the readiness of human beings to open themselves to hear, to unlock themselves; it is the willingness not to refuse.

3. The affirmations of the Gospel of John.[10] Note first that we find the same grounding relationships here in the Synoptics. In opposition to the Jews, the repeated and extensive witness of the Baptist, who was recognized by the Jews as a prophet, is brought up as the ground and argument for the claim of Jesus (John 1:19–38; 3:27–31). The same function is also served by the appeal to the Old Testament, to the Holy Scriptures, to the witness of Abraham and the claim of being children of Abraham.

These grounds are surpassed by the towering significance, accessible to all human beings, which is ascribed to the works of Jesus and their significance for the faith. To be sure, neither the singular nor the plural of *dynamis* is found in the Gospel of John. Rather, the substantive is replaced by the verb, which directs the gaze from the external work to the one performing it: to Him who has the power to bring about such things.

The Johannine word for the deeds of Jesus is the word *sign* or—less frequently—*work*. "Sign" in the sense of the Gospel of John says: In the signified lies an expression of the "capacity" and being-mighty which is reserved to God alone. It is a living and effective power in Jesus and his deeds, which is understood as the power of God. It is, moreover, an effective power which is especially revelatory of the glory of God. "No

10. Rudolf Schnackenburg, *The Gospel According to St. John*, vol. 1, trans. Kevin Smyth (New York: Herder and Herder, 1968) 357–63.

one can do these signs which you do unless God is with him" (John 3:2; cf. also 9:1–46). It is only another version of the unique unity of action between Jesus and God when the Gospel of John says that the works of Jesus are the witness of the Father for the Son. They function therefore as grounding for the exclusively and inclusively meant "I am" sayings found in this Gospel: Even though you do not believe me, believe the works, that you may know and understand that the Father is in me and I am in the Father" (John 10:38).

The purpose of these signs—the multiplication of the loaves, the healing of the blind, the raising of Lazarus—however interpreted, is to make a reference to the person of Him who, in community and unity with the Father, brings them about. Their purpose is to say that He who works the miracle of the feeding is the bread of life, that He who gave light to the blind is the light of the world; that He who raised Lazarus to life is the resurrection and the life.

The Gospel of John, which sees the works of Jesus in the horizon of sign and witness, as indication, grounding, confirmation, and justification, lays special emphasis also on the judging function that goes along with these works: "If I had not done among them the works which no one else did, they would not have sin; but now they have seen and hated both me and my Father" (John 15:24).

A special concern of the Gospel of John is to prove that a rejection of the signs and works of Jesus cannot appeal to Abraham, for Abraham's life stood under the sign of faith. In addition it is said that the rejection of the works of Jesus is an indication that those who reject Jesus do not know God (John 10:31–39), that they are confusing their own ideas and judgments with God's word. Thus the signs become not a help to faith but the occasion of crisis, scandal, unbelief.

This has pointed out the greatness and limitation of the deeds, signs, and works of Jesus and their function and significance. The function of the signs and works of Jesus in the context of the whole Gospel becomes clear in its conclusion:

Now Jesus did many other signs in the presence of the disciples, which are not written in this book; but these are written that you may believe that Jesus is the Christ, the Son of God, and that believing you may have life in his name (John 20:30-31).

Miracle-Signs and Faith

A glance at the biblical concept of miracle shows that what has been already said is not all there is to say. Indeed, there are not a few aspects that seem to contradict what we have said hitherto.

The theme still to be treated can be summed up in the oft-repeated thesis: *It is not miracles and the knowledge and recognition of them that constitute the presupposition and preparation for faith* in the divine revelation that has taken place in Jesus—it is the other way around: *faith is the presupposition for the knowledge and recognition of miracles as signs and works of God.*[11] Without faith, the miracles lose their function and sense of direction; they lead to the opposite of that to which the miracles are interiorly oriented. In other words, miracles are not criteria of revelation, not even its protection, grounding, or justification; they are rather an object of revelation and thus content of faith. There are many illustrations of this.

On the visit of Jesus to his home city, Mark relates: "He could do no mighty work there, except that he laid his hands upon a few sick people and healed them. And he marveled because of their unbelief" (Mark 6:5: Matt 13:58).

How often we find the phrases: "Your faith has helped you, made you well, saved you" (Mark 5:34). "Do not fear, only believe" (Mark 5:34). "Great is your faith! Be it done for you as you desire" (Matt 15:28). Still more moving are the words to Jesus of the father of a sick child: "'If you can do anything, have pity on us and help us.' And Jesus said to him, 'If you can! All things are possible to him who believes.' Immediately the father of the child cried out and said, 'I believe; help my unbelief!'" (Mark 9:22–24).

It is similar in the healing of the servant of the centurion of Capernaum: "Not even in Israel have I found such faith. . . . Go; be it done for you as you have believed" (Matt 8:1–13). In the storm at sea Jesus asks: "Have you no faith?" (Mark 4:40). These texts bring out the following connection. It is not through the mighty deeds Jesus performs that human beings come to faith in Jesus, but through their faith human beings come to expect Jesus' helping and healing power. For their faith Jesus works the signs of his power. There is a further point. Jesus repeatedly forbids the healed to report and tell of their healing (Mark 1:40–45; 7:35–37). How is it to be understood that the deeds and signs that are supposed to be a witness of the authority of Jesus and are supposed to document his mission to all human beings are accompanied with a command to silence: "Tell no one!"? Wouldn't it make more sense to declare: "Tell it to everyone!"?

Jesus repeatedly refuses to perform a miracle in the manner expected and demanded of him. "The Pharisees came and began to argue with him, seeking from him a sign from heaven, to test him. And he sighed deeply in his spirit, and said, 'Why does this generation seek a sign? Truly I say to you, no sign shall be given to this generation'" (Mark 8:11–12; cf. Matt 12:39; 16:1–4; Luke 11:29–32).

---

11. G. Söhngen, "Wunderzeichen und Glaube" in: *Die Einheit in der Theologie* (Munich, 1952) 265–85.

Why does Jesus refuse to give a sign? It is manifestly, because there is no faith corresponding to the desire for a sign, because even "a sign from heaven" does not lead to faith. Precisely this idea comes up repeatedly—for example, in the parable of the rich glutton and the poor Lazarus: "If they do not hear Moses and the prophets, neither will they be convinced if someone should rise from the dead" (Luke 16:31). Even more drastic is the scene at the crucifixion of Jesus: "Let the Christ, the King of Israel, come down now from the cross, that we may see and believe" (Mark 15:32).

Jesus rejects these demands for a sign from heaven. The reason is, as we see it, that unbelief prevents the signs from fulfilling their function and achieving their intended purpose of being signs that Jesus is the Messiah, the Revealer, Teacher, and Savior sent from God.

Of importance is also the judgment expressed in the Gospel of John—in the sense of a correction or reprimand: "Unless you see signs and wonders you will not believe" (John 4:48). Corresponding to this is the blessing for "those who have not seen and yet believe" (John 20:29). This means that to believe only in miracles and signs is a lack of faith, is an expression of weak faith. The Bible speaks ultimately of the fact that in the apocalyptic end time many a false Messiah and many false prophets will perform great signs and miracles, and that human beings will let themselves be led astray by them (Matt 24:24).

The severity of the situation here referred to is expressed above all in the proclamation of the gospel of Jesus the Christ. The most emphatic witness to it is Paul: "For Jews demand signs and Greeks seek wisdom, but we preach Christ crucified, a stumbling block to Jews and folly to Gentiles" (1 Cor 1:22–23).

The situation here addressed, which seems to be a dilemma in respect to the New Testament, can also be expressed, paradigmatically so to speak, in the following antitheses: Pascal declares: "Without miracles I would not be a Christian; without miracles it would not be a sin not to believe in Jesus."[12] Emil Brunner says, taking issue with this: No one believes in Christ because of miracles. Revelation is not directed to belief in miracles but to the conscience."

In response we can say that *faith*, which is presupposed for the coming and effective working of signs and miracles, must first be described negatively in view of the words of Jesus: "To this evil and adulterous generation no sign will be given." Such a desire for a sign does not come from an open readiness for which a sign could be of further assistance, but from a disposition which either denies the previous works of Jesus or attributes them to demonic influences, which sets, so to speak, a negative sign before everything that has to do with Jesus. As a consequence of this self-closing fundamental attitude, shutting oneself off, a

12. Pascal, *Pensées* 812 and 813.

sign is neither possible nor necessary; it changes nothing in one's fundamental constitution even if one should rise from the dead, even if the
Messiah should climb down from the cross. Only if a genuine metanoia,
i.e., the other side of faith, were to take its place, could signs fulfill
their intention and function. Faith as condition and presupposition of
the sign worked by Jesus is, accordingly, the [state of] *being free from
being closed off*, from hardness of heart and intellectual/spiritual
pride of possession. Faith is, positively, *openness and readiness* to want
to see and hear what Yahweh, the God of our Fathers, has manifested
and worked in Jesus.

A striking description of this behavior can be found in the Gospel of
Luke. Immediately after the pericope which reported the demand for
signs Jesus says: "Your eye is the lamp of your body; when your eye is
sound, your whole body is full of light; but when it is not sound, your
body is full of darkness. Therefore be careful lest the light in you be
darkness. If then your whole body is full of light, having no part dark,
it will be wholly bright, as when a lamp with its rays gives you light."
(Luke 11:34–36)

Light can be recognized only from light. From this fact the conclusion is drawn: "Therefore be careful lest the light in you be darkness."
In other words, human beings are responsible for their fundamental
attitude—Newman would say: for the "first principles."[13] All this
means that "the miraculous sign is directed not only to the external
light of the eye but also to the inner light of the heart." Gottlieb
Söhngen speaks of a rational witnessing function of the signs of
revelation and of a moral claiming function for personal conviction and
recognition.[14]

But could not this faith, faith as openness, as disposition, be awakened and made real also by a "sign from heaven" so that all misgivings
would be overcome? It must be said on this point that in matters of faith
and what leads to it, there should not be and may not be any overpow-
ering. This would contradict the freedom of the human being, which is
claimed for them and for the faith. Against unbelief, against an attitude of being closed off as a basic disposition of some human beings,
miracles are no help—on the contrary they bring that fundamental
disposition of human beings to light, [but] they leave the human beings
where and how they are.

As to the *specific relationship of faith and miracle*, this can be
said: Faith (in the sense described) is the presupposition of miracle, of
sign, of deed: "Your faith has made you healthy," to the extent that
through this faith the signs exercise the function and meaning that goes

---

13. Heirich Fries, *Die Religionsphilosophie Newmans* (Stuttgart, 1948).
14. G. Söhngen, "Wunderzeichen," 279.

with them and lead to the knowledge that Jesus is the one sent from God, in whom the *dynamis* of God is at work.

But one can also say—very much in the sense of the biblical message (and that is the other characterization of the relationship of miracle and faith)—Miracle is the presupposition of faith. The sign which is seen, known, and recognized in the right disposition, readiness, and openness can lead to faith in the specific sense: to the belief that Jesus is the Messiah, the Christ. In the Gospel of John it is written at the conclusion of the account of the wedding at Cana: "This, the first of his signs, Jesus did at Cana in Galilee, and manifested his glory; and his disciples believed in him" (John 2:11). This connection between seeing and believing is frequently pointed out in the Gospel of John at the end of accounts of the great signs of Jesus. At the same time it writes that the same sign (the multiplication of the loaves, the healing of the man born blind, the raising of Lazarus) according to the respective inner disposition of human beings, can lead to faith as well as to crisis, scandal, and division.

From all this we can say that Emil Brunner's thesis to the effect that revelation is oriented not to faith in miracles but to conscience is not at all antithetical to a supposed Catholic position. It actually expresses exactly what this position means. For how the revelation encountered in word and sign is answered and accepted does not depend on a facile, sensation-hungry faith in miracles; it depends on conscience, on faith.

The word, as Helmut Thielicke describes it, does not overpower the ears so that they must hear, but makes a claim: They who have ears to hear, let them hear! As the word is related to ears, so is miracle related to eyes. The miracle also does not overpower the eyes so that they are blinded. The miracle also makes a claim on the eyes: It stands there as a sign which no one can pass by without asking: in whose name, in whose power is this happening ? (Matt 21:23) This question is asked and must be decided. That is the claim of the miracle, no more, but also no less.[15]

Thus, just as word and miracle are the two sides of revelation, so too hearing and seeing belong together as the two functions of the same human being, that human being to whom God's revelation is directed.[16] The signs are there to be seen, and to be attended to. The signals are not the thing itself, but they should point out the thing, direct the attention to it.

Let us come back to the two propositions. First the proposition of Pascal: Without miracles I would not be a Christian. Such an affirmation does not contravene a path to faith and an attestation of faith of

---

15. H. Thielicke, "Das Wunder" in: *Theologie der Anfechtung* (Tübingen, 1949) 94–134.
16. Ibid. 114–15.

the kind witnessed to and recorded in the Bible. But one cannot declare Pascal's way to be the only legitimate way. The proposition of Emil Brunner—No one believes in Jesus because of miracles; miracles are not the reason why someone believes in Jesus—has in this extreme and exclusive version a biblically witnessed fact against it. Brunner's proposition is to be affirmed, that revelation is directed not to faith in miracles but to conscience. But the proposition leaves out a possibility: the possibility from conscience and in conscientiousness and in an act characterized by that and called faith, of being turned to the phenomenon of miracle, of connecting sign and conscience, and seeing therein a possible preparation for faith.

When evaluating and arranging the deeds of Jesus that are labeled with the word "miracle," one should keep in mind the following: One should consider the signs and works of Jesus not just individually, and thus in isolation; they must be seen together, in their *convergence*. The thinking of J. H. Newman on the argument from convergence[17] has its justification and significance precisely for this question too. An individual deed, an individual sign (miracle) alone and taken for itself is not sufficient to be effective as a guiding sign; but taken together, they carry a great deal of weight.

The miracles (signs) and works of Jesus are further to be seen in connection with the *word signifying* the signs and, above all, in connection with the *person* who does the deeds and who, in the deeds, expresses the unfolding and representation of himself. This means that Jesus is himself the great and decisive sign. J. H. Newman describes this connection in the following words:

The right way to come to faith in Christ is by way of the person and figure of our Lord as the Gospels describe him. Philip said to Nathaniel: Come and see! And it is of precisely this that our present-day rationalists want to deprive human beings. They confound and confuse them with preliminary questions so as not to let them come under the influence of the genuine eloquence of his divine life, his holy words and deeds.[18]

The Objection of Lessing

One thing are miracles which I see with my own eyes and have myself an opportunity to check, another thing are miracles of which I know only historically that others claim to have seen and checked them.

17. Karl Rahner and H. Vorgrimler, "Argument of Convergence," *DT* (1981) 26–27.
18. John Henry Newman, *Briefe und Tagebuchaufzeichnungen aus der Katholischen Zeit seines Lebens* (Mainz, 1957) 602 (= *Letters and Diaries*). On this theme, prominent in Newman's *Grammar of Assent* and numerous other works, see Thomas J. Norris, *Newman and His Theological Method* (Leiden: Brill, 1977) 19–22.

I don't deny that Christ performed miracles, but I deny that these miracles, since their truth has fully ceased, are proven by miracles still accessible in the present, since they are nothing but reports of miracles.

The problem is that this proof of spirit and power no longer has either spirit or power but has descended to human witnesses of spirit and power.[19]

The fact that some fact or event does not come to me through immediate inspection but through the mediation of others does not make the thing and the fact any different. The moment of mediation through report applies to all events not immediately accessible to me. Skepticism against mediation through report would be justified only if the report were to be proven false. A radical skepticism in that regard would reduce our knowledge and cognition to a minimum. Most of what we live from, on which we depend, we receive through mediation, through report; without report we would be in bottomless chaos. That does not dispense us from the obligation and task of checking the mediation for its credibility. But when this is produced, there is no reasonable ground to call into question the fact and reality mediated by it. It is not right that events, as soon as they become mediated, should have all power taken from them.

This applies to our question all the more so since, as has already been said, the signs and miracles witnessed in the New Testament are mediated not in isolation but in convergence, and also in connection with their context, i.e., of the word, and above all in connection with the person and figure of Jesus of Nazareth.

The objection of Lessing—that the proof of spirit and power is no longer valid today because no miracles are presently taking place that could verify the past—overlooks the fact that possible post-biblical miracles have a totally different value than the miracles connected with the person and work of Christ.

It is further to be noted that the signs witnessed in the New Testament that belong to the content of the preaching of the message of Jesus were directed, even in the times of the New Testament itself, not just to the immediate eyewitnesses. Most of the hearers of the message were no more witnesses of the events than we are. They were in fact, and above all after Jesus' death and resurrection, in the same situation we are: dependent on the witness and mediation of the proclaimers, dependent on their word, message, and report. The historical distance in space and time makes, in this consideration, no difference; it makes the question of interpretation and appropriation into a problem to be solved and a task to be performed.

Through the mediation of history by way of tradition and witness—and not without this mediation—there is a possibility of hand-

---

19. "Über den Beweis des Geistes und der Kraft" in: *Lessings Werke*, ed. K. Wölfel (Frankfurt, 1967), *Schriften* 2.307–12.

ing on to the living present the historical past of persons, their words and their deeds. In our case, this becomes the possibility of handing on faith and the credibility of faith. Looked at this way, the wide, ugly chasm between then and now of which Lessing speaks appears in another light. His fundamental objection, however ("Contingent truths of history can never become the proof of necessary truths of reason") overlooks the fact that the truth of faith is not mediated in any way except through history, and it is connected with history, that it is truth as history and in history, thus not a falsely understood necessary truth of reason, but truth connected with a person in the sense of the word "I am the truth" (John 14:6). The historically concrete does not render impossible the universality of some meaning; it actually brings about that universality of meaning in the sense of the *universale concretum* [concrete universal], in the sense of the "unconditioned concretion" we have already discussed (see § 29).

The Mode of Reality of Miracle

The more traditional, and to some extent still customary way of looking at this is as follows: A miracle is a perceivable event within the world that diverges from the customary course of nature and its laws and hence can be brought about only by God directly as its cause. The essence of a miracle lies in the fact that it surpasses the possibilities of nature and breaks through the laws of nature, as sign of God's sovereign power and freedom as well as in attestation of a revelation.

This description is inadequate for two reasons: We know neither the possibilities nor all the laws, conditions, and interrelationships of nature.

Even Augustine pointed out: "Miracles stand not against nature but against what we know of nature." That holds for today too, although we know a lot more about nature than Augustine could know. Fundamentally, therefore, we can never be exactly sure that a particular event or happening has not been caused by natural conditions, that it has taken place outside of or against the order of nature, and was caused immediately by God to the exclusion of immanent causes. What is violated in a miracle is the level of our knowledge of nature, not necessarily nature itself.

The natural science of today, with regard to the phenomenon of miracle, is opening up a new situation, at least to the extent that the earlier arguments brought forward in the name of natural science against the affirmations of theology with respect to God and God's possible action in the world, have largely been given up today. In the earlier conception, according to which space was infinitely great, matter infinite, space and time absolute and eternal and dependent on matter, when the world as world was seen as without beginning and without end, there was no possibility for the reality of God or for a possible divine activity in the world. What goes as natural-scientific knowledge nowadays is different: Space is finite, matter is finite and dissolvable into radiation; space and time had a beginning, they are relative and dependent on the condition of motion of matter. This knowledge signifies that one can no longer use natural science in principle as an argument against theological questions.

Quantum physics has opened up a new realm of nature, that of the microcosmos, in which causality has taken on the form of probability and of the calculation of probability under the guise of the uncertainty principle. But for all knowledge of nature Heisenberg's maxim holds that the laws of nature are not an image of nature but an image of our relation to nature.[20] This is, in turn, meaningful for our question. Even more important is the knowledge that natural science today does not identify the realm it can investigate with being as a whole, or identify its knowledge with knowledge in general, or register claim to an all-encompassing world view, but undertakes an explicit description of its field. To that belongs the recognition of limits and the knowledge of a beyond-the-limits, even if this no (longer) belongs in its own sphere of investigation and observation.

To see in miracle an immediate intervention of God into nature, i.e., into the order and activity established by God, is theologically not possible because God is thereby turned into a physical cause. God would then no longer be the all-determining reality different from the world as work of God. From this it follows that God does not take the place of physical causes; God's working, whatever and however it be (also God's working in the sense of a miracle) is mediated through immanent, created secondary causes; God works through them.

If that were not the case, then what was produced by God without immanent causes would stand like a relationless foreign body in the world. We cannot think a God who is not God, no more than we can think an event in the world which does not take place in the world and in its contexts of events (B. Weißmahr). Natural laws are parts of the creation of God who, in that creation, remains true to Himself.

Hence it follows: Miracle in the sense of an immediate, direct intervention of God nullifying nature, its order, its conditions and its laws is a theological non-concept. In a so-called miracle, the energies and laws of nature are not nullified but made use of.

---

20. On this, cf. H. Dolch, *Theologie und Physik* (Freiburg, 1951); W. Heisenberg, *Der Teil und das Ganze. Gespräch im Umkreis der Atomphysik* (Munich, 1969); *Schritte über die Grenzen. Gesammelte Reden und Aufsätze* (Munich, 1971).

But in what does the mode of reality of miracle consist? Does it consist in the fact that everything that is, that happens, that is encountered, also has the dimension of miracle, of the miraculous, so that everything is a miracle, or at least in the qualification: miracles are always happening; you only need eyes to see them? Is there besides this still something specific or special, which can be meant with the category "miracle"?

What happens in the world is, because it is the effect and representation of the fact that God is the creative ground of everything, the work of God. This does not hinder but frees up the proper significance and proper reality of the natural on all levels. The all-determining reality of God becomes recognizable in the variety of the creaturely and is made manifest therein in different ways, for example, in nature or in the free activity of human beings.

The power at work in everything, the action of God, becomes different due to the differences in nature and the world; it can therefore work and take on meaning in different ways. Therefore, a happening caused by natural causalities can become through them something special and extraordinary so that human beings come to wonderment, astonishment, questioning, that they are moved and challenged by the event and the circumstances surrounding it, that they recognize in some happening a call, a word, or a message that extends beyond what is factually present to them, which brings about a disclosure.

But that is possible only if human beings have a relationship to reality that goes beyond mere observation, a relationship characterized by the fact that meaningful effects can come from reality. In other words, we have here what we have called the revelational dimension of reality, the special expressive power of event. So-called miracles, which only take place but don't intend to say anything to anyone, are an absurd idea.

Miracles presuppose human beings who are willing, in the depths of their being, to let themselves be called in a willing openness for that which is in their lives the singularly wonderful, which is part of the whole perceivable world of experience and at the same time goes beyond it: i.e., in openness and receptivity for the "beyond" in their world of experience.[21]

A further perspective for our question can be gained by looking at the structure of all reality. No realm of being in reality is closed off and belongs exclusively to itself; everything that exists stands in an open relationship to everything else; without losing itself and its laws [of nature, etc.], it becomes present in a new way in this relationship, and is accepted in service and function by it. The inorganic is "superseded" (in the sense of preserving and surmounting) in the organically living, and

---

21. Karl Rahner, *Foundations of Christian Faith*, 263 .

this, in turn, in the psycho-spiritual reality of the human person. Nature on the whole is ordered to human beings not externally but internally. The world of the physical and chemical is taken up and preserved in the realm of the organic, biological and living. But the living is more; it is something new in relation to physics and chemistry and cannot be derived from them, although what is living consists of physical elements and chemical material. Human beings as persons in spirit, freedom, and love can, in turn, not be explained from the data of physics, chemistry, and biology, however much they are constituted by them. *Homo quodammodo est omnia* [The human being is, in a certain sense, everything].

On every level something new becomes manifest which stands in relation to what has preceded it and at the same time goes beyond it. From this comes the principle: It cannot be decided from a lower level what is possible on a higher level. The true image of the world is therefore always to be gained a posteriori not a priori. But the spirit-nature of human beings is itself open and receptive to a new, historical, free activity of God, which opens up a realm beyond creation. Creation and its order are not abrogated in this but find therein their true fulfillment. They are taken up into the sense-context of a "new creation," which, in turn, is sovereign.[22]

Jesus' works and deeds and his miracles are a sign that God's free, historical initiative, that the new, the new eon, has already begun, that it is turning out to be "in the world as if not in the world," a sign that the world is not a closed book, definitively determined, standing isolated over against its Creator, but that it is encompassed as a living happening by this living God, who does not break through its order and its laws—a formulation that indicates something destructive—but preserves them and employs and engages them for a new mode of activity.

Modern linguistics and philosophy of language can also make a contribution to the problem of miracle. One can keep the language of science and religious language separate from each other. Both forms of language can be related to the same thing, but produce a different context. Statements like "A low pressure area is causing an east wind" and "God made an east wind come up" are logically different, since they move in two different frames of reference.[23] But this asserts that affirmations on one level can never stand in direct contradiction with assertions on the other level. Contradiction presupposes identity of terms (categories of expression). Thus they move within different language sets, even if it is about one and the same thing, which can be presented

---

22. Basic ideas from R. Guardini, *Wunder und Zeichen* (Würzburg, 1959).
23. Example from W. Kasper, *Jesus the Christ*, 92.

at one time in the context of an explanation (science), and at another time in that of surprise (miracle).[24]

In conclusion: This way of looking at things enables us to see miracles once again as coming close to the mighty deeds and signs of the Bible and to the function assigned them there. That function neither forces nor replaces faith but raises questions, which leads into wonderment and astonishment and which, by the dynamic of sign, is put on the track of an answer. The miracles of Jesus are signs of the salvation of God's rule already entered into our world in Jesus. They are an expression of the bodily and worldly dimension of the rule of God.

An answer that solves all problems is certainly not provided with these manifold perspectives. But the variety of perspectives help put us on the track of an answer, an answer that, although always open to new questions, will, nevertheless, be able to give at least the beginning of an answer.

24. "Wunder in der Bibel,". in: *Bibel und Kirche* (1974 no. 1).

THE RESURRECTION (RAISING) OF JESUS FROM THE DEAD

The claim of Jesus to be the one who definitively reveals God seemed to have ended in the debacle of his death. If death had been the end of Jesus, there would be no history of the influence of Jesus, no reason to get involved with Jesus, no faith in Jesus the Christ and no community of those who believe in him, and there would be no Church, for Jesus would ultimately have been uninteresting for his contemporaries and his disciples. There would hardly have been any reason to say, one day: "It can't be all over with Jesus; the business of Jesus goes on," and then have the further question of what this business is.

The confirmation Jesus' claim to be the definitive revealer, Messiah, Son, lies, according to unanimous New Testament witness, in the message and in the faith ordered to it: The Crucified One has been raised from the dead; he is risen from the dead. Therefore the resurrection of Jesus, along with all the meanings associated with it, is also *the* sign and miracle. Karl Rahner says: The resurrection of Jesus is

the essential miracle in the life of Jesus, in which his real meaning is gathered up in radical unity and makes its appearance for us. The resurrection of Jesus calls to us in a more radical way than the individual miracles in the life of Jesus, since the resurrection has both the highest identity of saving sign and saving reality (more than all other conceivable miracles), and because it calls out to our hope of salvation and resurrection which is given us with transcendental necessity.[1]

In First Corinthians, the first chronological witness to the Easter message, this situation is just as unmistakably as radically formulated. Paul expressly appeals to a tradition he himself has received:

That he was raised on the third day in accordance with the Scriptures, and that he appeared to Cephas, then to the Twelve. Then he appeared to more than five hundred brethren at one time, most of whom are still alive. Then he appeared to James, then to all the apostles. Last of all, as to one untimely born, he appeared also to me. (1 Cor 15:4–8)

---

1. Karl Rahner, *Foundations of Christian Faith,* trans. William V. Dych (New York: Crossroad, 1994) 264.

If Christ has not been raised, then our preaching is in vain and your faith is in vain. We are even found to be misrepresenting God, because we testified of God that he raised Christ, whom he did not raise if it is true that the dead are not raised. (1 Cor 15:14–15)

The theme of the raising (resurrection) of Jesus needs only to be mentioned and immediately there bursts upon us today not only a flood of literature,[2] but—with it—also a plethora of questions and a whole palette of meanings of what the raising (resurrection) of Jesus from the dead is and means. It is in no way possible, however pressing and desirable, to present in the framework of this book the whole problematic as it is developing today. But the theme does come up again under the theme of the Church of Christ (see below § 50).

We will seek first to unfold the sense of the resurrection message and only then discuss the character of the resurrection event. For, from the sense of the Easter message, many questions that can and have been raised about the nature of the Easter event become superfluous.

The Meaning of the Resurrection Message

What the resurrection message of the New Testament says is this: God has affirmed the way in which Jesus traveled to the cross, and with that affirmed Jesus' death as the event through which His mission is not in any way disavowed but brought to completion as the way of the love of God for human beings.

The means by which God affirmed the way of Jesus was by not letting him fall into nothingness but precisely by bringing him through

2. Cf. the *Resurrection of Jesus Christ* in the theological dictionaries, handbooks, and reference works, and the presentations of this theme in the treatises on dogma and fundamental theology, the theologies of the New Testament, and the monographs on Jesus Christ. Walter Künneth, *The Theology of the Resurrection* (St. Louis: Concordia Publishing House, 1965); E. Hirsch, *Die Auferstehungsgeschichten und der christliche Glaube* (Tübingen, 1940); K. H. Rengstorf, *Die Auferstehung Jesu. Form und Sinn der Urchristlichen Botschaft* 2d ed. (Witten, 1954); H. von Campenhausen, *Der Ablauf der Osterereignisse und das leere Grab*, 2d ed. (Heidelberg, 1958); H. Graß, *Ostergeschehen und Ostergeschichte*, 3d ed. (Göttingen, 1964); Willi Marxsen, *The Beginnings of Christology, Together with the Lord's Supper as a Christological Problem*, trans. Paul J. Achtemeier and Lorenz Nieting (Philadelphia: Fortress Press, 1979); J. Kremer, *Das älteste Zeugnis von der Auferstehung Christi*, 2d ed. (Stuttgart, 1967); W. Marxsen—U. Wilckens—G. Delling—H. G. Geyer, *Die Bedeutung der Auferstehungsbotschaft für den Glauben an Jesus Christus* (Gütersloh, 1967); K. Lehmann, *Auferweckt am Dritten Tag nach der Schrift* (Freiburg—Basel—Vienna, 1968); H. Schlier, *Über die Auferstehung Jesu Christi* (Einsiedeln, 1968); F. Mußner, *Die Auferstehung Jesu* (Munich, 1969); W. Kern—G. O'Collins, "Paschal Mystery," DFT 758–76; A. Kolping, *Wunder und Auferstehung Jesu Christi* (Bergen–Enkheim, 1969); Ulrich Wilckens, *Resurrection: Biblical Testimony to the Resurrection: An Historical Examination and Explanation*, trans. A. M. Stewart (Atlanta: John Knox Press, 1978); A. Geense, *Auferstehung und Offenbarung* (Göttingen, 1971), also "Die Entstehung des Auferstehungsglauben," ThQ 153 (1973); L. Scheffczyk, Auferstehung, *Prinzip christlichen Glaubens* (Einsiedeln, 1975); K. Lienzler, *Logik der Auferstehung* (Freiburg—Basel—Vienna, 1976); E. Schillebeeckx, *Die Auferstehung Jesu als Grund der Erlösung* (Freiburg—Basel—Vienna, 1979); A. Vögtle—R. Pesch, *Wie kam es zum Osterglauben?* 2d ed. (Düsseldorf, 1984).

death to the living goal of this way. The Risen Christ is "in person" identical with Jesus of Nazareth, the Crucified.

The sense of the Easter message is thus not, Jesus is dead but the business of Jesus goes on, but, Jesus lives and therefore his business goes on. The business of Jesus is not to be separated from his person. But he lives not as one who comes back to life in order to die once again, but as one who has definitively overcome death and now has it behind him.

Jesus' resurrection asserts that he has entered into the future of the coming kingdom of God. We cannot "conceive" this eschatological future, since all human conception remains tied to the categories in which our present life, which remains "under way" towards this future, is constituted. It is qualified by the definitive victory of love and as the definitive secure place of the love that is lived in orientation towards this goal. The resurrection message asserts that God has made Jesus the Lord who brings humanity towards the future of God.

This makes clear the anthropological and existential sense of the resurrection message. We are disposed towards it and at the same time struck by it in the questions of life and death, and of sense and future. In the question of ourselves, in the question of the ground and content of our hope, in the question of our world and history, we have those conditions and presuppositions needed to perceive the resurrection message as word, as answer and as invitation as well as disclosure of our being (*Dasein*).[3]

The Question of the Resurrection Event

But there is the historical problematic of the biblical accounts of Easter. It is incontestable (above all, on the basis of 1 Corinthians 15) that persons from the circle of the followers of Jesus had experiences and encounters which they understood as self-manifestations of the risen Jesus. But these experiences are not uniformly described in the Easter accounts of the Gospels (cf. the synopsis of these accounts: about the day of the resurrection, about people going to the grave, about the appearances of the Risen One in Jerusalem, in Galilee).

In his writing *Eine Duplik* [A Rejoinder], Lessing takes issue with the thesis "The resurrection of Christ is not to be believed because the accounts of it in the Gospels are contradictory." Lessing replies: "The resurrection can be allowed its proper accuracy even though the accounts of the Gospels are contradictory"; he adds that in no secular history reported in different ways by different authors—even in a contradictory ways—would such a negative conclusion be drawn. In no wise would the event itself on which they agree be denied.[4] Lessing rejects textual

---

3. K. Rahner, *Foundations of Christian Faith*, 268–74.
4. G. E. Lessing, in: *Lessings Werke*, ed. K. Wölfel, vol. 3.323.

harmonizing and sees a proof of its truth precisely in the fact that it is not harmonizable. He discusses the textual contradictions—still studied today—but is not moved from his fundamental conviction.

There is also the factual problematic of the biblical accounts of Easter. The ideas about the bodiliness of the Risen One do not seem to be uniform. In the Gospels, especially in Luke and John, the "tangibility" of this body is in part strongly emphasized, even to the point of touchability and the taking of food. Paul on the other hand emphasizes the radical otherness of the "spiritual [pneumatikos] body" over against the earthly form of existence. Reflected here is the difficulty of describing what is new and special—the character of being absolutely without analogy—in the mode of being of the Risen One.

The resurrection event itself is not described anywhere in the New Testament. On the question of the resurrection event, there are different positions in contemporary theology and discussion:

—There took place in the spatio-temporal context only visions; and connected with them the inner process that they to whom they were communicated became certain of the abiding validity and future power of the word and business of Jesus despite his execution (E. Hirsch).

—There took place in the spatio-temporal context visions; but connected with them the inner process that they to whom they were communicated became certain of the presence of Jesus himself awakened from the dead to eschatological life. Thus, in the medium of visions took place the self-attestation of the Risen Jesus. However the presupposition for this cannot be placed as an event in the spatio-temporal context (H. Graß).

—There took place in the spatio-temporal context not only visions but a real seeing of the Risen One in new bodiliness. The presupposition here is that the body of the crucified was taken from the tomb and restored, if not in an earthly form of existence, then transformed into a pneumatic bodiliness. To that extent the raising up itself must be understood at least as an event breaking into the spatio-temporal context and being manifested therein by the emptied grave (W. Künneth).

—There took place nothing at all. The raising (resurrection) of Jesus from the dead is a metaphor. Resurrection is an interpretation for the fact that the business of Jesus goes on (W. Marxsen).

—There took place nothing. The raising (resurrection) of Jesus is an indication of the salvific significance of the cross, which alone can stand as an historical event: Jesus—that means resurrection—is risen in the word, in the kerygma (R. Bultmann).

The raising (resurrection) of Jesus is an *historical event* which took place in the apocalyptic-traditional context of the raising from the dead—in this context belongs also the tradition of the empty tomb.

The accounts of the empty tomb as confirmation of the resurrection of Jesus, as found above all in the Gospels, primarily in Mark 16, are, however, hard to harmonize in their differences; they don't admit of a historical reconstruction, and they represent an independent tradition of their own next to that of the appearances and encounters with the Risen One.

The empty tomb as such is not an adequate grounding for the resurrection of Jesus and the Easter faith of the disciples. The Gospels themselves report that the fact of the empty tomb can be explained in different ways (cf. Matt 28:11–15; John 20:15). Thus one can say that belief in the resurrection of Jesus took its beginning not from the so-called stories of the empty tomb, but from the proclamation, the confession and witness: "We have seen the Lord." This experience is the grounding for the phenomenon of the empty tomb; it makes clear why the tomb was empty.

"The empty tomb is for the faith not an indication, but rather a sign."[5] This sign was important above all for the proclamation of the resurrection message in Jerusalem.

In Jerusalem, at the place of the execution and tomb of Jesus, it was proclaimed, not long after his death, that he was risen. This fact requires that there was a reliable sign of this in the circle of the first community, that the tomb had been found empty. The kerygma of the resurrection could not have stood for a single day or for a single hour in Jerusalem if the emptiness of the tomb had not held fast as a fact for all concerned.[6]

The fact of the empty tomb was also never contested by hostile polemic.

If an historical event has to be characterized in such a way that an inner-historical analogy, an immanent causality and a protocol about the process of this causality belong to it, then the resurrection of Jesus cannot be a historical event. It is a process completely without parallel. Its only analogy is creation out of nothing (cf. Rom 4:17).

The raising (resurrection) of Jesus can, however, be called an historical event to the extent that it opens up a new horizon in the space of history and a new goal established as our future for historically living human beings, and thus became historically relevant in its effects. This is all the more true since what is new, unexpected, unforeseen, and not-determinable also belongs in principle to the reality of the historical— along with continuity and context.

Wolfhart Pannenberg speaks decisively of the resurrection as historical event and declares that it is not those who assert but those who dispute the resurrection as an historical event who have the burden of

5. Walter Kasper, *Jesus the Christ*, trans. V. Green (New York: Paulist Press, 1977) 135.
6. P. Althaus, in: Wolfhart Pannenberg, *Jesus: God and Man*, 2d ed., trans. Lewis L. Wilkins and Duane A Priebe (Philadelphia: Westminster Press, 1977).

proof. The objections against the fact of the resurrection come not so much from the accounts of the resurrection as from the presupposition that the historian cannot accept as fact such an unusual kind of event. But that is an unhistorical argument, an argument that rests on a quite specific world view in which, it is claimed, the dead remain dead. Pannenberg closes his reflections with the words:

If the origin of primitive Christianity which, apart from other traditions, even in Paul is traced back to appearances of the Risen One, and if, despite all critical examination of the content of the tradition, it becomes understandable only if one considers it in the light of the eschatological resurrection of the dead, and Jesus' resurrection from the dead within that, then the event so described is an historical event even if we don't know anything more about it. But without this historical base the Christian faith would lose it foundation. Thus, an event is to be asserted as historical which can be expressed only in [the context of] eschatological expectation.[7]

However one might describe the character of the so-called appearances, what they are all about is the attestation of Jesus who has been taken up into the future of God, into the future without death, into everlasting life. The causal ground of the resurrection experience, the seeing and the meeting with the Risen One, is not the productivity of the human power of imagination; it is rather the will of the resurrected Jesus to meet his disciples and let himself be seen as the Risen One. The experiences of the disciples, as witnesses of the Risen One and thereby witnesses of the resurrection, are the self-attestations of the Risen One.

How these experiences are represented in the disciples themselves is shown in their radical conversion, which turns out to be like a new creation: "From denyers have come confessors; from doubters, believers; from persecutors, followers and persecuted; from those running away, ambassadors; from failures, the called." They are the answer to what happened in and to Jesus: "From the rejected, he has become the accepted; from the abased, the exalted; from the dead, the living; from the past, the one who is coming; from the absent, the one abidingly present."[8]

Edward Schillebeeckx[9] says that the resurrection of Jesus is both a Jesus-event and a disciples-event. The resurrection of Jesus is for the disciples an inner process; their unbelief is overcome by an experience of conversion and grace. This conversion comes about by illumination, by seeing Jesus. The disciples have experienced a conversion: from disappointment in Jesus to metanoia and to the recognition that he is the eschatological prophet, the one who is to come, the Savior of the world, the Son of Man, the Son of God. Thus Schillebeeckx can also say: since

7. W. Pannenberg, *Jesus: God and Man*, 98.
8. G. Ebeling, *Dogmatik des christlichen Glaubens II* (Tübingen, 1979) 301–2
9. Edward Schillebeeckx, *Die Auferstehung Jesu als Grund der Erlösung*, 90–91

the resurrection of Jesus from the dead, the kingdom of God bears the face of Jesus Christ.[10]

Theology of the Resurrection

Jürgen Moltmann makes the resurrection of Jesus from the dead the starting point and middle point of his *Theology of Hope*; it is the ground of the hope of the Christian faith. His interpretation of the Easter event is clear and unambiguous. He declares that the Easter event is not an "expression of" but an "affirmation about." The words of the witnesses do not say: "I am certain," but "It is certain." The historical misgivings brought forward as an objection against the event-character of the resurrection of Jesus he answers with the indication that Easter, as absolute, new, future-opening beginning is to be described with other than the usual this-worldly categories. Thus, from immanent or historical experience no argument against the Easter event can be brought into play. It is rather from the Easter event that experience is to be understood in a new way. The resurrection of Jesus is no analogy to what always and otherwise can be experienced, but is "analogy to that which is to come." The resurrection is historical because it "instituted history in which one can and must live to the extent that it points out the road to what will happen in the future. It is historical because it opens up the eschatological future."[11]

If we ask what was revealed in the resurrection of Jesus from the dead, we can say: Revealed was the *being of God in the definitive sense*. What before shone in many beams is now brought together. If God really is God, then death can be no limit for God, but a mode of God's coming and a mode of God's revelation. Thus seen, resurrection faith is "no addition to faith in God and in Jesus Christ; it is the summing up and central concept of this faith."[12]

"The resurrection of Jesus is not only the decisive eschatological act of God, but an eschatological self-revelation; in it becomes definitively and unsurpassably manifest who God is: the one whose power encompasses life and death, being and non-being, who is creative love and fidelity, the power of new life, in whom therefore, even in the face of the shattering of all human possibilities, there is still unconditioned trust.

The raising of Jesus is the revelation and the proclamation of the kingdom of God proclaimed by Jesus. In the raising of Jesus from the dead God has proven His fidelity and love and definitively identified Himself with Jesus and his business.[13]

    10. E. Schillebeeckx, *Jesus: An Experiment in Christology*, trans. Herbert Hoskins (New York: Seabury Press, 1979) 320 .
    11. Jürgen Moltmann, *Theology of Hope: On the Ground and Implications of a Christian Eschatology* (New York: Harper & Row, 1967) 180–81.
    12. W. Kasper, *Jesus the Christ*, 145.
    13. Ibid.145.

Karl Rahner has made the impressive attempt to bring the message of the resurrection of Jesus and the content therein witnessed into relationship with human beings and their existence. He speaks of the "*transcendental resurrection-hope* as horizon for the experience of the resurrection of Jesus."

All human beings carry out with transcendental necessity, in the mode of either free acceptance or free rejection, the act of hope in their own resurrection. For all human beings want to be affirmed in definitiveness, and they experience this claim in the act of their own responsible freedom, whether or not they are able to thematize this implication of their exercise of freedom, whether they accept it believingly or reject it in doubt.[14]

This means:

We ourselves are not simply and absolutely outside the [circle of] witnesses of the resurrection of Jesus: We do not perceive something that lies totally outside of our horizon of experience. People experience their own resurrection, hoping to survive death, and do that in view of the Risen One standing before us in the apostolic witness. If this is taken into consideration, what ground would there be to forbid us, before our moral truth-conscience, from relying on the Easter experience of the first disciples? Nothing forces us against our will to believe them if we choose to remain skeptical. But much empowers us to believe them. Demanded of us is the boldest, and yet again the most self-evident thing: namely, to risk our existence on the fact that it is as a whole oriented to God, that it has a definitive sense, that it can be healed and saved, that this is precisely what took place in Jesus in an exemplary and productive manner, and that in view of him it is possible to believe this of ourselves just as the first disciples did, in whom that which we always wanted to do (i.e., believe) and for which we search from the depth of our being the historical objectivity, by which this faith can come in, has really happened with an absoluteness right up to death.

Do we have a better solution for the fundamental question of the sense of our existence? Is it really more honest, or simply on the deepest level more cowardly, to shrug our shoulders skeptically before this fundamental question and still go on (in that we live and try to live decently) as if everything still had a sense? It doesn't need to be maintained that those who think that they cannot believe in Jesus' resurrection would not like to live in an ultimately unqualified fidelity to their conscience. But we do maintain here that those who really do this, corresponding to or contradicting their own reflexive interpretation of their existence, believe in the—for them nameless—Risen One, whether they expressly know it or not. For it is also true of people such as this that, in the fundamental decision of their existence, they are tending towards healed, redeemed existence (with body and soul) as that which this earthly life itself transforms. They are thus moving into history and even at best don't yet know whether it has gotten to that point which even such a faith confesses to be the future of history. But then this faith, which is also our faith, bathes in the light of Jesus and the faith of his disciples, and does not need to shrink from confessing: It has already happened.[15]

14. Foundations of Faith 268.
15. K. Rahner—J. Schmitt—W. Bulst—J. Schmid—J. Ratzinger, "Resurrection," *SM* 5.323–42.

PART THREE

REVELATION AS THEME
OF CHURCH TRADITION AND OF
THEOLOGICAL REFLECTION

REVELATION AS THEME OF CHURCH TRADITION AND OF THEOLOGICAL REFLECTION

Ecclesiastical tradition is the tradition of the origin of Christianity, more exactly, Christianity's biblically witnessed origin. This origin is the content of tradition.

This is also true of the theme "revelation." And it is true in a special way because revelation encompasses all individual contents and presents them as contents of revelation. Hence one can also say: If church is faith community, if ecclesiastical tradition is tradition of faith, then the decisive and comprehensive point of reference is again revelation.

Tradition is nevertheless not a mere repetition of the origin, the handing on of some dead material, however precious that might still be. But such a handing on was never possible because the origin to be transmitted is an event which intends to bring something about, which has brought something about. But this is possible only if the origin is transmitted or transmits itself in historically living tradition. The vitality comes about through the mediation of revelation and faith into the respective time constituted by living human beings, who in turn are stamped by the spiritual, intellectual, cultural, social, political, and economic factors of an epoch. The tradition of the origin is to take place for human beings and their faith. It follows that the tradition of the origin must be a living handing-on. Therein lie both its constants and its transformations and variants. But only through a vitality that also includes transformation can fidelity to the origin be preserved. This means, with a view to language, that it is not by repetition of old words in old language and concepts from the past but by the effort to articulate the origin in new language and concepts that the origin is preserved.

For our theme, this means that if revelation is the comprehensive point of reference of faith, if the Church is understood as the community of faith and of the faithful, then revelation as theme of the origin must be the constant, abiding theme of this community and its history, of its revelation. Without this point of reference the community would lose its ground and the abiding orientation that lies within it.

It does not follow from this fact that the theme "revelation" has always been expressly articulated and reflected on in the faith community of the Church and its history of tradition.

The way of life that one takes for granted is not only preserved by life itself, by the life of faith and of the community of faith, it also achieves through this same life of faith its necessary continuity and adaptability. It is different when what one has received and taken for granted is challenged or attacked. What one took for granted must now be looked into, clarified, and defined over against denials and attacks. This is how most dogmas arose. They point to a situation of urgency in which a matter of faith was under attack.

Let us apply this situation to our theme. In a time that understood itself as self-evidently Christian, the comprehensive origin of what is Christian, revelation, was not a controversial theme but a likely point of origin and orientation. Within this horizon a controversy could be sparked only with respect to individual contents of faith, but not with respect to its comprehensive presuppositions, i.e., revelation.

This situation was not changed by the Reformation, except possibly in the sense of a different interpretation of something that, in its fact, was not controverted. The matter of the origin itself under the sign of *sola scriptura* [Scripture alone] was awakened anew, deepened, and brought to consciousness by the Reformation. Only with the onset of the so-called modern age did there come a change. This took place as the conflict between faith and knowledge broke out and was decided in favor of knowledge; it took place as human beings freed themselves from their previous bonds and authorities, emancipated themselves in thought and behavior, became responsible only to themselves and their own thought, and challenged revelation as a source of knowledge and a disclosure of reality, challenged it as orientation for behavior or as supernatural event, or simply called it inappropriate for enlightened human beings. Thus it is not surprising that the question of revelation as a theme expressly requiring theological articulation was first taken up in the modern age: concretely in Vatican I and—with notable differences—in the Second Vatican Council.

That it should become an object of theological reflection does not mean that theology is to present, repeat, or justify what has been said in, so to speak, official church language. But it is true that theology cannot pass over these data inattentively. If councils, as gatherings of bishops from the whole world, and their definitions or affirmations are a point of reference for the faith, then they are that for theology too, for reflection about the faith.

But first there is the task of understanding what has happened and what has been said. One gets this through knowledge of the context and the horizon of questioning to which the councils, in their answers, were referring.

From the situation of the questioning in which some content of the faith was expressly defined come the rules of a factual interpretation and hermeneutic. This hermeneutic must above all consider that an answer given for a specific situation of questioning cannot be an exhaustive, all-encompassing affirmation in the matter, and that it—this is a further conclusion—does not intend to be turned into that. That this has nevertheless been taking place is one of the reasons for the problems and difficulties encountered today in theology and Church.

REVELATION AS THEME OF TWO COUNCILS

The Contribution and Result of the First Vatican Council

It is indeed true that Vatican I focused specifically on fundamental-theological issues and that it had a defensive-apologetic way of formulating its questions. It treated the question "revelation and faith" as well as a part of the thematic connected with the Church as a fundamental-theological problem (the primacy of the pope and the infallibility of his *ex cathedra* decisions).

The dogmatic constitution *"Dei Filius" de fide catholica* [On the Catholic Faith] treats first of God, the Creator of all things. In the second chapter it treats of revelation, in the third chapter of faith, in the fourth chapter faith and reason. As one can see, these are the themes of this book.[1]

After the first chapter declares that God, as both ground and end (*principium et finis*) of all things, can be known from created things through the light of natural, human reason—this is a description of natural revelation, the revelation of God in reality understood as revelation—the constitution goes on to speak of God in the specific supernatural sense. It says:

It was pleasing to the wisdom and goodness [of God] to reveal Himself and the eternal decrees of God's will to the human race by a different way, a supernatural way. As the Apostle says: *At many times and in many ways God formerly spoke to the Fathers through the Prophets. But in these last days God has spoken to us in his Son* (Heb. 1:1f.).

The Latin phrasing brings out even more the precision of this assertion:

1. H. J. Pottmeyer, *Der Glaube vor dem Anspruch der Wissenschaft. Die Konstitution über den katholischen Glauben "Dei Filius" des I. Vatikanischen Konzils und die unveröffentlichten theologischen Voten der vorbereitended Kommision* (Freiburg—Basel—Vienna, 1968); P. Eicher, *Offenbarung. Prinzip Neuzeitlicher Theologie* (Munich 1977) 73–162.

Sancta mater Ecclesia tenet et docet . . . placuisse eius sapientiae et bonitati, alia eaque supernaturali via se ipsum ac aeterna voluntatis suae decreta humano generi revelare.[2]

The formulations contained in these words need to be explained and interpreted.

1. The text of the conciliar statement obviously speaks of different forms and modes of revelation. It speaks of another and specifically supernatural way, of an *"alia eaque supernaturalis via,"* in which the revelation of God is seen. Whoever speaks of an *"alia via*—another way," already presupposes one way. And if the *alia via* is called *"supernaturalis,"* then the one presupposed way can only be a *via naturalis*—natural way, even if it is not explicitly called that. In other words, supernatural revelation is contrasted with natural revelation. According to the words of the council, natural revelation takes place and is found in the work of creation: in the *"res creatae*—created things," in the *"creatura mundi*—created things of the world." It is said of these things that they allow God to be known and seen. The Epistle to the Romans (1:20) is quoted as the classical support for this affirmation. Finally, it is said that this revelation of God is accessible to the natural light of human reason: accessible in the form of knowledge.

Nothing is said about the *how* of this knowledge, nor is anything said about how many human beings actually have this knowledge. A very important sentence, however, does speak clearly about the concrete realization of this knowledge of God.[3] Revelation in the supernatural sense has its necessary function and meaning also in the fact that, as Aquinas put it, "that aspect of the divine things which is accessible to human reason as such can, even in the present situation of the human race, be easily known by all, with firm certitude and without any admittance of error."[4]

Therefore, in order to understand correctly these statements with respect to natural revelation and the knowledge of God corresponding to it, one must read both sentences together. This doesn't result in something contradictory; it rather describes the whole in a differentiated manner of speaking: the horizon of real possibility and the fact of the extent to which this horizon is factually, concretely, historically reached and fulfilled, or not reached and fulfilled. The council describes what human beings have factually made or not made of this possibility. It thus unites an abstract-metaphysical and a concrete-salvation historical consideration of human beings.

These characteristics correspond to the twofold structure of the affirmations of the Epistle to the Romans, to which the council appeals.

---

2. DS 3004.
3. DS 3005.
4. *STh* 1, q. 1, a. 1.

There, along with the clearly formulated statements about the knowledge of God, is placed the guilt of human beings: Human beings are culpable because they "by their wickedness suppress the truth" (Rom 1:18).

Building upon this text, theology speaks of the "natural revelation" of God. This is an interpretation of what the Bible and the teaching magisterium describe as revelation in and through creation and the work of creation. *Creation* and *nature*, concepts we are accustomed to put together and see together, stem by no means from the same roots and origins. *Natura, physis,* is a concept of Greek philosophy which has no place for creation by God out of nothing, and which even denies this if, by *physis* and *natura,* one understands that which has arisen and come to be from and of itself. Creation, *creatura,* is by contrast, a theological concept which expressly contradicts any self-actuated coming to be and any placing of the creature in the place of nature. But it is possible and legitimate—and this shows the possible change in form of the concepts—to integrate nature into creation, and thus to separate the concept "nature" from its original roots and to understand it as creation. "Nature," "natural," is meant in this way in the theological expression: "natural revelation." It is revelation of God in creation, revelation of God in His work.

To sum up: Under *natural revelation* we understand, objectively, creation. At the pinnacle of creation are first and foremost, human beings. On the basis of its creational being and consequent similarity with the being of the Creator (on the basis, therefore, of the analogy of being) creation makes known and points out the being and essence of the superworldly, otherworldly God. Insofar, then, as human beings can grasp, perceive, and know this making-known by the light of their natural reason, they can to that extent express it in their words. For it is in word that the openness that is there in being and is being pointed out there is made manifest. That is why human beings as spirit-endowed creatures are a revelation of God incomparably more than creation apart from humanity. Humanity is made after "God's image and likeness" and represents this dignity in its spirit-grounded lordship over creation and in its ability to give creatures their names (cf. Gen 1:26–27; 2:19).[5]

2. "Supernatural revelation" is to be distinguished from "natural revelation." Supernatural revelation is that form of divine disclosure which, objectively, is not given to human beings along with creation and which, subjectively, cannot be attained by the unaided powers of the human spirit.

---

5. G. Söhngen, "Die Biblische Lehre von der Gottebenbildlichkeit des Menschen" in: *Die Einheit in der Theologie* 173–211.

Revelation in its so-called supernatural mode leads beyond the revelation present in nature as work and creation of God. It consists in the fact that God makes known "Himself and the decrees of His will" in a way which cannot be disclosed and perceived by creation and by human beings: "*se ipsum ac aeterna voluntatis suae decreta revelare.*" This making-known has the fundamental structure of mediation through person and of the self-disclosure of person, the fundamental structure of word, and it takes place in the realm of history. Based on the beginning of the Epistle to the Hebrews, the council mentions above all two historical epochs for the actualization of this revelation: "in times past to the Fathers" through the prophets as bearers of divine messages, decisions, and mandates; and to us "in these last days," now, in the Son, who is the Word of God in person. Revelation in word is completed in revelation in person. It remains revelation in word because the Son is the word.

Supernatural revelation takes place in history, in specific epochs and moments, in the past and in the present. Connected with this is a concretion in a specific Here and Now, in a "Within" the world. Natural revelation stands at the beginning of history, insofar as history begins with creation. Within this beginning, natural revelation is in principle, from the outset, open to all human beings in every place and every time; it is *revelatio generalis* (general revelation). Apart from this, special supernatural revelation, which takes place through the Prophets and the Son, and thus takes place in a specific historical and personal concretion, and thus is *revelatio specialis* (special revelation), is intended for all human beings, for the human race.

For clarity's sake, since it is not a question of different levels of knowledge, it is both right and necessary to distinguish natural and supernatural revelation, to characterize them with the terms *revelatio generalis* and *specialis,* and to keep them separate in content. But, out of the same need for precise, differentiated knowledge, it is equally necessary to see the connection of the two modes of revelation: It is one and the same God who is self-revealing in creation and in word, deed, and history and finally, in personal, human form; and it is one and the same human being to whom, as knower and believer, revelation is given and to whom it is directed.

Revelation in creation, in work, in human beings, is the presupposition for the revelation of God in deed, word, history, and person. The well-known scholastic axiom sums it up in the phrase "*gratia praesupponit naturam* (grace presupposes nature)."[6] Supernatural revelation presupposes the world, creation and above all human beings in their

6. Joseph Ratzinger, "Gratia praesupponit naturam. Erwägungen über Sinn und Grenze eines scholastischen Axioms" in: J. Ratzinger—H. Fries, *Einsicht und Glaube* (Festschrift G. Söhngen), (Freiburg—Basel—Vienna, 1962) 135–49.

humanness as self-transcending created being. Supernatural revelation makes use of the language, means of expression, and instrumentality present in creation. On the other hand, it is also true that the natural is integrated in the supernatural and factually brought to its ultimate perfection: "*gratia perficit et complet naturam* (grace perfects and completes nature)." The revelation of creation is taken up in the revelation of word and person and brought to itself; it is made perfect as new creation, as new life, as rebirth. In a now-familiar formulation, Karl Barth speaks of creation as the external ground of the covenant and of the covenant as the inner ground of creation.[7]

Supernatural revelation encounters human beings not as an objective "in itself" and indifferent "over-against." It discloses to human beings something decisive about themselves: If human beings, from their origin, existence, and essence, are called to the self-transcending, thus supernatural, goal of their selves; if the human being infinitely surpasses the human being (Pascal); if God is the ultimate and exclusive satisfaction of the human spirit and the human heart—then it is not just for the sake of knowledge but for the sake of this ultimate goal-destination of human beings and for the sake of the meaning of human existence contained in it that supernatural revelation as personal self-disclosure of God and as opening up of God's eternal decrees of salvation is both called for and, in a certain sense, required. The First Vatican Council grounds this in the words: Supernatural revelation was necessary,

> because God in his boundless goodness has ordained human beings to a supernatural end, namely to participation in the divine realities which totally surpass the vision of the human spirit: for "no eye has seen, nor ear heard, nor the heart of man perceived, what God has prepared for those who love him. (1 Corinthians 2:9)

To know of this goal and its contents is absolutely decisive for the meaning of what it is to be human and for the orientation of human existence.

From these connections we can see how much supernatural revelation is related to human beings, and that it thus has existential meaning and significance for them—it both affects them and interprets their existence. And since human beings are actually constituted in their "supernatural existential" and their "*desiderium naturale videndi Deum* (natural desire of seeing God)," we can also see that human beings are the "nature" called to supernature, are not alienated by the truth and the event of this revelation, but are thereby brought to what they really are, in terms of uniqueness, actualization, and fulfillment. It is thus "inexistential," unnatural, to close off and refuse to acknowledge supernature thus understood.

7. Karl Barth, *Church Dogmatics*, 4 vols. (Louisville: John Knox Press 1994) III/1. 39, 42–329.

But what we are saying here need not be understood as if supernatural revelation represented total perfection for human beings and for human nature. For the concrete historical human being is defective nature. Nature thus constituted cannot, therefore, in itself, i.e., in its own fallen, perverted orientation, be brought to perfection; rather it must, in its own misguided self-glorification, be transformed, if human beings are to come into possession of their own perfection. Human beings must, therefore, be converted, in order to be able to become themselves. They must "deny themselves," they must break out of their self-centered existence, their "*cor incurvatum in se*," in order to recognize themselves in truth.[8]

3. Directly connected with the question of revelation is also the question of faith. Faith as answer to revelation thus belongs to the revelation event. On this point Vatican I comes out with a quite impressive description when it defines faith by starting from human beings, hence from a comprehensive anthropology. The proposition reads:

Since human beings are totally dependent on God, their Creator and Lord, and created reason is totally inferior to uncreated Wisdom, we are obliged to render to the self-revealing God through faith the full obediential service of understanding and will.[9]

Faith, it is said here, is the corresponding correlative to human beings who understand themselves as created, who recognize the total authority of God, and who, in faith, turn hearing into intensive hearing in the sense of faith. In faith as act of hearing and hearkening, human beings come to the truth about themselves. The refusal of faith, in the sense of an absolute autonomy demanded by human beings, totally misses what it means to be human.

Introducing a certain limiting specification, one that has become normative for the clarification and understanding of faith, Vatican I also states:

This faith, the beginning of human salvation, is, according to the teaching of the Catholic church, a supernatural virtue by whose power, with the inspiration and grace of God, *holds as true everything that God has revealed*(emphasis ours), and indeed not because we see into the inner truth of the matter by the natural light of reason, but because of the authority of the revealing God, who can neither be deceived nor deceive others. For, according to the claim of the Apostle, faith "is the assurance of things hoped for, the conviction of things not seen." (Heb. 11:1)[10]

The whole focus of this text is on the authority of God as corresponding to the hearing and hearkening of believing human beings, and this authority as both life-creating and faith-enabling source. This authority is spoken of as the reality that makes human beings what they

---

8. J. Ratzinger, "Gratia praesupponit naturam" 146–49.
9. DS 3008
10. Ibid.

are; it stands in opposition to a reason that recognizes nothing but what comes from itself. But this authority does not stand in opposition to knowledge as such. It is rather acknowledged as one way in which knowledge is opened up for human beings.[11]

From this starting point, faith is described as a "holding to be true what God has revealed." This sets up an "instruction-theoretic" (*instructionstheoretische*) specification of faith, of which it has been said with some justice—above all by [Lutheran] evangelical theology—that it is intellectualist and objectivist. What is presented here is an impersonal "It-" and "That-faith"; the "You-faith," truth as encounter, is left out.[12] That can be said only if one attends to the last quoted sentence and separates it from the interconnectedness of this faith in the full reality of human beings as creatures, as hearers of the Word, as receivers of salvation.

In response, we have to go back again to the theme of revelation: The specific description of special supernatural revelation by Vatican I in the words "God has revealed Himself and the eternal decrees of His salvific will" is, by all accounts, a classical description. It is a good expression of those aspects of revelation having to do with word, person, history, and event. There is no justification for accusing Vatican I of onesidedness and narrowness on this particular point. Vatican I is better than its reputation.

4. The statements of Vatican I have to be understood and evaluated in their own time; their purpose was to be of service to the faith and to the faithful.

They did this in the sense of the contradictions characterizing the situation at that time. Against the theses of the time, which were understood and expressly articulated as antitheses to faith and Church, the Council established its own theses, understood as antitheses to the spirit of the time. The possibility of thinking more synthetically—that perhaps the theses of the other side might contain something more than just error—was apparently not available to either side. They remained two hostile fronts, and the Council did its best to emphasize this opposition and to reject as confusion all attempts to break down the fronts. Since the spirit of the time was articulated mostly in the "isms" of the various world views, it was quite understandable that it would be encountered in this way and that faith was spoken of primarily as doctrine, as truth.

This kind of thinking was not restricted to the Church but was typical of the whole time. The practical way of doing things was to set one-

<hr>

11. H. G. Gadamer, *Truth and Method,* 2d ed., trans. Joel Weinsheimer and Donald G. Marshall (New York: Crossroad, 1989) 277–85.

12. Emil Brunner, *Truth as Encounter,* trans. Amandus W. Loos (London: S. C. M. Press, 1964).

self apart, to defend oneself, to be vigilant, and when necessary to flee from the other in order not to come into contact.

Those who think historically will concede the justice of this situation. They will not be able to charge Vatican I only with narrowness or fear, retreat or failure. All the more so when one considers the differentiations made at this council and the dialectical statements, for example between possibility as such and facticity, or when one recalls the attempts at synthesis between faith and reason, Church and culture, which, to be sure, were not given enough attention later on because an undifferentiated manner of speaking was in vogue. One also has to take note of the dialectical situation, the fact that Vatican I faced two fronts: over-against a radically conceived autonomy of human reason, which denied from the outset any possibility of faith, and over-against a rejection of reason in the name of a faith borne only by feeling, personal experience, or inner experience. Against the first position the council rightly spoke of faith and the limits of reason; against the second position the council explicitly made itself the advocate of reason in the realm of faith. This was done over-against the despisers of reason in the name of faith. In doing this the council upheld an astonishing epistemological optimism, something which these days is no longer achievable to the same extent.

But the same viewpoint of an historical justification leads to a second conclusion: to see that this historically conditioned perspective should not be explained in an unhistorically timeless stasis as the whole thing, as all of what faith means, or as all of what follows from faith for encounter with the world. Not to see the historical perspective of Vatican I, but to qualify it as a comprehensive, exhaustive statement—that is a fundamental misunderstanding. This council of a century ago had its point of reference, its addressees and its manner of dealing with them. It could thus express itself only in the orientation provided, in the orientation provided by the time—by and in which it was also confined. They who overlook this conditionedness and turn conditioned statements into universal theses not only do wrong to Vatican I, they also fall short in the matter of faith.[13]

Thus it is that these statements of Vatican I not only allow but demand that other perspectives be brought out, as for example in the signs of the times which turned out to be different in Vatican II than in the time of a hundred years ago. For the spirit of that age was characterized not only by its unfortunate opposition to faith, but also by an atmosphere that saw possibilities only in contradictions. One becomes aware of the possibility of these other persepectives when a time is understood not just in its "isms," but in its concrete human beings, who are always more than the incarnation of an "ism." This happens when one

13. G. Schwaiger, ed., *Hundert Jahre nach dem I. Vatikanum* (Regensburg, 1970).

talks not just dogmatically and theoretically, but pastorally and existentially, not in the form of anathemas but in the style of the Good
News, of dialogue and invitation. This will lead to the recognition
that faith is to be understood not only in the form of doctrine but—just
as important—as the existential specification of human beings; that
relationship to others can consist not just in defense, in condemnation, in
flight, or in protecting. To understand faith as only a No to the world is
as narrow and unacceptable as understanding the world as only a No to
faith. Faith should also and above all be mediated as offer, as light,
as help, as orientation, as the specification of the meaning of existence.
Only in this way will we ward off the danger, which lies in the purely
defensive attitude of faith, the danger that faith and Church become a
worldless ghetto, and thus alienated and misguided.

This is also the only to way to avoid what was not avoided in
Vatican I: exercising extensive criticism and passing judgment on the
situation and condition of the world and on the spirit of the time, but
refusing to subject to any criticism of its own the concrete Church itself,
its condition and its attitude in a falsely understood triumphalism, or
in an irrelevant timelessness, untouched and unmoved by any historical
fate, and thus failing to set up any presuppositions for a renewal of the
Church, but simply saying, with the general opinion of the time, that
the Church has no need of renewal.

Revelation as Theme of the Second Vatican Council

The Second Vatican Council, which is related not only in name but
also in issues with the context of Vatican I, without repeating it, did
this also with respect to the theme "Revelation." This was done in the
Dogmatic Constitution on Divine Revelation which is known under the
label of its beginning words, *Dei verbum*.[14]

This constitution is considered by not a few theologians, particularly Protestant theologians, as just as significant as the Constitution on
the Church (*Lumen gentium*) and the Constitution on the Church in the
Modern World (*Gaudium et spes*). Some, like Oscar Cullmann, even
hold it to be the most important declaration of the whole Council. One
sees the reason for this when one takes into consideration the theological and ecumenical significance of this text.

14. *Commentary on the Documents of Vatican II*, 5 vols., ed. by H. Vorgrimler, trans. Lalit
Adolphus (New York: Crossroad, 1989), "Dogmatic Constitution on Divine Revelation,"
3.155–72.; J. Ch. Hampe, ed., vol. 1, *Die Autoritat der Freiheit* (Munich, 1967) 109–239; E.
Stakemeier, *Die Konzilskonstitution uber die göttliche Offenbarung*, 2d ed. (Paderborn, 1967); P.
Eicher, *Offenbarung* (483–543); H. Sauer, "Von den 'Quellen der Offenbarung' zur
'Offenbarung selbst.' Zum theologischen Hintergrund der Auseinandersetzung um das
Schema 'Uber die göttliche Offenbarung' beim II. Vatikanischen Konzil" in: *Glaube im
Prozess. Christsein nach dem II. Vatikanum*, ed., E. Klinger and K. Wittstadt, 5th ed.
(Freiburg—Basel—Vienna, 1938) 514–45.

1. This constitution had a somewhat dramatic history at the council itself. Its composition produced no fewer than six different versions. We we can touch only briefly upon this history. First, the theological commission was given the job of working out a schema on the "Sources of Revelation." This was done according to the old method: that the sources of revelation are Scripture and Tradition as two complementary realities. The text of the schema was taken up two years later in the council hall and vigorously discussed. In this discussion the schema was attacked for precisely what the commission saw as the advantage of the text, that it repeated the old truth, that it said nothing new, that it—and this objection was even more serious—took into account neither the biblical nor the pastoral nor the ecumenical situation, and that it therefore represented a step backwards. Pope John XXIII personally made this criticism his own.

He ordered the discussion to be broken off and he set up a new so-called mixed commission, under the coequal presidency of Cardinals Ottaviani and Bea, and gave it the charge to prepare a new text, taking into consideration what had been omitted: the biblical, pastoral, and ecumenical dimension. On November 18, 1965, the dogmatic constitution was solemnly promulgated. It opened with the words *Dei verbum*—under which title it takes its place among the council texts.

In the *Kleinen Konzilskompendium* by Karl Rahner and Herbert Vorgrimler the observation is made that in what happened to this text the spirits were discerned and the council discovered therein its self-awareness.[15] Other experts confirm this when they explain that the decision of Pope John XXIII to have the text reworked and to have the pastoral, biblical, and ecumenical points of view brought into it became the decisive turning point of the Council. This gave the Council its normative orientation that, until then, had not been clearly present.

2. Let us now list its most important statements.

The proem of the constitution emphasized that it was moving in the footsteps of the council of Trent and Vatican I. But this *"vestigiis inhaerens"* meant not just an external, mechanical imitation but—as Karl Barth interpreted it—a "going forward from the footsteps of those councils."[16]

This going forward is to be seen first of all in the fact that the concept "revelation" was replaced by the personal designation *Word of God*. The Word of God has dominance over every speaking and doing of the Church. The Church is described as that which hears and proclaims the Word of God. The sense of this doing is, in the words of the

---

15. (Freiburg—Basel—Vienna, 1968) 361.
16. Karl Barth, *Ad limina Apostolorum : An Appraisal of Vatican II*, trans. Keith R. Crim (Richmond: John Knox Press, 1968).

Council, "so that the whole world in hearing the message of salvation may believe, in believing may hope, and in hoping may love" (no. 1). A different language is being spoken here than was spoken a hundred years before.

Vatican II does not take up the distinction between the two modes or paths of revelation (natural and supernatural), but describes the event of revelation and the activity of revelation in a more comprehensive way. Thus the Constitution on Revelation does not, like Vatican I, proceed from the qualities of God, from God's wisdom and goodness, but calls God Himself, in His wisdom and goodness, the origin of all revelation. In this way the theocentric and personal starting point is incomparably more strongly articulated than at Vatican I. Revelation is, as in Vatican I, described as God's self-communication, as a *"se ipsum revelare"*; but the former *"decreta voluntatis suae revelare"* is replaced by *"sacramentum voluntatis suae"*; in place of the legal view comes the sacramental perspective, which brings together law and grace, word and deed, message and sign, in the unity of the sacrament—mystery—in the biblical sense.

The theocentricity of revelation is even more clearly expressed in that we have described here a Trinitarian movement which goes forth from God the Father, comes to us through Christ, and in the Holy Spirit provides access to communion with God (no. 2).

The doctrinal accent of Vatican I's conception of revelation is expanded by the *dialogical and the presential element* of revelation: God speaks to human beings and seeks encounter with them—*"alloquitur, conversatur."* Human beings are understood as the dialogical beings, who can be described as hearers of the word, and who, through the word, receive communion with God.

The doctrinal narrowing of the concept of revelation is finally overcome in favor of a comprehensive conception, in that the historical dimension is included in which revelation is not characterized as a timeless compilation of doctrines and decrees, but is seen in the horizon of an *"oeconomia salutis"* (economy of salvation) and an *"historia salutis"* (history of salvation). This economy and history is expressly oriented to and connected with the history of humankind.

The revelation event takes place in deed and word which are internally connected with each other: The Works . . . reveal and reinforce the doctrine and the realities described by the words; the words proclaim the works and bring to light the mystery they contain. The depth of the truth disclosed by this revelation about God and about the salvation of human beings is illuminated for us in Christ, who is both the mediator and the fullness of all revelation" (no. 2).

Revelation is thus a series of events in which event, work, deed, and word interpenetrate each other: "The words proclaim the works and bring to light the mystery they contain." There is discussion here about signs and wonders as well. But this is done much more reservedly than in Vatican I and remains subordinate to a holistic consideration of the person and life of Jesus. The effect of this holistic view of revelation as word and history is that human beings are addressed and dealt with in their totality.

A further decisive aspect which was actually present in Vatican I with reference to Heb 1:1 is now explicitly drawn out: this is the *Christocentricity* of revelation. Jesus Christ, says the Constitution, is the "mediator and the fullness of all revelation."

Jesus Christ, the incarnate Word, sent as "human being to human beings," "speaks the words of God" (John 3:34) and fulfills the work of salvation whose accomplishment the Father had entrusted to him (cf. John 5:36; 17:4). Whoever sees Him sees also the Father (cf. John 14:9). He it is who through His whole being and His whole appearance, through words and works, through signs and miracles, but above all through His death and His glorious resurrection from the dead, finally through the sending of the Spirit of Truth, fulfills and completes revelation and through divine witness confirms that God is with us to free us from the darkness of sin and death and raise us to eternal life." (no. 4)

This brings out that Jesus Christ not only speaks to us about God, He is the very speaking of God (God speaking to us in person). Thus He is God's final word, because in Him, God has definitively spoken. He is in His person the final word and event of revelation.

The final goal of revelation is, accordingly, not information and instruction, but communion, union, and the transformation of human beings. Thus, in the midst and fullness of revelation in Jesus Christ there takes place a revelation about human beings; in Jesus, the human being who is God, is revealed what human beings are all about. On the basis of these statements, the revelation fulfilled in Jesus Christ is unsurpassable; "No new public revelation is to be expected before the appearance of our Lord Jesus Christ in glory (cf. 1 Tim 6:14 and Tit 2:13)" (no. 4).

Along with this fulfillment dimension of the revelation that has taken place in Jesus Christ, and along with the definitiveness claimed for it which constantly binds and orients faith to this origin, emphasis is given to the *future horizon* which was not articulated in Vatican I: The one who has come is the one who is to come. What has taken place in Jesus Christ is a constantly ongoing opening. As end it is also a beginning, a beginning and origin for all human beings in every moment of history. If Christ is the very speaking of God, this means that He is the constant "God with us," that in Him begins to open up the whole breadth of God's word which is to take place in history and through human beings.

3. This brings into view the conceptual definition of faith (*Bestimmung des Glaubens*) which is found in the Constitution on Revelation, *Dei verbum*. Here the council consciously takes over

Vatican I's basic idea of faith as obedience which comes from hearing and hearkening and lays claim on human beings in their entirety. But while Vatican I developed from this definition of wholeness a narrowing of the concept of faith in favor of a doctrinal formulation in the sense of *"revelata vera esse credimus"* (what is revealed we believe to be true), in which precisely this characteristic, without its comprehensive grounding, became normative and effective, Vatican II expands the formulation of faith as obedience into a much more comprehensive definition when it says:

The "obedience of faith" is to be given to God revealing. In doing this human beings totally and in freedom hand themselves over to God in that they "fully subject themselves with understanding and will to God revealing" and willingly consent to God's revelation. (no. 5)

The narrowing conceptions of faith as intellectual belief in dogmas or as fiducial faith are absorbed in the larger definition of faith as the total Yes of persons who, in the realization of their existence, give themselves over totally to God who is, in Jesus Christ, the way and truth of human beings. This total aspect of faith is brought to completion in the sense that faith is also described as hope, as promise grounded in the fulfillment in which is mirrored the already and the not-yet, the definitiveness and the ephemerality of faith. The risk of faith thus consists as much in its "nevertheless" over-against everything that can presently be seen and proven, as in a trust which sets out on a road whose end is not in sight.

4. The second chapter of the constitution treats of the handing on of divine revelation through Scripture, Tradition, and Church. We will meet this theme a bit later. Here we need say only that this chapter is not wholly successful. The relationship of Scripture, Tradition, and Church is indeed described—the question of a possible completion of the contents of Scripture remains open, but insufficiently clear expression is given to the fact that priority and normativity belong to Scripture to the extent that Tradition claims to be the authentic and binding interpretation of Scripture; the tradition-critical function of Scripture is not even mentioned.[17] Karl Barth, on this point, spoke of the council's "fainting spell."[18] Even so, one does find the important statement: "The teaching authority" [magisterium]—as organ of the tradition—

17.*Commentary on the Documents of Vatican II*, ed. H. Vorgrimler, 3.185–86: "The Second Vatican Council, for all practical purposes, completely passed over the tradition-critical moment. In doing so it failed to take advantage of an important opportunity for ecumenical dialogue; in fact, the working out of a positive possibility and necessity of an inner-Church critique of tradition would have been ecumenically more fruitful than the—quite fictitious—argument over the quantitative completeness of Scripture."

18. K. Barth, *Ad limina Apostolorum* 52; similarly O. Cullmann, in: J. Ch. Hampe, *Die Autorität der Freiheit*, 1.189–97.

is not above the word of God, but serves it in that it teaches nothing but what is handed on because, from its divine mission and with the assistance of the Holy Spirit, it hears the word of God full of reverence, preserves it in holiness, and interprets it faithfully, and because it draws from this one treasure of faith everything which it presents for belief as revealed by God. (no. 10)

The following chapters of the constitution are devoted to the Holy Scripture, thus giving factual expression to the priority of Scripture: Everything that the Church proclaims must be "nourished by the Holy Scripture and be oriented to it" (no. 21). "The Holy Scriptures contain the Word of God, and because they are inspired, they are truly God's word; thus the study of the Holy Book is, so to speak, the soul of sacred theology" (no. 24).

The way from Vatican I to Vatican II certainly has the marks of a trail, and thus a certain continuity. But this way sought to preserve continuity above all in a "forward." This "forward" was not only movement along the road but also and precisely progress in the reality signified by revelation and faith. It was progress inasmuch as the unquestionably good beginnings of Vatican I, which theologically had no great effect, were given better expression in Vatican II. To be mentioned here above all is the comprehensive definition of that which revelation and faith are. Analysis of the formulations found in the constitution *Dei verbum*, show that the results of theological reflection have been taken up and worked into it.[19] In its focus and openness, the conception of Vatican II is in position to make room for new aspects that have been subsequently articulated: the dimensions of the public, the social, and the political. This conception can also protect these dimensions from one-sidedness or exclusivity and thus help them to make their own rightful contribution.

In contrast with those of Vatican I, the statements of Vatican II are pastoral, that is, related to human beings. Further, they are biblically oriented. Never before had a council spoken so intensively, so openly, and in such detail about Holy Scripture as did Vatican II. In the constitution *Dei verbum*, four of the six chapters are taken up with this theme. They are ecumenically sensitive in that they take into account the whole theological effort on revelation and faith; they do not dig ditches or raise walls, but build bridges. They interpret revelation and faith not so much with the categories of law and doctrine but with the concept of the joyful, truth-making, and free-making Good News. This constitution thus makes one again the oppositions that had also broken out in the understanding of the faith between the confessions: faith as holding to be true—faith as self-giving and trust.

It has been objected that the statements of the last council express too great an optimism in view of human beings and the present situa-

19. On this see H. Waldenfels, *Offenbarung*.

tion. If this impression is given, then it was and is a long overdue obligation, since the road from the First to the Second Vatican Council was marked by pessimism, accusation, and condemnation.

Talk about the crisis of faith is in everyone's mouth today, and there are not a few who blame the last council for that. But nothing could be more false. If this crisis of faith that so many appeal to, and thereby perhaps also escalate, is to lead to life and not to death, it won't happen by looking back, by re-establishing the time, the world, the perspectives, and the methods of a hundred years ago. It will rather come about by the appropriation, realization and continuation of the orientation built into the foundations of Vatican II and its statements not as an end but as a beginning which stands under the sign of hope, of courage, and of life.

BOOK THREE

THE CHURCH

§ 39

THE CHURCH AS THEME OF FUNDAMENTAL THEOLOGY

To what extent is the Church[1] one of the themes of fundamental
theology? The answer is that Church is an object of fundamental
theology because it belongs to the presuppositions, and to the conditions

1. The literature on the theme of "Church" is limitless. One should consult the
theological lexicons and handbooks, and textbooks on dogmatics and fundamental
theology. In addition: J. Brinktrine, *Offenbarung und Kirche*, 2d ed. (Paderborn, 1949); J.
Salaverri, *De Ecclesia Christi* (Madrid, 1950); Emil Brunner, *Das Mißverständnis der Kirche*
(Stuttgart, 1951); L. Köster, *Die Kirche Unseres Glaubens*, 4th ed. (Freiburg, 1952); O.
Semmelroth, *Die Kirche als Ursakrament* (Frankfurt, 1953); also *Ich Glaube an die Kirche*
(Düsseldorf, 1959); St. Jacki, *Les tendences nouvelles de l'ecclésiologie* (Rome, 1957); M. Schmaus,
Katholische Dogmatik III/1: *Die Lehre von der Kirche* (Munich, 1958); also *Dogma* V/1
(Westminster, 1984); Heinrich Fries, *Kirche als Ereignis* (Düsseldorf, 1958); also, *Aspekte der
Kirche* (Stuttgart, 1963); M. A. Fahey, "Church" in: *Sytematic Theology: Roman Catholic
Perspectives*, ed. Francis Schüssler Fiorenza, John Galvin, 2 vols. (Minneapolis: Fortress Press,
1991) 2.4–74; E. Hill, "Church," *NDT* 185–201; E. Kinder, *Der Evangelische Glaube und die
Kirche* (Berlin, 1958); Rudolf Schnackenburg, trans. W. J. O'Hara, *The Church in the New
Testament* (New York: Herder and Herder, 1965); F. Holböck—Th. Sartory, *Mysterium der
Kirche in der Sicht der Theologischen Disziplinen*, vols. 1 and 2, (Salzburg, 1962); A. Lang, *Der
Auftrag der Kirche*, 3d. ed. (Munich, 1962); *Commentary on the Documents of Vatican II*, ed. H.
Vorgrimler, 1.105–297 (*Lumen gentium*), 5.1–370 (*Gaudium et spes*):
    In addition: G. Baraúna, ed., *De Ecclesia Christi. Beiträge zur Konstitution "über die
Kirche" des Zweiten Vatikanischen Konzils*, vols. 1 and 2 (Freiburg—Basel—Vienna—Frankfurt,
1966); G. Baraúna—V. Schnurr, *Die Kirche in der Welt von Heute* (Salzburg, 1967); Hans
Küng, *The Church*, trans. Edward Quinn (New York: Sheed and Ward, 1967); Walter
Kasper, *Die Heilssendung der Kirche in der Gegenwart* (Mainz, 1970); *Handbuch der
Dogmengeschichte*, vol. 3, fasc. a, b, c, d (Freiburg—Basel—Vienna, 1970/71); L. Boff, *Die
Kirche als Sakrament im Horizont der Welterfahrung* (Paderborn, 1972); H. Schlier, "Die
Ekklesiologie des Neuen Testaments" in: *MySal* IV/1.101–221; J. Finkenzeller, *Von der
Botschaft Jesu zur Kirche Jesu Christi* (Munich, 1974); Wolfhart Pannenberg, *Thesen zur
Theologie der Kirche*, 2d ed. (Munich, 1974); Jürgen Moltmann, *The Church in the Power of the
Spirit: A Contribution to Messianic Ecclesiology*, trans. Margaret Kohl (New York: Harper &
Row, 1977); U. Kühn, *Kirche* (Gütersloh, 1980); A. Kolping, *Fundamentaltheologie III. Die
Katholische Kirche als Sachwalterin der Offenbarung. 1. Teil: Die geschichtlichen Anfänge der Kirche
Jesu Christi* (Münster, 1981); also "Gemeinde—Kirche—Konfessionen—Ökumene" in:
Christliche Glaube in Moderner Gesellschaft 29 (Freiburg—Basel—Vienna, 1982); G. Alberigo—
Y. Congar—H. J. Pottmeyer, *Kirche im Wandel. Eine Kritische Bilanz nach dem Zweiten
Vatikanum* (Düsseldorf, 1982); Gerhard Lohfink, *Jesus and Community: The Social Dimension of
Christian Faith*, trans. John P. Galvin (Philadelphia: Fortress Press, 1984); J. Auer, *Die Kirche*
(Kleine Katholische Dogmatik VIII), (Regensburg, 1983).

of the possibility of faith, specifically of the Christian faith. It has this function because it is constitutive for the faith as communion of belief and of the believers, of communion in the faith that is related to Jesus Christ.[2]

This relationship between faith and Church can be made clear from the act of initiation within the Christian life, within Christian being, from the dialogue that takes place in baptism. The one to be baptized is asked: "What do you want of the Church?" The answer is not, as one would expect, "Baptism," but "Faith." Now this means that faith, as Christian faith, is primarily and originally not achieved, but sought for, asked for, received, bestowed. It is bestowed as gift of God and God's Spirit through the Church as a community which lives from this faith and is specified by it, and which thus can mediate it.

This becomes intelligible when, also in this context, one proceeds from the self-understanding of Christian faith and from that standpoint asks about the conditions of its possibility. We have already discussed this, but this new context requires us to take it up again.

The fundamental law, or better, the fundamental structure in the process of Christian faith, is formulated in Romans 10:13–15 as follows: Paul is quoting the prophet Joel: "Every one who calls upon the name of the Lord will be saved." Then follows his own reflection:

But how are men to call upon him in whom they have not believed? And how are they to believe in him of whom they have never heard? And how are they to hear without a preacher? And how can men preach unless they are sent? (Rom 10:14–15)

This does not mean a structure from ancient, primitive times when one could neither read nor write and when one was dependent on others through hearing and announcing, and in that way dependent for faith; nor does it mean a structure from a society that is passé or in the process of passing away, in which only the ruling class spoke and were allowed to speak while the underlings had to hear, to hearken, and to believe. This means rather a structure that is constitutive for faith and is thus abiding; this structure can therefore be replaced by no fundamentally different structure.[3]

Faith comes from hearing, not, like philosophy, from reflection. That must not be falsely understood as if faith had nothing to do with reflection and philosophy nothing to do with hearing. We are addressing here the question of origin and the question of priority. Faith is, as Joseph Ratzinger formulates it, not the thinking out of what can be

---

2. Cf. H. Fries, "Die Kirche als Träger und Vermittler der Offenbarung" in: Mysterium Kirche (F. Holböck—Th. Sartory) 1.1–36.

3. For what follows, see: Joseph Ratzinger, *Introduction to Christianity* (San Francisco, Calif.: Ignatius Press, 1990) 15–49.

thought out, and which, in the end, is at my disposition as the result of my thinking.[4]

Thinking within faith is fundamentally a reflection on what has been heard and received, to which also belongs reflection about its pre-suppositions and conditions of possibility. Thus there is in faith a pre-eminence, a priority of word over thought. This distinguishes faith structurally from the kind of structure found in philosophy.

There is a second element connected with this structure of faith: the communitarian, social relationship of faith; I mean the primacy of communion. That constitutes another difference from philosophy. Of course philosophy also takes place as philosophy within the sphere of a community-related school or academy—and yet philosophy is origi-nally and primarily the thought of the individual who knows as an individual, and in that seeks and finds truth, which then in word and speech becomes communicable and forms communion.

In contrast to this, there is in faith a primacy of community before the individual. If faith comes from hearing and proclaiming, the indi-vidual is lead by this process out of him/herself and into relationship with a community.

Whoever believes comes de facto out of the communion of belief and believers, and also belongs to it. These who want to come to faith must attach themselves to a community; they are taken up into it and become part of it: part of a community constituted by the word proclaimed and heard. Faith means to become a member of a community (Acts 2:41). And precisely this, the community defined this way, is called Church; it is alike *congregatio fidelium* and creation of the Word, *creatura Verbi*. The Greek word *ekklesia* (Latin *ecclesia*) says precisely this: Church is the communion of those who are called and assembled by the Word and who, in order to be and to be able to be this Word, are called and gath-ered ever anew. In this its constitution, the Church is the condition of the possibility of Christian faith for the individual.

This same fundamental structure—the primacy of the given before the given up, the primacy of receiving before doing—is expressed in sacrament, the other way in which the Church is represented and expressed in its activity: in the form of visibility, in the form of sign. In sacrament, word and sign, hearing and seeing, are connected. The word signifies the sign; at the same time the word within the sacramental event is an effective, a reality-creating, a performative word. That reality comes to be which is indicated in the sign.

In this perspective, along with the primacy of the given and the re-ceived, the primacy of community also comes into view. People don't confer sacraments on themselves, they receive them from others who, for their part, represent the community and are commissioned to do

4. Ibid. 56–61.

this. As Church of sacrament the Church is also the condition of the possibility of Christian faith, if faith is a description of all Christian being, if faith is also represented in sacrament which, for its part, is a sign of faith. The communion constituted by word and sacrament, and called Church, exists before the individual. It is at the same time the space in which individuals realize, make perfect, and live their own faith; it is the space which they, as the reality vivified by it, bring into and for the communion of believers.

These considerations on how it is that the Church belongs to the presuppositions, to the conditions of the possibility of Christian faith, are grounded in the uniqueness of this faith: primacy of word, primacy of communion. It was precisely this which was, in contrast to faith, formulated into a philosophy.

Furthermore, one can also describe and ground the community of faith, i.e., the Church, as condition of the possibility of faith if one emphasizes not only the difference between Christian faith and philosophy but also their inner connection and what they have in common. For this will also emphasize once again the anthropological involvement of faith.

Human beings are created in such a way that, in their existence and in its realization, in their activity, and also in the act of their thinking and philosophizing, they cannot prescind from the circumstances that have been described in a special way as characteristic of faith—thus from the circumstances that are determined by receiving and bestowing word and communion. Human existence is always coexistence, being is being with—the I recognizes itself in encounter with the You; and the You becomes known in giving itself to be known. Dialogue is the way to the Logos.

Language, education, culture, art, technology are built on the same circumstances: individuals being taken up into a context of community without which they would atrophy and fail to become themselves. Left to itself and purely isolated, human existence would not be possible in the sphere of thinking and philosophizing either. Thus it is that the communion which is there before the individual, and before the human in general—and in this sense institution as well—is not a hindrance to human beings but becomes the condition of the possibility of their becoming themselves.

In a time when the societal and communitarian dimension and the significance of institution in its function for the individual is becoming recognized, there is also a developing sense for the function of community and institution as condition of the possibility of faith for the individual.

To sum up: it is both from the special nature of Christian faith and from the fundamental structure of human beings in their being and activity that can one approach the Church from the fundamental theological point of view, namely as condition of the possibility of faith. The uniqueness of Christian faith is determined not only by pointing out how it contrasts with philosophy, but also by observing how the phenomenon of being given in advance, of receiving, of hearing, of community is a fundamental quality of human existence, and thus also of thinking and philosophy. This does not eliminate the differences between faith and philosophizing that still remain, but it does set up connections and analogies.

PART ONE

THE ORIGIN OF THE CHURCH FROM THE ORIGIN OF FAITH

CHURCH IN THE HORIZON OF REVELATION

ISRAEL AS COMMUNITY OF BELIEF AND BELIEVERS

Vatican II's conciliar constitution *Lumen gentium* described this theme as follows: Those who believe in Christ are called together in the Church. This Church was something that was beginning to take shape even from the beginning of the world: *ecclesia ab origine mundi praefigurata*; it was prepared for in marvelous ways in the history of the people of Israel and in the Old covenant: *ecclesia in historia populi Israel ac foedere antiquo mirabiliter praeparata* (no. 2).

Church from the Beginning

As for the prefiguration of the Church from the beginning of the world, one should note that even as early as the so-called "prehistory" (Genesis 1–11), which is placed before the history of Israel, the theme "Church as community of believers and of those united with God in faith" turns up.

It is not there thematically, of course, and in these precise words. But later theology has reflected on this beginning also under the theme "Church." If one can understand with one word the Church of Vatican II as sacrament, as visible and effective sign of the unity and unification of human beings with God and thereby also among themselves (no. 1), then it is not beside the point to talk about it already in view of the beginning of humanity in the way that it is presupposed in the Bible.

The so-called protology, what is said about the first beginnings as they are presented in Genesis 1–2, first describes human beings as work and creation of God, and even more, as God's image and likeness; thus, human beings in their original communion with God. From this idea the theology of the Church Fathers proposed the model of an *"ecclesia ab Adam,"* a Church founded with Adam.

Somewhat more known is the idea of an *"ecclesia ab Abel"*[1] developed by Augustine. What Augustine meant was the community of the devout and the just still possible after the Fall, which had its ancient biblical model in Abel.

Of course it is not possible to establish this "Church from the beginning," this *ecclesia ab Adam* or *Ab Abel* historically or geographically; but neither can one dismiss this conception as a vain imagining with no basis in reality.

One must first of all make clear that the statements in the so-called primitive history are "protology and etiology." The first is accordingly not only a temporal beginning but a reality being represented in history and effective in it. It is the reality of creation and salvation, of guilt and Fall; it is the reality that human beings are related to and dependent on God and remain so even after the Fall. These realities are—according to the Bible—factors at work in history and in the present.

For this reason a significance in reality accrues also to a Church of Humanity, an *"ecclesia ab Adam"* or *"ab Abel,"* inasmuch as one can say that human beings who live in orientation towards God, who are people of justice, love, and, reconciliation, the peacemakers, are connected with and related to that which Church will and should be: sign of unity of human beings with God and/or human beings among themselves. This statement is valid for today.

Augustine expressed this idea with a breadth and directness one doesn't expect to find in him:

All the just from the beginning of the world had Christ as their head. They believed in his future coming just as we have believed that he has already come; and in faith in him they have been redeemed just as we have been. . . . The times have changed, not the faith. Words are changed according to the specifics of the time according to which they are conjugated. . . . There is one sound for "He will come" and another for "He has come." The sound is different, but faith connects both, both those who believe that He will come and those who believe that He has come. In different times, but through the one door—Christ—we see human beings entering in. . . . We are all members of Christ and the same time are His body. Not only those who live in this place, but everyone all over the earth. Not only those who live in this time but, yes, what shall I say? From Abel the just until the end of time all human beings, who consistently go through life justly, form the one, whole body of Christ.[2]

Vatican II quoted the following text of Augustine, but only half of it: "Thus the Church strides between the persecutions of the world and the consolations of God on their pilgrimage towards God" (no. 8). Augustine continues: "And that has always been the case in this world,

---

1. Cf. Y. Congar, "Ecclesia ab Abel" in: *Abhandlungen über Theologie und Kirche. Festschrift for Karl Adam,* ed. M. Reding (Düsseldorf, 1952) 79–108; F. Hofmann, *Der Kirchenbegriff des heiligen Augustinus in seinen Grundlagen und in seiner Entwicklung* (Munich, 1933); M. Schmaus, *Katholische Dogmatik* III/1.64–71.

2. In M. Schmaus III/1, 64–66.

right from Abel on, whom, as the first just man, his brother slew, and so will it remain until the end of the world."

Use of the term "anonymous Christian" as a possible description to categorize people outside the visible Church also has its connection and foundation in the conception of a Church of Humanity.

Church in Israel

The Second Vatican Council says that the Church was prepared for in marvelous ways in the history of Israel and in the Old Covenant. We have already spoken at length about Israel's history of faith (see pp. 282–93). Therein lies the coordination of Israel and the Church. Both, i.e. the two together are a community of faith.

Israel is, as a people, a community of faith. If the contents of the credo of Israel is the history of this people brought about by Yahweh, then individuals can believe only as those who belong by way of generation to this people and who are inserted into the concrete history of this people. The community of the people is the living bearer and mediator of faith. Only those who belong to the community of this people belong to the community of faith; and those who want to join it can do so only if they are members of this people.

But that does mean that one can talk about an Old Testament collectivism in the sense that the individual is completely absorbed in the community. Individuals do not get lost, but find themselves in the midst of this community. The individual, not just Israel as community, is thus called Yahweh's Chosen One, son, and servant. Between individuals and community exists the relationship such that individuals are supported by the community and in their turn also support it because they are responsible for it. Their activity goes beyond the merely individual sphere and has its effect, for good and for ill, on the community.

In the course of the history of Israel, however, the idea grew stronger and stronger that belonging to the faith of Israel was determined not just by genetic belonging, but was possible and could be effective beyond the borders of the people of Israel. That meant that the horizon of the communion of faith can go beyond the actual community of the people. Thus there are just people also outside of Israel. And within Israel itself arose, ever more clearly, the distinction: belonging to the people is, as such, no guarantee for the integrity of faith in Israel as a community of faith. It was pointed out again and again, that not the people as a whole but its kernel, or remnant, was the bearer of the Yahweh-faith. At the time of the prophet Elijah, it was the seven thousand who did not bow their knee before Baal. The same was true for the prophets and the often-small group of their friends against which the majority of the people rose up. The situation was similar with the group of Maccabbees, while the greatest part of the people were no longer a faith community.

More important than belonging to Israel in a bodily way and having Abraham for one's father is, consequently, being a child of Abraham, which consists in the living out of the faith of Abraham (cf. Matthew 3:9). But the function of this kernel, this "remnant of Israel," was not that of closing itself off in a sectarian manner, but of being the power of the renewal and continuity of faith for all.

Israel as a faith community is and also should be a community of justice. Now that does not mean a formal-juridical kind of organization, but a community in which right rules in the form of righteousness, which is an image of the righteousness of Yahweh. The basis of this community of right are the *Ten Words*, the Decalogue, as Israel's constitution. The constant temptation of human beings to portray their own interests as a matter of righteousness and clothe it with the halo of right was also known and practiced in Israel, above all by those in power, the kings and priests.

It is not just our own critically-minded contemporaries who discover the misuse of justice. The prophets of the Old Covenant also pointed emphatically to it. From the counterimage of unrighteousness, they pointed out the meaning of right and righteousness.

And what unrighteousness means they labeled by name: It is not the failure to observe a paragraph of the law, but the wounding of human rights, the repression and exploitation of the poor, the helpless, the unprotected, the widows and orphans, the underprivileged. Righteousness is the renunciation of violence, and practical commitment to peace is praised as the fruit of righteousness.

Let us take a few examples of this passionate plea from the words of the prophets: Amos (about 760 B.C.) speaks in the name of Yahweh:

I hate, I despise your feasts, and I take no delight in your solemn assemblies. Even though you offer me your burnt offerings and cereal offerings, I will not accept them, and the peace offerings of your fatted beasts I will not look upon. Take away from me the noise of your songs; to the melody of your harps I will not listen. But let justice roll down like waters, and righteousness like an ever-flowing stream. (Amos 5:21–24)

The prophet Isaiah, about the year 740, complains about Jerusalem where the cult is strong but righteousness weak:

When you spread forth your hands, I will hide my eyes from you; even though you make many prayers, I will not listen; your hands are full of blood. Wash yourselves; make yourselves clean; remove the evil of your doings from before my eyes; cease to do evil, learn to do good; seek justice, correct oppression; defend the fatherless, plead for the widow. (Isa 1:15-17)

Micah, the contemporary of Isaiah, declares: the sign of conversion is not the number of cultic sacrifices but the fulfillment of the requirement:

He has shown you, O man, what is good; and what does the Lord require of you but to do justice, and to love kindness, and to walk humbly with your God? (Mic 6:8)

According to Alfons Deißler, these words are not only an adequate summing up of the fundamental message of the Old Testament, but an abiding commission also for that community of believers which is the Church of Jesus Christ.[3]

In Israel there is found also the phenomenon of the community of worship and community of ritual, the community which in ritual gives voice and expression to its faith in word and sign, above all in sacrifice. In the word, the acts of God are contemplated during worship: remembering, thanking, praising, making present, and petitioning for the future. In liturgical sign, above all in an extensive sacrificial rite, there is represented symbolically what moves and determines the faith of Israel from which it lives.

In sacrifice, acknowledgment and homage are expressed in the form of a gift and its offering. The fundamental idea here is that the sacrificial gift stands vicariously for those offering the sacrifice and for what moves them: thanksgiving, acknowledgment/recognition, self-giving, but also petition or atonement for guilt.

Against the sacrificial ideas of the Israelites one hears the objection, a common one among the philosophers of antiquity, that God has no need of gifts—God is Himself the giver of all gifts. It is not God but human beings who have need of sacrifice as symbolic expression of what can be said in word.

In sacrifice, a communion between God and human beings is symbolized and regarded as effective in a special way. The sacrificial gift is changed or transformed by its new definition of purpose; it is given over to God as an expression of self-giving. God's acceptance of the sacrifice creates a bond with those making the offering. This is represented by burning the gifts, or a part of them. A quite essential form of communion with God is represented by the table fellowship which comes from the sacrifice and the sacrificial gift, the sacrificial meal. Through it, communion among human beings is also established, vivified, and renewed. The sacred meal is a fundamental element in all religions.

3. A. Deißler, *Die Grundbotschaft des Alten Testaments*, 7th ed. (Freiburg—Basel—Vienna, 1979) 122, 156.

The prophets' criticism is directed not at sacrifice and ritual as such, but at their abuse: when life and ethos did not correspond to what the rite expressed, when one tried to use the ritual to buy out of the obligations of righteousness, or when one tried by way of the ritual, particularly by way of sacrifice, to exercise control over God, according to the measure *"do ut des"* (I give that you may give).

In the "prohibition of images" "Thou shalt make no image," it was expressly required of Old Testament ritual and worship that it worship without images. Expressly forbidden were human sacrifice, idolatry, charms and spells, magic, foretelling the future, ritual castration, and religious prostitution. In these practices, which were customary in the rituals of that time, Israel was not to be like the other nations. There were in addition the many ritual "purity requirements," which likewise served to define liturgical activity as well as to set it apart from other groups.

The place of divine worship in Israel varied considerably according to where one was in the course of the history of the people. The nomadic people of the early period used as their place of worship and liturgical assembly the tent, called the tent of meeting, holy tent, tent of the covenant. When the tent was taken down and carried away, Yahweh was thought of as accompanying and wandering with them.

In the sedentary period, more precisely in the time of the kingdom, in place of the tent came the solid house, the constant, abiding sanctuary of the people. This development found its high point in the shape of King Solomon's Temple built in Jerusalem (cf. 1 Kings 6–8). The Temple now seemed the form of liturgical assembly appropriate to the status of Israel, especially the kingdom, the fulfillment of what began in the Sinai event. Because of the Temple, Jerusalem becomes the holy city. The feasts of Israel are celebrated in the Temple; they are Temple feasts of the entire people.

The connection between Temple-building and faith-motivation is expressed in Solomon's prayer at the dedication of the Temple:

But will God indeed dwell on the earth? Behold, heaven and the highest heaven cannot contain thee; how much less this house which I have built! Yet have regard to the prayer of thy servant and to his supplication, O Lord my God, hearkening to the cry and to the prayer which thy servant prays before thee this day; that thy eyes may be open night and day toward this house, the place of which thou hast said, "My name shall be there." (1 Kings 8:27–29)

For the sake of completeness one still has to remember that after the destruction of the Solomonic Temple (586) came the Temple rebuilt after the exile, and finally the Temple built by King Herod which was the Temple at the time of the New Testament.

In exile a new form of liturgical place and space took shape: the synagogue. This was originally the community gathering, then the space in which the liturgical assembly met, the house of prayer. When, after the return, the Temple was rebuilt as the central place of worship and cult, and the service of the Temple was resumed, the form or institution of the synagogue survived, above all as the local community's place of assembly. The connection with Jerusalem, with the Temple, and with that of the whole nation as liturgical community took expression in the annual pilgrimage to the Temple, obligatory for all Israelites, to celebrate the great feasts of the nation.

The Hebrew expression for the liturgical assembly of the people of Israel is *kahal*; it is translated in the Greek translation of the Old Testament, the Septuagint, with the word *ekklesia*. This word *ekklesia* was already a quite well-known word in the hellenistic world; it meant "gathering of the people." It is enlightening to observe what structural elements are connected respectively with the Greek and Hebrew understanding of *ekklesia*, and how the same word means something different in a different context.

In the Greek understanding, the word *ekklesia* signifies a gathering of members with voting rights, the adult men in a polis who exercised lawgiving power in this polis. There *ekklesia* is the regularly meeting highest decision-making authority of the city or people; *ekklesia* is a political concept which has its home especially in democracy.

The meaning of *ekklesia* in the Hebrew understanding, as the word which translates *qahal*, is the assembled Israelite national community. But the difference from the Greek concept is considerable. The first difference consists in the fact that in the Greek popular assembly in which politics is discussed and carried out, only men are allowed, while in Israel the whole people is gathered, men, women, and children. The model of this assembly is the gathering of the whole people at Sinai. The day of the Sinai event is called the "Day of Assembly" (Deut 9:10; 18:26).

The assembly of the people in Israel did not come together for the purpose of political discussion or to make political decisions. Israel assembles with the intention of hearing the the Word of God, and of asking what directions and action would come from this, which indeed could have great political relevance. The Israelite *ekklesia*, the *qahal*, is primarily a liturgical assembly gathered to hear the Word of God and the law with the same readiness with which their fathers at Sinai did. But the hearing of the Word of God in the *ekklesia* becomes actualized for what is to be done here and now in Israel.

In Israel's situation during and after the Exile, in the time of the refoundation of the people of Israel, there is the new fact of the dispersion of the people—the *Diaspora*. It brings about the distinction between Diaspora Jews and Palestinian Jews. This difference also got stamped on the structure of their faith: in the greater openness of

Diaspora Judaism for the other: for Hellenism, and the more closed mentality of the Israelites in Palestine. In the liturgical assembly, along with the remembrance of the gathering of the people that once took place on Sinai, was also the articulation of the hope of a future gathering and assembly of the people of God from all the ends of the earth.

Israel as a cult community is determined not just by place as the location of ritual and worship, but also by time: as time for the liturgical assembly, for the praising and thanking remembrance of the great deeds of Yahweh. This specially set aside time is the Sabbath, the day of rest of the Creator, the day of rest of human beings, the day that is to be made holy, the day that is to be free for the remembering, for joy and thanksgiving, for one's obligations to other human beings, to establish a sign of freedom and social responsibility: "The Sabbath was made for man" (Mark 2:27). The times set aside are the festivals: the Passover feast (Easter) in memory of the Exodus, the feast of Pentecost in memory of the Sinai event, the feast of Tabernacles as thanksgiving for the journey through the desert, also as harvest feast, and the atonement festival (Yom Kippur), the great day of penance for the whole people. In these feasts of Israel, natural moments in the course of the year like sowing, harvest, equinox (Canaan) and historical moments are intertwined.

The meaning of the Sabbath and the feasts has already been mentioned as days of joy, memory, prayer, freedom, and of being free for service to Yahweh and other human beings. The special time is to be a sign of this and to remind the people that all time is God's time, that every day can and should be a day of the Lord—in the same way in which the time set aside for ritual and divine worship is to be a reminder that not only the Temple but the "whole earth is the Lord's."

§ 41

THE ORGANS OF THE COMMUNITY OF THE PEOPLE OF ISRAEL AS COMMUNITY OF FAITH

When one has a community of faith, a community of justice, a community of worship and of ritual, one also has, necessarily, structure. Structure, in turn, requires organs, i.e. the functions, roles and tasks of these organs in the service of the community. Such was the case also in Israel, and that indeed is a remarkable development which corresponds to the development of the people.[1]

The Patriarchs

In the beginning stands the father of the family, the head of the clan. He assumes the function of leadership, of establishing the arrangements for the community of the family and for the clan. In this position of authority, the father, as father of the house, as patriarch also assumes the religious functions: he prays, he offers sacrifice, he performs the religious practices.

Moses and the Priesthood

In the expansion to the still quite small nation of twelve tribes, Moses takes over the functions needed for the larger community. In his person he is the political speaker and leader of the people in the Exodus through the desert up to the borders of Canaan; he is the mediator of justice, of the law, and with that also the judge; he is finally the priest who represents his people before God: praying, interceding, sacrificing, and who turns to this people under Yahweh's mandate. In this Israelite community his is a threefold function of faith, justice, and

1. L. Rost, *Die Vorstufen von Kirche und Synagoge im Alten Testament* (Stuttgart, 1938); H. W. Hertzberg, *Werdende Kirche im Alten Testament* (Munich, 1950); N. Füglister, "Strukturen der Alttestamentlichen Ekklesiologie" in: *MySal* IV/1.23–99.

worship. But soon a differentiation of this structure in the course of Israel's history becomes noticeable, at least to the extent that the different functions are divided up among different persons.

According to the so-called priestly document, one of the four sources of the Pentateuch, Moses himself had appointed his brother Aaron and his sons as priests and ordained them in extensive ceremonies (Leviticus 8). The later priesthood in Jerusalem, which claimed a central position in its service of the central sanctuary, for which the high priesthood was established, claimed to be of the line of Aaron and his sons.

On the other hand, we hear from another tradition that at the time of Moses the tribe of Levi, which had proven itself in faith, had already been entrusted with priestly functions. These functions were connected with the development of ritual and worship in the tent, the Temple, and the synagogue, and were also quite varied in content.

The distinction between high priest, priest, and Levite comes from later, post-exilic times. The liturgical functions included prayer and sacrificial worship, but above all—and this in increasing measure in the Exile and Diaspora—instruction in the Law: the interpretation of the Law and its application to individual cases. Along with the figure of the priest appeared that of the scribe, i.e. the doctor of the Law, theologian, and, in a still later time, teacher of wisdom who taught not abstract theory but the wisdom of life.

The Judges

After Moses and Joshua the so-called Judges, also called saviors and leaders, took over the political functions. They are tribal heroes (Gideon, Sampson, Jephthah, Samuel). They are not institutions; they arise in times of special need and danger at the head of one tribe, of individual tribes, or of the people.

Their calling was seen in a special way as a free act of choice by Yahweh. The action of the judges served as proof of divine power, above all in the face of the often-depicted relationship of the over-whelming power of the enemies against the minimal strength of the tribes of Israel. The Book of Judges provides information about these events, but not in the sense of historical biographies or as an account of consecutive events, but in the framework of a theological schema (Jud 2:6–3:11): as a summing up of many individual traditions.

The time of the judges, as the time before the establishment of the monarchy, is described through the later, idealistically colored historical writing as an epoch in which immediacy with God, the freedom of the reign of God over his twelve-tribed people, was given spontaneous and charismatic expression.

The Kings

The last judge, Samuel, represents the transition to a broader stabilization, the establishment of the Monarchy. At first, the people's longing for a king (1 Sam 8) was interpreted as a rejection of Yahweh, as an expression of the wish that Yahweh should no longer be king over them (1 Sam 8:7). But the will of the people won out: "That we also may be like all the nations, and that our king may govern us and go out before us and fight our battles" (1 Sam 8:20). Samuel chooses and anoints Saul and later David as king, as king by God's grace. David succeeds in turning the twelve tribes into a political unity and in subjugating the Canaanite city states. This process was connected with the loss of the independence of the twelve tribes. What once were free nomads then became subjects of the king.

The kingdom is accepted if—biblically speaking—it is a kingdom after the "Heart of Yahweh," in such a way that it doesn't reject the lordship of Yahweh but makes it visible in the faith and obedience of the king towards Yahweh. When the monarchy was introduced in Israel, it was already an established institution in the Near East. The king was not only a political leader but a religious figure who for the most part was revered as a divinity. This was given expression in the court ceremonial, in the forms of ascending the throne, in the forms of homage. Although Israel's king as chosen one is also a religious figure, we nevertheless find no trace of a divinizing or divine veneration of the king. This was prevented by the way king and monarchy were part of the faith history of Israel, which was dominated by the theme: Yahweh is the king of his people. The king of Israel is the one who expressly acknowledges this.

The king acknowledged this fact as the reality of the faith of Israel and, with that, of his own faith. From this basis arose also the possibility of examination and criticism of the behavior of the king. Energetic use was made of the right of criticism; Saul was rejected as king and replaced by David.

This position of the king and of the kingdom in Israel grounded in faith was nevertheless unable to prevent a secularization from taking place, a turning of the monarchy towards worldliness. In the place of the election of the king, as was the case with Saul and David, was put inheritance; in the place of faith came political interests and calculation. Furthermore, political unification of the Israelite tribes with the inhabitants of Canaan became more important than unity and strengthening in faith.

The flowering of the monarchy did not last long. With Saul, David, and Solomon, it was finished. After the death of Solomon (about 930), the kingdom of David broke up, by popular decision, into the Northern Kingdom and the Southern Kingdom.

In the Northern Kingdom, with its later capital, Samaria, ten tribes were gathered. The Southern Kingdom with the city of Jerusalem consisted of the tribes of Judah and Benjamin. Jerusalem, as city of David, as the city of the Temple, had a special significance encompassing all the tribes.

There was a relationship of tension and rivalry between the Northern Kingdom and the Southern Kingdom and their kings. In order to affirm their independence, the kings of the Northern Kingdom, beginning with Jeroboam, tried to break loose from Jerusalem and the Temple; he made connections with the earlier sanctuaries of Canaan; along with the veneration of Yahweh, the kings also allowed the worship of Baal. Thus there was division, schism among the people of God. This explains the pluralism of the traditions of faith which found their way into the writing of the various sources and streams of tradition of the Old Testament.

Along with and despite the division of the people into two kingdoms, there existed between both a common bond: their faith in Yahweh, the God of the whole people, who guides the fate and history of both parts. With this lived on the hope that both parts would be united again. This unification—it is the idea above all of the great prophets Isaiah, Jeremiah, and Ezekiel—will be possible only by way of the renewal and the purification of both. The unification becomes then not just the restoration of an earlier condition, but a new creation.

Is not the division of the two parts of the one people of God—so might one ask—like the preview of the separation of the New Testament People of God? Attempts have even been made to divide the Northern Kingdom and the Southern Kingdom confessionally, so to speak; to see the Reformation churches modeled in the Northern Kingdom, and in the Southern Kingdom, with its developed cult, the Catholic Church. But something else is more important. It is already pointed out in the Old Testament how the road to unity looks: it is unity through union—and this leads over the road of renewal: through renewal to union—*ecclesia semper reformanda*. Also applicable here is the saying: *"Ecclesia praeparata in historia populi Israel"* (The Church is prepared for in the history of the People of Israel).

The Prophets

A further instance of authority in Israel as faith, justice, and liturgical community, and perhaps the most important, is the prophet. There has already been discussion of this in our presentation of revelation (see above pp. 290–92).

Prophets and prophetism have a long and differentiated history in Israel, and a function determined by that history. Prophets are found in

Israel's history especially at important turning points. Thus Moses is called a prophet, the one who was called and chosen, the one who, under God's direction and as the seer speaks, acts, and judges. He also sets the norm for the quality of the later prophets. At the beginning of the monarchy, Samuel plays a major role; he is called judge and prophet. His is the normative voice on the question of the introduction of the monarchy to Israel; he anoints Saul and David as kings. At the time of King David, around the year 1000, Nathan appears. In a memorable scene he charges the king with his great sin: his guilt in the death of Uriah (2 Sam 12:1–3). A constantly recurring motif in the history of Israel is the prophet before the king—and often against him, in contrast to the court prophets. It illustrates the fact that Israel is not to be like the other nations.

After the division of the kingdom, there arose in the North the most powerful of the prophets after Moses: Elijah. His very name is a program; it means: My God is Yahweh. He acts like a second Moses, turns against the priests of Baal, against King Ahab, and against the indifferent people, and calls them to decision.

In the Southern Kingdom and its capital, Jerusalem is the stage for the activity of Isaiah and King Ahab, where again a great decision is made. Isaiah warns the king against a disastrous policy of alliance. He appeals to the covenant of Yahweh and to the obligations of the faith in the classical words: "If you will not believe, surely you shall not be established" (Isa 7:9). A hundred years later the prophet Jeremiah appeared in the palace of the king and before the people. He is the prophet of doom who, in his Temple speech, warns against all false security, who sees the end coming without being able to stop it. During the Captivity the prophets Ezekiel (580) and Daniel (540) appear. Many of these prophets are called the written prophets, because their proclamation is handed on in their writings.

Alongside the king and monarchy are the priests and priesthood, over-against whom stands the prophet. Conflict arises in view of the dangers of a cult stylized to serve its own purposes. After his Temple speech the prophet Jeremiah is struck by the high priest in Jerusalem, put in the stocks, and subjected to public mockery and ridicule (Jer. 20).

Jeremiah gives impressive witness about prophets, the fate of the prophets, and about true and false prophets:

O Lord, thou hast deceived me, and I was deceived; thou art stronger than I, and thou hast prevailed. I have become a laughingstock all the day; every one mocks me. For whenever I cry out, I shout "Violence and destruction!" for the word of the Lord has become for me a reproach and derision all day long. If I say, "I will not mention him, or speak any more in his name," there is in my heart as it were a burning fire shut up in my bones, and I am weary with holding it in, and I cannot. For I hear many whispering. Terror is on every side! "Denounce him! Let us denounce him!" say all my familiar friends, watching for my fall. "Perhaps he will be deceived, then we can overcome him, and take our revenge on him." But the Lord is with me as a dread warrior; therefore my persecutors will stumble, they will not overcome me. They will be greatly shamed, for they will not succeed. Their eternal dishonor will never be forgotten. (Jer 20:7–11)

But in the prophets of Jerusalem I have seen a horrible thing: they commit adultery and walk in lies; they strengthen the hands of evildoers, so that no one turns from his wickedness. (Jer 23:14)

Thus says the Lord of hosts: "Do not listen to the words of the prophets who prophesy to you, filling you with vain hopes; they speak of visions of their own minds, not from the mouth of the Lord. They say continually to those who despise the word of the Lord, 'It shall be well with you'; and to everyone who stubbornly follows his own heart, they say, 'No evil shall come upon you.'" (Jer 23:16–17)

The Elders

There is an additional instance or organ in Israel's community of faith, law, and worship: the institution of the elders, the presbyters. First among these are the heads of the tribes and clans. The name "elder" signifies less a degree of age than an authority and dignity stemming from wisdom and experience of life.

The elders are already mentioned as a group along with Moses; they are the representatives of the people at the making of the Sinai covenant. After coming into the Land, the elders were the leading men in the communities and cities; they were a governing body authorized to carry out the tasks of administration, make decisions and passing legal judgments. In the time of the monarchy, for the sake of a unified and consistent organization, a centralized bureaucracy with a hierarchy of officials arose. It attempted to supplant as much as possible the elders as representatives of the people. But the institution of the elders survived.

In the time of the Exile this institution took on a new importance. They were the surviving instances of self-administration. They were in fact the leaders of the communities and of the synagogue worship, together with the rabbi, the Jewish teacher whose job was the interpretation and application of the Law. The organ and instance of the elders in Jewish synagogues as the representation of the laity exists to this day.

A council of the elders as a clearly defined highest Jewish governing body with its seat in Jerusalem arose only in later times. Together with the representatives of the priesthood, from whom the high priest was chosen, and together with the scribes, the official theologians, they constituted the supreme council, the Sanhedrin, in Jerusalem.

Thus one can say that Israel, as a community of people, as a community of faith, law, and worship, both on the whole and in particular is made up of specific structures, organs, and functions. They stand as much in coordination as in tension with each other, especially the prophetic in relation to the institutional. In all this is a *praeparatio ecclesiae* (preparation for the Church) as community of faith, law, and worship which, for the sake of the community, is dependent on organs and functions. These are represented in the Church as office which is connected with the performance of certain functions and tasks and attached to specific persons. In this—at least in the office of the presbyter—can still be recognized obvious traces of what once was.

§ 42

ISRAEL AND THE CHURCH

The direction of what we are saying goes something like this: In Israel and in the Old covenant, the Church of Jesus Christ was prepared. The Second Vatican council says: Israel is *"praeparatio ecclesiae"* (the preparation of/for the Church). This definition is to be carefully distinguished from other conceptions, some of which are defended even to this day.

Different Definitions of the Relationship

One conception claims: If the New Testament represents the fulfillment and goal of all previous ways and all preceding times, if it is the new, and at the same time the definitive, what further need has one for the old, the earlier? Is it not just ballast? This conception reaches its peak in the demand already made by the Gnostic, Marcion, and repeated by A. von Harnack, to do away with the Old Testament and concentrate just on the New.

In response it must be pointed out that the New Testament is also a Jewish book, that Jesus was a Jew, and so were all the apostles. If the claim is made that whoever has the fulfillment and goal of all paths as orientation has no further need of the Old Testament, that claim is missing the whole point that the category "fulfillment" cannot be understood when one is unable to explain what it is that constitutes fulfillment, and of whose expectation it is the fulfillment. The goal can be recognized only by someone who knows the way to it. The fundamental Christian affirmation is not understood without the Old Testament. For that is where one encounters this figure.

The proclamation of Jesus is determined by the ideas and contents of the Old Testament. The world in which Jesus lives is the world of the Old Testament and its people. The Scriptures Jesus knows, which he quotes and interprets, are the Old Testament books, the Law and the Prophets.

There is another approach too with relevance for assessing the ecclesiological significance of Israel. It is based on the argument just mentioned, which says that one cannot do without the Old Testament. This approach claims that Israel and the Church are to be considered equal. Israel and Church are to be considered as people of God; both are people of election, are *ecclesia* formed by Word and community; both are people on the way, both have the mandate not to be like other people, and at the same time to be there for all, and thus to understand their existence as "existence for." Both have as goal the coming of the kingdom of God.

Correct as these assertions may seem to be in view of what we have just mentioned, they do not do justice to what is special in the new and eschatological covenant, for they do not take account of the differences. They do not make sufficiently clear what fulfillment is, what it means that to say that Jesus is more than the prophet and the king of the Old Testament. They also do not make it sufficiently clear just how it is that the present, the today, that is witnessed in the New Testament, is the decisive moment in time.

There is also an approach that goes even further: it speaks not only of the equality of Israel and Church, but also of the idea that Israel and its history become the decisive criterion of what the Christian Church is, what it is to be and to do. The New Testament is thus seen as an appendix, a final book of the Old Testament; its value is measured by the extent to which it is brought into harmony with it. That is the favored theme in the present-day Jewish-Christian dialogue.[1] Martin Buber had already declared: What is valuable in the New Testament

---

1. Basic treatments: Franz Mußner, *Tractate on the Jews: The Significance of Judaism for Christian Faith,* trans. Leonard Swidler (Philadelphia: Fortress Press, 1984); Clemens Thoma, *A Christian Theology of Judaism,* trans. Helga Croner (New York: Paulist Press, 1980); H. Goldschmidt—H. J. Kraus, *Der Ungekündigte Bund,* 2d ed. (Stuttgart—Berlin, 1963); K. H. Rengstorf—K. Kortzfleisch, *Kirche und Synagoge,* 2 vols. (Stuttgart, 1968—1970); P. Lapide, *Ökumene aus Christen und Juden* (Neukirchen—Vluyn, 1972); F. Hammerstein, *Christian-Jewish Relations in Ecumenical Perspective* (Geneva, 1978); H. H. Henrix—M. Stöhr, *Exodus und Kreuz im ökumenischen Dialog Zwischen Juden und Christen* (Aachen, 1978); J. Maier—J. J. Petuchowski—C. Thoma, "Judentum und Christentum" in: *Christlicher Glaube in Moderner Gesellschaft* 26 (Freiburg—Basel—Vienna, 1980) 128–68; C. Thoma, *Die Theologischen Beziehungen Zwischen Christentum und Judentum* (Darmstadt, 1982); P. Lapide—K. Rahner, *Heil von den Juden? Ein Gespräch* (Mainz, 1983).

For recent work in English, cf.: J. H. Charlesworth, ed., *Jews and Christians: Exploring the Past, Present and Future* (New York: Crossroad, 1990); *Overcoming Fear between Jews and Christians* (New York: Crossroad, 1993); D. P. Effroymson—E. J. Fisher—L. Klenicki, eds., *Within Context: Essays on Jews and Judaism in the New Testament* (Collegeville, Minn.: Liturgical Press, 1993); C. A. Evans—D. A. Hagnet, eds., *Anti–Semitism and Early Christianity: Issues of Polemic and Faith* (Minneapolis: Fortress Press, 1993); *New Theology Review: An American Catholic Journal for Ministry:* vol. 7, no. 2 is devoted mostly to this theme.

takes its lineage from the Old Testament; what does not take its lineage from there is not good.[2]

It follows from this that Jesus is acknowledged insofar as he is prophet, brother of us all in faith,[3] insofar as he is a critic of the existing conditions and institutions of the establishment, a friend of tax collectors and sinners, for whom the idea of a Church was completely foreign.

In response, one must observe that all this does not do justice to the witness of the New Testament. The New Testament made it quite clear that Jesus of Nazareth is the Christ, that the messianic expectations are fulfilled in him, that we need to look for no one else as the One who is to come (Matthew 11:7–15). The New Testament makes a point of saying that the Jesus who is proclaiming becomes the one who is proclaimed, the one who believes becomes the one who is believed.

Karl Barth represents another contrasting concept of Israel and Church.[4] He says that the common element between Israel and the Church consists in the fact that both are the people of election, the election of the electing God. This people has a twofold figure: Israel and the Church, the Church as a people composed of Jews and Gentiles. Abraham, the father of Israel, is father of the Church because he is the father of faith; Jesus, the Lord of the Church, is, taking his lineage from Israel, the Messiah of this people. Both Israel and the Church have the common mandate to give witness to what God has done in them. Without Israel there would be no Church. The Church came to Israel, not Israel to the Church. It was grafted on as a branch (Rom. 9–11). The unity of the two is inseparable; it is often revealed in their common fate.

The difference between Israel and the Church consists, according to Barth, in the fact that Israel is the representation and reflection of the divine judgment, the representation also of human unwillingness and unworthiness over-against God's mercy. This is not Israel's past contribution, but its ongoing contribution to the Church, which needs precisely this mirror in order to be able to be and to do what it has been mandated. According to Barth, the Church is the representation of the

---

2. On this see Hans Urs von Balthasar, *Martin Buber and Christianity: A Dialogue between Israel and the Church*, trans. Alexander Dru (New York: Macmillan Press, 1961).

3. J. Klausner, *Jesus of Nazareth: His Life, Times, and Teaching* trans. Herbert Danby (New York: Menorah Pub. Co., 1979); F. Flusser, *Jesus* (rowohlts monographien), (Reinbeck, 1968); Schalom Ben Chorim, *Der Nazarener in jüdischer Sicht* (Munich, 1969); *Jesus im Judentum* (Wuppertal, 1970); P. Lapide, *Israelis, Jews, and Jesus*, trans. Peter Heinegg (Garden City, N. Y.: Doubleday, 1979); Heirich Fries, "Jesus in jüdischer Sicht" in: *Kirche und Religionen*, ed. H. Fries—F. Köster—F. Wolfinger, vol. 1: *Jesus in den Weltreligionen*, (St. Ottilien, 1981) 15–49.

4. Karl Barth, *Church Dogmatics* IV/1 und 2, ed., G. W. Bromiley—T. F. Torrence (Edinburgh: T. & T. Clark, 1956–75); on this cf. H. Fries, "Die Kirche als Ereignis. Zu Karl Barths Lehre von der Kirche" in: *Kirche als Ereignis* (Düsseldorf, 1958) 68–118, esp. 77–81.

divine mercy, that in which judgment is passed and overcome. To that extent the Church is the more perfect form of the community, of the people of God.

Furthermore, the special service of the Church is faith, while the service of Israel is hearing, the hearing of the words and the promises made to this people. According to Barth, this service too flows into the Church, for faith comes from hearing, faith is the actualized step of hearing. But it is precisely this step from hearing to faith which, according to Barth, Israel, as such and as a whole, does not take, and indeed at that point at which the promise is fulfilled: in Jesus Christ. Thus Israel, which in hearing becomes disobedient, gives the example of a beginning without continuation, of a present without future, in brief, the example of an opportunity missed. Here the ministry of the Church begins, the ministry of faith; to that extent the Church is the more perfect form of God's community. But even here Israel lives on in the Church, because its hearing lives on in faith and because faith even in the sphere of the Church can become small and weak; it can fail and be failed.

And finally: If God in Jesus Christ is preparing an end for human beings lost to death and judgment, and is giving them a new beginning in peace, safety, and life, then the one community of God exists in a twofold form: in a form that is passing away and in a form that is abiding and at the same time coming. These explanations represent in an original way the commonality and difference between Israel and the Church as well as its indissoluble bond, when this is seen in the history of faith.

To be sure, the differences are overemphasized here. For Israel is not just the representation of human disobedience, of sin and divine judgment. Israel is also not just the representation of a community that has not taken the step from hearing to believing. If this latter point is relevant with respect to the Messiah who has come in Jesus, it certainly isn't for the other contents of faith. For Israel also traveled the path from hearing to believing, to believing in God's actions, words, and promises. The difference lies in the difference that has come with the course of history which cannot be overlooked or leveled away.

In this at first astonishing comparison and contrast, Barth seems to yield to the tendency—as has already been indicated—to replace the schema of time and history with the schema of space. This comes out in the pregnant expression: the prophet and the apostle see the same thing: the prophet looking forward to what is coming, the apostle looking back to what has come. And precisely here lies the decisive difference conditioned by time and history. It is this: prophet and apostle do not see the same thing; they do not see the same in what they see. Time and history are also the coming of the new.

Therefore, in the matter of the relationship between Israel and the Church, we conclude that what is expressed by the category *praeparatio ecclesiae* in the history of Israel and in the Old Testament does more justice to the mutual relationships and connections between Israel and the Church.

The Historical Path

Paul, above all in chapters 9–11 of the Epistle to the Romans,[5] reflected on the relationship between Israel and the Church, and spoke expressly of the mystery of Israel. "They are Israelites, and to them belong the sonship, the glory, the covenants, the giving of the law, the worship, and the promises; to them belong the patriarchs, and of their race, according to the flesh, is the Christ" (Rom 9:4–5). Also, after Christ, God did not terminate his covenant with Israel, or withdraw his election. God did not reject his people. Israel remains beloved for the sake of the patriarchs; the gifts of grace and the callings of God remain irrevocable. In the image of the olive tree and its roots and branches, Paul says to the Romans: "It is not you that support the root, but the root that supports you" (Rom 11:18). Finally, Paul declares that God's salvific plan will be fulfilled only when all Israel, in the fulfillment of its faith and of the promises made to it, will have recognized the "Deliverer from Zion" (Rom 12:26).

In the interim, the Apostle recommends to Christians that they should set a convincing example by their witness in word and deed. As a result, Israel and the Church are to this day signs and witnesses to the fact that God has spoken and acted in history for the salvation of human beings. Israel and the Church live from the promise and fidelity of God. Belief in God's word and obedience to God's will are the ground of their existence. The Jews are thus to be characterized not as *infideles* (unbelievers) but as *fideles* (believers). Israel and the Church have the mandate not to be like other peoples; at the same time they are to be a sign raised up for all the world. Israel and the Church represent the fact, the fate, and the hope of the pilgrimaging people of God. This connection has often been forgotten in the course of the history of the Church.[6]

---

5. F. W. Maier, *Israel in der Heilsgeschichte nach Rom 9–11* (Munich, 1929); E. Peterson, "Die Kirche aus Juden und Heiden" in: *Theologische Traktate* (Munich, 1952) 241–92; John Oesterreicher, *The Israel of God: On the Old Testament Roots of the Church's Faith* (Englewood Cliffs, N.J.: Prentice Hall, 1963). In addition, the commentaries on Romans by K. Barth, J. Fitzmyer, O. Kuß, E. Käsemann, H. Schlier und U. Wilckens; D. Zeller, *Juden und Heiden in der Mission des Paulus* (Stuttgart, 1973); F. Mußner, *Tractate on the Jews* 52–74.

6. Material on the following to be found in: W. P. Eckert—E. L. Ehrlich, *Judenhaß— Schuld der Christen?* (Essen, 1964); H. Fries, "Überlegungen zum christlich–jüdischen Gespräch" in: *Wir und die andern* (Stuttgart, 1966) 208–39.

The Church understood itself as the New Israel and thus had no theological reason to bear enmity against Israel as such, even against post-Christian Israel. In addition, the Old Testament was present in the prayer and liturgy of the Church in numerous concrete ways. Despite this background, after the end of its own time of persecution and in the context of the Christian empire, Christianity made it almost its unique obligation to convert the supposedly obdurate and God-forsaken Jews, the progeny of those who cried out: "Let him be crucified!. . . His blood be on us and on our children" (Matthew 27:23, 25).

That, however, is a thesis which, used as a collective sentence, is utterly false. It doesn't even do justice to the simple fact that the condemnation of Jesus, on the face of it, was staged and carried out by Jewish officials of the time in consort with the Roman judiciary and military power: *Crucifixus sub Pontio Pilato*—crucified under Pontius Pilate.

But the theory of rejection remains. It grew out of an extensive *Adversus-Judaeos* literature. The Jews who refused to become Christians were accused of obstinacy and blindness. On the other hand, one finds in the Middle Ages, about the time from 800 to 1000, the concept—grounded in the *concordantia novi et veteris testamenti* , and getting expressed in older representations of Church and Synagogue under the cross—that Synagogue and Church symbolized the *ecclesia universalis.*[7] It is among the most astonishing facts that, in that particular time, not only were the Jews not subject to discrimination and persecution, but there existed an inner and outer harmony between Christian and Jews that was connected with legal equality. But soon the earlier conception of the *Adversus Judaeos* mentality gained the upper hand. Its new symbol was the representation of the Synagogue with blindfolded eyes and broken staff—in contrast to the radiant and victorious figure of the Church. In addition to that, there was the idea that, by the crucifixion of Jesus, the Jews had incurred the status of abiding servitude in the sense of slavery.

The Crusades opened wide the doors to open and brutal enmity towards the Jews—who were looked on simply as Christ-murderers—with the strange reasoning that it was necessary, when going to the Holy Land in order to win back the holy places for Christianity, first to kill the Jews in one's own homeland and take revenge on them. It was completely forgotten that the very blood of Christ does not cry out for vengeance by human hand. If one can also say that many popes, emperors, and bishops interceded for the rights of the Jews, they were still unable to prevent the atrocities against the Jews. The choice: baptism or death, was at that time nothing singular; baptism was often

---

7. Wolfgang Seiferth, *Synagogue and Church in the Middle Ages*, trans. Lee Chadeayne and Paul Gottwald (New York: Ungar, 1970).

accepted in order to escape death. But it was not unusual that the baptized Jews later fell into the hands of the Inquisition for suspicion of
heresy. The words of the crusade-preacher Bernard of Clairvaux to the
crusaders: "Go to Zion, defend the tomb of Christ your Lord, but lay no
hand on the Sons of Israel, and speak with them only in a friendly
manner, for they are the flesh and the bones of the Messiah, and if you
harm them, you run the risk of harming the Lord in the apple of his
eye," fell on deaf ears. Abelard, (1079-1142) otherwise the great oppo-
nent of Bernard, but in this matter in full agreement, depicted the situation of the Jews in these words:

> No nation has suffered the like for God. Dispersed among all nations, without
> king or secular princes, the Jews are oppressed with heavy taxes as if they were
> supposed to ransom their life anew each day. To mistreat Jews is considered a
> work pleasing to God. For such a captivity, such as the Jews suffer, the Christians
> were able to explain only from the extreme hatred of God. The life of the Jews is
> handed over to their most furious enemies. Even in sleep they are not left in peace
> by nightmares. Outside of heaven they have no secure place of refuge. When they
> want to travel to a neighboring locale, they must buy at great price the protection
> of those Christian princes who in truth wish them dead so as to confiscate their
> inheritance. The Jews cannot own fields and vineyards because there is no one
> there to guarantee their possession. Thus, the only occupation left to them was the
> business of money-lending, and this made them further hated among the Christians.

Expressed in these sentences is the agony, the incalculable entanglement of Jewish fate in the Christian realm. The Fourth Lateran
Council, under Innocent III (1215), ordained that Jews had to wear a visible sign of recognition, and on Good Friday remain in their homes.
Holy Week was for the Jews the worst time of the year. In the later
Middle Ages, supposed atrocities like ritual murder, desecration of
hosts, or—in the time of the great plague in the fourteenth century—
poisoning of wells, lead to the condemnation and killing of Jews.

The Reformation of the sixteenth century brought about no change
but, in some instances, a worsening of the situation. Of great importance
and consequence on this score is the position of Martin Luther.[8] First to
be mentioned is his work from the year 1523: That Jesus Christ was born
a Jew. In writing this, Luther was attending to the suspicion raised
against him that he was denying the truth of "Jesus, born of the Virgin
Mary."

Luther's presentations also had the intention of winning Jews for
Christ by friendly treatment. In doing so, Luther was consciously distancing himself from the treatment being inflicted on the Jews of his
time: "They have treated the Jews as if they were dogs and not human
beings."

His later works, above all his treatise against the Jews and their
lies (1543) was addressed not to Jews but to Christians. In order to

---

8. A basic study: J. Brosseder, *Luthers Stellung zu den Juden im Spiegel seiner Interpreten*
(Munich, 1972).

strengthen their faith, Luther drew a contrasting picture in view of the
Jews. They were depicted as human beings whom Jesus always and pur-
posely rejected and reviled. God preached to the Jews for 1500 years, so
they should know that. They who hear God's word for so long and say, I
do not want to know, their ignorance becomes not an excuse but sevenfold
guilt. One is dealing with ill-will, perversity, and stubbornness—those
symptoms which, in the views of the time, were characteristic of
heretics. Any hope that the Jews would convert was without prospect.
The question was, what concrete consequences were to be drawn according to the law of the time.

In his earlier writing, Luther was concerned to integrate the Jews
into the society of the time in order to convert them. As Luther came
more and more to the conviction that the conversion of the Jews to the
Christian faith would not succeed, he drew other consequences. He then
held the opinion that a tolerance of the Jews in Christian society was—
for the sake of the Christians—no longer justifiable; the toleration of
their religious practice, their worship in the synagogues, represented
blasphemy and a denial of the Christian faith. Christians, if they did
nothing, made themselves guilty of the sins of others.

Consequently Luther pleaded for what he called "harsh mercy."
He compared it with what physicians do who, in order to heal, have to
cause pain. Luther's proposal was: The synagogues and houses of the
Jews should be destroyed, for these are places where idolatry is practiced. The Jews should be gathered and put into ghettos so that they
would know that they are not the masters in our land. Their Talmud
and "Little Prayer Book" should be taken away, since they were all
stolen anyway. And finally, the Jews should emigrate to Palestine.

Should one say that Luther took over these counsels of "harsh
mercy" from the praxis of his time, that is correct; but it remains small
solace in view of the renewal from the Gospel for which the reformers
strove. Should one say that what Luther was doing in these arguments
was not anti-Semitism or a pamphlet against the Jews, or even persecution of the Jews, but a presentation of the Christian faith as he understood it in the sense of the doctrine of justification, in the sense of the
"through Christ alone," there remains the question: What follows from
this for an interpretation of the faith which leads to such consequences?

The effect of Luther's statements was that, later, the praxis recommended by him was adopted without attention to its theological
background. We cannot in this context pursue this troubling historical
development any further; but we must admit: Christian anti-Semitism
was one of the roots of present-day anti-Semitism, which certainly also
had other roots. The decisive impulses for the recognition of the Jews as

fellow human beings and fellow citizens came from Humanism and the Enlightenment. Lessing's *Nathan the Wise* is a moving witness to this.

It is only to be hoped that the experiences of our time, especially of the most recent German past, has opened or will definitively open the eyes of all human beings and Christians to the outrageous injustice of anti-Semitism. Christians must never again forget that anti-Semitism is a form of anti-Christianity. In the Time of National Socialism (Nazism), many did not understand, or did not want to understand, this connection. Otherwise, the solidarity would have been greater and more comprehensive; otherwise the confession and witness of the churches would have been more courageous, as the synagogues burned, and Jews were branded, persecuted, and deported, and finally so gruesomely annihilated. The horrible symbol of this is Auschwitz. The relationship of Jews and Christians can no longer, asserts J. B. Metz, be formulated and set down as if Auschwitz did not take place. "We Christians can never possibly put Auschwitz behind us; and we cannot possibly ever get over Auschwitz alone, but only along with the victims of Auschwitz. This is, in my eyes, the root of the Jewish-Christian ecumenical situation."

From this comes also the transition from missionizing to dialogue.[9] "We will come together with each other as Christians only when we, together, gain a new relationship to the Jewish people and their religion, not by turning our backs on Auschwitz but, by facing it give shape to the only form of Christianity that can be expected of us or allowed us after Auschwitz."[10]

The Statements of Vatican II

The relationship of Israel and the Church was also a theme of Vatican II. In the Declaration *Nostra aetate* (*Declaration on the Relationship of the Church to Non-Christian Religions*), it was given totally new fundamental expression.[11] The Declaration reads (no. 4):

As this sacred Synod searches into the mystery of the Church, it recalls the spiritual bond linking the people of the New Covenant with Abraham's stock.

For the Church of Christ acknowledges that, according to the mystery of God's saving design, the beginnings of her faith and her election are already found

9. Johannes Baptist Metz, "Ökumene nach Auschwitz. Zum Verhältnis von Christen und Juden in Deutschland" in: *Gott in Auschwitz. Dimensionen des Massenmords am jüdischen Volk* (Freiburg–Basel–Wien, 1979) 124. This discussion of the impact of the Holocaust on Christian theology has been a recurrent theme in the writing of Metz over the past two decades.

10. Ibid. 144

11. *Declaration on the Relationship of the Church to the Non–Christian Religions*. This context, the result of a difficult compromise, doesn't do justice to the matter. The theme itself is also found in the Dogmatic Constitution on the Church in: *Commentary on the Documents of Vatican II*, ed. H. Vorgrimler, 1.105–305.

among the patriarchs, Moses, and the prophets. She professes that all who believe in Christ, Abraham's sons according to faith (cf. Gal 3:7), are included in the same patriarch's call, and likewise that the salvation of the Church was mystically foreshadowed by the chosen people's exodus from the land of bondage.

The Church, therefore, cannot forget that she received the revelation of the Old Testament through the people with whom God in his inexpressible mercy deigned to establish the Ancient Covenant. Nor can she forget that she draws sustenance from the root of that good olive tree onto which have been grafted the wild olive branches of the Gentiles (cf. Rom.11:17–24). Indeed, the Church believes that by His cross Christ, our Peace, reconciled Jew and Gentile, making them both one in Himself (cf. Eph 2:14–16).

Also, the Church ever keeps in mind the words of the Apostle about his kinsmen, "who have the adoption as sons, and the glory and the covenant and the legislation and the worship and the promises; who have the fathers, and from whom is Christ according to the flesh" (Rom 9:4–5), the son of the Virgin Mary. The Church recalls too that from the Jewish people sprang the apostles, her foundation stones and pillars, as well as most of the early disciples who proclaimed Christ to the world.

As holy Scripture testifies, Jerusalem did not recognize the time of her visitation (cf. Luke 19:44), nor did the Jews in large number accept the Gospel; indeed not a few opposed the spreading of it (cf Rom. 11;28). Nevertheless, according to the apostle, the Jews still remain most dear to God because of their fathers, for he does not repent of the gifts he makes nor of the calls He issues (cf. Rom 11:28–29). In company with the prophets and the same Apostle, the Church awaits that day, known to God alone, on which all peoples will address the Lord in a single voice and "serve him with one accord" (Zeph 3:9, cf. Isa 66:23; Ps 65:4; Rom 11:11-32).

Since the spiritual patrimony common to Christians and Jews is so great, this sacred Synod wishes to foster and recommend that mutual understanding and respect which is the fruit above all of biblical and theological studies, and of brotherly dialogues.

True, authorities of the Jews and those who followed their lead pressed for the death of Christ (cf. Jn. 19:6), still, what happened in his passion cannot be blamed on all the Jews then living, without distinction, nor upon the Jews of today. Although the Church is the new people of God, the Jews should not be presented as repudiated or cursed by God, as if such views followed from the holy Scriptures. All should take pains, then, lest in catechetical instruction and in the preaching of God's word they teach anything out of harmony with the truth of the gospel and the spirit of Christ.

The Church repudiates all persecutions against any man. Moreover, mindful of her common patrimony with the Jews, and motivated by the gospel's spiritual love and by no political considerations, she deplores the hatred, persecutions, and displays of anit-Semitism directed against the Jews at any time and from any source.

Besides, as the Church has always held and continues to hold, Christ in his boundless love freely underwent his passion and death because of the sins of all men, so that all might attain salvation. It is, therefore, the duty of the Church's preaching to proclaim the cross of Christ as the sign of God's all-embracing love and as the fountain from which every grace flows.

PART TWO

JESUS AND THE CHURCH

JESUS' PROCLAMATION OF GOD'S RULE AND KINGDOM

What does Jesus' proclamation of God's Rule and Kingdom have to do with the theme "Jesus and the Church?" The question becomes acute when one takes into account that in the proclamation of Jesus, as far as it can be understood in the Synoptic Gospels, God's Rule and Kingdom stands in the center. The concept *basileia* (kingdom) occurs more than a hundred times, the word Church *(ekklesia)* only twice, and that from the same evangelist in exegetically strongly controverted places (Matthew 16:18 and 18:18). This is a remarkable state of affairs. It is easy to recognize in what direction will run the questions we have to ask. They are: Is the Church connected with Jesus' proclamation of God's Rule and Kingdom? Did it really happen the way the Constitution on the Church of Vatican II has it: "Jesus established the beginning of his Church by proclaiming the Good News, namely the arrival of the Kingdom of God that had been promised of old in the Scriptures" (no. 5)? Or is the Church the substitution, the embarrassment-avoiding solution for what was proclaimed but did not come about—namely, God's Rule? In other words, did it happen the way it is expressed in the classical statement of Alfred Loisy in his book *The Gospel and the Church*: "Jesus proclaimed the Kingdom of God, and what came was the church"? To get an orientation on these questions, it is important to speak first of God's Rule and Kingdom.

The Gospel of Mark, the oldest Gospel, depicts the beginning of the public activity of Jesus in Galilee with the words: "Now after John was arrested, Jesus came into Galilee, preaching the Gospel of God, and saying, 'The time is fulfilled, and the kingdom of God is at hand; repent, and believe in the Gospel'"(Mark 1:14–15).

Matthew 4:17 is similar: Jesus proclaimed: "Repent, for the Kingdom of Heaven is at hand." When the Gospel of Matthewhew says "Kingdom of Heaven" instead of kingdom of God, it is following a Jewish custom of that time not to speak the name of God but to use circumlocutions, e.g., by using the word heaven. In Matthew this account of the proclamation of Jesus is preceded by the account of the preaching of the Baptist: "Repent, for the Kingdom of Heaven is at hand" (Matthew 3:1).

What Is the Kingdom of God, the Kingdom of Heaven?[1]

It is not the kingdom that is or will be in heaven, but the rule and the kingdom of the One who is in heaven. The kingdom of God is no territory, no spatially clear, circumscribable region, but a condition, a situation, a mode of existence: that existence in which God, the lordship, and the divinity of God, is recognized as the all-decisive reality and gets actualized and comes to completion in the life of human beings, individually and in community.

The word used for God's Rule and Kingdom, *basileia,* is not an original creation of Jesus. With it he connects with statements and realities already found in the Old Testament, namely in the message, which is simultaneously promise and obligation, Yahweh is the Lord, the King of Israel. Yahweh's word and will are to be the foundation and basic order in Israel, Yahweh's people.

Let us ask more precisely what conceptions were connected with the idea of God's Rule and Kingdom within the Old Testament. They are the following:

1. The presential conception: Yahweh is Lord and king as the savior, helper, leader, and guide of the People of Israel. This is much more of a dynamic than a merely static conception: Yahweh rules in the history of his people, whose ways he effects and guides.

Yahweh—another presential concept—rules; Yahweh is King as Lord of heaven and earth. This being-Lord of Yahweh is grounded in the fact that Yahweh is the Creator of the world. This is not an act done just once, but an ongoing activity. For creation is, by its nature, dependent on the Creator as its ongoing ground of being. The identification of Yahweh with the Creator and Lord all is the special message of later Judaism and hence also the message of the prophets.

2. Next to the presential is the futuristic conception: Yahweh will come and establish His rule. It is the word of the coming, the eschatological kingdom. This becomes especially vital as hope in the midst of Israel's misery, in its situation of defeat, captivity, and exile.

---

1. On "Kingdom of God," consult the commentaries and theologies of the New Testament as well as the standard theological reference works. In addition: Martin Buber, *Kingship of God* (New York: Harper & Row, 1967); Rudolf Schnackenburg, *God's Rule and Kingdom,* trans. John Murray (New York: Herder and Herder, 1963); G. Gloege, *Reich Gottes und Kirche im Neuen Testament* (Darmstadt, 1961); Wolfhart Pannenberg, *Theologie und Reich Gottes* (Gütersloh, 1971); H. Merklein, *Jesu Botschaft von der Gottesherrschaft* (Stuttgart, 1983).

There is no contradiction between these two conceptions. The expectation of the coming does not signify the suspension of the rule of God in the present. The fact that God is coming takes on certainty from the fact that God has already proven Himself as present and active.

3. Connected with the conception of the coming rule, the coming kingdom, are various motifs and concepts about the manner in which God will establish his rule in the world. Yahweh comes as the victor over His enemies and exercises judgment over them. They are likewise the enemies of the People of Israel. The success and victory-theology from Israel's early years also acts as a leitmotif in the future and for it.

Along with this comes another conception of Yahweh's Rule and Kingdom: Yahweh will bring an end to all injustice and all oppression:

The Lord of hosts will make for all peoples a feast. He will destroy . . . . the covering that is cast over all peoples, the veil that is spread over all nations. He will swallow up death forever, and the Lord God will wipe away tears from all faces, and the reproach of his people he will take away from all the earth. (Isa 25:6–8)

In the description of the new exodus of Israel from exile and captivity, Yahweh is described as Savior, but not under the sign of power and glory. Yahweh is hoped for as Bringer of Peace, the kingdom of peace is to be the homeland of the nations (Isaiah 40—42). No earthly king will ever again be the representative of Yahweh.

After the Exile, the idea of Yahweh's Rule and Kingdom, of Yahweh's Kingship, again took on national, restorational traits. The memory of former national greatness, of the House of David, was awakened. Yahweh's Rule and Kingdom meant freedom from need and foreign rule, freedom for the Law and the worship of God.

Apocalyptic—as in the Book of Daniel—connected universal and cosmic traits with the future Kingdom of Yahweh. Yahweh comes in great power and glory, Yahweh comes in the clouds of heaven. The sign of this coming are cosmic disasters: earthquakes, darkness, famine, war, persecutions, being delivered up to evil hands. All this was described in the apocalyptic literature, and indeed according the conception favored at that time, when the measure of evil is full, when the power of evil has risen up worldwide, Yahweh will intervene and bring in the new time of salvation with the community of the elect. The mediator and bringer of this new and eternal Kingdom will be the Son of Man.

The standard figure for apocalyptic expectation is taken from the Book of Daniel, where the following vision is described:

I saw in the night visions, and behold, with the clouds of heaven there came one like a Son of Man, and he came to the Ancient of Days and was presented before him. And to him was given dominion and glory and kingdom, that all peoples, nations, and languages should serve him; his dominion is an everlasting dominion, which shall not pass away, and his kingdom one that shall not be destroyed. (Dan 7:13–14)

The Rabbinic Schools developed the idea of a present but hidden Rule of God. Connected with this was the belief that one could bring in the Rule and Kingdom of Yahweh by obedience and fidelity to the Law. Among the group of Essenes and the pious ones of Qumran, the kingdom of God is the Kingdom of the Elect, of the righteous, of the so-called Sons of Light, who can be this only if there is the kingdom of darkness and the sons of darkness, who are in battle against the light, but who will be annihilated in this battle.

In this rich stream of tradition, with its wealth of motifs relative to what is supposed to be the content of God's Rule and Kingdom, stands the proclamation of Jesus. It stands there both in connection and in contradiction.

Jesus' Proclamation of the Kingdom of God

The first statement in the proclamation of Jesus reads: The Kingdom of God, the Kingdom of Heaven is near at hand. This simple statement can be interpreted, and indeed it has been so interpreted, the Kingdom of God has come near—has indeed already come. Or, The Kingdom of God is in the vicinity, but is not yet here in full form.

Jesus does not mean, with the Rule of God proclaimed by him, that form of divine lordship that comes with the creation of the world and with divine governance, but a form different from that; he means the coming of a new form. Still less does the preaching of Jesus mean a condition brought about by human beings, which would then be called the Kingdom of God. The Kingdom of God will not be created, established, built, or brought about by human beings. It comes; it is the activity and work of God; it is the seed sown by him. Human beings can make themselves open for the coming of this kingdom, make and hold themselves ready for it. They can pray for the coming of the kingdom; they can seek it, the way one seeks for a precious pearl, for a treasure in the field.

God's Rule and Kingdom is the proclamation of a good news, it is the declaration of peace, joy, and salvation. This special quality of the message of Jesus becomes recognizable in comparison with the Kingdom-of-God preaching of the forerunner, John the Baptist (Matthew 3:1–12), which was a fire-and-brimstone preaching:

You brood of vipers! Who warned you to flee from the wrath to come? Bear fruit that befits repentance, and do not presume to say to yourselves, "We have Abraham as our father"; for I tell you, God is able from these stones to raise up children to Abraham. Even now the axe is laid to the root of the trees; every tree therefore that does `not bear good fruit is cut down and thrown into the fire. I baptize you with water for repentance, but he who is coming after me is mightier than I, whose sandals I am not worthy to carry: he will baptize you with the Holy Spirit and with fire. His winnowing fork is in his hand, and he will clear his threshing floor and gather his wheat into the granary, but the chaff he will burn with unquenchable fire. (Matthew 3:7–12).

Quite different is the sound of the proclamation of God's Rule and Kingdom by Jesus. It is the declaration of a rule of God in the form of joy, of hope, of consolation, of affirmation, and of the forgivenes of guilt— particularly for those on the darker side. In the language of the time, it was for tax collectors and sinners, for those plagued with suffering and sickness. The most beautiful and most moving parables in the preaching of Jesus have to do with pain over the lost and joy over the found. This motif varies in images from the lost and found coin, to the lost and con- fused sheep in the wilderness, but most strikingly in the inexhaustible depth of the parable of the lost son (Luke 15).

The word-proclamation becomes a sign-action and deed-action: Jesus practices table fellowship with tax collectors and sinners. In the community of the meal he assures them of community with himself and with his message, to the chagrin and anger of the pious and just. In or- der to recognize what is so special about this orientation of Jesus, one must keep in mind the kind of thing found in the rule of the monks from Qumran at the time of Jesus: "Fools, the insane, the simple-minded, the lame, the deformed, the deaf and the underage—none of these are permitted to be accepted into the community."

The so-called first sermon of Jesus in his home city of Nazareth is a fine example of Jesus' message and program (Luke 4:18):

> And he came to Nazareth, where he had been brought up; and he went to the synagogue, as his custom was, on the Sabbath day, and he stood up to read; and there was given to him the book of the prophet Isaiah. He opened the book and found the place where it was written, "The Spirit of the Lord is upon me, because he has anointed me to preach good news to the poor. He has sent me to proclaim re- lease to the captives and recovering sight to the blind, to set at liberty those who are oppressed, to proclaim the acceptable year of the Lord." And he closed the book and gave it back to the attendant, and sat down; and the eyes of all in the synagogue were fixed on him. And he began to say to them, "Today this scripture has been fulfilled in your hearing." And all spoke well of him, and wondered at the gracious words which proceeded from his mouth. (Luke 14:16–22)

The words of the Sermon on the Mount (Matthew 5–7), words about God's Rule and Kingdom, speak to those whom one normally thinks are excluded: those who are poor before God, the grieving, those who use no force, who hunger and thirst for justice, the merciful, the clean of heart, the peacemakers, those persecuted for the sake of justice.

God's Rule and Kingdom as invitation from God is the salvation of human beings. This invitation will establish that situation and mode of existence in which human beings reach perfect fulfillment, that situ- ation and mode of existence in which they are open for God, hearers of God's word, and receivers of God's favors. Constituent of this situation and mode of existence are poverty, suffering, persecution, readiness to forgive, and peacemaking, the very realities on which the beatitudes are grounded.

In Jesus' message of the Kingdom of God, the idea of judgment is not lacking. But judgment is not the first word, but a word spoken as answer to the conscious refusal or rejection of God's invitation.

It is clear that in the proclamation of Jesus there are various motifs of the traditional contents of God's Rule and Kingdom. But one thing is especially clear: Jesus' proclamation contradicts the conception of a kingdom of Yahweh understood in terms of the politics of national power, and manifesting itself in war, victory and success.

The sign of this contradiction is the refusal of Jesus to let himself be elevated to a political Messiah—according to the account of the Gospel of John—after the sign of the multiplication of the loaves (John 6:15). Add to this also Jesus' refusal to let himself be played out against the Roman emperor, with the familiar saying: "Give to Caesar what is Caesar's," a saying that at the same time contains a criticism, for he adds: "Give to God what is God's" (Matthew 22:21). Caesar cannot be given what is to be given to God, what is God's. A sign of this attitude of Jesus is the admonishment of Peter, who wanted to rescue Jesus with force when he was being taken captive (Matthew 26:51).

Especially filled with meaning is the sign-action with which Jesus surrounds his entry into Jerusalem: He is the fulfillment of the word (Zech 9:9): "Tell the daughter of Zion, Behold, your king is coming to you, humble, and mounted on an ass, and on a colt, the foal of an ass" (Matthew 21:5).

All these words and deeds of Jesus are unpolitical, if by "political" one understands power politics. But they are political, and indeed to the highest degree, inasmuch as they are applied not only to the isolated individuals but also to the public, to society and the nation, and also because they intend to be effective in the nation and for the nation and its activity and behavior. Included in their goal is the transformation of unjust conditions.

When Jesus rejects the limitation of God's Rule and Kingdom to the nation, to the People of Israel alone, to the descendants of Abraham, this is what it means: God's Rule and Kingdom is an invitation extended to all. The sign of this universality is Jesus' explicit invitation to the many who "will come from east and west and sit at table with Abraham, Isaac, and Jacob in the Kingdom of Heaven" (Matthew 8:11).

Jesus' proclamation of God's Rule and Kingdom which takes place as offer, invitation, and Gospel, calls forth an answer on the part of human beings in the form of a challenge and a decision. The first demand is: Reform! The earlier or otherwise customary word: Do Penance! contains, over-against that of Reform, a narrowing, connected with a negative aspect. Reform means, literally, strike out in another direction, on another course; do not remain where one is, but take care to become what one should be.

That means, in the sense of Jesus' preaching: Let God be God; recognize God as the all-determining reality. Put another way, it means: Break out of the self-centered aspect of being human; dismantle self-pride; see and make truly real their finite, creaturely, owed, and broken existence, i.e., their existence before God.

The second demand is, in the words of Mark: "Believe the Gospel" (Mark 1:15). Faith/belief is the positive side of reform. Faith is opening oneself up for the hearing and receiving of the message of salvation. It is the readiness to be drawn into that message, and to exist in and from that ground.

The third demand connected with the proclamation of Jesus reads: "Follow me!" From the literally understood "follow along behind him" there comes the greater meaning of the following or imitation of Christ. Following does not mean a slavish imitating, but signifies taking over the mind and the mode of existence of Jesus. It means to understand and make one's life real as Jesus did: as existence from God and for God and for human beings in the attitude of self-giving and freedom. To follow Jesus means to verify, in existence for others, existence for God; and in existence for others to open up the dimension of God.

This is expressed in the connection Jesus insisted on between love of God and love of neighbor, which is a basic theme of the New Testament. Love for God, its verification in love for human beings, for one's neighbor, for people in situations such as depicted in Jesus' judgment sermons: love for the hungry, the thirsty, the homeless, the naked, the sick, those in prison (Matthew 25:3–37)—that is not a past but an ever-present situation. Jesus pushes the demand for love of one's neighbor right up to love for one's enemy (Matthew 5:43–48). Love for human beings, however, especially in this extreme and radical form, is made possible by God's love for us and by our love as the readiness to be the completion of this divine gift to us. Schillebeeckx expresses this in the strikingly concentrated formulation: "God's rule is the power of God's love turned towards humankind."[2]

All these moments, above all the last-mentioned one of imitation/following, point to the fact that Jesus is the one who, like the prophets, proclaims and declares the message of God's Rule and Kingdom, and also that the nearness and the achieved presence of the kingdom is connected with him in a special way.

---

2. Edward Schillebeeckx, *Jesus, An Experiment in Christology*, trans. Herbert Hoskins (New York: Seabury Press, 1979) 140–54.

"IMMINENT EXPECTATION" AND THE
PROBLEM OF THE CHURCH

Many of the parables of God's Rule and Kingdom point to the fact that Jesus expected in an unqualified way the coming of this kingdom in the near future. The constantly recurring warnings to be watchful, to be ready for the imminent and surprising coming—"Like a thief in the night"—are expressions of this imminent expectation.[1] True enough, Jesus explicitly rejects any precise determination or calculation of the time. But there are some texts, which, because they indicate a time within Jesus' own generation, actually seem to point to the time of the end-event expected by Jesus. These are the so-called texts of imminent expectation.

Some read Jesus not only as speaking of the presence and the future of God's Rule and Kingdom, but also as reckoning with the immediate breaking in of God's rule in power and glory. If that is an accurate reading, then the idea of a Church as institution is excluded from the outset. Whoever is figuring on the immediately proximate end has no concern for a future which will already come to an end on the next day. And vice versa: Any appeal of the Church back to an institution by Jesus is impossible and inadmissible, because under the presupposition of an imminent expectation, there is no place for a phenomenon like Church to which, of course, institutions belong.

The Texts of Imminent Expectation

When they persecute you in one town, flee to the next; for truly, I say to you, you will not have gone through all the towns of Israel, before the Son of man comes. (Matthew 10:23)

1. E. Grasser, *Das Problem der Parusieverzögerung in den synoptischen Evangelien und in der Apostelgeschichte* (Berlin, 1957); Rudolf Schnackenburg, *God's Rule and Kingdom* (New York, 1963) 195–214; ibid., "Naherwartung" in: *LThK* 7.777–79; A. Strobel, *Untersuchungen zum eschatologischen Verzögerungsproblem* (Leiden, 1961).

And he said to them, "Truly I say to you, there are some standing here who will not taste death before they see the kingdom of God come with power." (Mark 9:1)

There are two variations of the following passage:

But I tell you truly, there are some standing here who will not taste death before they see the kingdom of God. (Luke 9:27)

Truly, I say to you, there are some standing here who will not taste death before they see the Son of man coming in his kingdom. (Matthew 16:28)

Rudolf Schnackenburg and Heinz Schürmann,[2] among others, explain that the interpretation of these texts is among the stickiest and most difficult tasks that New Testament exegetes have. On the one hand, nothing can be solved by sleight-of-hand, and on the other hand, a careful consideration of all the texts forbids them from being satisfied with the obvious explanation that Jesus was simply mistaken and that the primitive Church reinterpreted his imminent expectation. That would mean the confirmation of Loisy's statement: "What was proclaimed was the kingdom of God, what has come is the church" as a contradiction between the proclamation of Jesus and the factual reality of the Church.

Attempts at Interpretation

A certain aid to the interpretation of these texts comes from the fact, as we have already mentioned, that, in contrast to apocalyptic, setting a date for the imminent expectation is strictly rejected. And even more: in Mark 13:32 stands the likewise not easily explainable statement of Jesus: "But of that day or that hour no one knows, not even the angels in heaven, nor the Son, but only the Father"—a saying whose difficulty attests to its authority.

A second orientation is found in the fact that Jesus as prophet, as "more than a prophet," makes use of prophetic discourse and its style of speaking. Statements about a temporal proximity—in the prophets it takes the form of the declaration of the proximity of the Day of Yahweh—are not made in order to set down a length of time. Instead they serve the purpose of depicting the seriousness of the situation in order to lend emphasis to the appeal to reform, to being prepared, to watchfulness, and to the urgency of the decision.

The thesis that, in what he said about imminent expectation Jesus had succumbed to the apocalyptic trend and was deceived on this point, does not take into account those texts in which he is talking about the already-realized presence of the kingdom of God, as well as about its fate as an historical course of events. Such a thesis also gives too little weight to the many words that speak about perseverance and patience;

2. "Zur Traditions- und Redaktionsgeschichte von Mt 10, 23" in: *BZ* 3 (1959) 82–88.

it misses the point of the parables of the kingdom of God, which presuppose long durations of time (Matthew 25:19).

In other words, the real question is about the meaning to be given to the statements of imminent expectation in the whole context of the preaching of Jesus. This also raises the question of the (situation-in life/situation-in-the-gospel) context in which these statements of imminent expectation are found.

Matthew 10:23 stands in connection with the sermon commissioning the Twelve, the so-called small mission instruction. Jesus is sending out the Twelve. They are, like Jesus himself, to proclaim the message of the nearness of God's Rule and Kingdom; they are, like Jesus, to heal the sick and drive out demons.

Jesus gives the Twelve precise instructions and leaves them in no doubt about their fate. It stands under the motto: "I send you out as sheep in the midst of wolves; so be wise as serpents and innocent as doves" (Matthew 10:16). At the same time, Jesus wants to encourage and console them. He does this with the words: "You will not have gone through all the towns of Israel, before the Son of Man comes" (Matthew 10:23).

The exegetes, above all, as we have mentioned, R. Schnackenburg and H. Schürmann, ask whether these words from the commissioning speech originally stood in this context. To ask such a question is by no means an artificial procedure, but quite to the point. For Matthew does not make primarily biographical-historical references; he composes and shapes theologically, and arranges different layers of the tradition under an overall theme. That can be seen in the cycle of sayings of Matthew 5–7, or in the cycle of the parables (Matthew 13) or in the so-called miracle cycle.

From observations like these, and from a text and word comparison, it turns out that what Matthew presents as a text from a commissioning speech about the persecution of the disciples and their flight from city to city originally belonged to the judgment sermons. Explaining it this way falls back on the fact that the sentence which introduces and grounds the situation of persecution and flight ("You will be hated by all for my name's sake. But he who endures to the end will be saved" [Matthew 10:22]) stands word for word in the judgment sermon of Mark 13:13, and the same is true of Luke 21:17. Matthew takes over these words of Jesus from the tradition of the judgment sermons and the situation of persecution described there, in order to describe thereby the fate of the disciples being sent out by Jesus. Words from the eschatological judgment sermon are used to characterize the fate of the disciples: hate, persecution, and flight. For this reason, those words about the persecution of the disciples from city to city belong not in the mission sermon but in the judgment sermon. Matthew connects two originally different traditions of series of sayings from a Markan and non-Markan tradition, namely the sayings source (Q), and out of this shapes a sermon of consolation to the disciples in view of their difficult mission of being "sent like sheep among wolves."

Another interpretation of the same passage is give by Julius Schniewind.[3] This interpretation says that in Matthew 10:23 we have in fact a sermon about the mission of the disciples and the situation of persecution and flight connected with it. But what is really meant is the disciple of Jesus as such, the Christian missionary as such, who is represented by the disciple Matthew and who also, like the disciples of Jesus is not exempt from the fate of disciples—tribulation, flight, and persecution—with nothing left out.

The mission of the disciples of Jesus has its first and immediate partner in Israel, in the cities of Israel. Accordingly, what Matthew 10:23 says is: The mission in Israel will in fact not come to an end until the Son of Man comes at the end of time. This interpretation is not impossible in the New Testament when we keep in mind that the cities of Israel in their official representation rejected Jesus and his disciples, that the mission in the cities of Israel came to a standstill, and that finally the unification and the reconciliation of Israel with the message of Jesus was a living ecumenical hope of the Apostle Paul, which he expressed in the Epistle to the Romans 9–11.

As a result of these attempts at interpretation, one can conclude that even these passages, which are regarded as the classical expressions of Jesus' imminent expectation must not necessarily be interpreted as temporally limited in a narrow way and restricted to the expectation in the time of the Twelve of God's Rule and Kingdom in the form of power and fulfillment.

In conclusion, we adduce the judgment of Josef Schmid:[4] These words must keep their value as genuine words of Jesus because of their factual difficulty. Matthew took up these words in his universally intended Gospel, even though, as he wrote, the gospel had long since pressed out beyond Israel and thus contradicted the wording of this passage which, when kept in the context of the mission sermon, still said that the end of the world would come before the gospel had extended beyond Israel to the Gentiles. It is no longer possible for us to interpret these words in such a way as to do full justice to text, context, and wording, and still leave us with no other factual problems.

The text of Mark 9:1— "And he said to them, 'Truly, I say to you, there are some standing here who will not taste death before they see that the kingdom of God has come with power"—has already been

---

3. "Das Evangelium nach Matthäus" in: *Das Neue Testament Deutsch* (Göttingen, 1937) 125–28.

4. *Das Evangelium nach Matthäus*, 3d ed. (Regensburg, 1956) 179–81.

changed in Matthew 16:28 into the version "before they see the Son of Man coming in his kingdom," and in Luke 9:27 to "before they see the kingdom of God." This modification within the synoptic tradition is noteworthy. It shows that the text of Mark caused difficulties because it spoke of an imminent expectation that did not come about, or came about in a way different than one expected. But even the changes in Matthew and Luke leave open a broad range of interpretations. The version "before they see the kingdom of God" (Luke 9:27), thus without the addition "kingdom of God with power," without the verb "come," could be interpreted in such a way that Luke, who has been called the evangelist and theologian of salvation history, wanted to point out the "middle time" (*Mitte der Zeit*) which he emphasized in a special way. What he wanted to say was: In the person, life, word, and activity of Jesus is to be seen what the kingdom of God is.[5]

The passage itself of Mark 9:1 and the change in Matthew 16:28 to the version "Before they see the Son of Man coming in his kingdom" are interpreted by W. Pannenberg in the following way: The words about the coming of the Son of Man in his kingdom as words of Jesus' imminent expectation did not come about as an expectation of temporal proximity, but they did not remain unfulfilled. "It is fulfilled in the only way in which fulfillment can be spoken of anyway, namely, in such a way that the original meaning of the promise is changed by an event that corresponds to it and yet is different from what the prediction said." The resurrection of Jesus from the dead can be seen as the coming of the Son of Man, as the coming of his kingdom in power, and thus as fulfillment of the imminent expectation. For what happened in the resurrection of Jesus from the dead brought about something unheard of and uniquely new: the overcoming of death as the universal power over human beings.

What remains to come, what is not yet fulfilled, is the universal, cosmic dimension of this expectation: the general resurrection from the dead as the hope of human beings. "Nevertheless, the resurrection of Jesus justifies the imminent expectation which had moved him, and grounds anew for the rest of humanity the eschatological expectation already fulfilled in him."[6]

The final text needs a bit of attention: Mark 13:30 = Matthew 24:34 = Luke 21:22: "Truly, I say to you, this generation will not pass away before all these things take place." What "all these things" means is found in the whole of Mark 13. There one reads of the end and of the end of time, of the destruction of Jerusalem and the Temple, of great tribula-

5. Hans Conzelmann, *The Theology of St. Luke*, trans. Geoffrey Buswell (Philadelphia: Fortress Press, 1982).

6. Wolfhart Pannenberg, *Jesus: God and Man*, trans. Lewis L. Wilkins and Duane A. Priebe (Philadelphia: Westminster Press, 1977) 226.

tion, of persecutions, of cosmic disasters, of the temptations, hence, of the signs that will precede the end as the coming of the Son of Man. The interpretation of "This generation will not pass away before all these things take place" would be possible in view of those being immediately addressed, if only the destruction of Jerusalem were meant, but the end of all history is meant.

The interpretation of the text "This race, this generation will not pass away" would be quite simple, if it were talking not about the immediately addressed contemporary generation, but about the whole People of Israel. Then the meaning of the message would be: Israel will not pass away, Israel will last until all these things, the events at the end of history, take place. "The existence of the Jewish people through all periods of history is the great sign of the truth of Jesus' words."[7]

Another interpretation is given by the exegete M. Meinertz.[8] He says that the expression "this generation" is a technical term found frequently in the Old and New Testaments. It is an expression with an accusatory sense; it means not the contemporary generation, but human beings who refuse the call to reform and to faith, turn away, and close themselves off. These human beings will always be, even at the end as well. Those immediately addressed are, so to speak, the representatives of the human beings of this attitude.

A concluding remark: Jesus made use of contemporary conceptions for the preaching of his message. The matter of the message itself, the Gospel of God's Rule and Kingdom, however, in no way stands and falls with these apocalyptic conceptions, but can be separated from them. It retains its full meaning even in a changed horizon of expectation.

The Result

These interpretations are not only signs of careful exegesis, they are also, and even more so, signs of a consciousness of a problem, signs of difficulty that arise out of Christology as a whole, out of the Christology of the New Testament, and out of the Christology of ecclesiastical dogmas. Above all they arise from the problem: Was Jesus deceived, or was he mistaken? If Jesus had been mistaken, what would be the consequences? For systematic Christology these are very serious questions. They have massive implications for affirmations about Jesus as definitive revealer/revelation, as someone identical with His message.

How, on this point, is the tension between exegesis and dogmatics to be viewed; between an exegesis on the one hand which may not and cannot be forgotten, i.e., that there is a Christology that has come about

---

7. F. Mußner, *Was lehrt Jesus vom Ende der Welt?* (Munich, 1958) 64, ET: *What Did Jesus Teach about the End of the World?* (Ann Arbor, Mich.: Word of Life, 1974).

8. "Dieses Geschlecht im NT" in: *BZ* 3 (1959) 283.

historically, and which was understood as interpretation of Scripture; and a dogmatics on the other hand which today cannot act as if there were no exegesis or as if it could operate according to the motto: dogma commands history?

In his book *On Being a Christian* Hans Küng also treated this question.[9] He said, Jesus expected the Kingdom of God to come imminently—that is what the oldest texts say. But in the New Testament there is already recognizable a process of defusing and transition. The end of this development is found in the Second Letter of Peter, where it is asked: "Where is the promise of his coming? For ever since the fathers fell asleep, all things have continued as they were from the beginning of creation" (2 Pet 3:4). And then the answer comes: "Do not ignore this one fact, beloved, that with the Lord one day is as a thousand years, and a thousand years as one day" (2 Pet 3:8).

Examining Jesus, Küng asks the question: Was he not ultimately an apocalyptic enthusiast? Was he not caught in an illusion? In brief— wasn't he simply *mistaken?* "One doesn't necessarily have to have dogmatic reservations in order to concede this if necessary. To err is human. And if Jesus was truly human, he too could be mistaken." After this somewhat imprecise way of putting it, which would allow one to draw any conclusion whatever—anything and everything that is human must thus also be found in Jesus, otherwise he wouldn't be truly human—comes a revision: "In the sense of cosmic wisdom, it was a mistake—but the question remains whether the concept *error* is the right one in this context."

Küng asks a counter question: The narrator of Genesis, the narrarator of the six working days, and of the creation of human beings, was he in error because he was disavowed by the later scientific description of the coming to be of the world and of human beings—which for many Christians of the modern age signified no small disappointment and temptation, but which for most people today is taken for granted? But do we not find in this process of factual "demythologization" the very thing about which the author was most concerned—God as origin of everything, and not in competition with an evil counter-principle, the goodness of everything created and the greatness of the human being? Is not all this preserved, and indeed made even more clear by the stripping off of ideological wrappings? In this context of the beginning of the world, the concept of error comes across as undifferentiated and out of place. The same holds for the words about the end of the world.

Jesus spoke as a matter of course in the apocalyptic frame of reference and in the conceptual forms of his time. And even if he expressly rejected precise calculations of the eschatological fulfillment and severely limited the imaginative elabo-

9. Hans Küng, *On Being a Christian*, trans. Edward Quinn (Garden City, N.Y.: Doubleday & Co. Inc., 1976) 216–23.

ration of the Kingdom of God in comparison with early Jewish apocalyptic, he still remained fundamentally in the framework of understanding of imminent expectation, in the horizon of apocalyptic that is so foreign to us today. This framework of understanding has been superseded by historical development, the apocalyptic horizon has faded away—this must clearly be seen. From our present-day perspective, we have to say: In the matter of imminent expectation, one is dealing less with an error than with a time-conditioned, time-bound way of looking at the world, which Jesus shared with his contemporaries. It cannot be revived artificially. And indeed it shouldn't, since, in so-called apocalyptic times, the temptation arises again and again to have it revived for our so different horizon of experience. The apocalyptic framework of image and concept of that time, which has become so strange to us, would today only conceal and misrepresent the intended meaning.[10]

Today, it all comes down to the question whether the fundamental idea of Jesus, whether the agenda which Jesus had with his proclamation of the coming of the Kingdom of God, still has any meaning, i.e., in the completely changed horizon of experience of a humanity that has basically become used to the fact that the course of world history, at least for the time being, is going to continue. Or one can put the question positively: Just how is it that Jesus' message has remained so moving beyond his death and beyond the end that did not come about, and indeed only after that "end" got correctly formulated?

If everything rose and fell with the temporally fixed imminent expectation of the New Testament, such an outcome would be totally inexplicable. The whole process from which the Church grew would necessarily have ended after a short time. How the assertion of imminent expectation can be "translated" for our situation is explained by W. Pannenberg:[11] The imminent expectation of God's rule, which characterized the appearance and life of Jesus, is for us no longer realizable. The two thousand years that have intervened make this impossible. The mere progress of historical time makes any attitude that can be appropriated today into something somewhat different from the imminent expectation of Jesus. We can no longer take part in the imminent expectation of Jesus; we can, however, live and think in continuity with it and also with the appearance of Jesus, if we recognize the imminent expectation of Jesus as fulfilled in a preliminary way in Jesus' own resurrection, and as long as its still-awaited universal effect, the general resurrection from the dead as entrance into the Kingdom of God, also remains our expectation and hope. In contrast with the imminent expectation of the time of Jesus, this expectation is not related to a specific point in time, and it is therefore not superseded by the process of historical time; rather, as with all traditional ideas, it is seen in a new light. The continuation of Christian hope in the fu-

---

10. Ibid. 219–20 [translation ours].
11. W. Pannenberg, *Jesus: God and Man*, 242.

ture was the object of controversies which ended with its being held with unshakable firmness, but without further temporal specification.

According to Pannenberg, imminent expectation understood this way has set free an understanding of human beings that remains to this day the most profound revelation of the human situation in the world.

The message of Jesus about the nearness of God's rule has called human beings out of the assurances of their everyday forms of life and thereby exposed the ephemerality of every this-worldly form of life and fulfillment of life. In the light of the message of the nearness of God's rule it became clear, even independently of the term of its breaking in, what the destiny of human beings is: Human beings as human beings are always something more than the present situation; their meaning is not fulfilled in any already existing sphere of their life. It is through their orientation of openness to the future, and also to the world, that human beings realize the opening up of their existence for the future of God; but this opening up is independent of all more precise specifications of time.[12]

Summing up, we can say: If imminent expectation were the central and all-decisive element in the preaching of Jesus, then it would be understandable how the nonarrival of the parousia understood in this way would not have been without rather severe disturbances of faith. Consequently, the ground and content of belief in the message of the kingdom of God are not dissolved and lessened by the nonarrival of the parousia. Belief in an imminent Second Coming was understandable for many reasons—through that which already was: above all through the resurrection of Jesus from the dead as act of the power of God over death. What took place in Jesus is an understandable ground of imminent expectation. But isn't it true that the failure of imminent expectation was what first brought forth the idea of the fulfillment and presence of the Kingdom of God in Jesus and the Jesus-event? It is exactly the other way around.

Certainty of the future, i.e., that Jesus is coming as the Son of Man and judge of the world, lies in the fact that he has already come; the certainty of the future lies in the present. In the New Testament, "eschatology is the affirmation of the present as revealed towards a genuine future; eschatology is not the affirmation of an anticipated future back into the present." On the other hand, the question of *when* does play a psychologically understandable important role; but psychological intensity is not identical with theological significance. The eschatological statements are basically "statements of Christology and anthropology oriented towards fulfillment."[13]

From these considerations, Heinz Schürmann explains that the meaning and intention of the texts of imminent expectation could be ex-

---

12. Ibid. 226; cf. also Karl Rahner, "The Hermeneutics of Eschatological Assertions," *Theological Investigations 4* (New York, 1966) 323–46.
    13. Ibid. 346.

pressed with the concept "continual expectation."[14] Karl Rahner says that for him, imminent expectation is the true way in which he in his situation has to make real the nearness of God calling him to unconditioned decision. On the other hand, it is of the nature of human consciousness to have an unknown future before it.[15] More cannot be said, but nothing more needs to be said.

14. H. Schürmann, "Zur Traditions- und Redaktionsgeschichte von Mt 10, 23."
15. K. Rahner, *Foundations of Christian Faith* 250.

KINGDOM OF GOD AND CHURCH

The leitmotif of the theme "Kingdom of God and Church" can be expressed: "The Kingdom of God was proclaimed, the Church came." This statement is capable of very different interpretations.

Interpretations

The Church came because the fullness of the arrival of the Kingdom of God in power and glory, which was expected as imminent, was not accepted and taken up, and to that extent did not come. Church is the result not of an illusion but of an invitation rejected, a message refused, a faith refused; the result, in other words, of a failure.

The idea was represented by Romano Guardini. He asks: What would have happened if the People of Israel had accepted the message of the kingdom? He answers: Then

the glory of God would indeed have come in glory. As Jesus preached the Sermon on the Mount—and not that only, but quite a few others in the same powerful and self-assured manner—a great possibility stood behind that. Everything was related to "the Kingdom of God being near" (Matthew 3:2). Jesus even expressly said that it is near. This word cannot have meant only an enthusiastic formula or an expression of urgent exhortation; near means , in so many words, near. Thus, as far as God was concerned, it was possible that what the prophecies of Isaiah had proclaimed, the breakthrough of a new existence, would really come about . . . . This kingdom would have come if the message had been met with faith . . . . But that did not happen. Jesus was rejected by his people and put on the road to death.[1]

Two outlooks, according to Guardini, result from this situation: the texts along with the whole mood of imminent expectation take on an artless intelligibility. They mean what they say: the fulfillment of the Kingdom of God in the immediately proximate future. But precisely

---

1. Romano Guardini, *The Lord*, trans. Elinor Castendyk (London: Longmans, Green and Co. Ltd., 1956) 95–96. Taken up in his later book: *The Church of the Lord: On the Nature and Mission of the Church* (Chicago, 1967), these ideas are no longer accepted.

this was prevented by Israel's refusal. The Church, however, is not made impossible by this, but precisely by this made necessary.

The Church—this is a second consequence—takes on a marked form by this situation. Jesus maintains His demand for reform and faith, but creates a new ground and space for it: the Church. In Guardini's view, the Church was instituted on the last journey of Jesus to Jerusalem, after the decision of his death had been made. This thesis is connected with earlier conceptions which distinguish two phases in the life and activity of Jesus: first, there was the successful beginning, the so-called Galilean Spring; then came the increasing rejection and refusal, ending in the crucifixion in Jerusalem, which deprived that Spring of its fulfillment. The turning point is visible in Luke 9:51. "When the days drew near for him to be received up, he set his face to go to Jerusalem."

However, such a conception presupposes that we have on the basis of the Gospels a historically recoverable life of Jesus known down to individual details. Its interest was focused totally on the witness and the proclamation of what really was; but this witness does not have to proceed according to chronological sequence. Consequently,

as a result of the special character of the Gospel tradition it is not permitted to fix the individual logions according to time and situation. One can hardly recognize two stages of the preaching of Jesus, a first in which he, under the presupposition of the acceptance of his message and in view of his path to death, predicts the coming of the kingdom of glory for the near future, and a second in which, because of the unbelief of the people or its leaders, the fate of his death becomes a certainty and he announces a different divine plan of salvation which, despite the present rejection of the Messiah, indeed precisely on the basis of his death, foresees and promises the future glory.

Jesus nowhere expressed himself on what would have happened if the Jewish people had believed his message. A hypothetical theology is not to be found in the Gospels.

The revelation of divine sovereignty is governed wholly without any "if" and "when," and makes no provision for a twofold divine plan to be read from it. But it is connected to the law of promise and fulfillment recognizable in the whole Bible. The promise is absolute and still undifferentiated; only the fulfillment uncovers such and such new particulars. Thus, the proclamation of divine sovereignty through Jesus, which is at the same time a part of its realization, takes on new contours from the resonance and reaction it encounters in its hearers; and Jesus' answer to this brings us in turn new revelation of God's plan, how he will in the end, and completely, establish His lordship.[2]

---

2. Rudolf Schnackenburg, *God's Rule and Kingdom*, trans. John Murray (New York: Herder and Herder, 1963) 181–83.

Related to this thesis, but not identical with it, is the conception of Erik Peterson, which he presented in a very concentrated contribution under the title "The Church."[3] He offers three theses:

a. The messianic kingdom which Jesus proclaimed did not come. Why did it not come? Because the Jews as a people did not believe in the Son of Man. Thus, there is Church only under the presupposition that the people chosen by God did not believe in Jesus the Christ. It belongs to the concept of Church that it is Church of the Gentiles.

b. Church exists only under the presupposition that the coming of the Lord is not imminent. This is supported by the rejecting attitude of Israel against Jesus. This prevents the coming of the Kingdom and at the same time establishes the possibility of the continuance of the Church. Imminent eschatology is transposed into the "doctrine on the last things." That is not a falling away from the preaching of Jesus, but its transposition into a new situation. One consequence of this is that there are not Jews but Gentiles, that there is at the moment only Church, but not Kingdom of God. The new situation means that Jews are no longer called to the Kingdom of God, but Gentiles to the Church.

c. Church exists only under the presupposition that the Twelve Apostles were called by the Holy Spirit and consequently made the decision to go to the Gentiles.

This thesis of Peterson is also a possible interpretation of the proposition "What was preached was the Kingdom of God, what came was the Church," but not, to be sure, as the result of an illusion, but a necessary transposition (conditioned by Israel's attitude) which not only distinguishes Church and Kingdom of God, which is correct, but also almost separates them—which is problematic. For, it must be asked: How is it possible, according to these presuppositions, that in the Church to this day the message of God's Kingdom is proclaimed and that this message becomes the impulse and motive of its own praxis as well as of its activity in the world? Peterson's concept also overlooks the fact that the Church is essentially and originally Church of Jews and Gentiles (cf. Eph 2:14-22).

In addition, Gerhard Lohfink has pointed out that according to the Lukan tradition, Jesus does not want "to ground any new Church, but to gather together all Israel, and this for the reason that at the moment when the Church exists apparently as new community of faith, it does not stand next to or in Israel, but is identical with the true Israel." Luke

---

3. E. Peterson, "Die Kirche" in: *Theologische Traktate* (Munich, 1952) 411–29; Cf. on Peterson: Jürgen Moltmann, *The Church in the Power of the Spirit*, trans. Margaret Kohl (New York: Herder and Herder, 1977) 141–42.

conceives the Church as the true and authentic Israel, "which is the same as the old Israel—in its final salvation-historical phase."[4]

The Relationship between Kingdom of God and Church

The Church is not the Kingdom of God—Kingdom of God and Church are not identical. The Church of Jesus Christ, understood as the community of those who believe, whose faith is oriented to Jesus, the Christ, which lives from his word and from the word about him, who strive to imitate him, is a *sign* that the Kingdom of God is already present and near. It is present in the Church in the form of beginning, of provisionality, of hiddenness, and in part even of brokenness.

This comes from the fact that it calls itself Church of Jesus Christ; that it is related to Jesus as its source and origin; but in Jesus was given the proximity, even the presence of the Kingdom of God. The Church lives from Jesus' message, which it proclaims; it mediates Jesus' work in the service of healing in all kinds of ways, in the service of overcoming evil, of forgiveness and reconciliation. The Church lives from that new life that took its beginning in the resurrection of Jesus from the dead and appears both as indestructible hope and as comprehensive making sense of human existence. The Church is related to the message of God's Rule and Kingdom, to the Jesus proclaiming as well as the Jesus proclaimed, in whom imminent expectation becomes eventuated reality. This is the Church, the sign of God's dominion.

The Church is also not the Kingdom of God on earth, such that the promises and obligations of God's Rule and Kingdom as power of justice and love, which calls to reform, to faith, to confessing action in justice and love, were limited to the boundaries of the Church. God's Rule and Kingdom is in the world actively wherever there comes about factually what God's promises and demands contain. And even this is not limited to the Church, for it is possible in the world, among human beings. It becomes recognizable in acts of selflessness, of commitment to justice, reconciliation, freedom and peace. This is the application of the saying "Whoever is not against you is for you" (Luke 9:50). To say this does not reduce the significance of the Church, but acknowledges in it the power of affirmation to bring to bear its orientation to the world.

But even so it must be said that the Church of Jesus Christ in its history in no way always was, or even is, the place where the message of God's Rule and Kingdom became the standard orientation and obligation. How often, in place of this, has come complicity with the powers of the world, and in place of faith and witness, adaptation, diplomacy,

---

4. Gerhard Lohfink, "Hat Jesus eine Kirche gestiftet?" in *ThQ* 161 (1981) 81–97, at 91–92; ibid., *Jesus and Community: The Social Dimension of Christian Faith,* trans. John P. Galvin (Philadelphia: Fortress Press, 1984)

politics, success, evil and lazy compromise, yielding to the powerful, making do with the realities, and in the place of the Gospel, sermons about hell and the tortured conscience.

The Church is also not the Kingdom of God which we build, e.g., by any and all human efforts, no matter how extensive or brilliant. In spite of the many and great works, which fulfill the promises and demands of the message of the Kingdom of God, the fact remains: The Kingdom of God remains primarily gift which is supposed to become task, but which is not replaced by human activities, which cannot be equated with human works. All forms of human, Christian, churchly effort stand under the eschatological proviso. They are not the Kingdom of God; they point to it and are motivated by the idea of the Kingdom of God.

The Kingdom of God is—put positively—the goal, towards which the Church, in hope, is moving. Kingdom of God is the future of the Church and of the world. "Thy Kingdom come!" is understandable only as petition; likewise the exhortations to watchfulness, readiness, openness, patience, if the Church is not the Kingdom of God but awaits it, seeks it, is on the lookout for it.

It comes about from this tension of beginning and end of the Kingdom of God, of way and goal, of already and not yet, that the Church stands in the service of the Kingdom of God, that it is essentially a pilgrim Church, Church under way, wandering people of God, towards a goal, constantly striving to let the power that comes from the goal and the future become reality in the present. It is very characteristic, and of considerable importance precisely for the present-day understanding of Church, that the Second Vatican Council took over the dynamic concept "People of God" as the determining characteristic of Church over–against the otherwise customary static concepts like House of God, Temple of God, God's plant or flock, or Body of Christ.

The Kingdom of God in the form of beginning and presence, but also as goal and future, is the ever constant over–against of the Church; it is the motivating, mobilizing orientation, but also the critical instance of its activity and behavior. This has a number of consequences.

The Church cannot anachronistically anticipate the fact of its way and the fact of its hope for fulfillment. For this would mean that the Church is waiting for nothing more, that it already had everything, that it could take its ease, that it declares holy everything that is there, as it is, and everything that it does, that it considers every change an offense. It is on the basis of such false anticipations of the definitive, that is grounded that misplaced ecclesiastical triumphalism, that embarrassing pathos that can be connected with the well-known and popular hymn: "A house full of glory shines far across every land—built of eternal stone by the master-hand of God." Here the heavenly Jerusalem is brought down, so to speak, to this world—perhaps to that city which calls itself Eternal Rome, a title which, of course, does not come from the Gospel but from pre-Christian antiquity.

From the fact that the Church is under way, a wandering people of God, that it has history and with that a future which transcends and vivifies it, that the Kingdom of God is also its goal, there comes this consequence: The Church is an *"ecclesia semper reformanda,"* a Church in need of renewal, which is a sign of its finitude, its failure, and its guilt; but it is also a Church capable of renewal, which is a sign of its life and its future. From this has come one of the fundamental statements of Vatican II about the Church—in contrast to the earlier situation when such ideas were anathema to Catholic ears.

When it is asked where lie the points of orientation for renewal as the Church's task, the answer is: They are to be found in its orientation to the Kingdom of God, in its origin, and in its gift to be the presence of the Kingdom of God given in Jesus Christ; and they lie in its future, the goal and the fulfillment towards which it is moving.

From this orientation it is possible to understand and ground the orientation that the renewal must be true to origins, goal-oriented, and situation-related. From this program comes the necessity for the Church to take its leave from forms, structures, and models that were once historically adapted and justified in their time, perhaps even necessary. These may not be held onto at any price when a new time of the Church and for them has dawned. The Church must be ready for Exodus when what has come to be turns into hindrance and captivity.

The idea of the Church being under way, which means historicity, was formulated by Vatican II in some remarkable sentences: "The pilgrim Church bears in its sacraments and institutions, which still belong to this world, the form of this world which is passing away; and thus it belongs itself to that creation which still lies in groans and sighs and is awaiting the revelation of the children of God (cf. Rom 8:19-22)."[5] "The Church 'strides between the persecutions of the world and the consolations of God on its way of pilgrimage' (*Civ. Dei* 18.51)."[6] No trace of triumphalism or of anticipated glory is to be found here.

When the Kingdom of God is the goal of the Church's striving, then it cannot be there just for itself and its own institutional concerns, and thus fall into the practice ecclesiological narcissism. It becomes believable only when it passes on its directions, its explanations, its encouragements, not as the voice of its own ecclesiastical interests, but as the voice of the message of the Kingdom of God, which it is her task to make real in the realm of the Church, a message which at the same time signifies and brings about the full humanity of human beings. The

5. *Lumen Gentium* no. 48.
6. Ibid. no. 8.

Kingdom of God as the goal and destiny of the Church means that the existence of the Church must be an existence for—existence for others, a transparency of Jesus Christ whose whole life was an existence for others. Church is Church as it should be only when it is Church for the world. And that is precisely its most recent statement about itself: It is the sacrament, the effective sign of the unity of God and human beings and of human beings among each other.

If the Kingdom of God is also not identical with world and Church, they are still not without relationship to each other. Neither the world nor even the Church should become a caricature of the Kingdom of God. They should be signs of God's presence, and also set up such signs as hope for the world. The words, the promises as well as the obligations that proceed from God's Rule and Kingdom as present and future should bring forth fruit on the field of history, above all on the field of the Church which is connected with the Kingdom of God in this intensive way—in the already and the not-yet.

The Church which is not the Kingdom of God, not even the Kingdom of God on earth, which cannot build this Kingdom because it is God's gift, which when translated into mandate still remains gift, which nevertheless is related in such a comprehensive way to the already and the not-yet of the Kingdom, this Church is the community of those who pray for the coming of the Kingdom, who wait for its fulfillment, towards which they are on the way.

This community of the way is preserved on the way and kept directed towards the goal of its fulfillment by the fact that this community lives from the word, from the promises, from the powers and the ministries of what is the content of God's Rule and Kingdom. Church understood in this way is first and foremost a community of hope which is conscious of its provisionality, not only theoretically but also practically; at the same time it must mediate the power of this hope as consolation, as giving meaning to life, as liberation, and as provocation to men and women of the whole world. It must do this because it can do this.

This aspect of the Church as community comes above all from the fact that no one can hope only for oneself alone—and that holds for faith and love as well.

To dare to hope for God's Kingdom—that always means to hope for it with an eye for others, and therein to hope for ourselves. Only when our hope is a co-hope for others, when it takes on without fuss the shape and the movement of love and communion, only then does it cease being small and fearful, and cease pandering to our hapless egoism.[7]

7. "Unsere Hoffnung. Ein Bekenntnis zum Glauben in Dieser Zeit" in: *Gemeinsame Synode der Bistümer in der Bundesrepublik Deutschland* (Offizielle Gesamtausgabe, 1976) 99.

CHURCH AND KINGDOM OF GOD IN THE HORIZON OF THE "THEOLOGY OF HOPE"

These considerations afford us the opportunity to take up the theological outline of the Church found in the theology of Jürgen Moltmann, a theology marked in a central way by the idea of God's Kingdom, of the future, and thus of hope.[1]

Moltmann makes not only faith but also hope the central object of theology. The old motif of theology "*Credo ut intelligam*—I believe that I may understand" he changes into "*Spero ut intelligam.*"

The Basic Theses

Moltmann explains: For Christian theology today it could be of decisive significance "to follow the fundamental principle: *spero ut intelligam*. If it is hope that draws believers into the life of love, then it will also be hope that mobilizes and drives forward the thinking of faith, its recognition and consideration of human existence, of history, and of society. Human beings hope in order to know what they believe" (28).

Theology of hope has of course the essentially necessary orientation to faith. Hope is unfolded faith.

Faith binds human beings to Christ. Hope opens this faith for the all-encompassing future of Christ. Thus, in Christian life, faith is (temporally) prior, but hope has the (factual) primacy. Without faith's knowledge of Christ, hope turns into utopia reaching out into the empty air. But without hope, faith erodes, it becomes faint-hearted and finally dead faith. By faith human beings step into the footsteps of true life, but only hope keeps them on this track. Faith in Christ turns hope into assurance. Hope broadens faith in Christ and leads it to life (16).

Such a theology of hope obviously involves some implications and consequences. When hope and its presupposition, promise, are made

---

1. Jürgen Moltmann, *Theology of Hope*, trans. James W. Leitch (New York: Harper & Row, 1965). The numbers that follow refer to this edition.

the principle of theology, then the revelation event cannot be understood as epiphany, as the unveiling of doxa, or as an uncovering of the hidden God. According to Moltmann that would introduce categories in which Greek religion is made the criterion of biblical proclamation. The incontestably dominant theme of Old Testament witness, that God's self-revelation was done by way of promise, becomes for Moltmann the decisive horizon for biblical revelation in general and for its normative and guiding understanding: the salvation-event of the Old Testament can and should become the guide for our understanding of Christ (134).

This theological conception has a corollary and its suitable expression in theological language. The Logos corresponds to the epiphany of God, which announces, points out, and expresses in words what is, what is shown from the thing itself, which "experiences in the Logos the epiphany of the eternal presence of being and finds truth therein" (34), which can arrange them in the form of propositions, doctrine, and system. Theological speech proper is, however, to be done in such a way that "in the medium of hope theological concepts are not to become judgments which fixate reality on what it is, but to become anticipations which uncover for reality its prospects and future possibilities. Theological concepts do not fixate reality, they become rather expanded by hope and anticipate future being" (30).

The difference between Greek and Israelite-Christian thinking, between Logos and promise, between epiphany and apocalypse of truth, which was a basic phenomenon in the Old and New Testaments in its struggle with Greek thinking, is an ongoing task which, especially today, must be thought through and worked out anew. "The language of promise becomes an essential key for the liberation of Christian thought."

The Understanding of Church

The Church has to be placed in the framework and horizon of hope. It is, "as community of Christ, hope lived in community" (51). Its connection with Christ is its memory of him, in which the enthusiasm of fulfillment is not to be celebrated; in which, instead, the ground and the goal of all hope is given and the future of every promise has begun.

The Church is Exodus-Community, wandering People of God, whose way is a path through the desert. Its symbol is not the house but the tent. It takes part in the movement of the history of God with the world and is to be understood as a moment in this movement.

For this reason the Church is neither a force for order nor an institution of salvation which celebrates the epiphany of God in sacramental and cultic re-presentation. The Church is brotherhood. "She is the vehicle of the Gospel of freedom, not schoolmistress of the nations. It is not the Church which has the Gospel, but the Gospel makes for itself an Exodus people" (103). The important thing here is "not the spread of the Christian religion or the establishment of the Church, but the liberation of the people for Exodus in the name of the coming Kingdom" (103). The community of the Church serves the spread of the call of freedom in the world and is supposed to be, as itself a new community, the social form of hope. Church is Church for the world; without the world it is not Church.

The existence of the Church moved by this impulse will develop an especially active and creative power. It will not passively make do with realities or let things run their course; it will rather attempt to be active for and in the world, for and in society through its efforts for the reform of human beings and the renewal of circumstances, conditions, and structures. It will try anything in order to prepare itself and the world for the future which is called the Kingdom of God. It will acknowledge its responsibility for human beings and for the world and be active in all kinds of ways; it will be especially engaged for peace and justice. It will recognize in sickness, poverty, hunger, war, and death not divine arrangements but—in good biblical fashion—enemies of God, manifestations of the power of evil, which are there to be battled and overcome. It will no longer be concerned about healing wounds, but will work so that wounds will be prevented.

The Church therefore cannot stand in the place of hope, it must keep alive the fire of hope. This is where its present-day task and mission lie, this is where it recognizes the signs of the time. The mission of the Church consists in this, that in the widely dominant contemporary situation of failure, lack of courage, resignation, and despair, it fills human beings with the impulses and contents of Christian hope and spreads these abroad. The task of the Church today, says Moltmann, is the injection of humankind with hope.

Thus as Moltmann understands it, the Church is Church under the cross (116). There is where it will learn where Christians take up their cross—in common battle against inhumanity, in the common suffering of oppression and persecution. In this participation in the passion of Christ and in the passion of the people, the body of Christ and his freedom will become visible. Christian community is proven in opposition and resistance. Community with the crucified becomes further visible in Christians entering with solidarity into the brotherhoods of humankind which in their society live visibly in the shadow of the cross: the poor, the disabled, the rejected, the imprisoned. Community with the crucified is nothing other than to live in community with the least of the brothers and sisters of the Son of Man (Matthewhew 25). The Church as community of the cross, as Church under the cross, will come to know, especially by and in that (cross) that the word and act of forgiveness comes to reality within itself.

This consciousness is supported by the fact that in Christ, especially in his resurrection from the dead, as the overcoming of death, the most striking manifestation of the power of evil, is laid the ground and beginning of all hope. Through Easter, the lordship of Christ has become an actual event. However, without new life, without the power of love, without the courage of living hope coming from faith in the resurrection of Jesus,

resurrection faith would break down into a merely factual faith without consequences. But on the other hand, it is true that without resurrection faith, the new life in the lordship of Christ would lose its radical alternative to the dominant systems of humanity and would—adapted in various ways—lose its world-conquering power. Where there is certainty that death has lost its power, there is a genuine alternative to those systems of dominance which are built upon alliance with death. Depriving Death of its power brings to light a life which overcomes the system of dominance and oppression and demonstrates freedom in community (117).

This is also the reason why the Church, which is so understood and so understands itself, has every right and reason to celebrate the feast beginning with Easter as the celebration of freedom. With Easter, explains Moltmann, begins the laughing of the redeemed (129). Even before it becomes the content of faith, Easter is the content of a hymn of joy and jubilation: Death, where is your sting, hell, where is your victory? (1 Corinthians 15:55). When this freedom which is being grounded in the victory of Christ over death is celebrated as festival, it is lifted out of the manifold constrictions and compulsions of the everyday, for which it becomes effective at the same time.

According to Moltmann, the feast of freedom works in two ways: It effects the preservation of resistance against suffering, and it effects the preservation of consolation in suffering. "Without resistance, consolation in suffering can degenerate into false consolation. But without consolation in suffering, resistance against suffering can lead to the suppression, transference, and multiplication of suffering" (132).

"The liberating festival and life as festival without end mutually complement each other. Basically, everyday and festival day merge more into joy in freedom."

Evaluation

The advantages of this theology are obvious.[2] Hope can, in fact, be an embodiment of what Christian being, faith, and life mean. Hope is

2. The following considerations are connected with my work: "Spero ut intelligam. Bemerkungen zu einer Theologie der Hoffnung" in: *Wahrheit und Verkündigung*. Michael Schmaus zum 70. Geburtstag, ed. L. Scheffczyk—W. Dettloff—R. Heinzmann (Munich—

an unfolding of faith; it describes the face of faith turned towards the future. In addition, hope brings to expression the status of the Christian and the Church in a very impressive way: the state of being under way, of pilgrimage; the situation of the wandering People of God which knows about the goal of this way, but also does not forget that the goal is not yet reached.

In addition to this is the radical anchoring of this theology of hope in Jesus Christ. The awaited and hoped-for future is the future of Jesus Christ. Put more clearly, it is the future opened up for all human beings by the event of the resurrection from the dead, the future of life as victory over death, as the coming of the royal lordship of God no longer held back by anything.

The theology of hope also has special significance in that the theme "hope" has been until now a stepchild, so to speak, of theological reflection, which was devoted disproportionately to the themes "faith" (this above all) and "love." the treatise on hope was one among others. It was treated principally as one of the three "theological virtues," and there more or less cursorily. But there was hardly any attempt to make hope the principle of theology. In addition to that, the theology of hope presented here is able to raise hope out of the private and privatized sphere and, without loss of the personal, into the dimension of community, Church, and humanity. It is with this that hope gains its special, universal status. At the same time, it brings about the possibility to be an answer to the question of today's human beings, who are not moved by anything quite as strongly as the question of the future.

The theology of hope also facilitates in a special way an entering into conversation with the most clearly defined ideology of our day, Marxism, and especially with the *"Prinzip Hoffnung"* of Ernst Bloch.

Further inquiries: It is only under the express presupposition of the assessment and recognition we have just given that the following critical observations are to be viewed. These questions relate not so much to what Moltmann has said as to what was not said or to the rejected alternative.

In Moltmann's theology of hope, the promise is distinguished both from the statement of the Logos and from the announcement of the kerygma, because it is opposed to the promise of the epiphany as a category of Christian revelation. In reply, it must be said that it is not right to think alternatively in this context,' because such thinking easily leads to one-sidedness. Also, the matter of hope in no way requires such alternatives.

Paderborn—Vienna, 1967) 353-75; likewise in: *Diskussion über die Theologie der Hoffnung,* ed. W. D. Marsch (Munich, 1967) 81-105.

In contrast to Moltmann, one will, in accord with the New Testament, also speak of a fulfillment that has taken place in Jesus Christ, in his person and in his fate, and thus of an epiphany granted in Jesus Christ, a manner of presence which corresponds not only to anticipation but also to comprehension, which is ordered not only to hearing but also to seeing: "We have seen his glory" (John 1:14). This mode of revelation cannot be described satisfactorily in its entirety with the category of promise.

Moltmann questions whether New Testament revelation, which culminates in Jesus Christ and in the Christ-event, can be understood as a kind of epiphany. The incontestable New Testament statements supporting such an understanding Moltmann traces back to the influence of Greek religions characterized by logos and epiphany, especially to the mystery religions, which do not correspond to the real thrust of the New Testament witness.

In response, one has to ask the basic question whether an interpretation of the Christ-revelation in the categories of epiphany and logos is legitimate or not. Can the definitiveness, the last Word, "that became flesh and dwelt among us" (John 1:14), the fullness and the fulfillment by such an interpretation be legitimately expressed? Is such an interpretation necessary? This has nothing to do with "fulfillment enthusiasm" or with fixation on the "but still"; it has rather to do with the recognition that the New Testament represents another phase and dimension than the Old Testament, that the promised has come, that "we need wait for no other," that in Jesus Christ God has fulfilled and made true all promises, that God is thus the great and unlimited and irrevocable "Yes" (cf. 2 Corinthians 1:20).

These facts are not denied in principle by the theology of hope; it is simply a question of the right accents and emphases. For this reason, neither affirmation as corollary to epiphany nor address and kerygma as corollary to the here and now can be dispensed with—and of course, neither can promise as correlative to the future of Jesus Christ, for only together do they correspond to the totality of that to which the New Testament gives witness.

To the objection against the influence of Greek thinking as foreign to biblical categories, it must be pointed out that such clarity and linear singularity of biblical thinking or biblical language simply does not exist. Greek thought is in fact, and legitimately, found within the New Testament and the theology presented therein, and has its rightful place there. Only thus can the revelation event fulfilled in Jesus Christ become epiphany and promise for all; expressed in biblical terms, for "Jew and Gentile." If, for the bearers of the truth of the Gospel and of the preaching of Jesus the Christ and Lord, it is their task to be all to all, to the Jews a Jew and to the Greeks a Greek (Cf. 1 Corinthians 9:20), then Greek thinking, which is oriented to logos, epiphany, and presence, is not excluded, but admitted, even required, in order to articulate that of which the New Testament gives witness. What looks at first like an external influence is—when really looked at—the realization of universality, expansion in all dimensions.

The task is thus not to contest the category of promise in the New Testament and the reality of hope preordained to it; the task is to contest the need for exclusive alternatives in order to represent this principle. The task is to emphasize that the theology of hope can develop its true position and foundation and the power of its effectiveness not by exclusion but by its relationship to the whole: to the truth of the Logos, to epiphany, to announcement, to statement, to address, and to promise.

If it can be said in a thoroughly correct way that hope is unfolded faith, then this specification must be completed by saying that hope unfolds faith in a specific dimension, in the dimension of the future. But this dimension is not the whole of faith itself. Faith also has its unfolding back into the past and into its source and above all into the present, in which it realizes itself and the present it has. But because that is so, that is why faith is the comprehensive, all-encompassing principle of theology. One can—by all means—unfold hope from faith, but one cannot describe faith only in the horizon of hope. One cannot spell out and conjugate the Credo and its contents simply with the future. Faith is related to the whole, and thus also to hope.

The *"Spero ut intelligam"* is certainly in position to describe the situation, the inner and unitary thrust of salvation history and the connection between Old and New Testament. But at the same time, in the single category of hope and promise lies the danger of not sufficiently spelling out in their difference the distinctions between Old and New Testaments which, despite everything, are to be characterized by promise and fulfillment. What has taken place in Jesus is not just an event of promise, but is in fact, what Moltmann has doubts about (142), an event of fulfillment, to be specified in the indicative.

It must likewise be said: Important as it is to hold, along with Moltmann, that the Old Testament event can be a leitmotif for the Christ-event (134), it is just as important not to make an exclusive principle of it. It is just as important not to overlook the decisive point, that it is first of all from the overwhelmingly New and totally Other of the Christ-event that the Old Testament revelation-event gets its salvation-historical status and takes on its own unique value. In any case, this is the way the New Testament itself thought, wrote, and acted. The anticipatory certainly gives a preunderstanding of the definitive; but it is the definitive which brings the definitive understanding; and this can—as new—most certainly be a corrective of the anticipatory and of the preunderstanding. Thus, some questions have to be raised about this kind of a theology of hope. Can it adequately explain the definitiveness, the eschaton of the revelation granted in Christ? Is enough consideration given to the past and present, the here and now in its unique significance bestowed in Word and Sacrament?—for they would seem to be wholly taken up in being the occasion and ground of hope, and thus not seem to give sufficient expression to the salvation which is promised for and is effective in the here and now.

As for the phenomenon of Church in the horizon of the theology of hope, it is noteworthy that a whole series of Moltmann's characteristic affirmations about the Church are found, precisely in the form in which he expressed them, in the texts of Vatican II: Church as hope lived in community, as community of hope, as Church of Exodus, as wandering People of God journeying towards the Kingdom of God, Church as moment in the movement of the history of God with the world which itself expresses its provisional status, the Church as *ecclesia reformanda*, as sign of hope for the world, Church as advocate for human beings, especially for human beings who have no others to care for them, the Church as Church "under the cross," the Church as Church of the Risen One, the Church to whose definition the celebration of festival belongs.

The problem is the alternatives, which we have already mentioned. We repeat them here:

When Moltmann says that the Church is not an institution of salvation which is to celebrate the epiphany in cultic re-presentation, but is, instead, a brotherhood—it is hard to see how this alternative is legitimate. The problem is not with the word "institution of salvation," for one can instead say: The Church is sacrament, i.e., an effective sign of salvation, sign of unity between God and human beings, and thus sign of unity of human beings among themselves. If the Church is this sacrament, then it follows that this sacramental reality is subdivided into the sacraments, especially baptism and Eucharist. In sacrament an epiphany is celebrated in the form of *memoria*, of remembrance, of re-presentation, but nowhere is it written that this cultic or sacramental re-presentation blocks off the horizon of future and promise; instead it makes it manifest: "We proclaim your death, we praise your resurrection, until you come in glory" [eucharistic acclamation of the Roman Catholic Mass in German]. This mode of being Church is not an anti pode to the Church of brotherhood but the most profound ground of its possibility.

Important for the existence of the Church, according to Moltmann, is not the spread of the Christian religion, or its planting, but the liberation of the people for Exodus in the name of the Kingdom of God. Is that an antithesis? How can the Church lift up this cry of freedom if it is not made present as Church? And it really doesn't matter whether or not this is called a "planting of the Church."

Moltmann says: The Church is the vehicle of the gospel of freedom, not schoolmistress of the nations. It is not the Church that has the gospel but the gospel makes for itself its people of Exodus. What does this mean concretely: The gospel makes a people for itself? The gospel is not some freely swinging reality. Isn't the mediation of the gospel needed by human beings, by messengers, by preachers, by witnesses, by intersubjectivity? Can one say, as Moltmann does, the Church is the vehicle of the gospel, thus bearer and instrument, and on the other hand decree, it is not the Church that has the gospel? If that were so, how can it be the vehicle of the gospel? Moltmann's ecclesiology contains an impressive program. But it describes in an unequally more intensive manner what the Church is and should do, than what it concretely is and how it should concretely act.

The "should be" is certainly indispensable if the "is" position is not to be allowed to lead to ossification or indolence. On the other hand, however, if the mediation of *is* (reality) and *should* (program) is too distant, it could turn out that the situation, chance, and possibility coming from the here and now of the Church will receive too little attention. It could turn out that the fulfillment-enthusiasm rejected by Moltmann will be replaced by a future-enthusiasm—and this would be no less one-sided.

The function and task of the Church in its comprehensive liberating ministry to human beings is indispensable. This is true today more than ever. Nevertheless, the question has to be asked: is the freedom and liberation so understood, i.e., as social freedom and liberation, identical with the freedom and liberation of which the New Testament speaks, i.e., with the gospel of freedom? Or with Luther's program of the freedom of the Christian? Freedom there is understood essentially as freedom from the past, freedom from guilt, from the powers of fate, from fear, from being given up to the world; it is the freedom of reconciliation with God. Its primary purpose was not the overthrow of conditions and structural reform, but the renewal of human beings, of sentiment, of the spirit, which then—as with the slavery question—caused social consequences.

Further, it can and must be asked: Beside the socially liberating *diakonia* (ministry) as mission of the Church, should one not mention the equally indispensable task of *martyria* as proclamation, which can be not just proclamation of hope and future, which must also be interested in the Logos, in the truth, and likewise the function of the *leiturgia*—as designation of ritual, of sacramental action? These tasks cannot be allowed to fade into the background, especially since contemporary sociologists like Max Horkheimer and Peter L. Berger are looking for precisely this service from the Church; for this service cannot be provided by anyone else.

My critical remarks and further inquiries had no other purpose than to affirm, and indeed to support, the theology of hope. I believe they can do this by freeing its affirmations from the unnecessary alternatives and possible points of one-sidedness which could perhaps stand in the way of agreement with the theology of hope.[3]

3. In his *The Church in the Power of the Spirit*, J. Moltmann has taken up, furthered, and thematically unfolded the ecclesiology developed in his theology of hope. In doing this he also preserves the fundamental ideas of the theology of hope.

§47

THE HISTORICAL (EARTHLY) JESUS AND THE
POSSIBILITY OF THE CHURCH

What will now be presented has been prepared for in numerous ways: by what has been said about Jesus' proclamation of God's Rule and Kingdom, by our treatment of the problem of imminent expectation, by the theses on Kingdom of God and Church, and by our consideration of Church in the framework of the theology of hope.

Founding of the Church?

When we speak of the Church in connection with the earthly Jesus, we are not dealing with Church in its form laid down once and for all and preserved for us in every detail, but with the beginnings and foundation of Church, of Church as community of believers, whose faith is directed to Jesus Christ and whose life is oriented towards him. Thus, the controversy over the question: *Did Jesus Christ found or not found the Church?* can be a quarrel of words, because different meanings are at times connected with the same word: "Church" or "founding."

In the so-called *Oath against Modernism*, which Pope Pius X prescribed in defense against Modernism, there is the statement:

I believe with firm faith that the Church, the protector and teacher of the revealed Word, was immediately founded by Christ himself, and specifically by the historical Christ when he lived among us, and that it is built upon Peter, the first of the apostolic hierarchy, and his successors.[1]

A second position of the magisterium in this question is much more reserved and differentiated. It is found in the Dogmatic Constitution on the Church of Vatican II:

The mystery of the holy Church is manifest in her very foundation, for the Lord Jesus inaugurated her by preaching the good news, that is, the coming of God's Kingdom, which, for centuries, had been promised in the Scriptures: "The time is

---

1. DS 3540.

fulfilled, and the kingdom of God is at hand" (Mark 1:15; cf. Matt 4:17). In Christ's word, in His works, and in His presence this kingdom reveals itself to men. The word of the Lord is like a seed sown in a field (Mark 4:14). Those who hear the word with faith and become part of the little flock of Christ (Luke 12:32) have received the kingdom itself. Then, by its own power the seed sprouts and ripens until harvest time (cf. Mark 4:26-29). The miracles of Jesus also confirm that the kingdom has already arrived on earth: "If it is by the finger of God that I cast out demons, then the kingdom of God has come upon you" (Luke 11:21, cf. Matt 12:28). Before all things, however, the kingdom is clearly visible in the very person of Christ, Son of God and Son of Man, who came "to serve, and to give his life as a ransom for many (Mark 10:45). When Jesus rose up again after suffering death on the cross for mankind, He manifested that He had been appointed Lord, Messiah, and Priest forever (cf. Acts 2:36; Heb 5:6; 7:17–21), and He poured out on His disciples the Spirit promised by the Father (cf. Acts 2:33). The Church, consequently, equipped with the gifts of her Founder and faithfully guarding His precepts of charity, humility, and self-sacrifice, receives the mission to proclaim and to establish among all peoples the kingdom of Christ and of God. She becomes on earth the initial budding forth of that kingdom. While she slowly grows, the Church strains toward the consummation of the kingdom and, with all her strength, hopes and desires to be united in glory with her King. (*Lumen gentium* no. 5)

In amplification it was said (nos. 2 and 3) that the Church will be revealed by the outpouring of the Holy Spirit and made perfect at the end of the world. "Then, as one can read in the holy fathers, will all the just from Adam . . . . up to the last elect be gathered together with the Father in the all-embracing Church." Thus the universal Church in the beginning is connected with the Church at the end. Accordingly, the Church appears as "the people united by the unity of the Father and the Son and the Holy Spirit" (no. 4).[2]

The council does not speak of the Church as a ready-made reality, nor of its immediate grounding by the historical Jesus, nor of its hierarchy, but of its beginning. In addition, the Church is arranged into a rather large context, that of salvation history and the Kingdom of God. From this perspective, the question: Did Jesus found the Church or not? can also be brought to a solution. We can give an actual example of this.

In *On Being a Christian*, Hans Küng writes: "Not founded by Jesus, but after his death in reference to him as the crucified and yet risen Living One: the community of those who have committed themselves to the affair of Jesus and witness it as hope for all human beings."[3]

Karl Rahner says in response:

I'm not really sure if I should say that this statement contradicts the faith-conviction of all Christian churches, or whether I should only lament with all directness that Küng made this statement without any attempt to reconcile it in an under-

2. Cf. *Commentary on the Documents of Vatican II*, ed. H. Vorgrimler, 1.105–306; H. Ch. Hampe, ed., *Die Autorität der Freiheit. Gegenwart des Konzils und Zukunft der Kirche im ökumenischen Disput* I (Munich, 1967) 243–498.

3. Hans Küng, *On Being a Christian*, trans. Edward Quinn (Garden City, N. Y.: Doubleday, 1976) 478 [translation ours].

standable way with this faith-conviction . . . . Of course origin and foundation mean for us today a more complex reality, which also includes the resurrection itself, than could be attributed to a few instituting words of a juristic kind. The statement: Jesus founded the Church can and must be understood in a more differentiated way than it was in fundamental-theological ecclesiology up to and including Vatican II.[4]

Küng's answer to this, formulated as a question, is not to the point: "How can one explain this riddling theologizing which, fundamentally, and in a pseudo-dialectic way, can always say both: that Jesus founded the Church and yet didn't found it? How can one explain this double-grounded way of speaking?" Is this, as Küng calls it, an "accommodation by reinterpretation of church teaching"?[5] This misunderstands Karl Rahner; this is not pseudo-dialectic, but rather the effort to talk about a complex situation in a differentiated way.

But one point does become quite clear from all this: In the life of the earthly Jesus there is no recognizable single act of grounding, no founding document of the Church. There is a series of facts and events, from which it can be read that the earthly Jesus thought about a Church in the sense of a community connected with him, and he intended that.

Decisive Facts

Jesus' Proclamation of God's Rule and Kingdom is not directed to an individual but to a community, to a people, to the People of Israel. A community is the addressee of this proclamation; it is in a community that the beatitudes, the promises, and the obligations of God's Rule and Kingdom are to be accepted and made real. What is special in the community addressed is found in the fact that Jesus' word and invitation goes out to everyone; no one is excluded from community with Jesus. What Jesus speaks to with his offer of salvation through the Kingdom of God is thus no special group, no order like the Essenes, no secret religious organization, but Israel,[6] the People of God, which, to be sure, in the proclamation of the Kingdom of God by Jesus already points beyond the national boundaries of Israel: to men and women of a readiness and a faith which Jesus, as he says, did not find in Israel (Matthew 8:10).

With the claim of Jesus, as expressed in the titles Messiah, Son of Man, Servant of God, is included a community. Is the statement "Jesus is the Messiah, the Christ," a creation of the primitive community about Jesus who did not understand himself as Messiah? In response: Jesus did not call himself Messiah, but he is called Messiah by others, by the

---

4. In: *Diskussion über Hans Küngs "Christ sein"* (Mainz, 1976) 106.
5. In: *Frankfurter Allgemeine Zeitung*, 22 July 1976.
6. The basic thesis of Gerhard Lohfink's book: *Jesus and Community: The Social Dimension of Christian Faith*, trans. John P. Galvin (Philadelphia: Fortress Press, 1984).

Twelve, especially by Peter (Mark 8:29). Jesus does not reject this title, although he did explicitly add: "Tell this to no one!"

But it is equally correct that Jesus makes a messianic claim in his activity, for example, in his answer to the Baptist's: "Are you the one who is to come (i.e., the awaited Messiah, the anointed one), or are we to wait for another?" Jesus answered with reference to his deeds, which are "deeds of fulfillment" and thus messianic deeds (Matthew 11:2). A further indication can be taken from the trial of Jesus, in which the high priest asks Jesus: "Are you the Christ, the son of the Blessed?" And Jesus said, "I am.'" This answer is emphasized and surpassed by what follows: "And you will see the Son of Man seated at the right hand of Power, and coming with the clouds of heaven" (Mark 14:61–62).

The inscription on the cross: "King of the Jews" (Mark 15:26) is an indication and an indirect confirmation of the fact that Jesus was led before Pilate as Messiah.

In balance: The post-Easter confession "Jesus is the Christ" is certainly the confession of a belief in the Christ of faith, but this is of a faith which appeals to and knows that faith in Christ is connected with the earthly Jesus. For the fact that Jesus is the Christ is the mystery and paradox of this faith. But that means that the "Messiah," the "Christ," can be the content of faith only because this faith is already grounded in the mystery of the Messiah of the earthly Jesus. Without this, the confession—such as made by the primitive community, that Jesus is the Christ—would be inexplicable.

The Messiah, the Christ—an important fact—is no private person. To Messiah/Christ belongs, in the nature of things, community: the community of the Messiah. To Christ belongs, accordingly, an *ekklesia*—as a flock belongs to a shepherd.

As Josef Schmid says:

The answer to the question whether Jesus wanted and established a Church comes from his messianic consciousness. If one recognizes this as historical—and the texts suggest and justify this—then Jesus must have also gathered around himself a messianic community as the People of God of the end-time, which had begun with him.[7]

---

7. "Church," *SM* 1.313–37; More on this theme: J. Betz, "Die Gründung der Kirche Durch den Historischen Jesus," *ThQ* 138 (1958) 152–83; A. Vögtle, "Jesus und die Kirche" in: M. Roesle—O. Cullmann, *Begegnung der Christen*, Festschrift O. Karrer (Stuttgart—Frankfurt, 1959) 54–81; O. Kuss, "Jesus und die Kirche im Neuen Testament" in: *Auslegung und Verkündigung I* (Regensburg, 1963) 25–77; Rudolf Schnackenburg, *The Church in the New Testament*, trans. W. J. O'Hara (New York: Herder and Herder, 1965); H. Schlier, "Ekklesiologie des Neuen Testaments" in: *MySal* IV/1 (1972) 101–221. An important overview has been provided by G. Hainz, *Das problem der Kirchenentstehung in der deutschen protestantischen Theologie des 20. Jahrhunderts* (Mainz, 1974).

Not quite so clear as the relevance of the Messiah and his community is the ecclesiological implication of the titles "Son of Man" and "Servant of God." These are titles Jesus used of himself.

Jesus often and consciously called himself "Son of Man." He did this in view of his present activity: "The Son of Man is Lord over the Sabbath" (Mark 2:28); he does it especially in connection with His passion and judgment statements. The title "Son of Man" is, as it were, a protective title, which on the one hand is to express the messianic claim in Jesus' sense, but at the same time avoids that contemporary political misunderstanding connected with the messianic title at that time. The designation "Son of Man" is taken from the apocalyptic Book of Daniel (Dan 7:13). Described there is the figure to whom "was given dominion and glory and kingdom." In these designations, relationship to a community of human beings is included and expressed. In the Book of Daniel itself it is described as "the saints of the Most High" (7:18).

If Jesus claims the title "Son of Man" for himself, thisimplies, as many exegetes think, a community and people, a "corporate personality." This becomes even more clear in the further formation of the Son-of-Man concept in the apocalyptic literature of the time of Jesus: there, the Son of Man is called the Chosen One, the one around whom the chosen ones gather (Ethiopian Henoch).[8]

Similarly, to the concept of the Suffering Servant (Isa 49:6; 53:12), which Jesus used in order to specify his messianic task, belong community and following in the form of the many. Of the Servant of God in Isaiah it is said that the "many [are] his portion." This idea recurs in the words of Jesus when he explains the content of the image of the Son of Man: "The Son of Man came not to be served but to serve, and to give his life as a ransom for many" (Mark 10:45). This word is also found in Jesus' Last Supper in the formula over the cup: "This is my blood of the covenant, which is poured out for many" (Mark 14:24).

To conclude from all this: Connected with the titles "Son of Man" and "Servant of God" is the idea of a community in the form of the "elect," of the "many." The Son of Man coming as judge, which Jesus claims for and identifies with himself, gathers together his elect. These are they who have acknowledged him by the confession and witness of their life. The gathering at the end of time uncovers what is already there: the community of those who belong to the Son of Man.

Thus, the designations Messiah, Son of Man, Servant of God, and the claim connected these titles already contain the idea and the reality of a community belonging to Jesus, of a communion, of an *ekklesia*, understood as a community of those "called out" by him.

---

8. Representative of this idea: Oscar Cullmann, *The Christology of the New Testament*, trans. Shirely C. Guthrie and Charles A. M. Hall (Philadelphia: The Westminster Press, 1959) 137–92.

The Call of the Disciples

The call of the disciples by Jesus (Mark 1:16–20; Matthew 4:18–22; Luke 4:1–11) has a number of special characteristics.[9]

Entry into the discipleship of Jesus does not come about primarily by the will of the disciples themselves, but as answer to the word of the one calling in the stereotypical phrase: "Follow me!" This word is above all a word of calling or vocation, of being appointed for a task, similar to the way the calling of the prophets is witnessed. The calling includes the granting of the ability, the ability to follow the call and its task. This is expressed, for example, in the words: "I will make you fishers of men" (Mark 1:17). In this image is expressed the mission of those who are called for human beings, for human beings who, called in turn, are to be called out. The Greek word used for this has an inner relationship to *ekklesia*, the word for Church.

The call to follow is connected with the call to mission. Following does not mean mechanical imitation, but entering into the life conditions of him who calls to discipleship; it means sharing in his task, in his mission.

The discipleship to which Jesus calls and chooses is not a calling to a specific school, school orientation, or tradition, as with the rabbis, or with the schools of philosophers, but is a calling to be connected with and bound to his person—and this indeed in the sense of a decision that bears with it the sign of the unconditioned and the exclusive. There is also no possibility to choose someone else as master or teacher. The discipleship of Jesus does not allow for, as the Scripture says, reservations or "looking back." The discipleship of Jesus means what Peter says: "Lord, we have left everything and followed you" (Matthew 19:27).

Discipleship means "to follow Jesus," "to be with Jesus," to have communion with him, to share his life, to take on his fate. Discipleship means, as it is repeatedly summed up in the Gospels: "deny himself and take up his cross" (Mark 8:34). And if "cross" in word and image also includes death, then following means to be ready to venture and to give up one's life.

The Appointing of the Twelve

We are accustomed to connect the "Twelve" with the "Twelve Apostles." But one must keep in mind that the concept of apostle in the New Testament[10] is not at all univocal. The evidence is differentiated.

---

9. A. Schulz, *Nachfolgen und Nachahmen* (Munich, 1962); E. Neuhäusler, *Anspruch und Antwort Gottes* (Düsseldorf, 1962); H. Kahlfeld, *Der Jünger* (Frankfurt, 1962); K. H. Schelkle, *Discipleship and Priesthood* (New York: Herder and Herder, 1965).

10. Cf. the theological reference works and handbooks, esp. *TDNT* 1.407–47; H. von Campenhausen, *Der urchristliche Apostelbegriff* (Lund, 1948); W. Schmitthals, *The Office of Apostle in the Early Church* (Nashville, 1969); G. Klein, *Die Zölf Apostel* (Göttingen, 1964).

Mark 3:14 says: "Jesus appointed twelve"; Matthew 10:1ff: "He called to him his twelve disciples and gave them authority over unclean spirits, to cast them out, and to heal every disease and every infirmity. The names of the twelve apostles are . . ."; Luke 6:13: "He called his disciples, and chose from them twelve, whom he called apostles."

For Luke, the twelve are identical with the apostles, and this identification, is from Jesus himself. Matthew leaves it open whether the twelve were called apostles by Jesus himself, or only later. For Paul, who knows the concept "twelve" (1 Corinthians 15) and connects it with the resurrection witnesses, the concept "apostle" is not restricted to the twelve. Paul himself claims to be an apostle of Jesus. He labels (1 Thes 2:7) Timothy and Silvanus apostles, occasionally also Barnabas.

Even if one questions whether Jesus himself called the twelve "apostles" (Luke), even if the conditions for being an apostle in the New Testament changed (witness to the earthly life of Jesus—witness of the resurrection), it is certain that Jesus commissioned the twelve in the mode of "apostle," which went together with *sending* and *mission*.

The mission given by Jesus to the twelve has its preunderstanding not in the Greek use, where *apostolos* has a totally other meaning, and signifies bill of lading, passport, fleet expedition; it has its preunderstanding in Old Testament usage. In the Old Testament, to send means not simply to ship, but to send someone with a special assignment. Of importance in this is the fact of the sending in the connection with the person of the sender. The person of the one sent recedes behind that of the sender. In this process, the one commissioned receives specific powers and rights. These reside not in his own person but in the person of the one who commissions and sends. But to commission—and that is something further—can be done only by someone with the competence, authority, and power to do so. The commissioned is the representative of the one who gives the commission. It is from this context that the word and rule is to be understood: The one sent by someone is like that person: personally, factually, juridically.

It is clear from this that someone sent by Jesus stands in the series of sendings that come from God. It also becomes clear that Jesus himself can be called the one sent, the messenger of God, and the *apostolos* (Heb 3:1) and—finally—that the service of the one called by Jesus stands in the service of the great sending and commissioning which is revealed by God in Jesus.

Thus if Jesus called and sent part of his disciples in this way, if he perhaps himself called the twelve "apostles," he didn't make them either into simple messengers or into missionaries in the sense of early rabbinic Judaism, or into wandering preachers in the sense of the Stoa; he made them rather into his factual and personal "representatives." They were by word and deed to re-present [make present] Jesus where he himself was not present, but where he wanted his word and work, his "business," to be present.

In the calling and sending of the Twelve, it becomes clear what it is all about: Jesus makes himself represented and mediated: by others, by those commissioned and sent by him. But if this happens, that means that the idea of representation and mediation belongs to the original intention of Jesus. It is shown further that representation and mediation really make sense if Jesus thought about the continuation of his "business," of his mission in the future.

If, considering the Church fundamental-theologically, our goal is to describe it as that reality in which a function or service for the faith is taken into consideration for the following of Jesus, then the beginning of that is in the appointment of the Twelve and in their assignment that they are "to be with him and that he send them."

Now a word or two about the number *twelve*. The Twelve are the representatives of Israel as the twelve-tribed-people. This applies in a twofold direction: The Twelve make recognizable the continuity with Israel and represent it; at the same time, the Twelve are the progenitors going forth from this Israel to the new Israel, to which they are sent and for which they are commissioned.

According to the Synoptics, the sending of the Twelve is limited to Israel with the explicit addition: "Do not go to the Gentiles!" That is, however, not an exclusive prescription for all times. But it does correspond to the situation of the beginning and corresponds to the way of Jesus himself, who knows himself as son of David and son of Abraham, as sent to Israel, and who will gather it as the true Israel.

For this reason it is also understandable that the Twelve can claim no absolute value, and that this is all the more so when, in the further course of history, attention was directed less to the past than to the future, and the path of the disciples of Jesus after Easter leads from Jerusalem into the world and its political center, Rome.

From the history of the calling and appointment of the Twelve there are still some fundamental consequences to be drawn. The fundamental structure that Jesus gives to those called and appointed by him, the Twelve, the Apostles, the sending and the commissioning by one who has the power to give the commission, and the thus-specified qualification of those called, is not a structure dissoluble with time. This structure corresponds to the primacy of the word, which has the dominant position in faith, as well as to the primacy of community; it must therefore remain as constant.

In this sense, the apostolic, the being commissioned and sent, belongs to the fundamental structure of a community which is oriented to it. The apostolic in this sense is an identifying mark of itself. The concrete form in which this structure can be realized as an abiding constant is variable. But it has a criterion in the normative New Testament origin which was talked about in the description of the appointment of the Twelve by Jesus and in the details of the sending and being sent. This origin exercises of itself a critical function for what comes later.

Consequently, among the successors of the Twelve and the Apostles, apostolic structures whose transparency, in terms of the commissioning, mediation, and representation of the ministry required in the biblical origin, is overshadowed or misplaced, are as wrong as they are ruinous for the matter of the faith and the faith community. This applies where gospel commissioning and sending is mixed up with power and might, or where one equates the Kingdom of God with a territory.

Correspondence to the biblical origin would be just as lacking if, in the community related to Jesus and oriented to him, there were no structure whatsoever in which the fact of the sending and commissioning could be represented. The consequence of such a structureless, memberless community would be its dissolution, its melting down into any and every form, structure and community.

The Call of Simon Peter[11]

From the New Testament number of the disciples, the Twelve, and the Apostles, there is no one about whom we are given so much information detail as Simon, Peter, Cephas, who is called rock.

a. *The Call*: The Gospels tell of the call of Simon Peter the way they do of the other disciples and the Twelve. His name comes up again in connection with the listing of the others, in the framework of the "Catalogue of the Twelve." Simon Peter is always mentioned first or is called *"the first."* The decisive reason for this cannot be that he was the first in time to be called by Jesus—that cannot be determined with certainty—but that he is the first. This state of affairs is given special emphasis by the fact that Peter, according to unambiguous tradition, is the first witness of the resurrection of Jesus (1 Corinthians 15).

The function of the first, which is given to Peter, is demonstrated according to the Gospels by the fact that on many occasions and questions, he is the one who speaks, the spokesman—as in the situation of

---

11. Still quite important: O. Cullmann, *Peter: Disciple, Apostle, Martyr: A Historical and Theological Study*, 2nd ed. (Philadelphia: Westminster Press, 1962); J. Ringer, "Petrus der Fels. Das Felsenwort" in: M. Roesle—O. Cullmann, *Begegnung der Christen*, Festschrift O. Karrer (Stuttgart—Frankfurt, 1959) 271–347; J. Betz, "Christus—petra—Petrus" in: J. Betz—H. Fries, *Kirche und Überlieferung* (Freiburg—Basel—Vienna, 1960) 1–21; F. A. Sullivan, "Binding and Loosing," *NCE* 2.559–60; J. J. Castelot, "Peter, Apostle, St.," *NCE* 11.200–5; P. Hoffmann, "Der Petrusprimat im Matthäusevangelium" in: J. Gnilka, ed., *Neues Testament und Kirche* (Freiburg—Basel—Vienna, 1974) 94–114; E. Brown—K. Donfried—J. Reumann, *Der Petrus der Bibel. Eine ökumenische Untersuchung* (Stuttgart, 1976); J. Blank, "Petrus und Petrusamt im Neuen Testament" in: *Das Papsttum als ökumenische Frage*, ed. der Arbeitsgemeinschaft ökumenischer Universitätsinstitute, (Munich—Mainz, 1979) 59–103.

the confession of the Messiah (Matthew 16). To the question: "Who do men say that the Son of Man is?" Simon Peter answers: "You are the Christ, the son of the living God" (Matthew 16:13, 16). A similar scene is found in John 6. To the question of Jesus to the Twelve, "Do you also wish to go away?" Simon Peter answers, "To whom shall we go; you have the words of eternal life" (John 6:67–68). In the same way, Peter steps forward as the one to speak on the Mount of Transfiguration (Mark 9:5). Peter makes objections against the announcement of Jesus' passion (Mark 8:32) and is corrected by Jesus in the sharpest of words.

According to Acts, Peter is the authoritative spokesman at Pentecost. He is the leader of the community in Jerusalem. According to Luke, he is the one who accepted the first non-Jews the Roman centurion Cornelius, into the Church, and thus the one who initiated the mission to the Gentiles (Acts 10). Peter, along with James, is the leading figure of the Assembly in Jerusalem which dealt with the problem of the Church composed of Jews and Gentiles, especially with the question of whether the non-Jews had to be accepted into the Church by way of Judaism or not (Acts 15). The question was decided in favor of freedom.

b. *The Name*: Noteworthy is the fact that "Peter" is the new name of him who was originally called Simon. All the Gospels record that Jesus himself gave Simon the name Cephas, although there is no clarity about the occasion on which this name was conferred. "Peter" is the translation of the Aramaic word "Cephas," Stone, Rock. This was not a common given Jewish name; it is a noun, and thus a symbolic name. To help understand and assess the correct significance of the name "CephasPeter," we have an instructive parallel in the New Testament.

In Mark we read: "He appointed twelve to be with him, . . . Simon whom he surnamed Peter; James the son of Zeb´edee and John the brother of James, whom he surnamed Boaner´gees, that is, sons of thunder" (Mark 3:14, 16–17). Then follow the other names of the Twelve.

Important for our question now is the quite different history of these two surnames in the primitive Church. That of the Sons of Zeb´edee did not last because no special significance was seen in it. Quite different with Cephas-Petros! This one not only lasted but even pushed aside the original name of its bearer. Paul calls Peter regularly with the Aramaic name Cephas, which he obviously took over from the primitive community. Equally important is the witness that comes to us from Paul and especially from the Gospels, that the name Cephas was translated into the Greek "Petros." Because proper names are not usually translated (but transcribed), the Greek form "Petros" shows that this name was at first understood as a surname, an object-designation. It then became a proper name. These facts show what significance the new name "Cephas-Petros" had taken on for the primitive Church.

There is agreement today that Peter did not get this name from Jesus because of his character. For in his character he was not exactly a rock, but something much less stable. His enthusiastic love for his master, which he repeatedly proclaimed, was also possessed by the other disciples; it was thus no uniquely characterizing trait of his nature. He cannot, on that account, be explained as the most reliable of the Twelve. The reason Jesus himself gave this man the distinctive surname "Rock" lies in the special task for which he was destined.[12]

c. *Position and Task of Simon Peter:* These can be seen at first in the scene narrated in Luke 22:24–32. The text deals with the Twelve quarreling over their rank, over which of them was to be considered the greatest. Jesus' answer was: "The kings of the Gentiles exercise lordship over them; and those in authority over them are called benefactors. But not so with you; rather, let the greatest among you become as the youngest, and the leader as one who serves." Benefactor: that was the title by which the lords of antiquity, and not just of antiquity, liked to be addressed. After these words, Jesus turns immediately to Peter: "Simon, Simon, behold, Satan demanded to have you, that he might sift you like wheat, but I have prayed for you that your faith may not fail; and when you have turned again, strengthen your brethren" (Luke 22:31-32).

One can recognize in these words that the special position of Peter is being emphasized, but without letting that become an isolation from the rest of the Twelve. Rather, Peter is there for the sake of the others. The greatness and leadership talked about here consist in service and self-giving; they are a primacy of service.

The ministry of Peter to the faith of the others is to be done with a view to the temptation and danger that lie ahead. This situation faces all the disciples—it becomes immediately actual in view of the passion of Jesus. It is in view of this situation that Jesus intercedes for the disciples. He does this by praying for Simon Peter, that his faith will not fail. Peter, held up in the faith of Jesus, is to be strength and support for his brothers. The strength and support of the brothers is to be preserved in that Peter, in spite of his weakness, does not fall. But even this does not lie in the power and endurance of his faith, but in the fact that Jesus prays for him.

This text takes on special significance with the phrase: "When you have turned again." It alludes to the temptation of the faith of Peter, to his betrayal and denial—"I do not know the man" (Matthew 26:69–75)—but at the same time to the conversion he is to experience. The

---

12. J. Schmidt, "Petrus "der Fels" und die Petrusgestalt der Urgemeinde" in: M. Roesle—O. Cullmann, *Begegnung der Christen* 347–59.

words of Jesus are directed to the future: to the future position of Peter in the community of Jesus Christ.

This function of Peter is impressively depicted in Luke's Acts of the Apostles. Peter is the strength of his brothers as leader of the community in Jerusalem, as witness before the Sanhedrin, as first missionary to the Gentiles, as the decisive figure of authority at the apostolic assembly, and finally as martyr. Peter is to be the first by the fact that he exercises a special ministry to the faith of the community of believers.

This is what makes intelligible our customary present-day language about the ministry of Peter or Petrine function. But it is just as important to point out that the ministry of supporting the brethren in faith cannot be restricted to the historical Peter. This ministry is an abiding function in an abiding Church, and should above all be carried on by whoever succeeds Peter.

THE TEXT ON THE BUILDING OF THE CHURCH

The sixteenth chapter of the Gospel of Matthew describes the situation of the confessing of Jesus as the Messiah. It is a confession that Simon Peter makes in the name of the Twelve. The place is Caesarea Philippi in Northern Galilee. Jesus asks:

"Who do men say that the Son of Man is?" And they said, "Some say John the Baptist, others say Elijah, and others Jeremiah or one of the prophets." He said to them, "But who do you say that I am?" Simon Peter replied, "You are the Christ, the Son of the living God." And Jesus answered him, "Blessed are you, Simon Bar-Jona! For flesh and blood has not revealed this to you, but my Father who is in heaven. And I tell you, you are Peter, and on this rock I will build my church, and the powers of death shall not prevail against it. I will give you the keys of the Kingdom of Heaven, and whatever you bind on earth shall be bound in heaven, and whatever you loose on earth shall be loosed in heaven" (Matthew 16:13–19).

The Problematic of Matthew 16:17–19

A comparison of this passage with its parallels shows the following:

In Mark and Luke are found almost exactly the same question of Jesus: Who do people say that I am? The answer of Peter is also almost exactly the same: You are the Messiah; Luke adds: the Messiah of God. The addition of Matthew "Son of the living God," however, is lacking. In Mark and Luke one reads immediately: "He strictly forbade them to tell this to anyone."

The saying about the building of the Church on Simon as on a rock is found only in Matthew, not in Mark and Luke, who do indeed have the confession of the Messiah, but not the words about the Church. This creates a problem: If one assumes, as used to be the case, that the Gospel of Matthew is the earliest Gospel, it is hard to explain why Mark and Luke left out the words of Jesus to Peter about the building of the Church.

The situation becomes considerably different when one, as is customary today, proceeds from the fact that Mark was the first of the Gospels to be written and was a source along with the sayings source ("Q") for the Gospel of Matthew. One must further consider that Matthew doesn't give historical references, but *composes theologically.* In his effort to systematize, Matthew placed a saying of Jesus, a logion about the community ordered to him, about his *"qahal,"* in the context of the messianic confession of Peter. He did this with good reason and with high theological understanding. Factually, he fits it in superbly. For if the messianic community belongs to the Messiah, then the declaration of a community related to the Messiah fits in with the confession of the Messiah. The Messiah-proclamation of Peter corresponds to the answer of Jesus to the community belonging to the Messiah, and thus to him. It also follows from this that, over-against this factual relationship, the historical or geographical situation of this passage is not decisive.

From the theological composition of the Gospel of Matthew, from the fact that all the Gospels were composed or put together after the death of Jesus and in the light of faith in the Risen One, one can and indeed must reckon with the possibility and with the fact that post-Easter situations and words were projected back into the time of the earthly Jesus. For the question about Peter, this means: Some of his traits found in the Synoptic Gospels reflect his later leading role. And the words: "You are the Christ, the Son of the living God" is a reflection of post-Easter faith.

The matter itself, the question of the *ekklesia,* is not thereby dismissed, but only brought into a larger context. For one can and must say: The leading position of Peter can be made intelligible in the primitive community, and become acceptable, only because and if the reason for this goes back to Jesus himself. That remains established even if all its details and elements cannot be chronologically established with clarity. What came later demonstrates the power of an effective history that proceeds from this basis.

It is said, and this is a further problem, that the word *ekklesia* is found statistically within the Gospels only here and once more in Matthew 18:18. There it means assembly of the community for whom specific rules are laid down. For this reason, the saying about the building of the Church is suspected of being a later insertion. Such a suspicion of inauthenticity or later insertion would make sense if the matter which is spoken about with *ekklesia* never came up elsewhere; but that is not the case. It occurs in the Gospels in other images: in the image of the flock which belongs to the shepherd, in the image of the vineyard, in the image of the building and the cornerstone, in the image of the vine and the branches (John). Moreover, it is no objection that from a piece of so-called special material, as here in Matthew, a suspicion of inauthenticity is dredged up. In other cases, the special material is looked at as a sign of authenticity.

On the Interpretation of Matthew 16:17–19

The text of Matthew 16:17–19 is authentic. It is found in all the manuscripts of the Gospel of Matthew and in all translations. It corresponds to the style and the conception of this Gospel, which was originally written in Aramaic and directed to a Jewish audience. Even Matthew 16:17-19 has Semitic traits and contains typically Jewish conceptions. For instance the words: Bar-Jona, flesh and blood, powers of death, keys of the Kingdom of Heaven, binding and loosing; all these come not from the Greco-Roman circle of culture but from the Palestinian world.

Above all, the word play on "rock" and "man of rock" can only be conceived Aramaically; only there does it exactly fit; the word "cephas" can be used for both. In the translation into Greek, the play on words is only incompletely realized; there is a change from Petra to Petros.

For the interpretation of this so controverted and at the same time so important text, certain things need to be said. The interpretation is decided not just historically and by critical exegesis, but also by a previous understanding of faith, as well as by the question of what one thinks of the institution that claims to represent the office and ministry of Peter today, i.e., of the papacy and the pope.

How these particular a priori considerations can have an effect on the interpretation of the text is shown, e.g., in the interpretation of Martin Luther: The words "You are Peter, and on this rock I will build my community" are, according to him, in no way to be related to the person of Peter, whose successor the pope claims to be by appealing precisely to this text. Matthew 16:17–19 is, according to Luther, rather to be understood thus: that with the words "On this rock I will build my church" Jesus meant not Peter but himself, who is the rock and the cornerstone. With the words "on this rock" Jesus referred to himself; He did not mean Simon Peter.

The other interpretation of Luther, which is also found in Augustine, goes: The words "on this rock" do not apply to the person of Peter, but refer to the faith and the confession of Peter. Peter is meant only to the extent that Jesus recognized his faith as the rock. This faith in Jesus, the rock, was not limited to Peter; he only represented it.

In the interpretation of the words over Peter and the Church (Matthew 16:17–19), Roman Catholic and Reformational theology have, for some time, been coming closer to each other. They have done so in this way: The rock is neither Christ nor the faith of Peter, but Peter himself in his person, as the first.[1]

The controverted question concerns the historical situation of the text, which is not easy to unravel. Is it pre-Easter or post-Easter? But theologically, this is not terribly important. The controversy also concerns the further question of the succession of Peter and, finally, the question of the extent to which Matthew is talking about a constituted Church.

On this final point, we can say that it would contradict the situation of the beginning under way if one were already talking about a constituted *ekklesia*. Accordingly, one cannot say that there is no talk about Church, simply because one cannot speak about organization. Built up forms of organization are not elements of a beginning; they arise only when there is in a more comprehensive fashion that for which forms of organization are destined.

The Results

In the messianic confession of Peter, the *ekklesia* is singled out, too, as the community of this Messiah. Jesus says he will build it on Simon as the rock, the foundation.[2]

Jesus speaks of his *"qahal,"* of his *ekklesia,* which he will build or intends to build. This *"my ekklesia"* is intended as an expression of emphasis—perhaps analogous to the "but I say to you" found in Matthew 5—and intends to say something new: the building of a community, which is not intended to be a special community within the old People of God, but which continues the old and at the same time takes its place.

When Jesus speaks of *building* his *ekklesia,* he is presenting it under the image of a building, a house. This has its parallels in the way Jesus otherwise speaks. He speaks of the House of Israel (Matthew 10:5; 15:24), he speaks of the city on a mountain (Matthew 5:14). The self-description of the primitive Christian community as Temple of God (1 Corinthians 3:16; 2 Corinthians 6:16) and as house of God (Heb 3:6; 1 Pet 4:17) has its origin or basis in this manner of speaking.

This interpretation is illuminated by its relationship to the conceptions of the Old Testament where Yahweh is spoken of as the rock on which the People of Israel and its faith is grounded, and as the stone which the builders have rejected. There is also talk about the holy rock as the place of the presence of God, ultimately symbolized by the Temple on Mount Zion. These descriptions ascribed to Yahweh are

1. Oscar Cullmann, W. Kümmel, and Günther Bornkamm agree on this.
2. Cf. J. Betz, "Die Gründung der Kirche Durch den Historischen Jesus," *ThQ* 138 (1958) 152–83.

claimed by Jesus. Thus one can speak of a "Stone Christology." Jesus himself is the stone which the builders have rejected and which has become the cornerstone: Mark 12:10; Matthew 21:42; Luke 20:17; the stone which has become the stone of salvation: Acts 4:11; Rom 9:33. Related to this are the words of 1 Corinthians 3:11: "For no other foundation can anyone lay than that which is laid, which is Jesus Christ."

But now, according to the witness of Matthew 16:17–19, something further happens: Jesus establishes Simon in the *function of a foundation for the building of his ekklesia* and makes him share in his own function of foundation, ground, and rock. Jesus, the rock, has himself be represented by Simon, the rock; Simon, as Cephas-Peter, is to make present, mediate, and represent the rock-function of Jesus. He is not to upstage or replace the foundation which Christ himself is, but to point to it; he is to be its transparency. In Peter is to be represented the foundation, which Christ himself is: "Christus est petra, Petrus est vicarius petrae (Christ is the rock, Peter is the vicar of the rock)."

The words of Matthew 16:18 "On this rock I will build my church" are often understood as the laying of the Church's foundation stone; this action is unique and unrepeatable, for the foundation stone is laid once and for all. This image and function exclude from the outset any possibility of "succession."

Our response to this relies on what Anton Vögtle[3] has established in numerous writings. Matthew 16:18 does not mean "I will lay the foundation stone for the building of the Church" but "I will build the *ekklesia* upon a rock." Thus, accurately examined, one isn't talking about the laying of a foundation but about the building of the Church upon its rock foundation—or about the function of such a foundation for the building of the *ekklesia*. When one adds that the building of the *ekklesia* is neither a unique nor a past, completed action, but a continuing and abiding, living event, then it is not illegitimate to say: For this event, for the building of the *ekklesia*, we have its related function of the foundation not as a past but as a living, abiding, being-built *ekklesia*. It is a function that will remain as long as *ekklesia* remains. To be sure, the wording does not force one to draw this consequence, but it does allow for it and in no way excludes it from the outset.

It can be concluded from this: A foundation-function of the Petrine ministry in the Church of Jesus Christ that is both present and encounterable in history does not stand in contradiction to the normative origin which is found in the New Testament. What has taken place, therefore, is not historical decline but the completion and unfolding of something that has been grounded.

3. "Der Petrus der Verheißung und Erfüllung. Zum Petrusbuch von Oscar Cullmann," *MThZ* 7 (1954) 1–47; "Messiasbekenntnis und Petrusverheißung," *BZ* N. F. 1 (1957) 252–72; 2 (1958) 85–103.

When one finally moves from image to language, and when one asks what is meant to be said with the rock as foundation of a community of human beings, or with the Petrine office, Petrine function, or Petrine ministry, then it is this: It is supposed to be talking about the cohesion, the viability, the power of coordination, the constancy—functions connected with the leadership function, which are to be seen not as lordship and power but as service to the faith and to the community of the faith and the faithful.

The Keys of the Kingdom of Heaven

What is said in Matthew 16 about the foundation-function, about the so-called Petrine function, is expanded and illustrated by the words directed to Peter in Matthew 16:17–19: "I will give you the keys of the Kingdom of Heaven."

With the image of the keys and the power of the keys, Peter is not, as is often represented in pictures, being appointed the guardian of the gate or porter of heaven. The power of the keys means much more than that; as an ancient and common image, it signifies *authority and disposition* over a house. Power of the keys means to have the power to allow or to prohibit entry to the house.

The image of the keys of the Kingdom of Heaven has still another meaning. We get an understanding of it from Matthew. 23:13, where Jesus reproaches the Pharisees and scribes: "You shut the Kingdom of Heaven against men; for you neither enter yourselves nor allow those who would enter to go in." The scribes claimed to possess the power of keys for God's rule. This consisted, in their view, in their proclaiming, interpreting, "unlocking" the will of God laid down in the Scripture of the Old Testament, in the Law and the Prophets, and thus opened up to human beings access to the God's rule.

But they did this in such a way that they took the will of God, the Law, intended and praised as guidance, and developed it into 613 commands and prohibitions and made it an unfulfillable burden. Thus access to God's Rule and Kingdom was practically closed. In this view, whoever did not know the Law was subject to curse and contempt.

When Jesus gave over the keys of the Kingdom of Heaven to Simon Peter, what is meant is that Jesus himself lays claim to the authorization signified in the image of the keys to proclaim and interpret the will, the Law of God in the word of God's Rule, and that he has the authorization to hand on this authorization.

At the same time, another antithesis is contained in this passage: the function of proclamation and interpretation of the will of God expressed in the image of the keys of the Kingdom of Heaven is claimed by Jesus in sovereign fashion in this way: "It has been said to the men of old, but I say to you" as new orientation of the messianic community gathered about Jesus. In Matthew 16:17–19, Jesus hands on this function to Simon Peter. Concretely, this signifies the task, commissioned by Jesus, thus authentically, to proclaim the message of the *basileia* as embodiment of the Law and the Prophets in the form of the Gospel.

With the words of the keys of the Kingdom of Heaven, *ekklesia* is equated not with royal lordship, with God's Rule, but an inner ordering is expressed: the *ekklesia* of Jesus is the community of those who know about the mystery of God's Rule and Kingdom, about the presence of the lordship of God in Jesus, and at the same time are moving towards its definitive coming, and who in addition seek to make real the promises and obligations that come from it. Those commissioned and sent by Jesus, especially Simon Peter, to whom the keys of the Kingdom of Heaven are given, are introduced into this ministry of proclamation and interpretation.

Binding and Loosing

In the promise to Simon Peter, the words about the handing on of the keys of the Kingdom of Heaven say: "Whatever you bind on earth will be bound also in heaven, and whatever you loose on earth will be loosed also in heaven." These words too were common at that time,[4] especially in the language used by the rabbis. Binding and loosing meant to set down and determine something authentically, and in a binding and obligatory way; it also meant: to *oblige* something or to *free from an obligation*; and in extreme cases: to have control over exclusion to a community or admission to it.

The highest form of representation and realization of binding and loosing is found in the fact of forgiving sins, as this was claimed by Jesus and handed on to the disciples by the Risen One: "If you forgive the sins of any, they are forgiven; if you retain the sins of any, they are retained" (John 20:23). This passage makes particularly clear the message and presence of Jesus: The forgiveness of sins is the sign of the Kingdom of God which has arrived in Jesus.

When the power reserved to God and claimed by Jesus, to forgive the sins of human beings, is handed on with the power to bind and loose as a re-presentation of the power of the love of Jesus, what is getting expressed here is that the power of God's Rule is abiding and effective and has come to its realization in the messianic community. The words "Shall be bound/loosed also in heaven" mean: The forgiveness of sins, or its refusal, is effective; it is valid before God, authorized and thus accepted by God.

---

4. F. A. Sullivan, "Binding and Loosing," *NCE* 2.559–60.

Still to be expressly mentioned about binding and loosing is that the function and commissioning that goes with it is, according to Matthew 18:18, addressed in the so-called community rule of the community: "Whatever you bind on earth . . ." This passage too is controversial, and not just because of its exegetical aspects, but because of the significance ascribed to community in this or that understanding of Church. The Catholic conception leans towards saying that the heads of the community are addressed here. The Protestant conception relates the words to the community as such. The Gospel of Matthew itself saw no contradiction in the proximity of chapters 16 and 18.

If one can speak of a foundation-function as an abiding function that does not end with Peter but has its place in representation by living human beings in a Church that is abiding and constantly being built, then this also holds and is even more clearly recognizable from the other words: from the key of God's rule as commissioning to responsibility for authentic proclamation and teaching, and from the words of binding and loosing. Both words are related to a community which, as a faith community, is oriented by faith in Jesus.

Peter the Shepherd

In connection with our reflection on the building of the Church on Simon Peter, there is another important text, found in the Gospel of John, which, like Matthew 16 and Luke 22, is counted among the classical Peter-texts and adorns the gallery of St. Peter in Rome. This is in the so-called appendix chapter: John 21:15–19.

John 21 deals with the appearances, the self-manifestation of the Risen One and his words of commission,[5] one of which applies to Simon Peter in a special way. The passage reads:

When they had finished breakfast, Jesus said to Simon Peter, "Simon, son of John, do you love me more than these?" He said to him," Yes, Lord; you know that I love you." He said to him, "Feed my lambs." A second time he said to him, "Simon, son of John, do you love me?" He said to him, "Yes, Lord; you know that I love you." He said to him, "Tend my sheep." He said to him the third time, "Simon, son of John, do you love me?" Peter was grieved because he said to him the third time, "Do you love me?" And he said to him, "Lord, you know everything; you know that I love you." Jesus said to him, "Feed my sheep. Truly, truly, I say to you, when you were young, you girded yourself and walked where you would; but when you are old, you will stretch out your hands, and another will gird you and carry you where you do not wish to go." (This he said to show by what death he was to glorify God.) And after this he said to him, "Follow me."

These words express the calling of Peter to be the shepherd of the community of disciples. The image of the shepherd is a royal image,

---

5. A. Vögtle, "Ekklesiologische Auftragsworte des Auferstandenen" in: Sacra pagina II (Paris—Gembloux, 1959) 280–94.

and image of leadership and going ahead, and at the same time an image of care, of readiness to give up his life for his own. The image of the shepherd is filled out by Jesus himself in his Good Shepherd sermon (John 10): I am the good shepherd. His characteristic consists in the fact that he knows his own, that he doesn't abandon them in the situation of danger, that he is ready to give his life for them. The presupposition of the call of Peter as shepherd of the community is found in the question of Jesus to Peter: "Do you love me, do you love me more than these?" The greater self-dedication to Jesus is made the background of this primacy.

The threefold question of Jesus to Peter has to be seen in the context of his threefold denial. Remembering that was to introduce a salutary sobering; but at the same time, Peter is to be rehabilitated in his position and function after the experience of the denial. And also the overall general situation now created by Easter is also described—not least of all in the person of Peter who, with this confession, has given up all self-certitude and all self-praise.

By this commissioning of the Risen One, Peter is himself taken up into the mission of Jesus: in his care for the men and women who remained the flock of Christ. Thus, one can say: Also in the situation described in the Gospel of John there is not merely a Peter tradition, but a kind of primacy of Peter under the image of the "shepherd" in the pastoral office conferred on him.

The scene is concluded with its prophecy of the violent death Peter is to expect, which is part of the consequence of the following of the Shepherd who gave up his life. This is expressed in the image in which the earlier Peter "girded himself," i.e., hitched up his clothing to go wherever he himself wanted. But what will happen with the later Peter is that he will put out his hands for someone else to gird, i.e., tie or chain him—and the new, i.e., the older Peter will give himself over to his fate; he will let himself be led where he does not want to go. Thus, a prophecy of death is spoken as the final mode of the "Follow me!" said to Peter.

The Tension Present in Peter and His Ministry

In the New Testament and in the passages relating to Peter we find a remarkable antithesis. Along with the words of blessing and promise stand diametrically opposed words. Following the promise to Peter in Matthew 16:17–19, in connection with the prophecy of Jesus' passion, come the absolutely shocking words: "Get behind me, Satan! You are a hindrance to me; for you are not on the side of God, but of men" (Matthew 16:23). In Luke 22:32 are the words: "Strengthen your brethren" in connection with the immediately following prophecy: "I tell you, Peter, the cock will not crow this day, until you three times deny that you know me" (Luke 22:34). The conferral of the pastoral office in John 21 explicitly follows the remembrance of the triple denial of Peter. Whoever talks about Peter, the Petrine office, and the Petrine ministry, especially when doing so in the sense of an abiding re-presentation, should not overlook or be silent about this massive dialectic of *petra* and *skandalon*, of rock and stumbling stone.

Josef Ratzinger has called our attention to the fact[6] that in the figure of Peter we are confronted with an unmistakable paradox: his calling, his mandate in the service of Jesus and to the disciples, to the Twelve, to the community, and along with this the weakness that comes to light in him, the failure, the misunderstanding, that brings on him Jesus' harshest words.

Petra and *skandalon*—both are found in Peter according to the New Testament. Now one cannot, says Ratzinger, divide up the two characteristics in such a way that the Peter before Easter is the denyer, and the Peter after Easter the rock.

According to the indications of the New Testament, it is rather that Peter is both in both periods. According to the witness of the Synoptics, the pre-Easter Peter speaks the messianic confession and proclaims his readiness to follow Jesus in everything right up to death. But also the Peter after Easter and Pentecost, already appointed the shepherd, is still the one who, in fear, denies Christian freedom and offends against Christian love—as in Antioch when he cancelled table fellowship with the Gentile Christians and, as Paul says in Galatians 2:14, was "not straightforward about the truth of the Gospel," so that Paul "opposed him to his face, because he stood condemned" (Gal 2:11).

Ratzinger adds the remark:

Has it not remained this way throughout all church history, that the pope, the successor of Peter, has been *petra* and *skandalon*, rock of God and stumbling stone all in one? In fact it will be up to the faithful to endure this paradox of divine action, which continually shames its pride anew—this tension from rock to Satan, in which the most extreme opposites lay mysteriously side by side. Luther recognized the moment of Satan with compelling clarity, and was not wholly wrong in so doing; his mistake was not to have endured the biblical tension of *kepha (petra)* and Satan, which belongs to the fundamental tension of a faith that lives not from merit but from grace. Basically, no one should have understood this tension more than the man who put his mark on the formula of *simul iustus et peccator*, of human beings who are both just and sinners in one.

"If," Ratzinger continues,

it all depended on Peter, if flesh and blood are speaking from him, then he can be Satan and stumbling stone. But if he lets himself be taken completely into service by God, then, as God's instrument, he can really be a cosmic stone. But that is no expression of his achievement and his character but the name of an election and a

6. "Freimut und Gehorsam" in: *Das Neue Volk Gottes* (Düsseldorf, 1969) 249–66.

sending to which no one is competent by nature, least of all this Simon who in his natural character is anything but a rock. That he is the one who is declared to be the rock, that is the fundamental paradox of divine grace which works in weakness. It is always the promise of divine power into human weakness, so that God remains the savior and it doesn't become the human being. It is always the "nevertheless" of grace which is not disarmed by the incapacity of human beings, but precisely therein fulfills the victory of God's love, which doesn't let itself be overcome by the sins of human beings.[7]

However right and helpful are such reflections on the paradox of the Petrine office, they should not be used as a general pardon for all shortcomings and every failure. There could quite possibly arise the necessity and the obligation, which in turn already has a biblical paradigm, not only to endure this tension in faith, but from the power of faith to withstand Peter to his face as Paul did in Antioch, if his behavior does not correspond to the Gospel and thus to justice. Such an opposition is an expression of respect for the reality of this office, of this function represented in Peter. Such a protest can be a service to this office and above all to the reality for which this office exists.

Current Perspectives

As shown right from the beginning, the Church is not to be decided on by Peter, but Peter by the Church. But it would be insincere to say nothing about this ministry, this task of Peter in the *ekklesia*, just because the Petrine office has always been, as it is today, the subject of controversy.

The current position in view of the Petrine office can be described as follows—once again dialectically: There are people and groups that practically identify the Church with the Petrine office. In other words, they follow the motto: "*Ubi Petrus, ibi ecclesia*—where Peter, there the Church," or even: "*Papa, quod est ecclesia*—the Pope, which is the Church," and declare all critical questions as a falling away from the faith and from the Church. They also include in this condemnation those questions which do not contest the justification and significance of this office but only the mode and manner of its representation, exercise, and realization, and offer as answer to the questions only an escalation of this claim itself, as for example in the program: For Pope and Church.

There is a second group which even upon hearing the expressions "Rome," "Pope," and "Papacy," automatically reacts allergically and negatively. This group takes the occasion of criticism of the methods, procedures, and practices of Rome to reject and contest outright the justification and the sense of an institution like that of the Petrine office.

---

7. Ibid. 258–59.

Thus the biblical and historical context for the significance, the function, and the task of this office for the faith and for unity is overlooked. A criticism of the praxis of this ministry is possible only under the recognition of its reality and justification. The biblical foundations on which an office like the Petrine office is based give at the same time the best orientation whether the safeguarding and realization of this function and task—the ministry to unity, to strengthening faith, to the solving of conflicts—corresponds to the normativity of origin so decisive for function and task, and to the mission enunciated there.

Of course, the biblical foundations must be brought into a real relationship with the present possibilities and conditions for the realization of this office and with the present forms of social and political conditions: to a situation that has changed in many ways in comparison to what it once was. But one cannot take this one necessary and indispensable point of relationship, namely the present, and make it the one and only point of relationship, and merge together and dispense with the point of relationship from the origin in the past so that there is not more difference left.

Otherwise, one would be making formally the same mistake with which one charges the medieval or renaissance papacy. For it was precisely these popes who, without much consideration for its biblical origin, adapted their office to their time and to its conditions and models, so as to become contemporary. A fair criticism of this practice does not simply measure that age against our own, but notes the factual distance of those temporal-historical manifestations from those normative foundations encountered in the Scripture precisely for this office, the Petrine office. This contrast rightly qualifies the renaissance papacy as a betrayal of its origins, a betrayal which rightly called forth the protest of the Reformers and which explains the massive resonance which this protest elicited. For it is a resonance grounded not only in a mood of protest but also in a longing for a convincing nearness to the origin, thus for a genuine renewal.

The foundation words to Peter are thus freed of their isolation and brought to a new actuality today because they are now seen and read in the context of the building of the *ekklesia*, and hence understood from what is the major element in the *ekklesia*,. In addition, the New Testament talks not only about the promise to Simon Peter as foundation of the Church, but also about a foundation of apostles and prophets, although in a different context. This is articulated in the Letter to the Ephesians, where there is already a remarkable reflection about the Church as Church of Jews and Gentiles whose former enmity is to be overcome in the Church:

So then you are no longer strangers and sojourners, but you are fellow citizens with the saints and members of the household of God, built upon the foundation of the apostles and prophets, Christ Jesus himself being the cornerstone, in whom the whole structure is joined together and grows into a holy Temple in the Lord, in whom you also are built into it for a dwelling place of God in the Spirit. (Eph 2:19–22)[8]

Here too we find talk about the building of the Church. The Church appears as a building; its members are the stones of this building; they are built upon the foundation of the apostles and the prophets.

The prophets of the New Testament have, like those of the Old Covenant, the gifts and the tasks of seeing and saying, of rememberance, renewal, and criticism. These are oriented to the origin and to the respective concrete situation of the community of believers, of the People of God. With the doublet apostles and prophets, the matter of office and charism is brought into play. Then, in the fourth chapter of Ephesians, the gifts of the exalted Christ are mentioned: "His gifts were that some should be apostles, some prophets, some evangelists, some pastors and teachers" (Eph 4:11), to the end that the Body of Christ would thus be built up and that this body, by the reconciliation of the separated, as represented in Jews and Gentiles, would become "at home" in one house.

This makes it clear that the Church of Jesus Christ, built up of living stones, occupies a position which in the Old Testament was occupied by the Temple. For Jesus Christ is the place at which God has become accessible to human beings and through whom human beings have access to God. In this sense, then, wherever there is community in Jesus Christ, there is the house and Temple of God.

Consequently, the Christian places of worship that arose in the course of time were not called "house of God," and churches as church buildings have less significance than the Temple in the Old Testament or the holy places and sanctuaries in the other religions. The church building has the function of being a representation of the community which comes together in it; it is the community which is and remains the actual house, the actual Temple of God.

If, in dealing with the question of building and of the building of the Church, this passage from its different context in the Epistle to the Ephesians is brought into the discussion, the purpose is not to do away with Matthew 16:18 and its statement about the foundation on Peter. The purpose is to expand upon it in order to make clear that the foundation stone we have in Christ can be present and realized in all kinds of ways. So, too, if the passage from Ephesians does not talk about the Petrine foundation, that does not argue against it any more than the

---

8. On this passage see the commentaries of H. Schlier, *Der Brief an die Epheser* (Düsseldorf, 1937); R. Schnackenburg, *Der Brief and die Epheser* (Einsiedeln—Cologne—Neukirchen—Vluyn, 1982), Excursus: "Die Kirche in der Sicht des Epheserbriefes" 299–319.

lack of any mention of the foundation upon apostles and prophets argues against that foundation.

It is incontestable that, in the course of history, the full witness of Scripture about the foundation of the *ekklesia* has not always remained alive; choices were made, accents set, and preferences followed. That resulted in one-sidednesses, constrictions, and suppressions. There was, for example, a long time in the Western Church when the foundation in Peter was practically the only thing talked about. The foundation of the apostles and prophets was, to be sure, not theoretically denied, but it was not effective, or it was kept from becoming effective. *One* foundation claimed to contain the others in itself. Government is easier without prophets.

As I see it, our present-day situation is characterized by the fact that—in its difficulty, in its crisis, but also in its hope—a great deal reduces to the proper coordination and cooperation of the different forms of foundation: Peter—apostles—prophets. That this variety still brings numerous difficulties and tensions with it is understandable. For at present something is being tested and put into practice which is biblically grounded and was also a reality in the early history of the Church, but in the last centuries has fallen into forgetfulness or has been pushed aside in favor of the one and only foundation in the Petrine office.

But there is one question that comes up again and again: How could it come about that the Petrine office, whose being and purpose is for the unity of the *ekklesia* and for the strengthening of faith, has today become the most difficult obstacle to unity—even according to the admission of the pope himself? This can't be due to the office as such, nor simply to the resistance of those for whom it makes no sense. For it really should be something accessible. Historically viewed, it is due to the fact that time-conditioned historical, imperial, and feudal models of this office were looked upon as theological data. It is also due to the way this office was conceived, how it was organizationally structured, and how it worked. All this is still far too indebted to a model of earlier times. We see this in the way controversial questions of faith and theology are decided by directives or disciplinary measures, the way initiatives from individual churches and local churches, or from synods, are blocked on the basis that all this had to be regulated in a churchwide manner. But how can something be regulated when there is lacking precisely what there would be to regulate: life, experiences, initiatives?

The criticisms made today of the papacy, in its organization, measures, and methods reveal again and again that the most profound basis for such behavior and proceeding on the part of "Rome" lies in the fact that some believe that its indispensable ministry to the unity of the

Church can be carried out only by striving for and realizing unity as comprehensive standardization. The more this concept of unity changes in favor of a unity in plurality, so much the more could the function of the Petrine ministry become effective and find agreement. This would be happening in a world that is an eminently plural world but at the same time conscious of its unity as never before, a world that is creating forms, institutions, and representations for this unity and its ministry.[9]

9. H. Urs. von Balthasar, Der antirömische Affekt. Wie läßt sich das Papsttum in der Gesamtkirche integrieren? (Freiburg—Basel—Vienna, 1974); G. Denzler, Das Papsttum in der Diskussion (Regensburg, 1974); A. Brandenburg—H. J. Urban, ed., Petrus und Papst. Evangelium—Einheit der Kirche—Papstdienst, 2 vols., (Münster, 1977/78); J. Ratzinger, ed., Dienst an der Einheit. Zum Wesen und Auftrag des Petrusamtes (Düsseldorf, 1978); "Das Papsttum als ökumenische Frage," ed. Arbeitsgemeinschaft ökumenischer Universitätsinstitute, (Munich—Mainz, 1979); M. Hardt, Papsttum und Ökumene. Ansätze eines Neuverständnisses für einen Papstprimat in der protestantischen Theologie des 20. Jahrhunderts (Paderborn—Munich—Vienna—Zurich, 1981).

§49

THE LAST SUPPER OF JESUS AND THE CHURCH

Origin of the Last Supper

There are many problems connected with this theme. They begin with and are concentrated on the question of the origin of the Last Supper. There is already a whole library of writings on this, whose multiplicity is anything but an expression of a living unity.[1] This fullness can be very confusing and could easily make one lose heart. In any case, it clearly warns us against quick, harmonizing solutions. But we are still left with the task of searching for some orientations and guidelines.

In recent times, an idea has been catching on which, in contrast to earlier views, sees the Lord's Supper of Jesus not in isolation, but points out that the *meal* as such, as *primitive phenomenon* of human action and behavior, has a community dimension. The meal is an expression of a community of life and at the same time a means of founding, preserving, and vivifying community, perhaps even raising up again a broken one. In addition, it is a fact of the history of religions that the meal has a religious and cultic significance, as a sign of the community of human beings with the divinity and, precisely thereby, as grounding of a community of human beings amongst themselves.[2]

It is an incontestable fact that the earthly Jesus practiced table fellowship with His disciples, but he also did the same—this was what was new and experienced at the time as shocking—with tax collectors and sinners. These table fellowships are not mere happenstance; they indicate something fundamental and at the same time subversive. They bring a corrective to the concept of God customary at the time and its related praxis of keeping non-Jews and public sinners from taking part in Jewish meals. Which in the case of the Passover meal, was totally excluded.

---

1. Cf. H. Feld, *Das Verständnis des Abendmahls. Erträge der Forschung* (Darmstadt, 1976).
2. F. Bammel, *Das Heilige Mahl im Glauben der Völker* (Gütersloh, 1950).

That Jesus invites tax collectors and sinners to table with Him and allows Himself to be invited to table by them, this expresses the universality of His message and His invitation which is concentrated in the proclamation of the Kingdom of God. The table fellowships of Jesus climb to a high point and are at the same time a preparation for that which the Eucharist of Jesus means in an emphatic and differentiated sense. The Last Supper of Jesus thus has an inner connection with the Church, with the community of Jesus Christ, so much so that the Last Supper, a stage on the way to the becoming of the Church is in the view of many theologians, the very source of the idea of Church (Kattenbusch),[3] indeed, the actual founding action of the Church (Pannenberg).[4]

The texts of the Last Supper[5] are, like much of what we have in the New Testament, not historical protocols of the Last Supper of Jesus, but the statements, witnesses, and documentation of a living tradition taking shape in the Christian community after Jesus' death, resurrection, and exaltation, and of a praxis going back to this original time of tradition formation.

This means that there is a twofold illumination at work. The Eucharist of the community is explained and described in the light of the Last Supper of Jesus; the Last Supper of Jesus is depicted in the light of community liturgy. This is to be attended to in the interpretation of the Last Supper of Jesus. While this does not deny but explicit affirms the relationship to the earthly Jesus, it does put it into certain perspectives.

We have four accounts of the Last Supper: Matthew 26:26–29 and Mark 14:22–24, which agree almost word for word; likewise Luke 22:15–20 and Paul in 1 Corinthians 11:23–25 are very similar to each other. This latter is the oldest text, from about A.D. 54; it understands itself as tradition that Paul has "received from the Lord."

---

3. "Der Quellort der Kirchenidee" in: *Festgabe für Adolf von Harnack* (Tübingen, 1921) 143–72.

4. *Thesen zur Theologie der Kirche* (Munich, 1970) 34–76.

5. "Eucharist" in the theological reference works and in the theologies of the New Testament. In addition: Joachim Jeremias, *The Eucharistic Words of Jesus*, trans. Norman Perrin (New York: Scribner, 1966); H. Schürmann, *Der Passahmahlbericht Lk 22(7–14) 15–18*; ibid., *Die Einsetzungsberichte Lk 22, 19–20* (Münster, 1953); *Der Abendmahlsbericht Lk 22, 7–38*, 3d ed. (Leipzig, 1960); P. Neuenzeit, *Das Herrenmahl. Studien zur paulinischen Eucharistieauffassung* (Munich, 1960); "Eucharist," *SM* 2.257–67; R. Maloney, S.J., "Eucharist," *NDT*, 342–55; D. N. Power, "Eucharist," *Systematic Theology: Roman Catholic Perspectives*, ed. Francis Schüssler Fiorenza and John P. Galvin (Minneapolis: Fortress Press, 1991) 2.259–88; W. Marxsen, *The Beginnings of Christology, Together with the Lord's Supper as a Christological Problem*, trans. Paul J. Achtemeier and Lorenz Nieting (Philadelphia: Fortress Press, 1979); R. Feneberg, *Christliche Passahfeier und Abendmahl. Eine biblisch–hermeneutische Untersuchung der neutestamentlichen Einsetzungsworte* (Munich, 1971); H. Kahlefeld, *Das Abendmahl Jesu und die Eucharistie der Gemeinde* (Frankfurt, 1980).

The four texts contain two streams of tradition: the tradition of the Palestinian community in Mark and Matthew, and in Paul the practice of the Hellenistic community of Corinth.

The text of 1 Corinthians 11:23–26 reads:

For I received from the Lord what I also delivered to you, that the Lord Jesus on the night when he was betrayed took bread, and when he had given thanks, he broke it, and said, "This is my body which is for you. Do this in remembrance of me." In the same way also the cup, after supper, saying, "This cup is the new covenant in my blood. Do this, as often as you drink it, in remembrance of me." For as often as you eat this bread and drink the cup, you proclaim the Lord's death until he comes.

Many questions have to be asked about these and the other Eucharistic texts.

What does "I received from the Lord" mean? Is it, as Ernst Käsemann says,[6] that this is a "statement of holy law": that here, by the solemn appeal to the Lord's name, his authority is mentioned by name, the action of the Eucharist is grounded by the community, and the formula being handed on is sanctioned? Or is this a special revelation of the Risen Lord to Paul? Or is it claiming that the chain of tradition goes back without interruption to the very words of Jesus?

Other questions are: Is the Last Supper of Jesus the last in a series of table fellowships with the disciples, perhaps clothed with a special solemnity; is it a festive meal, a farewell meal?[7] This could be the meaning of the words: "I shall not drink again of the fruit of the vine until that day when I drink it new in the kingdom of God (Mark 14:25; cf. Luke 22:16–18).

Or is the Last Supper of Jesus, because of the temporal proximity to the Jewish feast of Easter, to be interpreted from the Jewish Passover meal, the cultic celebration of the Exodus from Egypt? Was the Last Supper of Jesus actually embedded within that feast? Does its understanding derive from that, especially the important words about the new covenant?

Further: What is being said by the indicatory (this is . . .) words that are spoken in the celebration of the Last Supper? It is notable that the indicatory words over the bread are always the same: "This is my body" (Matthew and Luke); 1 Corinthians adds: "for you"; Luke: "which is given for you." The cup formula in Mark reads: "This is my blood of the covenant, which is poured out for many"; Matthew adds: "for the forgiveness of sins"; 1 Corinthians 11:25: "This cup is the new covenant in my blood. Do this, as often as you drink it, in remembrance

---

6. E. Käsemann, *Sätze heiligen Rechtes im Neuen Testament* in: *Exegetische Versuche und Besinnungen*, 2d ed. (Gottingen, 1965) 69–82. Portions of this book have been translated into English as: *Essays on New Testament Themes*, trans. W. J. Montague (Naperville, Ill.: Alec R. Allenson, 1964).

7. On this see esp. H. Kahlefeld, *Das Abendmahl Jesu*.

of me!" Luke: "This cup is the new covenant in my blood which is poured
out for you."

Is There a History and a Development of the Eucharist? Are There Different Forms of the Eucharist?

These questions are to be taken up in relation to the well-known conception of Willi Marxsen: *Das Abendmahl als christologisches
Problem*—The Eucharist as Christological Problem. The title asserts:
The form and meaning of the Eucharist are connected with the development of Christology. Marxsen sees the matter in this way: In the
Eucharist of the Christian community there is a development in two
stages; likewise there are different forms of the Eucharist.

The first stage: In Paul, the oldest account, we find the Eucharistic
words and the Eucharistic event embedded in an ordinary meal celebration which is described in 1 Corinthians 11:17–34. This is indicated by
the words: "In the same way also the cup, *after supper.*" The principal
weight of this celebration, which connects Eucharist and meal celebration, and makes them one, lies in the fact that through this whole action the community recognizes, represents, and realizes itself. According
to Marxsen, in 1 Corinthians 11 it is not the elements of bread and wine
that are interpreted, rather it is *the community* celebrating the meal
which *is described.* Thus the whole thing is not about the meal, it is not
about the Eucharist. The celebration is interpreted in the following
way: the community celebrating the meal is, by virtue of their faith in
Christ, by virtue of the Christ-relationship of this faith, the Body of
Christ, the New Covenant. By its faith the community understands
itself as Body of Christ and finds in the overall celebration of the meal
a representation and realization of this existence of theirs as Body of
Christ. According to this interpretation of Marxsen, Christ himself
remains in 1 Corinthians 11 without relationship to the gifts of the
meal itself, i.e., the bread and wine.

The second stage, according to Marxsen, is recognizable in that already in Mark, Matthew, and Luke, the connection between a meal of
nourishment and the Eucharist, which led to abuses in Corinth, is no
longer there. Mark 14:17–28 recounts the meal, as does Matthew 26:20–
29, as the Eucharist of Jesus with the Twelve. The interpretation there
is not about a community celebrating a meal, but about the gifts of bread
and wine which are understood as Jesus' body and blood.

It is about Jesus and his re-presentation under the modes of bread and
wine and in the form of taking, eating, drinking. In this way the community of the Twelve is united with Jesus in the form of this sign. Body
and blood is to be understood not as parts of a human being, but as an indication of the concrete bodily person. The disciples become united with

Jesus under the mode of this sign and in the form of this meal, and have a unique community with him. This is a new mode in addition to the word. But the faith is related to both: to the word and the Lord's Supper/Eucharist of Jesus. This, according to Marxsen, was the form that prevailed in the time that followed. The conception of the Eucharist concentrated on the gifts corresponds, according to this, to the developed post-Easter Christology with its titles of sovereignty. The interpretation of the meal as description of the community understanding itself as Body of Christ, still recognizable in the first stage in 1 Corinthians, moves into the background in favor of the gifts given by Jesus the Christ, and of the community with him which they give, and which brings about that the community becomes Body of Christ. Marxsen admits this development as legitimate, even if one-sided.

There is also a third thesis: This form of the Eucharist which relates the Eucharist to the person of Jesus himself, was not instituted by Jesus himself. The reason is that the earthly Jesus neither demanded faith in his person, nor took over the traditional titles of sovereignty, nor wanted a Church. This raises the question of "The Last Supper of Jesus and the Church." For if Jesus had not wanted a Church, the Eucharist could have no relation to it.

Further Inquiries

Of especial concern is the third thesis. One has to ask about the meaning of the already-discussed words of the Synoptic Gospels about the unconditioned following and discipleship related to the person of Jesus; in addition the fact of the messianic actions of Jesus as well as the claim expressed in the words: "Whoever confesses me before human beings, him will I (him will the Son of Man) confess before his Father." Isn't this a confession? Doesn't it include a faith in the person of Jesus, especially when one considers how the message and the fact of the Kingdom of God are connected with the person, behavior, and activity of Jesus?

Marxsen puts too little value on the fact that, in the Eucharistic account of Paul, in spite of its being embedded in a meal of nourishment by which abuses arise, the Eucharist is emphasized and *discerned*. First by the express relationship to the action of Jesus "on the night when he was betrayed": "I received from the Lord what I also delivered to you. The Lord Jesus on the night when he was betrayed, took bread, gave thanks and said: This is my body for you."

It is likewise to be said that Paul speaks in this passage of the unworthy eating of the bread and unworthy drinking of the cup of the Lord, that he explicitly demands that all are to examine themselves, and indeed with the words that force towards discernment: "For anyone who eats and drinks without discerning the body eats and drinks judgment upon himself." These statements point beyond the fact of a community celebrating a meal which, as Marxsen thinks, understands itself as Body of Christ without relationship to the Eucharist.

But most of all, in Marxsen's interpretation, the core of the passage 1 Corinthians 11:24–26 carries too little weight: "This is my body for you—This cup is the new covenant in my blood. Do this, as often as you drink of it, in remembrance of me! For as often as you eat this bread and drink this cup, you proclaim the Lord's death until he comes."

These words cannot simply be said of an ordinary meal. They are, as intensively as they are extensively, *related* to Jesus, more exactly, *to his death.* These words also express the fact that through the eating of the bread and the drinking of the cup, the new covenant, i.e., the new community with God in Jesus, is established. Something new thereby happens in the community and for it; a reality is established which, without this meal, would not be.

Through its celebration of the Eucharist, the community is to constitute and represent itself, not just as interpretation of itself which, without relation to the Eucharist finds its symbolic expression as Body of Christ; but the community constitutes and discerns itself by the fact that in this action, in the eating of the bread broken and by the drinking from the cup, it proclaims in memory the death of the Lord until he comes. The *community is* thus *Body of Christ* and becomes this above all by participation in the body and blood of the Lord, by the Lord's Supper, in which anamnesis of Jesus is made and his death proclaimed until he comes. All this cannot be said just about a meal and about table fellowship as such.

The relationship suggested here of the Body of Christ as image of the community to the Body of Christ as content of the Eucharist and the Eucharistic event, is expressed once again in the same First Letter to the Corinthians with these words. "The cup of blessing which we bless, is it not a participation in the blood of Christ? The bread which we break, is it not a participation in the body of Christ? Because there is one bread, we who are many are one body, for we all partake of the one bread" (1 Corinthians 10:16–17).

Marxsen interprets this passage too as an interpretation of the community which is represented in image and in the parabolic power of the meal; the passage doesn't tell him anything about the Eucharist, but only about the community.

In response: Bread can only create a body if it has a special quality as mode of the re-presentation and presence of Christ. This is expressed in the words: the bread is (creates) participation in the Body of Christ. The unity of the celebrating community can be grounded by the unity of the bread only if the bread, as verse 16 says, is the Body of Christ, thus has a new meaning.

In these words—in the witness of 1 Corinthians, the witness about a community and its meal celebrations and Eucharistic celebrations, the witness about the abuses and misunderstandings arising there, and a witness of the interpretation of this event—the relationship of Eucharist and Church (understood as community) is represented.

This relationship can be summed up as follows: the Church, the community, understands itself as the Body of Christ. It becomes Body of Christ as an expression of itself by means of its participation in the Body of Christ as embodiment of the Eucharistic event. It becomes this in its recognition of the discernment of the Lord's Supper, in its remembering of the death of Jesus, in its proclamation—in the sign of the broken bread and poured-out wine—of the death of the Lord until He comes, in its receiving a share—which extends beyond earthly death—in the fruit of and salvific significance of this death, death for the many.

At the same time the Church recognizes here its existence as the community of the New Covenant. Through its participation in the event entrusted to it, it attains its own community. The Body of Christ (the Church) lives from the Body of Christ understood as the Lord's Supper. The community as Body of Christ fails in its calling if quarrels, egoism, and lack of love reign in it. Such behavior is the real obstacle to participation in the Eucharist; there is in addition—as obstacle—the "nondiscerning of the Body of the Lord."

Let us go back from here once again to the question with which we started: Is the Eucharist an institution of Jesus; can it be brought into relationship with the Church? Is the Lord's Supper witnessed and described by Paul with its relationship to the community with Jesus, in its relationship to the death of Jesus for the many, and with its ecclesiological implication, something quite different from what Jesus himself did and intended in the last meal witnessed in the Gospels? Connected with this is the question: Did Jesus bring the event of His last meal into relationship with His death as given for the many?

The first thing to be said is that the text of 1 Corinthians 11 from about the year A.D. 54 is not put forward as a Pauline conception, new creation, or interpretation, but as a tradition received by him and being handed on. Paul takes pains to give witness that the celebration of the Eucharist of the community in Corinth is based on the action of Jesus, his action on the night in which he was betrayed and handed over; that the celebration of the community re-presents in remembering the death of Jesus; that it proclaims it by its action; that it takes part in it by participation in bread and cup, which are characterized as Body of Christ and as cup of the covenant through the Blood of Christ. The community views the celebration of the Eucharist as fulfillment of the commission of Jesus and can recognize no other reason for its action than this, to do what Jesus did and what he commanded to be done. The community fulfills the command, the testament of Jesus. This is illustrated by the addition found in Paul (1 Cor 11:25): "Do this in memory of me!"

Therefore in 1 Corinthians 11, Paul has no intention of offering any practice of his own and no theory of this practice, in contrast, for example, to the practice of other communities, for example, of the Jerusalem community. His only apparent intention, which he takes pains to emphasize, is to hand on only that which in the tradition of all the communities lives on as Jesus' testament.

Over-against the thesis of Marxsen that no especially emphasized final meal, called Eucharist, can be witnessed about the historical Jesus, a number of other exegetes (J. Jeremias, P. Neuenzeit, J. Schmid, H. Schürmann) have explicitly emphasized precisely this. They have pointed to the fact that the Eucharist does not stand simply in the series of other celebrations of table fellowship of Jesus with his disciples and with tax collectors and sinners, but that it is distinguished from them as a *special meal*, and indeed, according to the opinion of Joachim Jeremias based on the Synoptics, by the fact that Jesus in the night before his death celebrated this last meal as a solemn Passover meal with readings, stories, prayers, and hymns, in which was celebrated the solemn remembrance of the departure and rescue from Egypt and the establishment of the covenant. The Lukan text talks explicitly about this: "I have earnestly desired to eat this Passover with you before I suffer" (Luke 2:15).

It is from within the Passover framework and context that the words and actions of Jesus take their meaning. They explain above all the words about the covenant and about the *new covenant*. They explain the words of self-giving in the sign of the broken bread and poured out wine as giving oneself up unto death.

But this death is interpreted as death for the many, or "for you," i.e., for Israel and the peoples of the world. This "for" has a twofold function: First, it has the function of *representation:* Jesus' death is a death in place of others. Further, it is a death whose fruit benefits others, thus a death that brings salvation, redemption, atonement, communion with God, a death that is the ground of the new covenant. The community of the meal in the form of taking, eating, and drinking, confers community with this event and community with the one who did, or does, this.

But even if the connection with the Passover meal were not provable, there is something else about the final meal of Jesus before his death that comes through loud and clear from all the witnesses as well as from the absolutely unique indicatory words over the bread and the cup. Jesus' death is not just foretold, it is also interpreted by the way in which he assumes the mission and fate of the Servant of God from Isaiah 42, by the way in which Jesus interprets his life and fate and recognizes the path he is to follow. The death of Jesus is an act of self-giving which founds something new. It founds a new order and existence, a new covenant into which they who belong to him are drawn by participation in this meal. In this way, and only in this way, is it possible that the celebration of the Lord's Supper be a proclamation of the Lord's death until he comes.

The Last Supper/Eucharist of Jesus is a sign of the fact that Jesus thought about a community of those connected with him, of those drawn into the fruit of his death, and about the people of a new covenant, and that he intended—beyond his existence and beyond his death—precisely what is meant by *Church*.

Result

The result of all this is that the different accounts of the Last Supper, which represent two traditions, leave the question of the Last Supper and the problem of its interpretation by no means completely unexplained. There is not only a formal convergence, but also a convergence in content in the following points—a convergence that remains verifiable in particulars despite all the differences.

All the accounts appeal to Jesus and his action "on the night he was betrayed." In all the accounts the Last Supper is a meal connected with the table fellowships held by Jesus, and at the same time a meal that is different, set apart. This is shown clearly as early as 1 Corinthians 11; and it is quite thoroughly shown in the other accounts of the Last Supper. This distinction is highlighted by the interpretative words over bread and wine into the Body and Blood of Christ; it is highlighted by the exhortation to self-examination before the reception, by the exhortation to the discernment of the Body and blood of the Lord from the other gifts of the meal, and finally—connected with this—by the warning against unworthy consumption. Thus, the theory of a development in two stages doesn't hold.

Additional support comes from the fact that this meal is connected with the death of Jesus understood as self-giving for the many. This is independent of the question: Last Supper—Passover meal? There are also the themes of sharing and participation in the person and fate of Jesus, and with that in the new life grounded therein which is conferred by Jesus through this meal and its gifts.

The convergence of the accounts of the Last Supper consists further in the fact that through this event something new is created and established: the eschatological New Covenant, being founded in the death of Jesus, whose bearer is the community of Jesus. The *ekklesia* exists and lives by its sharing and participation in this event in which the *memoria* of the death of Jesus is celebrated and through the celebration proclaimed, in which communion with Jesus, in the form of the gifts and signs, in the form of the meal, is conferred. The community of the disciples of Jesus has therewith an obligation to the attitude, the behavior, and the action of Jesus: to Jesus' existence for others. Where this dimension is lacking, or even seriously diminished, the Eucharist has not fulfilled its function.

In view of these dimensions, the Last Supper means that Jesus did think of a community—that is, of the community that was connected with him—and that this is what he intended. The community was to remain connected with him precisely through this celebration. But this understanding is possible and makes sense only if this memorial celebration is not for someone dead, not for someone who was definitively torn from his loved ones by death and whose irreplaceable loss can only be lamented. Such a lamentation for the dead must one day end, and indeed not all that long after death. If in the accounts of Last Supper we find words about proclaiming the death of Jesus until he comes, this implies that he can come only if he is alive, and has not remained in death.

Only so can it be understood that the celebration of the Lord's Supper was celebrated by the community with joy and jubilation, and that it was articulated as thanksgiving, as *Eucharist*. This would all be out of place as a memorial celebration of the dead. The celebration of the Lord's Supper is possible and makes sense only in the consciousness that the one whose memorial and self-giving death is being celebrated is not dead. And this is precisely the message of the resurrection of Jesus from the dead. Without the message of the raising of Jesus from the dead, there would be no Eucharist and no Church as community of those who ground their existence radically in Christ as someone present and living.

The situation of the Christian churches today is still represented as a broken church community. This is manifest in the broken eucharistic communion. There is a conclusion from this too: As long as there is no eucharistic community, there is no church community, and vice versa. The connection between eucharistic community and church community is indissoluble. It is of the utmost importance to recognize this and to act accordingly.

The question of the eucharistic community of the Church, which cannot be taken up in detail here, is among the most burning questions in present-day ecumenical dialogue. There is some astonishing documentation on this subject; for example, *Das Herrenmahl* (1979), a work of the

Common Roman Catholic and Evangelical Lutheran Commission, and the Convergence Declarations of the Commission for Faith and Order of the Ecumenical Council of Churches (1982) on Baptism, Eucharist, and Ministry.[8]

The developing dialectic on this theme can be expressed in the formula which still awaits full reception: The Eucharist demands and supports the community of faith; it is an expression of unity in faith, and at the same time a way of achieving this goal.

A good overview on the contemporary situation is mediated by the document of the Common Roman Catholic and Evangelical Lutheran Commission *Wege zur Gemeinschaft* (1980):

We are depressed by the fact that the state of the relationships of our churches with each other still does not allow for the opening of full eucharistic community. But we confess anew our longing for the goal of visible unity in the one faith and the one eucharistic community. The credibility of our witness before the world and of our celebration of the Eucharist itself is threatened by our separation in these celebrations. The great push towards eucharistic community which we presently experience suggests to us that this is not happening without the working of the Holy Spirit. We are not giving up the search for possibilities to grant even now a mutual admission to communion in special cases. (81)

8. *Das Herrenmahl*, Gemeinsame röm-kath./ev.-luth. Kommission (Paderborn—Frankfurt, 1978); *Baptism, Eucharist and Ministry (BEM)*, Faith and Order Paper No. 111 (Geneva: WCC, 1982); cf. Michael A. Fahey, ed., *Catholic Perspectives on Baptism, Eucharist and Ministry* (Lanham, Md.: University Press of America, 1986).

PART THREE

THE CHURCH OF CHRIST

After Jesus' death there was a new beginning. It is the beginning that is described with the word "resurrection/raising of Jesus from the dead," with the word "Easter" and with the new name "Christ" or "Kyrios, Lord," which is a title of sovereignty and is applied to Jesus: Jesus is the Christ and the Kyrios.

It would have been possible and reasonable to approach the theme "Church" with the new situation established with the raising of Jesus from the dead and to say something about the earthly Jesus, about his message and his action in the light of the risen Christ.

On the other hand, it is also possible and legitimate to take the path from the earthly Jesus to the Christ who was raised from the dead—this is Christology "from below." This is the way the Gospels did it, but incorporating it into their post-Easter perspective. It is both characteristic and significant that the New Testament, in the form in which we have it, begins with the Gospels of Jesus, or, that the Gospels were taken up into the canon, i.e., into the normative witness of the Church about Jesus the Christ. The community of believers was not satisfied simply with the message or the kerygma that Jesus, the Crucified, has been raised from the dead; not satisfied that this message alone was important. Instead, all importance was laid on giving witness to the Jesus who, through the pathway of his life, through death and resurrection, became the Christ and the Kyrios.

If the raising of Jesus from the dead represents something new in this sense, that Jesus is the Christ, this leads logically to the theme of this section: The Church of Christ.

§50

THE RAISING (RESURRECTION) OF JESUS AND THE CHURCH

The Significance of the Raising of Jesus

The message, the event, and the word about the raising of Jesus from the dead[1] signify that God has explicitly confirmed the pre-Easter activity of Jesus. The raising is thus also a new mode and new confirmation of God's rule, which has become effective in Jesus and which is realized in the resurrection in the sense that here, the overcoming of death has become reality and a new beginning, a new future for the world, and new hope has been established: the ground which determines history in a new way and gives it a new goal. It becomes clear that the divinity (the being God) of God consists in the fact that God makes the dead live. The Kingdom of God now bears the face of Jesus Christ (Schillebeeckx). By his raising from the dead, the proclaiming Jesus becomes the proclaimed Christ.

If the Church is the community of believers, of those who ground their faith in Jesus, then this faith is not just related to Jesus insofar as Jesus by his radical, God-grounded existence is, as the Epistle to the Hebrews says, "the pioneer and perfecter of our faith" (Heb 12:2)—the relatedness of faith is grounded in Jesus insofar as he, as the Christ and the Lord, is also the content of faith. In this way faith, in its comprehensive meaning, becomes Christian faith. The community of believers, who ground their faith in Jesus the Christ, is thus possible only and wholly because of Easter. For only there is the hope of faith directed to Jesus fulfilled. Easter thus has a completely special relationship to the community of believers which is called the Church.

We have already given considerable attention to the kind of change and conversion brought about in the Twelve and in the disciples by the raising of Jesus.

What it meant to be an apostle was also given a new dimension by Easter. An apostle is now the one who is the witness of the resurrection.

---

1. Cf. The expositions in our presentation of revelation above in Book Two.

A witness of the resurrection is whoever is a witness of the Risen One, and indeed not just an eye- and ear-witness, but a word- and deed-witness. That is why Paul can call himself an apostle. Whoever is a witness of the resurrection and the Risen One gives witness to the Lordship of Jesus unlimited by any power, even death. This opens up the ground and the right to mediate the message of life and salvation as message for all, for Jews and Gentiles. From the messenger commissioned for the twelve-tribed people, the apostle of Jesus Christ becomes the messenger and witness for the whole world. The apostles are taken up in the mission of Jesus: "As the Father has sent me, so I send you" (John 20:21). The words of the Risen One: "All authority in heaven and on earth has been given to me. Go therefore and make disciples of all nations" (Matt 28:18-19) correspond completely to the way of Jesus himself.

The Baptismal Commission

In the commissioning words of the Risen Lord in Mark and Matthew is found the word "baptism": "He who believes and is baptized" (Mark 16:16); "Baptize them in the name of the Father and of the Son and of the Holy Spirit" (Matt 28:19).[2]

Apart from these passages, nowhere in the Gospels is baptism looked upon as a condition for being a disciple of Jesus and for communion with him. The earthly Jesus speaks of conversion, faith, and following him. Jesus himself did not baptize; He was baptized. He received the baptism of John, which was a sign of conversion and repentance. Jesus' intention in doing this is to enter into the community of human beings and put Himself in solidarity with them. Baptism in the commissioning words of the risen One has another meaning.

The requirement of faith and conversion in no way gets lost in this change. It lives on in the statement: "He who believes" and "Make disciples of all nations!" On the other hand, it is clear that the practice of baptism existed from the beginning, that there are no unbaptized Christians. This is depicted in an exemplary way in the so-called Pentecost Sermon of Peter. When the hearers ask, "What shall we do?"

2. Cf. "Baptism" in the theological reference works, in the presentations of the theology of the New Testament, and in the textbooks on dogma and the history of dogma. In addition: Oscar Cullmann, *Baptism in the New Testament,* trans. J. K. S. Reid (London: S. C. M. Press, 1951); Rudolf Schnackenburg, *Baptism in the Thought of St. Paul: A Study in Pauline Theology,* trans. G. R. Beasley-Murray (New York: Herder and Herder, 1964); H. Schneider, *Die Taufe im Neuen Testament* (Stuttgart, 1952); B. Neunheuser, "Taufe und Firmung" in: *Handbuch der Dogmengeschichte IV/2* (Freiburg, 1956); O. Kuss, *Der Römerbrief* (Regensburg, 1957–1959) 307–381; likewise the commentaries on Romans by J. Fitzmyer, E. Käsemann, H. Schlier, and U. Wilckens; G. Delling, *Die Taufe im Neuen Testament* (Berlin, 1963); Karl Barth, *Church Dogmatics IV/4: Die Taufe als Begründung des christlichen Lebens* (Zurich, 1967); E. Schlink, *The Doctrine of Baptism,* trans. Herbert J. A. Bouman (St. Louis: Concordia Publishing House, 1972).

he answers, "Repent, and be baptized every one of you in the name of Jesus Christ for the forgiveness of your sins" (Acts 2:38). The summation reads: "So those who received his word were baptized, and there were added that day about three thousand souls" (Acts 2:41).

The practice of baptism present from the beginning can only be explained by the fact that one saw in this the fulfillment of the will and the commission of Jesus, even if, historically, it cannot be precisely determined when this took place. The passage in Matthew "Baptize them in the name of the Father and of the Son and of the Holy Spirit" repeats not the precise words of Jesus but the liturgical form of the baptismal formula either in the community of Matthew or as reflection within a certain development. Along with this formula there is, above all in Paul and in the Acts of the Apostles, baptism in the name of Jesus.

That the New Testament talks about baptism only after Easter is grounded in the fact that in the baptismal event a relationship to the death and resurrection of Jesus is represented. The one who receives baptism is given the gift of communion with the Crucified and Risen One and the life opened up by him. Whoever is baptized now belongs to Jesus Christ.

In addition, it was especially Paul who reflected profoundly in relation to the submerging ritual of the baptismal bath:

We were buried therefore with him by baptism into death, so that as Christ was raised from the dead by the glory of the Father, we too might walk in newness of life. For if we have been united with him in a death like his, we shall certainly be united with him in a resurrection like his. (Rom 6:4–5)

The being in Christ, the determining factor for the community of believers, which takes place in the act of faith, is realized on the level of visibility and symbol. That is, it comes about in baptism as the act of being grounded in Christ, similar to the way in which it comes about in the Lord's Supper, as life from the Body of Christ.

Baptism is, more precisely—this comes from biblical reflection on the matter—the sign of the new life, the "rebirth," the birth to being a new human being. Baptism is to be understood not at all in the sense of a naturalistic deification, but very much as the communication to human beings of the life opened up by Jesus Christ. The rejection of all magical ideas is assured by the fact that faith is the presupposition for the reception of baptism, and also by the fact that the gift bestowed in the sign of baptism does not work automatically but turns into an ongoing task, an imperative: the baptized must lead a new life, must "walk in the Spirit."

"Baptism," says Luther in the Small Catechism," is not simply water, but it is the water taken hold of in God's Word and united with

God."[3] Without God's Word, the water is only water and not baptism, but with the Word of God it is a baptism, a water of life and a bath of regeneration. Baptism with water means that the old human being is supposed to die in us by daily repentance, and, everyday, to rise again a new human being who lives in righteousness for God.[4]

Baptism in this view thus leads, as rite of initiation, into the community of those whose faith is defined by Jesus Christ. As initiation, baptism can be bestowed only once. This community is connected with Jesus Christ by baptism in a very special way, and it comes to be as unity in Christ by means of baptism. Paul expresses this in Galatians 3:27 in a somewhat strange, daring image: "For as many of you as were baptized into Christ have put on Christ. There is neither Jew nor Greek, there is neither slave nor free, there is neither male nor female; for you are all one in Christ Jesus" (Gal 3:27–28). To put on Christ like a garment means entering into a new situation and form, that of being Christ. It signifies the beginning of participation in the being of Christ himself, which is realized in the mode of the "Christ in me." There comes from this a new relationship to community and a new form of community. In the formulation of Paul, You are all "one" in Christ, and thus Body of Christ.

From this connection comes a new understanding of the baptism of Jesus. The passages belonging to this (Matthew 3:13–17; Luke 3:21; John 1:32–34) are, according to their literary genre, not biographical accounts of experience about, for example, the awakening of the messianic consciousness of Jesus or the description of a heavenly vision, but a piece of baptismal catechesis intended to give insight into the meaning of baptism. But factually it does give some connection between the baptism of John taken over by Jesus and the baptismal practice that was there from the [Christian] beginning.

In baptism and its interpretation as new birth, as connection with Jesus, as participation in his death and resurrection, is expressed in a very special way the fact that being a Christian is being in reception, that receiving comes before doing, that gift is the presupposition for every form of mandate. (It is in considerations like this that the possibility and justification of infant baptism is grounded.)

---

3. Martin Luther, *The Small Cathechism of Dr. Martin Luther* (St. Louis, 1940) 170.
4. Ibid. 177.

§51

THE CHURCH AS WORK OF THE SPIRIT

Jesus and the Spirit

Easter is the existential ground of the Church because here is brought to completion that to which faith is related: the person, the way, and the work of Jesus. To this completion, which is constitutive for the Church, belongs the coming of the Spirit. The Spirit as Spirit of God is the principle of creating life since the making of the world.[1]

According to the witness of the New Testament, the Spirit of God as power and life of God was active in Jesus in a special way: beginning with the Incarnation, manifest with the baptism of Jesus. Jesus' words and deeds are manifestations of the Spirit of God; by this Spirit He banishes the power of the evil one. In doing so Jesus is not seized as by an outside principle; He is Himself the bearer of the Spirit of God. That is why He can also mediate and share the Spirit. The Gospel of John talks about this explicitly: I will send you the helper, the Paraclete, "The Spirit of truth, who proceeds from the Father, He will bear witness to me" (John 15:26).

The realization of this promise takes place after Jesus' raising from the dead with the words "Receive the Holy Spirit" (John 20:22). The Spirit of God as life-giving, creating Spirit was active above all in the raising of Jesus from the dead. This is what the beginning of the Letter to the Romans says:

1. Basic works: Yves Congar, *I Believe in the Holy Spirit*, trans. David Smith (New York: Seabury Press, 1983); in addition: Johann Adam Möhler, *Unity in the Church or the Principle of Catholicism: Presented in the Spirit of the Church Fathers of the First Three Centuries*, ed. and trans. Peter C. Erb (Washington, D.C.: The Catholic University of America Press, 1996); E. Schweizer, *Geist und Gemeinde im Neuen Testament* (Munich, 1952); H. Mühlen, *Una mystica persona. Die Kirche als das Mysterium der Heilsgeschichtlichen Identität des Heiligen Geistes in Christus und den Christen* (Munich—Paderborn—Vienna, 1964); Hans Küng, *The Church* (New York: Sheed and Ward, 1967) 150–202; Jürgen Moltmann, *The Church in the Power of the Spirit* (New York: Harper & Row, 1977); Walter Kasper—G. Sauter, *Kirche—Ort des Geistes* (Freiburg—Basel—Vienna, 1976).

Paul, a servant of Jesus Christ, called to be an apostle, set apart for the gospel of God which he promised beforehand through his prophets in the Holy Scriptures, the gospel concerning his Son, who was descended from David according to the flesh and designated Son of God in power according to the Spirit of holiness by his resurrection from the dead, Jesus Christ our Lord, through whom we have received grace and apostleship [apostolic office]. . . . " (Rom 1:1–5)

The Pentecost narrative (Acts 2) contains some problems in individual aspects. But on the whole, what it intends to say is that the Spirit of God, the gift of the definitive time of salvation as expressed by the prophets (Joel), was conferred upon the apostles and those gathered with them: "They were all filled with the Holy Spirit and began to speak in other tongues, as the Spirit gave them utterance" (Acts 2:4). The effect of this conferral of the Spirit is experienced and becomes recognizable above all in the word and witness of Peter and the other apostles:

"Jesus of Nazareth, a man attested to you by God with mighty works and wonders and signs which God did through him in your midst, as you yourselves know— this Jesus, delivered up according to the definite plan and foreknowledge of God, you crucified and killed by the hands of lawless men. But God raised him up, having loosed the pangs of death, because it was not possible for him to be held by it." (Acts 2:22–24)

"Being therefore exalted at the right hand of God, and having received from the Father the promise of the Holy Spirit, he has poured out this which you see and hear." (Acts 2:33)

"Let all the house of Israel know assuredly that God has made him both Lord and Christ, this Jesus whom you crucified." (Acts 2:36)

The coordination of Christ and the Spirit is according to Paul so intensively visible that one can say: "The Lord is the Spirit. The Kyrios is the Pneuma" (2 Cor 3:17).[2] Through the Spirit of God, the Raised and Risen One will experience Himself as living presence and powerful reality beyond the distance of time and beyond the limits of space. Through the Spirit, then, a new belonging of Christians to Christ is effected. What significance the Spirit of Jesus has for the disciples is disclosed in the Gospel of John, in the so-called Paraclete sermons (John 14).[3] The Spirit, through whom Christ will remain as support (Paraclete) with His chosen ones, will remind them of Jesus, He will give witness of Him, He will lead to the truth, He will overcome the world. The Spirit is the guarantee that "his own" remain in the truth.

---

2. J. Hermann, *Kyrios und Pneuma* (Munich, 1961).
3. H. Schlier, *The Relevance of the New Testament* (New York: Herder and Herder, 1968) 239–48; Rudolf Schnackenburg, "Der Paraklet und die Parakletsprüche" in: *The Gospel According to St. John* (New York, 1990) 4 vols., 3.138–54.

The truth[4] which is connected with the Spirit as the Spirit of truth is to be understood not as propositional truth, but a sign of the fidelity of God which is fulfilled in the Jesus-event—according to John 14:6, "I am the truth." The reality of God and human beings is thereby disclosed and spoken in words. At the same time, the Johannine concept of truth includes not only that truth be taken cognizance of, but also that it be done. There is, consequently one—not the only—criterion for the presence and activity of this Spirit, a criterion for the discernment of spirits. This is found—and so closes the circle—in the statement related to Jesus, the Christ: "By this you know the Spirit of God: every spirit which confesses that Jesus Christ has come in the flesh is of God, and every spirit which does not confess Jesus is not of God" (1 John 4:2–3; cf. 1 Cor 12:2). The confession of Jesus, the Christ, is the criterion for the discernment of the Spirit and the spirits. This Spirit, the Spirit of Jesus, the Spirit whom Jesus sends, along with the Spirit's gifts and activity, are to be with them, are to determine, vivify, and characterize their existence whom the Johannine Christ calls "his own": as community of those who belong to him, which is a new name for the community of believers, for Church.

The Effects of the Spirit

Paul, especially, speaks of them as the fruits of the Spirit in the life of Christians (Gal 5:22). He calls them peace, joy, love, patience, friendliness, fidelity, and above all freedom. Freedom is for him the embodiment of Christian existence: "Where the Spirit of the Lord is, there is freedom" (2 Cor 3:17). For Paul, freedom is liberation from the manifold enslavements in the world and in all that is powerful in the world. Freedom is also empowerment to a life in Christ and from the Spirit.[5]

Paul also speaks of the fact that the Spirit of Christ lives in the Christian: "All who are led by the Spirit of God are sons of God. For you did not receive the spirit of slavery to fall back into fear, but you have received the spirit of sonship. When we cry, "Abba! Father!" it is the spirit himself bearing witness with our Spirit that we are children of God (Rom 8:14–16). "God's love has been poured out into our hearts through the Holy Spirit which has been given to us" (Rom 5:5). The Christian is the temple of the Holy Spirit (1 Cor 6:19). Christians are sealed with the Spirit of promise (cf. Eph 4:30). "God has sent the Spirit of His Son into our hearts" (Gal 4:6). Hence the admonition: "Do

---

4. Rudolf Schnackenburg, "Der Johanneische Wahrheitsbegriff" in: *The Gospel According to St. John* 2.225–37.

5. Ernst Käsemann, *Jesus Means Freedom: A Polemical Survey of the New Testament*, trans. Frank Clarke (Philadelphia: Fortress Press, 1970).

not grieve the Holy Spirit of God" (Eph 4:30). And on the other hand we also hear: Have no fear when you are led before kings and magistrates. "For it is not you who speak, but the Spirit of your Father speaking through you" (Matt 10:20). The Spirit thus means the inner definition of the Christian—with inner definition understood as source and origin for the actualization of faith and life.

The effects of the Spirit for the life of a community have been described by Paul in his First Letter to the Corinthians. This community was in no way an "ideal community." Instead, it was torn by strife and divisions. The Apostle lays before their eyes the image of a unity alive through the gifts of the Spirit, the charisms:

Now there are varieties of gifts, but the same Spirit; and there are varieties of service, but the same Lord; and there are varieties of working, but it is the same God who inspires them all in every one. To each is given the manifestation of the Spirit for the common good. To one is given through the Spirit the utterance of wisdom, and to another the utterance of knowledge according to the same Spirit, to another faith by the same Spirit, to another gifts of healing by the one Spirit, to another the working of miracles, to another prophecy, to another the ability to distinguish between spirits, to another various kinds of tongues, to another the interpretation of tongues. All these are inspired by one and the same Spirit, who apportions to each one individually as He wills. (1 Cor 12:4–11)

This description is not a representation of the community at Corinth as it actually is, but as it should be and should become. Paul says something in the Epistle to the Romans, as he views the community:

For as in one body we have many members, and all the members do not have the same function, so we, though many, are one body in Christ, and individually members one of another. Having gifts that differ according to the grace given to us, let us use them: if prophecy, in proportion to our faith; if service, in our serving; he who teaches, in his teaching; he who exhorts, in his exhortation; he who contributes, in liberality; he who gives aid, with zeal; he who does acts of mercy, with cheerfulness. (Rom 12:4–8)

From all this comes a further criterion for the discernment of spirits: Readiness for the building up of the community by service to its members, by the recognition of the gifts of the Spirit, by the knowledge of the interdependence of one upon the other. Like Christ, the Spirit, too, is a foundation of the unity of those who believe in Christ:

Be eager to maintain the unity of the Spirit in the bond of peace. There is one body and one Spirit, just as you were called to the one hope that belongs to your call, one Lord, one faith, one baptism, one God and Father of us all, who is above all and through all and in all (Eph 4:3-6).

In the situation constituted by the raising of Jesus, by the commissioning words of the Risen One, and by the sending of the Spirit, everything has come to fulfillment that belongs to revelation in the form of fulfillment, in the sense of the here and now. Also fulfilled is that which belongs to the community of those whose faith is defined by this revelation as fulfillment, i.e., the Church. It is therefore an apt definition when Hans Küng arranges his book on the Church under the three aspects: The Church as the New People of God—The Church as Body of Christ—The Church as Creation of the Spirit.

Through all of this, however, it is also being said that the Church is not identical with that to which it is related and on which it is grounded, that it does not have free power of disposition over it, but that God in Christ and in the Holy Spirit is the constant over-against of the orientation, the critique, the conversion, and the renewal of the Church. And so it is that the existence and task of the Church consists in constantly keeping open its transparency to its ground and its over-against.

As can be seen, it is theologically well grounded that the connection between Church and Holy Spirit is clearly expressed in the Apostles' Creed. I believe in the Church as work of the Holy Spirit in whom I believe. There are major theological systems which pneumatologically ground their representation of the Church as a whole, and understand it as work of the Holy Spirit. The works of Möhler, Mühlen, and Moltmann deserve special mention (see above, n. 1). Vatican II, in its Dogmatic Constitution on the Church, expressed the relationship of Church and Holy Spirit in this way:

When the work which the Father had given the Son to do on earth (cf. Jn. 17:4) was accomplished, the Holy Spirit was sent on the day of Pentecost in order that He might forever sanctify the Church, and thus all believers would have access to the Father through Christ in the one Spirit (cf. Eph. 2:18). He is the Spirit of life, a fountain of water springing up to life eternal (cf. Jn. 4:14; 7:38–39). Through Him the Father gives life to men who are dead from sin, till at last He revives in Christ even their mortal bodies (cf. Rom. 8:10–11).

The Spirit dwells in the Church and in the hearts of the faithful as in a temple (cf. 1 Cor. 3:16; 6:19). In them He prays and bears witness to the fact that they are adopted sons (cf. Gal. 4:6; Rom. 8:15–16 and 26). The Spirit guides the Church into the fullness of truth (cf. Jn. 16:13) and gives her a unity of fellowship and service. He furnishes and directs her with various gifts, both hierarchical and charismatic, and adorns her with the fruits of His grace (cf. Eph. 4:11–12; 1 Cor. 12:4; Gal. 5:22). By the power of the gospel He makes the Church grow, perpetually renews her, and leads her to perfect union with her Spouse. The Spirit and the Bride both say to the Lord Jesus, "Come!" (cf. Apoc. 22:17).

Thus the Church shines forth as "a people made one with the unity of the Father, the Son, and the Holy Spirit."[6]

---

6. *Lumen gentium* no. 4.

Signs of the Spirit Today

To believe in and understand the Church as work of the Spirit means to be mindful of its life and vitality, means to protect it from narrowness and inflexibility, and from fear and faintheartedness as well as from dissolution and lack of orientation. It means in addition that its own renewal is the Church's constant task, a task that is accomplished by the power of the Holy Spirit as the soul of the community of believers.

To believe in and understand the Church as work of the Spirit means to make a place in it for the new, the unexpected, the future, according to the injunction, "Do not quench the Spirit" (1 Thes 5:19); it means, further, to acknowledge that the Spirit of God blows when and where and how it wills, that it cannot be preordained, or chained, or manipulated and regimented. Amongs the signs of the activity of the Spirit in the Church are the prophets in the Church, the charismatics, often too the uncomfortable critics who understand criticism as faithful engagement, the ones who push towards new turning points and leave their mark on history. Signs of the activity of the Spirit are also the saints of every century and their heroic life of faith, their dedication, their love, and their following of Christ.

The working of the Holy Spirit is also recognizable today in a remarkable and unexpected manner in the midst of a wave of secularization, of departure from the Church, or resignation within the Church.[7] One can mention *Taizé* as a place of spiritual awakening, especially of a Christian awakening of youth, which is a special sign of hope. It is precisely the genuinely religious, the specifically Christian and "spiritual," that makes for the fascination of Taizé: its worship, the Eucharist, the silence, the contemplation, singing hymns in many languages and with one melody, the community, the mutual acceptance that grows of itself like the grain of wheat in the parable of Jesus. That all this is not just an ephemeral experience is shown by the fact that the young people there make the spirit of Taizé the form of their life, and that they seek to bring others to the same committment. The religious and the spiritual in Taizé by no means serve an individual self-edification. Taizé unites, as part of a work by Roger Schutz says, "meditation and commitment," meditation and battle, a battle against all forms of evil so that "human beings will be no more the sacrifice of human beings," as the program of the Council of Youth says.

The other inspiration is the ecumenical commitment of the Brothers of Taizé, and through them, also of those who come there. It is contained in this sentence of the rule: "Never be satisfied with the scandal of the separation of Christians. Have a passion for the unity of the

---

7. Cf. Heinrich Fries, "Aufbruch des religiösen Geistes" in: *Glaube und Kirche im ausgehenden 20. Jahrhundert* (Munich, 1979) 30–45.

Body of Christ!" The idea that ecumenical commitment is a sign of the working of the Holy Spirit was explicitly affirmed by Vatican II.

Something similar is seen in the movement of the *Focolarini* which, as a lay movement, has spread throughout the whole world. Here too is manifest an outbreak of the true Christian Spirit, above all in its readiness, in the Spirit of Jesus, to accept one's neighbor unconditionally and to carry the "revolution of love" to all countries. This movement perhaps does not have as much publicity as Taizé. But the living commitment in its many cells speaks for itself and is also a sign of great hope: In many places of the world shines the spark, the fire-place of the Focolarini. To be mentioned in this context—as a further sign—is the community of the Little Brothers and Sisters who, in the Spirit of Charles de Foucauld and through a life of poverty and simplicity, of selfless presence, of existence for others, give witness to the unconquerable Spirit of Jesus.

This brings up, as if automatically, a further remarkable sign. It is the charismatic movement in the Christian churches, which has dedicated itself to renewal.[8] Although it is not very easy to get an overall picture of the various groups and developments that make up this movement, it can still be said that in them lives a primitive Christian element, an experience of the Spirit manifested in the gifts and fruits of the Spirit: in the gifts of joy, spontaneity, prayer, spirituality, but also of healing and speaking in tongues.

Cardinal Suenens[9] became a special promoter of these charismatic movements and saw in them one of the great hopes for the future of the Church. With him on this are many theologians who hope to find through these movements solutions for the tasks of the Church and its ecumenical challenges, especially in those areas where efforts until now have gone nowhere. Pope Paul VI described the charismatic renewal as a chance for the Church, and then named the tasks connected with it: not to extinguish the Spirit and—on the other hand—to practice the discernment of spirits.

Joy over this movement should be greater than skepticism over some of its manifestations, such as ecstasy and speaking in tongues. If one is to recognize the quality of a tree from its fruit, then the fruits of this movement speak for it. They are the signs of breaking out and of confidence over against the many voices of concern, sorrow, lamentation, resignation, and pessimism, voices that are not helpful and certainly don't lead forward.

8. Cf. H. Mühlen, *Die Erneuerung des Christlichen Glaubens. Charisma—Geist—Befreiung* (Mainz, 1974); *Einübung in die Christliche Grunderfahrung*, 4th ed. (Mainz, 1978).

9. Joseph L. Cardinal Suenens, *A New Pentecost?*, trans. Frances Martin (New York: Seabury Press, 1975); *Ecumenism and Charismatic Renewal: Theological and Pastoral Orientations* (Ann Arbor, Mich.: Servant Books, 1978).

In these signs and phenomena as expressions of an outbreak of the religious, of the Christian Spirit, it has become clear that the location of this outbreak can be anywhere. "The Spirit blows where it will." That means: The place of this religious outbreak can lie with the bearer of an ecclesiastical office—for example, with a figure like Pope John XXIII. But it cannot be so understood that office and Spirit are co-extensive, that the Spirit of God has no possibility of being present outside of office and institution. These phenomena show that the outbreak of the religious Spirit takes place especially from below: with individuals, in groups, in communities, at the "base." This outbreak awakens spontaneously, with vitality, often perhaps over-enthusiastically, disorganizedly. But this belongs to the first moments of all outbreaks and movements.

Of course we have here the constant danger of "enthusiasm." That was already true in the community of Corinth. But one shouldn't be too ready with the qualification "enthusiast," so as not to suppress all sparks even of the smallest fire, and be mindful only of order and regimentation. God is no God of disorder, says Paul, but—not as one would expect, a God of order, either, but—"a God of peace" (1 Cor 14:33).

If we are accustomed to thinking about the situation of the Church primarily in terms of Europe and North America, it would be well to cast a glance at the World Church, as in Africa and South America. Walbert Bühlmann who, in his book *Where Faith Lives* (*Wo der Glaube lebt*), attempts to give insight into the situation of the World Church, and who brings with it a lifelong and world-encompassing experience, is full of confidence. He ends his book with the words: "I like to hope that in providential synchronization with the events of the world a new storm of Pentecost is blowing through the Church, and that the Church has never been more challenged, never had a greater chance to become Church of the world, than today."[10]

---

10. *Wo der Glaube lebt: Einblicke in die Lage der Weltkirche* (Freiburg—Basel—Vienna, 1974) 313. See also his *The Church of the Future: A Model for the Year 2001* (Maryknoll, N.Y.: Orbis Books, 1986).

PART FOUR

THE CHURCH AS MEDIATION
AND RE-PRESENTATION
OF REVELATION

§52

THE THEOLOGICAL PLACE OF THE QUESTION OF THE
STRUCTURE OF THE CHURCH

The word "structure" brings up a problem that is hotly discussed today, and we mean both a problem of the Church as well as in the Church.[1]

This problem is correctly approached only when one specifies it in terms of its reality and function. For our theme this means in terms of the reality and function of the Church, in terms of its tasks and ministries. The function of the Church consists in mediating the revelation event in word, event, deed, and action as its gift and task in history and for human beings. The structures of the Church have this as their purpose.

The Church is thus not the *ex post factum* collection of those who, each for themselves, have come to the faith, live from this faith, and then are given a corresponding structure. Faith, understood as Christian faith, comes from hearing and thus includes the primacy of the word. Thus, the presupposition of this faith is the Church as community of believers, as an intersubjectivity and the ministry or preaching which occurs therein and which comes from its mission. This indicates a basic structure in the service of the mediation of the faith. It includes differentiation and division into member parts: hearing, proclaiming, sending, and legitimation.

It is similar for the way in which especially the Christ-event is supposed to be mediated: (1) in the form of that effective remembering of what Jesus did—called sacrament—of a sign that effects what it signifies; (2) as communion with the person, the way and the fate of Jesus Christ, most significantly in baptism and Eucharist. Sacrament as gift presupposes the basic structure of giving and taking, of administering and receiving. The sacrament implies the one who administers it; this

---

1. Cf. H. Rombach, *Substanz, System, Struktur. Die Ontologie des Funktionalismus und der philosophische Hintergrund der Modernen Wissenschaft* (Freiburg—Munich, 1965).

person has a ministry of mediation which, in its turn, comes about because of a sending or commissioning, because of a legitimation.

The task of the Church as *diakonia*, as manifold ministry to human beings, as completing the intention and the action of Jesus, seems as such to require no structure; it is just as universal as it is situation and society-related. But it is just as clear that this ministry towards all needs those who will make people aware of them, who see and make others see, who initiate and who make known the appropriate possibilities. It needs, above all, those who not only verbally assert this, but complete it in act, existence, and life, not for others to be free of the ministry of service, but that living signs be established again and again for this ministry which is obligatory for all. And it needs definite forms, structures, and organizations so that the service provided can be comprehensively effective and helpful.

With these preliminary considerations, something fundamental has been said for and about the structure of the Church. Structure is a secondary phenomenon; it is not the primary reality, but is determined by the primary reality. To be sure, precisely in its service to the primary reality, structure takes on great significance. It is supposed to mediate the primary reality, make it become real. Put negatively: it must not overshadow or obstruct the primary reality.

This also clarifies by what factors and criteria this structure is determined. First by the task of the Church to be the historical, social, and societal mediator of the revelation-event culminating in Jesus Christ. The further specifications for the structure of the Church come from examining the human beings and the society for which this ministry is to be performed.

Consequently the principle "true to origins and adapted to the situation" applies also to the question of structure. Hence it follows that a look at the beginning is also indispensable for the question of the structure of the Church, both because this beginning and origin is supposed to be mediated to a living present and because this beginning is not only a temporal but also a normative, authoritative beginning. This beginning has at the same time a critical power and function over-against the further-developing history and the respective present. But also, the respective present is important for the question of structure, because the reality in whose service the structure exists, is supposed to become living and effective for the present, and for the human beings living therein, who, for their part, live in specific societal structures.

In addition to this general historical point, the present has an acute awareness of the problem of the significance of structure. It recognizes how much can depend on structure for any reality and its effects, but above all, how much structure and structures influence the individual, the person, in a helpful or hindering way.[2]

This fact cannot be and remain without effect on our consideration of the structures of the Church, because the mediation being done by the Church is supposed to take place in and for the present, and thus cannot overlook conditions which affect it. If the question of structures has become a hotly discussed theme in the framework of social criticism, it should come as no surprise that the intensity of the question does not spare the structures of the Church. This questioning is not satisfied with the factual as a taken-for-granted or definitive fact, but raises serious questions about whether it makes sense in terms of the reality in question and of the way it workds for the men and women of this time. In other words, there is an inescapable polarity between the origin, which is to be mediated and as such is to remain identical, and the present and human beings in the present, for whom this mediation is to be done. This makes clear how difficult and acute the problem is.

But there is also this consequence: The desire to decide the question of the structure of the Church theologically only according to the models and circumstances of the present, or, in brief, according to democratic pattern in contrast with earlier monarchical models can easily lead to what we blame on the past: to have committed ourselves to a falsely understood aggiornamento,[3] a falsely understood adaptation, to have kept and practiced too little distance, discernment, and criticism.

Along with the possible and justified criticism of structures when they make themselves the end, when they burden, confine, alienate, or oppress human beings, or when they distort what they are there for, it cannot be forgotten that structures also have an extremely positive significance. They can, when they are not coercive ordinances, be a great help to human beings. They can protect them from arbitrariness and confinements, they can help them to their rights and their freedom. Structures as legal structures have to a certain extent a protective function, which assures to human beings what is theirs.

Further, structures have a burden-easing function. They save human beings from having to do everything alone from having to make and decide everything anew every day. Structures offer human beings a catalogue of rules in which experiences, customs, directions, behavioral

---

2. So-called structuralism, developed above all in France (C. Levi-Strauss), is related in analysis and idea to the phenomenon of structure. It attempts "to proceed from substance to structure." Cf. G. Schiwy, *Der französische Strukturalismus* (Reinbeck, 1965); *Structuralism and Christianity* (Pittsburgh, 1971); "Structuralism," *SM* 5.182–83; O. Genest, "Exegesis and Structural Analysis,"*DFT* 298–306.

3. *Aggiornamento* = Italian, for "bringing up-to-date." In English the word refers to the work of renewal in the Roman Catholic Church during and after the Second Vatican Council *(The New Shortened Oxford English Dictionary* [Oxford, 1993] 40).

guidelines are summed up and laid down. Not to attend to these is foolish and injurious.

Structures have a protecting function. Metaphorically speaking, they keep the water of the source from drying up, getting aimlessly wasted, or becoming a dangerously raging wild stream; instead they insure that it is gathered and preserved. A system of regulation and drainage certainly takes away from the source its often fierce, sometimes foaming-over force. But at the same time structures and regulations see to it that the power and the life of the source do not get lost.

Channels and regulations make sense only when there is something to regulate: i.e., water, life. The regulation as such can never become its own end or replace the water of life. But on the other hand, if the source, the water, is to be guided to its functions, it needs such a regulatory system.

This basic knowledge and experience can be derived from many examples of history. The spontaneous new beginning that came with Francis of Assisi and was called forth by him could be preserved only in a rule serving this origin, even if falling short of its spontaneity. This holds for all religious orders.

As indicated, structures have to do with justice. The concepts "justice and order," in connection with the concepts "law and order," have for a long time had a negative sound. Right and order have often been seen as in opposition to freedom, to spontaneity or, above all in the sphere of the Church, as in opposition to Spirit, charism, and love. It is not to be contested that there are, can be, or will be laws and regulations where these oppositions apply. But the real opposition to justice is not love and Spirit; the opposite of justice is injustice, disorder, chaos, arbitrariness. Justice is the answer and counterposition to injustice, to oppression.

To help human beings get what is rightfully theirs, to bring them to the enjoyment of justice is the horizon and context into which the matter of justice is to be ordered and which the individual laws should serve as the application of right and justice to the concrete situation in history and society. This also means that all individual ordinances and items of law that one encounters must be oriented to this foundation: to serve justice, to make space for the right of human beings as the space of their very selves and of their freedom. It thus follows that all ordinances and laws can and should be measured by this. All this is also the horizon in which the question of structure in the Church and of the Church is to be considered.

If the structures of the Church are to be true to their origin and suited to the situation, as is the life and faith of the Church in general, then a look at this origin is necessary.

§53

STRUCTURES OF THE CHURCH AT THE BEGINNING OF THE CHURCH

Misunderstanding of the Church?

On the question of the structure of the Church at its beginning, the first thing to be attended to is the well-known and fascinating thesis that goes back to the work of Rudolf Sohm. We take it up as formulated by Emil Brunner in his book *Das mißverständnis der Kirche* (The Misunderstanding of the Church).[1] The title affirms that the Church, as we know it today, is a misunderstanding from the beginning. In this theory, the Church at its beginning was a community specified and constituted by nothing but Christ experienced alive in faith, by the Spirit, and by the gifts of the Spirit. It was a community of love, of agape, and of freedom. The Church at its beginning was free of every organization and institution.

What then developed from this beginning, the first traces of which are already recognizable in the late writings of the New Testament, is a falling away from this height. In the place of faith-decision as personal encounter with Christ came dogma; in the place of love, law; in the place of the Spirit, office. The subsequent history of the Church is thus to be qualified as a history of falling away. And the more dogma, law, and office mark a church, the more we have a misunderstanding of and fall from its origin. For Brunner, this applies above all to the Roman Catholic Church. The opposition was formulated by R. Sohm in this way: The essence of the Church and the essence of law and regulation are in opposition to each other. The essence of the Church is spiritual, the essence of law and regulation, on the other hand, secular. The Church is dependent on the factual (substance) truth; law and regulation, however, on its external form.

---

1. Emil Brunner, *Das Mißverständnis der Kirche* (Stuttgart, 1951); idem., *Die Lehre von der Kirche, vom Glauben und von der Vollendung. Dogmatik III* (Zurich—Stuttgart, 1960).

The Primitive Community

The Acts of the Apostles gives an account of the beginnings of the Christian community in Jerusalem. In response to the witness and preaching of the Apostles, above all, of the preaching of Peter, three thousand people were "added" on one day, the day of Easter. This was an addition to the already existing group and community of the disciples and apostles. They were "added" by faith, repentance, and baptism. Thus arose what is called the primitive Christian community in Jerusalem, the community of those "called out," the *ekklesia*.[2]

The Acts of the Apostles gives the following well-known description of this first community, the primitive community in Jerusalem:

They devoted themselves to the apostles' teaching and fellowship, to the breaking of bread and the prayers. . . . And all who believed were together and had all things in common. . . . And day by day, attending the Temple together and breaking bread in their homes, they partook of food with glad and generous hearts. (Acts 2:42–46)

The company of those who believed were of one heart and soul, and no one said that any of the things which he possessed was his own, but they had everything in common. (Acts 4:32)

It should be noted that this text sketches out not an historical account but an illuminating and ideal picture of the community. It is more of an "ought" than an "is." The reality, as one discovers from further reading in Acts, is not so ideal. For quarrels and tensions broke out in Jerusalem between the groups of the Hellenists and the Hebrews, i.e., between Jews from the Palestinian motherland and the Greek-speaking Jews from the cities of the Roman Empire, who had come back from there to Jerusalem.

The members of the primitive community in Jerusalem lived predominantly within the sphere of their Jewish origin. It was in the horizon of their Jewish faith and based on its practices of worship in the Temple and in the home that they attempted to represent what was new and particular in their *ekklesia* oriented to Jesus. In other words, the first Christians are Jews. Their Christian faith is understood not as a new religion which leads them away from Israel's faith, but as the confirmation of the promises to Israel. Precisely as Christians they are the true Jews.

Thus it is that in the addresses of the Acts of the Apostles, the theme "promise and fulfillment" is constantly addressed as an element of the faith of Israel, and that the first addressees of this preaching are Jews. On the behavior of the Jews relative to the crucifixion of Jesus,

---

2. K. Kertelge, *Gemeinde und Amt im Neuen Testament* (Munich, 1972); J. Hainz, ed., *Studien zum Thema Amt und Gemeinde im Neuen Testament* (Munich—Paderborn—Vienna, 1976).

the judgment was quite circumspect. Peter declares: "Now, brethren, I know that you acted in ignorance, as did also your rulers" (Acts 3:17).

But even here we see the beginning of distance and the separation that becomes manifest in the trial of the apostles Peter and John by the elders and the scribes and led to the prohibition against preaching in the name of Jesus Christ. It is intensified in the persecution of the Christian community by the Sanhedrin and reaches its first high point in the stoning of Stephen. These events resulted in the dispersal of the community; after the imprisonment of Peter, the apostles are generally no longer found as a group in Jersualem. The conflict was in fact sparked not so much by the fact that Jesus was proclaimed as Christ and Messiah, but by the confession that Jesus of Nazareth, handed over to death by the leaders of the people in the name of the Law, thus a cruci-fied man, was to be the origin and founder of a new covenant.

A conflict within the community itself was sparked by the new atti-tude towards the Law as the former path to salvation, and by the ques-tion of the path which non-Jews, addressees like the Jews of the Gospel of Jesus Christ, are to follow in coming to the community of the Church.

Structure of the Primitive Community

The structure of the community at Jerusalem had the apostles, with Peter as the first, standing at the head of the community as leaders, speakers, and representatives. They guide the community with an un-challenged authority which they derive from their sending and calling by Christ the Risen One. This is the source of their apostolate. But their authority also come from the witness and confession of their preaching and of their faith in Jesus the Christ before all the world, and finally from the gifts of the Spirit bestowed on them: the gifts of steadiness, sincerity, knowledge, and healing. In these leadership func-tions the apostles decide the concrete questions that come up in the community of Jerusalem.[3]

There followed, for example, the appointment of a group, the so-called Seven (Acts 6), who, in view of their later activity, were called deacons. Among the Seven, Stephen and Philip stood out. They were as-signed to the ministry of the proclamation of the word, and above all to the ministry to the poor. The Seven were chosen by the community. After their election they were introduced into their ministry by the apostles by prayer and the laying on of hands, an old gesture of the handing on of functions and authority.

---

3. E. Schweizer, *Gemeinde und Gemeindeordnung im Neuen Testament*, 2d ed. (Zurich, 1962).

A third group found in the community of Jerusalem were the *pres-byteroi*, the elders.[4] They are mentioned together with the apostles in the context: apostles and elders. The apostles and the elders are the decisive instances before whom and by whom the one important, basic question is clarified and decided, namely that acceptance into the community of the Church and to the way to salvation takes place not by way of the Law and circumcision, but by way of repentance, faith, and baptism.

The apostles and the elders pick out Paul and Barnabas to send them to Antioch, and to Syria and Cilicia. These two, we are told, went to Antioch, called the community together, and handed over to it the letter of recommendation of the apostles and the elders (Acts 15:30).

The elders of the Christian community are taken over from the Jewish institution of the *presbyteroi*, in the organization of the synagogue. What was originally an age designation has become a function designation for leading and guiding. The elders stand as a college at the head of the Jewish community. Their guiding function concerns the worship in the Temple, and the interpretation of the Torah with the primary task of its preservation. They have, besides this, judicial and administrative power (binding-loosing). The unity and order of the community is entrusted to them in a special way.

This structure of the Jewish local community was an accepted reality also for the community of those who believed in Jesus as the fulfiller of all promises and who found themselves in and with this faith and its consequences within the Jewish community, and who moved therein and were convinced that the existing forms and structures of community were quite suited to correspond to the new situation of faith oriented to Jesus and to the community living therefrom, the new *qahal*, the new People of God. For the new was to be considered as fulfillment and completion of the old.

In spite of this close connection of the Christian community with all that went before it, the emphasis on the new, and with that the difference, was unavoidable. The difference, which became clearer and clearer, was not so much found in the structure as in the way the content of the structure was filled out.

The elders of the Christian community were, despite formal and structural similarity, defined by what was new and different in their faith. The Jewish elders were bound to law and tradition and took their task from these. The Christian community, however, lives decidedly not from the Law and from the past, but from the experienced presence of the new, and from its hope in the return of their Lord. Prophecy,

---

4. W. Michaelis, *Das Ältestenamt der christlichen Gemeinde im Lichte der Heiligen Schrift* (Bern, 1953).

grown quiet within the synagogue, is awakened anew in the primitive community.

Consequently, the elders could not, simply by their knowledge and interpretation of the Scripture, be the authoritative teachers the way they used to be. The elders receive a new definition and task in the Christian community. This can be seen in the way the writings of the Old Testament, Law, and Prophets continue to be read and honored as Holy Scripture; they receive a new interpretation, however, as it were a new hermeneutical principle, by the message of Jesus crucified and risen.

The connection with the Old Covenant is preserved by the category of promise and fulfillment, but this now receives the dimension of preparation for the new and definitive. The community has a new connection of its own and a new tradition of its own which comes from Jesus Christ and is normatively bound to him, and which is to be kept alive and preserved in the community. From the witness of Acts, these three elements—the apostles with Peter at their head, the elders, and the Seven—constitute the structure of the primitive community of Jerusalem.

In general, the institution of the elders is protrayed in The Acts of the Apostles as the normal structure of the Christian communities. Where communities are founded—by apostles—elders and presbyters are subsequently appointed.

In a moving scene, Acts 20:28 relates that Paul, on his final journey to Jerusalem, no longer has time to go to Ephesus. He has the elders of the community come to Miletus in order to say goodbye to them. This speech is shaped by Luke as a kind of last will. It culminates in requiring of the elders: "Take heed to yourselves and to all the flock, in which the Holy Spirit has made you overseers, to care for the church of God" (Acts 20:28).

Mention of the elders is made towards the end of the first century in the Letter of James (5:14)—a description of the every-day life of a Christian community. It says there, in case of sickness, the elders of the community are to be called, that they might set the sick on their feet again by prayer in the name of the Lord and by anointing with oil. In the First Letter of Peter, in which the authority of Peter is claimed in order to lend authority to this writing to the communities in Asia Minor, one finds a community structure in which the author describes himself as a "fellow and witness of the sufferings of Christ" (1 Pet 5: 1). "Tend to the flock of God that is your charge, not by constraint but willingly, not for shameful gain but eagerly, not as domineering over those in your charge but being examples to the flock" (1 Pet 5: 2–3).

On this basis one has to say that the institution of the elders is a structural element found along with and under the authoritative apostolic office at the beginning of the Church. In addition, the appointment of the elders in the form of a liturgical action was carried out with prayer and the laying on of hands. This practice, which was taken over from Judaism, continues to this day—and not just in Judaism—as the sign of "ordination."

The Pauline Communities

In discussion of the Pauline communities,[5] the reference point is not the Acts of the Apostles which, in its second part, deals with the missionary activity of Paul and with the fact that he appointed elders in the communities he founded, thus taking over the structure of the Jerusalem community. The reference point is rather the communities about which Paul himself gives us an acccount and, in which he is concretely active. It is above all the community of Corinth, but also those of Thessalonica, Philippi, and Rome.

It is said that the picture of the communities as described by Paul is different from the one so far described. It is above all from the picture of the primitive Jerusalem community with its already described structure of "apostles and elders." In addition, the account of Luke (Acts) seems to be considerably different from what, for example, the First Letter to the Corinthians tells us about the life, behavior, buildup and structure of a very early Christian community.

Hans von Campenhausen gives this description of the community of Corinth: The Spirit is the organizational principle of the Christian community. Thus it needs no specific kind of order with its prescription, commands, and prohibitions. The Spirit who rules does not get actively involved in the framework of a specific church order or church constitution. In the community, freedom rules in principle because of immediacy to Christ, because of being filled with the Spirit. The community is not like any ordinarily constituted organization, but a living cosmos of free spiritual gifts, a community in which every coercion and every lasting power to command is clearly excluded.[6]

The community lives by the Spirit; its various members have many kinds of gifts. Where Spirit and love reign, no further order is needed; all regulations are really the working of the Spirit and the gifts of the Spirit. The most striking trait of the Pauline view of community is "the

5. K. Holl, "Der Kirchenbegriff des Paulus in seinem Verhältnis zu dem der Urgemeinde" in: Gesammelte Aufsätze zur Kirchengeschichte II (Tübingen, 1928) 44–67; J. Hainz, Ekklesia. Strukturen paulinischer Gemeindetheologie und Gemeindeordnung (Regensburg, 1972).

6. H. von Campenhausen, Ecclesiastical Authority and Spiritual Power in the Church of the First Three Centuries, trans. J. A. Baker (Stanford, Calif.: Stanford University Press, 1969) 58.

complete lack of a juridical order, the fundamental exclusion of every formal authority within the individual community."[7]

With this conception Campenhausen has taken over the thought of Emil Brunner, not, to be sure, for the New Testament Church in general, but for its Pauline form. He explicitly establishes that the Pauline personal-pneumatic, office-less form of church can claim a priority neither in time nor in idea over against the *ekklesia* of Jerusalem organized in members according to office and order. He further notes that the Pauline conception of Church manifests, along with the trait of the enthusiastic, also the trait of the utopian, and that it ultimately could neither hold nor survive; it led rather to tensions and conflicts. But the questions remain: Is the Church of the New Testament found in two differentiated if not contradictory forms: the Jewish-Christian and the Gentile-Christian; Is the Church in the Gentile-Christian sphere so constituted as Campenhausen says?[8]

Contradictory Structures?

Are the Jerusalem community, and the Corinthian community as type of the Pauline community, fundamentally different and contradictory in structure from the communities in the non-Jewish sphere?[9]

The problem of the constitutional and the juridical is not the problem of the beginning, of the first hour so to speak, but a matter of the second generation, whose concern was to keep the origin alive. The essential issue was continuity. Paul, as it seems, is by nature not primarily a man of constitutionally juridical "order" or of "organization," he is essentially a man of the "Spirit," of unusual charismatic gifts, a perfect witness of that earliest time overflowing with the fullness of the Spirit, if also with an alert sense for the necessities of sober, everyday reality. Paul is in addition mostly the "founder" of the communities to which he writes, and he possesses therein the authority of a "father," which does not need to be constituted "juridically," but which does contain a strong juridical element. He is essentially a "missionary" and thinks as a missionary; he wants to win people over and must avoid all harshness. He is a pastor of souls, accustomed to persuade, and to work things out with opposition and opponents in pastoral conversation. And finally, he expects the parousia to come soon and isn't at all reckoning—at least not at first—with the necessity of having to create a lasting order for the communities. What takes place in matters of constitu-

---

7. Ibid. 70.
8. O. Karrer, "Probleme der paulinischen Kirchenordnung nach H. von Campenhausen" in: *Um die Einheit der Christen* (Frankfurt, 1953) 69–86; O. Kuss, "Kirchliches Amt und geistliche Vollmacht" in: *Auslegung und Verkündigung I* (271–80).
9. The following material is dependent on O. Kuss, "Jesus und die Kirche im Neuen Testament" in: *Auslegung und Verkündigung* 1.25–77, esp. 49–55.

tion seems more like stopgap measures; nothing else is or should be needed, for the Lord is coming soon anyway.

But finally, one would not do justice to the real Paul if one tried to maintain that he knew nothing at all of "organization," of constitutional-juridical order, of an "office" or at least of elements of an "office." Even in the First Letter to the Thessalonians there is talk about those who "stand before" the faithful in the Lord. The same concept comes up in the Epistle to the Romans. The First Letter to the Corinthians speaks, instead of "piloting abilities," gifts for community-leading. At the beginning of the Letter to the Philippians *episkopoi* and *diakonoi* are mentioned, and although here too the community is mentioned first, it remains noteworthy that the community leaders are mentioned individually; they are apparently "officials." The matter becomes even clearer when we attend to how Paul's relationship to Jerusalem was established, i.e., to Peter, James, and John, who were "the pillars" (Gal 2:2).

Paul insisted with great emphasis that he received his calling not from human beings, also not by a human being, but by Jesus Christ and God, the Father, "who raised him from the dead." Nevertheless, however much he emphasized the immediacy of his apostolate, he didn't think much about developing a kind of independent special church. Rather he placed decisive importance on gaining the agreement/approval of the Jerusalem community, above all of "those in authority." When he is visiting Jerusalem for the second time after his conversion, he is undertaking the journey on the basis of a revelation. Thus he is not being summoned there, so to speak, but he is nevertheless going there in the consciousness that its yes or no would have the utmost broad-ranging consequences. It is a question of life and death; his purpose is nothing less than to learn from those in authority whether he is or has been running "in vain" with his gospel which he is preaching among the Gentiles. In his (monetary) collection Paul recognizes the position of Jerusalem as origin. Although it may be noteworthy that when he speaks of the collection its caritative aspect is prominent, it nevertheless cannot be denied that even in his version it is Jerusalem which took the initiative, and the character of the collection as a levy is quite clear. There can be no doubt that Paul depicts his meeting with those in Jerusalem with a certain between-the-lines reserve; he obviously wishes under all circumstances to avoid even the least limitation on his independence, on the revelation given him. But there can be just as little doubt that he lays decisive importance on receiving the fundamental approval of his gospel and his activity as apostle by those in authority in Jerusalem: Peter, James, and John. Thus it is not very likely that the structure of a community founded by him and later cared for by him would be totally different from that in Jerusalem.

When Paul later "opposed" Peter "to his face" (Gal 2:11) in Antioch, this argument was not over matters of principle. Paul is not opposing a Peter who is teaching something different, he is not pushing through "his gospel," or even "rebelling" instead, he is calling to order a Peter who—one with Paul in principle—is putting tactical considerations in the foreground at a time when, in Paul's view, an open confession for the single correct way of acting is necessary.

Purely Charismatic Communities?

In some recent Catholic presentations on the Church, above all by Hans Küng and Gotthold Hasenhüttl,[10] it is said that the community of Corinth was factually a purely charismatic community, because it was borne and marked uniquely by faith, love, Spirit, and the gifts of the Spirit. This community is then made into the exemplary picture and dominant model of Church in general. This forgets that the factual condition and the concrete life of this community were quite different.

The community of Corinth offers the picture of a very difficult, divided community, a community with struggling parties: "It has been reported to me," says Paul (1 Cor 1:11-13), "that there is quarreling among you, my brethren. What I mean is that each one of you says, 'I belong to Paul, ' or 'I belong to Apollos, ' or 'I belong to Cephas, ' or 'I belong to Christ.' Is Christ divided? Was Paul crucified for you? Or were you baptized in the name of Paul?" Besides, there is in the community of Corinth the case of incest, which the community is tolerating in its midst (chap. 5); there is the scandal of legal controversies before pagan courts (chap. 6); there is the practice of falsely understood or arbitrarily misused freedom (chap. 6); there are the abuses at the Eucharist (chap. 11), and the disorder in the liturgical assemblies (chap. 14). This is the reality of the community which the First Letter to the Corinthians has in mind and with which it sees itself confronted.

It is to this that the answer of the apostle is directed. It takes place in various stages: Paul claims that he can, indeed must, intervene, establish order, and decide—for he is the father of the community, which he, in his own words, begat by the gospel (1 Cor 4:15). This position of his contains a dominative authority, to which he also lays claim: authority grounded in being founder, in fatherhood.

In the questions that arise, Paul asserts his authority. He encourages, he wills, he commands. Paul makes clear regulations and gives concrete directions. Problems are definitely not left to the decision of a

---

10. Hans Küng, *The Church*, trans. Ray and Rosaleen Ockenden (New York: Sheed and Ward, 1967) 179–91; idem, "Die charismatische Struktur der Kirche" in: *Concilium* 1 (1965) 282-90; G. Hasenhüttl, *Charisma. Ordnungsprinzip der Kirche* (Freiburg—Basel—Vienna, 1969).

free charismatic regime in which matters as it were regulate themselves. Paul knows and realizes what is contained in power and authority.

In addition, Paul proposes as answer, possibility, and obligation his own picture of the way the community should be and the direction in which it must be led. Against the antagonism in Corinth which is leading to party loyalties and the building of fronts, he places the totally other picture of plurality in unity, of the plurality of the gifts of the Spirit and the unity of origin, of the principle of unity, and of the goal that encompasses them (1 Cor 12).

This connection and interplay are illustrated in the same chapter with the well-known image: the body with its many members together with their manifold functions. They are all dependent upon each other; the individual member must make good on its own specific gift and function without looking down on the other, which in its function and gift is irreplaceable and contributes to the building up of the whole. Thus: "If one member suffers, all suffer together; if one member is honored, all rejoice together. Now you are the body of Christ and individually members of it" (1 Cor 12:26–27).

Then comes the concrete application to the community:

And God has appointed in the church first apostles, second prophets, third teachers, then workers of miracles, then healers, helpers, administrators, speakers in various kinds of tongues. Are all apostles? Are all prophets? Are all teachers? Do all work miracles? Do all possess gifts of healing? Do all speak with tongues? Do all interpret? (1 Cor 12:28-30)

It follows from this text that charisms in the sense of 1 Corinthians 12 are gifts in the service of the building up of the community. Charisms include not only spectacular phenomena like ecstasies or talking in strange tongues—these are ranked in the lowest position—but the gifts of the every-day life of the community as well.

To one is given through the Spirit the utterance of wisdom, and to another the utterance of knowledge according to the same Spirit, to another faith by the same Spirit, to another gifts of healing by the one Spirit, to another the working of miracles, to another prophecy, to another the ability to distinguish between Spirits, to another various kinds of tongues, to another the interpretation of tongues. All these are inspired by one and the same Spirit, who apportions to each one individually as He wills. (1 Cor 12:8–11)

Chapter 14 of the same letter again takes up the subject of charisms, especially of prophetic and ecstatic speech. "He who prophesies is greater than he who speaks in tongues, unless someone interprets, so that the church may be edified" (1 Cor 14:5).

There are doubtless many different languages in the world, and none is without meaning; but if I do not know the meaning of a language, I shall be a foreigner to the speaker and the speaker a foreigner to me. So with yourselves; since you are eager for manifestations of the Spirit, strive to excel in building up the church. . . . In church I would rather speak five words with my mind, in order to instruct others, than ten thousand words in a tongue." (1 Cor 14:10–12, 19)

At the end of this chapter Paul promulgates concrete directives for the community assembly. He justifies them with these words: "God is not a God of confusion but of peace" (1 Cor 14:33). Now peace is not identical with any possible order, but it is surely incompatible with disorder; peace requires community, concord, and love. Ordinances that are understood as service are not opposed to this, but are intended to help secure peace.

Is the community of Corinth a charismatic community? This cannot be affirmed if one understands the charismatic in the sense of the extraordinary gifts, in the sense of ecstatic enthusiasm. Nor is it such if one understands the charismatic in such a way that every element of structure, arrangement, order, authority, and law is excluded because it would be in contradiction to charism. But one can understand the community at Corinth as charismatic community, and specify the Church in general as such, if by charism one understands the gift given to each and the call of that gift to a specific service in the community, which call empowers to this service. This comprehensive definition of charism sets it apart both from arbitrariness and disorder and against mere legality and uniformity.

§54

THE PLURIFORM DEVELOPMENT OF CHRISTIAN ORIGINS

Hans Conzelmann calls our attention to the fact that the nonarrival of the parousia did not cause any terribly great disturbances in the communities, that there were indeed questions about it, but no earth-shaking crisis.[1] It was relatively easy to integrate successfully the problems that arose from this in terms of the faith, to consolidate and stabilize the community and the communities, to give them form and structure, not to quench the fire of the origin but to preserve it and hand it on. We will now mention some of the moments in this process.

The Witness of the Acts of the Apostles

From the original situation in which the Jewish Christian and Gentile Christian communities existed side by side, there developed an ever more clear interrelationship. This can be seen from the way the Acts of the Apostles describes it as taken for granted that the communities founded by Paul and his companion Barnabas would have structure, and indeed a presbyteral structure. Presbyters, elders, form as a college the direction and leadership of the community. Their ministry is de-scribed as "pasturing the flock," with everything that goes with this according to the model of the Shepherd: "existence for it," care for its life as community of Jesus Christ, leadership, going ahead, protection, readiness to give up oneself.

Especially important is the already-mentioned passage of Acts 20:28, the so-called testament of Paul. Paul has the elders of Ephesus come to Miletus and he sums up their task with the words: "Take heed to yourselves and to all the flock, in which the Holy Spirit has made you overseers, to care for the church of God which he obtained with the blood of his own Son." The elders addressed here are called *episkopoi*/overseers. This joins together two concepts and structures: the

---

1. Hans Conzelmann, *History of Primitive Christianity*, trans. John E. Steely (New York: Abingdon Press, 1973) 100.

presbyter coming from the synagogue, and the *episkopos* coming from Greek law.

The task of the presbyters and elders is described with the category of *episkopos*.[2] Behind this is not the image of the slave overseer, but in general the function of the one who sees, who has the overview, who is aware of the whole picture and bears responsibility for it. In the Greek sphere, *episkopos* became a designation of office: a supervisory and administrative official. This formal structure is taken over for the Christian community and filled with a new content in view of the fact that the functions and tasks were those needed in a Christian community. The word episkopos comes close to the meaning of shepherd. In 1 Peter 2:25 Christ Himself is called "Shepherd and Episkopos."

Remarkable too is the great participation of the community in the responsibility for the ministries and tasks of the Church. According to the Acts of the Apostles, the community of Jerusalem collaborated in the election of Matthias as successor to Judas and in the election of the so-called "Seven." The account of the sending out of Paul and Barnabas on the first missionary journey is instructive. The mission is taken up in the community of Antioch: "In the church at Antioch there were prophets and teachers." They are obviously the leaders of the community; among them, Saul and Barnabas are also mentioned. "While they were worshipping the Lord and fasting, the Holy Spirit said, 'Set apart for me Barnabas and Saul for the work to which I have called them' Then after fasting and praying they laid their hands on them and sent them off" (Acts 13:1–3).

Here we have an incontestable form of an active collaboration of the community, even for the official tasks of Paul and Barnabas. The authority of the apostle was neither contested nor even lessened by this, any more than was the function of the elders as *episkopoi*, and of the *episkopoi* as elders. But these functions were incorporated into an extraordinarily remarkable activity of the community. To recall this is not only historically interesting but also of factual significance in our present-day discussion about structure and office, or in the question of a so-called "democratization of the Church," when what is to be meant by that is cooperation and co-responsibility.

The picture that comes from the beginning about community, structure, and community activity is certainly not univocal, closed, or in agreement in every point. That is in no way only a sign of the insecurity or lack of clarity in the beginning, which "ascends" from that unclarity to greater clarity, but an expression of how the necessary tasks and ministries in the Church were dealt with in different structures. This plurality is a sign of different possibilities to the communities and to the Church being realized by them.

2. Beyer, *TDNT* 2.599–622.

If the beginning is normative for all traditions, this also creates possibilities for history and the present. What in the beginning was a legitimate form and structure cannot later, even today, be simply declared impossible or illegitimate.

A third point is still to be considered: the function of Peter in the sphere of these communities. It consists, in a special way, in service to unity. According to the Acts of the Apostles, we find Peter in Jerusalem and Antioch, thus in Jewish-Christian and in Gentile-Christian space. According to the accounts of the Acts of the Apostles, it is Peter who accepts the Roman centurion Cornelius into the Church, and thereby gives the impulse to mission (Acts 10); it is Peter who, along with James, speaks the decisive word in the great assembly in Jerusalem (Acts 15). This was the specifically decisive word for the beginnings of the Church and for the Church in the beginning—for the way of the Gentiles to the Christian faith and to the community of believers. Joseph Ratzinger interprets the position of Peter in this way: Peter is the one who, by his presence and by his being there, represents the connection with the totality of Church at the time.[3]

Nothing essential changed in the position of Peter when, after his departure, James became the leader of the Jerusalem community. After its enthusiastic beginning and after the persecution (Acts 12), the primitive community seems to fall into an increasing narrowness and lose the importance which first and foremost fell to it as headquarters of all the churches.

One can say that the function of Peter travels with him. It is there where he is active, while the primacy function of James is tied to the community in Jerusalem. The departure of Peter from Jerusalem is also a sign that the issue was not just to preserve the old, but that as a consequence of the great missionary command, the path to venture leads into the universal world. But as new center for the universal Church, the obvious choice was the capital of the world at that time, Rome.

The Witness of the Pastoral Letters

The Pastoral Letters are documents from a later time. They are the letters to Timothy and Titus, which have Paul named as their author.[4] These are not letters to the communities, like the oldest and certainly genuine letters of Paul, but letters to individual persons who have a leading function in a community or in a group of communities. What is said in these letters is covered by claiming the authority of Paul as their author—as continuation of his activity in a differently devel-

3. *Das Neue Volk Gottes* (Düsseldorf, 1969) 115, 130–31.
4. H. Schlier, "Die Ordnung der Kirche nach den Pastoralbriefen" in: *Die Zeit der Kirche* (Freiburg, 1956) 129–47.

oped situation, in which the concern is, by using Pauline contents and motifs, to preserve and strengthen the foundation laid by his apostolic preaching.

There is practically unanimous agreement today that these are not authentic letters of Paul. The author could perhaps be a disciple of Paul or a missionary from post-Pauline time. The Pastoral Letters are Paul-anamnesis (N. Brox).[5] The personally stylized, concrete details belong to the stylistic means of pseudepigraphy; Paul is imitated as authentically as possible. Nevertheless the presumed concrete details are basically types of a constantly present situation for a post-apostolic community, for which Paul is to be actualized. The Gospel is not directly proclaimed in these letters, but presupposed as already known. For their factual and theological significance, the question of the author of the Pastoral Letters is not of great importance.

On the characterization of the situation presupposed in the Pastoral Letters, a few points are to be noted: The expectation of the parousia as immediately imminent event has, as in the authentic Pauline letters, not indeed been extinguished, but has noticeably receded. Regardless of this, the life of the community remains a life of hope: "Awaiting our blessed hope, the appearing of the glory of our great God and Savior Jesus Christ" (Tit 2:13). But the time factor has become secondary. They had taken their place in the world and looked to stabilize themselves therein.

The picture of the *ekklesia* addressed in the Pastoral Letters as local church is a picture with stable elements. The Church is encountered in the image of a house in which there has to be an ordering, still more exactly as support columns and foundation of truth. As expressed in 1 Timothy 3:15: "If I am delayed, you may know how one ought to behave in the household of God, which is the church of the living God, the pillar and bulwark of the truth."

The apostolic ministry and task includes the functions of the preacher, herald, missionary, and above all teacher. The message itself, the gospel, is found in the Pastorals in the form of teaching/doctrine, as the teaching of Jesus Christ. The conception of the gospel as teaching seems to have become necessary over against a confusion or lack of certainty coming from false teachers. Doctrinally speaking, the message is capable of better articulation, comprehension, and precision. But in this there is above all the duty of the protection of the entrusted good, the deposit, the "estate," connected with vigilance against false doctrine.

In the service of this task stand the duties which are claimed from the Apostle in the Pastorals and presented as apostolic responsibility.

5. Norbert Brox, *Die Pastoralbriefe; uebersetzt und erklaert,* Regensburger Neues Testament VII/2 (Regensburg, 1969).

In their formulation they assume the possession of decisive authority. One mark of this is the fullness of the vocabulary used to express it: "I exhort," "I charge you" (1 Tim 5:21); "I will," "I command" (2 Tim 4:1), or "must be" (1 Tim 3:2). According to the Pastoral Letters, Timothy and Titus are presented as disciples of Paul, as "my true child in a common faith" (Tit 1:4). There is also something special that characterizes Timothy and Titus, the expression "Rekindle the gift of God that is within you through the laying on of my hands" (2 Tim 1:6).

These disciples of the Apostle have thus been endowed with the grace of God by the laying on of hands. At the same time they are initiated into special duties and functions by the same laying on of hands. These are described in the Pastoral Letters as follows: They are the representatives of the apostles; they are the leaders of a group of individual communities; they have the right to appoint elders as leaders in the communities: "This is why I left you in Crete, that you might amend what was defective, and appoint elders in every town as I directed you" (Tit 1:5). In this function, Timothy and Titus are an instance of appeal in cases of complaints and disagreements that arise in the individual communities.

In addition, Timothy and Titus, under the mandate of the Apostle who is here presupposed as authority, give concrete directives for the communities, for the individual states in life: for men, women, and children, for slaves and for widows. There are further directions for their behavior in the face of dangers to come, especially with reference to persecution and false teaching. The most important task for Timothy and Titus, the disciples of the Apostle, is seen as preaching: "Preach the word!" The preaching takes primarily the form of doctrine, sound doctrine, the truth, as we see in the well-known words:

I charge you in the presence of God and of Christ Jesus who is to judge the living and the dead, and by his appearing and his kingdom: preach the word, be urgent in season and out of season, convince, rebuke, and exhort, be unfailing in patience and in teaching. For the time is coming when people will not endure sound teaching, but having itching ears they will accumulate for themselves teachers to suit their own likings, and will turn away from listening to the truth and wander into myths. (2 Tim 4:1–4)

The structure of the Church, according to the Pastoral Letters, includes the following offices: apostles, disciples of the apostles, presbyters, *episkopoi*, deacons. These letters have the following designations for the office in the community: episkopos, presbyter, deacon. It is striking that the concept episkopos occurs mostly in the singular, the concepts of presbyter and deacon mostly in the plural.

The duality of offices, from the Gentile-Christian sphere, episkopoi and deacons, and presbyter from the Jewish-Christian sphere have merged into a triad: episkopos—presbyter—deacon. The factual distinction between episkopos and presbyter is not yet complete, but it is under way.

Of the episkopos, the leader of the community, the following is required as presupposition:

If anyone aspires to the office of bishop, he desires a noble task. Now a bishop must be above reproach, the husband of one wife, temperate, sensible, dignified, hospitable, an apt teacher, no drunkard, not violent but gentle, not quarrelsome, and no lover of money. He must manage his own household well, keeping his children submissive and respectful in every way; for if a man does not know how to manage his own household, how can he care for God's church? (1 Tim 3:1–5)

Practically the same thing is said in the same words of the qualities of a presbyter and an elder: "He must hold firm to the sure word as taught, so that he may be able to give instruction in sound doctrine and also to confute those who contradict it" (Tit 1:9). Similar qualities are required of the deacon: "Deacons likewise must be serious, not double-tongued, not addicted to much wine, not greedy for gain; they must hold the mystery of the faith with a clear conscience. And let them also be tested first; then if they prove themselves blameless let them serve as deacons" (1 Tim 3:8–10).

We are doubtless dealing here with a schema being used in the framework of a current doctrine on duties. The qualities for various officials, for episkopos, presbyter, and deacon, are given in the form of a customary catalogue of virtues. They don't go beyond the average and leave out certain specific presuppositions for a specific office. It is a catalogue of the Christianly and humanly normal, of the everyday and the self-evident. It is important to note that in these developments, the activity of the episkopos or presbyter is not described; we are given instead the presuppositions for these activities. Norbert Brox explains the content of this catalogue as follows: The average level of the demands can perhaps be partly explained by the fact that the official is in an especially public position in the community and before the world and that certain types have to be excluded from the outset as candidates for the offices; thus, defining a lower limit (of qualifications) seems appropriate.[6]

All this points towards an old insight which, once again, is enjoying recognition: What has proven to be indispensable in neighborly, interhuman, and social relationships cannot be underestimated or neglected when it comes to order in God's house. Human inadequacy, deficient ethical quality, lack of testing in life, deficient leadership quality, lack of public reputation are no recommendation for the Christian life. This holds above all for those Christians who have an office or leading function in the community.

---

6. Ibid. 140.

The sobriety encountered here—the foregoing of the extraordinary—is not a deficiency but reveals a sense of everyday reality. We should note that this biblical description of community leadership, of presbyters, bishops, and deacons, obviously contains more possibilities than were thought possible. In our contemporary discussion about office in the Church, which is not a theoretical but an existential question, a reflection on this origin is helpful. It also seems to be quite suggestively significant—let this be said in conclusion—that the concept "priest," the sacrificing priest of the ancient religions, is nowhere used as a designation of those who take on leading functions and tasks—including worship, baptism, and Eucharist—in the community of Jesus Christ.

Gerhard Lohfink, in an article on the normativity of the concept of office in the Pastoral Letters, has refuted the conception of Heinrich Schlier that the principle of office dominates in the Pastoral Letters:

> The highest principle is the unfalsified handing on of the Gospel entrusted by God to the Church. Because the Pastoral Letters know that this handing on is not possible without an orderly situation of office in the local churches, they speak a great deal of office, not in order to lay down specific structures of office, but to assure the unfalsified handing on of the *paratheke* (what has been received). They presuppose as self-evident a firm web of relationship between office and gospel, but the prerogative clearly goes to the gospel. If we could ask the author of the Pastoral Letters, prescinding from all times and all language barriers and difficulties of understanding: Would you really want a very specific structure of office as norm for the Church, he would answer us: No, I would not want a specific office but the gospel as norm for the Church. Create for yourselves whatever office is the best guarantee for the unfalsified handing on and realization of the gospel![7]

The First Letter of Clement

This is a letter of the community of Rome to the community in Corinth about the years 96–98. In the letter itself the author is not mentioned by name; however the letter is ascribed to the Roman bishop Clement.[8]

The occasion of the letter was a conflict in the community of Corinth. It arose because in Corinth "old and proven presbyters" were "unjustly" deposed from their office. This resulted in a division in the community. The bishop of Rome as such, not their bishop, turned to the community in Corinth with the request to end the quarrel. The letter is not a directive, but a letter of appeal. As a guideline for order and structure in the community, the Letter of Clement in chapters 42–44 makes some noteworthy statements.

---

7. "Die Normativität der Amtsvorstellungen in den Pastoralbriefen,"*ThQ* 157 (1977) 93–106.

8. Text edition: *Die Apostolischen Väter*, ed. J. A. Fischer (Darmstadt, 1956) 1–107.

The apostles received the Good News for us from the Lord Jesus Christ. Jesus, the Christ, was sent by God. Christ comes from God, the apostles come from Christ. They were filled with certainty by the resurrection of our Lord and confirmed in fidelity by the Word of God. They preached in city and country and appointed their first fruits, after undergoing testing in the Spirit, as bishops and deacons for the future faithful." (1 Clem 42)

The apostles also knew that there would be conflict over the office of bishop; thus they gave exact instruction that when a bishop dies, other proven men would take over his office. That they who, with the agreement of the whole community, were appointed as bishops and blamelessly served the flock of Christ and receive good witness from all should now be deposed, that we hold to be unjust." (1 Clem 44)

Notice the way reference is made to the self-evidently described (and constitutive for office) chain of commission: God—Christ—apostles—episkopoi—deacons; note also the juridical, not sacramental, mode of argument. Injustice has been committed, it must be rectified. Equally noteworthy is the strong institution of the office of presbyter in the community of Corinth as well as in Rome in the decade of the nineties.

The Letters of Ignatius of Antioch

These letters[9] document the fact that the communities over which Ignatius himself has charge and the communities to which he writes—Ephesus, Magnesia, Rome, Philadelphia, Smyrna—have the following structure: At their head stands a bishop, and around him a college of presbyters and the deacons. Hence the terminology of a "monarchical episcopate" recognizable since Ignatius. This is not a felicitous expression; its meaning, however, is that the leadership of the community lies in one hand, that of the bishop. The interplay of bishop, presbyter, and deacons is illustrated by Ignatius with the musical images of the cithara and chords.

The Letters of Ignatius contain a highly developed theology of the episcopal office, which is grounded in concern for the unity of the Church. The original image of this unity is, said Ignatius, the one Christ in unity with the Father. This unity becomes visible in the one bishop. The bishop represents Christ in the community. The bishop is accordingly the center of the community; he is at the same time its constant alter ego. As he himself is borne by Christ, so shall he bear the community. Thus Ignatius can say: Where the bishop is, there is the community, the Church.

From this flows the concrete principle: "Do nothing without the bishop!" He alone is authorized to lead worship, above all to celebrate the Eucharist, and to administer the sacraments. If someone else wishes

---

9. Ibid. 111–225.

to do this, it can take place only with the approval of the bishop. "The Church is a people united in the bishop." In Ignatius the Spiritual, the pneumatic and the juridical moments of the episcopal office are united in a unique way. They work not in the attitude of an absolutist, authoritarian ruler, but in the manner of a man filled with Spirit, love, self-dedication, and responsibility. His life and his martyrdom are their existential confirmation and "verification."

His concern, his compulsion for unity in the form of a visible unity in the real community, in the form of a bishop, is to be understood against the background of Gnosticism, which wanted on the one hand to curse the Christian faith and on the other hand to melt it into a great syncretism and thus deprive it of what it really was. "It is one and the same passion which rejects gnostic docetism and affirms the real Church, which seeks for the Spiritual life and demands office" (H. von Campenhausen).

The Letters of Ignatius are an almost extravagantly exuberant witness and a spiritual confession from early Christianity. The Tübingen theologian Johann Adam Möhler wrote his first theological work *Die Einheit in der Kirche* under the strong impression he had received especially from the Letters of Ignatius, from their style, their pathos, and their enthusiasm.

With the theme "Unity in the Church," Möhler took up the theme of Ignatius and carried it through in his spirit. Möhler's division into the unity of the Spirit of the Church and the unity of the Body of the Church allows him to describe and acknowledge the connection between the inner life and the external structure of the Church. Möhler describes Church as the external, visible form of a holy, living power, the love which the Holy Spirit bestows. The Church is the Body of the Spirit of the faithful being formed from within. Möhler sees in doctrine the conceptual expression of the Christian Spirit. When he speaks of plurality without unity, he labels such people "ecclesiastical egoists." His theme is unity in plurality. "Even though all the faithful form one unity, they all maintain their individuality. All have the same faith, but possess the same thing in different forms." Accordingly there is diversity and freedom as well as legality (no contradiction) as an expression of the tension of life.

As did Ignatius seventeen centuries before him, Möhler sees the unity of the body of the Church primarily in the bishop. But he also sees it in the unity of the bishops, and so in the metropolitans, and in the bishop of Rome. Following Ignatius, Möhler says of Rome: "The bishop is thus the union of the faithful become visible in one place, their love for each other become a person, the manifestation and the living central point of the mind of Christ striving for unity, the love of the Christians themselves come to consciousness, and the means to hold on to it."[10] Certainly this is no "is" description, but a "should" prescription; but when this "should" becomes the orienting image, it is important and can also be effective. Möhler continues: "Whoever is eager for the episcopal honor is not capable of it, and whoever is capable of it is not eager for it."[11]

A final quotation from Möhler's writings: "There are clerics and laypersons; this means nothing other than that different gifts of grace are distributed, and they must [all] have points of connection to the community."[12]

Falling Away or Progress?

How are we to judge this path from the open structures of the beginning up to the ordered structures as they are found, soberly in the Pastoral Letters, and highly pneumatically and enthusiastically in the Letters of Ignatius? The question cannot be avoided: Is this a history of falling away from the living, Spirit-filled beginning, and thus a great misunderstanding (E. Brunner); or do we have here genuine progress to a continually more clarifying structure whose elements, episkopos, presbyter, deacon, we still have today, even if they are somewhat modified in content when we consider that the position of the bishop Ignatius roughly corresponded to that of a pastor of a community today?

It would be overly simplistic to think of falling away or progress as the applicable categories here, What happened was that the Church, in one historical epoch, created something that was representative of it and for it; and the organizational forms and structures available at the time, called "presbyter" and "episkopos" seemed possible and necessary. Grounded in the often-mentioned tension between "true to origins" and "adapted to the situation" is the principle that other situations can open up and require other possibilities, as long as the reality and the origin are preserved.

Some years ago (1969) the German bishops published a "Biblical-Dogmatic Guide" on the subject of the priestly office. In it are the following propositions which, for our theme, could not be formulated in a more pointed and focused fashion:

The New Testament is for the Church the document of its normative early history. Thus the Church must listen to these documents in order to show forth the essential characteristics which remain applicable for it until the Second Coming of Christ. This holds also for the offices that had their first form and shaping in the New Testament, and demonstrating a variability even then; nevertheless they

10. *Unity in the Church or The Principle of Catholicism*, ed Peter C. Erb (Washington, D.C.: The Catholic University of America Press, 1966) 218.
11. Ibid. 220.
12. Ibid. 209, 225.

stand in a factual continuity which allows questions to be asked about the essence of the priestly office and its significance for the structure of the Church. But since the Church is not beginning this conversation with the New Testament today for the first time, since it is a conversation which began quite early, a conversation to which it responded with an understanding of priesthood appropriate to the times, when it now continues with that always constantly necessary listening to and reflecting on the Scripture, it will also have to carry on the conversation with itself, that is, with its history and its tradition.

The inner reason we must include the historical development in our understanding of everything ecclesiastical, including ecclesiastical office, lies in the fact that the Church, in its founding by Jesus Christ, was historically grounded and dependent on historical development. The Church must always and inevitably realize its essence under different conditions, in the course of which time-conditioned elements become part of its reality. Hence, even within the New Testament, changes in the form of office are observable. Thus we too cannot avoid the historically conditioned and variable development of form in the Church and in church office. However careful may be our efforts with regard to the Church, and however profound our reforms, they never get to the point that what we are realizing is only its unchanged essence. It would thus be a misunderstanding to want to judge such changes, which do not involve its abiding nature, as always illegitimate or even as a falling away from the will and the mission of Christ.

But this variability requires precisely that we are constantly reflecting on the New Testament foundations, so that the connection with the original beginning of the Church and with Jesus Christ does not become obscured or even lost. For not every time-conditioned or every possible change is justified, and not every development means a step forward towards the full form of the Body of Christ (cf. Eph 4:12–13). In the [our] historically variable form in which we know the Church, we are constantly called upon to make this [full form of the Body] again visible by reflection on its origin.[13]

13. *Biblisch–dogmatische Handreichung* [über das priesterliche Amt] (Trier, 1969) 7–8.

TRADITION AND SUCCESSION

Tradition, (*paradosis, traditio*) is a basic word of theology and ecclesiology. It is already found in the New Testament, and indeed in its oldest writings, in 1 Corinthians 11:23: "I received from the Lord what I also delivered to you." What is received and delivered in this passage is the account of the Last Supper of Jesus with the testament: "Do this in memory of me. As often as you do it you proclaim the death of the Lord." Similarly in 1 Corinthians 15:3–5: "For I delivered to you as of first importance what I also received, that Christ died for our sins in accordance with the scriptures, that he was buried, that he was raised on the third day in accordance with the scriptures, and that he appeared to Cephas, then to the twelve." Here we are dealing with the heart of Christian proclamation, the message of Jesus crucified and risen.

In the tradition, in this "handing on," the purpose is not to let the Christ-event which has come to be in historical event, word, and action remain just as it is as a unique happening, but to carry it forward, to mediate it. The purpose is to pass it on from one person to another, from community to community, from generation to generation. For the Christ-event is not to remain something of the past; it is promise, directive, orientation, life, and salvation for all people and times; it is to be contemporaneous, as it were, with all times. The reality of this revelation-event is that it happened once, and at the same time happened once and for all.

The form of the tradition is also very appropriate because the Christ-event is given as gift which thus can be mediated only in the form of the handing on of the gift of tradition. In the Pastoral Letters the received and handed-on tradition is the constantly present gift and task to be preserved and protected, above all the tradition of the word, of doctrine, of the "truth."

Tradition of the Origin

The tradition presupposes an origin from which it comes and which is its constant source. The tradition is the tradition of the origin; the origin itself is thus the source of the tradition.[1] This origin is the revelation, which does not indeed begin with Jesus, but is fulfilled with Jesus, the Christ, and has received in him its definitiveness and unsurpassability. Thus the revelation culminating in Jesus is the source of the tradition; the tradition is the tradition of this revelation.

One can see this tradition also in other perspectives and call it the tradition residing in the apostles, the apostolic origin. For the apostles are the called, authentic, and legitimated witnesses of the Christ event. Everything else that follows is, as postapostolic reality connected with the apostolic, related to this Christ event. They belong to the original event itself. Thus, one can say that the apostles are the origin of the tradition, but the tradition itself is the tradition of the apostolic origin.

From this comprehensive definition—revelation, Christ-event, witness of the apostles—it becomes quite clear that tradition has to do certainly with tradition in the form of the word, the message, the teaching, the faith, but not only with these but also with the tradition of the whole reality that is named and is there with the origin/Christ-event: thus with *martyria, leitourgia*, and *diakonia*, with life, behavior, customs, structure, thus with being Christian, being Church as a whole. The whole Church is apostolic: *Credo ecclesiam apostolicam*.

From the relationship of origin and tradition flows the following consequence, when we designate the origin as source and the tradition as river and stream (the image is from Newman): The river cannot climb higher than its source. The tradition following revelation as its source cannot go beyond it in significance and effect.

1. G. Söhngen, "Überlieferung und apostolische Verkündigung" in: *Die Einheit in der Theologie* 315–23. On this theme: Oscar Cullmann, *Die Tradition als exegetisches, historisches und theologisches Problem* (Zurich, 1954); M. Schmaus, ed., *Die mündliche Überlieferung. Beiträge zum Begriff der Tradition von H. Bacht, H. Fries, J. R. Geiselmann* (Munich, 1957); J. Pieper, *Über den Begriff der Tradition* (Cologne—Opladen, 1958); H. Bacht, "Die Rolle der Tradition in der Kanonbildung," *Cath* 12 (1958) 16–37; J. Betz—H. Fries, ed., *Kirche und Überlieferung* (Freiburg—Basel—Vienna, 1960); P. Lengsfeld, *Überlieferung. Tradition und Schrift in der protestantischen und katholischen Theologie der Gegenwart* (Paderborn, 1960); Joseph R. Geiselmann, "Tradition" in : *Fragen der Theologie heute*, eds., Johannes Feiner—Josef Trutsch—Franz Böckle (Madrid, 1962); H. Weger, "Tradition," *SM* 6.269–74; Gerhard Ebeling, *The Word of God and Tradition: Historical Studies Interpreting the Divisions of Christianity*, trans. S. H. Hooke (Philadelphia: Fortress Press, 1968); Yves Congar, *Tradition and Traditions: An Historical and a Theological Essay* (New York: MacMillan, 1967); Walter Kasper, *Dogma Unter dem Wort Gottes* (Mainz, 1965); P. Lengsfeld, "Tradition innerhalb der konstitutiven Zeit der Offenbarung" in: *MySal* 1.239–88; J. A. Fichter, "Tradition," (in theology) *NCE* 14.225–28; J. Jensen, "Tradition," (in the Bible) *NCE* 14.223–25; J. Pieper, *Überlieferung. Begriff und Anspruch* (Munich, 1970).

Consequently, tradition as stream or river serves the preservation and further delivery of the water of the source. Speaking nonmetaphorically, it can turn out that the origin will be, in tradition, more and more understood, appropriated, disclosed, and unfolded in its richness—namely, in connection with the people and cultures through which the living origin is received. It is recognizable in the stream what wealth is contained in the source.[2]

Thus there can be progress, not of course in the revelation itself, but a growth in the grasping of the source, a growth in faith and understanding. The Constitution on Divine Revelation of Vatican II says:

> This tradition which comes from the apostles develops in the Church with the help of the Holy Spirit. For there is a growth in the understanding of the realities and the words which have been handed down. This happens through the contemplation and study made by the believers . . . through the intimate understanding of spiritual things they experience, and through the preaching of those who have received through episcopal succession the sure gift of truth. For, as the centuries succeed one another, the Church constantly moves forward toward the fullness of divine truth. . . . Through the same tradition the Church's full canon of the sacred books is known, and the sacred writings themselves are more profoundly understood and unceasingly made active in her. (*Dei verbum* no. 8)

Thus one can go on to say with the Council: "Scripture and tradition arise from the same divine source, are closely related to each other, and tend toward the same goal."

This all-too-harmonious picture needs to be enlarged. For it can turn out that the tradition does not always preserve and direct onwards the water of the source in full openness; that the tradition isn't always completely faithful to the tradition; that in the tradition some contents of the origin are not, of course, denied, but still covered over or not made sufficiently effective; that some contents of the origin are favored and others neglected, or, metaphorically speaking, diverted. This happens, for example when charism as gift of the Spirit to the Church is restricted to the charism of office; when the charism of the prophetic is seen as troublesome. This happens when, with the foundation of the Church, one thinks only of Peter and not of the foundation of the Church, which consists of apostles and prophets and above all of Christ himself; or when one prefers the Pastoral Letters and what they say about office and keeps silent about the open possibilities on this question in the early letters of Paul, or writes them off as an undeveloped stage.

---

2. Basic ideas from John Henry Newman's treatment of the development of Christian doctrine; *An Essay on the Development of Christian Doctrine* (Westminster, Md: Christian Classics, 1968); Cf. H. Fries, "J. H. Newman's Contribution to the Understanding of Tradition" in: M. Schmaus, ed., *Die mündliche Überlieferung*, 63–122; G. Biemer, *Newman on Tradition*, trans. Kevin Smyth (New York: Herder and Herder, 1967); J. Stern, *Bible et tradition chez Newman* (Paris: Aubier, 1967).

It can also happen that some things are carried along in the stream of the tradition, metaphorically speaking swept along with it, which do not come from the pure origin but are cultural and historical accretions. This apparently cannot be avoided, but it becomes a source of concern when these historical realizations and inculturations are clothed with the halo of the origin and thus with the quality of the normative and indispensable, such as certain models of ecclesiastical office, concretions of the office of the pope and the bishops in the course of history.

There is an important consequence from all this in the relationship of origin, i.e., source and tradition: The origin, the Christ-event, the apostolic has a liberating and critical power over-against the forms and articulations of the tradition. The origin has a normative power, it is the *norma normans* when the tradition has to mediate the origin.

This is the source of the Church's continual capacity for renewal, and also of the ongoing impulse for its need of renewal: *Ecclesia semper reformanda*. This means, concretely: Scripture exercises a traditional-critical function. For it is the witness of the origin, of the Christ-event, of the apostolic witness and faith. This holds even when the Scripture, for its part, is the result of a process of tradition, in which the preaching, the sending of the apostles, and the witness of the first believers are active. Nevertheless, Scripture remains the norming (*normans*) tradition; it is "canonical." It belongs in the Spirit-filled original event of the Church.[3]

In distinction from this, ecclesiastical tradition is primarily a history of the interpretation of Scripture, a process of dealing with Scripture; but again not only interpretation in the sense of an exegesis, a theory, but interpretation that interprets the reality dealt with in the Scripture as a comprehensive completion of life, thus also as praxis— true to origin and adapted to the situation.

Thus things like creeds, rites, dogmas, confessional writings, and also liturgies, devotional forms, juridical determinations, are understood as concrete interpretation of Scripture in the context of a particular historical situation. These traditions, too, are attributed a normativity, but a normativity that, for its part, is normed by the origin. These traditions are the *norma normata* as distinct from the *norma normans*.

It is clear then that tradition is a comprehensive process and that, with tradition, two things are meant: First, the objective taking down of a process of tradition in the form of dogmas, creeds, liturgy, structure, legal specifications, customs. These determine stations on the road of faith and on the road of life lived from faith. Hence the term of *traditio passiva* (passive tradition).

3. Karl Rahner, *Über die Schriftinterpretation* (Freiburg, 1958).

Along with this is tradition as living event, as completion, as act of the Church in its various concrete situations and in its attention to its ongoing tasks. The Tübingen School[4] puts it this way: Living faith as sanctified tradition. J. S. Drey speaks of the self-tradition of the origin to living presence. According to J. A. Möhler, tradition is "the living gospel proclaimed in the Church, the identity of the Christian consciousness with the consciousness of the whole Church." Tradition is thus, seen in terms of theological knowledge, at the same time the condition of the possibility of a faith which is oriented to Jesus Christ.[5] Tradition orients to the *norma normans* of the Scripture and frees from the curse of ideological dependence and from the hectic of the day and its actuality. Tradition can become the embodiment of a liberating and dangerous memory of Jesus Christ.

Contents and Form

Since the tradition in all stages does not take place by itself, it has need of organs and bearers through which it can take place. This connection is expressed in the category of succession, succession by human beings, succession in the apostolic faith and witness and in the carrying out of the apostolic mandate. This results in an inner coordination of tradition and succession. They define each other, so to speak, mutually. Joseph Ratzinger has given this dependence a well-known formulation: Succession is the form of the tradition. The tradition is the content of the succession.[6]

This can be made even more clear: If tradition can be described or paraphrased as content, as definition of the goal of succession, as apostolic tradition, then succession too can be described as form and structure of the tradition, as apostolic succession.

To clarify the concept: The apostles can have no successors in their being witnesses to the life of Jesus and to his words and deeds, especially his resurrection from the dead. Nor can they have successors in their being immediately sent and commissioned by Jesus. But the apostles can and must have a succession for their witness, preaching, faith, ministry. In other words, the apostolic ministry goes on and is further

4. J. R. Geiselmann, *Lebendiger Glaube aus geheiligter Überlieferung. Der Grundgedanke der Theologie Johann Adam Möhlers und der katholischen Tübinger Schule* (Mainz, 1942); *Die lebendige Überlieferung als Norm des christlichen Glaubens, dargestellt im Geiste der Traditionslehre Johannes Ev. Kuhns* (Freiburg—Basel—Vienna, 1958); *Die katholische Tübinger Schule. Ihre theologische Eigenart* (Freiburg—Basel—Vienna, 1964); M. B. Schepers, "Tübingen School," NCE 14, 339.
5. W. Kasper, "Tradition als Erkenntnisprinzip," *ThQ* 155 (1975) 198–215; *Die Lehre von der Tradition in der Römischen Schule* (Freiburg—Basel—Vienna, 1962).
6. Joseph Ratzinger, *Revelation and Tradition*, trans. W. J. O'Hara (London: Burns & Oates, 1966).

mediated in the community of the faithful. This takes place by apostolic succession and by successors to the apostles.

Not just individuals but the whole Church stands in the succession of the apostles. We believe and confess the apostolic Church. The whole Church is the People of God gathered by the apostles by the preaching of the gospel of Jesus Christ. The whole Church is the Spirit-temple built on the foundation of the apostles, the Christ-body held together by the ministry of the apostles. The whole Church is apostolic inasmuch as it stands in the succession of the apostolic faith.

For this apostolic succession ascribed to the Church as a whole to remain effective, it needs an even further concretion of succession as form and structure of the tradition. There is succession in the specific sense of succession in office, by which people are commissioned with the apostolic ministry in a special, official, and public way, and are initiated into it. The process is already found in the New Testament, where the apostles—the founders of the communities—appointed elders, presbyters, or episkopoi as leaders of the community. They did this with prayer and the laying on of hands, giving them the duty of a shepherd with the duties of special responsibility and care for the faith and life of a community.

This process is even more obvious in the (later) Pastoral Letters, where Timothy and Titus, the disciples of the Apostle, are entrusted with the specific tasks of leadership, preaching, and the preservation in the communities of the good news entrusted to them. As much as they are connected with the communities by the execution of special public tasks and as leader of the community, they still also stand over-against the community. Thus there is the special apostolic succession in the succession "in office" represented by persons. Specific persons, as successors of the apostles, take over the apostolic task in the post-apostolic age. In the New Testament they are called presbyters, episkopoi, directors, shepherds as respective leaders of the communities in which the gift of direction is counted among the charisms. This was done so that the Church as a whole would remain in the apostolic tradition. The appointment and commissioning of these persons, the bearers of an office for the performance of specific services and functions, is carried out according to biblical witness by prayer and the laying on of hands, in other words, by the act of ordination.[7] According to the New Testament (Acts of the Apostles), this is performed either by the apostles themselves or by disciples of the apostles like Titus and Timothy (Pastoral Letters).

This subsequently led, in the increasing distinction between presbyters and episkopoi, to the ordination by episkopoi, i.e., bishops, which in the early Church did not exclude ordination by presbyters. It

7. E. Lohse, *Die Ordination im Spätjudentum und im Neuen Testament* (Berlin, 1951).

is the rule today in most of the Christian churches that already-or-dained office holders do the ordaining. In the Roman Catholic and in the Orthodox Church, ordination is carried out by bishops. It follows that, that which is apostolic, apostolic succession, cannot be limited to succession in office. This is something, rather, that is encompassed by the whole Church; it has to serve the whole Church, and thus has its place there.

But it also remains true that specific succession in office and in public ministry to word and sacrament as special ministry to unity cannot be left out or be lacking. Thus succession in office is both a sign and a means to ensure the apostolic succession for the whole Church. Described more exactly: Succession in the form of ordination and in the form of the continuity contained therein is an essential sign and means for the continuity and identity of the apostolic faith.[8] This is why the question of office, which, of itself and qualitatively speaking, belongs among the secondary questions, is so vital in ecumenical discussion and so important ecclesiologically.

The Historical Development

In the course of time proof of succession in office, above all in the office of the bishop, became the predominant and characteristic guarantee of the true and authentic apostolic tradition. This took place above all in the second and third centuries in the struggle against Gnosticism, which threatened to supersede the apostolic faith with a knowledge and wisdom superior to it, and attempted to permeate it with elements from Greek philosophy and religion. The gnostics appealed to a secret tradition which they had received from the apostles. In response, it was especially Irenaeus (†202), the leader, the bishop of the community of Lyon, who in his writing *Adversus haereses* established the following principle: For the correct apostolic tradition of faith in the Church, one doesn't look to uncontrolled and uncontrollable secret traditions, but predominantly to the traditions in the churches grounded by the apostles. The uninterrupted succession of the bishops in these churches from the apostles, the bishops as successors of the apostles, vouches for the truth of their teaching. Succession in the bishop guarantees the continuity and identity of the tradition.

Then follows the oft-quoted remark by Irenaus: "Because it would be too much to count up the succession in office of all these bishops," it seems to him sufficient "to produce proof from the greatest, very old Church known to all, the Church founded by the apostles Peter and

---

8 W. Kasper, "Ökumenischer Fortschritt im Amtsverständnis?" in: *Amt in Widerstreit*, ed. K. Schuh (Berlin, 1975) 54–58, here 57. Cf. Yves Congar, ed., *Bischofsamt—Amt der Einheit* (Munich, 1983).

Paul in Rome, that the line of its bishops goes back to the apostles, and thus its teaching is also apostolic. Therefore all must agree with this Church" (*AdvHaer* 3.3.1-2). It is understandable that this passage is seen and claimed by the Catholic viewpoint as an important, indeed classic witness for succession in the office of the bishop, above all for a correspondence between tradition and succession: Succession in the office of the bishop is the form of the apostolic tradition which, in turn, is the substance of the succession.

There should be no objection to using the passage this way as long as one keeps in mind the place that such an emphatically emphasized succession in the office of bishop has in the apostolic tradition, and as long as one remembers that the emphasis on this visible, concrete, and thus also provable office corresponds to a specific context in historical time: the need to mount a defense against Gnosticism by means of a clear and recognizable counterposition: the *successio apostolica* of the bishops. Apostolicity as such and on the whole is not restricted to succession in office, even though there were, in times to follow, repeated tendencies to do this.

Nor was it thought that, in the coordination of episcopal succession and apostolic tradition, there was an automatic factor in the sense of an infallibly working guarantee. Were that the case, there would be no explanation for the fact that—even then—bishops were unfaithful to their mission and did not truly preserve the apostolic tradition. J. H. Newman, in a treatise that caused some excitement in his time, showed that during the Nicene controversies, the apostolic tradition relative to the person of Jesus Christ and his divine Sonship was preserved not by the majority of the bishops but by the sense of the faith of the Christian people (Jerome: "The world had become Arian").[9]

One will also not do justice to the meaning and intention of this text of Irenaeus if, to illustrate a generally valid situation with one obvious example, one makes it into a proof text for the primacy of the bishop of Rome in early times. This was done in the documents of Vatican I and, in its wake, in many textbooks of apologetics and dogmatics. Irenaeus does not speak thematically or directly about the bishop of Rome, but he speaks about the Roman community, which, because of its founding by Peter and Paul, had a special meaning and worth. The necessary agreement with the Church of Rome mentioned in this passage is accordingly to be understood in this sense, as agreement with apostolic tradition and succession, not in the sense of a special declaration of primacy with reference to the bishop of Rome, but as an example.

---

9. See Newman's discussion of the witness of the laity in questions of doctrine (quotation taken from: J. H. Newman, *Polemische Schriften* (Bd. IV der Ausgewählten Werke, ed. M. Laros and W. Becker), (Mainz, 1959) 255–92.

This tendency also resulted in a narrowing of the concept "apostolic." After Pope Gregory the Great (†604), the word *apostolicus* turned more and more into a designation applied to the occupants of the seat of the Roman bishop. In the wake of this development, the word "apostolic" took on the meaning "papal." Thus Gregory the Great himself calls the pope *"apostolicus pontifex."* That the meaning "apostolic" in the sense of "papal" has survived essentially to this day can be seen in many designations: apostolic see, apostolic legates and delegates, apostolic nuncios, apostolic vicars and prefects, apostolic blessing, apostolic indult, apostolic constitution, apostolic process. The emperor of Austria and Hungary was called "apostolic majesty."

The same development is found in an analogous way in the related expression *sedes apostolica*. The *Sedes apostolicae* are those sees where, at one time, the apostles were active, or which were the recipients of apostolic letters. This means, in the first instance, that not every episcopal see is a *sedes apostolica*, but only a certain number, which stand in a special relationship to the apostles. Among the *sedes apostolicae*, along with Antioch, Alexandria, Ephesus, and Jerusalem, the *sedes romana* takes a preferred position. The remaining episcopal sees are indirectly apostolic, inasmuch as they have community with a *sedes apostolica* in the proper and direct sense. In this understanding, all bishops are in the apostolic succession and can thus be witnesses of the apostolic tradition.

The concept of "apostle" and all that goes with it became more and more restricted in the course of history, since this designation, at the end of a development reaching up to the time before Vatican II, was applied only to certain persons and institutions, above all to the pope, the curia, the Church of Rome, and in a certain sense to the bishops who see their appointment in "the mercy of God and the grace of the Apostolic See." The *viri apostolici* become the *vir apostolicus*; the *sedes apostolicae* become the *sedes apostolica*; the apostolic work of Christians in Church and world becomes the apostolic activity of the hierarchy, the hierarchical apostolate with the assistance of laypersons.

The Layperson

Originally, lay signified the full membership to the totality of the people, also of the people of God. Its Christian specification and calling is expressed in an exemplary way in the First Letter of Peter: "You are a chosen race, a royal priesthood, a holy nation, God's own people, that you may declare the wonderful deeds of him who called you out of darkness into his marvelous light" (1 Pet 2:9). In the course of history in general, and especially in the course of the history of the Church, the layperson received more the predicate of the not qualified, or non-specialist.

Yves Congar, who in many writings has mediated the comprehensive sense of apostolic tradition and succession for Catholic theology and Church, has also brought the theological position of the layperson in the Church to an impressive new dignity.[10] It is especially due to him that the Second Vatican Council brought to life a completely new picture (fundamentally, a rediscovered old picture) of the layperson in the Church.

In its Dogmatic Constitution *Lumen gentium*, the Council designates as laypersons

all the faithful except those in holy orders and those in a religious state sanctioned by the Church. These faithful are by baptism made one body with Christ and are established among the People of God. They are in their own way made sharers in the priestly, prophetic, and kingly functions of Christ. They carry out their own part in the mission of the whole Christian people with respect to the Church and the world. (no. 31)

Further:

The chosen People of God is one: "one Lord, one faith, one baptism" (Eph. 4:5). As members, they share a common dignity from their rebirth in Christ. They have the same filial grace and the same vocation to perfection. They possess in common one salvation, one hope, and one undivided charity. (no. 32).

The activity of the laity in the Church is no longer called, as it was before, a "sharing in the hierarchical apostolate," so that they would be basically only the extended arm of the clergy or of those who receive the orders of the hierarchy. The mission of the laity is "a participation in the saving mission of the Church itself" (no 33) in and for the world, in its proper functioning, shaping, and ordering.

It is the business of the laity in virtue of their own calling to seek the kingdom of God in the administration and holy regulation of temporal things.

They live in the world, that is, in each and all of the secular professions and occupations. They live in the ordinary circumstances of family and social life from which the very web of their existence is woven. They are called there by God so that by exercising thier proper function and being led by the spirit of the gospel they can work for the sanctification of the world from within, in the manner of leaven. In this way they can make Christ known to others, especially by the testimony of a life resplendent in faith, hope, and love. (no. 31)

The laity have a special calling in the state of married and family life: "The Christian family loudly proclaims both the present virtues of the kingdom of God and the hope of a blessed life to come. Thus by its example and its witness, it accuses the world of sin and enlightens those

10. Y. Congar, *Lay People in the Church*, trans. Donald Attwater (Westminster, Md.: Newman Press, 1957).

who seek the truth" (no. 35). It is explicitly said that there are places and conditions where the Church as salt of the earth can be made present only by the laity (no. 33).

The relationship between clergy and laity is described this way: "The shepherds of the Church, following the example of the Lord, should serve each other and the rest of the faithful; but the faithful should work together closely, full of zeal, with the shepherds and teachers" (no. 32). Thus it is said that "the bishops should recognize and support the freedom, the dignity, and the responsibility of the laity in the Church" (no. 37). The laity have the right to receive in abundance of the Spiritual goods of the Church, above all the help of the Word of God and of the sacraments, from the ordained shepherds" (no. 37). The chapter on the laity closes with the moving words: "Every layperson must, before the world, be a witness to the resurrection and life of Jesus, our Lord, and a sign of the living God" (no. 38).

A great deal of these great and liberating words on the laity has been realized in the post-conciliar period: above all in the participation and engagement of the laity in the "councils" and boards on various levels, most concretely in their participation in the parish council. Especially impressive were the representation and engagement of the laity at the Catholic Synod in Würzburg.

The directives of the New Code of Canon Law on the laity (can. 224–231) take up some important motifs and ideas of Vatican II, and go far beyond the statements contained in the earlier Code of Canon Law (can. 682 and 683), as well as beyond the information in earlier theological reference works where, under the entry "Lay," one was referred to "Clergy."

In this time of decline in priestly vocations, more and more laypersons are called on for service to the Church and in it, most impressively in the vocation of pastoral assistants or pastoral consultants. Without this service of the laity, the life of the Catholic Church could no longer be maintained.

On the other hand, one cannot be silent about certain questions and concerns. There are efforts at present, to reduce as far as possible the influence of the laity in the Church, to leave their theological position as undefined as possible, and to limit their functions, e.g., in preaching. In all cases they want to put the ministry of the laity at the greatest possible distance from the office of the ordained leader of the community.

Obviously, there are and must be conditions and presuppositions for the taking on of a ministry in the Church. For example, in the guidelines issued in 1978 by the German Bishops' Conference for deacons and laypersons in pastoral office, one reads, with reference to marriage and family: "Whoever stands and lives in open contradiction to principles of the Catholic faith is not suitable for church ministry." With a view to marriage and family, these are some of the things said: "Any living together as if in marriage, i.e., a living together without a valid church marriage, and any remarrying of a divorced person without a valid church marriage, stands in contradiction to principles of the Catholic Church" Those living in such situations are not suitable for church ministry—they cannot do their job credibly.

But along with these very just impediments, a few others were also mentioned: interconfessional marriage, or the fact of a civil divorce, in which it is implied that the marriage in question is valid before the Church. If the divorced person avoids remarriage during the lifetime of the earlier partner, there is no opposition to Catholic principles, but an explicit respect for them. The interconfessional marriage as a general impediment for church service is difficult to reconcile with the proposition that was approved by the Würzburg Synod, that an interconfessional marriage can also be a chance and a fructification of the faith and thus a convincing realization of the ecumenical Church.[11]

One can only hope that, also on this point and in the face of this obvious step backwards, the opportunity and the obligation of *ecclesia semper reformanda* will be taken seriously.

---

11. Pastorale Zusammenarbeit der Kirchen im Dienst an der christlichen Einheit 7.1.2. Offizielle Gesamtausgabe (1978) 792.

THE QUESTION OF OFFICE IN CONTEMPORARY ECUMENICAL DISCUSSION

The question of church office is presently one of the most active themes in ecumenical dialogue. Of course, measured against the hierarchy of truths, this theme is not the most important. But, in the performance of the apostolic mission to be mediated in the present, it does take on a kind of key function, both as instance and instrument of the mediation of the Christian faith and as structural element of the Church.

On the Method of Ecumenical Dialogue

One method is that of convergence. It makes each confessional position understandable and perhaps acceptable to the ecumenical partner by a comprehensive and open interpretation of one's own position. Without any loss of one's own church identity, what is "other" in the other confessions is integrated into one's own as legitimate plurality. Thus what is one's own remains, but comes into possession of a greater reality, breadth and thus catholicity, without having to give up one's self in favor of a "third" entity without contours, a feared third confession.

This method is usually called a method of convergence. Its starting point is an open and well-intentioned view of the other from one's own position. Then, by means of a synoptic perspective, it seeks to focus on the lines of convergence and thus, as has already been explained, seeks to transform the problems, difficulties, and earlier contradictions into fruitful controversies.

There is an objection against this process: If one should ask only about what for example, is Evangelical in the Catholic Church and Catholic in the Evangelical Church, the horizon of the confessions is indeed being expanded. That is very nice and also by no means unimportant. But it runs the risk of simply taking up a position and refusing to move from it, despite the fact that the foundation beneath it is being broadened? Then the further question would be: In doing this, are not the churches again making themselves too much their own end and practicing a kind of ecclesiological narcissism as self-reflection and self-confirmation?

The other method tries to be a method of totality. It does not move from the present status as something definitively fixed, which can be enriched by convergence and integration; it seeks rather to integrate the present into a greater total horizon, and from there to ask further questions and take up new possibilities.

This can take place primarily by means of a reflection on the common normative origin. The New Testament is for the Christian Church the unique and founding document of its authoritative early history. Here, as the *norma normans*, is where we find the binding foundations of Christian faith and Christian reality. We move towards the further definition of horizon which is important for this method by reflecting on the history of faith and of Christian faith understanding as the history of something coming to be. This is as concrete as it is historical. It is, in other words, finite, perspectival, and situation-related; i.e., according to language, intellectual-historical status, and socio-cultural context. This history is a history of realization, but also a history of accentuation, possibly connected with one-sidedness, forgetfulness, and silence.

History also offers a fullness of realities that today can again come into their own. This happens according to the unassailable principle, That which, historically, was once legitimately real is in principle always possible again, possible today and possible tomorrow.

Reflection on history opens new and liberating perspectives. It liberates from the one-sided fixation on the immediately present as supposedly irreversible, and creates liberation from many dead ends, to say nothing of the courage and confidence that is given to the contemplator of history. Historical reflection also forces us not simply to repeat the historical, but to mediate, translate, re-present it. This brings a new moment into play: the *kairos*, the spcecial moment filled with grace and opportunity, the chance and the challenge to mediate the faith in such a way that it not only remains true to itself but is also experienced by people of a particular time and place as decisively liberating and illuminating.

By this method it becomes possible that long-established fronts are loosened and broken up, that new things in common are found, that the churches gain the power of a properly understood self-transcendence, and that the often suspiciously regarded "third confession" then means nothing more than the concrete form of the unity and unification of Christians, which represents a more comprehensive and fuller form of catholicity than is real and possible and even could be possible in the still-separated confessions—even in those which call themselves catholic. What church could or would be willing to do without that? The fact of separated Christianity signifies a lessening of catholicity even for the Catholic Church.

The Importance of the Question

After these preliminary remarks on method, we come to the matter itself: to the question of office in ecumenical dialogue today.

This question has been the theme of many discussions among the confessions in recent years. What is the reason for this? After achieving a rapprochement in many issues of content, at least in the sense that, although differences remain, they are no longer necessarily issues that separate the churches, there still remains one question about which it is not yet clear how it could lead to a rapprochement that would eventually lead to recognition. This is the question of ecclesiastical office. It is commonly recognized that church office in the Orthodox churches is assured by a chain of juridically sound ordinations. In the churches of the Reformation, however, this chain seems to have been lost and broken, and thus no longer exists. In the churches that have come from the Reformation, the pastor or the elders have taken the place of the bishops. And even if there is once again the office of bishop in the Evangelical churches, one has to say that such a bishop is basically a regional pastor, apart from the fact that the highest instance of authority in the Reformation churches was for a long time the respective ruler as the foremost layperson; he held a kind of "supreme episcopacy."

The question of office has consequences for the question of a possible eucharistic communion as sign and crown of the communion of churches. In the traditional Catholic view, the Eucharist can be celebrated validly only by an ordained priest. Since there is, in the words of the Council, a *defectus ordinis*, a lack of or defect in the Reformation churches, it is said of the Eucharist in these churches that they have not preserved the "original and complete reality" (*genuina et integra substantia*) of the eucharistic mystery.[1] This is why the question of office is of such paramount importance. Because this problem has not yet been solved, it seems to be a great obstacle on the ecumenical path. But if the call of the hour is not for the maintenance of separation but for efforts to overcome it or, positively, efforts for unity, then it was logical to give special attention to the theme "Eucharist and Office."

---

1. Decree on Ecumenism, no 22. On this, cf *Commentary on the Documents of Vatican II*, ed. H. Vorgrimler, 2.152–55.

The Council said explicitly that this theme should become the subject of theological dialogue.

This leads to the following consequences: Dialogue makes sense only when there is still lack of significant agreement in the matter under discussion. On the other hand, dialogue also makes sense only if one hopes that progress can be made on this issue: to a rapprochement, perhaps to a consensus leading to the possibility of recognition. This possible result can be all the more hoped for since agreement has been reached in other formerly controversial central questions, such as the doctrine of justification, not by way of silence but by exhaustively working through the problems.

Thus the theme of office was in the air, so to speak, and has since been taken up in many conferences and memoranda. A comprehensive overview is supplied by the work of Heinz Schütte: *Ordination and Succession in the Understanding of Evangelical and Catholic Exegetes and Theologians and in the Documents of Ecumenical Dialogue*[2]

The result of this study: Over the past three decades, documents of ecumenical discussion on various levels and in many countries between theologians of the World Council of Lutheran Churches (*Lutherischen Weltbundes*) and the Roman Catholic Church, beginning with the so-called Malta Paper on the Gospel and the Church (1971), have "produced a consensus in essential points regarding office, ordination, and succession, and convergence in other points. Apart from the doctrine of the Petrine Office, the dialogue partners agree that in their understanding of office (including ordination and succession), church-separating differences no longer exist.[3]

The Document "Spiritual Office in the Church"

A working group officially entitled "Common Roman-Catholic–Evangelical-Lutheran Commission" produced in 1981 an extensive study of *Spiritual Office in the Church*.[4] It weighs the balance of previous efforts. These can be summed up in the theses: "In the doctrine of the common priesthood of all the faithful and of the ministerial character of office in the Church and for the Church, there exists today for Lutherans and Catholics a common starting point for the clarification of the still-open questions in the understanding of the spiritual office in the Church" (15).

---

2. *Ordination und Sukzession im Verständnis evangelischer und katholischer Exegeten und Dogmatiker sowie in den Dokumenten ökumenischer Gespräche* (Düsseldorf, 1974).

3. Ibid. 428.

4. *Das Geistliche amt in der Kirche* (Paderborn—Frankfurt, 1981). Text also to be found in: *Dokumente wachsender Übereinstimmung. Sämtliche Berichte und Konsenstexte interkonfessioneller Gespräche auf Weltebene 1931-1982*, ed. H. Meyer—H. J. Urban—L. Vischer, (Paderborn—Frankfurt, 1983) 329–57.

Regarding special office in the Church as a carrying out of the apostolic task and ministry in the Church, as "succession from the apostles sent by Christ" (17), it is said that it is not just "purpose-related," nor is it delegation "from below," i.e., from the community, but is the establishment of Jesus Christ (20). This office stands both in the community as well as over against it: "To the extent that office is exercised under the mandate of and as re-presentation of Jesus Christ, it has full authority over against the community" (23). "Thus our churches can today say in unison that the essential and specific function of office-holder consists in gathering and building up the Christian community through the proclamation of the Word of God and the celebration of the sacraments, and of guiding the life of the community in its liturgical, missionary and diaconal spheres" (31). As constitutive as the existence of spiritual office is for the Church, it must, in its development, be open for every new form of actualization (18).

The open questions concern the point whether ordination, by which an office is conferred as it is in the Catholic ordination of priests, is a sacrament. This is the question of a strict or broad concept of sacrament, which makes it a question of theological rules of grammar. The document declares:

Where it is taught that by the act of ordination the Holy Spirit forever empowers the ordained with its gift of grace for service to word and sacrament, it must be asked whether formerly church-separating differences on this question have not been superseded. For Catholics as well as Lutherans, it is irreconcilable with this understanding of ordination to understand ordination only as a way of making church appointments and of installing into church office." (33)

The doctrine of the *character indelebilis*, of the indelible mark, which is conferred by ordination and which is characteristic of the Catholic conception, has no conceptual counterpart in Evangelical Lutheran thought, but it does have a factual convergence there. For "what is meant is that the call and the commissioning by God places the ordained person forever under the promise and the claim of God" (37). Consequently, ordination is never repeated. "Where this once-and-for-all understanding of ordination exists, and where the one-sidednesses and false developments have been overcome, one can speak of a factual convergence" (39).

The document then speaks of "office in its different manifestations" and presents Catholic doctrine in its tripartite division of office into episcopate, presbyterate, and diaconate, in which the episcopate is the basic office; according to Vatican II, it has the fullness of office. The Lutheran tradition, which originally wanted to maintain the episcopal constitution of the Church, was faced with an emergency situation when the Catholic bishops of that time refused to ordain those who confessed the Reformational faith. This resulted in the appointment of officials by nonepiscopal officials, ordinarily according to the principle: the ordained confer ordination. It was emphasized in this situation "that in the history of the Catholic Church there have been cases of ordination of priests by priests" (76). Recalling the New Testament coordination of presbyter and episkopos, it turned out that the Lutheran pastoral office took over practically the spiritual function of the episcopal office. Nevertheless, there was also the office of a supra regional leadership and supervision, the episcopate. "The Lutheran tradition recognizes, in view of the one apostolic office, the difference between bishop and pastor. It characterizes it as a distinction of human law" (47). Hence the conclusion: "When both churches recognize that this historical unfolding of the one apostolic office into a more local and a more regional office has happened for the faith with the help of the Holy Spirit, and that thereby something essential for the Church has arisen, then a high degree of consensus has been reached" (49).

Added to this are some reflections regarding the responsibility of the bishops for the preservation of faith and doctrine. Vatican II characterized the preaching of the gospel as one of the most important tasks of the bishops. "The bishops are both messengers of the faith as well as authentic teachers of the faith." "The bishops can fulfill this task only in community with the whole Church." The "carrying out of the episcopal teaching office takes place in the manifold exchange of the faith with the faithful, the priests, and the theologians" (51). "In controversies in which the unity of faith in the Church is in danger, the bishops have the right and the obligation to make binding decisions" (52).

In the Evangelical Lutheran Church, too, there is, according to the *Confessio Augustana* (art. 28), a responsibility of the bishops as supracommunity officeholders to watch over the purity of the gospel. Today this responsibility is carried out in various boards and panels, particularly in synods, where teachers of theology are represented along with holders of church office (55). There is no denying that from the traditional Roman Catholic point of view there are serious problems connected with this situation and that "there is insufficient clarity on the doctrinal competence of existing organs." It is added that this question has to be thought through in a new way. But the statement of the *Confessio Augustana* remains authoritative that the exercise of this teaching office "should take place not with human power but solely by God's word."

Thus, there is in both churches a supracommunitary doctrinal responsibility which is, to be sure, carried out in different ways, which still allows a certain parallelism between the two churches to be recognized. In both churches, doctrinal responsibility is tied up with the faith witness of the whole Church. Both churches know that they stand under the norm of the Gospel (57).

The Problem of Apostolic Succession

For a long time the Catholic understanding of apostolic succession was that of uninterrupted succession in the office of the bishops. When, as in the time of the Reformation, this chain was broken, apostolic succession was seen to have ceased. This is one of the precise points where there seemed to be a church-separating difference. Recently, the idea has more and more taken hold in all the churches that "apostolic" and apostolic succession belong to the essence of the Church as such, and that apostolic succession primarily means something with regard to content. It signifies "the succession of the whole Church in the apostolic faith" (61). It is in this overarching aspect that succession in the sense of succession in episcopal office is to be seen. The "witness of the gospel is bound to the witnesses of the gospel." Thus it can be said: Catholic doctrine understands apostolic succession in episcopal office as sign and as service to the apostolicity of the Church. The bishops, for their part, are "bound to the canon of Scripture and to the tradition of the apostolic faith, and must give living witness to it."

Because of the unanimous emphasis on the fact that "the content-understanding of apostolicity is primary," the road lies open for "a far-reaching agreement" (60). This is supported by the fact that for the Lutheran tradition as well, "apostolic succession [is] necessary and constitutive for the Church as well as for its office" (63). In the time of the Reformation, the preservation of historical succession in the office of bishop was interrupted. "Thus, for apostolic succession, all was concentrated on the right preaching of the gospel, which also always included office, faith, and the witness of life." Based on this, the ordination to office (or investment) of officeholder to officeholder has continued to be carried out in the Lutheran Church.

In view of this, some today hold the thesis not only that there is along with episcopal succession the so-called presbyteral succession, but that presbyteral succession is a legitimate form of episcopal succession, so that, strictly speaking, actual succession in office was not interrupted. This idea can be further strengthened by the concept represented by Walter Kasper that the Council of Trent did not take an explicit position on the question of the validity of office in the Evangelical Lutheran community. "The rejection of the validity of Lutheran offices is a widespread, practically common post-Tridentine doctrinal opinion which is based on the Council of Trent but by no means necessarily follows from it. We are not dealing with a binding Catholic doctrine, but rather with dominant praxis."[5] The question of validity is

5. Walter Kasper, "Zur Frage der Anerkennung der Ämter in der lutherischen Kirchen," ThQ 151 (1971) 97–109, at 103; H. Fries—K. Rahner, Unity of Churches—An Actual Possibility, trans. Ruth C. L. Gritsche and Eric W. Gritsche (Philadelphia: Fortress Press, 1985) 93–106.

to be separated from the question of orthodoxy and is by no means decided with that question. This is shown in the validity of baptism accepted by all the churches when it—no matter in what church—is correctly administered.

The document "Spiritual Office in the Church" draws the following consequences from reflections such as this: "The fact that, according to Catholic persuasion, standing in the apostolic succession belongs to the full status of the episcopal office, does not exclude the understanding that office in the Lutheran Church, even according to Catholic persuasion, carries out essential functions of the office that Jesus Christ instituted for his Church" (77).

This statement also casts light on the question as to how the often discussed statement from the Decree on Ecumenism (no. 22) on *defectus ordinis* (defect of orders) is to be understood. The official translation "because of the lack of the sacrament of orders," which threatened to block ecumenical dialogue in the question of office and ordination, has made room for a possible new interpretation. *Defectus* does not necessarily mean complete lack; it can also mean a deficiency in something existing. In our document, this formulation is proposed: "lack of the full form of ecclesiastical office." This is clearly a step forward, but the text, on the basis of all that has been said, could have taken a further step—namely, towards the possibility of a recognition of ecclesiastical offices. This possibility was expressed as a wish (81).

The document also reflects on the manner in which a mutual recognition of offices would be thinkable. A one-sided, isolated act, as has been variously proposed (additional ordination, acts of jurisdiction, reciprocal laying on of hands) is not considered suitable and satisfactory. The recognition of offices is seen rather as an overall church process in which the churches mutually accept each other. "In this view, the acceptance of full church communion would mean the recognition of offices." Against this rises the question: Is not full church community impossible to the extent that and as long as, there is no recognition of offices? And when it is said that a mutual recognition "must stand, in the context of the unity of the Church, in the confession of the one faith and in the celebration of the Lord's Supper," one has to agree. But it must still be asked—and that is the problem that is not solved here either: How can there be a unity of the Church in the celebration of the Lord's Supper as long as the question of the recognition of offices is not settled? For the celebration of the Lord's Supper requires official liturgical ministers, the ordained presider over the Eucharistic celebration. Or does the document intend to say that the Lord's supper as sacrament of unity is not only the expression of full church communion, but also a sign to prepare the way for full church communion—a function that in the possible Eucharistic communion with the Orthodox churches is factually recognized? Eucharistic community is possible there although full union in faith is not there (primacy of the pope, infallibility of his extraordinary magisterium).

Judging from the total content of this document, especially its theological assessment of its documentation of the ordination liturgies (57–101), it would have been quite appropriate in its conclusion to have spoken of somewhat more than of those steps of "mutual respect of offices about practical cooperation towards mutual recognition of the offices of the other church, which is identical with the acceptance of Eucharistic fellowship" (83). But in any case, the goal has been named, and the first steps taken towards it. And that is no small achievement. Apparently it is not possible at the moment to say more, if the theme "Office in the Church" is to be received on a churchwide basis. For not a few, what has been said here will go too far—to the extent that any attention at all is paid to the document.

The question of an office as service to the universal unity of the Church, the office of the bishop of Rome, the pope as successor in the office and ministry of Peter, is not treated extensively, but only indicated as a problem—but indicated with a noteworthy consciousness of the problem.

The extent to which a genuinely revolutionary reversal has been achieved in this question—remember Luther's statement about the pope as antiChrist—is also indicated in this document when it states:

In various dialogues the possibility has been established that even the Petrine Office of the bishop of Rome as visible sign of the unity of the whole Church does not need to be excluded by the Lutherans, as long as it is subordinated to the primacy of the gospel by theological reinterpretation and practical restructuring (73).

Convergence Declarations of the World Council of Churches

The convergence declarations of the Commission for Faith and Order of the World Council of Churches on baptism, Eucharist, and ministry, the so-called "Lima Document," the culmination of studies that began in Lucerne in 1927, rests on a broader ecumenical foundation. Roman Catholic theologians also worked on the Lima text. From this important document[6] we shall give special attention to the following texts on the theme of "office."

In order to fulfill its mission, the Church needs persons who are publicly and continually responsible for pointing to its fundamental dependence on Jesus Christ and who thereby provide, within a multiplicity of gifts, a focus of its unity. The ministry of such persons, who since very early times have been ordained, is constitutive for the life and witness of the Church. (BEM [Ministry] no. 8)

---

6. *Baptism, Eucharist and Ministry*, Faith and Order Paper No. 111 (Geneva: WCC, 1982).

Office is traced back to the will and testament of Jesus Christ:

As Christ chose and sent the apostles, Christ continues through the Holy Spirit to choose and call persons into the ordained ministry. As heralds and ambassadors, ordained ministers are representatives of Jesus Christ to the community, and they proclaim his message of reconciliation. As leaders and teachers they call the community to submit to the authority of Jesus Christ, the teacher and prophet, in whom Law and Prophets were fulfilled. As pastors, under Jesus Christ the chief shepherd, they assemble and guide the dispersed people of God, in anticipation of the coming Kingdom. (BEM [Ministry] no. 11)

The responsibility of this office is described as the task "to assemble and build up the body of Christ by proclaiming and teaching the Word of God, by celebrating the sacraments, and by guiding the life of the community in its worship, its mission and its caring ministry" (BEM [Ministry] no. 13).

It is expressly stated that in the Eucharistic celebration the ordained office is the visible focal point of the communion between Christ and the members of his body. It is Christ who invites to the meal and presides over it. It is in accordance with this that the celebration of the Eucharist is led and represented by an ordained official (no. 14). The presence of officials is mindful "of the divine initiative and the dependence of the Church on Jesus Christ" (no. 12).

A special authority is attributed to the ordained office. This is to be understood not as the possession of the ordained person, but as a gift for the ongoing building up of the body in which and for which the official has been ordained. Authority has the character of responsibility before God and is exercised in cooperation with the whole community. Accordingly, ordained officials must be neither autocrats nor impersonal functionaries. "Only when they seek the response and recognition of the community can their authority be protected from distortions due to isolation and dominance" (nos. 15 and 16).

The Lima Document takes up the question of office (ministry) and priesthood. It points out that the expressions "priesthood" or "priest" are used nowhere in the New Testament to signify the ordained office or the ordained official. This expression remains restricted, either to the unique priesthood of Jesus Christ or to the royal and prophetic priesthood of all the faithful.

In the early Church the terms "priesthood" and "priest" came to be used to designate the ordained ministry and minister as presiding at the Eucharist. They underline the fact that the ordained ministry is related to the priestly reality of Jesus Christ and the whole community. When the terms are used in connection with the ordained ministry, their meaning differs in appropriate ways from the sacrificial priesthood of Christ and from the corporate priesthood of the people of God. (Commentary to BEM [Ministry] no. 17)

At the same time, this is where the possibility and the right that ordained ministers be called priests is grounded.

On the office (ministry) of men and women in the Church, it says:

Where Christ is present, human barriers are being broken. The Church is called to convey to the world the image of a new community. There is in Christ no male or female (Gal. 3:28). Both women and men must discover together their contributions to the service of Christ in the Church. The Church must discover the ministry that can be provided by women as well as that which can be provided by men. . . . Though they agree on this need, the churches draw different conclusions as to the admission of women to the ordained ministry. An increasing number of churches have decided that there is no biblical or theological reason against ordaining women, and many of them have subsequently proceeded to do so. (BEM [Ministry] no. 18)

Those churches which do not ordain women hold that the force of a 1900-year tradition cannot simply be put in brackets. Discussion of these practical and theological questions was to be expanded in the different churches by common studies and reflections in ecumenical community of all churches.

On the question of the forms of ordained office, the document says:

The New Testament does not describe a single pattern of ministry which might serve as a blueprint or continuing norm for all future ministry in the Church. In the New Testament there appears rather a variety of forms which existed at different places and times. As the Holy Spirit continued to lead the Church in life, worship, and mission, certain elements from this early variety were further developed and became settled into a more universal pattern of ministry. During the second and third centuries, a threefold pattern of bishop, presbyter, and deacon became established as the pattern of ordained ministry throughout the Church. In succeeding centuries, the ministry by bishop, presbyter, and deacon underwent considerable changes in its practical exercise. (BEM [Ministry] no. 19)

It is expressly stated that, among these gifts and ministries, a ministry of *episkopé* is necessary in order to preserve the unity of the love of Christ. The office of the episkopos, the bishop, is ordered to this ministry. Under him, in the course of time, was gathered the *episkopé* (oversight) over more and more local communities. The presbyters become leaders of the local Eucharistic communities. The threefold office of bishop, priest, and deacon could be seen as an expression of the sought-for unity as well as the means to achieve it (no. 22).

The ecumenical relevance of this question is formulated in this way:

The threefold traditional pattern thus raises questions for all the churches. Churches maintaining the threefold pattern will need to ask how its potential can be fully developed for the most effective witness of the Church in this world. In this task, churches not having the threefold pattern should also participate. They will further need to ask themselves whether the threefold pattern as developed does not have a powerful claim to be accepted by them. (BEM [Ministry] no. 25)

The question of the apostolic tradition is described in the Lima Document in a way similar to the document on spiritual office:

Apostolic tradition in the Church means continuity in the permanent characteristics of the Church of the apostles: witness to the apostolic faith, proclamation and fresh interpretation of the gospel, celebration of baptism and the Eucharist, the transmission of ministerial responsibilities, communion in prayer, love, joy and suffering, service to the sick and the needy, unity among the local churches, and sharing the gifts the Lord has given to each. (BEM [Ministry] no. 34)

It is from this standpoint that the question of succession in apostolic office is also viewed:

Within the Church the ordained ministry has a particular task of preserving and actualizing the apostolic faith. The orderly transmission of the ordained ministry is therefore a powerful expression of the continuity of the Church throughout history; it also underlines the calling of the ordained minister as guardian of the faith. Where churches see little importance in orderly transmission, they should ask themselves whether they have not to change their conception of continuity in the apostolic tradition. On the other hand, where the ordained ministry does not adequately serve the proclamation of the apostolic faith, churches must ask themselves whether their ministerial structures are not in need of reform. (BEM [Ministry] no. 35)

And in this context the office of bishop and of episcopal succession is again taken up:

Under the particular historical circumstances of the growing Church in the early centuries, the succession of bishops became one of the ways, together with the transmission of the gospel and the life of the community, in which the apostolic tradition of the Church was expressed. This succession was understood as serving, symbolizing, and guarding the continuity of the apostolic faith and communion. (BEM [Ministry] no. 36)

The recognition of this fact is, to be sure, connected with an indication that a continuity in apostolic faith is also preserved in churches "which have not retained the form of historic episcopate." In many of these churches the reality and functions of the office of bishop are preserved "with or without the title 'bishop'" (no. 37).

But all this should not lessen the ecumenical significance of the question of the office of bishop. The Lima text explicitly says:

These considerations do not diminish the importance of the episcopal ministry. On the contrary, they enable churches which have not retained the episcopate to appreciate the episcopal succession as a sign, though not a guarantee, of the continuity and unity of the Church. Today churches, including those engaged in union negotiations, are expressing willingness to accept episcopal succession as a sign of the apostolicity of the life of the whole Church. Yet, at the same time, they cannot accept any suggestion that the ministry exercised in their own tradition should be invalid until the moment that it enters into an existing line of episcopal succession. Their acceptance of the episcopal succession will best further the unity of the whole Church if it is part of a wider process by which the episcopal churches themselves also regain their lost unity. (BEM [Ministry] no. 38)

Ordination is described as an action of God and of the community "through which ordained persons are strengthened by the Spirit for their task and supported by the recognition and prayer of the community" (no. 40). The act of ordination by laying on of hands "is, for the person so designated—simultaneously—the calling down of the Holy Spirit (*epiclesis*), sacramental sign, recognition of gifts, and obligation" (no. 41).

A comprehensive process of reception in the churches was to be introduced by the Lima Document. This marked a significant transition in the process of ecumenism, a shift from focusing on bilateral dialogue and discussion to focusing also on multilateral discussion. Consequently, the common Lima text was put before all the churches for their examination, and for them to decide about the extent to which they can find therein the faith of their own church, and to reflect on what concrete conclusions they would be prepared to draw from it.[7]

The Meaning of "Recognition"

Recognition has become a key concept in contemporary ecumenical discussion. It is, for the most part, not given its own precise exposition and definition, but introduced as if already well known.[8] Recognition

7. Expositions on the Lima Document: J. Dantine, "Zur Konvergenzerklärung über Taufe, Eucharistie und Amt" in: *Ökumenische Rundschau* 32 (1983) 12–27; Konfessionskundliches Institut, ed., *Kommentar zu den Lima-Erklärungen über Taufe, Eucharistie und Amt* (Bensheimer Hefte 59), (Göttingen, 1983); W. Kasper, "Taufe, Eucharistie und Amt in der gegenwärtigen ökumenischen Diskussion" in: *Präsentia Christi, Studien Johannes Betz zu Ehren* ed. L. Lies, (Düsseldorf, 1984) 293–308.; M. A. Fahey, ed., *Catholic Perspectives on Baptism, Eucharist and Ministry* (Lanham, Md.: University Press of America, 1986). The theme of office is found also in the document of the bilateral working group of the German Bishops' Conference and the leadership of the United Evangelical Lutheran Churches of Germany: *Kirchengemeinschaft in Wort und Sakrament* (Paderborn—Hannover, 1984) 62–90. There is mention of a high degree of agreement and mutual confirmation in the document *Das Geistliche Amt in der Kirche*, 102, note 25. Because of the work of E. Schillebeeckx, *Das kirchliche Amt* (Düsseldorf, 1981), the theme "office" again became the object of a lively discussion. Cf. W. Kasper, ThQ 163 (1983) 46–53.

Even before that, Joseph Ratzinger"s 1982 *Principles of Catholic Theology*, trans. Sister Mary Frances McCarthy (San Francisco: Ignatius Press, 1987) 299–311. We cannot here, and need not in the context of this ecumenical question, take up its specifically inner-Catholic aspects.

The concluding sentence of Ratzinger's book deserves to be quoted. "Theologians cannot and should not put themselves in the place of the pastoral leadership of the Church. They do have, precisely by reason of their responsibility as theologians, in critical service to the Church, the often-painful obligation to ask ecclesiastical authority whether, in its guidance, it is actually taking into account all the aspects of what is in reality a very complex problem. Although theologians too stand under the pastoral oversight of the church leadership, that should not make them cowardly and swallow the penultimate word. They must speak even if they are convinced that this church leadership will in all likelihood make different decisions. Each and all have here a special, inalienable responsibility to act honestly and conscientiously, while conscious of the possible ecclesiastical consequences, even for themselves" (203).

8. H. Fries, "Was heißt Anerkennung der kirchlichen Ämter?" StdZ 191 (1973) 505–15; Idem, in: *Amt und Widerstreit*, 110-121. These article relate to the criticism of the then highly controversial book: *Reform und Anerkennung kirchlicher Ämter. ein Memorandum der Arbeitsgemeinschaft ökumenischer Universitätsinstitute* (Munich—Mainz, 1973). The

does not mean a disrespect, denial, betrayal, or giving up of what is one's own. Thus recognition also does not mean turning into something else and letting oneself be absorbed by it. Recognition, rather, is something much more positive, It presupposes the fact of the one and the other, and thus the difference between them. Positively speaking, recognition means being related to others or the other: the other is seen and known (recognized) as reality. But much depends on how it is seen and known. Recognition means that what is known is, as recognized, not seen primarily as negative and of little value, and thus rejected; one does not also simply make do with it as something one can't get around; rather, the other is valued positively.

Recognition presupposes that, along with what is different, there is something common to which the acknowledgment and the recognition that possibly comes from it is related, something common whose affirmation is not contested. Recognition presupposes unity in legitimate plurality, and the de facto openness and possibility of affirmation contained therein. But this is possible only if the plurality is transparent to the unity of what is common, if the unity shines through in the many. Otherwise the multiplicity turns into an unconnected, atomized pluralism that is of no use to anything common or unity-building. These formal and general characteristics of recognition have the following consequences for our theme.

The possibility of a recognition of church office does not require a denial, loss, or dissolution of the concrete form of office found in one's own church, or of the manner and mode in which it is mediated. However, something quite significant can come about from reflection on the meaning and function of office, both from the openness and multiplicity found in the New Testament as well as from the plurality encountered in the history of the Church vis-à-vis the concrete shaping, mediating, and handing on of office. It can come about that this background not only offers a problem-free confirmation of the existing and of one's own, but also opens up a broader horizon of what is possible, and in which the other appears in a new light.

Recognition contributes in a special way to the possibility of what currently is repeatedly spoken of and striven for: special emphasis on what is particular to one's self, to one's own particular church tradition (earlier ecumenical efforts tended to focus on what was common). But this special emphasis, along with the already-mentioned fidelity to one's own tradition, raises the question of whether and how what is so emphasized will see the other: whether it will be seen that there is—to speak concretely—an office, an ordination, and a mode of apostolic

---

ecumenical development which has taken place in the interim has not contradicted but confirmed the intention and content of this memorandum.

succession in the Evangelical Lutheran Church. The next question concerns assessment of what is seen there. Will it be judged as the pure negation of, or as the complete contrary to what is constitutive in the Roman Catholic Church? Should this be the case, then from it would follow the right and even duty to ecclesiastical separation. Will it be judged as an overwhelmingly defective form of realization, or as a reality which, along with all the difference, is to be judged positively. The positivity will have to be judged according to whether the why and wherefore of office, of the special public ministry to word and sacrament as mediation of the manifold presence of Christ, is seen and recognized as present; and whether one can say yes to the presented and mediated reality of faith and Church.

If so, this also sheds light on the possible positivity and on the recognition of a form or office in which this continuity and identity, i.e., the content of the apostolic tradition, has been preserved. All this of course presupposes and requires that office and ordination in the Evangelical [German Lutheran] Church are not emptied of content and replaced by mere acts of administration, but that office preserves the rank and value which the New Testament and the confessional documents accord it.

Recognition includes that Christians are and remain at home in their concrete church, and live from their own concrete historical situation, which they intend neither to deny nor do away with; but recognition also means that they value, above all in their positivity, those others who are likewise part of a living history.

Thus recognition makes it appear quite possible that, from the Catholic side, for example, in the context of a common and more comprehensive understanding of the apostolicity of the Church, "one [would] accord special significance to episcopal succession, and deplore its absence in one's dialogue partner, but without denying an apostolic succession to the Evangelical [German Lutheran] tradition, since it has preserved other elements of this succession, and at times more faithfully than has the Catholic tradition." It would on the other hand be possible, from the Evangelical side, to emphasize their own conviction about the one office, "but without seeing a church-separating opposition in the historically developed three-level order of the Roman, Orthodox and Anglican Churches" (G. Gassmann).

To repeat: A recognition does not require but indeed excludes the elimination of all differences, the abrogation and leveling of profile. Rather, recognition means that this, which formerly signified an insuperable obstacle for the unity of the churches, is seen in a new light and with other eyes. This has become possible because the history of the churches has not stood still for four hundred years, because the situation from that time has changed. That is not to be regretted, but to be welcomed.

To mention an example no one could suspect, the offices of the Orthodox Church are recognized from the Catholic side. If, despite differences in the question of the Petrine office, even Eucharistic communion is possible, it does not follow from such recognition that the one who does the recognizing becomes an Orthodox Christian in the specific confessional sense. What really does follow is that this goal is seen and striven for in a new way. The confessions, formerly supporters of the division of Christendom, have been working out the problems that still remain and rediscovering their common cause in the face of the secular challenge and its opposition to everything Christian. The confessions are thus becoming subjects of a legitimate multiplicity, which is not a contradiction to but an expression of the unity that was there at the time of the New Testament; for in the New Testament Church we find a picture not of the established present but rather of what was to be striven for and become possible in the future. Achieved ecumenism is not to take the place of the confessions; confessions are to be the expression and form of achieved ecumenism.[9]

It has recently been proposed to replace the concept "recognition" with the concept of reconciliation and to speak of "reconciled difference," because recognition can easily be understood in the sense of "an after-the-fact justification of the status quo"—in other words, to connect recognition and reconciliation. There is no objection against this; the concept "reconciliation" contains elements of the dynamic and the future perhaps more than does the concept "recognition." But, as we can see from the connection of reform with recognition and from our attempt to describe recognition, this does not mean only the justification of what is already established: recognition is possible only through dynamic and movement.

9. H. Fries, Ökumene statt Konfessionen? (Frankfurt, 1977); H. Fries—K. Rahner, Unity of Churches—An Actual Possibility .

§ 57

THE PAPACY AS ECUMENICAL QUESTION

The question of office in the Church cannot pass over the question of a highest office. The Roman Catholic Church, of course, sees this office in the institution of the papacy. It has been describing it in recent years with the concepts "Petrine office" or "Petrine ministry," as a Petrine function.

The State of the Question

In the impressive array of documents presented up to this point, the question of the papacy has been excluded from consideration. This has repeatedly led to the objection that one cannot talk about office in the Church as theme of an ecumenical discussion without making clear statements about the papacy. That is all the less possible since the Roman Catholic Church specifies that by "Roman" is meant the office of the pope who is regarded as the successor of Peter, and who is the one who takes over and embodies the Petrine office, and Petrine ministry. This ministry is understood by Catholics, in connection with the well-known Petrine passages in the New Testament, as a rock-and-foundation function, a safeguarding of the power of the keys, a strengthening of the brethren in faith—as leadership in the sense of its pastoral commission.[1]

---

1 Cf. "Pope" and "Papacy" in the theological reference works, its treatments in church and papal history, in canon law, fundamental theology, and dogmatics. In addition: F. Heiler, *Altkirchlicher Autonomie und päpstlicher Zentralismus* (Munich, 1941); O. Karrer, *Peter and the Church: An Examination of Cullman's Thesis*, trans. Ronald Walls (New York: Herder and Herder, 1963); Karl Rahner—Joseph Ratzinger, *The Episcopate and the Primacy*, trans. Kenneth Barker and others (New York: Herder and Herder, 1962); Hans Küng, *Structures of the Church*, trans. Ray and Rosaleen Ockenden (New York: Crossroad, 1982) 201–351; *The Church* (New York: Sheed and Ward, 1967) 444–81; G. Denzler—F. Christ—W. Trilling—P. Stockmeier—W. de Vries—P. Lippert, *Zum Thema Petrusamt und Papsttum* (Stuttgart, 1970); G. Schwaiger, *Hundert Jahre nach dem Ersten Vatikanum* (Regensburg, 1970); Hans Urs von Balthasar, *Der antirömische Affekt. Wie läßt sich das Papsttum in der Gesamtkirche integrieren?* (Freiburg—Basel—Vienna, 1974); G. Denzler, *Das Papsttum in der Diskussion* (Regensburg, 1974); H. Stirnimann—L. Vischer, *Papsttum und*

However gratifying it is that there seems to be a growing consensus these days over the position of Peter in the New Testament—although even there quite a few difficulties still remain—the real difficulty consists in and begins with the understanding of and grounding of the papacy as successor of a Petrine office or Petrine ministry, as is current in Catholic thought. It is said that these functions could not cease with the person who first exercised them. A succession in the functions handed over to Simon Peter can thus make sense in the same way as does the succession of the apostolic task and mission through the successors of the apostles. An existing, contemporary Petrine office thus cannot be regarded as unbiblical.

We do not have the space to give here a comprehensive treatment of this many-sided problem. It is difficult to come to consensus on exegetical grounds. The reasons for the manifold differences lie, to be sure, not just in the textual material, but also in the factual and theological presuppositions, and also in the "interests," connected with the question of the papacy.

On the other hand—and this demonstrates the place of this question in the horizon of what we have now become conscious of as "hierarchy of truths"—the irresolution of precisely this problem, or the difference in this matter, is not an obstacle to a possible communion in the Eucharist. This is, by broad agreement, an expression of faith-community and Church-community, its seal so to speak. Eucharistic communion with the Orthodox churches and recently with the Old Catholics is considered, according to Vatican II, as possible under certain presuppositions, even though the question of the papacy is today no longer regarded as a matter of discipline, i.e., schism, but as a matter of faith.

A Look at History

In the beginnings of the history of the Church, we come across the fact that the community of Rome takes on a special significance among the other Christian communities. This significance does not consist first of all in the fact that the bishop of this community appeals to his posi-

---

Petrusdienst (Frankfurt, 1975); H. J. Mund, ed., *Das Petrusamt in der gegenwärtigen theologischen Diskussion* (Paderborn, 1976); Paul Misner, *Papacy and Development. Newman and the Primacy of the Pope* (Leiden: E. J. Brill, 1976); A. Brandenburg—H. J. Urban, ed., *Petrus und Papst. Evangelium—Einheit der Kirche—Papstdienst*, 2 vols. (Münster, 1977/78); G. Schwaiger, *Päpstlicher Primat und Autorität der Allgemeinen Konzilien im Spiegel der Geschichte* (Munich—Paderborn—Vienna, 1977); J. Ratzinger, ed., *Dienst an der Einheit. Zum Wesen und Auftrag des Petrusamtes* (Düsseldorf, 1978); *Das Papsttum als ökumenische Frage, hrsg. von der Arbeitsgemeinschaft ökumenischer Universitätsinstitute* (Munich—Mainz, 1979); M. Hardt, *Papsttum und Ökumene. Ansätze eines Neuverständnisses für einen Papstprimat in der protestantischen Theologie des 20. Jahrhunderts* (Paderborn—Munich—Zürich, 1981); H. Fries—K. Rahner, *Einigung und Wandel* (Münster, 1984).

tion as successor of Peter and stands on Matthew 16:17–19; it consists rather in the fact that the Roman community was founded by the apostles Peter and Paul, and that both apostles worked in Rome and died there. This community can thus lay special claim to be an "apostolic see" and thus bearer of the apostolic tradition.

Each in their own way, the First Letter of Clement, the Letter of Ignatius of Antioch to the Romans, and above all Irenaeus of Lyon, have highlighted this idea. In the battle against the secret teaching of Gnosticism, the community of Rome becomes for Irenaeus exemplary for the apostolic tradition of all churches—the locale of the normative tradition. In addition, even as early as the First Letter of Clement, decisions in this community were made regarding other communities. There developed in Rome a special charism of community leadership and charitable activity. The Apostles' Creed originated there and gained broad acceptance. The collection of the New Testament writings in preparation for a later canon took place in Rome. It was no wonder, then, that Rome took over first place among the churches, that it functioned in many cases as instance of orientation, arbitration, and appeal. In some well-known as well as obviously criticized decisions (as in the Easter date controversy and later in the controversy over heretical baptism) the bishop of Rome demanded obedience for his decision and recognition by the other churches.

That the bishop of Rome is successor of the apostle Peter, that the words of Jesus to Peter (Matt 16:18) thus also apply to the bishop of Rome, this was first expressed by Pope Callistus I (217–222) thus formulating the primacy of the bishop of Rome. This was recognized by the other bishops not in the juridical but in the symbolic sense: The holder of the see of Peter guarantees and embodies the unity of the bishops and thus of the whole Church.

For Cyprian, bishop of Carthage († 258) the totality of the bishops forms the foundation of the Church and its unity. The Roman Church is for this theologian the mother and root of the Catholic Church. He bases this on the view that the bishop of Rome possesses the chair of Peter and thus the primacy of Peter and is heir of the promise of Christ. To be sure, Cyprian understood this primacy in a representative and episcopal fashion. According to Cyprian, the founding of the Church on Peter is to be connected to the other idea that the Risen One gave all the apostles the same power as Peter. That is why Cyprian expressly opposed Pope Stephen who, appealing to Petrine succession, had demanded obedience of the other churches, especially of North Africa, for his—authoritative—decision by appealing to Petrine succession in the controversy over heretic baptism. In doing this Pope Stephen appealed to the primacy of the apostle Peter, now transferred to the bishop of Rome. But Cyprian, who rejected the decision of the pope in this particular question, had nevertheless in fact given expression to an idea which, in the course of further history, took on its own impressive legal reality: The bishop of Rome possesses a primacy over the whole Church.

The development beginning to take shape here was strengthened by a political motif: The local church of Rome in the capital of the empire occupies a special position. In the church-historical epoch ushered in by emperor Constantine, this was highlighted even further by the fact that the Christian religion became a permitted religion, and later even the state religion, and that the patrimony of Roman religion passed over to the Christian Church. This also touched upon matters of structure and sacred law. Because of the transference of the imperial capital from Rome to Byzantium-Constantinople, the political position of the bishop of Rome gained in influence and reputation, and all the more so as the downfall of the Western Roman Empire came closer and closer. In the time of the migrations and the fall of the capital city of Rome, which was a great shock for many Christians, the bishop of Rome took on an authority "which not only was characterized by spiritual categories but, in its assimilation to worldly power structures, also embodied secular power."[2] The figure and form of the empire got stamped on the shape of the Church. The *imitatio imperii* was set before the Church as problem and task.

In this situation the fate of towering personalities became associated with the chair of the bishop of Rome. Leo I († 461) was politically successful in his encounter with Attila and Genseric and thus made himself the advocate not only of the Christians but of all the citizens of Rome. At the same time he theologically intensified the previous [arguments for the] grounding of the Petrine office by transferring the special position of Peter as first among the other apostles also to his successor on the Roman chair, and by connecting its foundation function with the power of the keys and with the power to bind and loose. Leo's Christological doctrinal letter to the Council of Chalcedon (450) won the approval of the bishops assembled there with the well-known words: "Peter has spoken through Leo."

In the meantime, difficulties were also arising because of the political situation. At the same Council of Chalcedon, the same rights were granted to the bishop of New Rome, Byzantium, that the bishop of Old Rome in the West was exercising (canon 28). Thus was confirmed, or extended, what had already been expressed at the Council of Nicaea (325): that the *sedes apostolicae* in Rome, Alexandria, and Antioch all possessed patriarchal rights. The delegates of the pope did not accept

---

2. P. Stockmeier, "Das Petrusamt in der frühen Kirche," in: *Zum Thema Petrusamt und Papsttum*, 76; W. de Vries, "Die Entwicklung des Primats in den ersten drei Jahrhunderten," in: *Das Papsttum als ökumenische Frage* 114–58.

this decision quietly, but vigorously protested against it. It can be concluded from this turn of events that, "in Rome, the old apostolic responsibility, the core of the universal primacy, had by now become so tightly connected with the new patriarchal responsibilities that one could hardly distinguish them anymore. Consequently, one began to see in the formation of new, independent patriarchates, a danger for the primacy of Rome."[3] On the other hand, confusing the meaning of the apostolic chair with the idea of the patriarchate responsible for predominantly administrative tasks (stemming from later post-Constantinian times) had contributed to the difficulty of the situation and to misunderstanding even in the theological view of things. The foundation for differences, which led more and more to contradictions and alienations, was laid.

The later history of East and West, which we cannot go into here, only sharpened these tendencies, each in its own way. Let me but make this observation: Gregory the Great († 607), with Leo I the most convincing and most significant holder of the chair of Peter, saw in a special way the Petrine office as *diakonia*, as "care for all the communities," as care for the whole Church.[4] Into this care, as inaugurator of an extended mission, he drew the German-Roman people and the young churches developing in them. With the title *servus servorum Dei* he eloquently and consciously distanced himself from the designation "Ecumenical Patriarch" claimed by the bishop of Byzantium, which contained a claim to the direction of the whole Church. Historical hindsight illuminates how far-sighted this policy was. Had the papacy followed in the footsteps of this pope in ages to follow, a great deal of damage would have been prevented. But the difference between East and West, conditioned by many circumstances and events, led to ever-greater tensions and alienations in the course of the centuries, and ended finally with mutual excommunications in the anathemas of the year 1054. In this way, the churches in West and East were—although one, without being uniform, in practically all questions of faith, liturgy, and structure under a primacy of honor—in schism. In order to emphasize and justify the separation, differences in the understanding of the faith (e.g., The filioque controversy) and differences in custom and practice were turned into fundamental and dividing differences. Further differences were added on later. The schism, however, as expressed in the words of Y. Congar, is "not so much this alienation, but rather its acceptance."[5]

---

3. G. Schwaiger, "Der päpstliche Primat in der Geschichte der Kirche," *Zeitschrift für Kirchengeschichte* 82 (1971) 5.

4. Cf. J. Richards, *Gregor der Große. Sein Leben—seine Zeit* (Graz—Vienna—Cologne, 1983).

5. Y. Congar, *Zerrissene Christenheit. Wo trennten sich Ost und West?* (Vienna—Munich, 1969) 10.

And we have to add that the acceptance of the schism has lasted practically to the present day. Various attempts to eliminate the separation have not been successful. This situation was made even worse in the last century when the schism was given dogmatic relevance by the dogmas of Vatican I. For precisely that was dogmatically defined which was perceived by the churches of the East as obstacle and strongest reason for the schism: the universal, jurisdictional primacy, over all the churches, of the bishop of Rome who was explicitly not satisfied with a *primatus honoris et inspectionis* conceded by the Orthodox, but insisted on defining an explicit juridical primacy as "supreme power" and "full power."

The Reformation

Before we take up the situation in the present, we must say a word or two about the position of the churches of the Reformation on pope and papacy. In doing this it is not always easy to decide whether the statements are directed against the then-reigning occupier of the papacy or against the papacy as institution. In any case, the popes of that time were "renaissance popes" who, as they themselves put it, sought to "enjoy the papacy" and saw the image of their succession more in the emperor of Rome than in Peter the fisherman.

For our needs it may be enough to say how Luther reacted to the papacy.[6] But that is by no means all as clear as one might suppose, if one is talking about a denial or rejection of the papacy from the outset. With Luther, one can and must distinguish between different stages.

Even in his early writings Luther did indeed criticize the popes; but this did not distinguish him from many theologians before and during his own time. The criticism was of abuses: the worldliness and worldly power of the popes. This did not prevent Luther from recognizing the Roman Church and the papacy. He says, e.g.: All the works and merits of Christ and the Church are in the hand of the pope. He describes the Roman Church as protector of truth, a church that would never hold anything that was against the Holy Scripture. To be sure, the difference between Luther and the papacy becomes more clear and the criticism sharper and more fundamental in his indulgence theses. But even in the year 1519, Luther speaks out against the Bohemians who are rejecting the primacy of the Roman Church.

In the Resolutions on the Indulgence Theses are found, in the opinion of R. Bäumer, statements that are quite papalistic. They peak in the high-flown words: "Thus, most Holy Father, I prostrate myself at the

---

6. Documentation in: R. Bäumer, *Martin Luther und der Papst* (Münster, 1970); G. Müller, "Martin Luther und das Papsttum in lutherischer Sicht" in H. Stirnimann—L. Vischer, *Papsttum und Petrusdienst* 73–90.

foot of Your Holiness and dedicate myself to you with all that I am and all that I have. Let me live or let me die, approve my work or reject it as you please! I will recognize your voice as the voice of Christ, who rules and speaks in you. If I have merited death, I will not shrink from death." In a *protestatio* Luther solemnly testifies that he wishes to say and maintain nothing except only that which is contained in Holy Scripture, in the church fathers recognized by the Roman Church, and in papal canon law, and in what can be derived from them.[7]

The Luther of the year 1519 has been described, relative to the question of the papacy, as "Luther wrestling" with himself. He appeals from "the poorly informed to the better informed pope." The pope stands not over but under the Word of God. But under these presuppositions, Luther had no hesitation to speak of the pope as the mouth of Christ. In Luther's 1518 appeal to a general council he explicitly expressed—in common to be sure with many theologians of his time—the superiority of the council over the pope, and he thus brought up a new point of controversy. His fundamental criticism of the papacy becomes clear in the Leipzig disputation (1519), where Luther declares that he does not wish to be prisoner of just any authority. He will recognize only that which he has recognized as true, whether it be maintained by a Catholic or by a heretic, whether it be approved or rejected by a council; even councils can make mistakes.

In the writings "On the Babylonian Captivity of the Church" and "To the Christian Nobility of the German Nation," one finds the concept of the papacy as the kingdom of Babylon, or as an anti-Christian institution. After the publication of the bull threatening excommunication, Luther, in his "Against the Bull of the Antichrist," summons the faithful, for the sake of the faith, to consider the pope to be the Antichrist. If the threatened bull is not recalled (meaning, if the pope would not recognize the gospel of justification by faith), no one should have any doubt that the "pope is the enemy of God, persecutor of Christ, destroyer of Christianity, and the genuine Antichrist."[8] For the rest of his life Luther never moved away from this idea, that the pope is the Antichrist because he denied the gospel.

We don't have time to pursue the further course of this development, except to highlight that the "Smalkaldic Articles," which come from Luther and are numbered among the confessional writings of the Evangelical Lutheran Church, deal extensively with the papacy in the fourth article. According to this article, the pope possesses his power as head of all Christianity not *iure divino* or according to God's word. He is instead the bishop or pastor of the church of Rome and of those who, voluntarily or under the direction of worldly power, have joined up

---

7. In R. Bäumer, *Martin Luther und der Papst* 21.
8. Ibid. 56.

with him. But they do not stand under him as under a lord, but beside him as brothers and comrades. That is the way it was at the ancient councils; that is the way it was at the time of Cyprian. Now, however, no bishop dares call the pope brother; they talk about him as if about the all-gracious Lord. Everything that the pope has done and attempted on the basis of his assumed power has been a work of the devil for the purpose of ruining all Christian churches and destroying the first principal article of the redemption of Jesus Christ. History proves that the Church, for five hundred years, was without a pope. To this very day the churches of the East are not subject to him. Luther mentions the papal depositions at the Council of Constance, which deposed three popes and chose a fourth. The Church could never be better governed and protected than if we all lived under the one head of Christ and the bishops were all alike in office. But the pope has raised himself above the other bishops. That shows that he is the authentic Antichrist, who has placed himself above Christ and who will not allow Christians to be happy and blessed apart from his power.[9]

Melancthon, along with many other theologians, subscribed to the Smalkaldic Articles but added the following noteworthy addition: "I hold the articles to be correct and Christian; but of the pope I hold, as long as he is willing to accept the gospel, that for the sake of the peace and of the common unity of those Christians who are and in the future would like to be under him, that the superiority over the bishops which he has *iure divino* also be admitted by us."[10] In his treatise *De potestate papae* he described this in greater detail and tried to support it with biblical and historical indications, not without rejecting the claims that were, in his opinion, false: that the pope is the head over all Christianity, and has "by divine right" power over the two swords.[11] This not only points out that there remained, even then, some possibility of understanding, it is also being brought back into the discussion once again, and not just by Lutheran theologians. The important point is the distinction between *ius divinum* and *ius humanum* and the problem of the diverting of the functions which in the course of history have been added to this office: bishop of Rome, patriarch of the West, head over the Universal Catholic Church.

In conclusion, it should be mentioned that the [later] works of Luther—"On the Councils and Churches," "Against Hans Worst," and most of all, "Against the Papacy in Rome, Founded by the Devil"— make this polemic even sharper. The last-mentioned of these, in particular, transcends all measure of polemic, defamation, and hate and was subjected to sharp criticism even by Luther's friends. Shortly before

9. *Die Bekenntnisschriften der evangelisch-lutherischen Kirche* 427–33.
10. Ibid. 464 .
11. Ibid. 471-96.

his death, Luther is said to have written on the wall the words: "A plague was I to you in life, O Pope; in death will I be your death."

The criticism of Luther and the Reformation was not directed primarily against the papacy as institution as such, nor even primarily the bad moral image projected by the papacy of the time; the criticism that impelled to the judgment that the pope is the Antichrist was the fact that the pope refused to be a servant of the word of God and of the true gospel, as manifested, according to Luther, in his unwillingness to recognize the gospel of justification recently emphasized by Luther.

The Catholic Response

In consequence of the criticism and partial rejection of the papacy by the Reformation, there arose in the Roman Catholic Church a similarly colored polemic against Luther, above all by Cochlaeus.[12] In addition, the papacy itself was now emphasized in a special way and raised up as a specific mark of the Catholic Church. What was criticized and controverted took on a new relevance and value. At the same time, the reformers' criticism of the worldliness and secularization of the papacy was not without effect. It began in various ways in the Counter Reformation and the Catholic Renewal which—clearly recognizable in the art of the baroque—was adorned with triumphalism. An example of the newfound concept of Church is the classical and quite influential description of the Church by Robert Bellarmine in his work: *Disputationes de controversiis Christianae fidei*: "The Church is the community of human beings who, by confessing the same faith and by participation in the same sacraments are united under the leadership of the rightful shepherds, especially of the one representative of Christ on earth, the Roman Pope."

The Jesuit order, which arose in the course of the Counter Reformation and Catholic Renewal, took on the special task of being the *militia Christi* and made obedience to the pope its special mission and obligation. The more and more pronounced picture of the Roman Church as the papal church was by no means just the derogatory and one-sided view of others, but the self-articulation developed and consciously affirmed by the Catholic Church itself. In Catholic apologetics, *Romanitas* became a mark of the Church which included the others.[13] These tendencies were even further intensified under the pressures of difficult external circumstances—we can't go into details—which beset the popes in the eighteenth and nineteenth centuries, above all in the French Revolution and under Napoleon I.

---

12. A. Herte, *Die Lutherkommentare des Johannes Cochläus* (Münster, 1935).
13. On this cf. M. A. Fahey, "Church," *Sytematic Theology: Roman Catholic Perspectives* 2.4–74; E. Hill, "Church," *NDT* 185–201.

At the end of the nineteenth century, which brought the end of the imperial church, a pronounced papalism arose under the flag of restoration. Its most significant literary representative was Joseph de Maistre in his work *Du Pape* (On the Pope). Indeed, a substantial papal cult blossomed, and it not infrequently reached the borders of tastelessness and the blasphemous. These tendencies, through the entire nineteenth century, were part of an explicit defensive posture of the Catholic Church against the antifaith spirit of the time as the culmination of modernity. The roots of the antifaith modernity were, along with other factors, seen also and above all as stemming from the Reformation. This was qualified and thus disqualified as "so-called" Reformation, and regarded as one of the sources of modern corrosive subjectivism and confusing relativism. Against all this there seemed to be but one answer from the side of the Roman Catholic Church: an encompassing strengthening of the unity of the Church along with a comprehensive qualification of the highest office in the Church, the supreme pontificacy of the Roman bishop, the pope. The supreme and full jurisdiction over the whole Church united in him was to be the surety that was to guarantee unity by means of orientation to the Church's center and by means of the highest possible standardization in all spheres of church life. The First Vatican Council's (1869-1870) dogmatic definition of the pope's primacy as universal primacy of jurisdiction, and its related definition of the infallibility of his ex cathedra magisterium, had as its purpose to articulate what the highest office in the Church as center of unity is supposed to mean and bring about.[14]

The First Vatican Council

In the *Constitutio Dogmatica I "Pastor aeternus" de Ecclesia Christi*[15] it is said that Christ, the "eternal shepherd and bishop of our souls," installed Peter as the abiding bishop and priest-unifying principle and visible foundation, that the Petrine primacy was founded by Christ and that Peter received primacy of jurisdiction directly and immediately from Christ. As proof were cited John 1:42; Matthew 16:16ff.; John 21:15, but not Luke 22:32.

Then comes mention of *perpetuitas*, the abiding continuation of the Petrine primacy in the Roman popes. This reference is supported by three chosen historical witnesses: Leo I, Irenaeus, and Ambrose. Hence these particular documents require an in-depth discussion. For these

14. Cf. C. Butler—H. Lang, *The Vatican Council: The Story from Inside in Bishop Ullathorne's Letters* (New York: Longmans, Green, 1930); R. Aubert, *Vatikanum I* (Mainz, 1965); idem, "Die Ekklesiologie beim Vatikankonzil" in: *Das Konzil und die Konzile* (Stuttgart, 1962) 285–330; Y. Congar, *Handbuch der Dogmengeschichte* III/3 d (Freiburg—Basel—Vienna, 1971) 100–7.

15. DS 3050–3079.

witnesses, apart from their relatively late dating, are in their historical contexts by no means so obvious as the conciliar statement claims.

The content and nature of papal primacy are characterized by the bishop of Rome having preeminence over the whole world, that he is the "true representative of Christ, head of the whole Church and father and teacher of all Christians," that full power is given him to "pastor, rule and administer" the whole "Church." The Roman bishop "possesses the primacy of ordinary power over all other churches. This power of the legal jurisdiction of the Roman bishop, which has real episcopal character, is immediate." The pope is universal bishop. "The bishop of Rome is also the supreme judge of all the faithful." Since there is no higher official power, it is not permitted for anyone to pass judgment over this judgment.[16]

The concluding canon sums up the essence of the primacy in the following proposition:

Thus whoever says that the bishop of Rome has only the office of oversight and leadership and not the full and supreme power of legal jurisdiction over the entire Church—and not just in matters of faith and morals but also in whatever pertains to the order and governance of the Church spread over the whole world; or whoever says that he has only a larger share but not the whole fullness of this supreme power, or that this power of his is not ordinary and immediate power over the entire Church and the individual churches as well as over all and each and every shepherd and member of the faithful, let him be anathema.[17]

The definition of Vatican I on the primacy of the pope as *ius divinum* took place at the same hour in which the end of the church state (and with that the end of the political power of the pope) had come about. Before that there had been no lack of voices wanting to elevate to the level of dogma the necessity of the church state for the realization and exercise of the papacy. Theologians who warned against this, like I. Döllinger and J. H. Newman, were accused of a lack of loyalty to the Church. When the church state could no longer be maintained, it became all the more important for the pope's moral authority and innerchurch position of primacy to be emphasized and raised to an obligatory proposition of faith.

Bismarck's comparison of the Roman Church with an absolute monarchy, "more than any form of government in the world," was, to be sure, explicitly rejected, above all by a remarkable declaration (welcomed by Pius IX) of the German bishops in 1875,[18] but the compari

16. DS 3059–3063.

17 DS 3064.

18 DS 3112–3117. cf. Neuner—Roos 388a. This letter refers to a statement of Vatican I which reads: "So far is this power of the Supreme Pontiff from being any prejudice to the *ordinary and immediate power of the episcopal jurisdiction*, by which bishops who have been set by the Holy Spirit to succeed and hold the place of the Apostles, feed and govern, each his own flock, as true pastors, that this their episcopal authority is really asserted, strengthened and protected by the supreme and universal pastor" (DS 3061; Neuner—Roos 380).

son remained an unforgettable concept. All the more so since monarchy was considered the best form of constitution. Why should it not be for the Church, the perfect society?

The situation between the Christian confessions was saddled with a new burden by the dogmatic decisions of Vatican I. Men like J. H. Newman—but not just he—could see this coming and described the dogmatizing of the doctrine on the papacy as inopportune and superfluous. For in this case, in contrast to previous dogmatizing, a difficulty in the Church was not being met but being created. "What have we done to deserve to be treated as the faithful have never before been treated?"[19] Newman has never been wholly forgiven for this statement.

The Second Vatican Council

There has been considerable agreement throughout Christianity on many of the texts and intentions of Vatican II with regard to the Church. This "council of the Church about the Church" managed to achieve a great deal of defusing. It did this by giving prominence to a meditation on the Church as sacrament and mystery of unity and as people of God. It did this by emphasizing collegiality as a structural principle of the Church, which bound the pope with the bishops and them with him "with and under the pope." It did this by placing higher value on synodal elements, by explicitly affirming the priesthood of all the faithful, by stating that special spiritual office (distinct from the universal priesthood "in essence and not only in degree") is to be understood as ministry and as gift, and by its unmistakable emphasis on the Holy Spirit as normative source of judgment. Despite all this, the trajectory begun by Vatican I vis-à-vis the jurisdictional primacy of the pope remains in force. All the more so since the formulations of Vatican I, along with their openness to misunderstanding, were repeated in Vatican II. It has already been frequently pointed out that in the different texts of Vatican II that were supposed to complete [the work of] Vatican I—above all in regard to the bishops, the college of bishops, and the people of God—one finds more talk of the pope than in Vatican I. The *Nota praevia*, which in connection with the Constitution on the Church, *Lumen gentium*, was communicated to the council fathers from a "higher authority" by the general secretary, not only modified the concept of the council of bishops, but also formulated the following proposition which has a sharpness and ambiguity found not even in Vatican I: "The pope, as supreme shepherd of the

19. Letter of 18 January 1870 to Bishop Ullathorne, in: J. H. Newman, *Briefe und Tagebuchaufzeichnungen aus der katholischen Zeit seines Lebens*, 543 (cf. *The Letters and Diaries of John Henry Newman*, 31 vols. [London—New York: T. Nelson, Oxford: Clarendon, 1961-1984])

Church, can exercise his supreme power at any time at his discretion, as is required by his office" (no. 4).[20]

The New Code of Canon Law took up this statement in its full amplitude and sharpest pointedness and, looking to the Latin Church, declared: "The bishop of the Church of Rome, in whom resides the office given in a special way by the Lord to Peter, first of the Apostles and to be transmitted to his successors, is head of the college of bishops, the Vicar of Christ and Pastor of the universal Church on earth; therefore, in virtue of his office he enjoys supreme, full, immediate and universal ordinary power in the Church which he can always freely exercise" (canon 331).

So the situation remains that the question of the papacy is a still-unsolved ecumenical problem. It stands between the Roman Catholic and the Orthodox, Anglican, and Reformed churches, to say nothing of the so-called Free churches. The rejection of the papacy in the matter of his spiritual lordship as expressed in Vatican I and in the Church's book of laws seems to be a connecting bond which brings the otherwise so different forms of Christian churches and confessions into a certain unanimity and in a certain sense makes them one with each other. One must, of course, challenge that the "No" to Rome is in principle the only effective ecumenical basis.[21] This basis should be seen rather in the "Yes" to the central contents of the Christian faith. But the problematic connected with the theme "pope and papacy" still remains, even though one looks to the popes of today—in contrast to those of the sixteenth century—with respect, a respect that is never so great and so general as it was with regard to the compomise and transition pope, John XXIII. Under his pontificate and during the Second Vatican Council there was no anti-Roman feeling, either inside or outside the Catholic Church—and that was not so long ago.

The Dialogue with the Orthodox Churches

Now we must ask what, despite everything, has happened or perhaps can happen, in order not simply to repeat the, as always, a carefully nuanced No, *Non possumus*. We must take note of the following:

A great step forward with the Orthodox churches, in the question of the papacy, was taken when, on December 7, 1965, the 1054 bull of excommunication issued against the then-patriarch of Constantinople, Michael Caerularius, was solemnly revoked. It was, as stated in the

---

20. See especially: *Commentary on the Documents of Vatican II*, ed. H. Vorgrimler, 1.297–306.

21. H. U. von Balthasar, *The Office of Peter and the Structure of the Church*, trans. Andree Emery (San Francisco: Ignatius Press, 1986).

apostolic letter read by Cardinal Bea, "washed from memory and removed from the midst of the Church."

In St. Peter's, a common declaration of the Roman Catholic Church and the Orthodox Church of Constantinople was read. As a result, from now on, nothing more was to hinder fraternal reconciliation between the two churches. To be sure, both churches are conscious that old and new contradictions were not thereby overcome, but they could be wholly set aside by further examination of conscience and good will. The dialogue that is to lead to this goal was to be established on a new basis of trust, for hearts were to be purified by these events.

Patriarch Athenagoras caught up the meaning of this event in these words: "The Seventh of December signifies a light which dispels the darkness which cast gloom over a now-finished period of church history. This light illuminates the present and the future path of the Church."[22]

The result of this event, according to Joseph Ratzinger (who, ten years later, attempted to describe and interpret the situation), is to be characterized as follows: The situation of love grown cold, of the contradictions, the mistrust, and the antagonisms, is replaced by the relationship of love and fraternal affection. The symbol of division is replaced by the symbol of love. Now that the dialogue of love has reached its first goal, says Ratzinger, theological dialogue is needed, although this was never absent. But above all: the forgetting of the past must bring a new remembering which works on the healing of memory and which leads from the agape of ecclesiastical reality to the eucharistic agape.[23] This is even now possible and desired under certain circumstances; it is made explicit in the offer expressed in the Decree on Ecumenism.

Ten years after the revocation of the mutual excommunication, Pope Paul VI, during a liturgy in the Sistine Chapel devoted to this event, gave an impressive signal which caught the attention of the whole of Christianity. He dropped to his knees before Metropolitan Melito, the delegate of the Ecumenical Patriarch of Constantinople, and kissed his feet. What this means, when you really think about it, is that "*proskynesis*" has long been a papal claim. If, as this gesture was interpreted, the pope demands this "subjection of himself, it means that he is stepping to the limits of self-denial and demonstrating in extreme form how important to him reunion with the Orthodox Church is, how passionately he longs for the overcoming of the division of 1054." In his

---

22. H. Fries, "Sind die Christen einander nähergekommen?" in: K. Rahner—O. Cullmann—H. Fries, *Sind die Erwartungen erfüllt?* (Munich, 1966) 67–192, at 69–70.

23. J. Ratzinger, "Das Ende der Bannflüche von 1054. Folgen für Rom und die Ostkirchen," *Internationale Katholische Zeitschrift* 4 (1971) 280–303; *Principles of Catholic Theology*, trans. Sister Mary Frances McCarthy (San Francisco: Ignatius Press, 1987) 203–18.

address the pope said: "We are entering into a new phase of our reconciliation with the mutual will that it be the concluding phase."[24]

There is no doubt that in the current situation the Roman Catholic Church, through the special initiative of Pope John Paul II, is turning its ecumenical initiative towards the Orthodox churches and is attaching the greatest expectations to it. The pope spoke of a unification with the Church of the East at the beginning of the third millennium. There is not much time left before that, and one should not labor under any illusions about how difficult the discussions will be, especially on the question of the jurisdictional primacy of the pope. This has come out of the previous meetings of the International Orthodox–Catholic Commission, most recently in Munich in 1982: "We are just at the beginning." The Orthodox will not accept a primacy of the pope in the sense of an explicit taking over of the formulation of Vatican I and the new Codex of Canon Law. One can think of only one solution, as Joseph Ratzinger proposed it:

Those who stand on the ground of Catholic theology can certainly not simply declare the doctrine of primacy as null and void, even if they are attempting to understand the objections and are judging with open eyes the changing weight of what history can tell us. On the other hand, however, they cannot possibly regard the nineteenth and twentieth century form of primacy as the only possible one and as necessary for all Christians. The symbolic gestures of Paul VI, especially his prostration before the representative of the Ecumenical Patriarch, intended to express precisely this point and, by means of such signs, to lead us out of the bottleneck of past events. Although it is not in our power to do away with history, to take back the actions of centuries, one can still say: what was possible for a whole thousand years cannot be thought of as impossible for Christians today. After all, even in 1054, Humberto de Silva Candida, in the same bull in which he excommunicated Patriarch Caerularius and thus began the schism between East and West, also described the emperor and the citizens of Constantinople as "very Christian and orthodox," although their concept of Roman primacy was far less different from that of Caerularius than, for example, from that of Vatican I. In other words: Rome must not demand of the East this kind of a doctrine of primacy as if it were formulated and actually lived in the first millennium. When Patriarch Athenagoras in his July 25, 1967, visit with the pope in Phanar called him the successor of Peter, the first in honor among us, the presider in love, what was coming from the mouth of this great church leader was the essential content of the doctrine of primacy of the first millennium, and more must not be demanded by Rome. Unification could take place here on the basis that, on one side, the East gives up attacking the development of the second millennium as heretical, and accepts the Catholic Church as legal and orthodox in the shape it has taken in this development; the West, in turn, recognizes as orthodox and legal the shape that the Church of the East has preserved.[25]

24. *Her Korr* 30 (1976) 67.
25. "The Ecumenical Situation—Orthodoxy, Catholicism, and Protestantism" in: *Principles of Catholic Theology* 193–202, esp. 198–99.

The Dialogue with the Churches of the Reformation

The question of the papacy as ecumenical problem, in view of what was briefly described in our historical sketch, looks even more difficult when it becomes the theme of a dialogue between the Roman Catholic Church and the churches of the Reformation.

But even here, the question of the papacy has been decisively moved forward by the fact that, in our ecumenical efforts to work out the great questions of controversial theology—justification, the relationship of Scripture and tradition, the doctrine of the Eucharist and office, discussion about the proper understanding of "alone" and "and"—the doctrine of the papacy was always already there. It stands in an overarching relationship and context. That became manifest in the time of the Reformation and its criticism of the papacy. Hence, if

those fundamental reformational objections, which constitute the real core of the reformational antipapal polemic, are overcome or rendered moot by new agreements or convergences, this means that a decisive, if not indeed the decisive, step on the road to a solution of the papal problematic has been taken. Only now does it make sense to turn the question with any hope towards that of a church-wide office which can bring into serious consideration as one of the concrete possibilities the acceptance of the papacy even by the non-Catholic churches.[26]

Making this all the more feasible to think and move in this direction is the fact that the basic thought and praxis of the reformation churches on the concrete form of church offices is characterized by remarkable freedom and openness. The beginning of such an effort has by now taken place in some remarkable attempts.

Some important documents need to be mentioned: In the so-called Malta Document (1972), which the delegates appointed by the Lutheran World Union and the Roman Secretariat for Christian Unity composed under the title "The Gospel and the Church," the question of the papacy was briefly raised. It was said that jurisdictional primacy must "be understood" primarily "as service to the community and as bond of the unity of the Church." The office of the pope includes the responsibility of caring for the legitimate differences of the local churches. The concrete shape of this office can, corresponding to the respective historical conditions, be quite variable. From the Lutheran side it was recognized that no local church, because it is a manifestation of the universal Church, can isolate itself. It is in this sense that Lutherans see the importance of a ministry to the community of churches. The document also alludes to the problem this is for the

26. H. Meyer in: *Papsttum und Petrusdienst* 84.

Lutherans because of the lack of such an effective service to unity. The office of the pope as visible sign of the unity of the churches was thus not excluded, as long as it is made subordinate to the primacy of the gospel by theological reinterpretation and practical restructuring.

But disagreement remains between Catholics and Lutherans on the question whether the primacy of the pope is necessary for the Church or whether it represents only an in-priniciple possible function. However, it can indeed be said: If the primatial function of the pope is recognized as possible and this possibility is actually realized, then no explicit confession of the dogmatic necessity of the primacy of the pope need be required from the Evangelical sections of the one Church.[27]

The Lutheran–Roman Catholic Dialogue Group for the United States, an official dialogue group with theologians and bishops (1974), dealt much more extensively with the question of the papacy in its document: Ministry and Church Universal. Differing Attitudes Towards Papal Primacy.[28] The document carefully addresses the exegetical and historical problems connected with this question and rightly calls attention to the fact that the conditions and facts it brings to light are assessed in different ways from the Evangelical Lutheran and Catholic perspectives because of their different a priori presuppositions. The most important statements of the document concern its look into the future. They stand under the subtitle: "Outlook for the renewal of the structures of the papacy."

If the papacy present and future is taking on an ecumenical significance, if it is to serve the Church as a whole better and more effectively, then it is said that a renewal of its structure or structures is necessary. These must be oriented according to the principles of legitimate plurality, collegiality, and subsidiarity. It can be seen that these principles relate to the understanding and realization of the papacy "within" the Church. There is the correction conviction that a supreme office of unity can make good on its possibilities, and fulfill its duties only if it abandons the centralistic, isolated form that tries to do everything all by itself, and if it affirms that reality not only theoretically but also practically. It must, in other words, support the development of what fits the shape of the Church: a unity which finds in plurality not a hindrance to, but a living expression of, unity; a unity which can know the meaning of "first" only if there is statement and recognition of that for which the pope is to be first. What this means is collegiality in the various ranks and levels of the Church and in the Church. It also means the legitimate plurality of the Church whose unity the pope is supposed to protect.

---

27. Texts of the Malta Document in: *Dokumente wachsender Übereinstimmung*, 248-271, at 266.

28. Text in: H. Stirnimann—L. Vischer, *Papsttum und Petrusdienst* 91–140.

The principal of subsidiarity is the result of legitimate plurality and collegiality. It relieves the burden of the "top" and makes manifest the vitality and the wealth of the different parts. This is precisely what can contribute to the vitality and building up of the Church.

It is on the basis of these principles that a renewal in the structures of the papacy is to be striven for. The distinction between supreme authority and claiming supreme authority makes it possible for the pope to limit voluntarily the exercise of his jurisdiction. That would bring about a differentiation relative to the functions of the papacy, and would make a greater ecumenical reality thinkable. For the same reason, the primacy of the pope would be more a precedence in pastoral care than a juridical primacy with its typical questions of rights, powers, and competencies. One of the much needed effects of this would be that the abidingly juridical would be made more understandable in its necessity and (inner) limitation precisely from the pastoral responsibility of the pope.

Should these principles be recognized and put into practice, there would then exist, according to the views of the Lutheran members who helped produce this document, no reason to reject a supreme office of unity in the Church. The appropriateness, significance, and "blessing" of such an office is, precisely in today's Christianity in its striving for unity, more and more acknowledged and explicitly affirmed. The one necessary requirement is the demand by the Protestant participants that papal primacy be so conceived, understood, and put into practice— that this office unmistakably serve the gospel and the unity of Christians—and that the exercise of its power not be a hindrance to Christian freedom.[29] As one can see, this is the intention of the Reformation that is being expressed.

This consensus statement explicitly added that, over against this fundamental question, the issue of divine or human right in relation to the papacy is secondary. On the basis of a so-defined and so-limited statement of the question, no ecumenical progress is possible but only an endless discussion.

Then the authors of the document appeal to their churches to undertake concrete steps towards reconciliation:

Thus we ask the Lutheran churches if they are ready to confirm that papal primacy, renewed in the light of the gospel, need be no obstacle to reconciliation. We ask further whether they are in the position not only to recognize the legality of the papal office in the service of the Roman Catholic Church, but also the possibility and desirability of the papal office, renewed under the gospel in a more encompassing community which would also include the Lutheran churches.

But the Catholics Church is also asked whether it is willing to discuss possible structures for a reconciliation which would protect the le-

29. Ibid. 108.

gitimate traditions of the Lutheran churches and respect their spiritual heritage; and further, whether, in anticipation of an expected reconciliation, it is ready to recognize the Lutheran churches represented in our dialogue as sister churches which already possess the right to a certain degree of ecclesiastical commonness (no. 32 and 33).

The document concludes:

We believe that our common declaration reflects a convergence in the theological understanding of the papacy which makes a fruitful approach to these questions possible. Our churches should not let slip by this opportunity to answer to the will of Christ for the unity of His disciples. None of the churches should let stand a situation in which the members of one community consider another community as foreign. Our trust in the Lord who makes us into one body in Christ will help us to enter upon the still unknown paths to which His Holy Spirit is leading His Church. (no. 34)

To be sure, this astonishing document has still not received any official confirmation. That does not keep the dialogue group from remaining on the path and devoting itself to the theme of the infallibility of the pope and declaring "This apparently unsolved problem does not need to be an obstacle against reconciliation between the Lutheran and the Catholic Church." The document "Spiritual Office in the Church" speaks in similar fashion about the papacy under the title "Episcopal Office and Universal Unity of the Church" (67–73). The convergence statements from Lima do not take a position on the question.

In the Evangelical Catechism for Adults, which was published under the commission of the Evangelical Lutheran Church of Germany, one reads on our question:

All apostles have, according to the New Testament, fundamental significance for the Church. Peter is their representative. Even if the foundation was laid but once, one can still ask whether or not the ministry of a representative and spokesperson of all Christianity makes sense later as well. . . . To be sure, the non-Roman churches have until now come up with no convincing model as to how the unity of the church could take visible shape. . . . The position of the other church communities vis-à-vis the papacy will largely depend on how Rome succeeds in convincingly presenting the papacy as such a service to unity and as sign of unity.[30]

Wolfhart Pannenberg writes in the same vein: He proposes, with regard to the claim of the pope to serve the faith and to be the center of unity, shepherd, and teacher of all the faithful, to take him at his word and to call attention to a consequence which he thus formulates:

If a specially appropriate instance for the unity of all Christianity already exists in the form of the bishop of Rome, must not the unification of the separated churches be the first and most pressing business of the pope? Must he not, in all his decisions and statements, also take into consideration the needs and problems, but also the possible positive contribution of the Christians still separated from Rome today, instead of caring only for the preservation in the apostolic faith of

30. *Evangelischer Erwachsenenkatechismus* (Gütersloh, 1977) 916.

the church which presently calls itself Catholic and of its members? There would be a great deal, perhaps even something decisive, gained for the cause of Christian unity if, at every opportunity and in all openness, it became clear that the pope made his own the cause of all Christians, even the Christians still separated from Rome today, and made visible in his behavior the communion in Christ that binds all Christians together. To the degree in which the Roman bishop takes up in his thinking and decisions the present-day problems and mentalities, and the possible contribution of the other churches to the life of Christianity today, and also brings that to expression, to that same degree could his claim to be the representative of all Christianity gain in credibility even outside the present-day Roman Catholic Church. The example of John XXIII shows what possibilities really are open in this direction.[31]

The Dialogue with the Anglican Church

Without doubt, the final report of the official Commission for Anglican–Roman Catholic Dialogue, the Windsor Statement, the result of nine years of work, represents the most extensive rapprochement and understanding yet achieved by different churches on the question of the papacy.[32] The commission speaks of a "substantial agreement." The starting point and horizon of this statement is the idea of the Church as *koinonia*, as *communio*, which, for its part, is a fundamental characteristic of the ecclesiololgy of Vatican II.

In this context the Windsor Statement says: "All servants of the gospel must stand in communion with each other, for the one Church is a community of local churches. They must also be one in apostolic faith. Primacy as a burning point within the *koinonia* is a guarantee that what they teach and do is in harmony with the faith of the apostles." "Unity is the essence of the Church, and since the Church is visible, the unity must be visible. Fully visible unity between our churches cannot be achieved without mutual recognition of sacraments and office, together with the common acceptance of a universal primacy which, connected with the college of bishops, stands in the service of unity" (no. 9). "We are in agreement that a universal primacy in a reunited Church will be necessary, and appropriately should be the primacy of the bishop of Rome. In a reunited Church an office molded after the role of Peter will be a sign and guarantee of such a unity."

With regard to the thesis of Vatican I, which has become the thesis of the Catholic Church, that the primacy of the pope is based on divine law because it is founded by Jesus Christ, the text says:

---

31. "Einheit der Kirche als Glaubenswirklichkeit und als ökumenisches Ziel," *Una Sancta 30* (1975) 220–21.

32 Anglican-Roman Catholic International Commission, The Final Report, Windsor, 1981. German text in: *Dokumente wachsender Übereinstimmung* 177–98. Cf. H. Fries, "Das Petrusamt im anglikanisch-katholischen Dialog," *StdZ 107* (1982) 723–38.

He is the sign of the visible *koinonia* which God wills for His Church, [and] which will be realized through unity in multiplicity. The qualification *iure divino* can be applied to a universal primacy, conceived in this way, within the collegiality of the bishops and the collegiality of the whole church (no. 11). . . . In the past, Anglicans have considered as unacceptable the Roman Catholic doctrine that the bishop of Rome is the universal primate by divine right. Nevertheless we believe that the primacy of the Bishop of Rome can be understood as part of God's plan for the universal koinonia—in a way that can be harmonized with both our traditions. In view of this consensus, the language of divine right used by the First Vatican Council must no longer be considered a basis for a difference of opinion among us. (no. 15)

This proposition is then explained in the following way: "According to Christian doctrine, the unity of the Christian community demands visible expression. We agree that such a visible expression is the will of God and that the maintaining of visible unity on the universal level includes the episcopacy of a universal primate. This is a doctrinal statement."

The jurisdiction spoken of in the declaration of primacy is described as "fullness of power which is required for the exercise of an office." Connected with this are certain orientations that can go along with the exercise of the primacy. Hence the text demands:

The universal primate should carry out his office—and indeed recognizably to all—not in isolation but in collegial union with the bishops. This in no way lessens his own responsibility to speak and act upon occasion for the whole Church. The care for the universal jurisdiction of the universal primate is supported with every episcopal office. Yet the universal primate is not the source from which the diocesan bishops derive their authority, nor does his authority undermine that of the metropolitans or diocesan bishops. The primate is not an autocratic power over the Church, but a ministry within the Church and for the Church, which understands itself as a community of local churches in faith and love. (no. 19)

From this come also the moral limits in the exercise of the universal primacy:

The jurisdiction of the universal primacy has its sense in this authorization to further the catholicity as well as the unity and to care for and bring together the riches of the different traditions of the churches. The collegial and primatial responsibility for the preservation of the particular life of the local churches requires the appropriate reverence for their customs and traditions, as long as they do not contradict the faith or destroy the community. The striving for unity and the care for catholicity should not be separated from each other. (no. 21)

It is also required that the freedom of conscience not be endangered. If, as is done here, primacy is derived from the essence of the Church, and if this essence is seen as grounded in the will of God and by the cross and resurrection, one can see therein an origin of the primacy grounded in Jesus Christ; and one can call this origin divine, divine right, even if this divine right is not based on an explicit, juridically formulated, founding work of Jesus.

Whether one looks at the biblical and historical situation or at the state of current ecumenical theology, not a great deal more need be said in the dialogue of the churches regarding the grounding of papal primacy. What the Anglicans say about the meaning, right, and grounding of the primacy is not less but more than the churches of the East say. And if, as Joseph Ratzinger stated, the nineteenth- and twentieth-century form of the primacy is not seen as the only possible one and necessary for all Christians, then it is inadmissible (as happened in the first response of the Roman Congregation for the Doctrine of the Faith) to measure and judge the statements of the Anglican–Roman Catholic report only against the statements of Vatican I, and to ask whether they agree with its wording and requirements. To do this means elevating Vatican I to an absolute, ahistorical reality.

The Western maximum demand from the East would be, says Ratzinger, to demand a recognition of the primacy of the Roman bishop in the full range in which it was defined in 1870, and thereby to apply a practice of the primacy as it was accepted by the Uniates. He says, speaking of this and of other maximal demands, "None of the maximal solutions contain a real hope for unity." Should not what is right for the Orthodox also be approved for the Anglicans; and should we not especially refuse to impose as truth "what is in reality just an historically developed form which stands in a more or less close connection with the truth?"[33]

33. J. Ratzinger, *Principles of Catholic Theology* 198.

§ 58

THE PROBLEM OF INFALLIBILITY

The First Vatican Council

The Dogmatic Constitution on the Church of Jesus Christ, Chapter 4, from the First Vatican Council (1869-70) reads:

When the bishop of Rome speaks in virtue of his supreme teaching power (ex cathedra), that is, when in the exercise of his office as shepherd and teacher of all Christians, he definitively decides (*definit*) in virtue of his supreme apostolic authority that a doctrine on faith or morals is to be held by the whole Church, he possesses, on the basis of the divine assistance promised to him in Saint Peter, that infallibility with which the Divine Redeemer wished His Church to be endowed when making definitive decisions in matters of faith and morals. Consequently, these definitive decisions of the Bishop of Rome are, in themselves and not on the basis of the Church's consent, unchangeable (*Romani Pontificis definitiones ex sese, non autem ex consensu ecclesiae irreformabiles esse*).[1]

---

1. DS 3074 (Neuner–Roos 388); Heinrich Fries, "Ex sese, non ex consensu ecclesiae" in: R. Bäumer—H. Dolch, *Volk Gottes. Zum Kirchenverständnis der katholischen, evangelischen und anglikanischen Theologie* (Freiburg—Basel—Vienna, 1967) 480–500; H. Fries—J. Finsterhölzl, "Infallibility," *SM* 3.132–38; Hans Küng, *Infallibile? An Unresolved Enquiry* (Garden City, N. Y.: Doubleday, 1994); Karl Rahner, ed., *Zum Problem der Unfehlbarkeit. Antworten auf die Anfragen von Hans Küng* (Freiburg—Basel—Vienna, 1971); H. Küng, ed., *Fehlbar? Eine Bilanz* (Zurich—Einsideln—Cologne, 1973); M. Seybold, "Unfehlbarkeit des Papstes—Unfehlbarkeit der Kirche" in G. Denzler, ed., *Das Papsttum in der Diskussion* (Regensburg, 1974) 102–22; K. Schatz, *Kirchenbild und päpstliche Unfehlbarkeit bei den deutschsprachigen Minoritätsbischofen auf den 1. Vatikanum* (Rome, 1975); H. J. Pottmeyer, *Unfehlbarkeit und Souveränität. Die päpstliche Unfehlbarkeit im System der Ultramontanen Ekklesiologie des 19. Jahrhunderts* (Mainz, 1975); August B. Hasler, *Pius IX (1846–1878). Päpstliche Unfehlbarkeit und 1. Vatikanisches Konzil. Dogmatisierung und Durchsetzung einer Ideologie* (Stuttgart, 1977); also, *How the Pope Became Infallible: Pius IX and the Politics of Persuasion*, trans. Peter Heinegg (Garden City, N. Y.: Doubleday, 1981); M. Weitlauff, "Pius IX. und die Dogmatisierung der päpstlichen Unfehlbarkeit," *ZKG* 91 (1980) 94–105; W. Bienert, "Die Exzentrizität des Papstes. Über die Unfehlbarkeit des römischen Bischofs in der Kirche" in: A. Brandenburg—H. J. Urban, eds., *Petrus und Papst. Evangelium—Einheit der Kirche—Papstdienst* 2.56–86; O. H. Pesch—H. Ott, "Bilanz der diskussion um die vatikanische Primats- und Unfehlbarkeitsdiskussion," in: *Das Papsttum als ökumensiche Frage* 159–233; U. Horst, *Unfehlbarkeit und Geschichte. Studien zur Unfehlbarkeitsdiskussion von Melchior Cano bis zum I. Vatikanischen Konzil* (Mainz, 1982).

From the Protestant point of view, this declaration expresses not only the high point of the theological intention of the First Vatican Council's teaching on the Church, but also the clearest possible opposition to the Protestant faith and its understanding of the Church. Particularly because of this definitive formulation, Vatican I set off a very strong reaction. The difference from the faith of the Reformation expressed at the Council of Trent (1545–1563) was given a new accent by Vatican I, an accent which increased the contradictions by a further, decisive point and made the divisions between the confessions even deeper than they already were. In other words, the depth of the division was finally made clear by the declarations of the Roman Catholic Church at Vatican I. The necessity of the Reformation was confirmed anew, indeed was justified even more than ever.

In his *Church Dogmatics*, Karl Barth spoke of a "Vatican crime" against which one had to protest constantly.[2] He believed he could see this in the fact that, in this council—not to be sure as anything new, but as the end of a development that had already begun with Irenaeus of Lyon († ca. 202) and had steadily become stronger and stronger—the Church was declared to be that instance which determined and determines what the Scripture is and what belongs to it; even more critical, it makes itself the one and only authentic and legitimate interpreter of Scripture. But the decisive reason for protesting is that the remaining questions hitherto left open with regard to the Church and the critically important functions, responsibilities, and rights regarding the Scripture already long-acknowledged and attributed to her, are now precisely declared and concentrated by the definition of the primacy and by turning papal infallibility into dogma. This has brought about a "pantheistic identification of the Church with revelation." Thus, as Barth saw it, scriptural authority was changed into church authority—in a grandiose fulfillment of Augustine's words: "I would not believe in the Gospel if the authority of the Catholic Church did not move me to do so." And indeed, the identification of revelation and Church gets even stronger and becomes an elevation of the Church over Scripture. For whoever makes himself a judge over and has decision-making power over something, is setting himself over it, for he can do what he wants with it as its master. It is no wonder, then, that Barth speaks of anti-Christian and blasphemous declarations against which there is only one protection and defense: an Evangelical Church whose authority is not over but under the Word, whose existence means service and obedience, whose authority is validated because over her stands the authority of God with which it does not and could not ever become identical.

---

2. Karl Barth, *Church Dogmatics* I/2 (New York: Charles Scribner's Sons, 1956) 538–660 .

This protest and what it protested against could not possibly be expressed more sharply. Apparently we would be deceiving ourselves to think that this "No" has by now become merely a matter of history, even if every "No" doesn't make use of Barth's sharp language.

It is important to point out that the successor of Karl Barth at the University of Basel, Heinrich Ott, has written an astonishing "Evangelical Commentary" on the teaching of Vatican I, in which he comes to an essentially different interpretation of the same developments and the same text; he does not see in them an unbridgeable opposition between the confessions, but rather he sees in them a starting point for ecumenical discussion.[3] H. Ott finds it most remarkable that this text of the Council speaks about the infallibility of the Church, and that this constituted the comprehensive theme of the Council's declarations:

It is the will of Christ that the infallibility of the Church as such should be actualized in the *ex cathedra* decisions of the pope. There is a connecting point here: for, as Evangelical Christians, we can and must speak of the infallibility of the Church as such. The Spirit of God will indeed direct the community in all truth in accordance with the promise of Jesus Christ (John 16:13). It is impossible that the truth of the Gospel in the People of God on earth should ever be lost or be essentially changed. If this could happen, the People of God would cease to be the People of God. . . . If we really do count on the revelation of God unto our salvation, we must also count on the infallibility of the Church as a whole. The question is only (and this is where controversy begins): In what way does this infallibility get put into practice? From the Protestant point of view, the situation looks like this: through God's free activity in the Holy Spirit, the errors and aberrations in the history of the Church are corrected again and again; heresy—even if widespread for a long time—will always be overcome. The Catholic point of view, in contrast, sees the infallibility of the Church institutionally anchored in the Petrine office; it is visibly and bindingly actualized in the *ex cathedra* decisions of the papal magisterium.[4]

Here, as in all his writings, H. Ott pursues a factual interpretation of the Council and its intention. He also makes good use of the distinction between positive inspiration and negative assistance: "The magisterium is not given any new revelations; it stands under the Holy Scripture and only interprets it. But through the assistance of the Holy Spirit it is guaranteed that it will interpret it authentically, i.e., without error."

There is a different tone and a different atmosphere here than in the burning words and angry protest of Karl Barth. But that doesn't keep Ott from noting the Evangelical-Catholic differences and from formulating the objection and the fear "that by an infallibly deciding magisterium the conscience of the faithful will be violated, that its direct connection to God will be interrupted, and that it will be cut off

3. H. Ott, *Die Lehre des I. Vatikanischen Konzils* (Basel, 1963).
4. Ibid. 162–63.

from an ultimate, legitimate recourse from the representative of Christ to Christ himself."

There is no doubt, however, that we have here a welcome and laudable attempt to dismantle the frontal positions and enter on a new path. Ott's theological program of "unity through interpretation" merits most careful consideration.

The Meaning of the Text of the Council

Since the days of Vatican I there has not exactly been great enthusiasm, even within the Catholic Church, for the formulation that the definitive decisions of the pope are irreformable "in themselves, and not on the basis of their agreement with the Church." One of the major reasons for this was that this formulation has lead to misunderstandings. And these misunderstandings cannot be attributed merely to bad will and an intent to interpret tendentiously.

If one subjects to a broad analysis the theological and especially the ecumenical aspects of this "in themselves but not on the basis of their agreement with the Church," one has to take the following points into consideration: Even at Vatican I, this formulation was capable of a better interpretation than the one which it actually received and which later remained in effect. This is especially true when the formulation is turned into an isolated, self-explanatory formula without consideration for its textual context and its historical and church-historical background. The statements on the infallibility of the pope are in no sense a triumph of the so-called papalists and maximalists at the Council, but a recognizable corrective of them. That this is the case is clear from what happened at the Council itself, specifically in the following developments: The proposal to give chapter 4 of the dogmatic constitution *Pastor aeternus* the title "On the Infallibility of the Bishop of Rome" was rejected in favor of a considerably more factual formulation: "On the Infallible Magisterium of the Bishop of Rome." This was intended to bring out that it is not the person of the pope that is infallible, but that the unique, precisely described acts of his magisterium are infallible, free from error. As for the assistance of the Holy Spirit that is in force here, it is, as Cardinal Guidi, the archbishop of Bologna, explained, a matter of "assistance at a given moment," a "transitory illumination."[5] A specific act of the pope thus becomes infallible, but not his person; that is not changed. In addition, the compass of this infallible magisterium was given further precision by its restriction to "faith and morals." The pope cannot proclaim any new doctrine, but only that which has been accepted by the Church as a truth of faith.

---

5. Walter Kasper, "Primat und Episkopat nach dem Vatikanum I," *ThQ* 142 (1962) 69.

The mode of expressing an ex cathedra decision was given further precision. Infallibility comes into play when the pope, not as local bishop of Rome or as patriarch of the West, but "when he, exercising his office as shepherd and teacher of all Christians, in virtue of his supreme apostolic power of office, definitively decides that a teaching in faith or morals is to be firmly held by the whole Church." This describes an act which has been circumscribed as to its reality and goal in an extraordinarily clear way: it is a matter of an "extraordinary magisterium." This binds the pope to act in this way only for very serious reasons.

And finally: the infallibility of the papal magisterium is circumscribed by an encompassing perspective: It is the infallibility with which Christ endowed his Church, that it be in the truth and remain in it. This also means, and precisely according to Vatican I, that the pope and his office are described as deriving from the Church, and not the Church as deriving from the pope.

J. Pottmeyer, in his comprehensive study *Infallibility and Sovereignty*, has called attention to another, sometimes forgotten, perspective. He says: "The formulations of papal infallibility came about in the framework of a politically conscious ecclesiology which, after the breakup of the Christian universe, was struggling for an affirmation and strengthening of ecclesial-societal structures and their legitimation; external independence and internal integration were its concrete goals."[6]

The political intention and function of the definition was seen as follows: "It had a political function in three ways: First, it was to legitimate the principle of authority as the basis for the restoration of the societal system or—with the liberal Ultramontanists—the struggle of the people for freedom. Second, in the infallible authority of the pope was located the claim of the Church to be independent of the state. Finally, it stands in a necessary relationship with the primacy of jurisdiction, whose centralistic-autocratic praxis of leadership it legitimated."[7]

The dogmatic declaration on papal infallibility is not questioned by these historical perspectives; they only emphasize the relational framework, so to speak, of every affirmation of truth. If the external situation in which a doctrine is formulated, and thus its accompanying presuppositions, are changed, then the matter itself has to be given a "rereading" and a new form of appropriation as well as of factual interpretation. In this way the right and limits of every affirmation of truth can be recognized; this holds also, and specifically, for the definitions of Vatican I.

6. H. J. Pottmeyer, *Unfehlbarkeit und Souveränität* 18.
7. Ibid. 410.

Points of Orientation

There is a critical perspective that is vitally important for a proper understanding of infallibility. The inerrancy of ex cathedra papal decisions does not reside in those matters of faith and morals "in themselves" and alone. It has to be seen from the point of view of the Church as a whole—i.e. from the point of view of the "remaining in the truth" promised to the whole Church. Unfortunately, this has been far too neglected by theologians, whether Catholic or Protestant.

From the understanding of this broad view of the whole Church, it is theologically illuminating to point out that the "charism of truth" given to the extraordinary magisterium of the pope has a correspondence to the overall structure of revelation and represents an instance of the so-called *analogia fidei*. Throughout the phenomenon of revelation is found the structure of the "general in the particular" (*universale concretum*). In other words, the revelation that is applied to all and has become a reality for all always takes place concretely: in a historical event, to individual human beings, through a particular word, through a special act. The culmination and fulfillment of revelation in the person of Jesus of Nazareth and in the Christ-event is also the unsurpassable realization of the "general in the particular."

The application of this for our question is obvious: The promise given to the whole Church that it would be in the truth and remain in the truth does not require that all individual members of the Church have the "charism of truth" in the same way, but it does require that this charism is in the Church for the whole Church. Its specific concretization in a council or in an act of the extraordinary magisterium of the pope does not exclude this, but rather makes it—as a case of the "general in the particular"—possible and real. It also follows, according to the same law, that the infallibility given to the Church could be called into question if it weren't also concretized in a possible final word who is the first, the supreme shepherd, the rock, to whose ministry it belongs to strengthen his brethren in faith (cf. Luke 22:32).

The "in themselves" of Vatican I is thus taken up in the promise given to the whole Church to be the presence and place of the truth of Jesus Christ and thereby to enjoy the assistance of Christ and His Spirit. This definition thus remains protected from isolation.

The "in themselves" is also taken up under a properly understood agreement of the Church, even though the specific wording seems at first to signify the opposite of "not on the basis of the agreement of the Church." For the Council consciously wishes to express the agreement of the pope's ex cathedra decisions with the Church. A position was taken expressly against an isolated infallibility because with that, as was properly emphasized, the head of the Church would seem separated from the members, and it would no longer be clear to what extent the pope could be the head of the Church. This brings up—and this was clear at the Council—the relationship of the pope to the bishops. To mention this clearly was the concern of the minority at the council.

A long time was spent struggling over the formula: "The pope, who makes use of the counsel of the whole church and its assistance, cannot fall into error." Had it been accepted, the minority at the Council would have been fully satisfied.

Bishop Hefele of Rottenburg proposed to formulate the infallibility of the pope in such way that the Church would always remain included in it; to say in effect that "the pope is . . . infallible, supported by the ecclesiastical tradition or by the counsel and the help of the whole magisterium." He gave explanations of this which said that the second clause referred to the ordinary cases in which infallibility is exercised—for it is exercised by the antecedent or simultaneous consensus of the bishops. The first clause: "supported by the ecclesiastical tradition," referred to cases in which the tradition is so clear that the pope considers it to be justified to omit asking the rest of the magisterium.[8]

This position was supported by a sensational address of Cardinal Guidi, who explained that in the decree it should be made clear that it is not the pope alone who pronounces a definition, but the pope in agreement with the bishops. Thus he wanted to have included in the definition: "After he has carried out investigations relative to the tradition of the rest of the churches and has sought the counsel of a larger or smaller number of bishops, according to the nature of the case, and also after he has examined the matter himself and called on the assistance of the Holy Spirit," he cannot fall into error. The cardinal also proposed a canon: "If anyone holds that the pope of Rome, when he promulgates dogmatic decrees or constitutions, is acting from his own will and from a plenitude of power independently of the Church, i.e., apart from her and not on the basis of the counsel of the bishops who proclaim the tradition to their church, let him be anathema."[9]

There was always the hope that, within the different groups and tendencies of the Council, an agreement could be reached which would describe the special position of an ex cathedra decision of the pope and at the same time avert the misunderstanding of an isolated infallibility. In any case the following is noteworthy: The formulation proposed on the agreement of the Church was rejected by the majority on the grounds that this concept was ambiguous, for it could signify both factual agreement with the Church as well as the act of agreement of the

    8. Edward Cuthbert Butler—H. Lang, *The Vatican Council: The Story from Inside in Bishop Ullathorne's Letter,* vol. 1 (New York: Longmans, Green & Co., 1930) 145.
    9. Ibid. 96–97.

bishops to the decrees. Precisely this ambiguous concept was ultimately, especially (due to the efforts of Cardinal Manning at literally the last minute and in a not entirely unobjectionable procedural way) taken up into the final text, but in the formulation, equally ambiguous and even more difficult in interpretation, "but not on the basis of the agreement of the Church." The proposal of Bishop Dupanloup to delete these words and replace them with the formula "based on the witness of the churches,"[10] did not get approved. Equally unsuccessful was also the quite different proposal of a group of maximalists: "that the definitions are of themselves irrevocable without need of any further agreement on the part of the bishops, neither antecedent, nor simultaneous, nor subsequent."[11]

Why the various qualifying proposals of the minority on this point were not accepted is not easy to say. It was surely not to separate the pope from the Church, for the Council was of one mind in rejecting an isolated infallibility. But it was claimed that this kind of qualification would be hard to understand and apply (as if the rejection *non ex consensu ecclesiae* were more certain and more clear!). It was claimed that it didn't sufficiently emphasize the special position of the pope, and because it would be taken for granted that the pope, in a dogmatic decision, would do everything and make use of every means to realized his decision as a decision of the whole Church. These were understood to be moral obligations containing an elevated moral stringency which, as such, could not be juridically and dogmatically laid down.

That this is no mere surmise can be drawn from the fact that in the official text of the Council explicit reference was made to these facts: "The bishop of Rome, in accordance with the needs of the time and the circumstances, by calling general assemblies of churches or investigation of the view of the churches spread around the world, by partial synods or by other means such as Divine Providence made available, have set down as firm doctrine that which they, with God's help, have recognized to be in agreement with the Holy Scriptures and the apostolic traditions. For even to the successors of Peter the Holy Spirit is not promised in such a way that they, of their own authority, could publish a new teaching. Rather, they are, with the Spirit's assistance, to protect as holy and interpret faithfully the tradition handed on from the apostles, i.e., the deposit of faith they left behind."[12]

For this reason one has to reject the position of Hans Küng: "This is not the teaching of Vatican I: If he wants to, the pope can do anything, even without the Church."—"An arbitrary, authoritarian, single-handed action of the pope against the Church is a legitimate conse-

10. R. Aubert, *Vatikanum I* (Mainz, 1965) 274.
11. Ibid. 273.
12. DS 3069 (NR 385).

quence of the dogma of 1870." "For full validity, no antecedent, simultaneous or consequent agreement of the Church, no consultation, cooperation, or ratification of the episcopacy is necessary." Equally indefensible is Küng's thesis that it is the meaning of Vatican I that infallible propositions "not only are de facto not in error, but in principle it is not even possible for them to be in error." Kung's claim is that we are dealing with a priori infallible propositions. However, faith propositions are always a posteriori propositions.[13]

Küng's propositions are not to be found in what comes from the First Vatican Council but in the survival of the maximalists and papalists, who did not get what they wanted in the Council, were disappointed, and attempted to remedy this "defect" by a special program of subsequent interpretation and application. Consequently it must be said that such a manipulated post-Vatican program of interpretation and application is in no sense a mere legitimate consequence of the dogma of 1870; it is rather to be blamed on failures, on not attending to and not bringing to reality what really was the intention of Vatican I: to emphasize the relationship of pope and Church. This relationship was expressly emphasized in the collective declaration of the German bishops in 1875 in answer to the claim of Bismarck regarding the concept of the primacy of the pope as a sovereign, "who, because of his infallibility, is a totally absolute sovereign, more than any other absolute monarch in the world." This was characterized by the German bishops as a contradiction to the dogma of 1870, and Pius IX agreed.[14] Unfortunately, this letter of the German episcopacy remained quite unknown and had little practical effect. In the outcome, the point which was not denied but rather taken for granted and not so sharply accentuated, namely the relationship of pope and Church, was upstaged by the prerogatives of the papacy.

The Historical Background

If the words "not on the basis of the agreement of the Church" were added to the final formulation, then what preceded them cannot be adduced in contradiction. On the other hand, this formula cannot stand in contradiction to the textual context. As must be pointed out, this addition has an historical address: Gallicanism. It was believed, whether rightly or wrongly, that a barrier had to be set up against the fourth Gallican article, which says that the judgment of the pope is not definitive unless the Church has given its agreement. It follows that the *"non ex consensu ecclesiae"* means the so-called *consensus subsequens*, i.e., the subsequent agreement as additional and subsequent act of the

---

13. H. Küng, *Infallibile? An Unresolved Enquiry* 85, 83, 124..
14. DS 3112-3116 (NR 388a).

bishops. In other words, the "of themselves but not on the basis of the agreement of the Church" cannot mean that in his doctrinal decisions the pope is absolved from agreement with the Church; it can and does say only that a proclamation of a dogma by the pope as the supreme shepherd and teacher of the whole Church, which has come to pass under these presuppositions and conditions, is not subject in a formal-juridical way to any further act of agreement.

The formulation "of themselves, but not on the basis of the agreement of the Church" is explainable from its historical background. Because, however, by the time of Vatican I this background was no longer very present, and because it has by our own time quite faded away, the formula is easily misunderstandable. But when the textual context of the Council is taken account of and the perspectives we have been expounding are kept in mind, i.e., that the infallibility of the papal ex cathedra decisions derive from the promise given to the whole Church that she would be in the truth and the truth in her, it then becomes clear that it was a concern, even at Vatican I, to understand the office of the pope as deriving from the Church (and not vice versa) and thus to make his ex cathedra decisions into the voice of faith and acknowledgment of faith of the whole Church. This is impossible if he does not stand in constant contact with the faith-understanding of the Church (*sensus ecclesiae*), if he thus does not have the antecedent and simultaneous agreement of the Church (*consensus ecclesiae*) and, in whatever way, makes sure of that.

The comprehensive explanations that Bishop Gasser gave in the name of the Deputation for Faith, which was concerned above all with the explanation of the concepts involved and took into consideration the objections being raised, confirm this thesis in many details. Bishop Basser's report on the addition "but not on the basis of the agreement of the Church" reads: The intent here is to say something about the legal basis from which the binding power of a definition of the pope comes, but not about the basis of knowledge from which the pope draws. This "of themselves" is thus a "statement about the dogmatic definitions, not about the pope and about his obligation to draw his definitions from revelation and from the faith of the Church."[15]

The Second Vatican Council

In view of the questions and problems that stem from the dogma of the "infallible magisterium of the bishop of Rome" proclaimed at the First Vatican Council, the obvious next question is how this dogma is to be understood today, after the Second Vatican Council. The formula of Vatican I, that the solemn doctrinal decisions of the bishop of Rome are

---

15. K. Rahner, *Commentary on the Documents of Vatican II*, ed. H. Vorgrimler, 1.208–16.

irrevocable "of themselves, but not on the basis of the agreement of the Church" comes up again in Vatican II's Dogmatic Constitution on the Church. In the long third chapter "On the Hierarchical Structure of the Church, in Particular on the Office of Bishop," the decisive propositions from the constitution *Pastor aeternus* of 1869 are repeated. The statements on the bishops and the college of bishops are constantly brought face-to-face with the fact of the primacy of the pope and the infallibility of his ex cathedra decisions. In addition, the already-existing formulation that the definitive doctrinal decisions of the pope are irrevocable "of themselves and not on the basis of the agreement of the Church" is taken over word-for-word. They are moderated only to the extent that the "but not" is changed to an "and not." They are also expanded by the addition "They thus require no confirmation by others and are subject to no appeal to another judgment" (*Lumen gentium* no. 25).

Context is important for an understanding of this text. This third chapter on the hierarchical structure of the Church is placed after the great themes "On the Mystery of the Church" and "On the People of God" (chaps. 1 and 2). This can and should express in what context, in what function, and in whose service stand the hierarchical structure, the college of bishops and its head the pope, together with all their duties: they stand in the service of a mystery, a truth, and a reality of faith; they stand in the service of and in function of the people of God.

Infallibility is given to the Church as a defense provided by its divine Redeemer for the definitive grounding and support of doctrine on faith and morals (no. 25). The application and extent of this doctrine and its role in the service of the truth of revelation—as the previously made distinctions make clear—is specified: "It extends as far as does the treasure of divine revelation, which is to be protected intact and interpreted with fidelity." (This formulation is taken word-for-word from the first draft prepared at Vatican I for the Constitution on the Church of Christ.)[16] With the formulation "protect intact" are included also truths connected with the protection of the contents of revelation, even if they are themselves not formally revealed. The words "interpret with fidelity" refer to the development of a truth of faith which takes place in the course of history.

The infallibility of the Church thus described and limited is present in the bishop of Rome, "he enjoys it," in virtue of his being head of the college of bishops; it becomes effective "when the teacher of all the Christian faithful proclaims a doctrine of faith or morals in a definitive act." This gives clear expression to the real character of infallibility, which becomes actual only now and then; In specific moments and

---

16 F. van de Horst, *Das Schema über die Kirche auf dem 1. Vatikanischen Konzil* (Paderborn, 1963).

actions, the promise of the assistance of the Holy Spirit connected with the Petrine office becomes effective. In this case "the bishop of Rome makes his decision not as a private person, but, as supreme teacher of the whole Church, he interprets and protects Catholic doctrine." Take note, at this precise point, of the idea of the "general in the particular" mentioned above—not indeed in the language of power and official authority, but in that of charism: the grace "of the infallibility of the Church itself is then, in this decisive function of the bishop of Rome, present in a unique way" (no. 25).

The same relationship is clarified from still another perspective and starting point in the Dogmatic Constitution on the Church. It is said that the Holy People of God shares in the prophetic office of Christ. It is indeed affirmed that "the totality of the faithful who have the anointing of the Spirit (1 John 2:20 and 27) cannot err in faith. This special quality of theirs is made known through their supernatural sense of faith when they, from the bishops down to the last believing lay person, express their general agreement in matters of faith and morals" (no. 12). Here is express mention of the general agreement of the People of God—i.e. the Church.

The constitution *Lumen gentium* says something that wasn't as clearly expressed in Vatican I: "The infallibility promised to the Church is also given to the body of the bishops" (no. 25). Now it is always said of the college of bishops that it is a special college because of the position in it of the successor of Peter, that without him the function of the college cannot be fulfilled, because without its head the college is not full and present: "The college. . . . of bishops has authority only when understood to be in communion with the bishop of Rome, the successor of Peter, as its head and without encroachment on his primatial power over all shepherds and faithful" (no. 22).

The statements about the "full, supreme, and universal power" of the bishop of Rome are repeated in Vatican II, which also adds that the pope can always freely exercise this power. The new Code of Canon Law repeats this same statement (can. 331).

One must nevertheless keep in mind that in the context of our text (no. 25), the relationship of the college of bishops to the pope as the head of the college is not formulated as "under the Roman pope" but as "together with the successor of Peter." Another formulation in the same place speaks of the "bond of communion among themselves and with the successor of Peter." A further precision and clarification of Vatican I by the Second Vatican Council takes place when it is said that the bishop of Rome and the college of bishops, in their search for truth in the exercise of this office, have an obligation to revelation, "to accept which and to agree with which all are bound." "To investigate it [revelation] correctly and represent it properly, the bishop of Rome and the bishops take great pains with the appropriate means, as befits their obligation and the weight of the matter. However, they do not receive any new revelation pertaining to the divine content of faith." The phrase "take great pains" is, according to the commentary of Karl Rahner, "to be understood as a directive of the language of law: Their taking great pains must be directed to that." The "appropriate means" (*apta media*) are available today in theology and in the life of the Church to an incomparably greater degree than before, and they are to be made use of in an incomparably more comprehensive way in this common effort.[17]

A significant number of clarifications and emphases in *Lumen gentium* have the cumulative effect of considerably lessening the possibility of misunderstanding the formula of 1869. Among these are: (a) the location of the "ex sese, non ex consensu ecclesiae" in the overall understanding of the Church and of the infallibility promised to her; (b) the precision provided by the reference to infallibility as a grace granted for a particular, passing occasion; (c) the express mention of the infallibility of the body of the bishops; (d) the mention of the obligation to the word of truth of revelation and to the responsibility for the faith; (e) the repeatedly mentioned reference to the community which is made up of the whole Church, the People of God. It can also be said that the question of the bearers of the charism of infallibility can, after Vatican II, be answered even more clearly than before: the subject of infallibility is the "college of bishops," whose head is the pope and which, without this head, is not complete. On the other hand the pope, in definitive ex cathedra decisions, acts as head of the college of bishops.

If the pope defines at one time acting alone, at another time acting together with the council, we don't have two acts of two different subjects, but two modes of procedure of one and the same subject, which differ from each other only in the circumstance that in one case the one moral subject is spread over the face of the earth, and in the other case, is gathered in one place so that the cooperation and agreeing participation of the members of the college with its head are more obviously visible.[18]

In the book *Einigung der Kirche—Reale Möglichkeit* (Unification of the Church—Real Possibility) the attempt is made in one thesis (IV b) to mediate the ex cathedra teaching authority of the pope in such a way as to make sense of it today ecumenically. This proposal would

---

17. K. Rahner, *Commentary on the Documents of Vatican II*, edited by H. Vorgrimler, 1.208–16.

18. K. Rahner, "The *ius divinum* of the Individual Bishop" in: K. Rahner—J. Ratzinger, *The Episcopate and the Primacy*, trans. Kenneth Barker and others (New York: Herder and Herder, 1962) 109; L. Scheffczyk, "Träger der Unfehlbarkeit in Ekklesiologischer Sicht," *ThQ* 142 (1962) 310–28.

have the pope "declare (*iure humano*), that he will make use of his supreme (*ex cathedra*) teaching authority given him according to Catholic principles by Vatican I only in a way that, juridically or factually, corresponds to a general council of the whole Church, just as his previous ex cathedra decisions came about in agreement with and getting the sense of the whole Catholic episcopacy."

The Authentic Magisterium

For clarification, the *magisterium ordinarium* is also called the authentic magisterium of the pope ("*cum non ex cathedra loquitur*"). To it and to its statements is due a "religious obedience of the will and understanding," as well as a respectful acknowledgment and adherence, "according to the content and intention of the particular teaching." This can be recognized primarily "from the nature of the documents, the frequency of the occurrence of one and the same doctrine, and the manner of speaking" (no. 25). But one of the great problems with this is the frequent tendency also to attribute to these statements the additional quality of infallibility.

To this must also be added that this same magisterium has also made mistakes. The most spectacular case, the one with the worst consequences, is probably the condemnation of Galileo, which has since (but only quite recently) been reversed. The proposition of Martin Luther, that burning heretics contradicts the will of the Spirit (of God), was condemned by Pope Leo X. Pope Gregory XVI rejected in the sharpest possible terms the demand for religious freedom and freedom of conscience,[19] now explicitly professed and solemnly proclaimed at Vatican II. The ecumenical movement was dismissed by Pius XI in the encyclical *Mortalium animos* of 1928 as *Panchristianism* while Vatican II speaks of the same ecumenical movement as a work of the Holy Spirit. The modern theory of evolution was seen as a contradiction to the doctrine of creation, but today, their mutual correlation is acknowledged. The proposition "Extra ecclesiam nulla salus" is interpreted differently today than at the time of its formulation—or in the terrifying language of the Council of Florence.[20]

An example from most recent times is the continuing and still unresolved discussion about the encyclical of Paul VI *Humanae vitae* on the question of birth control, teachings that are being explicitly repeated by Pope John Paul II,[21] without even faithful Catholics fully agreeing with them.

19. DS.2731.
20. DS 1351.
21. F. Böckle—C. Holenstein, ed., *Die Enzyklika in der Diskussion* (Zürich, 1968); B. Häring, "Krise um *Humanae Vitae*," *ThQ* 149 (1969) 75–85; H. Fries, "Nach Humanae Vitae" in: *Ärgernis und Widerspruch*, 2d ed. (Würzburg, 1968) 175–90; K. Rahner, "On the

THE CHURCH AND REVELATION

One statement valid to this day was given by J. H. Newman in his comment on Vatican I.

But a pope is not infallible in his laws, nor in his commands, nor in his acts of state, nor in his administration, nor in his public policy. Let it be observed that the Vatican Council has left him just as it found him here. . . . Was St. Peter infallible on that occasion at Antioch when St. Paul withstood him? was St. Victor infallible when he separated from his communion the Asiatic Churches? or Liberius when in like manner he excommunicated Athanasius? And, to come to later times, was Gregory XIII, when he had a medal struck in honour of the Bartholomew massacre? or Paul IV. in his conduct towards Elizabeth? or Sixtus V. when he blessed the Armada? or Urban VII. when he persecuted Galileo? No Catholic ever pretends that these Popes were infallible in these acts. Since then infallibility alone could block the exercise of conscience, and the Pope is not infallible in that subjectmatter in which conscience is of supreme authority, no dead-lock, such as is implied in the objections which I am answering, can take place between conscience and the Pope.[22]

Critical Questions

As we look back on the First and Second Vatican councils, we can ask whether it made sense to take over a formulation that was burdened with many factual misunderstandings and that even now needs a great deal of interpretation. This applies both to the "in themselves" and to the "and not on the basis of the agreement of the Church"—for precisely this addition was and remains a cause of misunderstanding. It is not clear why, precisely in the spirit of Vatican II, one shouldn't have gone ahead to remove misunderstandings as far as possible. Now that doesn't mean concealing or denying the difference between the confessions which, precisely in the question of the Petrine office and its function, is given for the faith of the Church. What it is about is not burdening this difference with formulations or, perhaps, pushing them in a direction not at all intended by the truth and the meaning of the Petrine office.

The statement of the explanatory prenote: "The pope as supreme shepherd of the Church can exercise his power at any time as he sees fit, as is required by his office," is anything but a felicitous formulation, even if it can also be said that the maximalist-sounding "as he sees fit" is given some precision and limitation by the addition: "as is

---

Encyclical Humanae Vitae," *Theological Investigations* 11 (New York, 1974) 263–87. Recent discussion of this and related themes may be found in: J. T. Noonan, "Development in Moral Doctrine," *Theological Studies* 54 (1993) 662–77; G. Grisez and F. A. Sullivan, "Quaestio Disputata: The Ordinary Magisterium's Infallibility," *Theological Studies* 55 (1994) 720–38; J. E. Thiel, "Tradition and Authoratative Reasoning," *Theological Studies* 56 (1995) 627–51; R. F. Castigan, "Bossuet and the Consensus of the Church," *Theological Studies* 56 (1995) 652–72.

22. J. H. Newman, *Letter Addressed to His Grace the Duke of Norfolk* (London: B. M. Pickering, 1875) 62–63.

required by his office." What this in fact intends to say, and is indeed emphasized, is that "the activity of the pope stands under no external tribunal that can be brought up against him, but that he is also bound to the internal claim of his office: revelation and the Church. But this inner claim of his office also includes without doubt a moral bond to the voice of the whole Church."[23]

The question arises whether, in accordance with the intention of the Council, one should not have tried to express the ancient and irreformable truth, which goes with confession to the fact and function of the Petrine office, in a new language and formulation in order to protect this truth from misinterpretations and false associations.

There is, for the same reason, the question whether the certainly ancient and firmly established word *infallibilitas*, infallibility, is a good word which says what it intends, and which under all circumstances must be retained.[24] Whether we like it or not, the word infallibility contains, in the connotations of our contemporary language, a fullness of maximalist meanings extending from moral integrity to a faith-expressing and theological ne plus ultra. Precisely this is what is not meant by infallibility, but is denied by it.

The same Council explicitly says: Never will reason illuminated by faith become

capable of apprehending mysteries as it does those truths which constitute its proper object. For the divine mysteries by their own nature so far transcend the created intelligence that, even when delivered by revelation and received by faith, they remain coveredwith the veil of faith itself, and shrouded in a certain degree of darkness, so long as we are pilgrims in this mortal life, not yet with God; "for we walk by faith and not by sight" (2 Cor 5:7).[25]

But if this is the case and the word "infallibility" today calls forth the inappropriate associations we have mentioned, should one then not call to mind the law that one must sometimes seek new formulas and concepts to express what is intended in the old formulations? Must we not remind ourselves that mere repetitions of the formulations of the past can lead to misunderstanding of the matter in hand? Perhaps the concept "inerrancy," (or Möhler's "Unverirrlichkeit") might be more suitable—or simply the concept "true" and "truth" in connection with the concept "binding," which in the case of supreme engagement can become ultimately binding. Binding then means not an arbitrary but an authentic statement grounded in the reality of faith

23. J. Ratzinger, *Commentary on the Documents of Vatican II*, ed. H. Vorgrimler, 1.303–4.

24. H. Fries, "Das mißverständliche Wort" in: K. Rahner, ed., *Zum Problem der Unfehlbarkeit. Antworten auf den Anfragen von Hans Küng* 216–32; also, "Die nicht ausgehaltene Spannung. Überlegungen zur Auseinandersetzung um Hans Küng" in: *Dienst am Glauben* (Munich, 1981) 94–108.

25. DS 3016 (NR 43); also, H. Fries, "Das Problem der Vollständigkeit im Bereich von Glaube und Lehre" in: *Dienst am Glauben* 59–73.

and, for that reason, normative for the community of believers. Add to this that "binding" also has to do with connection in the sense of unification and grammatical rule.

"Infallible" means, therefore that what is said and decided in certain statements of the magisterium—statements that are precisely circumscribed as to their presuppositions, content, and form—is not false, is not erroneous and, to that extent, is true. But, within the context of truth as a possibility in human statement, what is thus said and decided still stands under the laws of the inadequate, finite, perspectival, analogous, and misunderstandable; for this is the law of faith and of all functions in the service of the faith as well as of all its articulations, to which doctrine and definition or definability belong. But all these just-named qualifications are not the same as "erroneous." It is precisely this distinction that is not found with sufficient clarity in Hans Küng. The lack of this distinction thus forms a new source of misunderstandings.

The quality of the not-false, and, to that extent, of infallibility, is found in such articulations of faith in the way which Küng himself explains under the basic thesis: The faith of the Church relies on propositions, because in its content it is a specific faith, because it is a faith that has to be able to communicate itself, has to be able to say and articulate what it means and whereof it speaks. The community of faith and of believers depends on there being a community of language, of understanding of language, and of grammar.[26]

It is a basic concern of Hans Küng to emphasize that the Church, despite all errors, abides in the truth. But if so, Küng asks, how can the Church abide in the truth, despite all errors, if, in its service to the faith there are not also—certainly not only—infallible propositions—infallible in the sense of binding, true propositions? To be fair, one must admit that Küng does explicitly say this. But because of his previous misunderstanding of infallibility as a "*superadditum*," as "infallible propositions guaranteed from the outset [a priori]," he comes to his dialectical formulation: The Church abides in the truth despite all errors. One must further ask: How is this abiding of the Church in the truth, despite all errors, to be recognized and realized if not also in true propositions? The same holds for abiding in the truth in the sense of the promise that God remains faithful to his work and Word in Jesus of Nazareth.

What the First Vatican Council defined and what was subsequently taken up in the second Vatican Council is the fact that, to the instances and acts through which a bindingly true statement can come about, thus to the dogmatic decisions of the councils, belongs also the magisterium of the bishop of Rome. It belongs there in a precisely cir-

---

26. H. Küng, *Infallible? An Unresolved Enquiry*, 118–23.

cumscribed way according to form and content as well as according to presuppositions and conditions. This represents the opposite of an a priori and is possible only a posteriori.

In the "Final Report" of the Anglican-Catholic dialogue one reads: The preservation of the Church in the truth makes it necessary "that the Church, in specific moments, be able to make a definitive decision on essential questions of doctrine, which then become a part of its abiding witness" (24). On the universal level, the Church can make such decisions at general ecumenical councils, but the universal primate can also speak in a binding way in the name of the whole Church (26). "If the responsibility to protect the Church from fundamental errors is a responsibility of the whole Church, it can still be carried out in its place [i.e. of the whole church] by a universal primate" (28).

These considerations are to be applied to a still-wider concept: the concept *"irreformabilis,"* irreformable, which is contained in the formula under discussion. In its apodictic version it will not properly fit into the program of a council which conceives its goal to be *reformatio* and which it so impressively realized in its proclamations; a council which repeatedly mentioned and set as its task the distinction between unchangeable truth and historical form of expression.[27] But the concept *"irreformabilis"* is also in extreme need of interpretation. So the question again arises whether a better-fitting formulation could not have, if not totally eliminated, at least alleviated this concern. For *"irreformabilis"* does indeed intend to exclude errors of faith from the definition, but it does not intend to say downright and absolute unchangeability. It includes the possibility of another, more suitable, or more comprehensive, or more complete version, which to be sure does not fall short of the truth already expressed in a definition, or which allows it to fall back into a state of unclarity, but which can open up an even deeper understanding of something formulated in a definition, and from that deeper understanding make a new formulation attainable. But will not this fact and possibility be more distorted than opened up by the word *"irreformabilis"*?

Magisterium and the Word of God

Ecumenically speaking, what is perhaps the most important accentuation and at the same time the strongest protection against a possible misunderstanding of the *"ex sese"* was provided by Vatican II's Dogmatic Constitution on Revelation, above all by the statement it

27. "Die Erklärung der römischen Glaubenskongregation 'Mysterium ecclesiae.'" German Text in *HerKorr* 27 (1973), 416–21; also K. Rahner, "Mysterium Ecclesiae," *Theological Investigations,* vol. 17, trans. Margaret Kohl (New York: Crossroad, 1981) 139–55; M. Seckler, in *ThQ* 153 (1973) 380–82.

made about the magisterium of the Church and in the Church: "The magisterium does not stand above the Word of God, but serves it, in that it teaches nothing but what has been handed on, because it reverently accepts the Word of God in divine commission and with the assistance of the Holy Spirit, protects it in holiness, and interprets it in fidelity" (*Dei verbum*, no. 10).

"Holy tradition" is so understood that it too is a way in which the Word of God is present, even if also not in the manner of the inspired Scripture. "Holy tradition and the Sacred Scripture form the one treasure of the Word of God given to the Church. Devoted to it, the whole People, united with its shepherd, perseveres with constancy in the teaching of the apostles and in community with them, in the breaking of the bread and in prayer, so that in this holding fast to the faith of the tradition, in its realization and in its confession, a unique unity reigns between the heads and the faithful." Thus "holy tradition, Sacred Scripture, and the magisterium of the Church are so connected and united with each other that no one of them exists without the other and that each together, each in its own way, under the influence of the one Holy Spirit, effectively serves the salvation of souls."

According to these words—which do not by any means clarify all questions regarding Scripture and Tradition, but do provide space for further theological reflection on them—it is established that there can be no doubt about the primacy and the incomparability of the Word of God in the Church. The Church knows and publicly proclaims that it is placed under the authority of the Word of God. It clearly understands its activity expressly as service to this Word, not as being in charge over it.[28]

Here is an unambiguous answer to Karl Barth's characterization of the Roman Catholic Church and its magisterium quoted at the beginning of this chapter, namely, his idea of the Church claiming to be identical with revelation and thus having control over the Word of God. The alternatives he set up at that time—Church of self-governance or Church of obedience, Church of claim or Church of humility—have now turned out to be quite impossible. It is worthy of note that Karl Barth himself finally recognized this. His repeated remarks on Vatican II support this assessment.[29]

It is of course important to place the correct interpretation of the "in themselves, not on the basis of the agreement of the Church" in the framework of the context and the whole text of the Council. But it is much more important to place it in the framework of the Council's fundamental structure and fundamental intention. And most important of

---

28. W. Kasper, *Dogma unter dem Wort Gottes* (Mainz, 1965).
29. K. Barth, *Ad limina Apostolorum: An Appraisal of Vatican II*, trans Keith R. Crim (Richmond: John Knox Press, 1968).

all for the credibility of the Church is the practical exercise of this magisterium as a ministry, a ministry in which it isn't the powerful formulation and choice of words that gets expressed with all solemnity, power and energy, but rather the humility of service to the faith, the responsibility and modesty which even in true statements remains conscious of itself, and which is part and parcel of our knowledge, a looking in mirrors and enigmas and not a knowledge as we ourselves are known (cf. 1 Cor 13:12). As Thomas Aquinas taught even and especially in matters of faith, all modes of the "expressible" fall short of the "reality."

In his answer to the declaration of the German Bishops' Conference, Hans Küng notes that in the declaration of the bishops, his question about the possibility of not only true but also of guaranteed infallible propositions was avoided. The word "infallible," significantly, does not even occur in the whole declaration. I see in this, in contrast to Küng, not as an avoidance of the reality under discussion, but a most welcome attempt, by leaving out and avoiding the easily misunderstood concept "infallible," to offer a new articulation of the matter, and thus, by getting away from what concretizes, narrows, and defends, to say something about the matter itself. What is meant by "infallible," and what this includes as gift and responsibility of the Church, also in view of infallible propositions, is thus formulated by the German bishops:

The binding quality proper to the revelational Word of God finds its concrete expression in the Credo of the Church with which, by way of answer, it takes up the revelation witnessed in the Bible. Although the faith of the Church must be constantly thought out anew, and hence remains unclosed until the end of history, it includes an unmistakeable Yes and an unmistakeable No which are both nonegotiable. Without this, an abiding of the Church in the truth of Jesus Christ is not possible. It is the right and obligation of the Church, in view of the new questions that arise in various historical situations, on the one hand to give room for a fundamental thinking out of the faith, but on the other hand, where necessary, to express anew in a binding way its nonegotiable Yes and No to these questions.[30]

---

30. As quoted in K. Rahner, ed., *Zum Problem der Unfehlbarkeit* 373.

THE ECCLESIASTICAL MAGISTERIUM AND HOLY SCRIPTURE

In the Catholic Church, the ecclesiastical magisterium is represented by the college of bishops, to which belongs the bishop of Rome as head of the college. It is in the bishops that we find the realizations of the mandate and mission of the apostles for the particular current situation of the Church. The apostolic witness, the apostolic teaching, and the binding orientation towards the whole Church which calls itself apostolic, are entrusted to the bishops in a special, "official" way, to be protected, preserved, and made present. Vatican II says:

The bishops are heralds of the faith who lead new disciples to Christ; they are authentic teachers, i.e., endowed with the authority of Christ. To the people entrusted to them they proclaim the message of faith and apply it to the moral life and expound it in the light of the Holy Spirit by bringing forth new and old from the treasure of revelation (cf. Matt 13:52). They thus make the faith become fruitful and they vigilantly keep their flock away from threatening errors (cf. 2 Tim 4:1-4—*Lumen gentium* 25).[1]

The liturgy of the ordination of bishops describes the obligations of the bishop. The first question addresses the most important task: "Will you make every effort to penetrate with all your wisdom into the understanding of Holy Scripture?" The second question is: "Will you in word and example teach what you have read in the study of Holy Scripture to the people for whom you are consecrated?"[2]

This duty is then expressed in an impressive symbol: the book of the Gospels is laid on the neck of the bishop being consecrated—an eloquent sign of who is the master and who the servant; then follows the laying on of hands. In doing so, the consecrators say: "Receive the Holy Spirit!" Towards the end of the ordination ceremony, the book of the Gospels is handed over with the words: "Take the Gospel! Go and

---

1. *Lumen gentium*, no. 25.
2. Cf. H. Fries,"Die Bedeutung der Heiligen Schrift für die Kirche nach katholischem Verständnis" in: *Zur Auferbauung des Leibes Christi*, Festgabe für Peter Brunner (Kassel, 1965) 28–40, at 28.

preach it to the people entrusted to you! God is powerful to give you His grace. He lives and reigns for ever."

At the councils and at conciliar meetings, the Bible is solemnly enthroned and placed in the middle of the council hall. This ceremony is doubtless intended to express the will and intention that all the considerations and decisions of a council are intended to stand in the service of Holy Scripture and, ultimately, of its interpretation.

All this constitutes a powerful expression of the extent to which bishops, in carrying out their office and their responsibility as witnesses of faith and of the teaching of the Holy Scripture, are obligated to its proclamation, communication, and interpretation.

Dogma and Holy Scripture

The ecclesiastical magisterium refers to sacred Scripture when it exercises its function in important matters: in its decisions in faith and doctrine as they are made, for example, in general councils, in the formulation of propositions of faith, and of dogmas, which claim to be the contents of the revelation of God and thus also the contents of faith.

Dogmas are statements of faith with the claim to be true and to be binding. If that is so, then dogmas must have a basis in the basic document of faith, Sacred Scripture. Accordingly, dogmas are also a consequence of the Church's connection with Scripture; they are an interpretation of Scripture in view of a concrete situation that requires a decision and needs clarity. Thus dogmas are an interpretation of Scripture in the language and in the concepts of a particular epoch.

In faith and doctrinal decisions, in dogmatic formulations of the ecclesiastical magisterium, one constantly finds references to Sacred Scripture and quotations from it. This is understandable and necessary if these decisions are to express that what is said in dogma—expressed often in unbiblical language and philosophical concepts—is related to the origin of faith and its basic document.

First of all, the texts from Holy Scripture found in the dogmas are only quoted; they are not presented by the magisterium in a kind of exegesis. They serve as factual evidence, as *"dicta probantia,"* i.e. as passages that confirm what is said by the magisterium. In other words, doctrinal decisions do not result from some kind of magisterial exegesis. Doctrinal decisions are statements about some aspect of the faith which has to be decided, or perhaps limited, here and now. These decisions concern some aspect of the content of faith that is now alive in the faith of the Church as a whole, i.e., present in the Church's confession of faith, in its preaching, in the liturgy, and also, primarily, in the witness of Scripture.

Several points must be underlined: There are very few bible texts whose meaning the magisterium has declared to be binding. There are twelve New Testament, passages about which it can be said that a doctrinal decision follows *de textu citato*, i.e. by appealing to the quoted biblical text. These passages are related (as, e.g., at the Council of Trent) to original sin, baptism, Eucharist, and confession. In Vatican I, Scripture is explicitly appealed to in support of so-called "natural revelation," as well as for the position of Peter, for his primacy and power of the keys. But even for these doctrines, no individual exegesis is given in the conciliar texts; it is said only that some specific content of doctrine and faith has its factual support and its "ultimate basis" in the scriptural text(s) referred to. Thus—on the part of Catholicism—no particular exegesis is either prescribed or forbidden.

One must also be aware of one of Catholic theology's valid principles of interpretation. This states that the claim to the binding quality, the claim to the truth, and, ultimately, to the "infallibility" of an aspect of faith present in a dogma is related to and limited to only that specific aspect of faith. This means that the grounding reasons of a biblical, historical, or even philosophical nature which are claimed as evidence and support for these statements of faith, do not, in their function as grounding reasons, share in the infallibility of the dogma itself. This means that the claiming of a specific biblical text as evidence and proof of a dogma does not say that we have here an infallible application of Scripture in the sense of a scriptural interpretation of the magisterium. This is, among other things, a demonstration of the primacy and superiority of praxis, of the lived faith, of faith existence, over its theoretical grounding—apart from the fact that the biblical texts on baptism and Eucharist describe a praxis. In this rule of interpretation, exegesis as scholarly interpretation of Scripture is left to, and confirmed in, its proper sphere of activity.

But this leads to another problem.

The Magisterium and the Interpretation of Scripture

The Councils of Trent as well as of Vatican I and II have made the following statements on the interpretation of Scripture. Trent decreed:

In order to keep irresponsible spirits in check: no one should presume, in matters of faith and morals which belong to the building up of Christian doctrine, trusting in his own cleverness, either to twist the Scripture to his own purpose against the meaning which Holy Mother the Church held and holds—she is the one to pass judgment on the true meaning and explanation of Sacred Scripture—or to interpret Sacred Scripture contrary to the unanimous opinion of the Fathers.[3]

3. DS 1507 (cf. NR 86).

This text had in mind specific abuses of the time; its purpose is to bring about a genuine renewal. The abuses of that time related to "irresponsible spirits": they also had in mind the poor theological and, above all, poor exegetical education of priests. This text is intended to counter such things as the proclamations of preachers who, relying on abstruse accounts of miracles and private revelations, were arbitrarily interpreting (twisting) the Scripture as they saw fit, and thus falsifying the gospel.

Against these people, attention was called to that rule of interpretation: The Scripture is to be interpreted in the sense to which the Church has held and still holds. That means, to be concrete—and this was specifically mentioned—in the sense of the *"doctores* and *magistri"* of Sacred Scripture whom the Church recognizes. This means not just the bishops but also theologians and lay people too. As the Council protocol shows, the idea of keeping the interpretation of Scripture solely a matter of the magisterium was explicitly rejected.[4] The sense which the Church has held, and holds means, further: It is the interpretation which is to be found in the authentic tradition, thus the decisions of the councils and also the unanimous witness of the Fathers and Doctors of the Church. Here unanimity is important—one single statement of one single theologian, however wise and important, clearly does not fulfill these conditions.[5]

A further precision is given to the proposition that the competency in interpretation claimed by the magisterium is related to the sphere of faith and morals: to *"fides et mores."* In the meaning of the Council of Trent, under *mores* are to be understood not so much ethical requirements but "customs and usages," i.e., rites and ordinances having to do with worship and the devotional life.

The proposition of the Council would thus have this meaning: As far as dogmatic formulations and ordinances for the Church's worship are concerned, and to the extent that these are affected by interpretation, no one may interpret Scripture against the meaning that is firmly held in the Church. This sets up a negative rule.

These directives were repeated at Vatican I. The Council specifically made its own the decision of Trent:

The blessed doctrinal decision of the assembly of the Church at Trent on the interpretation of Scripture, which was intended to keep irresponsible spirits in check, has been at times badly interpreted. But we renew this decision and declare its meaning to be, that in matters of faith and morals which belong to the building up of Christian doctrine, what is to be taken as the true meaning of Scripture is that

---

4. Cf. H. Kümmeringer, "Es ist Sache der Kirche, 'iudicare de vero sensu et interpretatione scripturarum sanctarum,'" *ThQ* 149 (1969) 282–96.
5. Ibid. 287

which (Holy Mother) the Church has held and still holds. The Church is the one to pass judgment on the true meaning and explanation of Sacred Scripture.[6]

In this text, too, the magisterium does not take charge of exegetical work, thus making it superfluous, or turn it into a mere helping hand for the magisterium. Not one single statement about exegesis is made, nor is any specific exegesis offered; it is instead a programmatic statement about the writings of the Bible—the whole of it.

Authority over Scripture?

Doesn't this still turn the ecclesiastical magisterium into a norm and instance above Scripture, giving it power over Scripture?

What must first be said is that the authority singled out by the ecclesiastical magisterium is not an authority over the Scripture but an authority over the individual and his/her subjectivity, and against possible arbitrariness. Trent explicitly mentioned the enthusiasts. In general terms, what it intends to say is that for the interpretation of Scripture, the community of the Church, its traditions, its interpretation of Scripture in the form of confessional formulas and liturgies, constitute a negative rule. One may not offend against this context and horizon; they must be respected.

In interpreting Scripture in this sense, the Church, in the form of the ecclesiastical magisterium, does not set itself over Scripture but is bound to it. In principle, whoever interprets—and precisely whoever does this authentically—is setting him/herself not over but under the text being interpreted, under the Word, under Scripture. A binding interpretation does not express control over what is being interpreted but expresses the most responsible service and dedication to and concern for it. Thus it can also be said: The Church, precisely as the Scripture-reading and Scripture-interpreting Church, remains subordinated to the witness of Scripture as witness of the Word of God. Its intention is to make effective the authority and saving power of the Word of God, not to assert itself.

In passing judgment on this, we must do so from the background of this basic intention, and not from the human failures, abuses, and mistakes that occur in carrying out this task. The originality and legitimacy of this mandate are not canceled by such failings.

The authority of the Church is thus an authority of interpretation, with a normative function and meaning for the individual. But the primary intention of the Church is not thereby to bind its members to itself or to "put them on a chain,"[7] but rather to "draw them into its own

---

6. DS 3007 (cf. NR 89).
7. H. Graß, *Die katholische lehre von der Heiligen Schrift und von der Tradition* (Lüneburg, 1954); K. G. Steck, *Das römische Lehramt und die Heilige Schrift* (Munich, 1963).

subordinate position under the Word of God in Scripture."[8] The authority of the Church is and remains subordinate to the witness of Scripture. The interpretive word of the Church is guided by the Word of Scripture and makes it present.

This means that the ecclesiastical magisterium is not the norm of Scripture but is itself the normed norm (*norma normata*) with regard to the understanding of Scripture of the individual Christian.

Holy Scripture is itself both the expression of and the witness of the faith and confession of the Church at its origins. Further, the process by which different writings become part of the canon of Holy Scripture, the process of separation from the apocryphal writings, was a process of development and testing. This culminated in the Church's making decisions ultimately on the basis of the faith alive in it, and on the basis of its orientation in its "rule of faith," in its confessing, and in its worship. Logically then, the interpretation of Scripture cannot be separated out from this inner context. There is nothing here that is inappropriate or forced, but a perfectly natural connection.

There is a further fact to be considered: The description of the road from the Council of Trent to Vatican I must include, among other things, the fact that in the living tradition of the Church the element of authority became stronger and stronger. In addition, the magisterium represented in the college of bishops became concentrated more and more in the magisterium of the Bishop of Rome. There was also the tendency to limit more and more the independence of scholarly theology. The task of the theologians, above all of the exegetes, was described as simply to provide the proof from Scripture and Tradition for the decisions of the ecclesiastical magisterium. Since Pius IX, it was seen as the most important task of theology to show how a doctrine, in the sense in which it is defined, is contained in the sources of revelation.[9] This came about for the fantastic [by hindsight] reason that it would be methodologically false if theology were to appeal to the sources against the magisterium. For one cannot explain what is clear (the current official teaching) from what is unclear (the sources of revelation); one must proceed inversely. It has been rightly said that this threatened to bring about a "disenfranchisement of the sources which would have finally eliminated the servant-aspect of the magisterium if one were to continue to move in this direction."[10]

8. P. Lengsfeld, *Überlieferung, Tradition und Schrift in der evangelischen und katholischen Theologie der Gegenwart* (Paderborn 1960) 196; also *Tradition und Heilige Schrift* in *MySal* 1.463–96; K. Rahner, "Scripture and Tradition," *SM* 6.54–57; W. Kasper, *Dogma under dem Wort Gottes* (Mainz, 1965).

9. M. Seckler, "Theologie als kirchliche Wissenschaft—ein römisches Modell" in: *Im Spannungsfeld von Wissenschaft und Kirche* (Freiburg—Basel—Vienna, 1980) 62, 84, at 79.

10. J. Ratzinger, *Commentary on the Documents of Vatican II*, ed. H. Vorgimler, 3.196–97.

The institution and the early activity of the so-called Biblical Commission has to be seen from the background of this mentality and this conception of theology. It is an establishment of the ecclesiastical magisterium, founded by Pope Leo XIII. This papal commission was to be a board consisting of "eminent scholars." Its task was to assure, by any means, that Catholics everywhere give to Holy Scripture the careful treatment required by the conditions of the time, and that Scripture be kept free not only from every "breath of error" but also from any excessively free opinion. The opening word of the papal writing "Vigilantiae" declares its program. Under Pius IX, further precision in the direction of this "watchfulness" was given to the tasks of the Biblical Commission: the commission took to answering questions on biblical problems. It did this above all in its decrees called "responsa," which treated the questions put to it mostly with only a negative or positive answer: "negative" or "affirmative." The series of responsa given between 1905 and 1915 dealt with the following questions: the theory of only apparently historical narratives; Moses as author of the Pentateuch; the author and historical reliability of the Gospel of John; Isaiah; the historicity of Genesis 1–3; the author and time of composition of the Psalms; the temporal priority of the Gospel of Matthew; the synoptic question; the Acts of the Apostles; Paul as author of the Pastoral letters and the Letter to the Hebrews; the so-called Johannine comma (1 John 5: 7-8) as authentic text.[11]

All the decisions made by the Biblical Commission on these questions have proven to be untenable. To be fair, one must add that the decisions of the Biblical commission referred primarily to the question of whether the historical arguments brought to bear up to that time were sufficient to reject traditional conceptions. The answer was, each time, No. The only decision to be revoked was that of 1897 on the Johannine comma. In 1927 the Biblical Commission wrote: "This decree was once promulgated in order to reign in the audacity of private scholars who presumed either to overthrow entirely the authenticity of the Johannine comma (1 John 5: 7-8)or, on the basis of their own ultimately valid judgment, to cast doubt upon it. But it did not intend in any way to keep Catholic exegetes from investigating the matter itself more comprehensively."[12]

Certainly, it can be said that the decisions of the Biblical Commission were more of a pastoral than of a doctrinal nature; they

---

11. The decisions of the Biblical Commission are contained in the *Enchiridion biblicum* (Rome, 1954). Among the errors of the Modernists, their ideas on magisterium and Bible, on inspiration, and on a series of other exegetical questions were condemned. Cf. also *DS* 3401–3419, (NR 104–7; 389–90; 108–18), 3505–3528. Cf. H. Fries,"Das Kirchliche Lehramt und die exegetische Arbeit" in H. Kahlefeld, ed., *Schriftauslegung dient dem Glauben* (Frankfurt, 1979) 56–90.

12. DS 3682.

were never at any time seen as "infallible." In addition, the time in which this commission worked—especially under Pius X—was one of excitement, uncertainty, worry, and fear. It was believed that the situation could be controlled only with clear statements and with the decisiveness of prohibitions. It was, after all, the time of Modernism, the time when the historical critical method was struggling to find its rightful place in Catholic theology. Its first representative however was a Catholic theologian, the Oratorian Richard Simon, whose writings, at the insistence of Bishop J. B. Bossuet, were put on the Index of Forbidden Books.[13]

The decisions of the Biblical Commission and the consequent indexing of the works of Catholic exegetes turned out to be a severe blow to Catholic exegesis. They crippled energies and deprived exegetes of the courage to publish findings based on historical-critical exegesis. As Joseph A. Fitzmyer described the situation: "As a result of these decrees, a dark cloud of reactionary conservatism overshadowed almost all of biblical science for the first half of our century."[14]

The New Situation

A change from this crippling, oppressive, and frustrating situation was brought about—astonishingly—by the ecclesiastical magisterium itself, by Pope Pius XII. His 1943 encyclical *Divino afflante spiritu*[15] on the up-to-date promotion of biblical studies stands as the Magna Charta of Catholic exegesis. It opened up and specified the exegetical task and liberated it from the pressures, curtailments, and investigations under which exegetes stood. It meant the emancipation of exegesis from the status of an auxiliary science relegated to supporting theological systems or legitimating ecclesiastical practices.

Here are some of the points made in this important document: The most important task of exegetes, using text criticism and their knowledge of ancient languages, is to discover and explain the true meaning of the sacred books. In doing so, those who expound Scripture should keep in mind that their primary concern must be to find out what is the literal sense of the biblical word. Above all they must point out the theological-doctrinal content of the individual books and texts in questions of faith and morals. Their explanation of Scripture is to be not just of use to theologians in their presentation and proof of the doctrines of faith, but also to be of assistance to priests in their preaching of Christian doctrine to the people, and finally to help all the faithful to lead holy

13. Cf. H. Graf Reventlow, "Richard Simon (1638-1760)" in: *Klassiker der Theologie*, ed. H. Fries—G. Kretschmar, (Munich, 1983) 2.9–21.

14. J. Fitzmyer, *Die Wahrheit der Evangelien* (Stuttgart, 1965).

15. Text in: *Enchiridion biblicum* 201–27; excerpts in DS 3825–31 (cf. NR 126a–c).

lives worthy of Christians. If Catholic exegetes provide that kind of an interpretation of Scripture, which is above all of a theological nature, they will effectively reduce to silence those who keep insisting that they can find in biblical commentaries hardly anything that raises the spirit to God, nourishes souls, and promotes the interior life—thus giving support to their claim that they must take refuge in a spiritual and, as they say, mystical explanation.

The text points out that in ancient Oriental authors the literal sense of a passage is often not as clear as it is with contemporary authors. What the ancient Orientals intend to say cannot be determined merely by the rules of grammar or philology, or just from the context. The exegete must travel back in spirit, so to speak, to those distant centuries of the Orient, and with the help of history, archaeology, ethnology, and other sciences, figure out precisely what literary forms the authors of that ancient age intended to use and in reality did use. What these modes of speech were cannot be determined a priori by the exegete, but only from a careful study of Oriental literature.

The Catholic exegete is expected to put all knowledge coming from archaeology, history, and literary studies at the service of a better explanation and interpretation of Scripture. Exegetes are also explicitly encouraged to use the secular sciences in their attempts to solve problems. The faithful for their part are urged to judge all these attempts not only as proper but also with great love. There is an explicit warning not to oppose or suspect the new just because it is new. This guiding document closes with the words: "The theological disciplines must be constantly rejuvenated and renewed from the study of the Bible as a sacred source."

Vatican II was also a council of renewal in this area. Renewal as program always also means renewal from the origin, from the normative witness of faith, concretely, from Holy Scripture. Its biblical orientation and perspective belongs, along with its pastoral and ecumenical dimension, to the characteristics of this council. More than in other councils, the Bible stands in the forefront—but again not as magisterial exegesis of individual passages, but as orientation to the reality to which Scripture gives witness.

The Dogmatic Constitution on the Church illustrates this. Not every passage it quotes fulfills, exegetically, an irrefutably probative function for what it teaches. But how very effective is its fundamental orientation to its origin in the New Testament is already visible in its description of the Church. It doesn't simply repeat and polish up the traditional, certainly biblical, image of the Church as Body of Christ; it is expanded by the now-fundamental biblical concept of Church as the People of God. And what still needs to be said about the Church is not done with socio-political models, e.g. of a *societas perfecta*, but clarified in the—to be sure, only briefly presented—use of many biblical images. Nor are these images replaced by a concept of the Church. The images remain there as images, each of them shedding light on some dimension of the Church. The purpose of the many images is to describe a differentiated reality: Church.

The Constitution on the Liturgy *(Sacrosanctum concilium)* speaks about the presence of Christ in the Word: "He is present in his Word, since it is he himself who is speaking, when Sacred Scripture is read in the Church" (no. 7). It says further that, for the benefit of the faithful, the table of the Word should be spread more richly and the treasury of the Bible opened further (no. 51). In the comparatives found here: "better, richer, deeper," is certainly also the admission that, in this matter, not enough was being done in the past.

Even more important than this is the fact that Vatican II, in its own constitution *Dei verbum,* On Divine Revelation, also took up the question of Scripture and the theme we have been discussing. It especially addresses the connections between Scripture, tradition, Church, and magisterium, and declares:

Sacred tradition and Sacred Scripture form the one sacred treasure of the Word of God given to the Church. In full devotion to this Word, the whole holy people, united with its shepherds, persevere constantly in the teaching and communion of the apostles, in the breaking of the bread and prayer (cf. Acts 2:42), so that in holding fast to the faith handed on to them, in living it out and confessing it, a unique harmony reigns between leaders and faithful. (no. 10)

The understanding of the definition of the content and the interrelationship of Scripture and tradition had been for some time a subject of lively discussion in Catholic theology. The Council of Trent had declared that the gospel which was promised by the prophets, proclaimed by Jesus Christ, and preached by the apostles as the source of all saving truth and moral order "is contained in written books and unwritten traditions which the apostles have received from the mouth of Christ, or which was handed on from hand to hand, so to speak, from the apostles themselves under the inspiration of the Holy Spirit, and thus come down to us."[16]

The question is: How is the "and" to be understood in "written books and unwritten traditions"? An indication of the importance of the question comes from the fact that the Latin *"et*—and" has taken the place of the originally proposed *"partim—partim*/partly—partly."

The interpretation offered by J. R. Geiselmann and developed by him in numerous investigations[17] which have met with widespread

---

16. DS 1501 (cf. NR 80–81).
17. Finally: *Die Heilige Schrift und die Tradition. Zu den neueren Controversen über das Verhältnis der Heiligen Schrift zu den nichtgeschriebenen Traditionen* (Freiburg—Basel—Vienna, 1962).

agreement in today's Catholic theology says that this change is not accidental but intentional. The intention is that the relationship between Scripture and tradition is not to be so determined that one part of the gospel is contained in Scripture and another part in tradition, which would mean that one would get the whole of the revealed Word by adding up the content of Scripture and tradition. The true description of the relationship between Scripture and tradition is to be understood in such a way that Scripture and tradition are two modes and means of communication, in each of which the whole gospel, the whole message of salvation, comes to us, even if in its own different mode of existence.

Vatican II left this question, and the possibility of a Catholic understanding of the *sola scriptura* principle, open. "But the task of explaining the written or handed-on Word of God in a binding manner is entrusted only to the living magisterium of the Church, whose authority is exercised in the name of Christ" (no. 10).

A correct understanding of what is said here can be gained by comparing it with a text of the Pius XII's 1950 encyclical *Humani generis*. One reads there that the divine Redeemer has entrusted his Word "neither to the individual faithful nor to the theologians as such for authentic interpretation, but only to the magisterium."[18] This "*soli magisterio*" is also taken up in Vatican II's constitution on revelation, but the context there makes it clear "that the function of authentic interpretation restricted to the magisterium is a specific service, which does not encompass all of the ways in which the Word is present; for among these is an irreplaceable function belonging also to the whole Church, bishops and laypeople together."[19]

But there is one question which we must raise. It is quite striking that in the documents of the magisterium the presumably Protestant "*particula exclusiva*" in the sense of the "alone" [faith alone, Scripture alone, etc.] are used repeatedly: e.g. "only to the magisterium." Wouldn't it have made good sense and also been quite appropriate in this context, to have also use the Catholic "and"? Are not, after all, the factual presuppositions for it already present?[20]

The Doctrine of Inspiration

Vatican I expressed the doctrine of the inspiration of Scripture in the following words: The Sacred Scriptures are "holy and canonical because, written under the inspiration of the Holy Spirit, they have God as their author and as such have been handed on to the Church."[21] Leo

---

18. DS 3886 (NR 398).
19. J. Ratzinger, *Commentary on the Documents of Vatican II*, ed. H. Vorgimler, 3.196–97.
20. Cf. M. Seckler, *ThQ* 153 (1973) 182.
21. DS 3006 (NR 87–88).

XIII's encyclical *Providentissimus Deus*, describes inspiration further by noting that the Holy Spirit "inspires [the hagiographers] with supernatural power to write so that they would correctly understand all that and only that which the Spirit willed, and write it down faithfully, suitably expressing it in infallible truth. Otherwise he [Holy Spirit] would not be the author of all of Sacred Scripture."[22]

The divine authorship does not exclude but includes the real authorship of the human hagiographers. This has customarily been explained by the concept—itself very much in need of explanation—of God as the principal cause and humans as the instrumental cause, in which the uniqueness, creativity, individuality, and freedom of the human authors, who are more than just "secretaries," is preserved.

In its Constitution on Revelation, Vatican II took over and developed further the earlier teaching of the magisterium:

In composing the sacred books, God chose men who while employed by Him made use of their powers and abilities so that with Him acting in them and through them, they as true authors consigned to writing everything and only those things which he wanted. Therefore, since everything asserted by the inspired authors or sacred writers must be held to be asserted by the Holy Spirit, it follows that the books of Scripture must be acknowledged as teaching firmly, faithfully, and without error that truth which God wanted put into the sacred writings for the sake of our salvation (no. 11).

The formula "for the sake of our salvation" is the decisive, new statement; in view of the distinction between saving truths and "secular truths," it admits the specification: "Everything in Sacred Scripture shares in the truth which God, for the sake of our salvation, wanted to have written down. It shares in this truth either immediately, in its contents, or mediately because of its service to the saving message."[23]

The council's text goes on:

Since God speaks in Sacred Scripture through human beings in human fashion, the interpreter of Sacred Scripture, in order to see clearly what God wanted to communicate to us, should carefully investigate what meaning the sacred writers really intended, and what God wanted to manifest by means of their words. Those who search out the intention of the sacred writers must among other things, have regard for the "literary forms." For truth is proposed and expressed in a variety of ways, depending on whether a text is history of one kind or another, or whether its form is that of prophecy, poetry, or some other type of speech. (no. 12)

The most illuminating interpretation of inspiration seems to me to be found in the considerations of Karl Rahner.[24] His starting point is that with Jesus Christ, as he is proclaimed and made present in the

---

22. DS 3293 (NR 100).

23. A. Grillmeier, in *Commentary on the Documents of Vatican II*, ed. by H. Vorgrimler, 200–25.

24. K. Rahner, *Inspiration in the Bible*, trans. Charles H. Henkey (New York: Herder and Herder, 1961); "Inspiration," in *HThG* 1. 717–25.

apostolic preaching, the absolute and definitive self-revelation of God has taken place. In this sense, revelation is closed off with the death of the apostles, i.e., with the end of the apostolic age—or, as one can also say, with the primitive Church. Christian revelation is designated for all times and all peoples and must always remain present. To make this possible, God so established the primitive Church, in its faith consciousness as source and norm of the faith of later times, in such a way that it can really exercise this function.

To this endowment of the primitive Church belongs also Scripture, as a record both of the apostolic kerygma constitutive of the primitive Church and of the faith consciousness grounded therein.

Since the Church concretizes in writing its paradosis, its faith, and its self-realization, thus forming Scripture in itself (per se), it orients itself as the normative primitive Church towards its own future. And conversely, since it is constituted for this future as its normative law, according to which the whole future of the Church has come about, it forms Scripture. Precisely in the formation of the Scripture it confirms that unique, distinguishing self-understanding that must belong to it in a special degree so that it can be the canon of the later Church.[25]

Scripture does not simply happen to come about in the course of the establishment of the primitive Church; rather, the active, inspiring, authorship of God is an inner moment of the church-building of the primitive Church, and it draws its distinguishing characteristics from the fact that this is what it is. God wills the Scripture and himself as its author, and established both of them because and to the extent that he wills to be active and effective as the originator of the Church. The inspiration of Scripture is really only God's founding of the Church at least in the sense that this divine founding is related as such to that constitutive element of the Church, which the Scripture actually is.[26]

It is from this point that Karl Rahner attempts also to explain the inspiration of the writings of the Old Testament:

Because and also to the extent that the Old Testament belongs from the outset to the formation of the Church (and not just of the Synagogue) as a part of its prehistory, and, to be sure, of that part which remains actual forever, what is true of the writings of the New Testament is true also of the Old Testament: as a moment in the formal, predefining Church, these writings are inspired by God.[27]

Of course, this principle by no means provides the answer to all particular problems. But it does set up a fundamental-theological framework within which concrete solutions can be sought.

25. K. Rahner, Inspiration in the Bible 48–49.
26. Ibid. 50–51.
27. Ibid. 54.

§ 60

CHURCH AND CHURCHES

The problem of "Church and Churches" occupies a different place in the fundamental theology of today than it did in earlier presentations of apologetics or fundamental theology.

The "demonstratio catholica"

In earlier times, the so-called *demonstratio catholica* went as follows: The Church of Jesus Christ exists only in the singular. There is, in other words, one and only one true Church. Reference was made to the numerous biblical references that speak of the Church in the singular, above all to Matthew 16:17–19, where Jesus speaks explicitly of "My Church." Consideration was given, in addition, to other biblical images for Church, such as flock, plant, building, temple, bride, body whose head is Christ; they all refer to the Church in the singular, to one Church. This impression is strengthened by the statements of the Captivity Epistles about the Church as the Body of Christ, as well as by recalling the urgent exhortations to unity, (above all from the mouth of Paul) connected with the struggle against division, dissension, and disturbances of unity (cf. 1 Cor 1:12–13; Eph 4:1–13).

But along with this we also have the sad and undeniable historical fact and experience that even very early, and precisely in reference to the idea of the one Church, there arose, divisions, mutual rejections, and excommunications. As a result, there were also, and almost from the very outset, churches in the plural. But this plural, as opposed to the plural of the local churches, was seen as illegitimate, something that shouldn't be. This held for both sides of the equation: the community from which the separation took place, but which was so to speak "*in possessione*" and saw itself as the old Church, as Church of the authentic tradition, knew itself at the same time as the one true Church of Jesus Christ from which the "newer" ones had separated and therefore had no right to call themselves Church of Jesus Christ. And from their side, the newer churches objected that the old church had not remained true to its origin, had lost continuity and identity, had withdrawn itself from the call to repentance and renewal, and had thus made separation from itself unavoidable; accordingly, only the new community can be the one true Church of Jesus Christ. But in any case, in terms of the legitimacy claimed by either side, there is only one Church, in the singular.

The growing distance from the old Church, and consequent division into parts, was accompanied by tensions right from the onset. On can see these tensions in the dogmatic controversies in Christological and Trinitarian questions, in the variety of church discipline and practice (controversy about the date of Easter, controversy about the baptism of heretics), and in the different theologies in the Western and Eastern Church. This kind of tension-producing separation, especially in the Middle Ages, in the now Christian West, in the *Imperium Christianum* as successor to the *Imperium Romanum*, also became a political issue. For despite the tensions between imperium and sacerdotium, between emperor and pope, it was important that this unity, which drew support and solidity above all from its unity of faith, its ecclesiastical unity, not be endangered. That there be one Church lay in the interest of both Church and state. Deviations from faith, dividing off into one's own group against the one Church—as happened after the Council of Chalcedon (450)—which in the meantime had become the great Church, the popular Church, these were not only of theological but also of political concern. They were therefore to be investigated, rejected, and fought against—and this with no less rigor than against an enemy from without.

Still, all this was not enough to prevent the 1054 division of the Church into the Church of the West and the Church of the East. After a long process of alienation, each side mutually condemned and excommunicated the other; each maintained for itself the claim to be the one, true, "orthodox" Church. Despite the schism, neither Church went so far as to dispute the other's claim to the predicate "Church." Unity in faith, sacrament, and hierarchical structure (with the exception of the recognition of the papacy as jurisdictional instance over the whole Church) remained intact. The differences between East and West, which did not justify any separation in faith, did in fact create that kind of a separation. The mutual excommunication and the schism connected with it did have, in fact, the same consequences as separation in faith: nonrecognition, alienation, hostility. The union councils of the Middle Ages did nothing to change this condition; their agreements were not met with reception.

So, there did arise church in the plural: Church of the West and Church of the East. No one felt this was satisfactory. It was seen as a misfortune, but possible.

This was changed by the divisions of Western Christendom in the sixteenth-century Reformation and its attendant movements. The Reformation originally intended no division into Church and churches; its concern was for the renewal of the existing Church with pope and bishops, for a renewal based on the normative source of Holy Scripture. The failure of these reform efforts led to the division of Christianity into different confessions: into the old Church and the Churches of the Reformation. In contrast to the separation of the Eastern and Western Church, there was now, here, a separation in faith; it was obviously deeper and more serious that the schism between the Eastern and Western Churches.

The old Church maintained its claim to be the one Church of Jesus Christ and to have preserved its unity in continuity, that unity from which the "newer" churches fell away. But these, for their part, maintained that the continuity of the original and still-existing Church is found in their own community, while the Roman Catholic Church is the one that fell away from its origin and distorted the form of the one true Church by "additions," and corrupted it even to the point of unrecognizability.

We have here churches in the plural which, in view of the will of Jesus and of his plea "that all who believe in him should be one" (John 17:21), and which, measured against the incessant exhortation of the Apostle Paul to the unity of the Body whose head is Christ, is certainly illegitimate—it should and must not be; it is wrong. But we also have here the respective claim of each of these churches to be the one Church of Jesus Christ, and thus to possess that singular of Church which belongs to the Church of Christ and is denied of the other churches. The fact of churches in the plural becomes a Christianity-wide scandal, a worldwide scandal. But the confessions declare, from their side, that the division is necessary for the sake of the truth, for the "sake of the salvation of souls," and must thus be maintained, if necessary even by force and by war.

The Signs of the Church

In this time of altercation caused by the Reformation, the question arose of the signs of the one, true Church of Jesus Christ, the question of the *notae ecclesiae*. It became a basic theme of theology.

According to the Reformers, the true Church of Jesus Christ is found where the gospel is preached in its purity and the holy sacraments are administered according to the gospel (*Confessio Augustana*, art. 7). To be added to this, according to the Reformational point of view is that, for the public ministry to gospel and sacrament, the "office of preaching" has been instituted by God (art. 5)., to which office one must be duly called (*"rite vocatus,"* art. 14). The other Reformers, especially Calvin, but also the Anglicans, have specified the signs of the Church in similar ways.

The same question was approached within the Catholic Church, but in a different way, in the context of the so-called *"demonstratio catholica."* The characteristics (*proprietates*) of the Church expressed in the Apostles' Creed—unity, holiness, catholicity, and apostolicity—were thus turned into *notae,* to marks of the Church. To be sure, as the explanation went, not every characteristic of the Church is a mark in the sense of a *nota;* but every *nota* is also a characteristic of the Church.

A characteristic of the Church can serve as a mark if it is easily recognizable, accessible to all, belongs exclusively to the Church, and belongs to the Church not intermittently but constantly and essentially. In the *demonstratio catholica,* the faith statements, "I believe in the one, holy, catholic and apostolic Church" become also signs accessible not only to faith but also to rational and historical reason. Now there are all kinds of difficulties and problems connected with this claim. For it is not clear how the same thing, the characteristics of the Church, are both to be believed by the faithful and at the same time to serve as marks accessible to everyone.

According to the *demonstratio catholica,* the argument goes as follows: The premise is: The Church of Jesus Christ was originally instituted with the four marks both as abiding characteristics and as signs of recognition. They are both the contents of faith and its signs of recognition. This thesis is understood as being drawn from the biblical sources and historically proven in such a way that everyone can understand it.

After the premise comes the minor proposition: These four signs of recognition are found, exclusively, in the Catholic Church—a proposition to be empirically established and proven. One has to admit, however, that it is not easy to prove this in a way totally convincing to everyone, so that an argument of credibility can be built on it. Such a proof presupposes extensive experience, and it has to face up to all kinds of opposite experiences, if one is not simply to be selectively comparing a luminous ideal from one's own side with quite different manifestations of reality from the other side.

The strengthening of the probative thrust of the *demonstratio catholica* did not content itself with claiming positively that these signs are found in the Catholic Church; it attempted also to prove negatively that these signs are not found in any of the other other churches, or at least not in the same pronounced way in which they are found in the Catholic Church.

As a result of the great difficulty of actually proving this, the argument of the *demonstratio catholica* was oversimplified, concentrated, and reduced to the so-called *via primatus* or *nota romanitatis*. Thus simplified, the argument unqualifiedly asserts that the true Church is where the pope is; the presence of the pope is what makes the Catholic Church Roman Catholic. Whichever church can claim this one, easily recognizable sign also, automatically so to speak, has the other signs. For, it was claimed (not argued, it must be noted): The Roman Church with the pope at its head possesses the four marks—one, holy, catholic, and apostolic—causatively; i.e., it is a causative source of these marks for the other churches, who possess them only participatively. The primacy, *Romanitas*, thus became an easily usable *nota characteristica et sufficiens*. But "since the process of proving this always drew back into territory unreachable by external argument, it became logically more and more cogent, and theologically more and more questionable."[1]

Briefly put, this results in the following argument: Only the Catholic Church possesses the marks which are at the same time the characteristics of the Church of Christ: unity, holiness, catholicity, apostolicity. It, therefore, is the one and only Church of Jesus Christ.[2] The other churches have no claim to the predicate "church," because the marks and characteristics are not found in them, or only partially, or in a fragmented way.

In this perspective the Catholic Church is

the broad stream which has borne through the centuries, and still bears, the movement that begins with Christ. The other churches are rivulets which have branched off from this stream and, to the extent that they have not petered out and dried up, or flowed back again into the great streambed, cannot compete with it in either external fullness or inner dynamic.[3]

The following consequences flow from this: The plural of churches is illegitimate; it contradicts the will of Jesus and the essence of the Church. Christian communities outside the one, true Church, the Roman Catholic Church, cannot be given the name "church," even if they claim it for themselves. With the exception of the Eastern Church, they are *"sectae acatholicae,"* heretical communities, "religious communities" (not churches) with "religious servants" (not ordained ministers).

1. M. Seckler, "Katholisch als Kofessionsbezeichnung" *ThQ* 145 (1965) 404. Cf. G. Thils, *Les notes de l'église dans l'apologétique catholique depuis la Reforme* (Gembloux, 1937).

2. Johanes Brunsman, *A Handbook of Fundamental Theology* (St. Louis: B. Herder Co., 1928); J. Brinktrine, *Offenbarung und Kirche* II (Paderborn, 1949) 232–84.

3. A. Lang, *Fundamentaltheologie* II. *Der Auftrag der Kirche* (Munich, 1958) 820–22.

Rightly seen, therefore, in this traditional Catholic view, one cannot say that the Church is separated and divided. The one, real Church is by no means divided, for it continually strengthens itself in that unity which, especially since Vatican I, is pushed to the point of unicity. From this viewpoint, one can say only that the others have broken away, have left the house of their father, like the prodigal son in the gospel parable of Luke 15.

The Church and the Question of Salvation

Since earliest times, the question of the true Church has been connected with the question of salvation. This was expressed in the proposition (since Cyprian no longer silent): "*Extra ecclesiam nulla salus*— Outside the Church there is no salvation." Cyprian applied this proposition to those who had broken off from the Church, or were in danger of doing so. He didn't quite turn it into a general principle. In addition, he understood under *salus* the means of salvation. But Cyprian's proposition subsequently took on an unrestricted meaning in the *Dictatus papae* of Gregory VII (1073-85), in the bull *Unam sanctam* of Boniface VIII in 1302, and in the 1442 Decree for the Jacobites. The bull *Unam sanctam* states: The

one and only Church does not have two heads like a monstrous birth, but only one body and one head, namely Christ and His representative, Peter and his successors. For the Lord said to Peter personally: "Feed my sheep" (John 21:17). "My" is what He said, and he meant it quite generally, not just an individual this one or that. It follows that He entrusts all of them to Peter. Thus, if Greeks or others say that they are not entrusted to Peter and his successors, they must then also necessarily admit that they are not among the sheep of Christ, since the Lord says in John: "There is only one sheepfold and only one shepherd" (John 10:16).[4]

"To subject oneself to the pope of Rome is for all human beings absolutely necessary for salvation: this we declare, maintain, define, and proclaim."[5] In its doctrinal decision for the Jacobites, the Council of Florence (1438-1443) pushed this axiom to the limit when it declared that "no one outside the Catholic Church, neither pagan, nor Jew, nor unbeliever, or anyone separated from the unity, will share in eternal life unless they join the Church before death." Even this proposition was essentially sharpened with a quotation from Fulgentius of Ruspe: "However much alms people may give, or even shed their blood for the name of Christ, they still cannot be saved unless they remain in the womb and in the unity of the Catholic Church."[6]

4. DS 872 (NR 341).
5. DS 875 (NR 342).
6. DS 1351.

However much the extraordinary and heroic missionary zeal of the Church may have been motivated by it, the consequences, for the salvation of those who were not members of this Church, of the axiom *Extra ecclesiam nulla salus* seemed unsupportable. For those who did not belong to this Church, as it seemed, would not be saved. But how can this be brought into line with God's universal salvific will that all human beings be saved (1 Tim 2:4)? And just as fraught with unsupportable misunderstanding is the opposite consequence, i.e., that belonging to the Roman Catholic Church is a sure guarantee, almost an infallible guarantee, of eternal salvation. But this proposition, certainly, was never expressed by any serious-minded Catholic theology.

Furthermore, it is practically impossible to bring the proposition "Outside the Church is no salvation" into line with the fundamentally contradictory, explicit condemnation of the proposition of Paschase Quesnel: "Outside the Church there is no grace.[7]

The dilemma of the proposition "Outside the Church is no salvation" called out for a solution. Pope Pius IX's formulation of it read:

We must hold in faith that outside of the Apostolic Roman Catholic Church no one can be saved. It is the sole ark of salvation, and everyone who does not enter into it must drown in the flood. But we must also firmly hold that in the eyes of the Lord, no one will be held guilty of this who lives in invincible ignorance of the true religion.[8]

This explanation, that because of guiltless, invincible ignorance, salvation can still be attained despite nonadherence to the Catholic Church , did not seem in the long run to be a satisfactory and adequate answer. That the basis of salvation should be only something negative and defective, an "error," was utterly inappropriate to the reality of salvation as grace and responsibility.

An attempt to deal with this was made by way of a concept presented in Pius XII's 1943 encyclical *Mystici corporis,* which opened up new paths in the theology of the Church. But even here we meet the crystal-clear declaration that the Mystical Body of Christ—the preeminent specification of the essence of the Church—is identical with the concrete Roman Catholic Church.

The relationship of non-Catholic Christians to the Church was described in this encyclical with the categories of the *desiderium inscium* and the *votum,* the unconscious desire and will/wish—thus positively, and not just on the basis of an error. In a clarifying explanation of the Holy Office to Archbishop Cushing of Boston [seeking clarification regarding Leonard Feeney's radical interpretation of the *extra ecclesiam*

---

7. DS 2429.
8. Neuner-Roos 367.

axiom] this *votum* was quite broadly extended to the point of being a *"votum implicitum*—implicit wish."[9]

In the interpretation of contemporary theology, the axiom *Extra ecclesiam nulla salus* is understood not as a personal principle but as an instrumental or reality principle. It does not declare which persons will be saved or not saved—no one can make such a judgment—but it intends to declare that through which salvation comes to human beings when it does come. It is a description of the way in which all are saved who will be saved: through Jesus Christ and through the Church in which he himself and his work are concretely present.[10]

There is accordingly no obstacle, suggests Henri de Lubac, to expressing the formula *Extra ecclesiam nulla salus* positively, and not to say to those of good will: Outside the Church you are damned, but through the Church and only through it are you saved. Salvation comes through the Church, through it salvation is already on the way to humanity. "Only the Christ who is at work in the Church brings about salvation. But his salvation-producing work is not restricted to the Church."[11]

Nevertheless, until Vatican II the question "Church and churches" was answered predominantly in the sense that comes from this brief historical sketch: The Church of Jesus Christ is exclusively identical with the Roman Catholic Church. Church exists only in the singular; a plural of churches is illegitimate. When "church" is spoken of in non-Catholic usage, it is an inexact manner of speaking. The other churches are not *"instrumenta salutis*—instruments of salvation"; only the Church of Christ is this, and this is identical with the Roman Catholic Church.

The New Situation from the Statements of Vatican II

The Second Vatican Council did not by any means elevate the Church to the center of the Christian faith. But in its comprehensive description of the Church, it did lay out its meaning and function and thus come to express that the Church is not the principal reality, but stands in the service of that reality.

Vatican II, which intended to be and was in fact a council for the renewal of the Church, and thus had a specifically ecumenical tone, had to take a new position with regard to the problem of Church and churches. The existing magisterial definitions turned out to be no longer useful. They had understood the unification of separated Christianity

---

9. DS 3866–3873 (NR 398g).

10. M. Schmaus, *Katholische Dogmatik* III/1: *Die Lehre von der Kirche* (Munich, 1958) 820–21.

11. *Katholizismus als Gemeinschaft* (Einsiedeln—Cologne, 1943) 207; cf. W. Kern, *Außerhalb der Kirche kein Heil?* (Freiburg—Basel—Vienna) 1979.

only as a return to the Roman Catholic Church, and thus as unconditional capitulation. The other churches were not prepared to do that.

In the question of "Church and churches," Vatican II found an approach to this problem that tried to find the preservation of identity and continuity not predominantly in negation and separation from everything not itself, but in a way of looking at things that connected fidelity to what is one's own with openness to the other.

The constitution *Lumen gentium* (no. 8) does indeed show its connection to the statements of the encyclical *Mystici corporis* of Pius XII. But it does this with differentiating nuances:

The society (*societas*) endowed with hierarchical organs and the Mystical Body of Christ, the visible assembly and the spiritual community, the earthly Church and the Church endowed with heavenly gifts, are not to be considered as two different realities; they form rather one, single, complex reality, which grows together from human and divine elements.

The basic idea is the analogy of the mystery of the Incarnation of God and of the Church as visible and spiritual community, as earthly Church endowed with heavenly gifts.

The text then continues:

This is the one and only Church of Christ, which we confess in the Creed as one, holy, Catholic, and apostolic. After His resurrection, our Redeemer gave it to Peter to feed; to him and to the rest of the apostles He entrusted its expansion and direction; He established them forever as "pillars and bulwarks of the truth" (1 Tim 3:5). This Church, constituted and set in the world as a society, has its concrete form of existence in the Catholic Church, which is led by the successor of Peter and by the bishops in communion with him. This does not exclude that outside of its structure various elements of sanctification and of truth are to be found which, as their own gifts of the Church of Christ, are pushing towards catholic unity.

In language and intention, these sentences reject any extreme understanding of exclusivity and identity, and at the same time make room for positivity and recognition. This is clearly indicated by an important textual variant. The original text read: "*Haec igitur ecclesia . . . est ecclesia Catholica, a romano Pontifice et Episcopis in eius communione gubernata*" (no. 8). In the final, official text, the *est* has been replaced by *subsistit*. The *est* is exclusive; the *subsistit* is positive and open.[12]

This *subsistit* has the function of "avoiding an uncontrolled identification of the Church of Christ with the Roman Catholic Church, and to remain open for the ecclesial reality in the other Christian confessions." The tenor of the statement is maintained in such a way, as an Evangelical (German Lutheran) commentary points out, "that not even

---

12. The original text read: " This Church... is the Catholic Church..."; the official final text reads "This Church... subsists in the Catholic Church..." See A. Grillmeier, *Commentary on the Documents of Vatican* II, 3. 200–25.

a trace of presumptuousness and self-satisfaction can be found in it."[13] Something further is to be noted in this text. It no longer talks about the Roman Catholic Church. In place of the local "Roman" and of the concept "*Romanus Pontifex*" is put the spiritual content of the Petrine office, and its unity with the community of bishops is explicitly added.

The question of the identification of the Church was taken up in another place in the Council and represented in the statements about the Church in the Decree on Ecumenism. Its reflections on the unity and uniqueness of the Church culminate in the statement: "The highest exemplar and source of this mystery is the unity, [of the Church] in the Trinity of Persons, of one God, the Father, the Son, and the Holy Spirit" (no. 2). The earthly and historical real presence of this—living and multiform—unity of the Church is the Holy Spirit, who is the one who effects the communion of the faithful in Christ and with Christ, and who is the giver of manifold gifts. This unity is articulated in the confession of the one faith, in the common celebration of the liturgy, and in the brotherly and sisterly unity of the family of God.

All this results in a clear expression that the unity of the Church and in the Church cannot consist in uniformity, but that it is living, rich, and pluriform. But there does exist a limit, where the unity necessary in essentials is threatened, where pluriformity leads to contradiction, opposition, and division.

The Question of Membership

In the light of what has been said on the question of identification, the relationship between Church and Churches also becomes approachable in a new way. If, according to the encyclical *Mystici corporis*, the relationship between Church of Christ and Roman Catholic Church is one of outright identity, the consequence is unavoidable that, in the strict sense, there really is no such thing as a division in the Church. For whoever doesn't belong to the Roman Catholic Church doesn't belong to the Church at all. The unity of the Church consists in the unity of the Roman Catholic Church itself. As long as this exists, it is not possible, theologically speaking, to talk about a division in the Church.

The question of what qualification is to be given to the incontestable Christian being of others, and of what one is to hold regarding the ecclesial dignity of those communities in which Christians outside the Roman Catholic Church are found, communities in which people realize their Christian faith and Christian life—there was an at-

---

13. W. Dietzfelbinger, "Die Grenzen der Kirche nach der dogmatischen Konstitution *De ecclesia*" in: *Kerygma und Dogma* (1965) 169.

tempt to bring these questions closer to an answer by asking the question of membership of the Church..

Before Vatican II, this question had two strands of tradition. The conception associated especially with canon law is based on canon 87 of the 1917 Code of Canon Law. This states that through baptism the human being becomes a *"persona"* in the Church of Christ with all the rights and obligations of a Christian as long as, in reference to the rights, no obstacle (*obex*) or penalty imposed by the Church stands in the way of the bond of ecclesial communion. The assertion of personhood, in the sense of a legal personality, also includes one's being in the Church, one's membership in it. It is through baptism then that membership is gained in the Church of Jesus Christ. "The being-person in the Church brought about by baptism is salvifically efficacious church membership."[14]

The question then arises: How is this general membership of all the baptized to be distinguished from the specific membership of the Catholic Christian? The Code of Canon Law does not devote much time to this, but it does suggest that there is a distinction between levels of membership: a constitutional membership of all Christians which is grounded in baptism and which distinguishes the Christian from the non-Christian, and an active membership which—as ever—can be hindered. In contrast to this strand of tradition, the encyclical *Mystici corporis*, in taking up an old dogmatic-apologetic position, proposes the thesis that only those belong to the Church *"reapse,"* i.e., in the proper sense, who have received baptism, confess the true faith, and have not separated themselves or been separated from the community of the Church.[15]

Thus three marks of membership are set up through which, all together, church membership is established: baptism—Catholic faith—being in one's proper place under the ecclesiastical hierarchy with the pope at its head. Accordingly, not belonging to the Church are those who live in schism (Eastern Church), those who live in heresy (Reformational Christianity), and those who live in apostasy. It is said that these three states of being, by their nature [i.e., "automatically"] separate human beings from the body of the Church. These determinations were concluded with the extraordinarily severe statement: "Those who are separated from each other in faith or in governance cannot live in this one body or from its divine Spirit." The status of non-Catholic Christians and non-Catholic communities is only indirectly approached by the encyclical *Mystici corporis*. It is said that these people are in a situation in which they cannot be sure of

14. Cf. K. Mörsdorf, *Lehrbuch des Kirchenrechts*, 11th ed. (Munich–Paderborn–Vienna, 1964) 175–84.
15. DS 3802 (NR 3986).

their eternal salvation; they are accordingly invited to free themselves from this situation.[16]

To this negative statement is added one that sounds a bit more positive, stating that non-Catholic Christians are related to the Church by
means of an "unconscious longing and wish," and that when they return
they do not come as strangers but as family members coming home to the
house of their father.

The criticism due this well-intentioned but unsatisfactory conception is formulated by Joseph Ratzinger:

> In projecting into the separated brethren a wish which they consciously and ex-
> plicitly reject, this Theory of an unconscious longing involves a fictitious psy-
> chology. In the matter of church membership, such a theory actually results in
> putting non-Catholic Christians on the same footing with heathens, to whom a
> "wishful" membership in the Church can also be attributed. The starting point of
> this whole attempted solution remains frozen on the subjective level; the salvation
> of non-Catholics is for all practical purposes reduced exclusively to the subjective
> factor of a wish which , furthermore, cannot even be consciously recognized.[17]

Vatican II attempted to solve these problems and the absurdities
arising from them with a new approach. The principal way in which it
did this was by not taking up again the image of member and membership as a description of the relationship of Catholic Church and non-
Catholic confessions, communities and churches, not even in the form of
distinguishing between levels of membership and nonmembership.
Similarly absent was the *Mystici corporis* idea of *votum* or *desiderium
inscium*. The Council placed the concept of the *votum* back where it
made some theological sense, i.e., related to the situation of the catechumens. There it means that catechumens, because of the conscious *votum* of their express will to be accepted into the Church, are connected
with the Church (*Lumen gentium* no. 14).

The key concepts that became all-important in the Council's reflection on the situation of Catholic and non-Catholic Christians were *in-
corporatio* and *coniunctio*. *Incorporari* or being incorporated corresponds
to the ecclesial state of the Catholic faithful; *coniunctum esse* specifies, in an open concept, the relationship of non-Catholics to the
Catholic Church.

Full membership, *plene incorporari*, consists in and is attributed to
those who—this is what is mentioned first and signifies an extraordinarily important ecclesiological [new] beginning—"have the Spirit of

---

16. DS 3821.
17. "Der Kirchenbegriff und die Frage nach der Gliedschaft der Kirche" in: *Das neue
Volk Gottes* (Düsseldorf, 1972) 101; cf. H. Fries, "Der ekklesiologische Status der
evangelischen Kirche in katholischer Sicht" in: *Aspekte der Kirche* (Stuttgart, 1963) 123–52;
W. Kasper,"Der ekklesiologische Charakter der nicht-katholicshen Kirchen," *ThQ* 145
(1965) 42–62.

Christ." Only after this is there mention of the other elements of membership in the Church:

They are fully incorporated into membership in the Church who, in the possession of the Spirit of Christ, accept the Church's entire discipline and all the means of salvation established in it, and are united in its visible bond with Christ who directs it through the pope and the bishops, and this by means of the bonds of the confession of faith, the sacraments, and the eccelsiastical leadership and community. (no. 14)

Belonging to the Church thus comes about in two ways: the internal, spiritual way, and the way of the visible level.

With this mention—along with its additional emphasis because of its prominent position in the text—of the spiritual criterion for belonging to the Church—"they who have the Spirit of Christ"—a quantum leap was made in the development of the understanding of the Church. Hitherto, one oriented the idea of Church only to what could be juridically established, and then sought to apply the decisive criteria only from that point of view. Through this decision, made in the sense of a *hierarchia veritatum*, hierarchy of truths, thinking on this question took on a new breadth and openness. This to be seen not as a betrayal but as a realization of what is truly Catholic. Just how important the idea of the criterion of the Spirit is can be seen from another point of view.

Sin does not take away one's membership in the Church. That sinners belong to the Church is an ancient theological proposition—but the membership affected by sin not only becomes ineffective, it also turns to the condemnation of the individual: "They will not be saved who, although incorporated into the Church, do not persevere in love and remain in the Church only with their bodies (*corpore*) but not with their hearts (*corde*)." The former, insufficiently clearly differentiated distinction between the question of salvation and that of membership in the Church, is now clarified: *plene incorporari* provides no grounds for presumption or false security.

Relationship to the other Christian communities is described with the words *coniunctum esse* and, within that reality, of *ordinari*—being ordered to the Catholic Church. The nature of this connectedness is described by the reference not to subjective conditions, but to Christian and ecclesial realities.

The history of this text is exciting. It reveals an intensive struggle for some progress beyond what was already established, and makes an attempt, right down to work done on individual words and concepts, to do justice to the ecumenical and pastoral intentions of the Council. Christian reality, which is constituted by baptism and its implications, is taken as the fundamental starting point. The important text reads:

With those who by baptism share in the honor of the Christian name, but do not confess the full faith or preserve unity of communion under the successor of Peter, the Church acknowledges itself to be connected in several ways. For many of them honor Scripture as the form of faith and of life, demonstrate genuine religious zeal, believe in the love of God, the Father Almighty, and in Christ the Son of God and Redeemer, receive the sign of baptism by which they are connected with Christ; indeed they recognize and receive other sacraments too in their own churches or ecclesial communities. . . . There is, in addition, community in prayer and in other spiritual goods; indeed even a true connection with the Holy Spirit, who in gifts and graces is active in them too with his sanctifying power and who has strengthened many of them even to the shedding of their blood. The Spirit arouses in all disciples of Christ such longing and activity that they would all like to be united in peace in the one flock under the one shepherd established by Christ. To achieve this, Holy Mother Church prays, hopes, and works unceasingly, and encourages her children to purification and renewal so that the sign of Christ might shine more clearly on the face of the Church. (*Lumen Gentium* no. 15)

From this new view of non-Catholic believers and their connection—even with all the still remaining separation and differences—with the Catholic Church, one is but a step away from a positive assessment of those communities in which individual Christians have received their Christian being and in which they live and make it real. If so many elements that represent a connection with the Catholic Church are attributed to the individual Christian, then the phenomenon of being connected also to their communities has to be admitted, and that in the sense that they be characterized by the name of Church.

The step to the explicit recognition of this consequence was taken at the Council in the Decree on Ecumenism (no. 3). It says, speaking of Christians living outside the Roman Catholic Churches:

All those justified by faith through baptism are incorporated into Christ. They therefore have a right to be honored by the title of Christian, and are properly regarded as brothers and sisters in the Lord by the sons and daughters of the Catholic Church. Moreover, some, indeed very many of the most significant elements or endowments which together, bo to build up and give life to the Church herself can exist outside the visible boundaries of the Catholic Church: the written word of God; the life of grace; faith, hope, and charity, along with other interior gifts of the Holy Spirit and visible elements. All of these, which come from Christ and lead back to Him, belong by right to the one Church of Christ. The brethren divided from us also carry out many of the sacred actions of the Christian religion. Undoubtedly, in that ways that vary, according to the different constitution of each Church and Community, these actions can truly engender a life of grace, and can be rightly described as capable of providing access to the community of salvation. It follows that these separated Churches and Communities, though we believe they suffer from defect already mentioned, have by no means been deprived of significance and importance in the mystery of salvation. For the Spirit of Christ has not refrained from using them as means of salvation, which derive their efficacy from the very fullness of grace and truth entrusted to the Catholic Church.

This text—going beyond *Lumen gentium*—declares: The Church is built up of the gifts of Christ. These gifts are found in their fullness in the Catholic Church. But they are found in varying degrees also in the other Christian communities, where they function as a community-building and community-preserving power. And the precise statement—"All this that proceeds from and leads back to Christ rightly belongs to the one, single Church of Christ"—doesn't just offer another open answer to the question of identification, but highlights and grounds the ecclesial character, the being-Church of the others. But there is also express emphasis here that through the churches living from these gifts of Christ, it is not division but the community of the Church of Christ that is made real.

The differences are thereby neither denied nor ignored, but they are ordered within a common unity that encompasses them. Thus it is that the word and concept "Church" is to be used in full justice and in truth, but at the same time, as the case may be, in an analogical sense. It connects unity and difference, difference and unity. Such a view does not require that the Catholic Church stop being the Church of Christ. But it is just as true that this affirmation does not require any denial of the ecclesial existence of the other churches for the sake of one's own ecclesiality; it rather allows ecclesiality to be recognized there as well, because the gifts from which the Church of Christ lives and is built up and which belong to the one, single Church are also alive there.

In the text we have quoted from the Decree on Ecumenism, there is mention of "Churches" and "ecclesial Communities"—no differentiations or subdivisions are given at this point, and one shouldn't force them after the fact. But it should still be noted that some of these communities themselves refuse to be Church. That is why the Decree on Ecumenism spoke of the "Oriental Churches" and "the separated Churches and church Communities in the West.'"

Finally, one should take note that the text gives a negative formulation to its positive statement that the Spirit of Christ uses the separated church communities as a means of salvation: *"Spiritus Christi uti non renuit*—the Spirit of Christ has not refrained. . . ." For the encyclical *Mystici corporis* "used this same manner of speaking when, with regard to the indwelling of the Holy Spirit for those fully separated from the Mystical Body, it explicitly maintains that the Spirit of God refuses to take up dwelling therein. In general, however, it is said there that they who in faith or leadership are separated from each other "cannot live in one Body and live from its one Divine Spirit."[18] The new view gained and articulated at the Council is a genuine, huge step forward; it is not just a development of medieval ecclesiology, but a clear corrective of it. Here we have a new theological starting point, which

18. DS 3808 (NR 398f).

calls for concrete and manifold realizations in the faith and existence of the Christian Churches.

Church and Churches in New Form

Taken together, these statements provide the possibility and create the needed presuppositions to see and appreciate the problem "Church and Churches" differently than in the past, i.e., in a positive, affirming sense. Churches in the plural can no longer be illegitimate if the Council explicitly talks of the other Christian communities and confessions as churches and church communities.

This erects a decisive ecumenical sign. While in the past the confessions, even in their essence, were mostly defined by that which distinguishes and separates them from the others:—"non-Catholic, non-Protestant"—today, conditioned by many external factors, we are mindful (and the Council explicitly said this) that there exists between the communities a binding common unity greater and more significant than the differences. While formerly, because of the differences, the greater common unity was almost lost sight of, today one is inclined to see the differences in the horizon of the greater common unity. This results in a viewpoint that not only does more justice to the reality, but also has ecumenical significance.

The non-Roman Catholic churches categorized as churches and church communities possess in that designation a decisive ecumenical basis and thus the presupposition for a more intensive common unity or union, now that the confessions, which clearly used to be the bearers of separation, are becoming more and more the subjects of a legitimate plurality in unity.[19] As a result, the once-separating contradictions are turning into a reconciling difference. In the formulation of Joseph Ratzinger, churches should remain churches and become one Church.

These statements invite us to submit biblical origins and history to a new examination. The same intensity with which the New Testament speaks of the unity of the Church, of the Church in the singular, is found there also in the way it speaks of the churches in the plural, in the sense of local churches, of liturgical assemblies in Corinth, Jerusalem, Rome, etc. These churches are not subsidiaries or mere substations of a central Church, they are Church in the full sense of the word, they are Church as event, as Church coming-to-be. For in them is done that which makes Church to be Church: the proclamation of Jesus' message and of the message of Jesus the Christ, the holding firm to the teaching of the apostles, the Breaking of the Bread as celebration of the Eucharist, the ministry of service.

19. H. Fries, *Ökumene statt Konfessionen?* (Frankfurt, 1977).

In doing these things, the communities thus mentioned manifest no uniformity in form and composition and, to some extent, in their organization as well. There were real differences between predominantly Jewish-Christian predominantly Gentile-Christian communities. The form of Church manifest in the New Testament was that of Church in churches, that of a unity of Church in its plurality, which was regarded not as a hindrance but as an expression of living unity being grounded in Christ and His Spirit and being obligated to the building up of that unity. In other words, the churches had their place in the one Church; the Church attains its realization in the churches.

Theoretically, this plurality has never been contested in the course of history. But one must immediately add (let it be said as Joseph Ratzinger put it): In the Catholic Church, this plurality has in fact been constantly forced more and more into a back seat over against a central system in which the local Church of Rome drew into itself, as it were, all the other local churches, thus curtailing the aspect of unity and making it uniform. In this fact lies on the one hand, some essential starting points for the Catholic Church in view of the current ecumenical movement. For the fact that the plurality of churches, which has its legitimate place in the Church, was constantly taking a back seat in the Catholic Church, was also caused by the fact that this plurality, not given sufficient room in the Church, had now unfolded outside of it in the independent development of the individual churches. If the Council recognizes this kind of reality, and it does, it is due to the insight that uniformity and unity are not identical, and that above all things the plurality of churches must again be brought to life in the unity of the Catholic Church.[20]

Here is a duty to be carried out, for which there is need of practical training in the Roman Catholic Church. Until Vatican II, and in the horizon of the aftereffects of Vatican I and its decision on the primacy and infallible magisterium of the pope, impulses that were consciously taken up and put into practice in a variety of ways by the so-called Pius popes according to the motto "the more uniform the better and more convincing for unity," the Catholic Church became practiced especially in those forms of unity which pushed towards the greatest possible uniformity, right up to a uniform liturgical language. Catholics still have no real practice in the legitimate multiplicity of the Church—affected perhaps by the alarming multiplicity, of the "denominations" which have arisen and still arise in the non-Roman Catholic churches.

Catholics will recognize that their own Church is not at all equipped to deal with the phenomenon of multiplicity in unity, and that it is the Church's duty to orient itself towards this possibility and reality. They will recognize that their own Church is faced with profound task of renewal, something that will not be accom-

---

20. "Die Kirche und die Kirchen," *Reformatio* 2 (1964) 104.

plished in a few days, but will require a process of patient self-opening, a process in which they will have no right whatsoever simply to absorb the others, because in the Church the place needed for the things to which they themselves have a legitimate right has still to be made.[21]

In place of the idea of conversion, which still has its meaning for individuals whose conscience so directs them, there is a fundamental shift to the idea of the community and unity of the churches; the churches remain and still become one Church. If Catholics dare to hope for something, then it is something like this: There will come a time in which the churches that exist outside the Church will finally be able to enter into their unity in such a way that while still remaining as churches they really take on only those modifications which are absolutely necessary for such a unity.

These modifications can be illustrated from that demand repeatedly encountered in inner-church and ecumenical discussion: The unification and unity of the Church can be only on the basis of the truth—not by circumventing it. Hence the validity of Ratzinger's words:

The claim of truth may not be eliminated where it is not pressing and irreversible. One may not take as truth what in reality is a historically developed form which stands in a more or less close connection with the truth. Thus precisely when the weight of truth and its indispensability is brought into play, it must also be accompanied by a manner of speaking that guards against overly hasty truth claims and is ready to search with the eyes of love after the inner breadth of what is true.[22]

Thus one can say: The form of Church and churches that one finds in the New Testament is not the mirror image of the present situation of the Church. To that extent, the well-known thesis of Ernst Käsemann— that the New Testament canon grounds not the unity of the Church but the plurality of confessions[23]—is acceptable if one thereby understands not the present status of separated, mutually excommunicating confessions, but that hoped-for and striven-for situation which is the goal of ecumenical unity: Confessions not as bearers of separation but as subjects of legitimate and reconciled multiplicity in unity.

As the importance of the local churches "in which and of which the Church consists," is given more recognition within the Catholic Church, the former mission churches become increasingly independent in genuine form and character, for example the Church in Africa, in Latin America, and in the Far East, so much the more will the Catholic Church be equipped and ready for the task ahead: namely, that churches should remain churches and become one Church.

---

21. Ibid. 106.

22. J. Ratzinger, *Principles of Catholic Theology*, trans. Sister Mary Frances McCarthy (San Francisco: Ignatius Press, 1987) 198.

23. "Begründet der neutestamentliche Kanon die Einheit der Kirche?" in: *Exegetische Versuche und Besinnungen I* 214-223.

It follows from all this that the ecumenical Church cannot take the place of the confessions; rather the confessions, faithfully to the core of what they are should become an expression and sign of the ecumenical Church. That is when, by carrying out a process of properly understood recognition as a realization of the responsibility and the promise *Ecclesia semper reformanda*, the reality "Church and Churches" will have come to fulfillment.[24]

24. Cf. H. Fries—K. Rahner, *Unity of Church—An Actual Possibility* (Philadelphia—New York, 1985) ; W. Bühlmann, *The Church of the Future: A Model for the Year 2001* (Maryknoll, N.Y.: 1986).

§61

EPILOGUE

THE CHALLENGE OF POSTMODERNISM AND
FUNDAMENTAL THEOLOGY

The purpose of this epilogue[1] is to provide the English-language reader with an update of recent developments most directly affecting fundamental theology since the German publication of *Fundamental-theologie* in 1985. Therefore, the focus of this final chapter will be threefold. First, it will give a general overview and explication of what has been termed "postmodernism." Postmodernism, perhaps more than any other movement in the past fifteen years, seeks to undercut the "fundamental" or foundational aspect of theology that Heinrich Fries puts forth. Due to the limited nature of this overview, general characterizations of postmodernist thought will have to suffice. Second, an example bearing some resemblance to this philosophical approach will be given as it is developed in George Lindbeck's *The Nature of Doctrine*,[2] a study of religion and theology. Lindbeck's work is not explicitly located in the postmodern movement—he defines it as "postliberal," but certain anthropological and methodological approaches he proposes for analyzing the nature of religion do emerge from postmodernism—especially his cultural-linguistic approach.[3] These approaches should be identified as such. Finally, a discussion of two critical points of disagreement will set Fries's *Fundamental*

1. This epilogue was written under my direction and with the assistance of several of my theological colleagues in the Boston area, by Thomas M. Kelly, who was my primary assistant in this translation project over the past two years.—R. J. Daly, S.J.

2. George Lindbeck, *The Nature of Doctrine: Religion and Theology in a Postliberal Age* (Philadelphia: Westminster, 1984).

3. Lindbeck is post-liberal inasmuch as he avoids locating the methodological starting point for theology in the "subject." He is post-modern inasmuch as he confines truth claims and epistemological realism solely to concrete historical contexts bound by culture and language; i.e. he avoids making transcendent truth claims.

Theology apart from Lindbeck's approach and much of the postmodern movement.

Postmodernism: A General Overview[4]

In his article "Between Foundations and Nihilism: Is Phronesis the Via Media for Theology?"[5] Thomas Guarino begins with the question "What type of rationality is proper to theology as a discipline?" This question today is greeted by a spectrum of answers ranging from nihilism to fundamentalism. It is a question that has serious consequences for any theological inquiry. While admitting that rationality is not a univocal term, Guarino adds that "a particular understanding of the way reason is used or a denial of reason's capacities, will affect one's conception of revelation, how it is received, and the type of truth or falsity predicated for it."[6] It is here that he introduces the first point of his article: The postmodernist critique of "foundationalism" is undercutting the traditional approach to the human in general, and to human knowing in particular.

Traditional "foundationalist" thought, whether of the classical metaphysical or modern transcendental variety, has come on hard times of late. Its critics resist the foundationalist compulsion to establish some first principle, Archimdean point, or

---

4. For background on postmodernism as well as its influence on theology and philosophy see: Richard Bernstein, *The New Constellation: The Ethical-Political Horizons of Modernity/Postmodernity* (Cambridge, Mass. MIT, 1992); Jean Francois Lyotard, *The Postmodern Condition: A Report on Knowledge*, trans. Geoff Bennington and Brian Massumi (Minneapolis: University of Minnesota, 1984); Rodolphe Gasche, *The Tain of the Mirro: Derrida and the Philosophy of Reflection* (Cambridge, Mass.: Harvard University, 1986); Mark Taylor, *Erring: A Postmodern A/Theology* (Chicago: University of Chicago, 1984); *Nots* (Chicago: University of Chicago, 1993); Gregory Bruce Smith, *Nietzsche, Heidegger, and the Transition to Postmodernity* (Chicago: University of Chicago, 1995); Kevin Hart, *The Trespass of the Sign: Deconstruction, Theology and Philosophy* (New York: Cambridge University, 1989); Jeffery Barash, *Martin Heidegger and the Problem of Historical Meaning* (Dordrecht: Martinus Nijhoff, 1988); Gianni Vattimo, *The End of Modernity: Nihilism and Hermeneutics*, trans. Jon R. Snyder (Baltimore: Johns Hopkins University, 1988); *Paradigm Change in Theology*, ed. Hans Kung and David Tracy (New York, Crossroad, 1989); David Tracy, *Plurality and Ambiguity: Hermeneutics, Religion, Hope* (San Francisco: Harper and Row, 1987); *On Naming the Present: Reflections on God, Hermeneutics, and Church* (Maryknoll, N.Y., Orbis, 1994); *Dialogue and Deconstruction: The Gadamer-Derrida Encounter*, ed. Diane P. Michelfelder and Richard E. Palmer (Albany: SUNY, 1989); Hans–Georg Gadamer, *Truth and Method*, 2d rev. ed., J. Weinsheimer and D. G. Marshall, eds. (New York: Crossroad, 1991); Michel Foucault, *The Foucault Reader*, ed. P. Rabinow (New York: Pantheon, 1984); Jacques Derrida, *Speech and Phenomena* (Evanston: Northwestern University, 1973); *Of Grammatology*, trans. G. C. Spivak (Baltimore: Johns Hopkins University, 1979); *New Essays on Religious Language*, ed. D. M. High (New York: Oxford University, 1969); Robert J. Fogelin, *Wittgenstein* (London: Routledge & Kegan Paul, 1980); Tilman Kuchler, *Postmodern Gaming: Heidegger, Duchamp, Derrida* (New York: P. Lang, 1994); David Ray Griffin et al., *Founders of Constructive Postmodern Philosophy: Peirce, James, Bergson, Whithead, and Hartshorne* (Albany: SUNY, 1993); *Varieties of Postmodern Theology* (Albany: SUNY, 1989); *Postmodernism and the Social Sciences*, ed. J. Doherty, E. Graham, and M. Malek (New York: St. Martin's, 1992).

5. Thomas Guarino, *Theological Studies* 54 (1993) 37–54.

6. Ibid. 37, n. 1.

ahistorical matrix from which to begin the search for rigorous and objective knowledge. The search for ultimate and determinate ontological or epistemological grounds guides virtually the entire tradition of Western thought, wholly enveloping the Platonic-Thomistic-Cartesian-Kantian-Husserlian axis. It attempts, once and for all, to "stop the show" by means of assorted foundational *archai* or *principia* such as *esse, ousia, eidos, res cogitans, Wille zur Macht,* etc.[7]

According to Guarino, foundationalism and similar hermeneutical trajectories have grounded much of traditional Catholic systematic thought, especially as it relates to doctrinal statements and the transmittal of "Truth" through history in tradition (*Dei verbum* 7-8). Some well-known contemporary examples of "foundationalists" in the Roman Catholic tradition include Bernard Lonergan, Karl Rahner, and Walter Kasper. All of these theologians utilize "a foundationalist ontology in order to undergird a theology which supports both the referential nature of doctrinal statements as well as their integral and continuous transmission."[8]

Opposed to this foundationalism, which has traditionally undergirded Catholicism—a foundationalism implicit in any universal claim regarding human nature—is the postmodern position. Guarino gives a very general synopsis of postmodernism ranging from the thought of Derrida and Foucault through Gadamer to Habermas. Within this spectrum he makes a distinction between moderate and strong postmodernism. "As I will use the terms, 'moderate postmodernism' indicates nonfoundationalist thought which seeks a rationality appropriate to our postmetaphysical, posttranscendental age; 'strong postmodernism' is more radical inasmuch as it appears to involve an outright rejection of rationality of any kind."[9] These two degrees of postmodernism define themselves over against "modernism," which Guarino defines as any attempt "to construct some grand narrative or over-arching theoretical system, one of the *grand recits* of history such as the 'dialectics of the Spirit' or the 'emancipation of the rational.'" The strong postmodern trajectory is defined, in part, by Jean-Francois Lyotard with the following assertions:

The postmodern rebels against all onto-theological metanarratives and protological-eschatological schemas. It accentuates and celebrates the heteromorphous nature of discourse and life.

Epistemic systematizations and totalizing visions are, at base, ontotheological and isomorphic illusions which ultimately seek the obliteration of heterogeneity and differ(a)nce. Metaphysics in particular and foundationalism in general are unblinking attempts at congruency and commensurability. . . . [10]

7. Ibid. 38.
8. Ibid. 39.
9. Ibid. 40.
10. Ibid. 40–41 including n. 16.

The very concept of "truth" itself is part of the (now discarded) metaphysical baggage. . . . There exists only sheer heteronomy and the emergence of random and unrelated subsystems of all kinds.[11]

Due to such extreme claims, it would seem that very little dialogue or even consideration of dialogue for theological purposes can be proposed with such an approach, for it undercuts itself. If there is no meaning or rationality, how can one reasonably assert that there is no meaning or rationality? The moderate postmodern position attempts to utilize some form of rationality. Its critique is more specifically concerned with the very real problem of history. The following assertions generally characterize moderate postmodernism:

What is here termed the moderate postmodern position takes into serious consideration fundamental postmodern concerns such as the radicalness of historicity, the pervasiveness of ideology, the decentered subject, the rejection of transcendentalism, the encompassing horizons of absence, and the subsequent avoidance of *Identitätsphilosophie*.

The moderate postmodern position has its roots in Heidegger and Wittgenstein.

Because all theories and forms of life are not equally true, criteria must be developed so as to distinguish coherency from incoherency and rationality from irrationality. Of course, it must be unceasingly stated that reason is exercised in circumstances which are thoroughly finite, conditioned, and historical. Nonetheless, it is truly reason which is exercised. The irrational and deconstructionist tendencies of strong postmodernism, then, are as ontologically inappropriate as are the naive and truncated forms of foundationalism.[12]

It is quite clear from these assertions that even the less radical moderate postmodernism presents serious difficulties for theology, for it calls into question two integral parts of any theological enterprise. The first pertains to basic affirmations about human nature. The second pertains to the possibility and meaning of the transmittal of doctrinal truth through history. Guarino concludes his article with a call for a nuanced theological foundationalism which incorporates "the broad horizons of historicity, facticity and paradigm-bound rationality even while maintaining the metaphysical/transcendental subject."[13] The specifics of how that may be worked out cannot be elaborated upon here, for there are many suggested approaches from various "schools" of theology.

This call for taking history, and hence the post-modernist critique, seriously is also a concern for David Tracy.

If theology is to continue to have a systematically apologetic task, and if that task is to prove adequate to the contemporary postmodern situation, then new criteria for the task are needed. Traditional modern fundamental theologies relied too ex-

---

11. Frederic Jameson, *Postmodernism* (Durham: Duke University, 1990) 12, 342.
12. Guarino 42–44.
13. Ibid. 54.

clusively on transcendental inquiry—and, too, often, models of that inquiry not explicitly related to the questions of language (and thereby plurality and historicity) and questions of history (and thereby ambiguity and postmodern suspicion, not merely modern critique).[14]

The basis of Tracy's acceptance of parts of the postmodernist critique is the need to attend to the specifics of history, historicity, and language. It is only in this way that one can understand oneself "as a subject active in history."[15] Anything less than this fails to take into account the human being as being human in history. Tracy also sees much danger in what he views to be the faults of an all-encompassing foundationalism which fails to take into account any difference—i.e., fundamentalism. It is against this fundamentalism that he describes postmodernity as an "ethics of resistance—resistance, above all, to more of the same, the same unquestioned sameness of the modern turn to the subject, the modern over-belief in the search for a perfect method, the modern social evolutionary narrative whereby all is finally and endlessly more of the self-same."[16] What now determines all intellectual categories is the post-modern turn to the other and the different. This emphasis on the other and the different calls into question the grand narrative of the dominant culture—in our case the "social evolutionary narrative of modernity." The postmodern critique, for Tracy, is a much-needed wake-up call for theologians to respond to the problem of history, in difference and otherness, and to utilize contemporary intellectual movements for the benefit of theology.

God's shattering otherness, the neighbor's irreducible otherness, the othering reality of "revelation," not the consoling modern communality of "religion," all these expressions of otherness come now in new postmodern and post-neoorthodox forms to demand the serious attention of all thoughtful theologians.[17]

Tracy's embrace of aspects of the postmodernist critique of theology ultimately benefits theology, for as he states, "Any transcendental mode of inquiry (like Husserl's) will function well if, and only if, it can account for its own linguistic and historical essence."[18]

---

14. David Tracy, "The Uneasy Alliance Reconceived: Catholic Theological Method, Modernity, and Postmodernity," *Theological Studies* 50 (1989) 560. Tracy further suggests: Paul Ricoeur, "Hermeneutics and the Critique of Ideology," in: *Hermeneutics and the Human Sciences* (Cambridge, Harvard Univ. Press 1981).

15. David Tracy, "Theology and the Many Faces of Postmodernity," *Theology Today* 51 (1995) 108.

16. Ibid.

17. Ibid. Cf. Jack A. Bonsor, "History, Dogma, and Nature: Further Reflections on Postmodernism and Theology," *Theological Studies* 55 (1994) 295–313. Bonsor states that "foundationalist thinking legitimates the hegemony of a particular perspective" (297). For this reason he suggests that theologians withhold judgment on postmodernism until its benefits for dealing with history and historicity become more evident.

18. Tracy, "The Uneasy Alliance," 560.

With this very brief overview in mind, it is now possible to present an example of a theological attempt to utilize some moderate postmodern principles in constructing a methodological approach to religion and theology. The following presentation of George Lindbeck's views on the nature of religion and, therefore, of human nature, and his views on the relation of language and experience will serve to highlight some problems I have characterized as postmodern.

A Postmodern Theological Attempt

George Lindbeck proposes a new framework for conceiving religion and religious doctrine in his book *The Nature of Doctrine*. It is evident in the Foreword of this work that two main concerns underlie his project. First, his ecumenical endeavors, both past and present, move him to seek new concepts to remove anomalies present in the doctrinal disputes among particular Christian denominations. These anomalies of concern include the "interrelationship of doctrinal permanence and change, conflict and compatibility, unity and disunity, and variety and uniformity among, but especially within religions."[19] The second concern for Lindbeck is the academic status of the study of religion. He seems particularly concerned that religion and religious discourse is slowly removing itself from current intellectual movements in the academy. He repeatedly stresses that "other sciences" employ this kind of method in their approach to their respective fields of study—and from this he infers that any other approach to the nature of religion and doctrine will prove to be either provincial or relativistic. Consequently, a theoretical framework for religion is of primary concern for Lindbeck, and "theology" is defined as a subset of this field (theory of religion) that includes "scholarly activity of second-order reflection on the data of religion (including doctrinal data) and of formulating arguments for or against material positions (including doctrinal ones)."[20] He states clearly that his inquiry intends to be both strictly theoretical and religiously neutral. This assertion is much more than simply a starting point for his new system. At issue in this approach are the presuppositions upon which the cultural-linguistic framework stands.[21]

This epilogue will concentrate on Lindbeck's assertions concerning the foundations of religion, especially as they relate to its experiential

---

19. Lindbeck, *The Nature of Doctrine* 9.

20. Ibid. 10.

21. It is here where one must ask if there exists a strictly theoretical and religiously neutral starting point for the study of religion. Is it possible to remove confessional "baggage" from theoretical inquiry? Paradoxically, Lindbeck points out that "the motivations for this book are ultimately more substantively theological than purely theoretical" (18). The issue then becomes whether a "religiously neutral" approach is possible for dealing with theologically substantive problems as he would define them.

foundation. This will obviously include mention of doctrine, for it is closely related, but the focus will not be upon doctrine. First I will summarize Lindbeck's understanding of current theological theories of religion and doctrine. Second, I will present his analysis of religion and experience followed by the cultural-linguistic framework that he proposes as a solution to current doctrinal reconciliation efforts. This will be followed by a discussion of what I view to be the two most important points of disagreement between Lindbeck and Fries. The first issue is the methodological difference between a theoretical investigation of religion and a theological investigation. This difference highlights the purpose of doing theology for each author. The second issue is concerned with the function of language and its relation to the anatomy of "experience."

Current Theological Theories of Religion and Doctrine

Lindbeck presents current theological theories of religion and doctrine in three broad categories. The first of these theories "emphasizes the cognitive aspects"[22] of religion and is generally referred to as "propositionalist." The second theory is termed "experiential-expressive" and emphasizes the experiential aspect of religion. The final theory is actually a combination of the first two. For Lindbeck, all three approaches remain tied to a specific and unsatisfactory formulation of doctrine which is unable to achieve "doctrinal reconciliation without capitulation."[23]

The propositional approach, according to Lindbeck, "stresses the ways in which church doctrines function as informative propositions or truth claims about objective realities."[24] It is mainly concerned with the meaningfulness of religious utterances and, as will subsequently be discussed, possesses a particularly unsatisfactory understanding of how language functions. Lindbeck clearly states that "doctrinal reconciliation without capitulation" is impossible in this propositional approach because, "if a doctrine is once true, it is always true, and if it is once false, it is always false."[25] This is an impossibility because the meanings of doctrines remain inflexible and therefore cannot change "while remaining the same."[26]

The experiential-expressive approach to religion "interprets doctrines as noninformative and nondiscursive symbols of inner feelings, attitudes, or existential orientations."[27] Put differently, for an experien-

22. *The Nature of Doctrine* 16.
23. Ibid.
24. Ibid.
25. Ibid.
26. Ibid. 17.
27. Ibid. 16.

tial-expressive approach, doctrines express and are continually evaluated against a prereflexive experience or existential orientation. According to Lindbeck, this approach began with Schleiermacher and is equally unsatisfactory for doctrinal reconciliation. The elasticity of the meaning of doctrines is quite pronounced under some uses (i.e., Schleiermacher) of this starting point—and doctrinal constancy becomes a very real problem.

The general principle is that insofar as doctrines function as nondiscursive symbols, they are polyvalent in import and therefore subject to changes of meaning or even to a total loss of meaningfulness, to what Tillich calls their death. They are not crucial for religious agreement or disagreement, because these are constituted by harmony or conflict in underlying feelings, attitudes, existential orientations, or practices, rather than by what happens on the level of symbolic (including doctrinal) objectifications.[28]

The third theoretical approach combines the cognitively-propositional and experiential-expressive approaches. Karl Rahner and Bernard Lonergan serve as representatives of this approach for Lindbeck. And while this approach is better able to "account more fully . . . .for both variable and invariable aspects of religious traditions,"[29] the practical application of such an approach continually falls short of his goals. This is so for two reasons. First, they supposedly lack the criteria with which to determine "when a given doctrinal development is consistent with the sources of faith,"[30] and therefore must rely on the magisterium more than is desirable. Secondly, "their explanations of how this reconciliation is possible tend to be too awkward and complex to be easily intelligible or convincing." The point remains that, for Lindbeck, the third (hybrid) theory is also unacceptable.[31]

With the previous three categories of theory determined to be either too rigid in doctrinal meaning, too elastic in doctrinal meaning, or simply too complex to be easily intelligible, Lindbeck has effectively cleared the theological landscape of viable options for his project. It is here that he proposes an alternate approach to address the anomalies of doctrinal permanency and change.

It has become customary in a considerable body of anthropological, sociological, and philosophical literature (about which more will be said later) to emphasize neither the cognitive nor the experiential-expressive aspects of religion; rather,

---

28. Ibid. 17.
29. Ibid.
30. Ibid.
31. Lindbeck does not give this third "hybrid" approach more than a passing glance, and in fact states that "for our purposes it will generally be subsumed under the earlier approaches" (16). This approach warrants a greater and more exhaustive analysis, for it is quite different than pure experiential-expressivism as defined by Lindbeck. For this epilogue, I will bracket this "hybrid" approach or refer to it with the names of the theologians (i.e., Rahner or Lonergan, etc.). Henceforth the three approaches are referred to as (1) cognitive-propositional, (2) experiential-expressive, (3) cultural-linguistic.

emphasis is placed on those respects in which religions resemble languages together with their correlative forms of life and are thus similar to cultures (insofar as these are understood semiotically as reality and value systems—that is, as idioms for the construing of reality and the living of life). The function of church doctrines that becomes most prominent in this perspective is their use, not as expressive symbols or as truth claims, but as communally authoritative rules of discourse, attitude and action. This general way of conceptualizing religion will be called in what follows a "cultural-linguistic" approach, and the implied view of church doctrine will be referred to as a "regulative" or "rule" theory.[32]

This regulative approach, for Lindbeck, accomplishes his goal of doctrinal reconciliation without capitulation because rules "retain an invariant meaning under changing conditions of compatibility and conflict."[33] Opposition between rules can sometimes be solved by specifying their contextual application.[34]

Lindbeck concludes this first chapter by defining some of the reasons why the experiential-expressive approach is prevalent today. He reduces many of the reasons for the prevalence of this approach to psychological hypotheses concerned with fulfilling the modern psyche. It is also interesting to note that while academic methods have bypassed this approach in favor of a cultural-linguistic approach, those "commending religion to society at large"[35] have employed the experiential-expressivist approach. Lindbeck surmises that the reason for this unsatisfactory situation is that the experiential-expressive approach sells better in the modern theological marketplace, "while the cultural and linguistic approaches are better suited to the nontheological study of religion."[36] He obviously views with disappointment the fact that religion is being commended to society in a framework and manner that is not theoretically and academically sound and will probably lead to doctrinal provincialism or relativism.[37] Two questions then surface. Is the religious community-at-large quite out of touch with the academy, or is it the other way around? Secondly, does the content of a subject determine, to any degree, the method of studying it? It would seem that, unlike most other disciplines in the academy, the discipline of "religious studies" is concerned with the human experience to an "other" that is somehow relational to us. That is certainly the case in terms of the study of theology. A cultural-linguistic paradigm would appear insufficient to provide meaningful categories for this

32. Ibid. 1718.
33. Ibid. 18.
34. The question should be introduced here as to whether context and a given rule can be separated or whether context is, in fact, part of a rule, and vice versa. To answer this question adequately would require an emphasis on the doctrinal aspect of this work which is interesting enough, though not the focus of this epilogue.
35. Ibid. 23.
36. Ibid 25.
37. I assert this here, somewhat strongly, given Lindbeck's understanding of the relationship between language and reality soon to be addressed.

relationality. Lindbeck understands this problem and its importance, for in chapter two he discusses the relationship between religion and experience.

Religion and Experience

In chapter two of *The Nature of Doctrine*, Lindbeck proposes to evaluate whether an experiential-expressive approach to religion (which views itself as a *product* of experience) is better suited as a framework for understanding religion than a cultural-linguistic approach (which views itself as a *producer* of experience). He brackets, for the time being, a theological inquiry and states that the aim of the chapter "is to give a nontheological account of the relations of religion and experience."[38] In one sense he has already answered the question he posed. By bracketing the theological question, he avoids any discussion of an inner relation to an outer reality (a "material" point) and is able to focus on the "theoretical" aspects of a methodology that by its very name works *from* various cultural and linguistic influences *to* the individual. Lindbeck then presents his interpretation of what is characteristic of experiential-expressivism in general.

Experiential-Expressivism

The one-page exposition of the experiential-expressive approach to religion given by Lindbeck begins with five of the six theses Lonergan puts forth in his theory of religion.[39] They are as follows: 1) Different religions are diverse expressions or objectifications of a common core experience. 2) The experience, while conscious, may be unknown on the level of self-conscious reflection. 3) This experience is present in all human beings. 4) In most religions, the experience is the source and norm of objectifications. 5) The primordial religious experience is God's gift of love.[40] It is important to note that problems with this approach begin to surface for Lindbeck when the "term" of this experience is mentioned in a confessional sense. Having bracketed any "material" points from the discussion, Lindbeck avoids any mention of God, except to criticize

38. Ibid. 30.

39. Lindbeck was subsequently criticized on this exposition by Charles C. Hefling, "Turning Liberalism Inside-Out," *Method: Journal of Lonergan Studies* 3 (1985) 51–69, and by Dennis M. Doyle, "Lindbeck's Appropriation of Lonergan," ibid., 4 (1986) 18–28.

40. Lindbeck 31. He follows this last point with the comment that "in this thesis, Lonergan is obviously speaking as a Christian theologian rather than simply a theorist of religion. This is one of the real issues in this work—is it possible to divorce a theory of religion from any theological presuppositions? Is there an objective corner from which one can evaluate theological methods? For a very helpful dialogue between Lonergan and postmodernism see Fred Lawrence, "The Fragility of Consciousness: Lonergan and the Postmodern Concern for the Other," *Theological Studies* 54 (1993) 55–94.

Lonergan's approach which specifically names God as the author of this primordial experience of love. In part it is unacceptable for Lindbeck because "it is difficult or impossible to specify"[41] the distinctive features of this core experience. This of course is true, since the term of this experience is not an object alongside other objects and it also includes quite a few unknowns. But is this a sufficient reason to dispense with a theology that begins from such an experience? The characterizations of this experience seem to create more problems for Lindbeck than it solves, and so he offers the alternative of a cultural-linguistic approach.

A Cultural-Linguistic Alternative

According to Lindbeck, religions are "comprehensive interpretive schemes," which structure human experience and understanding of self and world. Religion is a kind of cultural framework "that shapes the entirety of life and thought."[42] It is not primarily (though it may well be so secondarily secondarily) an array of beliefs concerning the truth, or a symbolism of attitudes, feelings, or sentiments. "Rather, it is similar to an idiom that makes possible the description of realities, the formulation of beliefs, and the experiencing of inner attitudes, feelings, and sentiments."[43] It is in this sense that religion "shapes the subjectivities of individuals rather than being primarily a manifestation of those subjectivities."[44] And so, in effect, a cultural-linguistic model reverses the traditional experiential-expressive conception of the "inner" and the "outer." "Instead of deriving external features of a religion from inner experience, it is the inner experiences which are viewed as derivative."[45]

It is clear from this very brief sketch of the cultural-linguistic approach that experience *qua* experience still has a very important role. The difference now is that experience is viewed as a product of religion as opposed to its producer. As one progresses through Lindbeck's comparison of the two models, it becomes evident that the nature of experience on the one hand and its relation to expression are construed differently from each other. For traditional experiential-expressivists such as Schleiermacher, and for theologians such as Rahner and Lonergan who combine approaches, experience *qua* experience, and the subsequent

41. Lindbeck 32.
42. Ibid. 32–33.
43. Ibid. 33.
44. Ibid.
45. Ibid. 33.

reflection upon it are two different realities.[46] This does not seem to be the case for Lindbeck.

When one pictures inner experiences as prior to expression and communication, it is natural to think of them in their most basic and elemental form as also prior to conceptualization or symbolization. If, in contrast, expressive and communicative symbols, whether linguistic or non-linguistic, are primary—then, while there are of course nonreflective experiences, there are no uninterpreted or unschematized ones. On this view, the means of communication and expression are a precondition, a kind of quasi-transcendental (i.e., culturally formed) *a priori* for the possibility of experience.[47]

Towards the end of his second chapter, Lindbeck uses various illustrations as examples of the truth for this theory of experience. From color interpretations among various tribal peoples to the reasons why prophets discover new concepts, he attempts to construct a case for this view of experience. Two definitions of great importance should not be missed among these examples. The first of these pertains to limitations on his definition of experience, the second concerns the order of "mental activities." Both points are vital for understanding his approach. First, experience separated from its communication or symbolization is not possible for Lindbeck. That is, experience and the ability to express or communicate it simply cannot be separated. Practically applied, there are no private experiences because "all symbol systems have their origin in interpersonal relations and social interactions."[48] Second, the order of mental activities is important to note. The first intention "is the act whereby we grasp objects." The second intention "is the reflex act of grasping or reflecting on first formal intentions."[49] The obvious result of this assertion is that one cannot grasp anything without certain tools, which are possessed only by being culturally communicated. This applies to religious experience as well. "They can be construed as by-products of linguistically or conceptually structured cognitive activities of which we are not directly aware because they are first intentional."[50]

With this understanding of experience, shaped by a particular view of language and epistemology, Lindbeck asserts his thesis toward the end of chapter two. "First come the objectivities of the religion, its language, doctrines, liturgies, and modes of action, and it is through these that passions are shaped into various kinds of what is called religious experience."[51] This has direct consequences for the definition of

46. This is clear from Fries's remarks above in §24, Rahner's Introduction to the *Foundations of Christian Faith*, and Lonergan's two sub-sections in *Method in Theology* titled "Religious Experience" (105–7) and "Expressions of Religious Experience" (108–9).
47. Lindbeck 36.
48. Ibid. 38.
49. Ibid.
50. Ibid.
51. Ibid. 39.

religion he proposes. Religion is no longer something universal "arising from within the depths of individuals," but instead it is "a variegated set of cultural-linguistic systems that, at least in some cases, differentially shape and produce our most profound sentiments, attitudes, and awareness."[52] He is careful in concluding this chapter to state that the "scientific study" of religion and the "theological study" may be better served by different approaches. The cultural-linguistic approach could best serve theorists of religion while the experiential-expressive may best serve theology.

For our purpose here, the doctrine question will be bracketed and the focus will be on the question of experience. It is evident that Fries views experience, language, epistemology, and the purpose of theology quite differently from Lindbeck.

Theory of Religion vs. Theology, and the Purpose of Theology

Thus far our method has been to discuss the nature of what it is to be human which then serves as a basis for understanding doctrine as both intelligible and formative. Even if, as in Lindbeck's case, one starts methodologically in a cultural-linguistic system, a corresponding view of human nature must be at least presupposed which is appropriate to that approach. Fries would find that Lindbeck has a different starting point for a theory of religion (cultural linguistic framework in general) and for theology (biblical narrative in particular). These are not easily reconcilable, for a different starting point negates either one or the other—for the term and goal of both is the same—God. A twofold approach to theory and theology is unacceptable because for Fries, the universal theological and anthropological presuppositions for theology are authoritative and take precedence over all other aspects or agendas related to religion and doctrine. Put differently, Fries's starting point allows him to engage those who do not share his particular religious or cultural language—i.e., *those who do not share his particular approach to religion.* As Fries states in his Foreword, "It is precisely fundamental theology that has the duty of being both true to origins and adapted to contemporary situations, or attending to the message of faith as well as to the needs of concrete human beings."[53] And, because the theological anthropology that presupposes such a duty contains universals, so does the starting point for such a project. Theory and theology are not separate realities. This ability to engage others outside one's reality system does not seem possible for Lindbeck.

When Lindbeck chooses a cultural-linguistic starting point for his theory of religion, the inevitable question arises as to which culture

52. Ibid. 40.
53. Above, page 1.

and which language? The answer of course is as varied as the subject-matter. The Arabic/Middle Eastern/Koranic paradigm is the structure of reality for Muslims. The Pacific Rim/Oriental/Buddhist paradigm offers a structure of reality for inhabitants of that area, culture, and language. Understood at a theoretical level, every religion is simply a different set of historically bound cultural and linguistic factors structured in ways that produce very different reality systems and experiences. Thus in Lindbeck's theory, characterized by his moderate postmodern understanding of history, there is no right and wrong, revealed or contrived religion—just different (quasi self-contained) structures of reality stemming from various cultural and linguistic factors. But is this kind of "neutrality" possible for a theological investigation? The answer to this question is possible only when one discerns what is authoritative for Lindbeck, and why. Before addressing what is authoritative for Lindbeck, one further point needs to be mentioned here. One cannot deny that Lindbeck would make truth claims or that he would hold for an eptistemological realism. The key point is to understand that these claims and this realism are confined *solely to the particular historical context*—i.e., bound by space and time. Absolute truth claims transcending cultures and history or a transcendental epistemological realism would not be acceptable for Lindbeck. Put diffferently, Lindbeck can make truth claims *within* a particular cultural-linguistic construct, but not *between* them.[54]

Given his emphasis on language as capable of constructing reality, it comes as no surprise that Lindbeck utilizes the Bible as *the* narrative par excellence for Christianity. "A scriptural world is thus able to absorb the universe. It supplies the interpretive framework within which believers seek to live their lives and understand reality."[55] For the strictly theological enterprise, he does not rely on propositional truth claims or an "undefinable" experience, but on Scripture. His particular interpretation of Scripture fits neatly into a cultural-linguistic paradigm.

It is important to note the direction of interpretation. Typology does not make scriptural contents into metaphors for extra-scriptural realities, but the other way around. It does not suggest, as is often said in our day, that believers find their stories in the Bible, but rather that they make the story of the Bible their story. The cross is not viewed as a figurative representation of suffering nor the

---

54. This is basically the same conclusion reached by David H. Kelsey, *The Uses of Scripture in Recent Theology* (Philadelphia: Fortress, 1975) esp. 57–58. In other words, once one has identified one's fundamental discrimen (Kelsey) or cultural-linguistic world view (Lindbeck), one can go no further. In contrast, the approach of Fries (and foundational thinkers generally) commits one, by a careful use of dialectic, as e.g. developed by B. Lonergan, to try to distinguish between more or less authentic discrimina/cultural-linguistic world views. Cf. Robert J. Daly, ed., *Christian Biblical Ethics* (New York—Ramsey: Paulist, 1984) 94–97, 125–30, esp. at 130.

55. Lindbeck 117.

messianic kingdom as a symbol for hope in the future; rather, suffering should be cruciform, and hopes for the future messianic. More generally stated, it is the religion instantiated in Scripture which defines being, truth, goodness, and beauty, and the nonscriptural exemplifications of these realities need to be transformed into figures (or types or antitypes) of the scriptural ones. Intratextual theology redescribes reality within the scriptural framework rather than translating Scripture into extrascriptural categories. It is the text, so to speak, which absorbs the world, rather than the world the text.[56]

This interpretive framework emphasizes how life is to be lived in light of what the Bible says about God in stories concerning Israel and ultimately Jesus. When extrascriptural categories are imported into reading Scripture, that reality within it is corrupted.[57] Says Lindbeck:

The believer, so an intratextual approach would maintain, is not told primarily to be conformed to a reconstructed Jesus of history (as Hans Küng maintains), nor to a metaphysical Christ of faith (as in much of the propositionalist tradition), nor to an abba experience of God (as for Schillebeeckx), nor to an agapeic way of being in the world (as for David Tracy), but he or she is rather to be conformed to the Jesus Christ depicted in the narrative. An intratextual reading tries to derive the interpretive framework that designates the theologically controlling sense from the literary structure of the text itself.[58]

There are numerous problems with this approach; in large part they are subsumed under the hermeneutical question concerning whether written words or recorded deeds in one culture and time can simply be understood, in themselves, (i.e., unmediated) when transposed into another culture and time. What conditions of possibility exist for one to enter into a framework that is outside of our own horizon? This is the problem of history. If these historical occurrences cannot be understood in themselves (i.e., ahistorically, without context), and disclosing the correct interpretation is in fact the job of the theologian, whose interpretation, whose reality structure, would prevail in such a task?

There is another problem which is also very important. If Scripture, understood in Lindbeck's sense, is the authoritative point of reference for Christians in general, it seems that those outside the Christian cultural-linguistic reality system are simply cut off. John Thiel's *Imagination and Authority*[59] sums up this very point.

Lindbeck sees the crisis of Christian faith in the modern world as nothing less than the threat of its extinction. His notion of constrained authorship addresses

---

56. Lindbeck 118.

57. This seems to overlook the fact that Greek thought exists in the New Testament (see above § 46). Does Lindbeck really mean extra-scriptural or extra-cultural? That brings up another problem. Understood in a cultural-linguistic framework, the message and truth of the Bible would be confined to that period and time in which it is written. Yet Lindbeck seems to make the biblical Word immune to problems of historical transmission.

58. Lindbeck 120.

59. John E. Thiel, *Imagination and Authority: Theological Authorship in the Modern Tradition* (Minneapolis: Fortress, 1991).

that threat through the theologian's efforts to describe the meaning of the biblical text not for the culture at large but for the community of faith and in so doing to instruct the community in authentic speaking and acting. One might say that Lindbeck's alternative to the "modern" theologian very much resembles the ancient Christian catechist living in a pagan world.[60]

Fries would view any starting point that is unable to engage contemporary society as detrimental to theology and the theory of religion in general. This is especially detrimental to religion with regard to its opponents today. For these opponents, the entire notion of revelation, especially as embodied by the Bible, is part of the problem. Jesus of Nazareth, as depicted in Scripture, is also part of the problem. For others, even "religious" people, the word "God" is part of the problem. The only common ground that theology shares with much of "secular" culture is the question of what it means to be a human being. This is where the dialogue must begin—this is where the theologian engages culture. Thiel speaks of this approach, and its description includes the fundamental theological approach of Fries.

Foundational theologies seek theoretical grounding in a nonscriptural anthropology, epistemology, or method because they assume the need to engage culture in and through theological reflection and they find the possibility of rapprochement in an appropriate secular theory. For Lindbeck the possibility of such rapprochement has evaporated.[61]

One final point regarding a theory of religion and doing theology deserves to be mentioned. Lindbeck stresses at the beginning of his book that his theory is strictly theory—one that can be religiously neutral. But given the nature of human inquiry and the history from which each individual emerges, a religiously neutral inquiry is simply an illusion. There is no "neutral" (i.e., acontextual) corner from which the religious landscape can be evaluated, for every human being has been affected by opinions or lack thereof on the subject and has internalized these to various degrees. That is not to say that a "Truth" or set of truths does not exist, but it does mean that this "Truth" or set of truths is mediated in history through human beings. It is no surprise that Lindbeck's theory disregards any human authorship as normative for theology when one takes into account Lindbeck's confessional views on the authoritative nature of Scripture. John Thiel puts it well:

The antifoundationalist argument of *The Nature of Doctrine* may appear on the surface as the use of relatively recent philosophical conclusions to further the ends of a new theological proposal. But one need not look much beneath the surface of Lindbeck's argument to consider whether his confessional commitment to the Lutheran tradition makes its antifoundationalist perspective theologically attractive. Of itself, antifoundationalism is a philosophical stance reached through sophisticated arguments against the integrity of naively inductive logic. From the

60. Ibid. 161.
61. Ibid.

perspective of classical Lutheran doctrine, however, it supports a confessional judgment regarding the inability of the innate power of reason to know God or to foster an understanding of things spiritual.[62]

Thiel's criticism, which connects Lindbeck's confessional presuppositions regarding human nature to his project is not, to be sure, an *ad hominem* argument; rather, it points quite convincingly to the fact that no "strictly theoretical" approach to religion exists. Perhaps Lindbeck is drawn to Wittgenstein's theory of language not for what it says about language *qua* language, but for what it says about human nature. And this is the real issue: the logic of fundamental theology contradicts the faith claims of Lindbeck the Lutheran. This statement about human nature is in agreement with the core assertions of post-modernism.

Each stands, theologically or philosophically, against the assumption that reason can fashion a truthful complex of knowledge based on inherent abilities of the mind. Both render harsh judgments on reason's creative capacity to function apart from traditions or communities of meaning, whether ecclesial or philosophical.[63]

In one sense, a response by Fries to *The Nature of Doctrine* is doomed before it even begins. For to give Fries or anyone who grounds the conditions for the possibility of faith in human experience a fair hearing would be to admit the possibility of human creativity usurping Scripture for the structuring of Christian reality as opposed to Scripture using human creativity to structure reality. The opposition to Fries is most evident when taken against Fries's definition of fundamental theology found in his Foreword. "The term 'fundamental theology' is intended to express that the apologetic task can and should be integrated in a comprehensive theological reflection in the believing reason's self-examination of its foundations and presuppositions." Thiel asserts that this is unacceptable for Lindbeck, for "an exercise of theological authorship not constrained by the cultural-linguistic approach will produce theological works that bespeak a fallen nature's anthropocentricity rather than God's promise of salvation revealed in scriptural tradition."[64]

Language and Experience

Perhaps one point to begin a discussion on the topic of language and experience is to list a number of assertions held by traditional Catholic theological anthropologies. For Lindbeck, these assertions would belong to the third or hybrid method of theology. Representative of this contemporary transcendental approach within fundamental theology is

62. Ibid. 183–84.
63. Ibid. 184.
64. Thiel, 187.

Gerald O'Collins. The following is a general list of the characteristics of human experience. Many, if not all, are found in Fries's work.

(a) The human subject displays an openness and tendency toward an ultimate horizon of unconditioned being, that furthest limit which circles and encloses all our experiences. Against such a horizon we experience some *particular* being, grasp some *specific* meaning, know this *particular truth* and desire some *specific* good thing [italics mine].

(b) The ultimate horizon is not one determined object among others. Knowing it is not just one more instance of knowledge in general. It is there as an unthematized and unreflective element. Even when through subsequent reflection it becomes the object of explicit attention, it can never be totally and adequately thought through and objectivized.

(c) The human subject enjoys a "transcendental" experience of his horizon, in the sense that the experience goes beyond any particular acts of knowing and willing.

(d) The ultimate horizon is always affirmed, even in the explicit act of denying it.

(e) This ultimate horizon is the *a priori* condition for the possibility of any human experience. When, for instance, some specific act of knowledge occurs, that is because there already exists a knowing subject oriented toward this horizon.

(f) As the absolute fullness of being, meaning, truth, and goodness, this absolute horizon is to be identified with God.

(g) Hence we can speak of transcendental experience as transcendental revelation.

(h) The divine self-communication involved in transcendental experience is a gratuitous, supernatural gift from God.

(i) As the ultimate horizon needed to create the possibility for any experience, God is known to every human person. Whether or not they realize this consciously and accept it willingly, all human beings receive the transcendental experience of God's primordial self-communication.

(j) Finally, transcendental experience/revelation establishes the presupposition and condition for receiving divine revelation and salvation in the specific forms of *historical existence*—above all through the *historical experience* of Israel and the life, death, and resurrection of Jesus Christ.[65]

These points have set out the specific transcendental method most at odds with Lindbeck's view of human nature. It is now possible to understand the contrast that Lindbeck offers regarding the relationship of language to experience.

A full and complete response to Lindbeck's use of language and its consequences for "experience" would require an extended exposition and response to his interpretation of the language theory of Ludwig Wittgenstein. For the purpose of this epilogue, it will suffice to point

---

65. Gerald O'Collins, *Fundamental Theology* (New York: Crossroad 1981) 48–49. I have highlighted the main points of the more extensive summaries given by O'Collins. Many of these points are explicitly developed above in §23, "The Human Being as Revelation."

out some differences in Fries's and Lindbeck's views of language and some of the underlying presuppositions that support those views.[66]

That creation is intelligible and that language is both descriptive and formative are two presuppositions that Fries works with. One experiences that creation at an original or primary level through dependence and consequently transcendence. Language describes that reality and allows for its communication and description. Says Fries:

Through the power and the powerlessness of word and language, language possesses dimensions of revelation. It opens up in very special ways the reality of human beings as creatures in power and helplessness, and keeps awake and alive the question of the ground of created being. Thus its revelational relationship is described as relationship to transcendence.[67]

This description discloses and, in this sense, shapes the reality of human experience; it does not construct this reality. Reality and the description of reality are two separate moments in human rationality. And while it never completely recaptures the original experience itself, it must be attempted by the theologian anyway. Once this universal common denominator (experience) of human nature is established, the specifics of faith and doctrine can then be articulated. At issue here is not really the use of language as much as the human nature's innate ability, as God's creation, to grasp creation as intelligible. This does not seem to be the view of human nature held by Lindbeck.

Lindbeck's use of language mainly stresses its constructive role in actually creating a reality that is given as unintelligible. This seems to be a statement more about human nature than about language, and, given the previous illumination on Lindbeck's view of human nature, the role of language could not really be any different. Armed with an antifoundationalist (postmodern) position advocated by Wittgenstein, Lindbeck can de-emphasize human agency and emphasize the biblical Word as the main author of theology. His extremely brief explication of mental activities attempts to support this position but fails due to his presuppositions regarding human nature. Following a critique of "some professed Thomists such as Lonergan and Rahner,"[68] Lindbeck asserts that Aristotelians, including Aquinas, would agree with his rendering of mental activities.

---

66. Fries would agree with Rahner's remarks regarding language and the distinction between an experience and subsequent reflection upon that experience. This is evident in the introduction to *Foundations of Christian Faith* under the subheading "Epistemological Problems." I also believe Fries would concur with Lonergan's comments on Edward MacKinnon's statement concerning language as affected by Wittgenstein. There is specific agreement when Lonergan states, "The discovery of a new usage is a mental act expressed by the new usage," *Method in Theology*, "The Dialectic of Method: Part One," 255.

67. Above §24, p. 222.

68. Lindbeck 39.

For the Aristotelians, affective experiences (in which would be included a sense of the holy or of absolute dependence) always depend on prior cognition of objects, and the objects available to us in this life *are all in some fashion constructed out of conceptually or linguistically structured sense experience* (italics mine).[69]

This could be correct only if Aquinas believed that language actually structured what was otherwise unintelligible reality. In fact, however, Aquinas viewed creation in itself as intelligible. Furthermore, Lindbeck's analysis of mental activities is seriously underdeveloped. What does it mean to "grasp" something? What level of knowing does that correspond to in Aquinas? Does Aristotle presuppose sense experience as "conceptually and linguistically structured?" While this has not been the place for a full epistemological critique, some major differences have been highlighted between the two authors.

Conclusion

One may disagree with Lindbeck's approach to theology and still appreciate the problems he seeks to solve. The vacuous nature of doctrine in many Christian denominations and the absolutely rigid nature of doctrine in some others points to a major problem in Christian ecumenical efforts. But regardless of how divided this house may be, theological frameworks that fail to engage society-at-large fail in their specifically Christian mission as well. In large part, the debate regarding issues of belief and unbelief with "secular" culture centers on the meaning of human existence. Nietzsche, for example, may assert that humankind's primordial urge is the "will to power," while Freud may think it is narcissistic satisfaction. With Jesus Christ as the Revelation from which we begin, theology must respond by demonstrating convincingly that the human condition, in its very constitution and in history, is oriented to the infinite in radical dependence and drawn toward the infinite through the historical experience of transcendence. The question is not: revelation or experience? The question is: how is historical experience a revelation? How is the human being a self-communication of God?

In an age when the nature of the human seems to be understood solidly apart from the horizon of the infinite, the role of fundamental theology as the explication of the presuppositions and conditions for the possibility of faith becomes increasingly important. Heinrich Fries and others with foundational starting points serve as constant reminders that effective contemporary theology must first address the existential, historical question: What is it to be human? The content of faith can then be mediated "as answer to the question and the questions

69. Ibid.

of human beings, to the questions which human beings ask, to the question which human beings themselves are."[70]

In spite of all the pressing contemporary ecumenical theological issues, at the root of any experiential-expressivist dissatisfaction with Lindbeck is a fundamentally opposite view of human nature. Fries's *Fundamental Theology* is a thorough response to the kind of position outlined by Lindbeck and to the presuppositions of the postmodern critique. It provides a clear and accurate foundational starting point for theology today with a nuanced understanding of the importance of history and historicity. The inability of a cultural-linguistic model to accept any foundation has little to do with theological frameworks and ecumenical issues and even less to do with language—it has to do with anthropology. The necessity of addressing contemporary movements such as postmodernism is summed up for the theologian in the conclusion to Fries's Introduction:

It is no longer enough merely to proclaim or solemnly assert the Christian faith. One has to lay out its grounds in the face of the overwhelming power of the contemporary experience of world and existence and of the challenges which accompany this experience. It is a massive task, but also a great opportunity.[71]

70. Above §11, p. 129.
71. Above, p. 5.

INDEX OF NAMES

This index includes only the names of authors and persons mentioned in the main text. Biblical names and places are listed in the Subject Index.

SUBJECT INDEX

This index includes the names of biblical personages, all place names (Council cities, however, under the heading "Council"), as well as Latin and Greek word-concepts. The Latin expressions which occur in the text—e.g *ecclesia semper reformanda"; "credo ut intelligam"*—are also listed. Frequent cross references to parallel or analogous concepts are listed in individual detail in order to give, even in the index, an indication of the specific fields of connotation and association. This has the added advantage of somewhat lessening the number of times frequently-occuring concepts must be listed. Although the concepts "reality" and "New Testament" are not listed, the individual New Testament authors are, as well as the concepts "Scripture: Holy Scripture" and "Old Testament."

[In view of the needs of English readers, we have made this is a somewhat edited translation of the subject index of *Fundamentaltheologie*. It is an attempt to preserve the merits of the original despite the occasionally unavoidable awkwardness of concepts which cannot be translated exactly into English.—RJD]